# THE
# SOCIOLOGY
# OF LAW

CHANDLER PUBLICATIONS IN

ANTHROPOLOGY AND SOCIOLOGY

LEONARD BROOM, *Editor*

 Science Research Associates, Inc.
259 East Erie Street, Chicago, Illinois 60611

A Subsidiary of IBM          Distributors

# THE
# SOCIOLOGY
# OF LAW

## Interdisciplinary Readings

*Edited by*

## RITA JAMES SIMON

UNIVERSITY OF ILLINOIS

CHANDLER PUBLISHING COMPANY
124 Spear Street · San Francisco, California 94105

Copyright © 1968 by Chandler Publishing Company
Library of Congress Catalog Card No. 68–10343
Printed in the United States of America

For Julian, David, and Judith

# CONTENTS

Preface     xi

**PART I. Sociological Jurisprudence: Stage One**     3

The Need of a Sociological Jurisprudence ROSCOE POUND     9

The Path of the Law OLIVER WENDELL HOLMES     19

Some Realism about Realism KARL N. LLEWELLYN     29

The Sociological Concept of Law MAX WEBER     46

What Is "Sociology of Law"? NICHOLAS S. TIMASHEFF     56

The Value of Sociology to Law ROBERT C. ANGELL     65

**PART II. Early Empirical Research**     79

A Study of the Way in Which a Verdict Is Reached by a Jury H. P. WELD
AND E. R. DANZIG     83

The Business Failures Project—II, An Analysis of Methods of Investigation WILLIAM O. DOUGLAS AND DOROTHY S. THOMAS     94

Crime and Custom in Savage Society BRONISLAW MALINOWSKI     110

Studies in Testimony WILLIAM M. MARSTON     117

## PART III. Sociological Jurisprudence: Stage Two                    137

The Relation of Law to Experimental Social Science THOMAS A. COWAN    141
The Essence of Experimental Jurisprudence FREDERICK K. BEUTEL        163
Jurimetrics: The Next Step Forward LEE LOEVINGER                     178
The Sociology of Law PHILIP SELZNICK                                 190
Political Jurisprudence MARTIN SHAPIRO                               201
The Anthropological Study of Law LAURA NADER                         220

## PART IV. Contemporary Empirical Research                           243

*Section One. The Legal Profession*                                   253
  The Road to Individual Practice JEROME E. CARLIN          255
  Work of the Wall Street Lawyer ERWIN O. SMIGEL            264
  Careers of Lawyers, Law Practice and Legal Institutions JACK LADINSKY   275

*Section Two. The Jury System*                                        291
  The Dignity of the Civil Jury HARRY KALVEN, JR.           293
  Jurors' Evaluation of Expert Psychiatric Testimony RITA JAMES SIMON   314
  The Jury, the Law and the Personal Injury Damage Award HARRY
    KALVEN, JR.                                    329
  Plaintiff's Family Status As Affecting Juror Behavior: Some Tentative
    Insights DALE W. BROEDER                       339
  Supreme Court Behavior in Racial Exclusion Cases: 1935–1960
    S. SIDNEY ULMER                                353

*Section Three. The Courts*                                           365
  Accidents, Money, and the Law: A Study of the Economics of Personal
    Injury Litigation MARC A. FRANKLIN, ROBERT H. CHANIN, AND IRVING
    MARK                                           367
  Pleading Guilty for Considerations: A Study of Bargain Justice DONALD
    J. NEWMAN                                      392
  The Analysis of Behavior Patterns on the United States Supreme Court
    S. SIDNEY ULMER                                407

*Section Four. Law and the Police*                                          431

  Police Practices and the Law—From Arrest to Release or Charge
    EDWARD J. BARRETT                                       433
  A Study of Police Isolation JOHN P. CLARK                     449

*Section Five. Law and Psychiatry*                                          461

  The Defense of Insanity: A Survey of Legal and Psychiatric Opinion
    RITA JAMES SIMON AND WENDELL SHACKELFORD             463
  The Homosexual in Court MANFRED S. GUTTMACHER               478

*Section Six. Law and Desegregation*                                        493

  Schools in Transition ROBIN M. WILLIAMS, JR., AND MARGARET W. RYAN   495
  Southern Judges and Negro Voting Rights: The Judicial Approach to
    the Solution of Controversial Social Problems CHARLES V. HAMILTON   506
  Constituency Versus Constitutionalism: The Desegregation Issue and
    Tensions and Aspirations of Southern Attorneys General SAMUEL
    KRISLOV                                                  537

*Section Seven. Legal Ethics*                                               551

  Professional Ethics Among Criminal Lawyers ARTHUR LEWIS WOOD   553
  An Evaluation of the Effectiveness of Some Curriculum Innovations in
    Law Schools RITA JAMES SIMON                            573
  Account of a Field Study in a Rural Area of the Representation of In-
    digents Accused of Crime BERTRAM F. WILLCOX AND EDWARD J.
    BLOUSTEIN                                                591

*Section Eight. Law, Public Opinion, and Mass Media*                        615

  The Effects of Newspapers on the Verdicts of Potential Jurors RITA
    JAMES SIMON                                              617
  Parental Authority: The Community and the Law JULIUS COHEN, REGI-
    NALD A. H. ROBSON, AND ALAN BATES                       628
  Trial by Mass Media? MARTIN MILLSPAUGH                       641

*Section Nine. Law and Social Change*                                       645

  Legal Evolution and Societal Complexity RICHARD D. SCHWARTZ AND
    JAMES C. MILLER                                          647
  Law and Social Change YEHEZKEL DROR                          663

Index                                                                       681

# PREFACE

The purpose of this collection is to present an overview of the major trends in the sociology of law in the United States during the past half century or so. The book is divided into four parts. Parts I and III excerpt major theoretical trends in the field, and Parts II and IV describe empirical research. The first half of Parts I and III represents the contributions of legal scholars; and the second half, those of social scientists.

The earlier materials, represented in Parts I and II, are included in order to provide a more comprehensive picture of where the field has been and of the origins of some of the current ideas and research—in other words, to serve as historical landmarks. Another and perhaps more important reason for including the earlier materials—at the cost of a more comprehensive review of current work—was to permit better evaluation of the significance of the current materials.

An adequate understanding of the kinds of problems researchers encountered in a previous era is helpful background for an informed evaluation of current work. When looking at the excerpts in the earlier and later theoretical parts, the reader might ask: Have the definitions and boundaries of the field remained relatively stable, and do the same problems appear in both eras; or have there been important changes in the field's definition? Comparably, the reader might find it useful to look at the research selections with an eye on the preceding theoretical part and ask: What kinds of relationships exist between the problems posed by the theorists and the topics selected for empirical study?

As I indicate in the introductions to the various parts, the specific selections do not exhaust all areas of past or current research. For example, in the early period, while the work of Underhill Moore is referred to in a footnote, I have not included an excerpt of any of his studies. Also omitted from this period are excerpts from work done at Johns Hopkins and Columbia Law Schools in the early 1920's and 1930's. In the part on current research the absence of materials on Law and Economics and Law and Poverty are perhaps the most serious omissions. But even with these omissions, the book should serve as a useful source both for students in the field and for those just entering.

I want, finally, to express my gratitude to the Institute of Communications Research at the University of Illinois for providing me with excellent secretarial and clerical services. The help that the staff of the Institute gave me in collecting and editing the excerpts made the preparation of this volume a much less arduous task than it might have been.

RITA JAMES SIMON

# THE
# SOCIOLOGY
# OF LAW

# PART I | SOCIOLOGICAL JURISPRUDENCE: STAGE ONE

ROSCOE POUND · OLIVER WENDELL HOLMES · KARL N. LLEWELLYN · MAX WEBER · NICHOLAS S. TIMASHEFF · ROBERT C. ANGELL

FOUNDERS OF THE "SOCIOLOGICAL-JURISPRUDENCE" MOVEment in the United States were among the most eminent members of the legal profession: they were primarily judges on the appellate bench and professors at the most prestigious law schools. Names which come to mind immediately are Oliver Wendell Holmes, Benjamin Cardozo, Louis Brandeis, Roscoe Pound, Karl Llewellyn, and William O. Douglas.

Having been profoundly influenced by the teaching and writings of one of the founders of American sociology, E. A. Ross, Roscoe Pound urged his colleagues in the law to convert to the faith of sociological research. As is often the tendency of the convert, Pound went about his task with the zeal of a missionary saving souls in a pagan society. He called upon the teachers of law as well as the practitioners to shift from the standard of "legal justice" to that of "social justice"—rules which are consistent with public standards and values. In the article reprinted here, Pound used as his illustration for attacking the individualistic approach of the common law the lack of compensation to laborers for injuries sustained in the course of their employment. Social justice demands that laborers be insured against such accidents.

A flavor of Pound's criticism of individualistic theories and the standards of legal justice comes through clearly in the following excerpt from the selection reprinted here:

A Bench and Bar trained in individualist theories and firm in the persuasion that the so-called legal justice is an absolute and a necessary standard, from which there may be no departure without the destruction of the legal order, may retard but cannot prevent progress to the newer standard recognized by the sociologist.

Comparing research in the law with research in other disciplines, such as the social and natural sciences, Pound bemoaned the lack of institutional resources for stimulating empirical research on legal matters. Specifically, he noted the absence of financial support, research institutes, and personnel.

Pound was also critical of the value orientation of the law professor for his emphasis on legal justice and "pure law" and his failure to discuss the rules by which the courts actually decide cases and the social, political, and economic consequences of legal rules. More than any other legal scholar of his time, Roscoe Pound wanted to adopt the perspective and techniques of sociological research as the paradigm for legal research. He stressed the importance of collecting empirical data from which to deduce the principles of judicial administration. He was concerned about the practical implication of legal rules, the relationship between legal rules and behavior, and the extent to which formal rules were supported by the public. Influenced as he was by Ross, he saw the need for research in law as one type of social control and in the relationship between social changes and changes in the law.

In the excerpt from "The Path of the Law," Oliver Wendell Holmes stresses two points which are most relevant to sociological jurisprudence:

1. The law is what the courts will do. It is not a system of abstract principles, nor a state of mind. It is behavior. More specifically, it is the decisions handed down by the appellate courts.

2. It is important to consider the social consequences of legal rules. In speaking to judges, Holmes emphasized the desirability of having them state explicitly and definitively the social advantages of the rule of law that they

were making or enforcing. In discussing legal education, he stressed the importance of having lawyers recognize that they are engaged in a partisan struggle and that the questions involved in the debate have important practical implications. As part of their legal education, students of the law should not only understand the meaning of the law and be able to apply it in the appropriate context, but should be equally concerned about understanding the social consequences of a law in any given dispute.

In writing about Justice Holmes on the occasion of his ninetieth birthday, Benjamin Cardozo said: "Who else has been able to pack a whole philosophy of legal method into a fragment of a paragraph?" Cardozo was referring to the opening sentences in Holmes' lectures on *The Common Law* (Boston: Little, Brown, 1881, p. 1):

The life of the law has not been logic; it has been experience. The felt necessities of the time, the prevalent moral and political theories, institutions of public policy, avowed or unconscious, even the prejudices which judges share with their fellowmen have had a good deal more to do than the syllogism in determining the rules by which men should be governed. The law embodies the story of a nation's development through many centuries and it cannot be dealt with as if it contained only the axioms and corollaries of a book of mathematics.

The next selection is an excerpt from a longer piece by Karl Llewellyn, who had been a distinguished member of two law-school faculties, Columbia and Chicago. "Some Realism about Realism," which appeared in 1931 in the *Harvard Law Review*, was written only a few years after Llewellyn had been both an instigator and participator in "the Columbia experiment." This was an experiment in the reorganization of a law-school curriculum along functional lines that Brainerd Currie (a former colleague of Llewellyn) described some forty years ago as one of the most significant events in the history of American legal education. As a faculty member at the Columbia University Law School during the period of the experiment (1926–1928), Llewellyn worked closely with specialists in the social sciences to compile new materials for legal study, to plan new courses, and to reorganize existing ones with an emphasis on the social functions of the law in each of the areas under study.

Llewellyn's article reflects some of the concerns of the Columbia project, although its explicit aim was to rebut a series of criticisms offered by Roscoe Pound against a group of legal scholars whom Pound labeled as "the school of realists." In the longer piece, Llewellyn listed each of Pound's thirteen criticisms and described the evidence supporting or negating each of the charges. Using an inductive, empirical approach, Llewellyn demonstrated that the evidence in support of Pound's criticism was at best slight, and on about half of the points, nonexistent.

The excerpt included here, picks up at the point where Llewellyn is defining what in fact are the dominant characteristics of the approach of the men associated with the realist movement. He discusses such general characteristics as conceiving of law and society as being in a state of flux and thinking of law as a means to a social end, rather than an end in itself. In addition, he emphasizes the separation of "Is and Ought for purposes of study," by which he means the importance of producing detailed, objective descriptions of how legal institutions actually operate before any consideration can be given to how they ought to function. He urges a constant evaluation of the law in terms of its effects, with a careful analysis of what the effects are.

By way of illustration, Llewellyn concludes with a list of problems to which he urges scholars interested in applying this approach to direct their efforts. If Llewellyn's topics are compared with the topics proposed for research in the selections by Martin Shapiro and Lee Loevinger (in Part III) written a quarter of a century later, it will be found that there is considerable overlap. In part, the overlap should be attributed to the basic importance of the topics, but probably more importantly to the slowness with which scholars have accepted the challenge for research in these areas.

Comparison of the contributions of the sociologists who were writing in approximately the same period reveals that their interests and efforts were directed toward similar objectives. Max Weber, in the excerpt from his unfinished work, *Law and Economy in Society*, discusses two issues which were major concerns of Holmes and Llewellyn. In distinguishing between the judicial and the sociological point of view, Weber stresses that the judicial view is aimed at "the correct meaning of propositions." The legal scholar, "taking for granted the empirical validity of the legal propositions, examines each of them and tries to determine its logically correct meaning in such a way that all of them can be combined in a system which is logically coherent, i.e., free from internal contradictions." The sociological point of view "contemplates the interconnections of human activities as they actually take place." Thus, when the legal order is used in a sociological sense, it refers not to a set of norms of logically demonstrable correctness but to a complex of determinants of actual human conduct. Holmes' statement, "The life of the law has not been logic; it has been experience," makes essentially the same distinction.

Weber also writes: "The 'ideal legal order' of legal theory has nothing directly to do with the world of real economic conduct [substitute *social* for *economic,* and the point still applies], since both exist on different levels. One exists in the ideal realm of the 'ought,' while the other deals with the real world of the 'is.'" Llewellyn's distinction between the "is" and the "ought" is comparable.

For Weber, the most useful definition of law is a system of norms which are directly guaranteed by legal coercion. By the term "legal coercion," Weber means that law embodies much more than physical coercion or violence; it includes all of the coercive apparatuses represented by the court, the police, and administrative bodies and organizations. Thus, when a citizen is said to have a "right," it means, in Weber's words, "He has a chance, factually guaranteed to him by the consensually accepted interpretation of a legal norm, of invoking in favor of his ideal or material interests the aid of a 'coercive apparatus' which is in special readiness for this purpose."

Like Pound, Holmes, and Llewellyn, Weber describes the essence of law, places great stress on experience over logic, and emphasizes the distinction between law and other internal or subjective normative phenomena such as ethics and beliefs. They differed in that for Holmes law and judicial decisions were one and the same, and for Weber law and a particular form of social control were one and the same. In Weber's first distinction between law and internal or subjective norms, he is very much in the main stream of sociological jurisprudence, sharing the orientation of both earlier and later legal and sociological scholars. But in his emphasis on law as a type of social control, Weber offers a narrower definition than those used by contemporary or later writers.

The work of Nicholas Timasheff, another European scholar, in part represents interests somewhat outside the growing experiential tradition characteristic of the American school. For example, he disagrees with Llewellyn and Holmes on a crucial issue concerning the distinction between "is" and "ought." For Timasheff, legal rules are a type of ethical rule (ethico-imperatives); they are "ought" statements which are enforced by a centralized power. But in claiming as he does that the sociology of law is the study of how human behavior adheres to legal norms or fails to adhere to such norms and in distinguishing jurisprudence (the study of legal norms) from sociological jurisprudence (the study of how legal norms determine human behavior within a given social structure), Timasheff establishes intellectual boundaries which have proved useful.

On the whole, Timasheff's contributions have been to the school of "grand theory." And as has been true of other subfields within sociology, the more "grand" or "all-encompassing" the questions, the less fruitful have they proved as seedbeds for empirical research. In the sociology of law, as indeed in most of the other subareas of sociology, research has been more responsive to theories of the "middle range."

The last selection in Part I, by Robert Angell, is significant primarily because it advocates a division of labor between law and sociology which has in fact been adopted and proved workable for those engaged in empirical research. Angell recognized earlier than most that the important contribution which sociologists can bring to the partnership is research techniques, not substance. He points out that there are relatively few sociological findings which would bear directly upon legal problems. Thus, rather than emphasize the pertinence or availability of collected data, sociologists should make the research methods they have developed their distinctive contribution.

By "method," Angell means something as broad as an approach or orientation to a discipline and as specific as how to run an opinion survey or experiment. An example of the breadth he intends is the recognition that law operates within a social milieu and that there is an interdependence between law and other institutions, such as the family, the occupational system, and the church.

Angell, like Llewellyn, was also associated with the interdisciplinary project on curriculum innovation at the Columbia University Law School in the 1920's. He too had an opportunity to observe firsthand the difficulties which develop when social scientists try to teach lawyers substance in areas about which lawyers feel themselves to be experts. He also probably observed that when a lawyer is actually working on a specific, concrete problem, the knowledge which social scientists can contribute is not of the caliber of the "factual testimony" lawyers expect to obtain from experts. In stressing method rather than substance, Angell opened the door to a fruitful relationship in which both disciplines could respect the special skills which the other brought to the endeavor.

# THE NEED
# OF A SOCIOLOGICAL
# JURISPRUDENCE

*Roscoe Pound*

\*    \*    \*    \*

Political and juridical development were necessary before industrial and social development. Government and law created the environment of peace and order and stability in which alone the industrial and social organization of to-day could grow. Hence legal theory and doctrine reached a degree of fixity before the conditions with which law must deal to-day had come into existence. And at this point where legal principles were taking a final shape the growing point in human progress began to shift to the natural and physical sciences and their applications in engineering, in the arts, and in scientific cultivation of the soil and development of its resources. Titius and Seius, who in their day had driven philosophy from the schools, are not unlikely to be driven out in turn. The changed order of things has been felt in legal science. Research of almost every other sort has been endowed. Laboratories are set up to investigate every other human interest. A flood of bulletins goes forth annually to spread far and wide the latest results in the application of natural and physical science to health and wealth, in the application of economic theory to our material well-being, in the application of sociological principles to problems of state and municipal life. In all these things the public shows an enduring interest. It ought to be someone's duty to advise the people of the progress of juridical science and to make its results public property. It ought to be someone's duty to gather and preserve statistics of

Reprinted from 19 *The Green Bag* (October 1907), 607–615. Footnotes have been renumbered to run in sequence throughout the selection.

the administration of justice and to apply thereto or deduce therefrom the proper principles of judicial administration. Law teachers ought to be making clear to the public what law is and why law is and what law does and why it does so. But no one can obtain statistics at all complete nor at all authoritative upon the most everyday points in judicial administration. No one is studying seriously or scientifically how to make our huge output of legislation effective. There are no endowments for juridical research. There are no laboratories dedicated to legal science whose bulletins shall make it possible for the scholar to obtain authoritative data and for the lay public to reach sound conclusions. No one thinks of establishing them. In state universities where one may be trained gratuitously in the most specialized applications of science, where an engineer may obtain his technical training without expense, students of law are charged a heavy tuition. The obvious reason is that the people do not feel that jurisprudence is doing anything for them. Legal science must first exhibit some practical results. It must show that it has something to offer before it may hope for public recognition. But it should not be suffered to remain stricken with sterility in face of the fruitful tasks that await it in this era of transition.

\*     \*     \*     \*

Law is no longer anything sacred or mysterious. Judicial decisions are investigated and discussed freely by historians, economists, and sociologists. The doctrines announced by the courts are debated by the press, and have even been dealt with in political platforms. Laymen know full well that they may make laws, and that knowledge of the law is no necessary prerequisite of far-reaching legislation. The legislative steam roller levels the just rule with the unjust in the public anxiety to lay out a new road. The introduction of the doctrine of comparative negligence in employer's liability statutes and recent statutes leaving questions of negligence wholly to juries or, in other words, cutting off all assurance that like cases involving negligence will receive a like decision, afford interesting examples. The common-law doctrines, at least as explained to the people, did not commend themselves to the public intelligence. In such cases, something is to be done; and it is done too often with but little understanding of old law, mischief, or remedy. But we have no right to rail at such miscarriages. The public must move in such legal light as the luminaries of the law afford. Those who practice and those who teach the law should be in a position to command the popular ear. We must reinvestigate the theories of justice, of law, and of rights. We must seek the basis of doctrines, not in Blackstone's wisdom of our ancestors, not in the apocryphal reasons of the beginnings of legal science, not in their history, useful as that is in enabling us to appraise doctrines at their true value, but in a scientific apprehension of the relations of law to society and of the needs and interests and opinions of society of to-day.

Ample reason for the present condition of jurisprudence in America is to be found in the dominance of practitioners and of the ideas and ideals of practitioners in legal education. So long as the one object is to train practitioners who can make money at the Bar, and so long as schools are judged chiefly by their success in affording such training, we may expect nothing better. Yet this is an explanation rather than an excuse. The schools must teach the rules by which the courts decide cases. They cannot teach a different law from that which is recognized and enforced by the courts. But they are not bound to teach traditional legal pseudo-science. They are not bound to teach the practitioner's philosophy of law, however much he may think it involved in the very idea of a legal system. It is not long ago that a fictitious legal history was equally orthodox. Freeman tells us of a law-teacher who "required the candidates for degrees to say that William the Conqueror introduced the feudal system at the great Gemot of Salisbury in 1086,"[1] and when remonstrance was made by the historian, replied that he was examiner in law; that "facts might be found in chronicles, but law was to be found in Blackstone; it was to be found in Blackstone as an infallible source; what Blackstone said, he, as a law-examiner, could not dispute."[2] But courts and law books can no more make authoritative philosophy than they can make authoritative history.

I do not advocate the adding of any new course or new courses to our curricula. Doubtless the schools are offering now all the courses that students may take with profit. But law schools not only make tough law,[3] they make tough legal science, as the long postponement of the German code through dominance of the historical school, the persistence of eighteenth-century theories in American legal thought, long after they had been abandoned in all other fields, and the sturdy resistance of com-

---

[1] *It is interesting to note that this statement is still with us in law-teaching. Mordecai, Law Lectures, 24 (1907).*

[2] *Freeman, Methods of Historical Study, 73–74.*

[3] *Maitland, English Law and the Renaissance, 25.*

mon-law individualism to the collectivist tendencies of modern thought abundantly witness. We must not make the mistake in American legal education of creating a permanent gulf between legal thought and popular thought. But we may commit this mistake not merely by teaching legal pseudo-science and obsolete philosophy but quite as much by the more prevalent method of saying nothing about these matters at all, leaving the student to pick up what he may here and there in the cases and texts, with no hint that there are other conceptions and other theories entertained by scholars of no small authority, and to go forth in the belief that he is completely trained.[4] I have little faith in abstract courses, even if our schools had room for any new courses. Instruction of the sort required must be concrete. It must lie in the point of view from which concrete legal problems are discussed, concrete doctrines are expounded, and actual decisions are investigated and criticized. The modern teacher of law should be a student of sociology, economics, and politics as well. He should know not only what the courts decide and the principles by which they decide, but quite as much the circumstances and conditions, social and economic, to which these principles are to be applied; he should know the state of popular thought and feeling which makes the environment in which the principles must operate in practice. Legal monks who passed their lives in an atmosphere of pure law, from which every worldly and human element is excluded, cannot shape practical principles to be applied to a restless world of flesh and blood. The most logical and skillfully reasoned rules may defeat the end of law in their practical administration because not adapted to the environment in which they are to be enforced.[5] It is, therefore, the duty of American teachers of law to investigate the sociological foundations, not of law alone, but of the common law and of the special topics in which they give instruction, and, while teaching the actual law by which courts decide, to give to their teaching the color which will fit new generations of lawyers to lead the people as they should, instead of giving up their legitimate hegemony in legislation and politics to engineers and naturalists and economists.

Without trenching upon points of controversy, it may be assumed that the practical end of the administration of justice according to law, is

---

[4] *Complaint has been made in France to the same effect. Vareilles-Som-mières, Principes Fondamentaux du Droit, preface.*

[5] *See Brunner's comment upon the effect of the reception of Roman law in Germany on peasant possessions. Grundzuge der Deutschen Rechtsgeschichte, 216.*

such adjustment of the relations of men to each other and to society as conforms to the moral sense of the community. In the past this adjustment has conformed to the general moral sense by proceeding along lines of strict individualism. The idea has been, so far as possible, to allow everyone to do and to acquire all that he can. The individualist conception of justice as the liberty of each limited only by the like liberties of all has been the legal conception. So completely has this been true that sociologists speak of this conception as "legal justice," and it is sometimes assumed that law must needs aim at a different kind of justice from what is commonly understood and regarded by the community. But this cannot be. Law is a means, not an end. Such a divergence cannot endure unless the law is in the hands of a progressive and enlightened caste whose conceptions are in advance of the public and whose leadership is bringing popular thought to a higher level.[6] When, instead, law is in the hands of a highly cautious and conservative profession, whose thought on such matters lags behind, the divergence provokes irritation at law and disregard of its mandates. To-day, while jurists in America are repeating individualist formulas of justice, sociologists are speaking rather of "the enforcement by society of an artificial equality in social conditions which are naturally unequal."[7] They are defining justice as the satisfaction of everyone's wants so far as they are not outweighed by others' wants.[8] That this is the direction of popular thought is shown by the unconscious drift of the law in the same direction. It is true we still harp upon the sacredness of property before the law. The leader of our profession tells us that a fundamental object is, "preservation of the rights of private property."[9] A text book used in more than one law school advises us that "the right of property is of divine origin derived by title-deed from the universal creator of all things and attested by universal intuition."[10] The highest court of one of the states tells us in eloquent words that the right to take property

---

[6] *An excellent example may be seen in the history of equity in England. Equity was unpopular, but it was in the right line of progress. The chancellors, however, developed doctrines of an ultra-ethical character which went beyond the requirements of common sense, and these refinements of equity have been largely swept away. For instances of this, the doctrine as to compensation of trustees, precatory trusts, and the rules as to clogging the equity of redemption may suffice.*

[7] *Ward, Applied Sociology, 23.*

[8] *Ward, Applied Sociology, 22–24, Willoughby, Social Justice, 20–25.*

[9] *Argument of Mr. Choate in the Income Tax Cases, 157 U.S. 429, 534.*

[10] *Smith, Personal Property, Sec. 33.*

by will is an absolute and inherent right, not depending upon legislation.[11] But the steady progress of the law is in another direction. Ihering lays down this as the difference between the new and the old: "Formerly high valuing of property, lower valuing of the person; now, lower valuing of property, higher valuing of the person."[12] He says the line of legal growth of the future is "weakening of the sense of property, strengthening of the feeling of honor."[13] And that this is true for our law in America, the continual complaints that modern legislation deprives men of the power to regulate their own affairs and to manage their own property bear abundant witness.

The progress of law away from the older individualism is not confined to property rights. A passing of ultra-individualist phases of common-law doctrines on every hand, both through legislation and through judicial decision, is sufficiently obvious. Let us note a few cases. One of the so-called natural rights, which is still insisted upon, is freedom of contract, the right of each man to say for himself what engagements he will undertake and to settle the details thereof for himself. But modern legislation is constantly abridging this right by creating classes of persons and classes of subjects, with respect to which rights and obligations are defined by law "and made conclusive upon the parties, irrespective of stipulations attempting to set them aside;"[14] and such statutes are now held constitutional within wide limits. Nor is this tendency confined to legislation. The contract of insurance has been so dealt with by the courts that it is no longer an ordinary contract, to be judged as such, but the law of insurance has become a specialized body of doctrine.[15] The older decisions were extremely strict in insisting upon the right of a surety to make his own contract in every respect. The slightest deviations, which had the effect of varying in some degree the obligation for which he engaged to become answerable, sufficed to relieve him. He and he alone could determine for what he would bind himself, and he could do so as arbitrarily as he chose, for it was his affair.[16] But the advent of the surety company has already

---

[11] *Nunnemacher v. State, 108 N. W. 627.*

[12] *Ihering, Scherz und Ernst in der Jurisprudenz (9 ed.) 418.*

[13] *Ihering, Scherz und Ernst in der Jurisprudenz (9 ed.) 429.*

[14] *Freund, Police Power, Sec. 503.*

[15] *Wambaugh, Cases on Insurance, preface.*

[16] *Hence if the king died, surety for the peace was released "for 'tis to observe his peace, and when he is dead, 'tis not his peace." Anonymous. Brook's New Cas. 172. A typical modern case is U.S. v. Boecker, 21 Wall. 652.*

produced a change. It was felt that the right of every person to make his own contracts for himself must give way to a public demand for enforcement of contracts of insurance unless some substantial injury to the insurer appeared, and this feeling has led to a line of judicial decisions with respect to contracts of surety companies that cannot well be reconciled with the settled course of adjudication as to natural persons.[17] Professor Gray has noted a similar phenomenon in the matter of spendthrift trusts.[18] The common law insisted rigorously on individual responsibility. It was not possible for a debtor through any device to enjoy the whole substantial benefit of property free from claims of his creditors. The American decisions which permit such trusts are, as he points out, at clear variance with the spirit of the common law. They are another sign of the drift toward equality in the satisfaction of wants rather than equality in freedom of action as the standard of justice; and the decisions which Professor Gray justly stigmatizes as "snobbish"[19] are but crude attempts to apply this standard before it has been recognized clearly or has taken definite shape. Probably nowhere is the individualism of the common law expressed more characteristically than in the doctrines as to contributory negligence. Recent legislation with respect to employer's liability is almost wiping out those doctrines. It seems to be felt that nothing short of fraud, or disregard of life or limb so gross as to amount to fraud, should preclude recovery. No less characteristic is the view which the common law takes of industrial accidents. It insists that such accidents must be due either to wholly unpreventible conditions or to the negligence of some person. Either the employer, it holds, was negligent or the employee. That the business itself, and not the negligence of some person operating therein, may be responsible for the accident, is a situation which it cannot conceive of and for which it makes no provision beyond laying down that the employee assumes the incidental risks. But it is coming to be well understood by all who have studied the circumstances of modern industrial employment that the supposed contributory negligence of employees is in effect a result of the mechanical conditions imposed on them by the nature of their employment, and that by reason of these conditions the individual vigilance and responsibility contemplated by the common law are impossi-

---

[17] See for instance, American Bonding Co. v. City of Ottumwa, 137 Fed. 572, Segari v. Mazzei (La.) 41 So. 245.

[18] Gray, Restraints on the Alienation of Property (2 ed.) viii–x.

[19] Restraints on the Alienation of Property, xi.

ble in practice. Hence, while the common law insists upon the workman taking the ordinary risks of his occupation, requires him to show negligence on the part of his employer as a prerequisite of recovery, and holds him to account rigidly for negligence of his own contributing to the accident, the public has been coming more and more to think that the employer should take the risk of accidents to his men, as of accidents to his plant and machinery, and that contributory negligence—where there is no willful self-injury and no fraud—is one of these ordinary risks. As the President put it recently in his address at the Georgia Day celebration at the Jamestown Exposition: "It is neither just, expedient, nor humane; it is revolting to judgment and sentiment alike that the financial burden of accidents occurring because of the necessary exigencies of their daily occupation should be thrust upon those sufferers who are least able to bear it. . . . When the employer . . . starts in motion agencies which create risks for others, he should take all the ordinary and extraordinary risks involved." Juries have perceived this dimly for years and have rendered verdicts accordingly. Legislation is now fast introducing rules founded avowedly upon this theory. If this legislation is constructed and applied by men thoroughly imbued with the common-law doctrine and with common-law prejudices, the divergence between legal rules and popular thought, if it does not produce legislation still more radical, will add to existing disrespect for the law. But we must note here once more that higher regard for the person and regard for equality in the satisfaction of wants are the controlling elements in the newer doctrine.

Another noteworthy sign of the shifting from the standard of so-called legal justice to that of social justice is to be seen in the tendency of modern legislation to reintroduce *status* or something very like it. The conception that rights should belong or duties attach to a person of full age and natural capacity because of the position he occupies in society or of the occupation in which he is engaged, is repugnant to the spirit of the common law. Hence courts, imbued strongly with common-law notions of this matter, have tended to hold statutes which carry out this idea unconstitutional whenever possible. But the conception is perfectly reconcilable with, and indeed is demanded by the idea of social justice. When the standard is equality of freedom of action, all classes other than those few and simple ones, based on so-called natural incapacities, such as infancy and lunacy, are repugnant to the idea of justice. When the standard is equality in the satisfaction of wants, such classification and such return in part to the idea of *status* are inevitable.

Even more marked and of longer standing is the weakening of extreme doctrines of *fides est servanda* through the shifting to the idea of social justice. Here again the point of view of the common law was extremely individualist. It left the individual free to assume whatever obligation he chose and to determine its details for himself. But here, as elsewhere, it imposed a responsibility corresponding to this freedom. If he chose to assume an obligation, the common law held him to it jealously. He had weighed the risk and had taken it. As he was allowed to incur it like a man, he must bear its consequences like a man. Hence common-law judges were extremely reluctant to permit contract debtors to escape by availing themselves of the statute of limitations, and for a time very nearly nullified that statute so far as it applied to debts.[20] But to-day exemption, homestead, and appraisement statutes, not to speak of bankruptcy and insolvency laws, greatly restrict the power of the creditor to enforce the liability assumed.[21] There is a growing sentiment that the creditor who extends credit should assume a risk. The principle that promises must be kept yields to the demand that satisfaction of the reasonable wants of the debtor be first reasonably provided for.

In all cases of divergence between the standard of the common law and the standard of the public, it goes without saying that the latter will prevail in the end. Sooner or later what public opinion demands will be recognized and enforced by the courts. A Bench and Bar trained in individualist theories and firm in the persuasion that the so-called legal justice is an absolute and a necessary standard, from which there may be no departure without the destruction of the legal order, may retard but cannot prevent progress to the newer standard recognized by the sociologist. In this progress lawyers should be conscious factors, not unconscious followers of popular thought, not conscious obstructors of the course of legal development. To this end it is the duty of teachers of law, while they teach scrupulously the law that the courts administer, to teach it in the

---

[20] *See an interesting discussion of this in Pritchard v. Howell, 1 Wis. 131.*

[21] *See also the recent attempt of the federal circuit court to force a scheme of reorganization upon reluctant creditors of a public service company in the Chicago Traction Cases. Whatever view may be taken of this decree, it is a sign of the times.*

spirit and from the standpoint of the political, economic, and sociological learning of to-day. It is their task to create in this country a true sociological jurisprudence, to develop a thorough understanding between the people and the law, to insure that the common law remain, what its exponents have always insisted it is—the custom of the people, the expression of their habits of thought and action as to the relations of men with each other. . . .

# THE PATH
# OF THE LAW[1]

## Oliver Wendell Holmes

\*    \*    \*    \*

I wish, if I can, to lay down some first principles for the study of this body of dogma or systematized prediction which we call the law, for men who want to use it as the instrument of their business to enable them to prophesy in their turn, and, as bearing upon the study, I wish to point out an ideal which as yet our law has not attained.

The first thing for a business-like understanding of the matter is to understand its limits, and therefore I think it desirable at once to point out and dispel a confusion between morality and law, which sometimes rises to the height of conscious theory, and more often and indeed constantly is making trouble in detail without reaching the point of consciousness. You can see very plainly that a bad man has as much reason as a good one for wishing to avoid an encounter with the public force, and therefore you can see the practical importance of the distinction between morality and law. A man who cares nothing for an ethical rule which is believed and practised by his neighbors is likely nevertheless to care a good deal to avoid being made to pay money, and will want to keep out of jail if he can.

I take it for granted that no hearer of mine will misinterpret what I have to say as the language of cynicism. The law is the witness and external deposit of our moral life. Its history is the history of the moral

---

[1] *An Address delivered by Mr. Justice Holmes, of the Supreme Judicial Court of Massachusetts, at the dedication of the new hall of the Boston University School of Law, on January 8, 1897. Copyrighted by O. W. Holmes, 1897.*

Reprinted from 10 *Harvard Law Review* (1897), 457–478. Footnotes have been renumbered to run in sequence throughout the selection.

development of the race. The practice of it, in spite of popular jests, tends to make good citizens and good men. When I emphasize the difference between law and morals I do so with reference to a single end, that of learning and understanding the law. For that purpose you must definitely master its specific marks, and it is for that that I ask you for the moment to imagine yourselves indifferent to other and greater things.

I do not say that there is not a wider point of view from which the distinction between law and morals becomes of secondary or no importance, as all mathematical distinctions vanish in presence of the infinite. But I do say that that distinction is of the first importance for the object which we are here to consider,—a right study and mastery of the law as a business with well understood limits, a body of dogma enclosed within definite lines. I have just shown the practical reason for saying so. If you want to know the law and nothing else, you must look at it as a bad man, who cares only for the material consequences which such knowledge enables him to predict, not as a good one, who finds his reasons for conduct, whether inside the law or outside of it, in the vaguer sanctions of conscience. The theoretical importance of the distinction is no less, if you would reason on your subject aright. The law is full of phraseology drawn from morals, and by the mere force of language continually invites us to pass from one domain to the other without perceiving it, as we are sure to do unless we have the boundary constantly before our minds. The law talks about rights, and duties, and malice, and intent, and negligence, and so forth, and nothing is easier, or, I may say, more common in legal reasoning, than to take these words in their moral sense, at some stage of the argument, and so to drop into fallacy. For instance, when we speak of the rights of man in a moral sense, we mean to mark the limits of interference with individual freedom which we think are prescribed by conscience, or by our ideal, however reached. Yet it is certain that many laws have been enforced in the past, and it is likely that some are enforced now, which are condemned by the most enlightened opinion of the time, or which at all events pass the limit of interference as many consciences would draw it. Manifestly, therefore, nothing but confusion of thought can result from assuming that the rights of man in a moral sense are equally rights in the sense of the Constitution and the law. No doubt simple and extreme cases can be put of imaginable laws which the statute-making power would not dare to enact, even in the absence of written constitutional prohibitions, because the community would rise in rebellion and fight; and this gives some plausibility to the proposition that the law, if not a part of morality, is limited by it. But this limit of power is not coextensive with any system of morals. For the most part it falls far within the lines of any such system, and in some cases may extend beyond them, for reasons drawn from the habits of a particular people at a particular time. I once heard the late Professor Agassiz say that a German population would rise if you added two cents to the price of a glass of beer. A statute in such a case would be empty words, not because it was wrong, but because it could not be enforced. No one will deny that wrong statutes can be and are enforced, and we should not all agree as to which were the wrong ones.

The confusion with which I am dealing besets confessedly legal conceptions. Take the fundamental question, What constitutes the law? You will find some text writers telling you that it is something different from what is decided by the courts of Massachusetts or England, that it is a system of reason, that it is a deduction from principles of ethics or admitted axioms or what not, which may or may not coincide with the decisions. But if we take the view of our friend the bad man we shall find that he does not care two straws for the axioms or deductions, but that he does want to know what the Massachusetts or English courts are likely to do in fact. I am much of his mind. The prophecies of what the courts will do in fact, and nothing more pretentious, are what I mean by the law.

Take again a notion which as popularly understood is the widest conception which the law contains;—the notion of legal duty, to which already I have referred. We fill the word with all the content which we draw from morals. But what does it mean to a bad man? Mainly, and in the first place, a prophecy that if he does certain things he will be subjected to disagreeable consequences by way of imprisonment or com-pulsory payment of money. But from his point of view, what is the difference betwcen being fined and being taxed a certain sum for doing a certain thing? That his point of view is the test of legal principles is shown by the many discussions which have arisen in the courts on the very question whether a given statutory liability is a penalty or a tax. On the answer to this question depends the decision whether conduct is legally wrong or right, and also whether a man is under compulsion or free. Leaving the criminal law on one side, what is the difference between the liability under the mill acts or statutes authorizing a taking by eminent domain and the liability for what we call a wrongful conversion of property where restoration is out of the question? In both cases the party taking another man's property has to pay its fair value as assessed by a jury, and no more. What significance is there in calling one taking right and another wrong from the point of view of the law? It does not matter, so far as the given consequence, the compulsory payment, is concerned, whether the act to which it is attached is described in terms of praise or in terms of blame, or whether the law purports to prohibit it or to allow it. If it matters at all, still speaking from the bad man's point of view, it must be because in one case and not in the other some further disadvantages, or at least some further consequences, are attached to the act by the law. The only other disadvantages thus attached to it which I ever have been able to think of are to be found in two somewhat insignificant legal doctrines, both of which might be abolished without much disturbance. One is, that a contract to do a prohibited act is unlawful, and the other, that, if one of two or more joint wrongdoers has to pay all the damages, he cannot recover contribution from his fellows. And that I believe is all. You see how the vague circumference of the notion of duty shrinks and at the same time grows more precise when we wash it with cynical acid and expel everything except the object of our study, the operations of the law.

Nowhere is the confusion between legal and moral ideas more manifest than in the law of contract. Among other things, here again the so called primary rights and duties are invested with a mystic significance beyond what can be assigned and explained. The duty to keep a contract at common law means a prediction that you must pay damages if you do not keep it,—and nothing else. If you commit a tort, you are liable to pay a compensatory sum. If you commit a contract, you are liable to pay a compensatory sum unless the promised event comes to pass, and that is all the difference. But such a mode of looking at the matter stinks in the nostrils of those who think it advantageous to get as much ethics into the law as they can. It was good enough for Lord Coke, however, and here, as in many other cases, I am content to abide with him. In Bromage *v.* Genning,[2] a prohibition was sought in the King's Bench against a suit in the marches of Wales for the specific performance of a covenant to grant a lease, and Coke said that it would subvert the intention of the covenantor, since he intends it to be at his election either to lose the damages or to make the lease. Sergeant Harris for the plaintiff confessed that he moved the

---

[2] *1 Roll. Rep. 368.*

matter against his conscience, and a prohibition was granted. This goes further than we should go now, but it shows what I venture to say has been the common law point of view from the beginning, although Mr. Harriman, in his very able little book upon Contracts has been misled, as I humbly think, to a different conclusion.

I have spoken only of the common law, because there are some cases in which a logical justification can be found for speaking of civil liabilities as imposing duties in an intelligible sense. These are the relatively few in which equity will grant an injunction, and will enforce it by putting the defendant in prison or otherwise punishing him unless he complies with the order of the court. But I hardly think it advisable to shape general theory from the exception, and I think it would be better to cease troubling ourselves about primary rights and sanctions altogether, than to describe our prophecies concerning the liabilities commonly imposed by the law in those inappropriate terms.

I mentioned, as other examples of the use by the law of words drawn from morals, malice, intent, and negligence. It is enough to take malice as it is used in the law of civil liability for wrongs,—what we lawyers call the law of torts,—to show you that it means something different in law from what it means in morals, and also to show how the difference has been obscured by giving to principles which have little or nothing to do with each other the same name. Three hundred years ago a parson preached a sermon and told a story out of Fox's Book of Martyrs of a man who had assisted at the torture of one of the saints, and afterward died, suffering compensatory inward torment. It happened that Fox was wrong. The man was alive and chanced to hear the sermon, and thereupon he sued the parson. Chief Justice Wray instructed the jury that the defendant was not liable, because the story was told innocently, without malice. He took malice in the moral sense, as importing a malevolent motive. But nowadays no one doubts that a man may be liable, without any malevolent motive at all, for false statements manifestly calculated to inflict temporal damage. In stating the case in pleading, we still should call the defendant's conduct malicious; but, in my opinion at least, the word means nothing about motives, or even about the defendant's attitude toward the future, but only signifies that the tendency of his conduct under the known circumstances was very plainly to cause the plaintiff temporal harm.[3]

---

[3] See *Hanson v. Globe Newspaper Co., 159 Mass. 293, 302.*

In the law of contract the use of moral phraseology has led to equal confusion, as I have shown in part already, but only in part. Morals deal with the actual internal state of the individual's mind, what he actually intends. From the time of the Romans down to now, this mode of dealing has affected the language of the law as to contract, and the language used has reacted upon the thought. We talk about a contract as a meeting of the minds of the parties, and thence it is inferred in various cases that there is no contract because their minds have not met; that is, because they have intended different things or because one party has not known of the assent of the other. Yet nothing is more certain than that parties may be bound by a contract to things which neither of them intended, and when one does not know of the other's assent. Suppose a contract is executed in due form and in writing to deliver a lecture, mentioning no time. One of the parties thinks that the promise will be construed to mean at once, within a week. The other thinks that it means when he is ready. The court says that it means within a reasonable time. The parties are bound by the contract as it is interpreted by the court, yet neither of them meant what the court declares that they have said. In my opinion no one will understand the true theory of contract or be able even to discuss some fundamental questions intelligently until he has understood that all contracts are formal, that the making of a contract depends not on the agreement of two minds in one intention, but on the agreement of two sets of external signs,—not on the parties' having *meant* the same thing but on their having *said* the same thing. Furthermore, as the signs may be addressed to one sense or another,—to sight or to hearing,—on the nature of the sign will depend the moment when the contract is made. If the sign is tangible, for instance, a letter, the contract is made when the letter of acceptance is delivered. If it is necessary that the minds of the parties meet, there will be no contract until the acceptance can be read,—none, for example, if the acceptance be snatched from the hand of the offerer by a third person.

This is not the time to work out a theory in detail, or to answer many obvious doubts and questions which are suggested by these general views. I know of none which are not easy to answer, but what I am trying to do now is only by a series of hints to throw some light on the narrow path of legal doctrine, and upon two pitfalls which, as it seems to me, lie perilously near to it. Of the first of these I have said enough. I hope that my illustrations have shown the danger, both to speculation and to practice, of confounding morality with law, and the trap which legal language lays for us on that side of our way. For my own part, I often doubt whether it would not be a gain if every word of moral significance could be banished from the law altogether, and other words adopted which should convey legal ideas uncolored by anything outside the law. We should lose the fossil records of a good deal of history and the majesty got from ethical associations, but by ridding ourselves of an unnecessary confusion we should gain very much in the clearness of our thought.

So much for the limits of the law. The next thing which I wish to consider is what are the forces which determine its content and its growth. You may assume, with Hobbes and Bentham and Austin, that all law emanates from the sovereign, even when the first human beings to enunciate it are the judges, or you may think that law is the voice of the Zeitgeist, or what you like. It is all one to my present purpose. Even if every decision required the sanction of an emperor with despotic power and a whimsical turn of mind, we should be interested none the less, still with a view of prediction, in discovering some order, some rational explanation, and some principle of growth for the rules which he laid down. In every system there are such explanations and principles to be found. It is with regard to them that a second fallacy comes in, which I think it important to expose.

The fallacy to which I refer is the notion that the only force at work in the development of the law is logic. In the broadest sense, indeed, that notion would be true. The postulate on which we think about the universe is that there is a fixed quantitative relation between every phenomenon and its antecedents and consequents. If there is such a thing as a phenomenon without these fixed quantitative relations, it is a miracle. It is outside the law of cause and effect, and as such transcends our power of thought, or at least is something to or from which we cannot reason. The condition of our thinking about the universe is that it is capable of being thought about rationally, or, in other words, that every part of it is effect and cause in the same sense in which those parts are with which we are most familiar. So in the broadest sense it is true that the law is a logical development, like everything else. The danger of which I speak is not the admission that the principles governing other phenomena also govern the law, but the notion that a given system, ours, for instance, can be worked out like mathematics from some general axioms of conduct. This is the natural error of the schools, but it is not confined to them. I once heard a very eminent judge say that he never let a decision go until he was absolutely sure that it was right. So judicial dissent often is blamed, as if it meant simply that one side or the other were not doing their sums right, and, if they would take more trouble, agreement inevitably would come.

This mode of thinking is entirely natural. The training of lawyers is a training in logic. The processes of analogy, discrimination, and deduction are those in which they are most at home. The language of judicial decision is mainly the language of logic. And the logical method and form flatter that longing for certainty and for repose which is in every human mind. But certainty generally is illusion, and repose is not the destiny of man. Behind the logical form lies a judgment as to the relative worth and importance of competing legislative grounds, often an inarticulate and unconscious judgment, it is true, and yet the very root and nerve of the whole proceeding. You can give any conclusion a logical form. You always can imply a condition in a contract. But why do you imply it? It is because of some belief as to the practice of the community or of a class, or because of some opinion as to policy, or, in short, because of some attitude of yours upon a matter not capable of exact quantitative measurement, and therefore not capable of founding exact logical conclusions. Such matters really are battle grounds where the means do not exist for determinations that shall be good for all time, and where the decision can do no more than embody the preference of a given body in a given time and place. We do not realize how large a part of our law is open to reconsideration upon a slight change in the habit of the public mind. No concrete proposition is self-evident, no matter how ready we may be to accept it, not even Mr. Herbert Spencer's Every man has a right to do what he wills, provided he interferes not with a like right on the part of his neighbors.

Why is a false and injurious statement privileged, if it is made honestly in giving information about a servant? It is because it has been thought more important that information should be given freely, than that a man should be protected from what under other circumstances would be an actionable wrong. Why is a man at liberty to set up a business which he knows will ruin his neighbor? It is because the public good is supposed to be best subserved by free competition. Obviously such judgments of relative importance may vary in different times and places. Why does a judge instruct a jury that an employer is not liable to an employee for an injury received in the course of his employment unless he is negligent, and why do the jury generally find for the plaintiff if the case is allowed to go to them? It is because the traditional policy of our law is to confine liability to cases where a prudent man might have foreseen the injury, or at least the danger, while the inclination of a very large part of the community is to make certain classes of persons insure the safety of those with whom they deal. Since the last words were written, I have seen the requirement of such insurance put forth as part of the programme of one of the best known labor organizations. There is a concealed, half conscious battle on the question of legislative policy, and if any one thinks that it can be settled deductively, or once for all, I only can say that I think he is theoretically wrong, and that I am certain that his conclusion will not be accepted in practice *semper ubique et ab omnibus*.

Indeed, I think that even now our theory upon this matter is open to reconsideration, although I am not prepared to say how I should decide if a reconsideration were proposed. Our law of torts comes from the old days of isolated, ungeneralized wrongs, assaults, slanders, and the like, where the damages might be taken to lie where they fell by legal judgment. But the torts with which our courts are kept busy to-day are mainly the incidents of certain well known businesses. They are injuries to person or property by railroads, factories, and the like. The liability for them is estimated, and sooner or later goes into the price paid by the public. The public really pays the damages, and the question of liability, if pressed far enough, is really the question how far it is desirable that the public should insure the safety of those whose work it uses. It might be said that in such cases the chance of a jury finding for the defendant is merely a chance, once in a while rather arbitrarily interrupting the regular course of recovery, most likely in the case of an unusually conscientious plaintiff, and therefore better done away with. On the other hand, the economic value even of a life to the community can be estimated, and no recovery, it may be said, ought to go beyond that amount. It is conceivable that some day in certain cases we may find ourselves imitating, on a higher plane, the tariff for life and limb which we see in the Leges Barbarorum.

I think that the judges themselves have failed adequately to recognize their duty of weighing considerations of social advantage. The duty is inevitable, and the result of the often proclaimed judicial aversion to deal with such considerations is simply to leave the very ground and foundation of judgments inarticulate, and often unconscious, as I have said. When socialism first began to be talked about, the comfortable classes of the community were a good deal frightened. I suspect that this fear has influenced judicial action both here and in England, yet it is certain that it is not a conscious factor in the decisions to which I refer. I think that something similar has led people who no longer hope to control the legislatures to look to the courts as expounders of the Constitutions, and that in some courts new principles have been discovered outside the bodies of those instruments, which may be generalized into acceptance of the economic doctrines which prevailed about fifty years ago, and a wholesale prohibition of what a tribunal of lawyers does not think about right. I cannot but believe that if the training of lawyers led them habitually to consider more definitely and explicitly the social advantage on which the rule they lay down must be justified, they sometimes would hesitate where now they are confident, and see that really they were taking sides upon debatable and often burning questions.

\*　\*　\*　\*

# SOME REALISM
# ABOUT REALISM*

## Karl N. Llewellyn

Ferment is abroad in the law. The sphere of interest widens; men become interested again in the life that swirls around things legal. Before rules, were facts; in the beginning was not a Word, but a Doing. Behind decisions stand judges; judges are men; as men they have human backgrounds. Beyond rules, again, lie effects: beyond decisions stand people whom rules and decisions directly or indirectly touch. The field of Law reaches both forward and back from the Substantive Law of school and doctrine. The sphere of interest is widening; so, too, is the scope of doubt. *Beyond rules lie effects*—but do they? Are some rules mere paper? And if effects, what effects? Hearsay, unbuttressed guess, assumption or assertion unchecked by test—can such be trusted on this matter of what law is *doing*?

The ferment is proper to the time. The law of schools threatened at the close of the century to turn into words—placid, clear-seeming, lifeless,

---

*\* Jerome Frank refused me permission to sign his name as joint author to this paper, on the ground that it was my fist which pushed the pen. But his generosity does not alter the fact that the paper could not have been written without his help. I therefore write the first sections, in partial recognition, as "We," meaning thereby Frank and myself. In the description of the realists, I turn to the first person singular, partly because any alignment of such diverse work is individually colored; partly because any phrasing which would seem to suggest a non-existent school would be unfortunate.*

---

Reprinted from "Some Realism about Realism—Responding to Dean Pound," 44 *Harvard Law Review* (1931), 1222–1264, by permission of the publisher. Copyright 1931 by The Harvard Law Review Association. Footnotes have been renumbered to run in sequence throughout the selection. The author's appendixes have been omitted, as have references to them.

like some old canal. Practice rolled on, muddy, turbulent, vigorous. It is now spilling, flooding, into the canal of stagnant words. It brings ferment and trouble. So other fields of thought have spilled their waters in: the stress on behavior in the social sciences; their drive toward integration; the physicists' reëxamination of final-seeming premises; the challenge of war and revolution. These stir. They stir the law. Interests of practice claim attention. Methods of work unfamiliar to lawyers make their way in, beside traditional techniques. Traditional techniques themselves are reëxamined, checked against fact, stripped somewhat of confusion. And always there is this restless questing: what *difference* does statute, or rule, or court-decision, make?

Whether this ferment is one thing or twenty is a question; if one thing, it is twenty things in one. But it is with us. It spreads. It is no mere talk. It shows results, results enough through the past decade to demonstrate its value.

And those involved are folk of modest ideals. They want law to deal, they themselves want to deal, with things, with people, with tangibles, with *definite* tangibles, and *observable* relations between definite tangibles—not with words alone; when law deals with words, they want the words to represent tangibles which can be got at beneath the words, and observable relations between those tangibles. They want to check ideas, and rules, and formulas by facts, to keep them close to facts. They view rules, they view law, as means to ends; as only means to ends; as having meaning only insofar as they are means to ends. They suspect, with law moving slowly and the life around them moving fast, that some law may have gotten out of joint with life. This is a question in first instance of fact: what does law *do,* to people, or for people? In the second instance, it is a question of ends: what *ought* law to do to people, or for them? But there is no reaching a judgment as to whether any specific part of present law does what it ought, until you can first answer what it is doing now. To see this, and to be ignorant of the answer, is to start fermenting, is to start trying to find out.

All this is, we say, a simple-hearted point of view, and often philosophically naïve—though it has in it elements enough of intellectual sophistication. It denies very little, except the completeness of the teachings handed down. It knows too little to care about denying much. It affirms ignorance, pitched within and without. It affirms the need to know. Its call is for intelligent effort to dispel the ignorance. Intelligent effort to cut beneath old rules, old words, to get sight of current things. It is not a new point of view; it is as old as man. But its rediscovery in any age, by any man, in any discipline, is joyous.

*   *   *   *

What are the characteristics of the new fermenters? The common points of departure are several.

(1) The conception of law in flux, of moving law, and of judicial creation of law.

(2) The conception of law as a means to social ends and not as an end in itself; so that any part needs constantly to be examined for its purpose, and for its effect, and to be judged in the light of both and of their relation to each other.

(3) The conception of society in flux, and in flux typically faster than the law, so that the probability is always given that any portion of law needs reëxamination to determine how far it fits the society it purports to serve.

(4) The *temporary* divorce of Is and Ought for purposes of study. By this I mean that whereas value judgments must always be appealed to in order to set objectives for inquiry, yet during the inquiry itself into what Is, the observation, the description, and the establishment of relations between the things described are to remain *as largely as possible* uncontaminated by the desires of the observer or by what he wishes might be or thinks ought (ethically) to be. More particularly, this involves during the study of what courts are doing the effort to disregard the question what they ought to do. Such divorce of Is and Ought is, of course, not conceived as permanent. To men who begin with a suspicion that change is needed, a permanent divorce would be impossible. The argument is simply that no judgment of what Ought to be done in the future with respect to any part of law can be intelligently made without knowing objectively, as far as possible, what that part of law is now doing. And realists believe that experience shows the intrusion of Ought-spectacles *during the investigation of the facts* to make it very difficult to see what is being done. On the Ought side this means an insistence on informed evaluations instead of armchair speculations. Its full implications on the side of Is-investigation can be appreciated only when one follows the contributions to objective description in business law and practice made by realists whose social philosophy rejects many of the accepted foundations of the existing eco-

nomic order. (*E.g.,* Handler *re* trade-marks and advertising; Klaus *re* marketing and banking; Llewellyn *re* sales; Moore *re* banking; Patterson *re* risk-bearing.)

(5) Distrust of traditional legal rules and concepts insofar as they purport to *describe* what either courts or people are actually doing. Hence the constant emphasis on rules as "generalized predictions of what courts will do." This is much more widespread as yet than its counterpart: the careful severance of rules *for* doing (precepts) from rules *of* doing (practices).

(6) Hand in hand with this distrust of traditional rules (on the descriptive side) goes a distrust of the theory that traditional prescriptive rule-formulations are *the* heavily operative factor in producing court decisions. This involves the tentative adoption of the theory of rationalization for the study of opinions. It will be noted that "distrust" in this and the preceding point is not at all equivalent to "negation in any given instance."

(7) The belief in the worthwhileness of grouping cases and legal situations into narrower categories than has been the practice in the past. This is connected with the distrust of verbally simple rules—which so often cover dissimilar and non-simple fact situations (dissimilarity being tested partly by the way cases come out, and partly by the observer's judgment as to how they ought to come out; but a realist tries to indicate explicitly which criterion he is applying).

(8) An insistence on evaluation of any part of law in terms of its effects, and an insistence on the worthwhileness of trying to find these effects.

(9) Insistence on *sustained and programmatic attack* on the problems of law along any of these lines. None of the ideas set forth in this list is new. Each can be matched from somewhere; each can be matched from recent orthodox work in law. New twists and combinations do appear here and there. What is as novel as it is vital is for a goodly number of men to pick up ideas which have been expressed and dropped, used for an hour and dropped, played with from time to time and dropped—to pick up such ideas and set about *consistently, persistently, insistently to carry them through*. Grant that the idea or point of view is familiar—the results of steady, sustained, systematic work with it are not familiar. Not hit-or-miss stuff, not the insight which flashes and is forgotten, but sustained

effort to force an old insight into its full bearing, to exploit it to the point where it laps over upon an apparently inconsistent insight, to explore their bearing on each other by the test of fact. This urge, in law, is quite new enough over the last decades to excuse a touch of frenzy among the locust-eaters.[1]

The first, second, third and fifth of the above items, while common to the workers of the newer movement, are not peculiar to them. But the other items (4, 6, 7, 8 and 9) are to me the characteristic marks of the movement. Men or work fitting those specifications are to me "realistic" whatever label they may wear. Such, and none other, are the perfect fauna of this new land. Not all the work cited below fits my peculiar definition in all points. All such work fits most of the points.

Bound, as all "innovators" are, by prior thinking, these innovating "realists" brought their batteries to bear in first instance on the work of appellate courts. Still wholly within the tradition of our law, they strove to improve on that tradition.

(a) An early and fruitful line of attack borrowed from psychology the concept of *rationalization* already mentioned. To recanvass the opinions, viewing them no longer as mirroring the process of deciding cases, but rather as trained lawyers' arguments made by the judges (after the decision has been reached), intended to make the decision seem plausible, legally decent, legally right, to make it seem, indeed, legally inevitable—this was to open up new vision. It was assumed that the deductive logic of opinions need by no means be either a *description* of the process of decision, or an *explanation* of how the decision was reached. Indeed over-enthusiasm has at times assumed that the logic of the opinion *could* be neither; and similar over-enthusiasm, perceiving case after case in which the opinion is clearly almost valueless as an indication of how that case came to decision, has worked at times almost as if the opinion were equally valueless in predicting what a later court will do.[2]

---

[1] *Since everyone who reads the manuscript in this sad age finds this allusion blind, but I still like it, I insert the passage: ". . . Preaching in the wilderness of Judea, And saying, Repent ye. . . . And the same John had his raiment of camel's hair, and a leathern girdle about his loins;* and his meat was locusts *and wild honey." Matthew III, 1, 2, 4.*

[2] E.g., *Tulin*, The Role of Penalties in Criminal Law (*1928*) 37 YALE L. J. *1048; Douglas*, Vicarious Liability and Administration of Risk (*1929*) 38 id. *584*,

But the line of inquiry via rationalization has come close to demonstrating that in any case doubtful enough to make litigation respectable the available authoritative premises—*i.e.*, premises legitimate and impeccable under the traditional legal techniques—are at least two, and that the two are mutually contradictory as applied to the case in hand.[3] Which opens the question of what made the court select the one available premise rather than the other. And which raises the greatest of doubts as to *how far* that supposed certainty in decision which derives merely from the presence of accepted rules really goes.

(b) A second line of attack has been to discriminate among rules with reference to their relative significance. Too much is written and thought about "law" and "rules," lump-wise. Which part of law? Which rule? Iron rules of policy, and rules "in the absence of agreement"; rules which keep a case from the jury, and rules as to the etiquette of instructions necessary to make a verdict stick—if one can get it; rules "of pure decision" for hospital cases, and rules which counsellors rely on in their counselling; rules which affect many (and which many, and how?) and rules which affect few.[4] Such discriminations affect the traditional law curriculum, the traditional organization of law books and, above all, the orientation of study: to drive into the most important fields of ignorance.

(c) A further line of attack on the apparent conflict and uncertainty among the decisions in appellate courts has been to seek more understandable statement of them by grouping the facts in new—and typically but

---

720; *Corbin*, Contracts for the Benefit of Third Persons (*1930*) *46* L. Q. REV. *12*.

*Moore and Oliphant certainly, and I think Sturges, would differ from me, to a greater or less extent, as to how far this is "over-enthusiasm." Moore's three years' quest reached for some more objective technique of prediction. Moore and Sussman, Legal and Institutional Methods Applied to the Debiting of Direct Discounts (1931) 40 YALE L. J. 381, 555, 752, 928. And Oliphant, A Return to Stare Decisis (1928) 14 A. B. A. J. 71, 159, n.5.*

[3] *For a series of examples, see Cook,* The Utility of Jurisprudence in the Solution of Legal Problems *in 5* LECTURES ON LEGAL TOPICS, ASSOCIATION OF THE BAR OF THE CITY OF NEW YORK (*1923–24*) *335; Powell,* Current Conflicts Between the Commerce Clause and State Police Power, 1922–1927 (*1928*) *12* MINN. L. REV. *470, 491, 607, 631.*

[4] *Compare the work of Bohlen and Green on torts; Llewellyn on contracts, for attempts to carry this type of old insight through more consistently.*

not always narrower—categories. The search is for correlations of fact-situation and outcome which (aided by common sense) may reveal *when* courts seize on one rather than another of the available competing premises. One may even stumble on the trail of *why* they do. Perhaps, *e.g.*, third party beneficiary difficulties simply fail to get applied to promises to make provision for dependents;[5] perhaps the preëxisting duty rule goes by the board when the agreement is one for a marriage-settlement.[6] Perhaps, indeed, contracts in what we may broadly call family relations do not work out in general as they do in business.[7] If so, the rules—viewed as statements of the course of judicial behavior—as *predictions* of what will happen—need to be restated. Sometimes it is a question of carving out hitherto unnoticed exceptions. But sometimes the results force the worker to reclassify an area altogether.[8] Typically, as stated, the classes of situations which result are narrower, much narrower than the traditional classes. The process is in essence the orthodox technique of making distinctions, and reformulating—but undertaken systematically; exploited consciously, instead of being reserved until facts which refuse to be twisted by "interpretation" force action.[9] The departure from orthodox procedure lies chiefly in distrust of, instead of search for, the widest sweep

---

[5] *Note* (*1931*) *31* Col. L. Rev. *117*.

[6] *An unpublished study by Moore. Another example is Handler and Pickett,* Trade Marks and Trade Names—An Analysis and Synthesis (*1930*) *30* Col. L. Rev. *168, 759.*

[7] *Perhaps they should not—but that is an Ought question. One will be forced to raise it, if he finds courts in their results persistently evading the consequences of what accepted doctrine declares to be the general rule. Compare Moore and Sussman,* supra *note* [2], *at 555, 557; Oliphant,* supra *note* [2], *at 159, 160.*

[8] *Sometimes the effort fails. Durfee and Duffy,* Foreclosure of Land Contracts in Michigan: Equitable Suit and Summary Proceeding (*1928*) *7 Mich. St. B. J. 166, 221, 236. It is a grateful sign of a growing scientific spirit when* negative *results of investigation come into print.*

[9] *It may not be* convenient *to draw rules for courts to use in terms of these narrower categories. Williston argues that the set of official formulas must not be too complex; they are for "application" by ordinary men, not intellectual giants.* Williston, Some Modern Tendencies in the Law (*1929*) *127. That does not touch the present point. Even with broad formulas prevailing, as at present, one still gets better results in* describing *where courts get to if he thinks in terms of narrower classifications of the facts. But a fair portion of present unpredictability is certainly attributable to the fact that the courts are using official formulas which fit, only part of the time, what the facts seem to call for. Sometimes the facts win, sometimes the formula. See note* [10], *infra.*

of generalization words permit.[10] Not that such sweeping generalizations are not desired—*if they can be made so as to state what judges do.*

All of these three earliest lines of attack converge to a single conclusion: *there is less possibility of accurate prediction of what courts will do than the traditional rules would lead us to suppose*[11] (and what possibility there is must be found in good measure outside these same traditional rules). The particular kind of certainty that men have thus far thought to find in law is in good measure an illusion. Realistic workers have sometimes insisted on this truth so hard that they have been thought pleased with it. (The danger lies close, for one thinking indiscriminately of Is and

---

[10] *When this procedure results in a formulation along lines strikingly unorthodox* (cf. *my own approach to title*—CASES AND MATERIALS ON THE LAW OF SALES (1930)) *but one which the worker finds helpful in prediction or in generalizing results, Dean Pound's query as to* how far *courts achieve certainty by traditional rule and form becomes pressing. At times Moore* (chiefly in conversation), *Oliphant* (supra note [2], *conversation, and theory of contracts*), *and Sturges* (Legal Theory and Real Property Mortgages (1928) 37 YALE L. J. 691), *seem to me to verge upon a position which escapes my understanding: that the judges' reactions to the facts in such cases are only negligibly influenced by the orthodox rules. My experience is that when measures* (here "the rule") *do not fit purposes* (here *the line of discrimination discovered by the fact-issue-judgment approach*) *the result is* always *some inadequacy in accomplishing purposes. And my experience is that when purposes do not become conscious, there is commonly inadequacy at times in locating a measure for their adequate accomplishment.* (Compare Corbin's results on the English cases: *Corbin*, Contracts for the Benefit of Third Persons (1930) 46 L. Q. REV. 12.) *What one has gained by the new formulation, if it proves significant, seems to me to be a tool for clarifying the situation and the purposes; a means of bringing a hidden factor, perhaps* the hidden factor in past uncertainty, *into view; perhaps also a new insight into wise objectives, and so a key for reform. Compare Llewellyn*, What Price Contract?—An Essay in Perspective (1931) 40 YALE L. J. 704, 732, n.62.

[11] *Partly, as I have tried to develop elsewhere* (Llewellyn, Legal Illusion (1931) 31 COL. L. REV. 82, 87; PRÄJUDIZIENRECHT U. RECHTSPRECHUNG IN AMERIKA (1931) § 52 et seq.), *because the "certainty" sought is conceived verbally, and in terms of lawyers, not factually and in terms of laymen. Neither can commonly be had save at the cost of the other. We get enough of each to upset the other. One effect of the realist approach is to center on certainty for laymen and improve the machinery for attaining it. The present dilemma is quickly stated: if there is no certainty in law* (rules and concepts plus *intuition* plus *lawmen's practices*) *why is not any layman qualified to practice or to judge? But if the certainty is what the rule-believers claim, how can two good lawyers disagree about an appealed case? Cf. also . . . Isaacs*, [How Lawyers Think (1923) 23 COL. L. REV. 555], *at 890 et seq.; Isaacs, infra note* [25], *at 211–12.*

Ought, to suspect announcements of fact to reflect preferences, ethically normative judgments, on the part of those who do the announcing.)

But announcements of fact are not appraisals of worth. The contrary holds. The immediate result of the preliminary work thus far described has been a further, varied series of endeavors; *the focussing of conscious attack on discovering the factors thus far unpredictable, in good part with a view to their control.* Not wholly with a view to such elimination; part of the conscious attack is directed to finding where and when and how far *un*certainty has value. Much of what has been taken as insistence on the exclusive significance of the particular (with supposed implicit denial of the existence of valid or apposite generalizations) represents in fact a clearing of the ground for such attack. Close study of particular unpredictables may lessen unpredictability. It may increase the value of what remains. It certainly makes clearer what the present situation is. "Link by link is chain-mail made."

(i) There is the question of the personality of the judge. (Little has as yet been attempted in study of the jury; Frank, *Law and the Modern Mind,* makes a beginning.) Within this field, again, attempts diverge. Some have attempted study of the particular judge[12]—a line that will certainly lead to inquiry into his social conditioning.[13] Some have attempted to bring various psychological hypotheses to bear.[14] All that has

---

[12] E.g., *Powell's insistence on the particular judges in successions of decisions.* Supra *note [3]*; Commerce, Congress, and the Supreme Court, 1922–1925 (*1926*) 26 Col. L. Rev. *396, 521;* . . . The Judiciality of Minimum Wage Legislation (*1924*) 37 Harv. L. Rev. *545;* The Nature of a Patent Right (*1917*) 17 Col. L. Rev. *663; Haines,* General Observations on the Effects of Personal, Political, and Economic Influences in the Decisions of Judges (*1922*) 17 Ill. L. Rev. *96; Brown,* Police Power—Legislation for Health and Personal Safety (*1929*) 42 Harv. L. Rev. *866; Cushman,* The Social and Economic Interpretation of the Fourteenth Amendment (*1922*) 20 Mich. L. Rev. *737;* Frankfurter and Landis, The Business of the Supreme Court (*1928*), *and the supplementary series of articles in* (*1928*) 42 Harv. L. Rev. *1;* (*1929*) 43 id. *1;* (*1930*) 44 id. *1.*

To be added, especially, is the growing volume of judicial self-revelation: Cardozo's work: . . . ; Judge Amidon's beautiful opinion in Great Northern Ry. v. Brousseau, 286 Fed. 414 (D. N. D. 1923); and parts of such earlier work as Young, The Law as an Expression of Community Ideals and the Law Making Functions of Courts (1917) 27 Yale L. J. 1.

[13] *Nelles, Book Review* (*1931*) 40 Yale L. J. *998.*

[14] *Freudian: beginnings in Frank,* Law and the Modern Mind (*1930*). *Behaviorist: an attempt in Patterson,* Equitable Relief for Unilateral Mistake (*1928*) 28 Col. L. Rev. *859. Semi-behaviorist, via cultural anthropology: Moore and Sussman,* supra *note* [2].

become clear is that our government is not a government of laws, but one of laws through men.

(ii) There has been some attempt to work out the varieties of interaction between the traditional concepts (the judge's "legal" equipment for thinking, seeing, judging) and the fact-pressures of the cases.[15] This is a question not—as above—of getting at results on particular facts, but of studying the effect, *e.g.*, of a series of cases in which the facts either press successively in the one direction, or alternate in their pressures and counteract each other. Closely related in substance, but wholly diverse in both method and aim, is study of the machinery by which fact-pressures can under our procedure be brought to bear upon the court.[16]

(iii) First efforts have been made to capitalize the wealth of our reported cases to make large-scale quantitative studies of facts and outcome; the hope has been that these might develop lines of prediction more sure, or at least capable of adding further certainty to the predictions based as hitherto on intensive study of smaller bodies of cases. This represents a more ambitious development of the procedure described above, under (c); I know of no published results.

(iv) Repeated effort has been made to work with the cases of single states, to see how far additional predictability might thus be gained.[17]

---

[15] *Llewellyn in* 3 ENCYCLOPAEDIA OF THE SOCIAL SCIENCES (*1930*) 249; LLEWELLYN, CASES AND MATERIALS ON THE LAW OF SALES (*1930*); PRÄJUDIZIENRECHT U. RECHTSPRECHUNG IN AMERIKA (*1931*). *With which last compare Pound,* A Theory of Judicial Decision (*1923*) 36 HARV. L. REV. *641, 802, esp. 940;* HENDERSON, THE POSITION OF FOREIGN CORPORATIONS IN AMERICAN CONSTITUTIONAL LAW (*1918*); CARDOZO, THE NATURE OF THE JUDICIAL PROCESS (*1925*); *Corbin,* supra *note* [2]; *Haines,* supra *note* [2]; *Berle,* Investors and the Revised Delaware Corporation Act (*1929*) 29 COL. L. REV. *563; Finkelstein,* [Further Notes on Self-Limitation (*1925*) 39 HARV. L. REV. *221*]; *Hamilton,* Judicial Tolerance of Farmers' Cooperatives (*1929*) 38 YALE L. J. *936; . . . .*

[16] *The famous Brandeis brief and its successors mark the beginning. In commercial cases both Germany and England have evolved effective machinery.*

[17] *Here, as throughout, one notes the contact of the realist movement with a tradition of practice (single state law, interest in procedure, "automobile jurisprudence" and the like, damage and procedure points treated in conjunction with the relevant substantive law, interest in the facts and atmosphere) which the older academic tradition was prone to scorn. But this progress backwards takes with it, and fertilizes the practical tradition with, the interest in theory, generality of outlook, and long-range thinking of the older academic tradition. Fortunate media for this type of work are the local law reviews. Such work, long continued, will force a radical revision of thought about "the common law" and, one may*

(v) Study has been attempted of "substantive rules" in the particular light of the available remedial procedure; the hope being to discover in the court's unmentioned knowledge of the immediate consequences of this rule or that, in the case at hand, a motivation for decision which cuts deeper than any shown by the opinion.[18] Related, but distinct, is the reassertion of the fundamental quality of remedy, and the general approach to restating "what the law is" (on the side of prediction) in terms not of rights, but of what can be done: Not only "no remedy, no right," but "precisely as much right as remedy."[19]

(vi) The set-up of men's ways and practices and ideas on the subject matter of the controversy has been studied, in the hope that this might yield a further or even final[0] basis for prediction. The work here ranges from more or less indefinite reference to custom (the historical school), or mores (Corbin),[21] through rough or more careful canvasses[22] of business[3]

---

hope, educate the "national" reviews. See also . . . Kales, An Unsolicited Report on Legal Education (1918) 18 COL. L. REV. 21.

[18] E.g., Tulin, supra note [2], Pound, supra note [15], at 649 et seq. on the art of administrating justice through damages. And cf. the remedy canvass in Patterson, Equitable Relief for Unilateral Mistake (1928) 28 COL. L. REV. 859; Durfee and Duffy, supra note [8].

[19] E.g., Klaus, Identification of the Holder and Tender of Receipt on the Counter Presentation of Checks (1929) 13 MINN. L. REV. 281; Handler, False and Misleading Advertising (1929) 39 YALE L. J. 22; Handler and Pickett, supra note [6]; cf. . . . ; LLEWELLYN, CASES AND MATERIALS ON THE LAW OF SALES c. III.

[20] Moore, An Institutional Approach to the Law of Commercial Banking (1929) 38 YALE L. J. 703; Moore and Sussman, supra note [2], might be so read; or rather, so misread. His study of behavior is not based on a belief that it will by itself lead to final results; it is rather (as is the intelligent behaviorist program in psychology) a "Let us see how far we can get with this" approach. And it is hard to justify a quarrel with that. See Moore and Sussman, supra note [2], at 556–64, esp. 561. And though prediction should be achieved, there still remains the question of Ought—if in no other guise, then as a legislative matter. Compare also L. K. Frank, An Institutional Analysis of the Law (1924) 24 COL. L. REV. 480 (a magnificent example of what the outsider can contribute); . . . ; Ketcham, Law as a Body of Subjective Rules (1929) 23 ILL. L. REV. 360.

[21] Recently becoming much more specific—see Third Parties as Beneficiaries of Contractors' Surety Bonds (1928) 38 YALE L. J. 1.

[22] Ideals here largely outstrip scholarly achievement. But most realist scholars are in their work materially ahead of what they have printed. It should be noted that Douglas' business failures study, [Douglas and Thomas, The Business Failures Project—II, An Analysis of Investigation (1931) 40 YALE L. J. 1034], proceeds to a level comparable to Klaus or Moore.

[23] Or practice in criminal law administration, as in the crime surveys; or on family matters: JACOBS AND ANGELL, A RESEARCH IN FAMILY LAW (1930); Powell

practice and ideology (*e.g.*, Berle, Sturges, Isaacs, Handler, Bogert, Durfee and Duffy, Breckenridge, Turner, Douglas, Shanks, Oliphant, and indeed Holmes) to painstaking and detailed studies in which practice is much more considered than is any prevailing set of ideas about what the practices are (Klaus) or—even—to studies in which the concept of "practice" is itself broken up into behavior-sequences presented with careful note of the degree of their frequency and recurrence, and in which all reference to the actor's own ideas is deprecated or excluded (Moore and Sussman). While grouped here together, under one formula, these workers show differences in degree and manner of interest in the background-ways which range from one pole to the other. Corbin's main interest is the appellate case; most of the second group mentioned rely on semi-special information and readily available material from economics, sociology, etc., with occasional careful studies of their own, and carry a strong interest into drafting or counselling work; Klaus insists on full canvass of all relevant literature, buttressed by and viewed in the light of intensive personal investigation; Moore's canvass and study is so original and thorough in technique as to offer as vital and important a contribution to ethnology and sociology as to banking practice. This is not one "school"; here alone are the germs of many "schools."

(vii) Another line of attack, hardly begun, is that on the effect of the lawyer on the outcome of cases, as an element in prediction. The lawyer *in litigation* has been the subject thus far only of desultory comment.[24] Groping approach has been made to the counsellor as field general, in the business field: in drafting, and in counselling (and so in the building of practices and professional understandings which influence court action later), and in the strategy of presenting cases in favorable series, settling the unfavorable cases, etc.[25]

---

*and Looker,* Decedents' Estates—Illumination from Probate and Tax Records (*1930*) 30 Col. L. Rev. 919.

[24] *One exception is Sturges,* Law's Delays, Lawyers' Delays, and Forwarded Cases (*1928*) 12 Minn. L. Rev. 351; cf. *Wickser,* Bar Associations (*1930*) 15 Corn. L. Q. 390. *Yet no more vital field exists. Consider merely the effect of skilful or dumb-skulled presentation on the growth of case-law.*

[25] *Something of this in Elizabeth Sanford's forthcoming* The Unit Rule; *something in* Llewellyn, Bramble Bush (*1930*) *c. X; and Frederick,* The Trust Receipt as Security (*1922*) 22 Col. L. Rev. 395, 546, *is not only itself a step in such a sequence, but esp. at 409 et seq. presents, in the Farmers and Mechanics Bank cases, thence to importing, and thence to the automobile line, both materials and suggestion for such a study. And see Isaacs,* Business Security and Legal

All of the above has focussed on how to tell what appellate courts will do, however far afield any new scent may have led the individual hunter. But the interest in *effects* on laymen of what the courts will do leads rapidly from this still respectably traditional sphere of legal discussion into a series of further inquiries whose legal decorum is more dubious. They soon extend far beyond what has in recent years been conceived (in regard to the developed state) as law at all. I can not stop to consider these inquiries in detail. Space presses. Each of the following phases could be, and should be, elaborated at least into such a rough sketch as the foregoing. Through each would continue to run interest in what actually eventuates; interest in accurate description of what eventuates; interest in attempting, where prediction becomes uncertain, some conscious attack on hidden factors whose study might lessen the uncertainty; and interest in effects—on laymen. Finally, insistence that Ought-judgment should be bottomed on knowledge. And that action should be bottomed on all the knowledge that can be got in time to act.

I. *There is first the question of what lower courts and especially trial courts are doing, and what relation their doing has to the sayings and doings of upper courts and legislatures.*

Here the question has been to begin to find out, to find some way, some ways, of getting the hitherto unavailable facts, to find some significant way or ways of classifying what business is done, how long it takes, how various parts of the procedural machinery work. (*E.g.,* Warner, Sunderland, Millar, Clark, Yntema, Marshall, Oliphant, Douglas, Arnold, Morgan, Frankfurter, Greene, and Swazie.) Another attack begins by inquiry not into records, but into the process of trial and their effects on the outcome of cases. (Frank, Green.) This, on the civil side, where we have (save for memoirs) been wholly in the dark. On the criminal side, beginnings lie further back. (Pound, Frankfurter, Moley and the Crime Surveys; where lawyers have drawn on the criminologists.) All that is really clear to date is that until we know more here our "rules" give us no remote suggestion of *what law means* to persons in the lower income brackets,[26] and give us misleading suggestions as to the whole body of

---

Security (*1923*) 37 Harv. L. Rev. *201;* . . . Isaacs, How Lawyers Think (*1923*) 23 Col. L. Rev. *555.*

[26] *Little has been done in print to follow up* Reginald Smith's *path-breaking* Justice and the Poor (*1924*); *but allied is the growing literature on poor man's financing and Bradway's work.*

cases unappealed. Meantime, the techniques of the social sciences are being drawn upon and modified to make the work possible.[27]

II. *There is the question of administrative bodies*—not merely on the side of administrative law (itself a novel concept recently enough)—but including all the action which state officials take "under the law" so far as it proves to affect people.[28] And with this we begin departing from the orthodox. To be sure, the practicing lawyer today knows his commission as he knows his court. But the trail thus broken leads into the wilds of government, and politics, and queer events in both.

III. *There is the question of legislative regulation*—in terms of what it *means in action, and to whom,* not merely in terms of what it says. And with that, the question of what goes into producing legislative change—or blocking it[29]—especially so far as the profession participates therein; legislative history on the official record; but as well the background of fact and interest and need. And, no less vital, there is the fact-inquiry into areas of life where maladjustment capable of legal remedy exists.[30]

IV. Finally, and cutting now completely beyond the tradition-bounded area of law, there is the matter not of describing or predicting the action of officials—be they appellate courts, trial courts, legislators, administrators—but of describing and predicting *the effects of their action on the laymen of the community.*[31] "Law" without effect approaches zero

---

[27] *Especially useful W. Clark, Douglas and Thomas* [The Business Failures Project—A Problem in Methodology (*1930*), YALE L. J. *1013*] . . . .

[28] *One may cite generally Freund, Frankfurter, Henderson, Dickinson, Landis, Magill. Also* PATTERSON, THE INSURANCE COMMISSIONER (*1927*); cf. *Stason,* Judicial Review of Tax Errors—Effect of Failure to Resort to Administrative Remedies (*1930*) 28 MICH. L. REV. *637. And much of the Crime Survey and criminological work fits here. So, e.g., Sheldon Glueck, Fosdick.*

[29] *See . . . Berle,* supra *note* [15]; CHILDS, LABOR AND CAPITAL IN NATIONAL POLITICS (*1930*).

[30] *In general* cf. *Berle and Weiner in the corporate field;* FRANKFURTER AND GREENE, THE LABOR INJUNCTION (*1930*); . . . ; *Sunderland. In brief, who not, realist or non-realist, who has ever touched facts and found no solution in case-law? What the realist offers is only thirst for more facts, better gathered, more clearly interpreted. And* not *selected (though accurate) to point an argument. For which reason not all the work just mentioned, despite its value, can count as fully "realistic."*

[31] *I quote Felix Cohen: "In the economic analysis of judicial rules and theories much valuable work has been done by Hale, Bonbright, Richberg, Henderson, Julius Cohen, Goddard and Weiner, particularly in the field of public utility valuation. Otherwise there is simply the call for facts, e.g., Weiner,* Payment of Dissent-

in its meaning. To be ignorant of its effect is to be ignorant of its meaning. To know its effect without study of the persons whom it affects is impossible. Here the antecedents of court action touch its results. To know law, then, to know *anything* of what is necessary to judge or evaluate law, we must proceed into these areas which have traditionally been conceived (save by the historical school) as not-law. Not only what courts do instead of what courts say, but also what difference it makes to anybody that they do it. And no sooner does one begin such a study than it becomes clear that there can be no broad talk of "law" nor of "the community"; but that it is a question of reaching the particular part of the community relevant to some particular part of law. There are persons

---

ing Stockholders *(1927) 27* Col. L. Rev. *547." Except that the "otherwise" comes several lines too soon, I concur in toto. As to the point of difference, before I even open the books to search I think, e.g., of Breckenridge, J. M. Clark, J. R. Commons, Douglas, Fredericks, Herman Finkelstein, Handler, Kidd, Klaus, Patterson, Radin, Ripley, Roscoe Turner, Vold, Wilbert Ward, all (save Clark and Commons) as to work inside the field of private commercial law.*

*Such analysis seems to be on the increase. Comparing e.g., the Cornell Law Quarterly, vols. 14–16 with vols. 4–6, and the Michigan Law Review, vols. 27–29 with vols. 17–19, one finds both reference to facts and analysis of effects of rules of private law increasing—not so much in frequency as in scope and care and objectivity, and integration into the essential framework of the papers. (On public law the older material often rivals the recent; the fact-impetus developed there earlier.) Striking in the earlier materials is Rogers,* An Account of Some Psychological Experiments on the Subject of Trade-Mark Infringement *(1919) 18* Mich. L. Rev. *75; but perhaps even more striking is that in the later, Billig,* What Price Bankruptcy: A Plea for "Friendly Adjustment" *(1929) 14* Corn. L. Q. *413 (and compare Billig,* Extra-Judicial Administration of Insolvent Estates: A Study of Recent Cases *(1930) 78* U. of Pa. L. Rev. *293) using figures and more systematic approach to facts and effects, does not stand alone, but stirs up prompt and competent discussion of his data, not merely of his conclusions; Gamer,* On Comparing "Friendly Adjustment" and Bankruptcy *(1930) 16* Corn L. Q. *35. Competent discussion is to the single study what the incorporation of a new tool of approach into a thinker's standard working kit is to the insight which once came and then was forgotten. Compare my own use of risk-allocation as early as 1920, Implied Warranties of Wholesomeness Again (1920) 29* Yale L. J. *782, only to wholly overlook it in 1922 in a problem that shrieked for its use (*Certified Altered Checks Under the Negotiable Instruments Law *(1922) 31 id. 522) and to almost disregard it in two papers in 1923, both in fields where it yields results.* Supervening Impossibility of Performing Conditions Precedent in the Law of Negotiable Paper *(1923) 23* Col. L. Rev. *142;* C. I. F. Contracts in American Law *(1923) 32* Yale L. J. *711. In short I did not have the idea in 1920; I had had it then—once. Contrast its consistent employment, wherever it promised help, since 1925. It is the growing normality of appeal to facts and of their critical use which marks the intrusion of this aspect of realism into the literature.*

sought to be affected, and persons not sought to be affected. Of the former, some are not in fact materially affected (the gangster-feud); of the latter, some are (depositors in a failing bank which the banking laws have *not* controlled). . . . There is the range of questions as to those legal "helpful devices" (corporation,[32] contract, lease) designed to make it easier for men to get where they want and what they want. There is all the information social scientists have gathered to be explored, in its bearings on the law. There is all the information they have not been interested in gathering, likewise to be explored—but first, to be gathered.

Here are the matters one or another of the new fermenters is ploughing into. Even the sketchy citations here are enough to make clear that their lines of work organize curiously into a whole.

But again rises the query: are the matters *new?* What realist knows so little of law or the ways of human thought as to make such a claim? Which of the inquiries has not been made, or started, or adumbrated in the past? Which of the techniques does not rest on our prior culture? New, I repeat, is one thing only: the *systematic* effort to carry one problem through, to carry a succession of problems through, to *consistently,* not occasionally, choose the best available technique, to *consistently* keep description on the descriptive level, to *consistently* distinguish the fact basis which will feed evaluation from the evaluation which it will later feed, to *consistently* seek *all* the relevant data one can find to *add* to the haphazard single-life experience, to *add* to general common sense.

Is it not obvious that—if this be realism—realism is a mass of trends in legal work and thinking? (1) They have their common core, present to some extent wherever realistic work is done: recognition of law as means; recognition of change in society that may call for change in law; interest in what happens; interest in effects; recognition of the need for effort toward keeping perception of the facts uncolored by one's views on Ought; a distrust of the received set of rules and concepts as adequate indications of what is happening in the courts; a drive toward narrowing the categories of description. (2) They have grown out of the study of the

---

[32] *The literature here is vast. Peculiarly striking Weiner,* Conflictng Functions of the Upset Price in a Corporate Reorganization *(1927)* 27 Col. L. Rev. 132; *Douglas and Shanks,* Insulation from Liability Through Subsidiary Corporations *(1930)* 39 Yale L. J. *193; Posner,* Liability of the Trustee Under the Corporate Indenture *(1928)* 42 Harv. L. Rev. *198; Berle,* Corporate Powers as Powers in Trust *(1931)* 44 Harv. L. Rev. *1049.*

action of appellate courts, and that study still remains their potent stimulus. Uncertainty in the action of such courts is one main problem: to find the why of it; to find means to reduce it, where it needs reduction; to find where it needs reduction, where expansion. (3) But into the work of lower courts, of administrative bodies, of legislatures, of the life which lies before and behind law, the ferment of investigation spreads.

\*　\*　\*　\*

# THE SOCIOLOGICAL
# CONCEPT OF LAW

*Max Weber*

1. *The Sociological Concept of Law.* When we speak of
"law," "legal order," or "legal proposition" (*Rechtssatz*), close attention
must be paid to the distinction between the legal and the sociological
points of view. Taking the former, we ask: What is intrinsically valid as
law? That is to say: What significance or, in other words, what *normative*
meaning ought to be attributed in correct logic to a verbal pattern having
the form of a legal proposition. But if we take the latter point of view, we
ask: What *actually* happens in a community owing to the *probability* that
persons participating in the communal activity (*Gemeinschaftshandeln*),
especially those wielding a socially relevant amount of power over the
communal activity, subjectively consider certain norms as valid and practically act according to them, in other words, orient their own conduct
towards these norms? This distinction also determines, in principle, the
relationship between *law* and *economy*.

The juridical point of view, or, more precisely, that of legal dogmatics[1] aims at the correct meaning of propositions the content of which
constitutes an order supposedly determinative for the conduct of a defined

---

[1] *Legal dogmatics* (dogmatische Rechtswissenschaft)—*the term frequently used
in German to mean the legal science of the law itself as distinguished from such
ways of looking upon law from the outside as philosophy, history, or sociology of
law.*

---

Reprinted by permission of the editor and of the publishers from Max Rheinstein, editor,
*Max Weber Law and Economy in Society,* pp. 11–20 (Section 1 of Chapter II), Cambridge, Mass.: Harvard University Press, Copyright, 1956, by the President and Fellows
of Harvard College. Editor's selection title. Footnotes have been renumbered to run in
sequence throughout the selection.

group of persons: in other words, it tries to define the facts to which this order applies and the way in which it bears upon them. Toward this end, the jurist, taking for granted the empirical validity of the legal propositions, examines each of them and tries to determine its logically correct meaning in such a way that all of them can be combined in a system which is logically coherent, i.e., free from internal contradictions.

Sociological economics,[2] on the other hand, contemplates the interconnections of human activities as they actually take place and as they are conditioned by their necessary orientation toward the "economic situation of facts." We shall thus use the term "economic order" for the situation which arises from the combination of the following two factors, viz., first, the mode of distribution of factual power over goods and economic services as it emerges consensually from the process of balancing conflicting interests; and, second, the mode in which both goods and services are actually used by virtue of that power and the underlying intentions.

It is obvious that these two approaches deal with entirely different problems and that their "objectives" cannot come directly into contact with one another. The ideal "legal order" of legal theory has nothing directly to do with the world of real economic conduct, since both exist on different levels. One exists in the ideal realm of the "ought," while the other deals with the real world of the "is." If it is nevertheless said that the economic and the legal order are intimately related to one another, the latter is understood, not in the legal, but in the sociological sense, i.e., as being *empirically* valid. In this context "legal order" thus assumes a totally different meaning. It refers, not to a set of norms of logically demonstrable correctness, but rather to a complex of actual determinants (*Bestimmungsgründe*) of actual human conduct. This point requires further elaboration.

The fact that some persons act in a certain way because they regard it as prescribed by legal propositions (*Rechtssaetze*) is, of course, an essential element in the actual emergence and continued operation of a "legal order." But . . . it is by no means necessary that all, or even a majority, of those who engage in such conduct, do so from this motivation. As a matter of fact, such a situation has never occurred. The broad mass of the

---

[2] Sozialökonomie—*the term used in the title of the encyclopedic series of which* WEBER's ECONOMY AND SOCIETY *forms part, and meant to indicate the author's endeavor to present the economic order as a constituent part of the phenomena of social life. . . .*

participants act in a way corresponding to legal norms, not out of obedience regarded as a legal obligation, but either because the environment approves of the conduct and disapproves of its opposite, or merely as a result of unreflective habituation to a regularity of life that has engraved itself as a custom. If the latter attitude were universal, the law would no longer "subjectively" be regarded as such, but would be observed as custom. However slight, objectively, may be the chance of the coercive apparatus . . . enforcing, in a given situation, compliance with those norms, we nevertheless have to consider them as "law." Neither is it necessary—according to what was said above—that all those who share a belief in certain norms of behavior, actually live in accordance with that belief at all times. Such a situation, likewise, has never obtained, nor need it obtain, since, according to our general definition, it is the "orientation" of an action toward a norm, rather than the "success" of that norm that is decisive for its validity. "Law," as understood by us, is simply an "order system" endowed with certain specific guarantees of the probability of its empirical validity.

The term "guaranteed law" shall be understood to mean that there exists a "coercive apparatus," i.e., that there are one or more persons whose special task it is to hold themselves ready to apply specially provided means of coercion (legal coercion) for the purpose of norm enforcement. The means of coercion may be physical or psychological, they may be direct or indirect in their operation, and they may be directed, as the case may require, against the participants in the consensual community (*Einverstaendnisgemeinschaft*), the consociation, the corporate body or the institution within which the order system is (empirically) valid; or they may be aimed at those outside. They are the "legal norms" of the community in question.

By no means all norms which are consensually valid in a community—as we shall see later—are "legal norms." Nor are all official functions of the persons constituting the coercive apparatus of a community concerned with legal coercion; we shall rather consider as legal coercion only those actions whose intention is the enforcement of conformity to a norm as such, i.e., because of its being formally accepted as binding. The term will not be applied, however, where conformity of conduct to a norm is sought to be produced because of considerations of expediency or other material circumstances. It is obvious that the effectuation of the validity of a norm may in fact be pursued for the most diverse motives. However, we shall designate it as "guaranteed law" only in those cases where there exists the probability that coercion, that is, legal coercion, will be applied "for its own sake." As we shall have opportunity to see, not all law is guaranteed law. We shall speak of law—albeit in the sense of "indirectly guaranteed" or "unguaranteed" law—also in all those cases where the validity of a norm consists in the fact that the mode of orientation of an action toward it has some "legal consequences"; i.e., that there are other norms which associate with the "observance" or "infringement" of the primary norm certain probabilities of consensual action guaranteed, in their turn, by legal coercion.

We shall have occasion to illustrate this case, which occurs in a large area of legal life. However, in order to avoid further complication, whenever we shall use the term "law" without qualification, we shall mean norms which are directly guaranteed by legal coercion. Such "guaranteed law" is by no means in all cases guaranteed by "violence" in the sense of the prospect of physical coercion. In our terminology, law, including "guaranteed law" is not characterized sociologically by violence or, even less, by that modern technique of effectuating claims of private law through bringing "suit" in a "court," followed by coercive execution of the judgment obtained. The sphere of "public" law, i.e., the norms governing the conduct of the organs of the state and the activities carried on within the framework of public administration and in relation to itself . . . recognizes numerous rights and legal norms, upon the infringement of which a coercive apparatus can be set in motion only through the "remonstrance" by members of a limited group of persons, and often without any means of physical coercion. Sociologically, the question of whether or not guaranteed law exists in such a situation depends on the availability of an organized coercive apparatus for the nonviolent exercise of legal coercion. This apparatus must also possess such power that there is in fact a significant probability that the norm will be respected because of the possibility of recourse to such legal coercion.

Today legal coercion by violence is the monopoly of the state. All other consociations applying legal coercion by violence are today considered as heteronomous and mostly also as heterocephalous.[3] This view is

---

[3] *Heteronomous—receiving its order from the outside; opposite—autonomous; heterocephalous—headed by one who is not chosen by the members of the group in question, as, for instance, the Governor of the Territory of Hawaii, who is appointed by the President of the United States.*

characteristic, however, only of certain stages of development. We shall speak of "state" law, i.e., of law guaranteed by the state, only when, and to the extent that, the guaranty for it, that is, legal coercion, is exercised through the specific, i.e., normally direct and *physical,* means of coercion of the political community. Thus, the existence of a "legal norm" in the sense of "state law" means that the following situation obtains: In the case of certain events occurring there is general agreement that certain organs of the community can be expected to go into official action, and the very expectation of such action is apt to induce conformity with the commands derived from the generally accepted interpretation of that legal norm; or, where such conformity has become unattainable, at least to effect reparation or "indemnification." The event inducing this consequence, the legal coercion by the state, may consist in certain human acts, for instance, the conclusion or the breach of a contract, or the commission of a tort. But this type of occurrence constitutes only a special instance, since, upon the basis of some empirically valid legal proposition, the coercive instruments of the political powers against persons and things may also be applied where, for example, a river has risen above a certain level. It is in no way inherent, however, in the validity of a legal norm as normally conceived, that those who obey do so, predominantly or in any way, because of the availability of such a coercive apparatus as defined above. The motives for obedience may rather be of many different kinds. In the majority of cases, they are predominantly utilitarian or ethical or subjectively conventional, i.e., consisting of the fear of disapproval by the environment. The nature of these motives is highly relevant in determining the kind and the degree of validity of the law itself. But in so far as the formal sociological concept of guaranteed law, as we intend to use it, is concerned, these psychological facts are irrelevant. In this connection nothing matters except that there be a sufficiently high probability of intervention on the part of a specially designated group of persons, even in those cases where nothing has occurred but the sheer fact of a norm infringement, i.e., on purely formal grounds.

The empirical validity of a norm as a legal norm affects the interests of an individual in many respects. In particular, it may convey to an individual certain calculable chances of having economic goods available or of acquiring them under certain conditions in the future. Obviously, the creation or protection of such chances is normally one of the aims of law enactment by those who agree upon a norm or impose it upon others.

There are two ways in which such a "chance" may be attributed. The attribution may be a mere by-product of the empirical validity of the norm; in that case the norm is not *meant* to guarantee to an individual the chance which happens to fall to him. It may also be, however, that the norm is specifically meant to provide to the individual such a guaranty, in other words, to grant him a "right." Sociologically, the statement that someone has a right by virtue of the legal order of the state thus normally means the following: He has a chance, factually guaranteed to him by the consensually accepted interpretation of a legal norm, of invoking in favor of his ideal or material interests the aid of a "coercive apparatus" which is in special readiness for this purpose. This aid consists, at least normally, in the readiness of certain persons to come to his support in the event that they are approached in the proper way, and that it is shown that the recourse to such aid is actually guaranteed to him by a "legal norm." Such guaranty is based simply upon the "validity" of the legal proposition, and does not depend upon questions of expediency, discretion, grace, or arbitrary pleasure.

A law, thus, is valid wherever legal help in this sense can be obtained in a relevant measure, even though without recourse to physical or other drastic coercive means. A law can also be said to be valid, viz., in the case of unguaranteed law, if its violation, as, for instance, that of an electoral law, induces, on the ground of some empirically valid norm, legal consequences, for instance, the invalidation of the election, for the execution of which an agency with coercive powers has been established.

For purposes of simplification we shall pass by those "chances" which are produced as mere "by-products." A "right," in the context of the "state," is guaranteed by the coercive power of the political authorities. Wherever the means of coercion which constitute the guaranty of a "right" belong to some authority other than the political, for instance, a hierocracy, we shall speak of "extra-state law."

A discussion of the various categories of such extra-state law would be out of place in the present context. All we need to recall is that there exist nonviolent means of coercion which may have the same or, under certain conditions, even greater effectiveness than the violent ones. Frequently, and in fairly large areas even regularly, the threat of such measures as the exclusion from an organization or a boycott, or the prospect of magically conditioned advantages or disadvantages in this world or of reward and punishment in the next, are under certain cultural conditions more effective in producing certain behavior than a political apparatus whose coercive functioning is not always predictable with certainty. Legal forcible coercion exercised by the coercive apparatus of the political community has often come off badly as compared with the coercive power of other, e.g., religious, authorities. In general, the actual scope of its efficiency depends on the circumstances of each concrete case. Within the realm of sociological reality, legal coercion continues to exist, however, as long as some socially *relevant* effects are produced by its power machinery.

2. *State Law and Extra-State Law.* The assumption that a state "exists" only if and when the coercive means of the political community are superior to *all* others, is anti-sociological. "Ecclesiastical law" is still law even where it comes into conflict with "state" law, as it has happened many times and as it is bound to happen again in the case of the relations between the modern state and certain churches, for instance, the Roman-Catholic. In imperial Austria, the Slavic *Zadruga* not only lacked any kind of legal guaranty by the state, but some of its norms were outright contradictory to the official law. . . . Since the consensual action constituting a *Zadruga* has at its disposal its own coercive apparatus for the enforcement of its norms, these norms are to be considered as "law." Only the state, if invoked, would refuse recognition and proceed, through its coercive power, to break it up.

Outside the sphere of the European-Continental legal system, it is no rare occurrence at all that modern state law explicitly treats as "valid" the norms of other corporate groups and reviews their concrete decisions. American law thus protects labor union labels or regulates the conditions under which a candidate is to be regarded as "validly" nominated by a party. English judges intervene, on appeal, in the judicial proceedings of a club. Even on the continent German judges investigate, in defamation cases, the propriety of the rejection of a challenge to a duel, even though duelling is forbidden by law.[4] We shall not enter into a casuistic inquiry into the extent to which such norms thus become "state law." For all the reasons given above and, in particular, for the sake of terminological consistency, we categorically deny that "law" exists only where legal

---

[4] *Weber was himself involved in a suit of this kind when, in 1911, he brought action against a faculty colleague at the University of Heidelberg who had spread the—false—rumor that Weber, when insulted, had rejected a challenge to a duel;* see MARIANNE WEBER, MAX WEBER, EIN LEBENSBILD (*2nd ed. 1951*) 472.

coercion is guaranteed by the political authority. There is no practical reason for such a terminology. A "legal order" shall rather be said to exist wherever coercive means, of a physical or psychological kind, are available; i.e., wherever they are at the disposal of one or more persons who hold themselves ready to use them for this purpose in the case of certain events; in other words, wherever we find a consociation specifically dedicated to the purpose of "legal coercion." The possession of such an apparatus for the exercise of physical coercion has not always been the monopoly of the political community. As far as psychological coercion is concerned, there is no such monopoly even today, as demonstrated by the importance of law guaranteed only by the church.

We have also indicated already that direct guaranty of law and of rights by a coercive apparatus constitutes only one instance of the existence of "law" and of "rights." Even within this limited sphere the coercive apparatus can take on a great variety of forms. In marginal cases, it may consist in the consensually valid chance of coercive intervention by *all* the members of the community in the event of an infringement of a valid norm. However, in that case one cannot properly speak of a "coercive apparatus" unless the conditions under which participation in such coercive intervention is to be obligatory, are firmly fixed. In those cases where the protection of rights is guaranteed by the organs of the political authority, the coercive apparatus may be reinforced by pressure groups: the strict regulations of associations of creditors and landlords, especially their blacklists of unreliable debtors or tenants, often operate more effectively than the prospect of a lawsuit. It goes without saying that this kind of coercion may be extended to claims which the state does not guarantee at all; such claims are nevertheless based on *rights* even though they are guaranteed by authorities other than the state. The law of the state often tries to obstruct the coercive means of other consociations; the English Libel Act thus tries to preclude blacklisting by excluding the defense of truth. But the state is not always successful. There are groups stronger than the state in this respect, for instance, those groups and associations, usually based on social class, which rely on the "honor code" of the duel as the means of resolving conflicts. With courts of honor and boycott as the coercive means at their disposal, they usually succeed in compelling, with particular emphasis, the fulfillment of obligations as "debts of honor," for instance, gambling debts or the duty to engage in a duel; such debts are intrinsically connected with the specific purposes of the group in question, but, as far as the state is concerned, they are not recognized, or are even proscribed. But the state has been forced, at least partially, to trim its sails.

It would indeed be bad legal reasoning to demand that such a specific delict as duelling be punished as "attempted murder" or assault and battery. Those crimes are of a quite different character. But it remains a fact that in Germany the readiness to participate in a duel is still a *legal* obligation imposed by the state upon its army officers even though the duel is expressly forbidden by the Criminal Code.[5] The State itself has connected legal consequences with an officer's failure to comply with the honor code. Outside of the class of army officers the situation is different, however. The typical means of statutory coercion applied by "private" organizations against refractory members is exclusion from the corporate body and its tangible or intangible advantages. In the professional organizations of physicians and lawyers as well as in social or political clubs, it is the *ultima ratio*. The modern political organization has to a large extent usurped the application of these measures of coercion. Thus, recourse to them has been denied to the physicians and lawyers in Germany; in England the state courts have been given jurisdiction to review, on appeal, exclusions from clubs; and in America the courts have power over political parties as well as the right of reviewing, on appeal, the legality of the use of a union label.

This conflict between the means of coercion of the various corporate groups is as old as the law itself. In the past it has not always ended with the triumph of the coercive means of the political body, and even today this has not always been the outcome. A party, for instance, who has violated the code of the group, has no remedy against a systematic attempt to drive him out of business by underselling. Similarly, there is no protection against being blacklisted for having availed oneself of the plea of illegality of a contract in futures. In the Middle Ages the prohibitions of resorting to the ecclesiastical court contained in the statutes of certain merchants' guilds were clearly invalid from the point of view of canon law, but they persisted nonetheless. . . .

To a considerable extent the state must tolerate the coercive power of organizations even in cases where it is directed not only against members, but also against outsiders on whom the organization tries to impose its own norms. Illustrations are afforded by the efforts of cartels to force

---

[5] *Written before the Revolution of 1918.*

outsiders into membership, or by the measures taken by creditors' associations against debtors and tenants.

An important marginal case of coercively guaranteed law, in the sociological sense, is presented by that situation which may be regarded as the very opposite of that which is presented by the modern political communities as well as by those religious communities which apply their own "laws." In the modern communities the law is guaranteed by a "judge" or some other "organ" who is an impartial and disinterested umpire rather than a person who would be characterized by a special relationship with one or the other of the parties. In the situation which we have in mind the means of coercion are provided by those very persons who are linked to the party by close personal relationship, for example, as members of his kinship group. Just as war under modern international law, so under these conditions "vengeance" and "feud" are the only, or at least, the normal, forms of law enforcement. In this case, the "right" of the individual consists, sociologically seen, in the mere probability that the members of his kinship group will respond to their obligation of supporting his feud and blood vengeance (an obligation primarily guaranteed by fear of the wrath of supernatural authorities) and that they will possess strength sufficient to support the right claimed by him even though out necessarily to achieve its final triumph.

The term "legal relationship" will be applied to designate that situation in which the content of a right is constituted by a relationship, i.e., the actual or potential actions of concrete persons or of persons to be identified by concrete criteria. The rights contained in a legal relationship may vary in accordance with the actually occurring actions. In this sense a state can be designated as a legal relationship, even in the hypothetical marginal case in which the ruler alone is regarded as endowed with rights (the right to give orders) and where, accordingly, the opportunities of all the other individuals are reduced to reflexes of his regulations.

# WHAT IS "SOCIOLOGY OF LAW"?

*Nicholas S. Timasheff*

[Abstract omitted.]

Since olden times, law has been the object of a science called "jurisprudence." This science has had a glorious record, numbering in its annals many famous names and immortal treatises. It is a many-branched science, which has developed into a network of numerous special sciences called "civil law," "criminal law," "constitutional law," and so forth. Is there room in this field for still another science, that of "sociology of law"? Or is "sociology of law" only a new name for a science known for centuries?

Yes, there is room. No, it is not a new name for an old science. Law is, of course, the center of interest for both; but the points of view are quite different and therefore also the knowledge gained by them.

Law is a cultural force. Its function is that of imposing norms of conduct or patterns of social behavior on the individual will. It is the aim of jurisprudence to study these norms. This study may be carried out with regard to norms in force in a certain country at a given time. Each single norm has to be explained and elucidated: for very often they appear in forms far from clear. Different norms have to be brought into correlation

Reprinted from 43 *American Journal of Sociology* (1937), 225–235, by permission of the author and of The University of Chicago Press. Copyright 1937 by The University of Chicago Press. Footnotes have been renumbered to run in sequence throughout the selection.

with one another: for their true meaning appears only by comparison and contrast. Classifying them and working them into precise systems forms another task of jurisprudence. Finally, the norms of conduct included in law are sometimes not directly expressed, but only indirectly mentioned in other norms; therefore true juridical discoveries are possible. Such are the tasks of positive or analytical jurisprudence. They are, of course, arduous but attractive tasks.

The concrete norms of conduct forming law may be also studied from the historical point of view. Instead of describing in detail the norms applied today in a certain country, we may analyze the gradual development of the principal norms within certain periods in a given country. Such a study is undertaken by historical jurisprudence.

In both analytical and historical jurisprudence the comparative method may be applied: legal norms are studied with regard to a group of countries the social structures of which present or presented some similitude. This is the task of comparative jurisprudence.

Finally, the structure of the legal norms presents, at all times and places, some unchangeable features which may be considered as belonging to the very essence of law. Studying this unchangeable form of the patterns, their natural elements, is the task of theoretical jurisprudence.

In all these cases the norms of conduct as such remain the object of study. This is, in spite of the opinion of many scientists,[1] a study of actuality, and not a study belonging to the domain of evaluation—for the social patterns of behavior included in law actually exist, forming a part of culture. Rules of evaluation are the objects of jurisprudence, but in their relation to actuality. Finding out the logical interdependence between various individual norms is the main task of this science; logical analysis is therefore its chief method.

There is another actuality, closely related to these norms, but not studied in jurisprudence. This is human behavior in society, in so far as it is determined by these norms and in so far as it determines these norms or patterns of behavior.

In general, legal norms actually determine human behavior in society: the triumph of law is the rule, its defeat in a concrete case an exception.

---

[1] For instance, H. Kelsen, Der juristische und der soziologische Staatsbegriff (Tübingen, 1922).

Why is this so? What is the force of law? How does law determine human behavior in society? What are the conditions for the efficacy or nonefficacy of legal norms—in other words, of adjusting or not adjusting human behavior to the particular social patterns of behavior forming law? This is the first group of questions which stand outside the true domain of jurisprudence and which form the first field for the sociological investigation of law.

On the other hand, the legal norms or social patterns of behavior are creations of human will, of the corporate will of social groups. What are the forces determining the creation, the transformation, and the destruction of the juridical patterns of behavior? This is a second group of questions related to law, but standing outside the true domain of jurisprudence and forming another field for the sociological investigation of law. Chains of human actions and reactions must be searched for, chains in which legal norms and configurations of human behavior determined by these norms play alternately the roles corresponding to the active and the passive voices of verbs.

When such chains of action have been discovered and accurately described, a third task may be undertaken: that of establishing correlations, causal or logico-meaningful,[2] between changes in law and changes in other social phenomena, as well as between certain legal structures and certain social structures. Searching for such correlations without an accurate knowledge of law as an actual social phenomenon would be a hopeless enterprise. The absence of precise causal knowledge of many social phenomena is one of the reasons why the study of social correlations results in rather negative or indeterminate statements.[3] Especially in criminology, where knowledge of the factors correlated with crime is essential, the idea is sometimes expressed that, without a scientific knowledge of legal behavior and of its factors, scientific statements concerning the genesis of crime are almost impossible.

Human behavior in society, in so far as it is related to law, is the object of the new science, called "sociology of law." Causal investigation is its chief method.

*　　*　　*　　*

---

[2] P. A. Sorokin, Social and Cultural Dynamics (New York, 1937), Vol. 1, chap. 1.

[3] P. A. Sorokin, Contemporary Sociological Theories (New York, and London 1928), pp. 279, 326, 403, 422, 598, and passim.

But the sociological approach forms necessarily only a kind of adjunct to the analytical, historical, comparative, or theoretical study of legal norms: for it is impossible to construct a system of knowledge which would, in an accurate way, combine the formal study of norms and the causal study of human behavior related to these norms. Such a study needs a place by the side of jurisprudence, but not within jurisprudence.

Very instructive, from this point of view, is the recent history of the science of criminal law. C. Lombroso's revolutionary accomplishments[4] resulted in attempts to rebuild this science completely, to replace the formal study of patterns of prohibited behavior described in criminal statutes by a causal study of crime and the effects of punishment, and later in attempts to combine both points of view into one system. All attempts of the latter kind were a complete failure, and today a resolute separation is again prevailing—there is a science of criminal law, studying in an analytical, historical, or comparative way the patterns of prohibited behavior, and another science called criminology, studying actual human behavior in so far as it is related to crime and punishment.[5] Both should, of course, occupy definite and honorable places on the general map of scientific knowledge.

The content of the sociology of law depends on the structure of the social phenomenon called law. This is a complex, secondary phenomenon. Two primary social phenomena, those of ethics and of power, are united in it. Norms of conduct imposed upon the individual will are included not only in law, but also in morals and custom; morals, custom, and law are the ethical forces, together forming ethics. On the other hand, the strength of law, the juridical pressure on human behavior, may be considered as the display of the social energy concentrated in organized social power. But the display of this energy is not peculiar to law: social power may dominate over individuals by means of law as well as outside law, forming in that case despotical rule.[6] Social power may act without any connection with ethics, just as ethics may exist without any connection with social power. Therefore the notions of ethics and power are not two co-ordinated

---

[4] C. Lombroso, L'Uomo delinquente (1st ed., 1876).

[5] In spite of this conclusive experience, M. Rumpf proposes to include the sociology of law in a "total" jurisprudence. ("Was ist Rechtssoziologie?" Archiv für zivilistische Praxis [1924], pp. 36–51.)

[6] R. von Stammler, Recht und Wilkür (Halle, 1895); Die Lehre vom richtigen Rechte (2d ed.; Halle, 1926).

or subordinated notions. They may be considered as two circles which cross each other. The overlapping section is law.[7]

Were a sociology of ethics and a sociology of power already in existence, the sociology of law might be based upon the results of these sciences and be limited to the study of the joint action of ethics and of power, of ethics supported by power, or of power limited by ethics. But neither of these sciences yet exists. Therefore the sociology of law has to begin by studying, from the causal point of view, the phenomenon of ethics, to continue by studying, from the same point of view, the phenomenon of power, and to conclude by an analysis of the complex phenomenon formed by the joint action of both.

What are the materials to be used and the methods to be applied when constructing a scientific theory of law as of an actual social phenomenon?

In the first place, important material may be collected by means of observation, which may be of two types. The first is introspection, i.e., accurate subsequent analysis of one's state of consciousness in so far as it is related to law (acting according to law, acting against the law, acting with the intent of transforming law, reaction produced by another's acting in accordance with or against law). A prominent representative of the theoretical trend in jurisprudence, Professor G. Gurvitch, insists in his latest work on the necessity of studying the specific actuality presented by law and of beginning this study with the analysis of the "immediate juridical experience." This experience is given in acts of legislators, of authorities, of electors, of persons contracting settlements, of persons taking part in the juridical life of corporate bodies—only this interpretation gives to these acts the character of being related to law. But this type of experience is, according to his opinion, veiled in the minds of the actors by too much reflection and conceptual formulation. Gradual reduction and "inversion" have to be applied in order to gain the needed knowledge.[8] This is, I may add, a method analogous to that applied by Freud's school when investigating subconscious psychic currents.

---

[7] For a more detailed exposition of the relation of law to ethics and to power see my article, "Le Droit, l'éthique, le pouvoir," Archives de philosophie du droit et de sociologie juridique (1936), Nos. 1–2.

[8] G. Gurvitch, L'Expérience juridique et la philosophie pluraliste du droit (Paris, 1935), pp. 13, 63.

The second type of observation studies human behavior determined by law or relative to law. Material collected by those pursuing the sociological trend in jurisprudence may be very useful in so far as it shows how rigid legal formulas are transformed in actual life, or how (for example) unjust or antiquated laws are avoided. For jurisprudence with this sociological tendency the transformed norms are the objects of study, replacing the dead rules included in written law.[9] For the sociology of law—not the transformed norms of conduct, but the fact of their transformation—is interesting, and thus creates an incentive for studying, in general, the process of modifying patterns of written law by means of conflicts with other social phenomena and structures. The sociology of law does not have to be limited by data of such a type. Direct and special observation may also be applied in order to investigate such problems as, for instance, the role of conditioned reflexes in securing the triumph of law. The idea that social control, especially control by means of law, is based upon conditioned reflexes, is sometimes expressed in social psychology.[10] But there is no precise study of how this control is effected, and which are the unconditioned reflexes forming the basis of the conditioned. I. Pavlov suggests especially the study of the reflexes of freedom and submission.[11]

Experiment has to join observation. Introspective experiments are proposed by Professor L. Petrajitsky. According to him, juridical or (in general) ethical impulses may be successfully studied, applying the methods of contradiction and of teasing; impulses increase in force if attempts are made to hinder their normal running, or if rapid changes of the situation occur, alternately decreasing and increasing the chances for realizing the impulses. In such cases these impulses, which are almost imperceptible when they develop in a normal way, become dominating and therefore may be described with great accuracy.[12]

Experiments by means of tests are also possible. J. Piaget[13] and I.

---

[9] For instance, Ehrlich, [Grundlegung einer Soziologie des Rechts (Munich, 1913). English translation by Harvard University Press], pp. 298, 396.

[10] F. H. Allport, Social Psychology, passim.

[11] Twenty-five Years of Objective Study of the Higher Nervous Activity of Animals (Leningrad, 1925), pp. 306–8 (Eng. trans., 1928); cf. also Conditioned Reflexes (Eng. trans., 1927), pp. 395–96, and K. Platonow, Hypnosis and Suggestion (Kharkow, 1925), pp. 41–42 (in Russian).

[12] Petrajitsky, [Theory of Law and of State, in Russian (2d ed., Petrograd, 1909), I], p. 5.

[13] Le Jugement moral des enfants (Paris, 1931).

Caruso[14] have applied an ingenious system of tests in order to study the growth of the retributive emotion in children. Their point of view was that of morals rather than law, but, in spite of this, their results are of great help when studying the "immediate juridical experience." On the other hand it would be very useful to apply the same method in order to investigate the juridical mentality of adults. Such questions as the survival of the primitive revenge mentality, or the role of the retributive emotion as one of the roots of criminal law even today,[15] or the relative force of norms of conduct belonging to the domains of law, morals, and custom, could be studied in a large number of different situations.

Just as pathology gives valuable data when studying biology, so psychopathology when studying psychology. Criminology, the study of abnormal behavior in human society, or of *not* adapting the individual will to social patterns, may, together with the sociology of revolutions, give a great number of valuable insights in constructing the sociology of law. The sociology of law and criminology must each assist the other.

Data collected by observation and by experiments of the above-mentioned types, and by using the results of criminological research, refer to the conduct of modern civilized men. In order to control the general validity of the data obtained in these ways, the data of ethnology and of historical jurisprudence have to be included, as well as data of child psychology.[16] Of course, these data should not be given an exaggerated place in the system—the sociology of law should not become a theory of primitive law, just as sociology in general should not be merely a science of primitive human behavior.

As with criminology, the support of the sociology of law on the one hand and of ethnology and historical jurisprudence on the other hand must be a mutual one.

---

[14] La Notion de la responsabilité et de la justice immanente chez l'enfant. (*This book is to appear next year in Louvain. The author kindly gave me permission to use his manuscript.*)

[15] *The question of whether the retributive emotion plays and ought to play a part in modern criminal law was amply debated during the preparation of a new criminal code for Germany. The best work concerning the above-mentioned question is that of E. Beling,* Die Vergeltung und ihre Bedeutung für das Strafrecht (*Leipzig, 1908*).

[16] *Petrajitsky* (op. cit., *pp. 95–99*) *makes very ingenious remarks concerning the importance of studying children at play as an aid in understanding the growth of the juridical mentality.*

The sociology of law is the only science which might discover objective and not purely subjective and conjectural limits for the phenomenon of law; the limit is given by differences in social interaction. In law the "equal interaction" forming the essence of the recognition of norms by group members is combined with an "unequal interaction" related to power.[17]

The absence of such considerations often hinders authors from putting correctly the problems of primitive or of historical jurisprudence. For instance, when trying to prove that law already existed at very early stages of social evolution, B. Malinowski invokes the fact that there were already rules "conceived and acted upon as binding obligations."[18] But custom and social morals (in opposition to personal moral conviction) are also binding, endowed with social pressure, and therefore the existence of compulsory rules is insufficient to prove the existence of law. Further, according to A. S. Diamond, "among the tribes, which have not yet evolved courts . . . . we may observe . . . . settled rules of conduct as to marriage and inheritance and perhaps property, and these might well be described as law."[19] Why? For these rules "are in the direct line of the history of law." On the contrary, the legal character of other rules, which were in force together with that named above, but later on disappeared, is denied.[20] In other words, the author separates early rules into two classes from the viewpoint of their later fate. The lack of any actual criterion for legal rules is obvious.

Last but not least, brilliant remarks of sociological character have been made by philosophers of law, historians of law, and students of positive law. These remarks in their totality are not able to replace sociology of law; for, made without any relation to a general sociological system, sometimes without knowing that sociology may exist or in conscious opposition to any sociology, especially to sociology of law, these remarks have almost without exception been conjectures rather than scientific theories. But it is not the task of the sociology of law to replace, but only to complete, the points of view of analytical, historical, comparative, and theoretical jurisprudence. Every attempt to construct a sociology

---

[17] Cf. my above-quoted article, "Le Droit, l'éthique, le pouvoir."
[18] B. Malinowski, Crime and Custom in Savage Society (London, 1926), p. 15.
[19] A. S. Diamond, Primitive Law (London and New York, 1935), p. 219.
[20] Op. cit., pp. 191–92.

of law without possessing sufficient knowledge in jurisprudence would be a failure.

There is room for a new science of the sociology of law; there are sufficient materials and methods to help us gain new knowledge; and there exist already brilliant attempts to solve the problem of the sociology of law. Continuing these efforts is an important task, not only from the theoretical but also from the practical point of view. For the sociology of law might become a basis for an applied science of legislation. And, in opposition to the belief of Savigny and the other founders of the historical school of jurisprudence, our time is called to a more rational settlement of human relations by means of consciously elaborated legislation.

# THE VALUE
# OF SOCIOLOGY
# TO LAW*

*Robert C. Angell*

There has been a good deal said about a sociological approach to law and, as time goes by, more and more attempts are being made to turn words into action. There is a definite trend toward the use of the sociologist, his research methods, his findings, or his body of principles by those concerned with the law. It may not be amiss, therefore, for a sociologist to inquire what the possibilities of this trend really are. Though, in certain respects, he may be less well equipped for this task than the student of law, he at least has the advantage of seeing clearly the shortcomings of contemporary sociology and is not as likely as optimistic outsiders to exaggerate its value to law.

## PRESENT STATUS OF SOCIOLOGY

It is difficult to characterize in brief compass the status of a whole scientific discipline because general statements about the situation are likely to prove meaningless to those not in touch with the actual scientific work which such statements attempt to summarize. However, perhaps we

* To Professor John P. Dawson of the Michigan Law School I owe a debt, which I gratefully acknowledge, for his repeated discussion with me of many points in this paper.

Reprinted by permission of the author and of the publishers from 31 *Michigan Law Review* (1933), 512–525. Author's list of suggested readings has been omitted.

may point out that, roughly speaking, sociology has had two main periods. In the first, discerning scholars formulated large generalizations or hypotheses regarding social relationships on the basis of their own experience and observation, supplemented by history, anthropology, and other enlightened comment upon human life. Many of these hypotheses have since proven inaccurate, but others of them have well withstood the test of more searching analysis. Such, for instance, are Cooley's general notion of the tentative character of all social growth, his theory of the enormous and fundamental influence of intimate, face-to-face groups like the family, and his hypothesis of the institutional character of pecuniary valuation. The second period has been marked by a swing of the pendulum toward more systematic induction. Although a necessary antidote to uncritical "armchair" speculation, this movement has undoubtedly restricted unduly the play of scientific imagination, so that we have had great accumulations of ill-assorted and undigested facts with little theory to illumine them. Case histories have been gathered in great numbers, social surveys of various kinds have been made, and statistical studies of all sorts have been carried on. All these methods give us important information about social facts but they do not give us generalizations or laws of social relation and function unless further work is done in the way of setting up hypotheses and testing them. This procedure has been approximated in some instances but, unfortunately, only in a relatively few.

Sociology, then, presents the spectacle of a considerable number of seemingly valid generalizations, rather sweeping and rather vague, on the one hand, and great masses of descriptive data on the other, with little achieved in the way of detailed and specific theory which can be used for prediction and control. There remains to be mentioned the research techniques which sociologists, along with other social scientists, are gradually evolving. Without making any claims of startling success in this field, it is certainly true that sociologists are exhibiting considerable ingenuity in devising research methods and that steady progress may be expected.

## THE SOCIOLOGIST'S APPROACH TO LAW

Despite its undeveloped character, however, sociology may be expected to have considerable influence on law. Before discussing its possibilities in this respect, it will perhaps be well to appreciate the point of view with which a sociologist naturally approaches the law. He is accustomed to studying the mutual adaptations of various social entities—personalities, groups, institutions, etc. He thinks of each of these entities as evolving under the influence of all the others with which it is in contact, and he regards it as his job to disclose these relationships, to understand their significance, and, where possible, to measure them. To him, therefore, the law naturally appears as one functional system or institution working in interaction with hundreds of others in our complex life. What goes on within the legal order appears as a series of adaptations to a great variety of conditions; and conversely, the other organized social wholes are adjusting in one way or another to the legal order. These mutual influences are all part of the vast system of interstimulation and response which constitutes the social process.

## SOCIOLOGY IN LEGAL EDUCATION

First, then, what is the potential worth of contemporary sociology to the teaching and learning of the law? The answer, in general terms, is rather obvious. Sociology, together with economics and political science, should give the law student a greater comprehension of the *milieu* in which the law operates. It should enable him to realize the interdependence of law and other social institutions, such as the family and the church, and to understand what are the contemporary trends in such institutions to which the law is adapting. It should enable him to appreciate law's necessarily evolutionary character. And, finally, it should enable him to see that the law is only one means of social control and that education, public sentiment, and other means may be equally effective and less painful. Already something is being done in these directions. Many law students have taken sociology as undergraduates, though it must be acknowledged that little attention is usually paid to law as a factor in social life except in criminology courses. For the most part the students must, on their own initiative, make the application of general sociological principles to legal phenomena and bring to bear any pertinent factual information acquired. This is a stimulating and fruitful intellectual procedure, but it is not an easy one, so that the chances are that it is commonly done very imperfectly. If sociology is really to illuminate the work of most law students, the task of bringing the two together should not be left wholly to individual insight and initiative. Four ways of helping the student in this matter have been, or are being tried: (1) Courses in the sociology of law such as the course now being given in the sociology department at Michigan. (2) Orientation courses of a broad, sociological character in the law schools as at Yale and Columbia. (3) The reorganization of the law school curriculum into courses integrated on the basis of social institutions rather than abstract legal principles. This method of introducing sociological theory has been much discussed, under the designation "functional approach," and, in a limited degree, has been attempted at Columbia.[1] (4) The teaching of the conventional law courses by men sufficiently acquainted with the social sciences to use their generalizations and findings of fact wherever pertinent. This is probably being realized more and more everywhere as younger men, more familiar with the social sciences than their elders, become members of law faculties. It is this method which will probably be most widely adopted since it represents no serious wrench from past procedure; whether it will be sufficient for the purpose without supplementation by other methods, time alone can tell.

The acquaintance with sociological principles and findings which will make for a broader understanding during law school days is of course intended to serve the individual to advantage in later life, be he practitioner, judge, legislator, administrative official, or teacher. In these days when rapid social changes require rapid readjustment of the law, those vitally concerned with the law need far more, in order to be effective, than a common-sense knowledge of what is going on in the wider sphere of social relationships. Further, they may perhaps become accustomed to drawing upon contemporary sociological research where there are pertinent findings bearing upon particular legal problems. Ever since the famous Brandeis brief in *Muller v. Oregon* there has been a greater realization of the possible importance of sociological evidence in constitutional cases where the ultimate appeal must after all be to social and economic facts. Another sphere where findings of this character are surely coming into greater use is in the hearings on and framing of statutes by legislatures. Interested parties are seeing to it that any results of social

---

[1] *See* SUMMARY OF STUDIES IN LEGAL EDUCATION, *by the Faculty of Law of Columbia University* (1928); *and* JACOBS AND ANGELL, A RESEARCH IN FAMILY LAW (*1930*).

research which tend to substantiate their viewpoints are brought to the attention of the legislators.

## SOCIOLOGICAL RESEARCH IN THE LEGAL FIELD

In spite of what has just been said, however, there are relatively few sociological findings which bear directly upon specific problems with which these law men are concerned. The sociologist has more to offer at present in the way of research method than of pertinent collected data. If the full value of sociology is to be had, many new investigations will have to be undertaken, investigations framed with precisely the object of throwing light upon legal questions. I am not concerned here with the auspices under which these research projects will be undertaken. Very likely legislatures, administrative bureaus, and even appellate courts will come to employ research staffs; certainly law schools and other research institutions will carry forward the work, once promising studies begin to be made. And I believe such studies can be made even with the present research techniques of sociology.

### Functional Studies of Legal Machinery

The sort of research in the legal field which would most readily tap the sociologist's distinctive resources would be the study of the actual operation of various parts of the legal machinery. By the gathering of statistics, planned observation, interviews, and personal documents secured for the purpose, the working of procedural agencies might be thoroughly analyzed. Almost all sorts of units can be investigated in this way—legislative committees, courts, judges, prosecutors, or administrative officers. Beginnings have been made in this direction but most of the studies have not gone beyond the stage of gathering statistics regarding the obvious facts, such as the number of different types of cases, the percentage of acquittals, the frequency with which certain procedural situations recur, etc.[2] These statistical studies are of undoubted value in

---

[2] See Wayne L. Morse, "A Survey of the Grand Jury," 10 Or. L. Rev. 101–160 (1930); William M. Wherry, "A Study of the Organization of Litigation and of the

showing trends and are of great practical value for administrative purposes, but they throw little light on fundamental causal relationships. We find out that certain things are happening but we are not brought to understand why. Other studies have attempted to supplement the statistical evidence by more intimate information and interpretation,[3] but much more could and should be done in this direction. Practicing lawyers know a great deal regarding such matters and, if their help could be enlisted, would prove invaluable in getting at the relationships which make our procedural agencies behave as they do. Judge Hutcheson has given us a slight indication of what might be accomplished if judges could be brought to write personal documents concerning their official activities.[4] There seems to be no legitimate way to obtain information upon how juries actually deal with the matters before them, though this would be an illuminating study. In the field of criminal justice, however, there are many officials and agencies which could well be subjected to intensive, systematic investigation. When a number of such studies of the same sort have been secured they could be analyzed to discover differences due to local customs, to personality traits of officials involved, to pressures from particular groups, and so on.

### Difficulties in Research Focused Upon Legal Rules

However, we not only wish to know how our procedural devices function and why, but we are extremely interested in knowing the sources of the legal rules which are supposedly being applied, and their effects in life at large. The minute we begin planning research in this field we are

---

Jury Trial in the Supreme Court of New York County," 8 N. Y. L. Q. Rev. 396–427 (1930); Hessel E. Yntema and George H. Jaffin, "Preliminary Analysis of Concurrent Jurisdiction," 79 U. Pa. L. Rev. 869–919 (1930); George Everson, "The Human Element in Justice," 10 J. of Crim. and Criminol. 90–99 (1919); and many studies of criminal justice.

[3] Ruth Bloodgood, "The Federal Courts and the Delinquent Child," United States Children's Bureau Publication No. 103 (1922); Katherine Lenroot and Emma O. Lundberg, "Juvenile Courts at Work," United States Children's Bureau Publication No. 141 (1925); Bernard Flexner, Reuben Oppenliemer, and Katherine Lenroot, "Child, Family and Court," United States Children's Bureau Publication No. 193 (1929); and several of the reports of the Wickersham Commission on Law Enforcement. See also Leon Tulin, "The Role of Penalties in Criminal Law," 37 Yale L. J. 1048–1069 (1927).

[4] Hutcheson, "The Judgment Intuitive: The Function of the 'Hunch' in Judicial Decision," 14 Corn. L. Q. 274–288 (1928).

plunged in a quagmire of difficulties. First, it is not always easy to fix upon the rule. Decisions of appellate courts are directed toward particular disputes and yet are universally assumed to govern future decisions. The traditional occupation of the lawyer has been to draw out legal norms from the particulars of decided cases, and the job is often a ticklish one. Experts often disagree as to what is the local rule upon an apparently simple question. The second obstacle is the fact that the rule, even when clearly formulated, may not be adhered to in the actual administration of the law. When practice diverges from the abstract rule in this sense, we no longer have one definite social influence whose causes and effects may be investigated. For example, if the legal grounds of divorce in a particular jurisdiction are not identical with the grounds on which divorces are actually given in practice, the sociologist will need to consider the influence of both the rule and the actual practice. The third difficulty revolves about the long-standing and nation-wide acceptance of many of our legal rules. Although this might seem to be an advantage because it makes it easier to fix upon the rule, it is a drawback because social research must have variation to work with. Since sociologists can not artificially vary conditions as the physical scientist can, we must observe instances where life itself is, as it were, experimenting. The variation may occur in time within a single jurisdiction or may occur as between two contemporary jurisdictions. As long as there are differences in rule associated with other social differences, there is some hope that research can achieve something; but not otherwise. Imagine trying to discover the conditions of American life which have led to the acceptance of the requirement of consideration in contract law, or imagine trying to trace out the social effects of such a rule. The only possible way to make any headway would be either to compare our situation with that obtaining in European jurisdictions having a different rule or to go back for the necessary contrast to a time in English law when the rule did not obtain. As a matter of fact this is usually what legal scholars who are interested in the significance of some well-established rule have done. Some valuable studies have been made in this way,[5] and doubtless much more could be done through new investiga-

---

[5] *Three examples from the work of the Columbia Law School are Goebel's treatment of the English corporation* (CASES AND MATERIALS ON THE DEVELOPMENT OF LEGAL INSTITUTIONS 539–653), JACOBS, DOMESTIC RELATIONS (1932), *and the economic background built up in* LLEWELLYN, CASES AND MATERIALS ON THE LAW OF SALES (1930).

tions. Such research would be particularly significant to the lawyer because it would promote his own special aims of understanding and interpreting legal rules. But work of this kind must remain highly speculative, so that the sociologist, who wishes to get at the forces behind legal doctrine and the effect of the legal mechanism upon organized society by more empirical methods, will have to devote his attention to rules not so uniform. The limitations of his own techniques are what bind him.

### Studies of Social Causes of Legal Rules

With these difficulties in mind we may now turn to the first type of research which might be undertaken, the study of the general social forces back of particular rules. The above discussion has indicated that we must find diverging situations which may be compared. This requirement is fulfilled when the law of a particular jurisdiction is changed or when two jurisdictions have different rules on the same point. In the first instance the change in the law may be a reflection of changes in the conditions of life in that jurisdiction. In the long run, and taking legal changes in the mass, this must be so, for social forces are bound to affect the law ultimately, though any particular change may be due to some temporary circumstance such as the personality of a judge or the accidents of litigation or, in the case of legislation, a whole complex of personal and political factors. It would be worth while to determine in any event whether or not the legal change was a response to a changing set of fundamental social conditions. This method would probably prove especially fruitful in the case of statutes. By careful study at the time of a new statute's consideration by the legislature we could probably obtain a fairly accurate picture of what needs, felt and voiced by what groups, were bringing about the legal change. With common law rules the matter would be more difficult, but even here appellate courts are recognizing in their decisions more frankly than ever before the factors of social expediency which lie back of changes. Constitutional interpretation likewise lends itself to investigation of this character.[6] It is probable that studies of this kind, based on legal changes in one jurisdiction, would be more successful than comparison of two

---

[6] See Robert E. Cushman, "The Social and Economic Interpretation of the Fourteenth Amendment," 20 MICH. L. REV. 737–764 (1921); and Walter Nelles, "A Strike and its Legal Consequences," 40 YALE L. J. 507–554 (1930).

jurisdictions having diverging rules. There are so many possible influences making for divergence between two jurisdictions that the problem of running down the significant ones in any particular instance would be tremendous. Broad generalizations such as those made by anthropologists and legal historians are possible, but there is some doubt whether more refined analysis would yield much. Professor Underhill Moore has produced a very interesting and very elaborate investigation testing the hypothesis that divergent banking decisions are due to differences in the banking practices in the several jurisdictions.[7] The amount of labor spent upon the study appears to have been enormous and it is undoubtedly worth the effort expended to have a type investigation of this kind made. Yet even if the hypothesis were proved perfectly valid the result would simply aid in predicting future decisions in various jurisdictions. One might still wonder why the differences in banking practice.

### Research Comparing Law With Custom

This leads to the general question of the value of research which attempts to compare law with custom. No doubt such investigations can be made. I have even participated in the making of one.[8] But the difficulty is, when we secure our results, to decide what they mean. We may find out that the law either does or does not tend to parallel custom in the jurisdiction in question. But surely this does not take us far.[9] We can not assume that the law should always follow custom, for, on the one hand, there are in some quarters bad customs which public opinion would not wish incorporated in the law, and, on the other, many of the friction situations which reach the courts for settlement are precisely the ones in which the customary adjustments have failed to work. There is the further difficulty that usually in modern life we find no one custom generally accepted, but several quite different practices or, if a recent invention has just come in to create the situation, no settled practice at all.

An approach to law and custom which recognizes more explicitly

---

[7] *Underhill Moore and Gilbert Sussman, "Legal and Institutional Methods Applied to the Debiting of Direct Discounts,"* 40 YALE L. J. 381–400, 555–575, 752–778, 928–953, 1055–1073, 1219–1272 (1930).

[8] JACOBS AND ANGELL, A RESEARCH IN FAMILY LAW, *part IV* (1930).

[9] *Pound makes the same point in "The Call for a Realist Jurisprudence,"* 44 HARV. L. REV. 697 *at* 708–709 (1930); *also Dickinson in "The Law Behind Law,"* 29 COL. L. REV. 113 *at* 125–141 (1929).

their interactive character would perhaps prove more fruitful. Such an approach would of necessity use the historical method. One might take some small segment of life in a field such as commercial contracts, and trace the continuous action and reaction between the institutional ways and the law. In the field mentioned we know that courts have taken judicial notice of the customs of a particular trade on many occasions, and frequently refer to custom in the interpretation of ambiguous transactions. Certainly the reverse process also takes place. The law, influenced as it is by the interests of those outside the immediate transaction, modifies from time to time the institutional ways.

### Research Upon the Divergence Between Rules and Their Administration

So far in our discussion of the social influences producing particular rules we have said nothing concerning the administration of these rules by officials, commissions, lower courts, etc. Where the administration is practically identical with the rules themselves, as, for instance, with intestate succession to property, no further problem arises. Where, however, the administration diverges markedly from the verbal formula, there arises the additional question as to why the divergence occurs. Both the divergence and the reason for it are proper matters for research. An interesting attempt in this direction has recently been made with reference to divorce rules in Wisconsin.[10] Here again, the comparative procedure is highly desirable. If the situation changes in one jurisdiction from a rigid and unvarying administration to one which diverges either consistently or intermittently from the verbal rule, we would perhaps be able to trace the causes of the shift; or if there are two jurisdictions, in one of which administration is practically identical with the rule while in the other it is not, the comparison of the two sets of relevant factors might prove illuminating.

### Studying the Social Effects of Legal Rules

Let us turn now from the social influences producing the rules to the social effects produced by the rules. The former is of special interest to the

---

[10] N. P. Feinsinger and Kimball Young, "Recrimination and Related Doctrines in the Wisconsin Law of Divorce as Administered in Dane County," 6 WIS. L. REV. 195–216 (1930).

practicing lawyer who might thereby be able to make a better prediction as to what new rules will shortly emerge, and to the scholar who wishes to understand how social processes work. The latter is of interest to almost everyone, for we all wish to know what our laws are doing to us. However, we are desiring something which will tax our present methods of social research to the utmost. Law is but one small segment in the whole realm of life. It is difficult enough to determine what forces converging from the surrounding life account for the changes and contrasts in legal rules; it is much harder to determine what are the effects of the ripples set up by law on the vast sea of human relationships. So many other centers of influence are sending forth larger waves that the effect of law is largely obscured.

There is, however, one small group of people whose conduct is definitely influenced by particular rules—the officials charged with administering them. Several studies have already been made from this angle.[11] Investigations of this kind are closely allied to the procedural studies previously discussed, the only difference being that, instead of subjecting all the official behavior of those concerned to scrutiny, only those activities which have to do with a particular law are observed and analyzed. This is one of the simplest types of research to carry through and sometimes, as with child labor laws, it reveals much of the wider social influence of the particular rules.

But when we attempt to go beyond the effect of the law upon those charged with administering it and inquire what its effects are upon the community at large, we are faced with a far more difficult task. The easiest situation to deal with is where there is a one-to-one correspondence between the verbal rule and its administration. Here once more it would be necessary to use a comparative technique. In general, it appears that a study in one jurisdiction before and after the coming into force of a new rule would be more fruitful than the comparison of the effects of two different rules in two jurisdictions. There would probably be a greater

---

[11] *Edith Abbott and Sophonisba Breckenridge, "The Administration of the Aid to Mothers Law in Illinois," United States Children's Bureau Publication No. 82 (1921); "Administration of Child Labor Laws," United States Children's Bureau Publications No's 12 (1915), 17 (1930), 41 (1919), 78 (1921), 85 (1921), 133 (1924); "The Promotion of the Welfare and Hygiene of Maternity and Infancy," United States Children's Bureau Publications No's 137 (1924), 146 (1925), 156 (1926), 178 (1927); and several of the reports of the Wickersham Commission on Law Enforcement.*

similarity of other forces at work at successive periods in the same jurisdiction than in two jurisdictions at the same time, so that the effects of the law would be thrown into sharper relief. We shall probably, therefore, wish to undertake careful studies of how persons and institutions behave prior to the creation of a new rule as compared with their behavior subsequent thereto. A very able investigation employing this technique has been carried out by the Children's Bureau.[12] The more important the legal rule is in the causation of behavior the more likely it is that the other method of comparison—that of two jurisdictions at the same time—will prove fruitful. For instance, housing laws, through a rigid system of inspection and enforcement, have very definite effects upon the construction of new buildings. Thus the influence of different laws might be rather easily ascertained. Again, the rules for the distribution among heirs of intestate estates are of such importance to the subsequent lives of the heirs that case histories which followed their careers might reveal differing effects of different rules.

Unfortunately in many, if not most, instances there is not the one-to-one correspondence between the verbal rule and its administration that has been assumed above. This leads to further complications and further difficulties. Take, for instance, a municipal ordinance setting twenty miles an hour as a maximum speed for motor vehicles. In the first place there is perhaps an understanding among police officials that arrests will not be made for driving at a speed of less than 25 miles an hour. This is known to some drivers but not to all. Therefore some believe that there is one real limit, some another; and many perhaps do not know what either of these limits is. Added to this confusion, we have reason to believe that some people consistently observe the limit which they recognize, that some disregard it only in emergencies, and that still others obey it only when they suspect the approach of an officer. Under these conditions what can sociological research accomplish in the direction of determining the effects of the ordinance? Evidently the task is not one to be undertaken lightly. One could, conceivably through interviews and close observation, get some light upon the frequency of all the causal sequences enumerated above. But then one would have, not the influence of the verbal rule nor of

---

[12] *"The Welfare of Infants of Illegitimate Birth in Baltimore as Affected by a Maryland Law of 1916 Governing the Separation from their Mothers of Children Under 6 Months Old,"* United States Children's Bureau Publication No. 144 (1925).

the rule-as-administered, but the influence of the two jumbled together. Whether this would be of much value even if it could be accurately ascertained is doubtful.

### Studies of How Knowledge of Law is Diffused

A wholly different subject for investigation would be the channels by which people learn what the law is. In transactions which are commonly engineered and shaped from the start by lawyers, such as the formation of corporations, legal technical knowledge is brought to bear directly. In other transactions the legal skills of the lawyer are appropriated at second hand, through the use of forms, stereotyped contracts, etc. In other fields of law, where conduct is not so commonly guided by foresight and plan, future courses of action may be shaped by particular experiences, such as the previously unappreciated liability of oneself or a neighbor for negligence. In still other fields, of which family law is the most obvious example, legal doctrine may be almost unknown to interested parties and, even if known, of little influence on conduct. In the case of legislation which aims at imposing a course of conduct on persons more or less unwilling (factory acts, desertion and non-support legislation), and in most of the criminal law, it would be extremely useful to know the agencies by which knowledge of the law is diffused. Among the agencies which we might expect to find important here are the newspaper accounts of legislative action and judicial decision, trade association activities and journals, neighborhood gossip and non-official contact with officials. There can be no doubt that new and more effective agencies for this purpose could be devised at many points, once research has revealed the inadequacies of present channels.

Perhaps the starting point for such a study should be an attempt to discover how much or little people actually know about the formulated law in different fields. Existing techniques of interview and questionnaire would be adequate for the purpose. The results would probably demonstrate that non-legal types of adjustment prevail throughout most of the social field to which private law relates. The resulting picture would probably be a surprise to most lawyers,[13] though not to many sociologists.

---

[13] *Though Llewellyn shows himself in* THE BRAMBLE BUSH *to be fully aware of the conclusions here suggested.*

We should undoubtedly find large groups of persons pursuing their daily affairs in an orderly way almost oblivious to legal rules which are theoretically supposed to affect their acts.[14]

Such, then, is a sketch of some of the potential values of contemporary sociology to law. The outlook may be discouraging to the lawyer, if not to the sociologist. I make this qualification because sociologists have long been familiar with the factors which preclude any rapid and sure advance toward precise knowledge in their field. Like the lawyers they must deal with social data which are extremely variable and infinitely complex; unlike the lawyers they are not accustomed to results that are in any considerable degree predictable or that can be framed in logically symmetrical terms. Perhaps the prime lesson which the sociologist, with his mass of conflicting and variable data, can teach the lawyer and legislator is to proceed with care in framing and acting on hypotheses in social matters.

---

[14] *A type of research which is a little farther afield but which nevertheless might have some significance for law is the investigation of why certain persons become entangled in the legal web. Such are the numerous studies of the causes of juvenile delinquency and adult criminality. Another of the same kind in the civil field is that attempted at Yale dealing with the bankgrounds of bankruptcy. (William O. Douglas and Dorothy S. Thomas, "The Business Failures Project—II. An Analysis of Methods of Investigation," 40* YALE L. J. *1034–1054 (1930).)*

# PART II | EARLY EMPIRICAL RESEARCH

H. P. WELD AND E. R. DANZIG ·
WILLIAM O. DOUGLAS AND DOROTHY S.
THOMAS · BRONISLAW MALINOWSKI ·
WILLIAM M. MARSTON

PART II DESCRIBES SOME OF THE EARLY EMPIRICAL STUDIES in sociological jurisprudence. It represents both the interests and the quality of work done in the period preceding the contemporary blossoming of research in the law and the behavioral sciences. This early period is distinctive from the contemporary one in at least two important respects:

1. The theoretical and practical implications of the findings were described in more grandiose terms. For example, Underhill Moore, a leading figure of this early empirical school, saw in the design and results of his studies of parking-ordinance violations, check processing, banking practices, and other

areas, significant contributions to psychological learning theory. In reporting the quantity and degree of conformity to rules of law pertaining to parking and driving ordinances, Moore and his associate Callahan wrote that they "had no particular interest in parking and driving or in generalizations applicable to traffic alone." They chose to observe such behavior because they could make relatively accurate observations of behavior yielding quantitative data and because behavior studied under such conditions could be fitted into a stimulus-response learning theory paradigm.[1] William Marston, on the basis of his experiments on the accuracy and reliability of testimony, was willing to advocate significant changes in the manner in which evidence is presented.

2. The choice of problems tended to be determined primarily by the legal partner, and the research was conducted in the law school. It is interesting, in light of this second characteristic, that there were so few studies of the legal profession or of the relationship between the law and other professional groups with whom lawyers interact.[2] Lawyers, at least the ones who did research, apparently were not self-conscious about their occupational role. They preferred to concentrate their research on substantive problems. It was not until sociologists became partners or research entrepreneurs that the work lawyers do and the values of the profession became research targets.

The excerpt from Weld and Danzig's "A Study of the Way in Which a Verdict Is Reached by a Jury" reports some of the findings from a study carried on at Cornell University Law School in the middle 1930's. Separated as they were by some twenty years, nevertheless, the studies of the jury system conducted at Cornell and those conducted later at the University of Chicago Law School, mark the two main attempts at finding out how the jury functions. (Excerpts from the later jury research are included in Section 2 of Part IV.) At this time I wish to call attention, very briefly, to the major differences between the two approaches.

The Cornell studies were modeled along the lines of the "opinion formation and change experiments" which are part of the traditional experimental-psychology literature. They made little attempt to analyze substantive legal issues or to look at the jury as a sociolegal institution. They emphasized individual reactions and responses, paying little attention to group interaction or institutional relationships. On the other hand, the Chicago studies have been criticized for being primarily vehicles for extending research into decision making by small groups. The Chicago studies emphasized the processes of

---

[1] *Underhill Moore and Charles Callahan, "Law and Learning Theory: A Study in Legal Control,"* Yale Law Journal, 53 (1943), 1–87.

[2] *The study by E. W. Robinson,* Law and the Lawyers (*New York: Macmillan, 1935*), *is a rare exception.*

social interaction more than they did the reactions of the individual juror. But the excerpts included in Part IV do describe jurors' reactions to such basic substantive issues as rules of law, expert testimony, the insurance status of the defendant, the amount of damages sought, and the social characteristics of the defendant. Reading the excerpt from the Cornell study included in this part, and then reading excerpts from the more recent Chicago study should make more obvious some of the differences alluded to here.

The article by Douglas and Thomas differs from the others in this part because the authors' main purpose is to describe the methods of the project rather than the results. As part of their larger interest in why businesses fail, Douglas and Thomas describe the social and economic data which they tried to collect from businessmen who had gone bankrupt.[3] They then offer an explanation for the differential rate of responses that they received from different items on the interview schedule. Using a step-by-step approach and offering an explanation for why each step was taken, the article is a useful yardstick for measuring the degree of sophistication that characterized empirical legal research in this period.

An excerpt from one of the early works by the anthropologist, Bronislaw Malinowski, is included in this part because it serves as an interesting comparison to the type of research that was being done in traditional and non-Western societies as opposed to the studies conducted in the United States during the same period. The excerpt describes how the legal principle of "Mother-right, which rules that a child is bodily related and morally beholden by kinship to its mother and to her only," is *actually* enforced and how violations are treated in the Trobriand Islands.

The concluding selection in Part II, Marston's "Studies in Testimony," is of the same genre as the Weld and Danzig piece. Like the Cornell jury studies, it used as its model the psychological prestimulus and poststimulus experiment. The substantive issue in the Marston article is the psycholegal causes of testimonial error. The paper reports the completeness and accuracy to which respondents can testify about events that they personally witnessed. Marston makes two types of comparison: (1) He examined the completeness and accuracy of verbal versus written testimony; and (2) he compared the completeness and accuracy of reports as between men and women and as between lay witnesses and judges.

Marston defines the major purpose of his research as an opportunity to

---

[3] *Douglas and Thomas' research on business failures was done at the Yale Law School, which pioneered much of the interdisciplinary legal research in the 1930's and 1940's. Underhill Moore and his associates were also members of the Yale faculty during the same period.*

accumulate evidence that would serve as the basis for introducing policy changes in existing trial procedures. In his concern for "reforming" the law, Marston affiliates himself with an important theme in legal research not found in the other excerpts. This concern with "legal reform" was a significant factor that influenced many scholars engaged in research during this period. It certainly influenced the work of Hutchins and Schlesinger in their studies of the law of evidence, and that of Lasswell and McDougall in their assessment of the professional training of lawyers for the public interest.

# A STUDY OF THE WAY
# IN WHICH A VERDICT
# IS REACHED
# BY A JURY

*H. P. Weld and E. R. Danzig*

Little is known about the manner in which the evidence in a court-trial is received, weighed, and accepted by a jury. Weld and Roff have made a study in which a large number of individuals listened to the report of the evidence in a criminal trial and, as individuals, reached a verdict concerning the relative guilt or innocence of the prisoner. Since the witnesses themselves were not heard in either direct or cross-examination, since there were neither opening nor summing up statements by the attorneys, and since the individual subjects had no opportunity of discussing the case with each other, no claim was made that the experiment showed what would happen in an actual trial.[1]

In the present study we were able to overcome these omissions, to some extent at least, by availing ourselves of a trial in a moot court, one of a series conducted by Professor Lyman Wilson of the Cornell Law School. The case was prepared by Professor Wilson who also acted as Judge.[2] The counsel for the plaintiff and the defendant were students in the Law

---

[1] H. P. Weld and M. F. Roff, *A study in the formation of opinion based upon legal evidence*, this JOURNAL, 51, 1938, 609–628.

[2] *We are grateful to Professor Wilson for his hearty coöperation. It was his sympathetic interest and cordial support that made the experiment possible.*

---

Reprinted by permission of the publishers from 53 *American Journal of Psychology* (1940), 518–536. Footnotes have been renumbered to run in sequence throughout the selection.

School, and three juries were selected from students who were taking courses in psychology. All of the proceedings were recorded by a professional court stenographer. The trial was held in the Moot Court Room of the Cornell Law School on two successive Tuesday afternoons, April 9th and 16th, 1940. The evidential details of the case were presented by witnesses who had been selected and coached by the attorneys.

The entire trial was conducted in the manner of a real trial, with several minor exceptions. The most important of these were that the jurors were not examined and no oaths were administered. The excellent acting by the witnesses, the introduction in evidence of photographs and blueprints, and the earnestness of all participants in the trial gave an air of reality to the proceedings such as to simulate an actual suit at law.

The three juries consisted (A) of twelve men, another (B) of twelve women, and a third (C) of seventeen men and women.[3]

## METHOD AND PROCEDURE

The trial in the court room was divided into 18 stages, which hereinafter will be indicated by roman numerals. Every member of the jury was given a data sheet on which the stages were printed in order and the juror was directed to record his judgment for the plaintiff or defendant in terms of a 9-point scale, after each stage had been presented to the court. This scale was as follows: *1*, conviction that the defendant is not liable for damages; *2*, strong belief that the defendant is not liable; *3*, fair belief that the defendant is not liable; *4*, slight belief that the defendant is not liable; *5*, doubt that the defendant is liable; *6*, slight belief that the defendant is liable; *7*, fair belief that the defendant is liable; *8*, strong belief that the defendant is liable; *9*, conviction that the defendant is liable.

After the judge had finished his instructions to the jury, the three juries retired to separate jury rooms under charge of a foreman who previously had been selected as one having prestige with his particular group. On reaching the jury room the foreman immediately instructed every juror to record on his data sheet his vote or judgment on the following statement: "I find by a preponderance of the evidence that the

---

[3] *This jury originally had 24 members divided into 2 juries of 12 each, but 7 members were unable to attend throughout the trial.*

defendant is liable." After the judgments were recorded the foreman polled the vote. The foreman had previously been instructed that if the poll was not unanimous he should make sure that the points at issue as expressed by the judge were clearly understood by every member of the jury, and then proceed to a discussion. When he thought it advisable he could take a second poll in the same manner as the first, and further polls as necessary. The jury was to be dismissed if unanimity was not reached at the end of thirty minutes.

*   *   *   *

## RESULTS

*In the court room.* The results fall into two groups: those obtained in the court room, and those found in the jury room. The numerical results showing the distribution of the jurors' judgments in the court room on the 9-point scale for each of the installments are shown in Table I. A graph showing the mass tendencies of their judgments for each of the installments is shown in Fig. 1. We have taken the median value as representing the central tendency, and the quartile deviation on each side of the median as representing the variation. The heavy central line in the figure represents the course of the median value of the jurors' judgments; the width of the figure shows the quartile deviation above and below the median. A summary statement of the results shown in table and figure at each stage of the trial follows.

I. Plaintiff's opening statement resulted in a slight belief that the defendant was liable. Six of the 41 jurors had a strong belief that he was liable, 16 expressed doubt, and 6 felt some degree of belief that the defendant was not liable. Of the jurors, 19 had, however, some belief in the liability of the defendant.

II. Defendant's opening statement brought the median down toward doubt. Only 6 jurors had any belief in the liability of defendant, 22 expressed doubt; and 13 had some belief in his non-liability. Thus it appears that the opening statements of the attorneys left the jurors relatively open-minded.

III. The direct examination of the plaintiff brought the median to the highest point in the plaintiff's favor that was reached throughout the

## TABLE I. THE DISTRIBUTION OF JUDGMENTS ON THE 9-POINT SCALE.

| Scale Values | | | | | | | | Stages of the Trial | | | | | | | | | | | |
|---|---|---|---|---|---|---|---|---|---|---|---|---|---|---|---|---|---|---|
| | I | II | III | IV | V | VI | VII | VIII | IX | X | XI | XII | XIII | XIV | XV | XVI | XVII | XVIII |
| 9 | | | | | | | | | | | | | | | | | 1 | 1 |
| 8 | 6 | 1 | 1 | | 1 | 2 | 4 | 6 | 2 | 3 | 3 | 3 | | 1 | 2 | | 1 | 2 |
| 7 | 6 | 2 | 12 | 3 | 5 | 5 | 6 | 9 | 5 | 4 | 3 | 6 | | 3 | 6 | 1 | 4 | 5 |
| 6 | 7 | 3 | 14 | 4 | 11 | 6 | 14 | 10 | 5 | 3 | 7 | 6 | 3 | 3 | 3 | | 3 | 3 |
| 5 | 16 | 22 | 5 | 9 | 16 | 14 | 9 | 12 | 10 | 13 | 14 | 13 | 4 | 4 | 11 | 7 | 8 | 9 |
| 4 | 3 | 4 | 5 | 14 | 2 | 9 | 6 | 3 | 8 | 5 | 6 | 7 | 7 | 9 | 7 | 3 | 9 | 2 |
| 3 | 2 | 7 | 1 | 7 | 2 | 1 | 1 | 1 | 8 | 10 | 5 | 4 | 16 | 5 | 5 | 4 | 8 | 7 |
| 2 | | 1 | 2 | 1 | 3 | 3 | 1 | | 1 | 1 | 3 | 2 | 6 | 3 | 2 | 19 | 4 | 5 |
| 1 | 1 | 1 | 1 | 3 | 1 | 1 | | | 2 | 2 | | | 5 | 2 | | 7 | 7 | 7 |
| Median | 5.9 | 5.3 | 6.4 | 4.6 | 5.7 | 5.4 | 6.2 | 6.4 | 5.1 | 5.1 | 4.4 | 4.5 | 3.5 | 4.5 | 5.3 | 2.7 | 3.9 | 4.7 |
| $Q_1$ | 5.2 | 4.3 | 5.2 | 3.8 | 5.1 | 4.5 | 5.2 | 5.5 | 3.9 | 3.7 | 3.3 | 3.6 | 2.8 | 3.5 | 4.2 | 2.1 | 2.7 | 2.6 |
| $Q_2$ | 7.2 | 5.7 | 7.2 | 5.6 | 6.6 | 6.4 | 6.9 | 7.5 | 6.3 | 5.9 | 5.3 | 5.7 | 4.5 | 5.8 | 6.6 | 4.2 | 5.8 | 6.2 |

trial—a slight to fair belief in liability of defendant. The judgments of 26 jurors fell in this category, with one convinced of liability. Only 5 remained doubtful, with 9 jurors holding to some belief of non-liability.

IV. Defendant's cross-examination of the plaintiff was very effective, not only neutralizing the effect of the plaintiff's testimony but also bringing the median judgments down below the middle rating of doubt to slight belief in non-liability. Of the 41 jurors, 25 expressed doubt and 3 were convinced that the defendant was not liable.

V. Plaintiff's second witness brought the median back to almost the

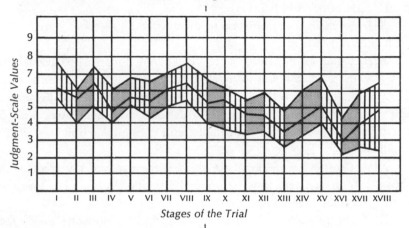

FIGURE 1. THE COURSE OF THE JUDGMENTS AT EVERY STAGE OF THE TRIAL. *The central black line represents the median value of all the judgments for each stage. The width of the figure represents the quartile deviation above and below the median. The barred portion shows the effect of the evidence for the defendant; the stippled portion that for the plaintiff.*

same position that was reached after plaintiff's opening—16 jurors were doubtful, and 17 had some degree of belief in the defendant's liability.

VI. Defendant's cross-examination of plaintiff's second witness had only a slight effect, moving downward in the direction of doubt.

VII. Direct examination of plaintiff's third witness moved the median above slight belief in liability, with 4 jurors holding a strong belief in liability, and 20 with a slight to fair belief in liability. Only 8 had any belief in non-liability.

VIII. Defendant's cross-examination of the plaintiff's third witness proved harmful to the defendant. The trend was toward liability, with only 4 jurors showing any degree of belief that the defendant was not liable. This is the second highest point in the plaintiff's favor, the median being only 0.01 below its position following plaintiff's first witness (Stage III).

IX. Defendant's first witness was effective, bringing the median down a whole step, to doubt.

X. Plaintiff's cross-examination of defendant's first witness had little effect, moving the median up only 0.04.

XI. Direct examination of the second witness for the defendant resulted in 28 ratings of some belief in non-liability. Only 6 at this point had some degree of belief in liability.

XII. Again cross-examination by plaintiff had little effect, moving the median up only 0.10.

XIII. Direct examination of the defendant's third witness brought a new low, the median going to slight to fair belief in the defendant's case. Three jurors had fair belief in liability, and 4 were doubtful. All the rest had some degree of belief that the defendant was not liable, with 5 convinced of defendant's non-liability and 6 with a strong belief in non-liability.

XIV. Cross-examination of the third witness moved the median up almost a complete step, thus restoring the position held just before the third witness took the stand.

XV. The rebuttal testimony of [the plaintiff's husband] raised the median another step in plaintiff's favor, to a bit above doubt.

XVI. The summing up by the defendant's counsel was the most effective stage of the entire trial. The median was brought down to between fair and strong belief in non-liability, and only one juror expressed any belief whatsoever in liability. Seven were convinced of non-liability, and 19 had strong belief.

XVII. Plaintiff's summing up, though effective, did not restore the median to the position held at the conclusion of the testimony. It brought the median up to slight belief in non-liability.

XVIII. The judge's charge to the jury proved helpful to the plaintiff's case, raising the median almost a step but leaving it still in the defendant's favor. The ratings had greater scatter at this point than at any other stage. At this final stage only 11 jurors had any degree of belief in liability, 9 were doubtful, and 21 had some belief that the defendant is not liable. Of the latter, 7 were convinced and 5 had a strong belief in non-liability.

*In the jury room.* None of the juries reached a unanimous decision on the first poll, so that three more polls were taken. Only one juror out of the 41 changed his vote on subsequent polls. That juror, in Jury A, voted for the plaintiff on the first poll and for the defendant thereafter. Thus the final vote at the end of the 30-min. period was as follows: Jury A (men), 10 to 2 in favor of the defendant;[4] Jury B (women), 8 to 4 in favor of the defendant; Jury C (mixed), 11 to 6 in favor of the defendant.

In the jury room all votes, with four exceptions, were forecast by the final judgments in the court room. Of the exceptions three had expressed doubt in their final rating but on every poll in the jury room voted for the plaintiff. These three explained that despite their expression of doubt they had had a slight leaning toward the plaintiff. The other exception was the one juror who changed his vote as a result of the discussion. He explained that this was because he accepted the contention of the other jurors that the testimony of the [plaintiff and her husband] was unsubstantiated by other proof.

It should be realized that the judgments in the court room were not based on "the preponderance of the evidence." Consequently, a juror who had indicated a judgment of only slight or fair belief in liability could still say there was a preponderance of evidence to establish the defendant's liability. Likewise, a juror who left the court room with a judgment of doubt might in the jury room contend that there was no preponderance of the evidence for the plaintiff. In point of fact, there were 5 jurors who voted for the defendant on this basis.

*Individual differences.* Thus far our study of the results has been limited solely to the trends of the mass judgments. The quartile deviation has, it is true, given some idea of the relative distribution and [Table I has] shown the actual distribution of the judgments. We have, however, not questioned how any individual member of our jury reached his particular judgment. The only way in which anything like complete knowledge of this question could be reached would be either by questioning every member or by asking him to write a commentary on his judgment at the time every judgment was made. Neither could have been done without interfering with the progress of the trial. We can, however,

---

[4] *The vote of Jury A is in New York State sufficient for a decision in a civil case. See 463 A of the Code of Civil Procedure.*

study the complete report of an individual and by judicious questions after the trial get some insight into the basis of his ratings and votes. We have done this in some instances. Whenever we found a report that differed markedly from the others it was put aside for further study. Our findings for some of these cases are informative.

Five of the jurors seldom, if ever, made a judgment below 5. Most of their judgments were either 7 or 8, thus showing a fair or strong belief that the defendant was liable for damages. These jurors formed a slight belief in liability after the opening statement of the plaintiff. For one juror this judgment was strengthened by the opening statement of the defendant because, as he said, "If the defendant should prove what he claimed he would prove he would still be liable." For this group of jurors, all subsequent evidence, the summing up, and the judge's instructions only slightly increased or decreased the certainty of their original judgment, and in the jury room all five voted consistently for the plaintiff.

Four jurors were with the opening statement of the plaintiff left with a slight to fair belief that the defendant was *not* liable; thereafter they never at any time felt that a preponderance of the evidence was in favor of the plaintiff. In the jury room they consistently voted for the defendant.

In one case a juror who began with a conviction of non-liability maintained her belief in the defendant's case until the summing up by the plaintiff, when she was convinced of liability. Her vote in the jury room was for the plaintiff.

Individuals often react differently to the same testimony. Thus, testimony which some considered helpful to the plaintiff was thought by others to strengthen the defendant's case, and still others thought it to be of no importance one way or the other. In the same manner, the reaction to the personality and behavior of some of the lawyers varied markedly with individual jurors. According to statements of the jurors, judgments were sometimes affected by admiration for or antagonism toward certain members of counsel.

All the jurors did not reach decisions through a logical analysis of the case; some could not explain or justify their conclusions. Thus several reported that they voted as they did because the party "just didn't have any business recovering in a case like that," or "it just didn't seem right to me." An examination of the reports of the jury foremen reveals, however, that the juries as a whole were well aware of the important issues in the case as set forth by the judge.

*Sex differences.* No outstanding differences were found between the men and the women jurors. When the medians of the men's judgments were plotted on the same graph with the medians of the women's judgments, the curves were found to coincide in most places and to be quite similar throughout. In the jury room, 13 out of 19 girls, and 16 out of 22 boys voted for the defendant; the ratio is almost exactly the same.

*Discussion of results.* We cannot assume of course, that other juries would, in all respects, give the same results as our juries did. We may, we think, dismiss the possibility that our jurors were influenced in some unusual way because the trial was a moot and not a real trial. It was held in a room designed and furnished like a conventional court room, and the proceedings were conducted with the decorum and seriousness of an actual trial. There are, however, two factors which might have distinguished the work of our juries from that of other juries. In the first place our jurors were probably superior in intelligence and education to the average juror. In the second place, the fact that the case was in part fabricated and the small number of witnesses may have simplified the task.

On the other hand, when we consider the psychological processes involved in reaching a verdict, certain of our results which agree with the results of other experiments, may be regarded as typical of the average juror. We have substantiated the finding of Weld and Roff that "the direction of the mass tendency as represented by the median is in general a function of the testimony,"[5] *i.e.* the judgments of the jurors tend to support the contention of the plaintiff or of the defendant as the testimony favors the one or the other side. The first witness for a side is usually the most effective; and although we found that subsequent witnesses were usually less we did not find with Weld and Roff that they tended to become progressively less effective. It is probable that our number of witnesses was too small to show this result, and it is possible that the cross-examination interfered with the trend.

Our results show, however, that the oscillation of the judgments during the course of the trial is influenced not only by the testimony but also both by the opening and closing statements of counsel and by the personality of the witnesses or of members of counsel. As instance of the former, the opening statement of the plaintiff set up a belief in the liability

[5] Op. cit. *622.*

of the defendant exactly as the testimony of a witness for the plaintiff would have done. Similarly when the defendant summed up his case he did more for it than any one of his witnesses had done; and he did it in part by laying less stress upon his proof and more upon the fact that the [plaintiff and her husband] had no proof that they had in fact deposited valuables at the desk, thus casting suspicion on the honesty of the [plaintiff and her husband]—a bit of strategy for which the plaintiff apparently had no defense.

As regards the influence of personalities, from the first some jurors were convinced of the sincerity and honesty of the [plaintiff and her husband], whereas others mistrusted them; the men were slightly more influenced by [the plaintiff's] testimony than were the women jurors; the attorney for the plaintiff who made the opening statement was by voice and manner more persuasive than was his colleague who did the summing up.

We also found, as Weld and Roff found that early in the trial many jurors reached a fairly definite decision, and that thereafter the effect of the testimony was merely to change their certainty. This happened with at least 25% of our jurors, half of whom were disposed in the one, and half in the other way. Even those who as the trial progressed developed an attitude of doubt were still inclined to favor the one side or the other and in the jury room did so. We found no juror who attempted to maintain an attitude of doubt on the theory that he should make no decision until he had heard all the evidence, but we can substantiate the earlier findings of the cautious juror, and of the juror who is easily swayed by the testimony. In addition we discovered jurors who were influenced in reaching their verdict less by the proof than by their notion of what under the circumstances seemed to them to be "right" or just.

The fact that our results show no significant sex differences need occasion no surprise. They agree with Burtt[6] as against Münsterberg that women are no more tenacious than men in maintaining their opinions during discussion. Our results from the jury room do not agree with those of several experiments made on the formation of opinion by discussion. As we have shown, only one of our 41 jurors changed his vote in the jury

---

[6] H. E. Burtt, Sex-differences in the effect of discussion, J. Exper. Psychol., 3, 1920, 390–395; Legal Psychology, 1931, 159 f.; H. Münsterberg, Psychology of Social Sanity, 1914, 181–202.

room whereas in most if not all experiments on group opinion changes in opinion resulting from discussion are frequent.[7] The reason for our result is probably due to the fact that our jurors had already reached a decision when they came to the jury room and they were prepared to defend their opinion. Our results also give positive evidence in support of those advocates who question the value of cross-examination except for special reasons.[8]

Finally we agree with Weld and Roff as regards the general nature of the thinking process in reaching a trial-verdict. In addition we have discovered the existence of personal standards of evaluation which the juror brings to the trial . . . , and we also have evidence that if the prestige of a member of counsel is sufficient, some members of a jury may accept his opinion and maintain it as their own. In no other way can we explain the effect on some jurors of the summing up by the defendant counsel.

## SUMMARY

(*1*) The judgments rose and fell with the evidence.

(*2*) The opening and closing statements of the attorneys were important.

(*3*) The effect of cross-examination was variable. In some instances it weakened or even nullified, and at one point (Stage VIII) it strengthened, the effect of the testimony given in the direct examination.

(*4*) No significant sex differences were revealed.

(*5*) Some opinions were formed on the basis of the opening statements. In some cases a decision was reached early in the trial and all subsequent evidence was interpreted in the light of that decision. In others, decisions were not reached until the end of the trial. The weight given to any particular testimony was influenced by all the preceding judgments, and particularly, by the immediately preceding judgment.

(*6*) The juror reached a decision before going into the jury room and the arguments of his fellow jurors who did not agree with him were not effective in changing his decision.

---

[7] *For references see Weld and Roff*, op. cit., *610.*
[8] *See J. H. Wigmore*, Science of Judicial Proof, *1937, 279 ff.*

# THE BUSINESS FAILURES
# PROJECT—II,
# AN ANALYSIS OF METHODS
# OF INVESTIGATION

*William O. Douglas*
*and Dorothy S. Thomas*

In a previous article various problems in procedure and methodology arising out of an investigation into the antecedents of business failures were presented.[1] The techniques employed to obtain the data were described and the immediate and more remote objectives were outlined. Since that time 598 bankruptcies from the District of New Jersey, comprising about two-thirds of all the bankruptcy cases in that District between October, 1929, and July, 1930, have been studied. The analysis of the results of these cases throws light on some of the methodological problems raised in the previous article.

As indicated in the earlier article, the method of securing the information from the bankrupts was by means of a weekly or bi-weekly clinic in the bankruptcy court. Pursuant to court notice those bankrupts whose petitions were filed during the week or two weeks preceding the date set for the clinic appeared in open court, together with their attorneys, and were examined by a staff of investigators, averaging eight in number. Each investigator examined one bankrupt at a time. The clinics lasted

---

[1] *Clark, Douglas and Thomas,* The Business Failures Project—A Problem in Methodology *(1930)* 39 YALE L. J. *1013.*

Reprinted by permission of the Yale Law Journal Company and Fred B. Rothman & Company from the *Yale Law Journal,* vol. 40 (1931), pp. 1034–1054.

between two and three hours each and the investigators averaged two examinations each per clinic. After 58 cases had been covered it was found necessary to abandon the clinic.

The impossibility of continuing the clinic produced a dilemma. Sufficient information was not at hand to provide a basis for any adequate revision of the work-sheet, or to further the development of more adequate techniques for controlling errors and securing data from which inferences could be drawn as to the causal connection between bankruptcy and the various factors under investigation. Furthermore, the administrative machinery had been set up for a continuance of the study along the lines already indicated. The exigencies of the whole situation made it necessary to use several methods for collecting the work-sheet data. Some of the methods, as we will indicate, have produced data of little value. All of them, however, contributed toward the development of a new work-sheet, in which the most obvious sources of unreliability have been eliminated. This article describes the abortive attempts to collect data after the clinic had broken up, compares the clinic data with these others, and outlines the method of data collection now in operation, and the revisions in the new work-sheet. . . .

The methods other than the clinic that were developed to meet the situation were: (1) a personal interview with the bankrupt; (2) mailing of the questionnaire to the bankrupt, together with a letter from the staff, indicating the purpose of the study and asking the bankrupt to fill out the questionnaire and return it by mail; (3) mailing of the questionnaire to the bankrupt, together with a letter from the court directing and soliciting the bankrupt to fill out the questionnaire and return it by mail. These four methods are referred to hereafter as (a) the clinic, (b) the personal interview, (c) the personal letter, and (d) the court letter. The number of cases covered by each method were:

| | |
|---|---|
| Clinic | 58 |
| Personal interview | 91 |
| Personal letter | 90 |
| Court letter | 359 |
| Total | 598 |

Because of the heterogeneity of the total, two classes of cases were taken out for special analysis in this article. They were 278 cases of retailers, and

104 cases of contractors (including partnership cases). The cases excluded from the analysis consisted of small groups of wholesalers and manufacturers and a larger group of wage-earners. An attempt was made to insure that the computations in Table I (below) were based on relevant cases only. All questions relating to the personal characteristics of the bankrupts were relevant for both partners in a partnership, and were, of course, irrelevant for corporations, except for the obvious one-man corporation. Certain questions were irrelevant for special cases only, *e. g. "grade reached"* was irrelevant when there had been no schooling, "inventory" was irrelevant when no stock was held, etc. All questions relating to the firm rather than the individual included one partner's schedule only in partnership cases.

It was felt that no analysis of the frequency of presumably "causal" factors could be made, and no control group could be set up to test these causal factors, until some estimate could be made of the definiteness, completeness, and accuracy of the data obtained. Accuracy, of course, can be tested only by external checks, although it can be inferred from internal evidence in some cases. Even though the information be highly accurate, however, the study is inadequate unless a large proportion of the answers are complete and definite with regard to the essential questions. Unless such definiteness is obtained, the final frequency tables will be based on a sample of cases almost certainly selective and unrepresentative of the total group.

Ideally, the investigations of causal factors in bankruptcy should attempt two things: (1) An analysis by the case method of all probably relevant matters pertaining to the entire situation converging at bankruptcy. This would cover a wide range and would consider a variety of factors in the environment in which the bankrupt lived. It would entail a study of the adjustment or lack of adjustment of the bankrupt to society and would include such matters as physical and mental health, mental capacity and training, and economic factors. (2) A statistical study of the association of the factors found to be relevant, by comparison of bankrupts with a control group.

At this stage of such research it is quite obvious that inclusive analyses of the first sort would be impracticable. The project aimed at something less complete and was restricted almost entirely to sociological and economic factors. It was not possible to use existing methods for measuring intelligence, though an attempt was made. Nor did the situation warrant physical and psychiatric examinations, though efforts were made to develop that phase of the study.

The sociological data pertained to the individual and his family. The educational and vocational career of the bankrupt were covered in an attempt to produce qualitative data throwing some light on his capacity as a business man. While inconclusive by themselves, they added to the total situation significant factors aiding particular case analyses. For the same reason, age, nationality and language were covered. Questions respecting the family of the bankrupt were designed largely with the view of obtaining information concerning the economic strain produced by the bankruptcy. Such matters as size of family, number of contributors, medical expense, amount of rent or mortgage payments on the home were included.

The balance of the questions related for the most part to business practices. Capitalization of the business was sought for the purpose of discovering cases of obvious under-financing which would handicap the business from the start. Subsequent financing was investigated to ascertain if the fixed charges were so heavy as to place a strain on the business. Questions pertaining to insurance were included, not only to discover if the lack of insurance was producing losses from which the business could not recover, but also as some earmark of prudent or unwise management. The kinds of books kept obviously would indicate whether the individual was operating by guess work or was attempting to order his business affairs efficiently. Data respecting credit extension and credit losses were also included not only because of their relevance to the quality of the management but also to reveal those cases in which such losses were so high as to be dangerous to successful operation. Other economic questions covered a wide range and included such questions as inventory, advertising practices and overhead.

In all there were 136 questions to be answered by the bankrupt and in addition about fifty more to be obtained from other sources. To answer these questions completely and intelligently the average bankrupt needed at least an hour. No doubt mere length tended to produce a large number of failures to answer or partial answers when the bankrupt was left to his own devices, as in the personal letter, or felt under no compulsion to answer, as in the personal interview. In view of the limitations of the methods used it probably would have been more satisfactory to have asked fewer questions and to have restricted their range.

The following analysis deals with the degree of definiteness and completeness obtained by the methods, and touches slightly the question of accuracy, but does not even approach the question of the frequency of occurrence of various factors in the several bankrupt groups. The answers have been classified as complete, partial and ambiguous, and no answer. By complete answer is meant one which on its face is responsive to the question and apparently definite and complete, while partial and ambiguous describe those answers which do not make sense or are so sketchy as to leave one in doubt as to the meaning. A crude example of the latter is the answer "yes" to the question, "Did the language used help or hinder the business?"

Certain typical questions were selected for analysis in order to discover the proportion of complete and definite answers to the other types of answers. The selection was made to include (1) simple questions calling for a categorical, short answer; (2) possibly misleading or ambiguous questions calling for judgment on the part of investigator or informant; (3) questions calling for detailed information depending on memory or access to records. These questions related both to economic and to sociological matters and to events both far distant and near. All of the information for these questions was derived from the bankrupts. While numerous other questions might have been analyzed in the same manner it is felt that such analysis probably would not alter the conclusions materially, in view of the representativeness of these questions.

Of the questions calling for answers in terms of a single date, place, etc. or in terms of a simple choice between clear-cut alternatives or among several well-defined possibilities, an analysis was made of the one relating to the form of organization. This question was as follows:

> Form of organization: (a) individual
> (b) partnership
> (c) corporation

In both the retail and contractors' groups the question was answered definitely and completely by 98% of the firms. There can be no criticism of this question from the point of view of bringing out the definite information for which it was designed.

Of the questions formulated to elicit pertinent personal data about the bankrupts, perhaps the most essential were those relating to his education, vocational career, familial status and dependents. The question relating to education was as follows:

a. Length of formal school attendance
   1. Number of years at school_____
   2. Grade reached_____
   3. Location of schools_____

     _____
     _____
     _____
     _____

   4. Name of schools_____
b. Character of higher education—cultural, vocational

     _____
     _____
     _____

c. Correspondence courses, night school, etc.

     _____
     _____
     _____

The questions regarding location and name of school were asked merely as a possible check on the other information, and therefore have no relevance to the present problem. It may be stated, parenthetically, that they were answered so infrequently as to be worthless as a check. This analysis concerns (1) the number of years in school, (2) the grade reached, (3) whether or not there was any higher education, irrespective of its character, and (4) whether or not there was any education through correspondence courses or night school, irrespective of its character. The number of years in school brought a complete reply in 36% of the relevant cases of retailers and 89% of the contractors. From the point of view of the methods used in the inquiry, then, this question may be considered moderately successful. There are probably several reasons for failure to answer. Memory probably played some part, resentment because of the apparent irrelevance of the question, another part, etc. These factors almost certainly operated selectively to exclude the least well-educated group, and raise the suspicion that averages based on these data may be too high to be representative of the whole group.

With regard to the other parts of the question, the replies were distinctly less definite and the proportion of "no answers" larger. The grade reached was indicated definitely in only 60% of the cases of retailers and *68%* of the contractors, the part regarding higher education in *53%* of the retailers, and *60%* of the contractors, and the part regarding correspondence and night schools in *59%* of the retailers and *66%* of the contractors. Several possible explanations occur.

Most people might be expected to remember more clearly the grade reached rather than the number of years spent in school, because of the frequent discontinuity of the latter. Yet a much larger proportion indicated the number of years spent in school than gave an answer regarding the grade reached. It is possible that persons retarded in grade as compared to years spent in school would resent having that fact known. The falling off of *25* to *30%* complete answers in the parts of the question relating to higher education and night schools may have been due to a feeling that the answer to the first part in many cases carried an implicit answer to these parts. The slightly greater percentage of replies to the correspondence and night school question than to the higher education question seems to be due to a tendency to leave a question unanswered rather than record a negative, since the extra percentage can be accounted for by the greater proportion of affirmative replies in the correspondence-night school part of the question.

The question relating to the vocational career was as follows:

Vocational career (Describe job, name occupation, name employer, give dates, places, etc.)
a. In other occupations_____

b. Apprenticeship in present business_____

c. As an independent business man in present business_____

d. Length of time in business which failed_____
   Dates _____

e. Present occupation_____

The data obtained on the first part were unsuited to this analysis because of the complexity of the factors involved and the almost universal incompleteness of the answers, taken as a whole. Parts b, c and d were selected for analysis in terms of whether or not the bankrupt had served an apprenticeship, how long he had been an independent business man, and the length of time he had been in the business which failed. The apprenticeship question brought only 58% complete replies for retailers, and 79% for contractors; the question relating to his career as an independent business man 55% for retailers, and 65% for contractors; and the question relating to the length of time in the business which failed 94% for retailers, and 96% for contractors. Probably the uncertainty in the bankrupt's mind as to the exact meaning of "apprenticeship" led to the small number of complete replies. In 92% of the retail cases, for example, where there had been an apprenticeship, a definite number of years was indicated. The range was from 1 to 24 years, and the high average of 7 years for these cases suggests some misunderstanding of the meaning of the question, since it is highly improbable, under modern industrial conditions, that apprenticeship would last so long. There is every reason to believe the time in the business which failed could be stated accurately, and would be so stated because of the extreme relevance of that question to the court proceedings. The failure to answer the question in 4 to 6% of the cases may have been due to carelessness.

Other questions, though calling for definite information which a bankrupt would be able to furnish from his memory without consulting records, were phrased so inartistically as to elicit information on only a part of the question or to render the entire answer ambiguous. Such a question was:

Do you carry life or health insurance?_____ When was it taken? _____ What amount?_____ What is the annual premium?_____ Who is the beneficiary?_____

As should have been expected the tendency was to reply on either life or health and not both because of the ambiguous wording of the question.

The results obtained on this question are interesting. In respect to the groups mentioned, there were 93% definite, clear, and complete answers to life insurance for the retailers and 89% for the contractors. These high percentages are in contrast to the 34% of the complete answers respecting health insurance for the retailers and 49% for the contractors.

Data collected on fire and burglary insurance for these groups brought very high percentages of complete answers—*94%* for fire insurance for the retailers and *88%* for the contractors. For burglary insurance the percentages were *92%* for the retailers and *82%* for the contractors. These questions were simple and concise, calling merely for a yes or no answer and a statement of the amount.

Somewhat less satisfactory answers were obtained to the questions:

Did the debtor make use of a local credit bureau? (Yes or no)_____ At what intervals were inventory taken?_____ What books were kept?_____

The complete answers on the use of a credit bureau were *88%* for the retailers, and *82%* for the contractors; on inventory *71%* for the retailers, and *58%* for the contractors; and on books *81%* for the retailers, and *88%* for the contractors. This may have been due to less familiarity on the part of the bankrupts with the meaning of the terms or to the fact that the answer might have to be qualified or lengthy. Such could be true if the bankrupt's practice in respect to any of them had varied or had not been systematized or regular. It seems doubtful that with the use of the questionnaire method any more extended qualitative analysis could have been obtained of the debtor's method of credit investigation, in view of the fact that it would require more thoughtful answers, would take a great deal of time and therefore would be apt to be neglected. Thus the question calling for a categorical yes-no answer was probably the best one under the circumstances even though qualitative deficiencies may result.

One of the most important economic questions called for the following information:

(1) Total net sales, open credit (last year in business)
(2) Total net sales, deferred payments (last year in business)
(3) Total net sales, all accounts (cash, open credit, deferred payments) (last year in business)
(4) Net losses for bad debts, open credit (last year in business)
(5) Net losses on deferred payments (last year in business).

The importance of these questions has been indicated above. The percentages of complete answers were:

|     | Retailers | Contractors |
| --- | --- | --- |
| (2) | 42% | 45% |
| (3) | 42% | 40% |
| (4) | 44% | 48% |
| (5) | 42% | 47% |

These low percentages of complete answers may have been due, to a large extent, to the fact that they required recourse to the books and accounts for complete and accurate answers. Even if the bankrupt desired to give full and accurate replies and was willing to spend time on them, he might not have been able to consult the books, since they were probably in the hands of one of the bankruptcy officials. Perhaps in other cases no books showing the information had been kept. In either event probably in the vast majority of cases the complete answers were furnished from memory alone. The difficulty of remembering these details no doubt was so great as to discourage the attempt. In addition, the discrimination necessary to distinguish between "open credit" and "deferred payments" may also have contributed to the giving of no answers.

The percentages of complete answers to the question, "Did the debtor fail in business before?" were consistently high, being 93% for the retailers and 87% for the contractors.

In the first part of this article, attention was drawn to the different methods of data collection. An analysis in terms of the different results obtained for each of these methods will indicate the extent to which the work-sheet itself was at fault in its failure to elicit definite replies. If the differential is very great between any of the methods, there will be an indication of the extent to which the work-sheet can function under favorable as compared with unfavorable circumstances. Unfortunately, however, the distribution of cases among methods was quite uneven, running as low as 41 retailers and 10 contractors in the personal letter group and 23 retailers and 14 contractors in the clinic group. No attempt was made to treat the retailers and contractors separately in the comparison of methods because of this deficiency in the number of cases. Even so, the number of cases in the last two groups is so small as to make an accurate comparison between the various methods somewhat difficult and percentages will be unreliable. But where there appear great differences in percentages of complete answers, these are taken as indicative of the differential, even though the actual numerical expression of this differential is not accurate. Before discussing the results obtained by these various methods it might be well to make some general observations about each.

The "clinic" was theoretically the most ideal of the four for a scientific study. It necessarily brought the interviewer and the bankrupt together, permitted an extensive cross-examination of the bankrupt, and enabled the interviewer to fill out the questionnaire and make copious notes of matters not covered by the questionnaire. As actually used, however, it had certain distinct limitations. With eight examinations going on at one time in one small courtroom and twelve or more bankrupts and their attorneys waiting in the same room, the tendency to hurry the examination was almost unavoidable. Consequently the examinations did not seem as thorough and effective as they could have been if the interview had been held in private with no requirements for haste and without the disconcerting features of a semi-public examination. Secondly, the kind of examination used was not the traditional bankruptcy examination, and though legal, it was unfamiliar. The tendency on the part of the bankrupts and their attorneys was either to treat it lightly or to look on it with suspicion. While there was apparent cooperation, this attitude militated against effectiveness. Coupled with the physical conditions attendant on the examination it made that technique considerably less valuable than originally contemplated.

The personal interview method was an extremely difficult one to use. It was expensive and time consuming and few bankrupts would consent to an examination without approval of counsel. To convince an attorney of the appropriateness of an examination was difficult, as he was naturally suspicious. The general attitude was that if an examination was desired the regularly constituted bankruptcy officials could order one. Even if counsel consented it was usual for him to require the examination in his presence so that he could protect his client if occasion arose. This meant a hurried examination as the counsel's time was valuable and the examiner was under great pressure to complete it with dispatch. If a personal interview were obtained without the presence of counsel the conditions normally were not conducive to thoroughness. It might be late at night, or at lunch hour, or while the bankrupt was being constantly interrupted. Further, being under no compulsion the bankrupt usually ruled the situation. Occasionally, a bankrupt with leisure and unusual cooperation was found and the examiner could take his time. Normally great persistence was required and an extreme amount of cajoling was necessary to approximate a thorough examination.

Both the personal letter and court letter methods had all of the disadvantages of having schedules filled out by the subjects under investigation rather than by the investigator or with the aid of the investigator. Thus observational errors would be increased—perhaps to great proportions. There was present in the court letter, however, an element of compulsion absent from the personal letter, because of the fact that the former was official. In this sense the court letter method was more comparable to the clinic than the others. For complete answers it might be expected that the court letter would produce higher percentages than the personal letter and even might exceed the personal interview. For reliability of data, however, the personal interview and clinic theoretically would be better.

The following paragraphs compare the four methods with respect to the specific questions analyzed above, in light of the data set forth in Table I.

The percentages of complete answers on the form of organization were all very high, irrespective of method, personal letter showing up least well with 92% complete answers compared with 99% for court letter, 95% for personal interview and 100% for clinic.

The clinic had again the most marked success with the education questions: For years in school, it was the only method bringing over 90% complete replies, and the personal letter brought only 75%. On grade reached, the clinic brought 84% complete replies, with the other methods markedly inferior and the personal interview as low as 35%. The clinic was still superior on the higher education question, but all four methods seem quite inadequate, the range in percentage of complete replies being from 47% to 69%. On correspondence courses, also, the replies were inadequate, averaging about 60% for all except the clinic which brought 80%.

The low percentage on the personal interview on three out of four of these questions may be explained in part by the fact that the field workers as well as the bankrupts rated the question as unimportant or regarded a complete answer on the first point sufficient. Furthermore, the field workers were working under pressure and fearful of not being able to finish all of the answers. They therefore probably made a selection of economic questions which they regarded as more important. This hunch is partly substantiated by the relatively higher percentage of answers by the personal interview method on the economic questions.

A curious difference in methods is shown by the percentages on apprenticeship and length of time as an independent business man. On apprenticeship the court letter has 61% complete answers, the personal letter 53% and the clinic only 63%. On length of time as independent business man the court letter has 53%, personal letter 46% and clinic

TABLE I. BANKRUPTCY CASES AMONG RETAILERS AND CONTRACTORS IN NEW JERSEY, OCTOBER, 1929–JULY, 1930. ANALYZED BY METHOD OF INQUIRY AND COMPLETENESS OF ANSWERS TO SPECIFIC QUESTIONS.

| | Method of Inquiry | | | | | | | |
| | Court Letter | | | | Personal Interview | | | |
| Question Relating to | No. of Relevant Cases | Percentage of Answers That Are | | | No. of Relevant Cases | Percentage of Answers That Are | | |
| | | Complete | Partial & Ambiguous | No Answer | | Complete | Partial & Ambiguous | No Answer |
|---|---|---|---|---|---|---|---|---|
| Life insurance | 238 | 95 | 1 | 4 | 53 | 91 | 6 | 3 |
| Health insurance | 238 | 40 | 1 | 59 | 53 | 30 | 6 | 64 |
| Fire insurance | 222 | 92 | 1 | 7 | 54 | 100 | 0 | 0 |
| Burglary insurance | 222 | 86 | 0 | 14 | 54 | 96 | 0 | 4 |
| Use of credit bureau | 222 | 84 | 0 | 16 | 53 | 96 | 0 | 4 |
| Inventory | 222 | 63 | 2 | 35 | 54 | 80 | 2 | 18 |
| Books kept | 222 | 81 | 6 | 13 | 54 | 89 | 11 | 0 |
| Net sales, open credit | 222 | 29 | 9 | 62 | 54 | 63 | 6 | 31 |
| Net sales, deferred pay't | 222 | 29 | 5 | 66 | 54 | 69 | 5 | 26 |
| Net losses, open credit | 222 | 35 | 11 | 54 | 54 | 59 | 19 | 22 |
| Net losses, deferred pay't | 222 | 33 | 6 | 61 | 54 | 60 | 7 | 33 |
| Apprenticeship | 238 | 61 | 11 | 28 | 53 | 80 | 7 | 13 |
| Time ind. bus. man | 238 | 53 | 15 | 32 | 53 | 73 | 0 | 27 |
| Time in bus. which failed | 238 | 96 | 1 | 3 | 53 | 96 | 0 | 4 |
| Years in school | 238 | 89 | 2 | 9 | 53 | 87 | 4 | 9 |
| Grade reached | 219 | 67 | 16 | 17 | 50 | 35 | 12 | 53 |
| Higher education, etc. | 238 | 54 | 5 | 41 | 53 | 47 | 0 | 53 |
| Correspondence school, etc. | 238 | 62 | 0 | 38 | 53 | 57 | 2 | 41 |
| Previous failure | 238 | 96 | 0 | 4 | 53 | 96 | 0 | 4 |
| Type of organization | 222 | 99 | 1 | 0 | 54 | 95 | 0 | 5 |

| | Personal Letter | | | | Clinic | | | |
|---|---|---|---|---|---|---|---|---|
| | No. of Relevant Cases | Percentage of Answers That Are | | | No. of Relevant Cases | Percentage of Answers That Are | | |
| Question Relating to | | Complete | Partial & Ambiguous | No Answer | | Complete | Partial & Ambiguous | No Answer |
| Life insurance | 51 | 90 | 0 | 10 | 37 | 77 | 17 | 6 |
| Health insurance | 51 | 34 | 0 | 66 | 37 | 44 | 19 | 37 |
| Fire insurance | 49 | 82 | 2 | 16 | 37 | 85 | 3 | 12 |
| Burglary insurance | 49 | 90 | 0 | 10 | 37 | 92 | 5 | 3 |
| Use of credit bureau | 49 | 80 | 0 | 20 | 37 | 92 | 0 | 8 |
| Inventory | 49 | 57 | 10 | 33 | 36 | 83 | 3 | 14 |
| Books kept | 49 | 73 | 2 | 25 | 37 | 97 | 3 | 0 |
| Net sales, open credit | 49 | 58 | 6 | 36 | 37 | 76 | 3 | 21 |
| Net sales, deferred pay't | 49 | 51 | 4 | 45 | 37 | 59 | 3 | 38 |
| Net losses, open credit | 49 | 54 | 6 | 40 | 37 | 78 | 8 | 14 |
| Net losses, deferred pay't | 49 | 53 | 4 | 43 | 37 | 68 | 0 | 32 |
| Apprenticeship | 51 | 53 | 12 | 35 | 37 | 63 | 11 | 26 |
| Time ind. bus. man | 51 | 46 | 20 | 34 | 37 | 54 | 29 | 17 |
| Time in bus. which failed | 51 | 86 | 2 | 12 | 37 | 94 | 0 | 6 |
| Years in school | 51 | 75 | 4 | 21 | 37 | 92 | 3 | 5 |
| Grade reached | 45 | 50 | 21 | 29 | 37 | 84 | 8 | 8 |
| Higher education, etc. | 51 | 56 | 4 | 40 | 37 | 69 | 3 | 28 |
| Correspondence school, etc. | 51 | 61 | 0 | 39 | 37 | 80 | 0 | 20 |
| Previous failure | 51 | 87 | 0 | 13 | 37 | 59 | 0 | 41 |
| Type of organization | 49 | 92 | 3 | 5 | 37 | 100 | 0 | 0 |

*54%*. This lack of substantial differences between the first two methods and the last is surprising, not that the percentages for the court letters and personal letters were unusually low but that the clinic was not higher. The ascendency of the personal interview group (*80%* for apprenticeship and *73%* for independent business man) is difficult to explain.

The insurance questions, primarily economic, were quite uniformly successful irrespective of the method employed, with the exception of health insurance, although the clinic has only *77%* complete on life insurance.

On the questions relating to the use of the credit bureau, the differences in methods probably are not significant and do not show any inferiority of the court letter method. The same is true for books kept. In regard to inventory, however, the inferior showing of the court letter and personal letter method is striking (*63%* and *57%*, as compared with *80%* and *83%* for personal interview and clinic). A hunch that the term "inventory" was not understood might be justified by these percentages, since in the personal interview and clinic groups the examiner could explain the term.

In respect to the questions pertaining to business done on credit and credit losses, the percentages for the court letter and personal letter are consistently below those for the personal interview and the clinic. The court letter is especially inferior, ranging from *29%* to *35%*. The personal letter ranges from *51%* to *58%*. The personal interview is slightly superior, ranging from *59%* to *69%*, and the clinic superior to these others with a range of *59%* to *78%*.

It is difficult to explain the higher percentage in personal letter cases than in court letter cases. As noted above, the element of compulsion was lacking with the personal letters and was present with the court letters. Therefore, a lower percentage of complete answers might be expected in the former. The differential may be due to the fact that there was too small a number of cases in the personal letter group to test adequately the efficiency of that method.

The higher percentage in the clinic cases in comparison with the other methods may well reflect the superiority of that method. But the percentages in the questions referring to deferred payments hardly justify this conclusion, even in view of the somewhat unfavorable circumstances in which the examiners were working in the clinic. The mediocre showing of the personal interview may be explained in part by the disadvantages the field workers were under in the examination. The low percentage in the court letter cases might tend to support the contention that this method is distinctly inferior. However, on other questions . . . , the percentage of complete answers by that method showed some superiority.

*　　*　　*　　*

This somewhat pedantic and perhaps over-detailed account of the meagreness of data obtained by various uses of the questionnaire is given for several reasons. Perhaps the most important is its educative value to those interested in socio-legal research. Unless hypotheses can be so formed as to elicit definite information from the group under investigation, very little light will be thrown on the validity of these hypotheses. It is easy to neglect this factor in this type of research. Questionnaires are broadcast, incomparable methods of data collection are employed, and a final analysis is made on the basis of a fraction of the cases under investigation, or of some questions from one group of schedules, other questions from an overlapping group, etc. The uncertainties inherent in such data are completely lost sight of in the frequency tables which are usually presented with all the false definiteness that mere numbers can attain. The fallacy involved in such a procedure is indicated by this analysis of the types of replies received in a preliminary study of bankruptcy. Although frequency tables will be presented in a subsequent article, they will be presented only because, incomplete as the data are, they represent the most adequate in this almost untouched field.

A further reason for this detailed consideration is that it indicates the improvement that results when due regard is given to a careful phrasing of questions, training of field workers, and control of the conditions of investigation. The Boston situation, while still imperfect in many respects, is producing definite and complete answers to an extent that will make frequency tables more truly representative of the groups studied.

*　　*　　*　　*

The general aim is to avoid two pitfalls: (1) the production of a large body of complete and definite data which may nevertheless be highly inaccurate, and (2) to avoid the production of a small, unrepresentative body of data, which may nevertheless be highly accurate.

# CRIME AND CUSTOM
# IN SAVAGE SOCIETY

## Bronislaw Malinowski

\*    \*    \*    \*

Anthropology, still a young science, is now on the way to free itself from the control of pre-scientific interest, though certain recent attempts at offering extremely simple and, at the same time, sensational solutions of all the riddles of Culture are still dominated by crude curiosity. In the study of primitive law we can perceive this sound tendency in the gradual but definite recognition that savagery is not ruled by moods, passions, and accidents, but by tradition and order. Even then there remains something of the old 'shocker' interest in the over-emphasis of criminal justice, in the attention devoted to the breaches of the law and their punishment. Law in modern Anthropology is still almost exclusively studied in its singular and sensational manipulations, in cases of blood-curdling crime, followed by tribal vendetta, in accounts of criminal sorcery with retaliation, of incest, adultery, breach of taboo or murder. In all this, besides the dramatic piquancy of the incidents, the anthropologist can, or thinks he can, trace certain unexpected, exotic, astonishing features of primitive law: a transcending solidarity of the kindred group, excluding all sense of self-interest; a legal and economic Communism; a submission to a rigid, undifferentiated tribal law.[1]

---

[1] *Thus Rivers speaks of a "group sentiment of the clan system with its accompanying communistic practices", supposed to exist in Melanesia, and he adds that to such natives the "principle 'each man for himself' is beyond the reach of understanding"* (Social Organization, p. 170). *Sidney Hartland imagines that in savagery "The same code in the same Divine Name, and with equal authority, may make*

Reprinted by permission of the publishers from *Crime and Custom in Savage Society*, Chap. I, at pp. 72–84 (London: Routledge & Kegan Paul, Ltd., 1926). Footnotes have been renumbered to run in sequence throughout the selection.

As a reaction against the method and the principles just stated, I have tried to approach the facts of primitive law in the Trobriands from the other end. I have started with the description of the ordinary, not the singular; of the law obeyed and not the law broken; of the permanent currents and tides in their social life and not its adventitious storms. From the account given, I have been able to conclude that contrary to most established views civil law—or its savage equivalent—is extremely well developed, and that it rules all aspects of social organization. We also found that it is clearly distinguishable, and distinguished by the natives, from the other types of norm, whether morals or manners, rules of art or commands of religion. The rules of their law, far from being rigid, absolute or issued in the Divine Name, are maintained by social forces, understood as rational and necessary, elastic and capable of adjustment. Far also from being exclusively a group affair, his rights and his duties are in the main the concern of the individual, who knows perfectly well how to look after his interests and realizes that he has to redeem his obligations. We found indeed that the native's attitude towards duty and privilege is very much the same as in a civilized community—to the extent in fact that he not only stretches but also at times breaks the law. . . . It would be a very one-sided picture indeed of the law in the Trobriands, if the rules were shown only in good working order, if the system were only described in equilibrium! That law functions only very imperfectly, that there are many hitches and breakdowns, I have now and again indicated, but a full description of the criminal and dramatic issues is necessary, though, as I have said, it should not be unduly emphasized.

There is still one reason why we must have a close look at native life in disorder. We found that in the Trobriands, social relations are governed by a number of legal principles. The most important of these is Mother-right, which rules that a child is bodily related and morally beholden by kinship to its mother and to her only. This principle governs succession to rank, power and dignities, economic inheritance, the rights to soil and to local citizenship and membership in the totemic clan. The status between brother and sister, the relations between the sexes and most

*regulations for the conduct of commercial transactions and of the most intimate conjugal relations, as well as for a complex and splendid ceremonial of divine worship"* (Primitive Law, p. 214). *Both statements are misleading. . . .*

of their private and public social intercourse is defined by rules forming part of matriarchal law. The economic duties of a man towards his married sister and her household constitute a strange and important feature of this law. The whole system is based on mythology, on the native theory of procreation, on certain of their magico-religious beliefs and it pervades all the institutions and customs of the tribe.

But, side by side with the system of Mother-right, in its shadow so to speak, there exist certain other, minor systems of legal rules. The law of marriage, defining the status of husband and wife, with its patrilocal arrangements, with its limited but clear bestowal of authority on the man and of guardianship over his wife and children in certain specified matters, is based on legal principles independent of Mother-right, though on several points intertwined with it and adjusted to it. The constitution of a village community, the position of the headman in his village and of the chief in his district, the privileges and duties of the public magician—all these are independent legal systems.

Now since we know that primitive law is not perfect, the problem emerges: how does this composite body of systems behave under the strain of circumstances? Is each system well harmonized within its own limits? Does such a system, moreover, keep within its limits or has it a tendency to encroach upon alien ground? Do the systems then come into conflict, and what is the character of such conflict? Here once more we have to appeal to the criminal, disorderly, disloyal elements of the community to furnish us with material from which we can answer our questions.

In the accounts to which we now proceed—and which will be given concretely and with some detail—we shall keep before us the main problems still unsolved: the nature of criminal acts and procedure and their relation to civil law; the main factors active in the restitution of the disturbed equilibrium; the relations and the possible conflicts between the several systems of native law.

While engaged in my field-work in the Trobriands, I used always to live right among the natives, pitching my tent in the village, and being thus forcibly present at all that happened, trivial or solemn, hum-drum or dramatic. The event which I now proceed to relate happened during my first visit in the Trobriands, a few months only after I had started my field-work in the archipelago.

One day an outbreak of wailing and a great commotion told me that a death had occurred somewhere in the neighbourhood. I was informed that Kima'i, a young lad of my acquaintance, of sixteen or so, had fallen from a coco-nut palm and killed himself.

I hastened to the next village where this had occurred, only to find the whole mortuary proceedings in progress. This was my first case of death, mourning, and burial, so that in my concern with the ethno-graphical aspects of the ceremonial, I forgot the circumstances of the tragedy even though one or two singular facts occurred at the same time in the village which should have aroused my suspicions. I found that another youth had been severely wounded by some mysterious coincidence. And at the funeral there was obviously a general feeling of hostility between the village where the boy died and that into which his body was carried for burial.

Only much later was I able to discover the real meaning of these events: the boy had committed suicide. The truth was that he had broken the rules of exogamy, the partner in his crime being his maternal cousin, the daughter of his mother's sister. This had been known and generally disapproved of, but nothing was done until the girl's discarded lover, who had wanted to marry her and who felt personally injured, took the initiative. This rival threatened first to use black magic against the guilty youth, but this had not much effect. Then one evening he insulted the culprit in public—accusing him in the hearing of the whole community of incest and hurling at him certain expressions intolerable to a native.

For this there was only one remedy; only one means of escape remained to the unfortunate youth. Next morning he put on festive attire and ornamentation, climbed a coco-nut palm and addressed the community, speaking from among the palm leaves and bidding them farewell. He explained the reasons for his desperate deed and also launched forth a veiled accusation against the man who had driven him to his death, upon which it became the duty of his clansmen to avenge him. Then he wailed aloud, as is the custom, jumped from a palm some sixty feet high and was killed on the spot. There followed a fight within the village in which the rival was wounded; and the quarrel was repeated during the funeral.

Now this case opened up a number of important lines of inquiry. I was here in the presence of a pronounced crime: the breach of totemic clan exogamy. The exogamous prohibition is one of the corner-stones of totemism, Mother-right, and the classificatory system of kinship. All females of his clan are called sisters by a man and forbidden as such. It is an axiom of Anthropology that nothing arouses a greater horror than the breach of this prohibition, and that besides a strong reaction of public opinion, there are also supernatural punishments, which visit this crime. Nor is this axiom devoid of foundation in fact. If you were to inquire into the matter among the Trobrianders, you would find that all statements confirm the axiom, that the natives show horror at the idea of violating the rules of exogamy and that they believe that sores, disease and even death might follow clan incest. This is the ideal of native law, and in moral matters it is easy and pleasant strictly to adhere to the ideal—when judging the conduct of others or expressing an opinion about conduct in general.

When it comes to the application of morality and ideals to real life, however, things take on a different complexion. In the case described it was obvious that the facts would not tally with the ideal of conduct. Public opinion was neither outraged by the knowledge of the crime to any extent, nor did it react directly—it had to be mobilized by a public statement of the crime and by insults being hurled at the culprit by an interested party. Even then he had to carry out the punishment himself. The 'group-reaction' and the 'supernatural sanction' were not therefore the active principles. Probing further into the matter and collecting concrete information, I found that the breach of exogamy—as regards intercourse and not marriage—is by no means a rare occurrence, and public opinion is lenient, though decidedly hypocritical. If the affair is carried on *sub rosa* with a certain amount of decorum, and if no one in particular stirs up trouble—'public opinion' will gossip, but not demand any harsh punishment. If, on the contrary, scandal breaks out—every one turns against the guilty pair and by ostracism and insults one or the other may be driven to suicide.

As regards the supernatural sanction, this case led me to an interesting and important discovery. I learned that there is a perfectly well established remedy against any pathological consequences of this trespass, a remedy considered practically infallible, if properly executed. That is to say the natives possess a system of magic consisting of spells and rites performed over water, herbs, and stones, which when correctly carried out, is completely efficient in undoing the bad results of clan incest.

That was the first time in my field-work that I came across what could be called a well-established system of evasion and that in the case of one of the most fundamental laws of the tribe. Later on I discovered that such parasitic growths upon the main branches of tribal order exist in several other cases, besides the counteraction of incest. The importance of this fact is obvious. It shows clearly that a supernatural sanction need not safeguard a rule of conduct with an automatic effect. Against magical influence there may be counter-magic. It is no doubt better not to run the risk—the counter-magic may have been imperfectly learned or faultily performed—but the risk is not great. The supernatural sanction shows then a considerable elasticity, in conjunction with a suitable antidote.

This methodical antidote teaches us another lesson. In a community where laws are not only occasionally broken, but systematically circumvented by well-established methods, there can be no question of a 'spontaneous' obedience to law, of slavish adherence to tradition. For this tradition teaches man surreptitiously how to evade some of its sterner commands—and you cannot be *spontaneously* pushed forwards and pulled back at the same time!

Magic to undo the consequences of clan incest is perhaps the most definite instance of methodical evasion of law, but there are other cases besides. Thus a system of magic to estrange the affections of a woman from her husband and to induce her to commit adultery is a traditional way of flouting the institution of marriage and the prohibition of adultery. To a slightly different category perhaps belong the various forms of deleterious and malicious magic: to destroy the crops, to thwart a fisherman, to drive the pigs into the jungle, to blight bananas, coco-nuts or areca palms, to spoil a feast or a *Kula* expedition. Such magic, being levelled at established institutions and important pursuits, is really an instrument of crime, supplied by tradition. As such it is a department of tradition, which works against law and is directly in conflict with it, since law in various forms safeguards these pursuits and institutions. . . .

The law of exogamy, the prohibition of marriage and intercourse within the clan is often quoted as one of the most rigid and wholesale commandments of primitive law, in that it forbids sexual relations within the clan with the same stringency, regardless of the degree of kinship between the two people concerned. The unity of the clan and the reality of the 'classificatory system of relationship' are—it is urged—most fully vindicated in the taboo of clan incest. It lumps together all the men and all the women of the clan as 'brothers' and 'sisters' to each other and debars them absolutely from sexual intimacy. A careful analysis of the relevant facts in the Trobriands completely disposes of this view. It is again one of these figments of native tradition, taken over at its face value by anthropology and bodily incorporated into its teachings.[2] In the Trobriands, the breach of exogamy is regarded quite differently according to whether the guilty pair are closely related or whether they are only united by bonds of common clanship. Incest with a sister is to the natives an unspeakable, almost unthinkable crime—which again does not mean that it is never committed. The breach in the case of a matrilineal first cousin is a very serious offence, and it can have, as we have seen, tragic consequences. As kinship recedes, the stringency lessens and, when committed with one who merely belongs to the same clan, the breach of exogamy is but a venial offence, easily condoned. Thus, as regards this prohibition, the females of his clan are to a man not one compact group, not one homogeneous 'clan', but a well-differentiated set of individuals, each standing in a special relation, according to her place in his genealogy.

From the point of view of the native libertine, *suvasova* (the breach of exogamy) is indeed a specially interesting and spicy form of erotic experience. Most of my informants would not only admit but actually did boast about having committed this offence or that of adultery (*kaylasi*); and I have many concrete, well-attested cases on record.

*　*　*　*

---

[2] *To give an illustration, reversing the rôle of savage and civilized, of ethnographer and informant: many of my Melanesian friends, taking at its face value the doctrine of 'brotherly love' preached by Christian Missionaries and the taboo on warfare and killing preached and promulgated by Government officials, were unable to reconcile the stories about the Great War, reaching—through planters, traders, overseers, plantation hands—the remotest Melanesian or Papuan village. They were really puzzled at hearing that in one day white men were wiping out as many of their own kind as would make up several of the biggest Melanesian tribes. They forcibly concluded that the White Man was a tremendous liar, but they were not certain at which end the lie lay—whether in the moral pretence or in his bragging about war achievements.*

# STUDIES
# IN TESTIMONY

*William M. Marston*

## 1. PROBLEMS

It seems to be a regrettable fact that little systematic psychological experimentation is being carried on in the field of normal adult testimony. Much valuable material is being produced by psychiatrists, sociologists, and criminologists from time to time; but the subjects of such studies are, for the most part, either psychopathic or criminal variants from the mental or social norms. On the other hand, much constructive work is being done by statistical and educational psychologists toward the development of intelligence and fitness tests; but the direct application of such psycho-statistical procedures to everyday legal problems of testimony seems a long way off.

Such work as has been reported in the legal field proper lies almost wholly in the line of the "Aussage," or "fidelity of report" tests.[1] An incident is performed, or an object presented, before experimental subjects whose immediate, written report is scored as to accuracy and completeness by the experimenter. "The question has been asked," says Wigmore,[2] "whether the alleged percentages of testimonial error, as found in the laboratory experiments, do really, in trials, produce misleading results in the verdicts. The way to answer this is to include a jury (or judge of fact)

---

[1] For summary, see Wigmore: "Principles of Judicial Proof," p. 575 ff.

[2] Wigmore, Ill. Law Review, 1909, p. 426. Cited in summary, reference [1], above.

---

in the experiment, and observe whether the findings of fact follow the testimonial errors or whether they succeed in avoiding them and in reaching the actual facts." The problem, thus stated, is, from a psychological point of view, such a broad one that preliminary studies are indicated for the purpose of roughly determining, first, where lie the possible psycho-legal causes of testimonial error; and, secondly, as suggested by Wigmore, what possible psychological relations may exist between the findings of judge and jury and the original testimony upon which such findings were based. Such were the purposes, then, of the preliminary studies herein reported.

## 2. COMPARISON OF METHODS OF ELICITING TESTIMONY

The most obvious analytical modification of the older method, which consisted of testimony written without questioning, and of written responses to questions, would seem to be a closer approximation of the typical conditions obtaining in actual cases. Three different methods of eliciting testimony for use in the courtroom exist. First, under certain conditions, the witness may refresh his memory from notes made by himself. Such notes are written, according to usual rule, immediately following the occurrence. Psychologically, it is safe to assume, as a working premise, that perusal of such notes, on the stand, substitutes the notes for present memory. Therefore, an account of the incident witnessed, written by the observer himself without questioning, immediately after the occurrence in issue, almost exactly reproduces the actual condition of notes of this sort used on the witness stand. I have called this "Free Narration."

Secondly, the witness is subjected to direct examination. No leading questions may be asked, and the witness does not fear legal trickery, or attempts to entangle his testimony by "catch" questions, since he is examined by an attorney whose purpose is to co-operate in every way possible with his own witness. To be sure, in actual court procedure, the testimony is orally given, and is recorded verbatim by the court stenographer—a condition not practicable in experiments where a number of witnesses must be examined simultaneously. Moreover, no trial is ever held immediately after the occurrence of the incidents in issue; whereas, for the sake of experimental uniformity between witnesses in Aussage tests, it is advisable to take all testimony immediately upon conclusion of the incident, before the witnesses leave the room. In the present experiment, I was able to frame questions conforming, with sufficient accuracy, to a comprehensive direct examination of witnesses in actual practice; but it should be borne in mind that the answers were written by each witness, instead of being given orally; and that the writing was done immediately, instead of after the usual interval intervening between incident and trial. This series of immediate, written responses to non-leading questions I have called "Direct Examination."

Thirdly, witnesses actually on the stand are subjected to cross-examination. The witness knows that the examining counsel is antagonistic, and that every device will be used to entangle and obscure his testimony. Leading questions may be asked freely, and queries of a leading nature based upon deliberately erroneous suggestions are commonly introduced for the purpose of influencing the jury, and of suggesting a doubt, or a contradictory answer, to the witness. These conditions may readily be reproduced in experimental procedure, subject to the qualifications of answers being written immediately, by the witnesses, instead of being given orally, after an interval, as in actual trials. I introduced several deliberately suggestive leading questions of the nature above mentioned into this portion of the test, and 40 questions were propounded, as against 10 in the Direct Examination. This longer series, as described, I have called "Cross-Examination."

### Method

The incident to be observed and reported was performed before a group of 18 students, who were attending a lecture in Legal Psychology at American University, Washington, D. C. All 18 subjects were lawyers, either practising in the District of Columbia or employed by the Government. None of the subjects received any intimation that an experiment was to be performed, nor were they aware that any test was in progress until the incident had been concluded and the experimenter began to issue instructions for recording of testimony.

\*　　\*　　\*　　\*

The incident used was that of an unknown youth rapping on the door of the lecture room, soon after the beginning of the lecture; entering on the lecturer's request, and delivering an envelope to the lecturer. The latter removed a yellow paper from the envelope, pretended to read a message, and exchanged remarks with the stranger, who thereafter left the room. There were no deliberately false suggestions in the affair to lead witnesses astray, and the actions were of such a usual nature that no emotion beyond mild surprise or curiosity could be evoked from the witnesses.

There were a large number of details, however, of possible and connected legal significance. The predetermined plot was trial of the strange youth for the knifing of a person of his acquaintance. In strict adherence to realism, the youth chosen was a Texan, very quick of hand and temper. He possessed a long, green-handled pocket-knife, the blade of which might well be used for stabbing purposes. With one hand the young Texan could draw and open this knife, all in the same motion. Under his left arm he carried three books, one red, one green, and one blue (colors to furnish psychological primaries), and the predetermined plot included the finding of these books at the scene of the crime. Besides the envelope handed the lecturer, the young man carried a second envelope in the same hand, which might have contained a taunting letter, just received from the murdered acquaintance. While the lecturer read his supposed message, the Texan faced the audience, drew and opened his knife, and scraped at his gloved thumb with it, in supposed embarrassment. The points of usual legal significance, therefore, would be all those details serving to identify the Texan, his books, his envelope, and his knife—a not unusual type of legal meaning for any testimony offered. I may anticipate the results by stating that not a single witness noticed the knife at all!

### Results

Each observable detail in the above outlined incident was allotted a score of one point, summing into a total of 147. Similarly, the number of possible points scorable in answering direct and cross-examinations were separately compiled, giving a total of 120 points for direct, and 107 points for cross-examination. Most of these points, of course, were included in the original 147 which might have been obtained, as a perfect score, in the free narration; but for the purpose of comparison of the three methods of eliciting testimony, it was necessary to score each part of the test separately. Table I, following, gives the results:

TABLE I. SCORES OF WITNESSES REPORTING AN UNEXPECTED INCIDENT.

| | Free Narration | Direct Exam. | Cross Exam. |
|---|---|---|---|
| Average of all witnesses— | | | |
| Completeness | 23.2 | 31.2 | 28.7 |
| Accuracy | 94.05 | 83.2 | 75.7 |
| Caution | — | 40.1 | 51.8 |
| Highest witness— | | | |
| Completeness | 31.9 | 48.7 | 43.9 |
| Accuracy | 100. | 94.5 | 97.2 |
| Caution | — | 77.7 | 88.8 |
| Lowest witness— | | | |
| Completeness | 6.4 | 7.5 | 19.6 |
| Accuracy | 83.7 | 64.2 | 61.9 |
| Caution | — | 15.3 | 10. |

The figures in Table I, above, represent percentages. The per cent "Completeness" means the completeness of the correct points given by the witness. Thus the first figure given in Table I, which is 23.2 per cent completeness as the average for all witnesses in free narration, means that the 18 witnesses testified, correctly, to an average of a little over 34 points during this portion of their testimony. Since the total they might have given correctly was 147, $\frac{34+}{147}$, or 23.2%, represents the completeness of their correct findings.

The figure for these witnesses' average "accuracy" in free narration, which is 94.05%, signifies the percentage which their correct points are of their total points given. That means that, whereas these subjects, on an average, gave 34+ points correctly, they actually gave a total average of 36+ points 2 of which were erroneous. The handling of errors in figuring Aussage results seems to me another fertile source of possible confusion. If a witness gives 34 points correctly and 2 points erroneously, how can it have any meaning to figure his total, 36, as the number representing his completeness? Surely the 2 erroneous points are not, in any sense, a portion or fraction of the possible number of 147 points to be given.

Rather, it seems to me, he has gotten $\frac{34}{147}$ of his job done; and, in addition, he has volunteered 2 extra, wrong facts. These 2 mistakes will not tend to impair the completeness of what he has found correctly; but they will tend to mislead the jury into possible additional erroneous findings. The two errors should, therefore, be used as a basis for figuring the percentage of said witness' reliability, or the accuracy of all his testimony taken as a unit, and should be given a negative rather than a positive value in the estimation of the worth of each witness' testimony.

The percentage of "caution," as used in Table I and succeeding tables, signifies that percentage of the total times the witness really didn't know a point, in answer to a question, when that witness declined to answer, or said, "I don't know." The figure is arrived at by totaling the number of errors, "don't know's," and no-answer responses, which total clearly represents the actual total of points unknown to the witness, and then figuring what fraction or percentage of this total is represented by the number of "don't know's" and no-answers, which clearly constitutes the actual total of points the witness knew he didn't know. To take an hypothetical case, suppose a given witness made 6 erroneous answers and replied "I don't know" to 4 queries. Then 4 plus 6 shows that the witness actually did not know the answers to 10 inquiries. But he took a chance on 6 answers and got them wrong, while on 4 he exercised caution and declined to respond. His index of caution, then, would be $\frac{4}{10}$, or 40%. Of course, there is always the possibility that the witness also took chances in answering some of the questions to which he responded correctly; but on this we can obtain no objective check. The value of the index, or percentage of caution, is largely interpretive, as may be seen by a glance at the results in Table I.

### Summary

Careful inspection of these results reveals data which may be summarized as follows:

A—Free narration is uniformly less complete and more accurate than either direct or cross examination.

B—Direct examination is both more complete and more accurate than cross examination. The "low" witness, put into the table to show the range of variation in results, does not conform to the average or to the "high" witness in this particular, and the explanation would seem to lie in an individual eccentricity which leads this man not to respond to any inquiry unless pressed or irritated. The "high" witness, on the other hand, proved even more accurate on cross examination than on direct, this increase in accuracy evidently being at the expense of completeness.

C—Cross examination shows greater caution than direct examination, though without any corresponding gain in either completeness or accuracy on the average. From study of individual records, however, I would suggest that the added caution in cross examination has a vital influence in holding the accuracy percentages up to a figure at all comparable with that obtaining in direct examination. Added caution does an important, though hidden, work, in short, in redeeming cross examination from a degree of inaccuracy which would render it almost wholly worthless.

D—The percentage of caution, in individual results, shows a close correlation with both completeness and accuracy. It seems a rough but certain indicator of the probable value of any witness' testimony.

## 3. COMPARISON OF UNEXPECTED AND EXPECTED INCIDENTS

The lawyer-witnesses in my first experiment were very much dissatisfied with their scores. It seemed to them incredible that not one subject had observed the large, green-handled knife which had been the crux or point of maximum legal meaning in the incident presented. They advanced the theory that the very usualness of the actions involved had cut their perceptions in half; and I countered with the judgment that if they were to see the same incident over again, fully cognizant that it was to occur, their scores would not be improved more than fifteen or twenty per cent. The point was worth investigating, however, since if knowledge that something to be especially observed is about to occur should noticeably increase completeness and accuracy of report, it would mean that the state of witnesses' attention at the time their observations were made is the controlling factor in the resulting value of their testimony. This was the problem, therefore, which I next sought to investigate.

## Method

The same incident, with different actor, costume, knife, envelopes, and conversation, was performed before another class in legal psychology at American University, all members of which had been fully informed as to the details and results of the first experiment. This second class, moreover, which was composed of 12 lawyers, contained two of the same witnesses who had reported on the first incident. No special announcement was made when this second incident was performed that a test was in progress; but, according to later report, every member of the class knew from the moment knocks were heard upon the door of the lecture-room that an Aussage experiment was contemplated. In this way a general study of the importance of witnesses' initial state of attention could be made without interposing that artificial setting which must always arise when subjects are told: "Here is a picture, look at it." As nearly as the actual conditions usually obtaining in observations of actions especially attracting witnesses' attention, and on which they knew while making the observation that they would be called upon to report later, could be reproduced experimentally, this second experiment reproduced them. The two men who had seen the same incident, with differing details, previously performed enjoyed, of course, a considerable advantage over witnesses in actual cases under otherwise corresponding conditions. A separate study of the results obtained by these two witnesses, therefore, was made, as well as a study of the average scores of the whole group, including the two men in question.

## Results

Since the plot of the second incident remained identical with that of the first, including all the actions of knocking, entering the room, giving an envelope to the lecturer, removing a yellow paper, reading a supposed message, stranger's putting second envelope in pocket, taking out knife and scraping at gloved thumb, exchange of almost identical remarks, and stranger's leaving the room, it might certainly be expected that the scores of the two witnesses who had seen the first incident, at least, would show a remarkable improvement. No tricks were introduced, even in the details changed, the new actor being an obviously different individual, with obviously different clothes; his second envelope being very large, and his knife a very large, white-handled affair. The colors of the books were kept the same as in the first experiment. Despite all these favorable conditions for an improved score, Table II, following, shows that the two witnesses reporting on both incidents, one of whom was next to the high man in the second group, failed to exhibit any significant improvement whatever, except in completeness of free narration.

A glance at Table II shows that the only notable improvement in score was obtained, by both subjects, in the completeness of their free narration, their average gain being 22%. This is slightly more of an increase in score than I had predicted, basing my guess upon the general psychological factors involved. When we continue our inspection, however, we soon discover that only one other gain was made, and that was an average improvement of only 7.2% in cross examination completeness. On the other hand, the most consistent difference between the scores of the first and second experiments seems to be a diminution in accuracy in all types of report, varying from .2% in Mr. H's cross examination to 15.9% in the same subject's free narration. This loss in accuracy is uniform except for a gain of 1.1% during the direct examination of Mr. H. The explanation clearly lies in the tremendous diminution of caution which both subjects showed, this loss running as high as 44.5% during the cross examination of Mr. W. In short, the gain which might have been expected to result from repetition of identical perceptions and report of identical observations in the second experiment was largely counteracted, and, during a considerable part of the testimony was completely reversed by the overconfidence or self-assurance of subjects witnessing the same incident for the second time. This result once more emphasizes the apparent close relationship between the caution of the witness and the general reliability of his testimony; and I venture the suggestion that caution plays its part during the observation of an incident as well as during the reporting thereof.

Table III . . . gives the comparative scores of the 18 witnesses to the first incident under unexpected conditions, and the scores of the 12 witnesses to the second incident, who did expect it, from the initial knocks on the lecture-room door, and who knew it was a test incident throughout. The two witnesses who had also seen the first incident are averaged into the second, or "Expected" group, in order to emphasize any possible differences between the scores resulting from the difference in the state of witnesses' expectations.

TABLE II. SCORES OF WITNESSES TWICE REPORTING SAME INCIDENT. U = UNEXPECTED INCIDENT. E = EXPECTED INCIDENT.

| | Mr. W. | | | | Mr. H. | | | | Average Superiority | |
| | Score | | Superiority | | Score | | Superiority | | | |
| | U | E | U | E | U | E | U | E | U | E |
|---|---|---|---|---|---|---|---|---|---|---|
| **Free Narration** | | | | | | | | | | |
| Completeness | 25.5 | 52.5 | | | 22.4 | 39.4 | | | | |
| Accuracy | 92.5 | 85.9 | 6.6 | 27. | 100. | 84.1 | 15.9 | 17. | 11.2 | 22. |
| **Direct Exam.** | | | | | | | | | | |
| Completeness | 48.7 | 34.5 | 14.2 | | 37.5 | 45.4 | | 7.9 | | 3.1 |
| Accuracy | 92.1 | 79. | 13.1 | | 83.3 | 84.4 | 5. | 1.1 | 16. | |
| Caution | 54.5 | 13.3 | 41.2 | 16. | 25. | 20. | | | 23.1 | |
| **Cross Exam.** | | | | | | | | | | |
| Completeness | 24.2 | 40.2 | 5.3 | | 31.7 | 30.2 | 1.5 | | 27. | 7.2 |
| Accuracy | 81.2 | 75.9 | | | 73.9 | 73.7 | .2 | | | |
| Caution | 71.4 | 26.9 | 44.5 | | 45.4 | 23.8 | 21.6 | | 33. | |

TABLE III. SCORES OF WITNESSES REPORTING UNEXPECTED AND EXPECTED INCIDENTS.

| | Free Narration | | Direct Exam. | | Cross Exam. | | Total Average | | Superiority of Higher Average | |
| | U | E | U | E | U | E | U | E | U | E |
|---|---|---|---|---|---|---|---|---|---|---|
| **Average of all Witnesses** | | | | | | | | | | |
| Completeness | 23.2 | 35.2 | 31.2 | 33.7 | 28.7 | 32.3 | 27.6 | 33.7 | | 6.1 |
| Accuracy | 94. | 81.2 | 83.2 | 73.9 | 75.7 | 74.3 | 84.3 | 76.4 | 7.9 | |
| Caution | | | 40.1 | 8.3 | 51.8 | 18.6 | 45.9 | 13.4 | 32.5 | |
| **Highest Witness** | | | | | | | | | | |
| Completeness | 31.9 | 52.5 | 48.7 | 45.4 | 43.9 | 40.2 | 41.5 | 46. | | 4.5 |
| Accuracy | 100. | 91.1 | 94.5 | 92.2 | 97.2 | 86.6 | 97.2 | 89.9 | 7.3 | |
| Caution | | | 77.7 | 25. | 88.8 | 35.7 | 83.2 | 30.3 | 52.9 | |
| **Lowest Witness** | | | | | | | | | | |
| Completeness | 6.4 | 18.2 | 7.5 | 23. | 19.6 | 18.7 | 11.1 | 19.9 | | 8.8 |
| Accuracy | 83.7 | 68.4 | 64.2 | 57.3 | 61.9 | 57.1 | 69.9 | 60.9 | 9. | |
| Caution | | | 15.3 | 0. | 10. | 0. | 12.6 | 0. | 12.6 | |

## Summary

Analysis of Tables II and III, above, shows:

A—Messrs. W. and H., repeating witnesses, manifest great improvement in the completeness of their free narration when the incident is expected; they show slight, but consistent, loss of accuracy under these same conditions; and they show great loss of caution throughout all reports of the expected incident.

B—The entire group of witnesses under expected conditions, as contrasted with the whole group under unexpected conditions, shows slight gain in completeness during all types of report (ranging from 4.5% to 8.8%); they show slight loss in accuracy in all types of testimony (averaging 7.9%); and they show considerable loss of caution in all three types of report (ranging from 12.6% to 52.9%). It is to be noted that most of the gain in completeness in the total group scores, just as in the repeating witnesses' scores, was achieved during free narration, only average gains of 2.5% and 3.6% being registered in direct and cross examinations, respectively.

## 4. COMPARISON OF FINDINGS OF FACT BY JUDGE, MALE JURY, AND FEMALE JURY

The second part of the original problem, it will be remembered, consisted of opening up the psychological analysis of relations existing between the findings of judge or jury, and the testimony upon which such findings were based. A preliminary complication immediately made itself manifest. Which finder of fact can produce most accurate results for purposes of comparison with witnesses' testimony, judge or jury? And, since we have both male and female jurors in most jurisdictions since the adoption of the Nineteenth Amendment, which sex shall we assume to be most reliable in the exercise of this function? It would seem, in light of these complications, that a preliminary comparison of judge, male jury, and female jury, as finders of fact, was indicated before any attempt could be made to compare the respective values of findings of fact and testimony.

## Method

The testimony of each witness in both experiments was, it will be remembered, written out by the witness himself. It was only necessary, therefore, to have this testimony typed, with individual copies for each judge and juror. Diagrams of the lecture-room were also prepared for the judge in the first experiment, and for two of the juries in the second experiment, who were unable to make a personal inspection of the scene where the incident occurred.

. . . Views of the lecture-room where the incident occurred were arranged for both juries, and each individual juror was furnished with a copy of all the evidence several days in advance of the meeting at which they made their final findings. Notes on the methods and general procedure in the jury-room were kept by the foreman and forewoman of male and female juries, respectively. . . .

\*     \*     \*     \*

## Results

. . . [B]oth judge and juries, in rendering their findings, followed the three forms in which the testimony was elicited; that is, they made one finding in the form of free narration, another in form of answers to direct examination, and a third in form of answers to cross examination questions. It is impossible to state, with complete accuracy, to what extent the direct and cross examination testimony influenced the free narration findings; but it may be judged, from careful inspection of all results, that the finders of fact adhered rather strictly to the actual content of testimony in each part to which their report corresponded. In Table IV, following, the completeness, accuracy, and caution of the judge, of the male jury, and of the female jury are compared separately for free narration, direct examination, and cross examination.

The interesting, and to many jurists unexpected, result of superiority of female jury findings over those of the male jury is manifest in Table IV. The judge, as might, perhaps, be predicted, scored approximately 10% higher, on the average, than the highest jury in the completeness of his findings, while the judge's average accuracy was also slightly higher than that of the juries. For the first time, however, in these experiments, we

TABLE IV. SCORES OF JUDGE, FEMALE JURY, AND MALE JURY.

|  | Completeness | Accuracy | Caution |
|---|---|---|---|
| Free narration— | | | |
| Judge | 31.2 | 88.4 | — |
| Female jury | 16.3 | 92.3 | — |
| Male jury | 20.4 | 75. | — |
| Direct examination— | | | |
| Judge | 40.8 | 72. | 17.3 |
| Female jury | 33.3 | 71.4 | 23.8 |
| Male jury | 21.6 | 59. | 14.2 |
| Cross examination— | | | |
| Judge | 38.3 | 82. | 30.7 |
| Female jury | 30.8 | 71.7 | 23.5 |
| Male jury | 27.1 | 68.1 | 36.3 |
| Total averages— | | | |
| Judge | 36.7 | 80.8 | 24. |
| Female jury | 26.8 | 78.4 | 23.6 |
| Male jury | 23.4 | 67.3 | 25.2 |

find that the index of caution seems to have little or no correlation with successful results. The differences between the percentages of caution manifest in the reports of these three finders of fact was negligible, and the very slight difference which existed, on the average, was shown to be in favor of the least successful jury. The explanation of the judge's superiority over both juries, therefore, and of the superiority of the women's jury over that composed of men, is not to be sought in native conservatism, or in added suspiciousness of attitude on the part of those finders of fact who turned in the best results. It is frequently assumed by trial judges and lawyers that the "hardboiled" attitude so quickly acquired in the courtroom is conducive to increased success in evaluating witnesses' testimony; but such a conclusion is not indicated by the results of this preliminary experiment.

\*　\*　\*　\*

## 5. COMPARISON OF FINDINGS OF FACT BY JURIES, BASED UPON WRITTEN AND ORAL TESTIMONY

It is frequently asserted by presiding justices at actual trials that much fact-finding value is to be derived from the opportunity given a jury, in the court-room, of observing each witness, face to face, as he gives his testimony on the witness stand. This value, if any, must have been totally lacking in the findings of fact made by judges and juries in the experiments reported above, since all testimony was presented to them in typewritten form, and the witnesses were not even known by sight to the finders of fact . . . . Such, indeed, is the usual condition obtaining in Aussage tests, since it is difficult and often impracticable to arrange for a dozen or more witnesses to give their testimony, orally, before an experimental court. However, this problem should not be overlooked in outlining the field for further psycho-legal investigation, since if a material loss of testimonial value were indicated as a result of failure on the part of the finders of fact to observe the witnesses while they testified, routine Aussage procedure must be radically revised to permit such observation during testimony orally given. This was the final problem, therefore, which I undertook to investigate before attempting a comparison of the values of findings of judges and juries with the value of the original testimony upon which such findings were based.

### Methods

Two juries, male and female, were assembled simultaneously . . . . The jurors were all of mature age, advanced education, and unimpaired perceptual abilities. The 12 witnesses to the second experimental incident were brought before the juries, one at a time, in the same lecture-room where the incident had originally occurred. Each witness was asked, first, to tell what happened in his own way, without questioning. He was thereafter examined in both direct and leading form, just as he had been questioned when he wrote out his report, immediately after the occurrence in issue. All witnesses remained in a separate witness-room, across the hall from the lecture-room, until called to the stand, in accordance with strictest trial procedure. Jurors were allowed to take such notes as they wished during testimony, and the testimony was taken down verbatim by stenographers who were present. The transcript of testimony was not furnished the juries during their deliberations, since this would have necessitated impracticable delay, and since juries in actual trials usually make little, if any, use of the testimonial record.

Necessarily, as in actual cases, court did not sit, as above described, until three months after the incident in issue occurred. It is to be noted, however, that every witness had written out his complete testimony immediately after the incident. This might well tend, psychologically, to fix the memory in his mind, since kinæsthetic and visual imagery of the testimony thus set down would be added to perceptual imagery of the original incident. Moreover, the real incident was reviewed at the lecture following its occurrence, and witnesses spent much time discussing together their individual errors. In view of these memory reinforcements and corrections, and in light of the fact that actual trials often take place several years after the occurrences which are testified to thereat, a higher percentage of oral testimonial value might well be expected than that obtaining in actual cases. E. H. Marston . . . sat, as an observer, with the female jury after it had retired to the jury-room to make its findings; and I sat, similarly, with the male jury while its report was decided upon. Results of these observations proved valuable in suggesting a possible explanation of sex differences in fact-finding success.

### Results

One of the most interesting details of the results of this experiment was the extraordinary testimony given by one of the witnesses, based, as was afterward revealed, upon deliberate suggestions made to him in the witness-room by the other witnesses awaiting their turn to testify. The men were evidently comparing their memories of the incident, to start with, and began to exaggerate and make fun of each other's alleged mistakes. Finding Mr. A. hypersuggestible, they combined to put into his mind the most absurd and improbable details. When called before the juries, in fact, Mr. A. actually testified that the actor in the incident in issue wore one high, black shoe, and one low, tan shoe; that he had some sort of gold medal in the buttonhole of a bright scarlet coat, and that he wore a flaming red tie, knotted in spread-eagle fashion, outside coat and vest! More significant than the mere fact of this witness' unusual suggestibility to mischievously motivated "coaching," however, was the resulting effect upon certain jurors. One woman juror was so impressed by the extreme self-confidence shown by Mr. A. on the stand that she came to the conclusion that he was the only reliable witness out of the 12 men called. As a result of her insistence upon this point, at least two erroneous findings were introduced into the female jury's report. A member of the male jury argued, also, that such extraordinary statements would never have been made by any witness unless he had actually seen details which the other witnesses were not in position to observe. After extended discussion, several of Mr. A.'s statements were adopted as correct by the male jury, thus materially reducing both their completeness and accuracy ratings. Such disproportionate and erroneous importance given by jurors to prejudiced witnesses' self-assertiveness on the stand may well play an important role in many a jury's final findings.

Table VII, following, [Tables V and VI omitted] compares the scores of male and female jury findings of fact based upon oral testimony, as above described, with similar scores of findings of fact reported by the University of Maryland juries, and based solely upon the written testimony of the same witnesses to the same incident. In order to make these jury scores fairly comparable, both were figured by the second method described above.

TABLE VII. COMPARATIVE SCORES OF JURY FINDINGS BASED UPON ORAL AND WRITTEN TESTIMONY.

| | *Oral* | *Written* | *Superiority When Based on Written Testimony* |
|---|---|---|---|
| Completeness— | | | |
| Female jury | 38.6 | 48.9 | 10.3 |
| Male jury | 33.6 | 44.8 | 11.2 |
| Average | 36.1 | 46.8 | 10.7 |
| Accuracy— | | | |
| Female jury | 80.6 | 77.4 | −3.2 |
| Male jury | 68.8 | 92.6 | 23.8 |
| Average | 74.7 | 85. | 10.3 |

It is to be noted, in Table VII, that the accuracy percentage of the male jury, which was discussed at length above, is actually based upon the written testimony of a single witness, instead of upon the written testimony of all 12 witnesses. While this accidental variation must invalidate direct comparison of male jury accuracy with the accuracy scores of corresponding finders of fact, as noted in the foregoing discussion, it has no serious bearing upon comparison of average accuracy of written testimony method with average accuracy of oral testimony method. Since all the testimony furnished both Maryland University juries was written, all their findings must have been based solely upon material received in written form. It may well be, however, that accidental outside knowledge of a single witness' reliability might also have raised the total average accuracy percentage of findings based upon oral testimony. I suggest, nevertheless, that such previous confidence in a witness would probably be found to have less effect, in the oral procedure, since fresh perceptions of each witness as he testifies might be expected, psychologically, to supplant or materially modify previous estimates of the particular witness' accuracy.

## Summary

The results and observations in this experiment may be summarized as follows:

A—Jury findings based upon testimony written out by witnesses immediately following the occurrence are superior in both completeness and accuracy to jury findings based upon oral testimony of the same witnesses heard by a jury some time after the event in issue. What proportion of this superiority, if any, is due to the mere lapse of time between incident and oral testimony is not indicated by this experimental procedure, and should be made the subject of subsequent investigation.

B—The self-confidence, or self-assertiveness, of a witness on the stand, even though that witness be the most obviously unreliable and improbable of all those heard, may have a greater influence upon jurors of both sexes than does the logical or psychological probability of other testimony.

C—Careful comparison of the observations of E. H. Marston and myself upon the jury-room deliberations of female and male juries, respectively, gave the following results:

(1) The female jury exercised much greater care in considering detailed testimony than did the male jury. The women jurors were more painstaking, and manifested a thoroughness and a willingness to put themselves to more trouble and to do more work in considering all the testimony submitted, no matter how trivial or obviously erroneous it seemed, than the men jurors.

(2) Both juries pursued, without previous discussion or consultation, the same method of compiling their final findings; that is, separate consideration, discussion, and vote upon each moot point, with subsequent revision of previously agreed on findings, where this became necessary.

(3) Individual jurors of both sexes appeared equally prejudiced and illogical in discussion of certain points; and both juries, taken as units,

seemed equally unable to "size up" or psychologically analyze the behavior and responses of witnesses on the stand which had been especially noted.

\* \* \* \*

In conclusion, I would point out various concrete examples of results herein reported which, if verified, might be utilized to bring about practical improvements in courtroom procedure without any prerequisite change in basic law. Judges, for instance, have wide discretion in limitation of cross examination, and granting of broad latitude in direct examination. If psycho-legal research should finally establish the fact that testimonial results in response to direct questioning have preponderantly greater completeness and accuracy, the bench would already possess sufficient power to put this conclusion into practice to a considerable extent.

Again, it is possible, under our present procedure, to take immediate, written statements from witnesses who have been present during accidents and other occurrences of ultimate trial importance. Such statements may be used in various ways during actual trial and are so used very frequently. If it were established as a definite, scientific fact that such immediate, written testimony has several times the value of oral testimony given later, at the trial, the court and counsel, knowing this fact, might add much emphasis and weight to the immediately written statements, in many ways, without departing materially from our present trial system. Indeed, it would not necessitate a very radical departure in legal procedure to provide official machinery for the eliciting and recording of crucial testimony, in important cases, as soon after the occurrence as the witnesses could be summoned; and the establishment of subsequent admissibility of such testimony, as a check upon the witnesses' later testimony, at the trial, would merely require an extension of the rule under which previous sworn testimony may be used at the present time to discredit a witness in cross examination. The official, immediate eliciting of testimony might, moreover, be conducted according to that form which psycho-legal research had proved productive of most complete and accurate results.

In the matter of women jurors, in jurisdictions where sex is no longer a bar to jury service, both counsel and court possess the power to influence the proportion of female representation on any panel. Excusing of jurors, disqualification for cause, and the arbitrary right of challenge may all be used, legitimately, to effect the result of securing women on every jury, if this result turns out to be desirable in the interests of justice. Only continued psycho-legal investigation can establish the desirability of such procedure; but the preliminary experiments reported above certainly indicate a possible value of women as jurors which is wholly contrary to the older practice of deliberate exclusion of women from the jury, whenever possible.

If properly guarded scientific researches should establish the fact, which already seems obvious to many psychologists, that an ordinary jury has lamentable absence of ability and skill in analyzing, psychologically, the reliability of the witnesses appearing before it, and of analyzing, both logically and psychologically the testimony of those witnesses, upon which the case must be decided, much may be done in the way of producing expert analysis of testimony for the jury's assistance. Counsel may procure properly qualified experts in various aspects of testimonial analysis; the court has a wide discretion in admitting such expert testimony; and the jury may be required, by the court's charge, to give due consideration to all the testimony before it, with the possibility of a new trial should expert analysis of crucial evidence be patently disregarded. Nor is the plan of a testimonial expert officially retained in capacity of "friend of the court" so foreign to a modern practice which thus utilizes the sociological advice of probation officers and the psychiatric services of medical examiners.

Finally, if it can be conclusively demonstrated that a single, trained individual greatly excels any jury in fact-finding ability, parties to any cause, civil or criminal, who honestly desire efficient findings of fact may, in most instances, waive the right to jury trial and thus secure that result most in accordance with justice. Also, in the appointment of masters, commissioners, and other non-judicial fact-finding agents, the court or other appointing official may be directly guided by the results of adequate psycho-legal investigations indicating what types of training and experience are most conducive to completeness and accuracy of report upon the testimony submitted.

All these possibilities for practical improvement in the handling of human testimony as a result of psycho-legal experimentation are cited, not because of their supreme intrinsic importance, but merely to illustrate the possibilities of immediate co-operation between the psychological laboratory and the courtroom. Juristic theory and practice have profited enormously from scientific treatment of abnormalities; why should not a similar profit be derived from psycho-legal solution of normal problems?

# PART III | SOCIOLOGICAL JURISPRUDENCE: STAGE TWO

THOMAS A. COWAN · FREDERICK K. BEUTEL
· LEE LOEVINGER · PHILIP SELZNICK ·
MARTIN SHAPIRO · LAURA NADER

THE THEORETICAL ESSAYS IN SOCIOLOGICAL JURISPRUDENCE which preceded the contemporary empirical research, represented in Part IV, differ from the essays of the earlier period in at least two important respects. First, the leading contributors were on law-school faculties, not on the appellate bench. Second, they were less concerned with "grand theory" or with "speculation about the nature of the universe" and more concerned with *method*. They emphasize the importance of training legal researchers in the methods of scientific inquiry, in the meaning of experimentation, in the importance of replication, and in the usefulness and limitations of statistical analysis. They claim that unless such training is undertaken, empirical legal research will continue to be practiced outside the mainstream of scientific inquiry.

Because these writers stress the necessity of rigorous scientific inquiry and of training men to carry out such research, the substantive problems they raise are narrower and more specific than those considered earlier. To borrow Robert Merton's phrase, they are problems primarily of the "middle range." And, as Loevinger writes in his article on jurimetrics, they are questions and problems that are capable not only of being debated, but of being investigated and answered.

The legal scholars in this period who advocated an orientation toward sociological jurisprudence did not see themselves as pioneers faced with the task of clearing the wilderness and establishing the first intellectual beachhead. Instead, they saw themselves as leaders of a second generation. As such, their concerns were with refinements and with more specific and limited problems.

The excerpts included in Part III illustrate different aspects of this perspective. Thomas Cowan compares law to medicine, claiming that both are bodies of applied scientific learning around which have clustered folklore, superstitions, traditional practices, and myths—as well as science. For him, the relationship between the social sciences and the law parallels the division of labor which exists between the natural sciences and medicine. Although the social sciences are only "emerging" sciences (they are not experimental enough), both law and the social sciences can help each other in their mutual striving to develop into mature sciences. The law can help by its willingness to accept relevant findings about society obtained through experimental research and by so formulating its own questions and problems that the social sciences will be stimulated to conduct research on those matters.

Frederick Beutel is more specific than Cowan in delineating the questions that a science of law should try to answer. In addition to listing eight steps which should be followed in exacting a method of experimental jurisprudence, Beutel stresses the practical implications of such an approach: namely, in order to serve as the basis for changes in public policy which are in keeping with scientific evidence and not merely in response to political pressures and upheavals, as has traditionally been the case.

Lee Loevinger stresses even more than Cowan and Beutel the importance of scientific method and discipline for legal research. Not only does he insist on attaching a new name to the discipline, "jurimetrics," in place of the traditional "jurisprudence," but he also claims that the types of problems and the orientations to the problems, as well as the techniques for studying the problems, must be altered if legal research is to become truly scientific. Whereas students of jurisprudence considered problems broadly and generally, students of jurimetrics must learn how to specify and narrow their areas of inquiry; they must learn how to operationalize questions for research. Whereas students of jurisprudence used "debate" as their medium for finding answers, students of jurimetrics must use "empirical investigation"; and they must be prepared to discard answers or to modify positions and principles as the data demand. Loevinger not only describes method and approach, but also outlines nine major topics to which students of jurimetrics might address themselves, immediately. In keeping with his insistence on the importance of operationalizing problems for investigation, under each topic he asks how we can measure it, how reliable and valid our present information on the problem is, and what techniques will improve the present state of knowledge.

In this period, as in the earlier one, the sociologists who are interested in legal sociology are developing ideas around the same general problems. In an article which Philip Selznick wrote in 1959 and which is today the piece most often cited as the best statement of where the field is and where it might go, Selznick argues along the lines advocated by Loevinger.

Selznick reviews the field by dividing it into three stages of development. The first stage is concerned with "communicating a perspective," that perspective being a sociological approach to the study of legal phenomenon. This approach is substantive in orientation. It explains how a sociologist views the functioning of communities and groups, what the significance of group membership to individual behavior is, and how such an orientation can be applied usefully to the study of legal institutions. It is concerned with creating a *geist*. Robert Angell, Nicholas Timasheff, and others represented in Part I made important contributions to that perspective.

The second stage is one in which researchers bring to bear specific sociological techniques and findings to the study of particular legal problems or institutions. It is this stage which Selznick, writing in 1959, saw us entering, and the research conducted since that year—on the legal profession, the jury system, court delay, and judicial decision making—bear witness to the reality of that prophecy. The problems selected represent research of the "middle range."[1]

---

[1] *An article by Arnold Rose which appeared a few years before the piece by Selznick illustrates the kind of theory that is offered during this second, or "middle-range," period. In his article, "Problems in the Sociology of Law and Law Enforcement,"* 6 Journal of Legal Education (1953), 191–202, *Rose lists four areas in which he believes it would be mutually beneficial for lawyers and social scientists to do empirical research: (1) the formulation of legislative measures, (2) the formulation of judicial decisions, (3) the consequences of law and judicial decisions, and (4) the function of law in the legal process. It would be mutually beneficial because the problems are of substantive interest to the law and because the social scientists have devised techniques and skills applicable to such problems. In urging what might appear as a marriage of convenience, Rose pointed out that the problems he suggests for research have important practical value in contributing toward the functioning of a moral social order.*

It is not until the third stage of development, which is yet to come, that the field of sociological jurisprudence will develop an "intellectual autonomy and maturity." In this last stage, scholars will engage in empirical research on problems about which they only speculated in the first stage. They will have acquired the necessary technological skills and will be ready to tackle empirically such basic issues as the legality of justice and the function of law. Selznick, unfortunately, hazards no guess as to how long it will be before this final period of development is entered.

As his title, "Political Jurisprudence," suggests, Martin Shapiro makes a case for the extension of sociological jurisprudence by combining its orientation with the substantive knowledge of political science. It is a plea for concentration on the specifically political aspects of the law's interaction with society, for concern with the impact of "legal arrangements" on the distribution of power and rewards among the various elements in a given society.

By way of illustration, Shapiro cites the need for research on the courts as political institutions, on the interrelationships among different levels of courts, on the attitudes of judges, and on the relationship between attitudes and judicial decisions. The excerpt by Shapiro serves at least two functions. (1) It points up interesting areas for research not only by providing general questions, but also by placing those questions into a body of literature which includes theoretical as well as empirical work. (2) It calls upon political scientists to recognize that a new subfield is in the making and asks them either to shift what has previously been *ad hoc* research into the domain of the new subfield or to embark on research which has as its focus legal phenomena and institutions as a political process.

The final selection in Part III, by anthropologist Laura Nader, which in its entirety reviews "the main themes and questions about law that have concerned anthropologists," describes "relevant studies in . . . the sociology of law and anthropological conflict studies," and discusses "present trends and new directions in anthropological studies of law." Only the last section appears in this volume. It contains a brief but excellent summary of recent ethnographic research and compares legal systems and institutions in complex Western societies with those in isolated and traditional non-Western societies. In concluding, the author lists half a dozen specific questions which she urges ethnographers to find answers to, because in so doing they will provide the basis for a truly comparative study of the law.

# THE RELATION OF LAW
# TO EXPERIMENTAL
# SOCIAL SCIENCE

## Thomas A. Cowan

In medicine all the sciences grouped round the art of treatment had to be liberated from the commercial casuistry of the profession before sound biology and scientific pathology could produce hygiene and preventive medicine. In the same way, in law, the jurisprudent must first of all free himself from the trammels and impediments of expediency, and then perhaps he will be able to build up an effective technique of safeguards against possible breach and incentives to good citizenship.[1]

Malinowski's analogy is instructive. It is well-known that as the biological sciences became experimental they separated off from the art of treatment, were developed in the laboratory quite apart from immediate application, and entered medicine proper as applied science. The result is that modern medicine has progressed further in the last hundred years than in all the previous millennia during which the art of healing had engaged the sustained attention of the human race. Jurisprudence today is in a position comparable to that which medicine occupied a century ago. That is, it is a hodge-podge of science, philosophy and technical art. The books are full of references to the "science of law," the "philosophy of law," and to the various aspects of the technical legal process.

---

[1] B. Malinowski, Introduction to HOGBIN, LAW AND ORDER IN POLYNESIA LXVIII (1934).

---

Reprinted by permission of the author and of the publishers from 96 University of Pennsylvania Law Review (1948), 484–502.

It is the purpose of this paper to suggest that the familiar tripartite division of jurisprudence should undergo change. In brief, it is the writer's position that the "science of law" should become a part of an expanded social science as the latter is placed more firmly on an experimental basis. An attempt will also be made to indicate very briefly at the end of the article how philosophy of law should merge with philosophy of the social sciences, or as this last subject is coming to be called, the methodology of the social sciences.[2] The result to be anticipated from these developments, of course, is a vast enrichment of the third part of jurisprudence, that is, the technical legal art, law proper, with "legal science" and "legal philosophy" as we know them today things of the past. This is a very large order indeed. It calls for a certain amount of "crystal-gazing" if we are to be able to discern something of the dim outline of the jurisprudence of the future. The effort will be worth while if it does no more than indicate new areas and lines of research.

We shall begin then with the statement that law stands to social science in some sense as medicine stands to biological science. This view assumes that neither law nor medicine is science. Rather each is a body of applied scientific learning; a focus round which clusters, to greater or less degree, a curious admixture of science, myth, superstition, folklore, and the traditional practices of centuries-old craft. It has been the homely wisdom of the ages that only the priesthood could compete with medicine and law in encysted isolation from current progressive notions and in stout resistance to change under impact of the science of the day. For the past century, however, medicine has broken sharply with tradition and has incorporated more and more of the results of the experimental sciences. The term "scientific medicine" has become a barbarism, since "non-scientific medicine" is now recognized as magic or superstition. How goes it with law? Why are the terms "science of law" or "scientific law" not recognized as solecisms?

It is perhaps unnecessary to emphasize that these conceptions *should* be recognized as outmoded. That they are in fact not so regarded is made abundantly clear by a reference to almost any modern work on jurisprudence. Indeed, the conviction that law is a science, or that the body of legal materials is or should be a scientific corpus is well-nigh universal. Idealists

---

[2] *See, for example*, KAUFMANN, METHODOLOGY OF THE SOCIAL SCIENCES (*1944*).

and empiricists alike share this conviction. From the starry idealism of the Kantian Stammler[3] or the mystic Radbruch,[4] through the double way of the life of reason and faith of the neo-Scholastics,[5] to the present day phenomenologism of Kelsen[6] and his followers runs a common assumption that an idealist basis for an autonomous science of law exists or can be made to exist. The same is true for the empiricists past and present. Whether it be John Austin's[7] dry-as-dust narrow analysis of the body of the matured systems of modern law or Roscoe Pound's[8] multi-faceted system of sociological jurisprudence[9] embracing as it does the newest conceptions of pragmatism, the assumption is always implicit and generally expressed that law should be a science coordinate with the other sciences and that the central problem of the student of jurisprudence is to lay the foundations of a modern science of law. The only serious challenge to this widely-held conviction is the negativistic attack of the sceptics whose efforts are largely directed to exposing the pretensions of legal "scientists" and "philosophers." This work, while a necessary propedeutic, must not be left to stand alone. For it leads to cynicism and frustration, and experience indicates that rather than remain indefinitely unsatisfied with sceptical "solutions," most people end by returning to an even more intrenched position of dogmatism.

Suppose we take it for granted for the moment, then, that the "science of law" is still permitted to flourish because social science has not absorbed

---

[3] STAMMLER, SYSTEMATISCHE THEORIE DER RECHTSWISSENSCHAFT (*1923*); LEHRBUCH DER RECHTSPHILOSOPHIE (*1928*); Fundamental Tendencies in Modern Jurisprudence, *21* MICH. L. REV. *623* (*1923*).

[4] RADBRUCH, RECHTSPHILOSOPHIE (*3d ed. 1935*).

[5] GENY, METHODE D'INTERPRETATION EN DROIT PRIVE POSITIF (*2d ed. 1919*); SCIENCE ET TECHNIQUE EN DROIT PRIVE POSITIF, *vol. I* (*1913*), *vol. II* (*1915*), *vol. III* (*1912*), *vol. IV* (*1924*).

[6] KELSEN, REINE RECHTSLEHRE (*1934*); KELSEN, GENERAL THEORY OF LAW AND STATE (*Wedberg's trans. 1945*); EBENSTEIN, THE PURE THEORY OF LAW (*1945*); *55* HARV. L. REV. *44* (*1942*); *51* L. Q. REV. *517* (*1935*); *50* L. Q. REV. *474* (*1934*).

[7] AUSTIN, JURISPRUDENCE (*1911*).

[8] *Pound*, The Scope and Purpose of Sociological Jurisprudence, *25* HARV. L. REV. *140* (*1912*); Fifty Years of Jurisprudence, *50* HARV. L. REV. *557* (*1937*); *51* HARV. L. REV. *444, 777* (*1938*).

[9] *See Pound*, Sociology of Law and Sociological Jurisprudence, *5* U. OF TORONTO L. J. *1, 2–3* (*1944*): "*Sociological jurisprudence is in another line of development. It proceeds from historical and philosophical jurisprudence to utilization of the social sciences, and particularly of sociology, toward a broader and more effective science of law.*"

it; and that this absorption has not taken place because social science is not experimental enough. On this assumption, law can aid the development of an emerging social science in two ways. First by preparing to accept as much as possible of the newer developments of these embryonic sciences; and second (but this is only an extension of the first) by so formulating its own body of doctrine that the social sciences will be stimulated to research and will be encouraged to meet the demands of an expanding system of law for more and more intensive development of the science of society.

Let us now examine a few instances to illustrate the effects of the developing social disciplines on law. If we turn to anthropology we can see in short compass the effect of prevailing legal theories on field investigations and the correlative influence of such investigations on law after the inadequacies of legal theory become manifest. Under the influence of English and continental doctrines of the nature of law based on analysis of matured systems, amateur anthropologists (usually missionaries) were able to report an almost total absence of law in primitive society.[10] The simple savages, unrestrained by the onerous bonds of legal obligations, were supposed to have worked out the affairs of their everyday lives in happy innocence reminiscent of the golden days of the Garden of Eden. With the development of positivism, however, and the growth of the notion that the foundation of the legal system is the body of restraints imposed by political or social authority as the outgrowth of custom, the pendulum swung the other way, and the primitives were conceived as a group of tradition-bound law-ridden wretches, too ignorant to break through the "cake of custom" to a more progressive life.[11] Both views were, of course, one-sided and inadequate, stemming from narrowly conceived theories of the nature of law. When, therefore, stimulated by a pragmatic theory of knowledge, anthropology broke with the legal tradition and commenced to investigate the jural relations of primitive communities as they actually function,[12] a counter influence on jurisprudence was set up with salutary effects on legal thinking. It is now no longer fashionable in legal circles to speak of fundamental principles of law governing the whole of human society. In anthropology, the field worker now knows that the data on law which one gets from an investigation of a primitive

---

[10] *See* MALINOWSKI, CRIME AND CUSTOM IN SAVAGE SOCIETY *11–12 (1926)*.

[11] Id. *at 9–10.*

[12] *For examples of functional analysis of law in non-literate societies, See* HOGBIN, *note 1* supra; LLEWELLYN AND HOEBEL, THE CHEYENNE WAY *(1941)*.

society is conditioned by the jural assumptions and postulates he takes with him to the investigation.[13] In other words, anthropologists have reached the Kantian stage in the study of law and by comparison legal theories often seem unsophisticated.

All primitive tribes still extant are undergoing a process of acculturation[14] as a result of the impact of modern civilization. These changes are the subject of investigation by modern anthropologists who are able to observe the effects of modern systems of social control on native ways of life. One of the most important aspects of such control is, of course, law. Studies by Malinowski[15] and his school show the actual effects to be observed from different types of control imposed by colonial administrators on so-called primitive peoples.

More elaborate than these, and more in accordance with scientific methodology are the researches of Kardiner,[16] Du Bois[17] and others. Working toward designed experiments incorporating psychoanalytic techniques, these investigators are attempting to set up "controls" in the scientific sense. They seem to be groping toward a newer and more significant notion of what a "social laboratory" should be and their results, if they can be developed, should be of vast importance to law.

In the field of psychology, we need only note how much of the law of evidence has come into wide disrepute by the general realization of the

---

[13] *See, for example,* MALINOWSKI, A SCIENTIFIC THEORY OF CULTURE 7 (*1944*): "*As I shall try to point out, a genuine scientific method has been inherent in all historic work, in all chronicling, in every argument used in jurisprudence, economics, and linguistics. There is no such thing as description completely devoid of theory. Whether you reconstruct historic scenes, carry out a field investigation in savage tribe or a civilized community, analyze statistics, or make inferences from an archaeological monument or a prehistoric find—every statement and every argument has to be made in words, that is, in concepts. Each concept, in turn, is the result of a theory which declares that some facts are relevant and others adventitious, that some factors determine the course of events and others are merely accidental by-play; that things happen as they do because personalities, masses, and material agencies of the environment produced them.*"

[14] HERSHKOWITZ, ACCULTURATION: THE STUDY OF CULTURE CONTACT (*1938*).

[15] MALINOWSKI, THE DYNAMICS OF CULTURE CHANGE (*1945*); THE PRESENT STATE OF STUDIES IN CULTURE CONTACT, AFRICA, *Vol. xl* (*1938*), *Vol. xii* (*1939*); HOGBIN, EXPERIMENTS IN CIVILIZATION (*1939*).

[16] KARDINER, THE INDIVIDUAL AND HIS SOCIETY (*1939*); THE PSYCHOLOGICAL FRONTIERS OF SOCIETY (*1945*).

[17] DU BOIS, THE PEOPLE OF ALOR (*1944*).

gross unreliability of witnesses in testifying even to the simplest facts. Our famed jury trial was a device which gradually substituted rational examination of evidence for the mechanical trials of an earlier period. These early systems had been rigid, formal, crude. Their evident effect was to settle disputes on the basis of agreed upon ritualistic performances irrespective of the merits of the controversy as we would see those "merits" today. Compared with these ceremonies, jury trials were scientific. Now, however, we must admit that the all too frequent result of trials is the ceremonious disposition of controversies without serious attempt to discover scientifically the facts which form the basis of the dispute.

Thus far, the finding of psychology as to the reliability of testimony has had only a negative effect on the law. We have had demonstrated for us beyond cavil that the senses, which once were thought of as the only reliable source of knowledge of the outside world, are quite unreliable. To be sure, this is merely scientific confirmation of an opinion stoutly held on the basis of common sense and of philosophic doctrine since Greek times. Now, however, we have highly developed methods for measuring deviations from a norm of sensitivity in stimulus and response in the field of sensations.[18]

A half century of experimental work on the organs of sight, sound, taste, smell and touch has accumulated a sophisticated body of doctrine concerning bodily sensations. But only a small fraction of this learning is serviceable to the law. What the evidence expert is really interested in is not so much the reliability of the powers of observation of witnesses, but rather their general *credibility*. To repeat, common sense is well acquainted with the fallibility of the organs of sensation. Indeed, the etymological distinction between "common sense" on the one hand, and your "sensations" and mine on the other shows that this conviction is deeply rooted in the language. General credibility is much more than this. It is the answer to the question: What accounts for the fact that different individuals give different degrees of assent to one and the same proposition? Its answering involves among other things a way of measuring degrees of assent. We know now that the problem is vastly more complicated than the eighteenth and nineteenth century mathematical statisti-

---

[18] *Cowan,* Credibility, Probability, and Social Science, 4 BULL. INSTITUTE OF EXPERIMENTAL METHOD 18 (1947).

cians took it to be. The studies of Nicholas Bernouilli, Laplace, Condorcet, Poisson, and Quetelet are interesting examples of how very naive much of the work of genius may appear to informed lay opinion of a later era.[19] Nevertheless, what for them was the result of inspiration must become for our psychologists hard work. The beginning of a psychology of general credibility is at hand. It takes the form of an attempt to put on an experimental basis the study of human personality.[20] In this field, law is in the position not so much of accepting advances in psychology as of demanding that psychology devise credibility scales so that some of the fruits of this science of the future may be available to it.

The development of psychoanalysis and its "deviates" is having a potent though often undiscerned effect on legal theory. This fundamental re-orientation of the nature of the human mind brings into prominence the unconscious as distinguished from the conscious aspects of mental behavior. And as might be expected all disciplines based upon the assumption that only conscious behavior fully deserves the description "mental" must, as this new viewpoint makes headway, recast their foundations. It is inviting to speculate on the effect this new insight could have on the law's theory of mental behavior. In the *Psychopathology of Every Day Life,* Freud advanced the theory that all slips of speech and of memory, however "accidental" they may appear, really serve some unconscious purpose. The notion of "unconscious intentions" is given meaning and the forceful analogy between the mind and the iceberg is suggested. That is, it is intimated that only a small fraction of mental behavior reaches the level of consciousness. Much the most important part remains submerged, inaccessible to the individual, and open only to "analysis" by the expert.

The idea of "unconscious intention" as applied to the legal notion of intent is interesting. As now constituted intent in law refers to conscious purpose. What does negligence mean? Why, evidently "unconscious purpose." Negligence is not absence of a state of mind, but presence of unconscious purpose of an anti-social character. This notion interpolates a third possibility between the theory of subjective (conscious) intent of the classical variety, and the theory of objective intent of the Holmesian mold. Each of these as presently constituted is unsatisfactory. Subjective intent is

---

[19] *Jaffin,* Prologue to Nomostatistics, 35 COL. L. REV. *1, 15* et seq. *(1935).*
[20] CHURCHMAN AND ACKOFF, PSYCHOLOGISTICS, *Chapters 4–8 (to appear).*

largely abandoned except in the criminal law while objective intent reduces the actor to an automaton, rewarded for mechanical obedience to legal rule, punished equally mechanically for infraction thereof.

Psychoanalytical knowledge is becoming very widespread as a result of keen interest on the part of the general public in the workings of the unconscious mind. Doubtless other instances of its possible effect on the law can be readily supplied by the reader. The law of evidence, for example, is bound to feel its effects some day. Criminal administration is in the thick of it, at least at the medical end of the subject. The criminal law itself, not only in the case of crimes of a sexual nature, but in other crimes as well could conceivably be re-organized on a "psychoanalytical" basis. In fact the whole subject of reform respecting crime and punishment could well advance beyond the stage of outraged protest of novelists and humanitarians and be placed in a scientific setting as a study in sado-masochism. Thus viewed, the criminal law and its administration would be regarded as a branch of medicine rather than law. Then treatment could be substituted for force, the law could be spared the brutalizing effect of resort to physical coercion in its most hideous form, and humanitarian judges could really dispense justice, that is, the settling of disputes on a rational peaceable basis.

In the realm of politico-legal theory, the old quarrel as to whether law takes its sanction from morality (often called "the law of nature") or whether on the contrary all law is nothing other than the command of the political sovereign could receive from psycho-analysis a re-orientation that would outmode completely the older formulation of the problem. Conscience re-appears as the super-ego. Account could then be taken of the evidence, becoming overwhelming, that the habits of obedience to law and order are internalized commands of such potency and vigor as to make negligible by comparison the claim that behind every law and alone efficacious for its observance is the political power of the state. One who obeys too much, too readily, is a neurotic! In this formulation the voice of conscience (the super-ego) as the foundation of the legal order reasserts itself over the notion, now become academic, that only the external force of society guarantees obedience to the law.

The psychoanalytic insight that the use of force, brutalizing alike to victim and "avenger," is always some form of sado-masochism throws light on one of the most harrowing dilemmas the law has to face. For undoubtedly law is society's alternative to war, the supreme instance of the resolution of controversies on the basis of sado-masochism. But when the law too resorts to force, the sadism and the masochism merely change their form. They still remain pathological. Hence, the perversity of those legal theorists of the analytical school who insist that the very foundation of law and its sole sanction is the politically organized force of society. As well say, law is society's politically organized sado-masochism. This change of perspective would insist that the "force" aspect of analytical jurisprudence recognizes itself as pathological, that is, a lamentable condition to be cured if possible.

In social psychology, experimental work shows the persistence of native habits of observance or violation of rules of behavior.[21] For example, apparently no known correlation exists between the response of law observance or violation on the one hand, and legal stimulus in the form of the criminal law on the other. Interests or psychological drives, which now are the foundation of law for the pragmatists, notably Pound, call for social psychology to carry legal theory further on. The day is coming when consultation with the social psychologist will be a necessary prerequisite to legislation designed as most of it is to regulate human behavior in conflict situations.

In economics, Marxism as well as non-Marxian views of the nature of human society have had a revolutionary effect on legal theories. Under the materialistic attack on the exploitative character of human society and the laying bare of the conflict of interests among various groups, the older ideal of the law as the expression of eternal principles of justice, above class and creed alike, gave way to newer interpretations of law as the expression of the various interests, economic, political, social, religious in the community. This type of analysis often of the order of exposé or (more shallowly) debunking, rests on the position that the legal order as now imperfectly constituted exists to arbitrate differentially the conflicting demands of the various classes in society. This is a frank recognition that the interests of the community are not homogeneous, that they do in fact conflict. We might take as an example of the above the following "stylized," "hypothetical" or "composite" interpretation of the materialistic view. Let us assume that in the period during and immediately after a successful revolution, for example, the interests of all important sectors of

---

[21] KATZ AND SCHANCK, SOCIAL PSYCHOLOGY, 3–34 (1938).

the ranks of the insurgents are united against a common externalized enemy. When, however, the harmony of purpose born of the revolution is over and counter-revolutionary activities are no longer to be feared, the source of conflict is recognized as internal. Government assumes the role of arbitrator, expands the scope of its activities, makes justiciable more and more controversies, and grows in bulk.

If and when internal conflict becomes wide-spread and the economy threatens to be disrupted, government assumes a more active role and provides social service to meet the rising demands which the non-governmental economy cannot fill. Then law needs a complete re-orientation. Its adversary method of settling disputes no longer suffices. The executive branch of the government is dominant and law becomes executive, that is, administrative. Once more exposé becomes popular. For in a class society the administration of positive services cannot be impartial. One class is served at the expense of another. What one gets, the other must do without. Administrative law, the response of the legal order to the needs of a service government, cannot avoid laying bare the conflict of interests among those who compete for its services. By the materialistic view, administrative law (in its widest possible sense) must pave the way for its own destruction since it contains within itself the seeds of contradiction. Either it becomes judicial justice on the basis of purported attempts to deal impartially with controversies, in the outcome of which it has no interest; or else it is forced openly to betray itself as the instrument of a particular class and disappears from law into the general economy as a service agency devoid of legal character.

The above is but a brief illustration of many possible materialistic interpretations of the relation of law to the economic structure of modern society. Theories of the economic character of law rise and fall with the ebb and flow of general theories of economics.

Thus far we have been interested in the effect of social science on law. The reciprocal effect of law on social science will be analogous. The present body of doctrine, developed by those having a joint interest in law and some branch of social science likewise awaits the emergence of genuine experimental science. The studies known as psychology of law,[22]

---

[22] *Britt,* The Lawyer as the Psychologist, *36* ILL. L. REV. *621 (1942), The Social* Psychology of Law, *34* ILL. L. REV. *919 (1940)*; FRANK, LAW AND THE MODERN MIND *(1930)*.

sociology of law,[23] legal anthropology,[24] as well as the even more diffuse bodies of learning called law and statistics,[25] law and economics,[26] law and politics,[27] and the like, will presumably all be subsumed under the aegis of experimental social science.

## AN EXAMPLE FROM THE LAW OF EVIDENCE

So far we have been dealing with over-all effects of the reciprocal impact of law and the social sciences. In this section we turn to an attempt to show in what way these views of the relation of law to social science could affect and influence a particular branch of the law, namely the law of evidence.

The dependence of any branch of "evidence" upon science is obvious to modern readers, and the close connection between any branch of the law, including the law of evidence, and morality is likewise readily admitted. But what of aesthetics? What is its connection with the law of evidence? Why, evidently, aesthetics deals with art, whether fine art or technical art. And the law (at least the law in action) is a technical art, and the rules of evidence are a most important part of the law's technique. Hence, aesthetics must ultimately be taken account of in any thoughtful consideration of the nature of the law of evidence.

Morality makes its demands on the law of evidence by virtue of the fact that the primary end of the law of evidence, as of all law, is to secure

---

[23] POUND, SOCIOLOGY OF LAW, TWENTIETH CENTURY SOCIOLOGY (1945); GURVITCH, SOCIOLOGY OF LAW (1942); EHRLICH, FUNDAMENTAL PRINCIPLES OF SOCIOLOGY OF LAW (Moll's trans. 1936); TIMASHEFF, AN INTRODUCTION TO THE SOCIOLOGY OF LAW (1939).

[24] Malinowski, A New Instrument for the Interpretation of Law, 51 YALE L. J. 1235 (1942); Hoebel, Fundamental Legal Concepts as Applied in the Study of Primitive Law, 51 YALE L. J. 951 (1942); note 12, supra.

[25] Jaffin, Prologue to Nomostatistics, 35 COL. L. REV. 1 (1935).

[26] Robinson, Law and Economics, 2 MOD. L. REV. 257 (1939); STONE, THE PROVINCE AND FUNCTION OF LAW 607–609 (1946); COMMONS, LEGAL FOUNDATIONS OF CAPITALISM (1924); ARNOLD, THE SYMBOLS OF GOVERNMENT 72–104 (1937).

[27] FRANKFURTER, LAW AND POLITICS (1939); LASKI, STUDIES IN LAW AND POLITICS (1932); Pound, Law and the State—Jurisprudence and Politics, 57 HARV. L. REV. 1193 (1944).

the *just* settlement of conflicts. And settlements are generally not deemed to be just unless they accord with the long-range scheme of values the community and the culture prizes. But one of the values most highly prized by the present culture is "scientific truth." Occasionally the demands for the recognition of this value become so exigent that they subordinate all other values for the time being. Finally, the ensemble of the ways in which conflicting values compete and find their resolution is the *art* of judicial administration; and the rules of evidence (indeed all procedural devices) have much to say about how this art shall be practiced.

To press this notion a little farther: art (technical art) deals with form, style, manner of doing things. It too is a value. Skill, craft, technique are "good." Thus, into the conflict of values between norms of just decision and standards of truth must go the claims of skill, craft, and technique. We have mentioned the fact that on occasion the demands of science are recognized as paramount. Justice and art yield to truth; sometimes gracefully, and then the decision is often discovered in fact to be both just and artful; sometimes with manifest reluctance, and then we should be on guard lest the decision is either not just or not technically sound.

Again, strange to say, "justice" may take the center of the stage, subordinating truth and art. The outcome may well be a fortunate one—perhaps truth and art should yield, that "justice may prevail." But perhaps, on the contrary, demands urged in the name of justice do such violence to truth or to art that injustice in fact results. The balance must be restored, for a morality that outruns one of its prime values, truth, is apt to be tyranny. To outrun another of its values—skill, art—is to defeat in action its own ultimate purpose.

Lastly, the demands of art may quite evidently dominate to the exclusion of the others. If the outcome is well and happily founded, older notions of truth and justice may be expected to yield. If not, then we may well suspect that art, craft, technique (let us now call the result "ceremony") have sacrificed either justice or truth on their altar.

This much said it is time to reflect that despite its apparent newness, the methodological question of the relation of art, science and morality to the law of evidence is really old, as such things go. Particularly is this true with reference to science and morality. The basic outlines of the problem were laid down half a century ago in Thayer's *Preliminary Treatise on Evidence.*[28]

Thayer undertook the pioneering task of precipitating the law of evidence out of the complex substances which had theretofore held it in solution. His job was to trace the origin and development of the jury system as the efficient cause of the law of evidence; to mark law off from fact in order to make plainer the functions of judge and jury; and (as concerns us here) on the one hand, to show the difference between legal proof and proof in general, and on the other to distinguish the body of the rules of evidence from the whole process of legal reasoning or proof. So well and carefully was this work of delimiting the proper area of legal evidence done and so pressing was the necessity for doing it, that it is perhaps not too much to say of this patient and subtle legal analyst that he created the modern law of evidence.

Two notions of paramount importance stand out in his exposition of the nature of legal reasoning. These are first that "legal reasoning" is an art whose primary function is to seek justice, not truth; and second that despite this accommodation of a mental process to a particular end, the art of reasoning and the laws of thought remain constant for legal as well as for all other human pursuits. Such a "functional" or "pragmatic" view of the nature of reasoning runs counter, of course, to all modern rationalistic views of truth as autonomous, and therefore unaffected by social purpose. For Thayer, it is clear, truth is something that exists "for a purpose"; and, in law, this purpose is evidently justice. And still this leaves us with the dilemma of "legal reasoning" unresolved. Is reasoning an autonomous activity of the mind or is it not? If reasoning is a constant then how can it be subordinated to justice? Is "legal reasoning" merely a convenient label to designate the particular activity at which the mind is directed? No, legal reasoning or more specifically legal proof is meant to be a body of doctrine which can be studied by itself. Indeed, the task of studying is taken by Thayer as representing a challenge to legal scholarship that cannot be indefinitely deferred.[29]

Wigmore had high hopes that the science of judicial proof would soon displace the rules of admissibility, although ironically enough his

---

[28] THAYER, A PRELIMINARY TREATISE ON EVIDENCE AT THE COMMON LAW (*1898*).

[29] Id. *at 273.*

own life work was dedicated to the rules and his writings on science of proof remained substantially unchanged as they first appeared in 1904.[30] For example in the *Introduction to the Principles of Judicial Proof* (1913) he writes:

The judicial rules of Admissibility are destined to lessen in relative importance during the next generation or later. Proof will assume the important place; and we must therefore prepare ourselves for this shift of emphasis.[31]

What contribution, we may now ask, can the social sciences make to the problem of the nature of judicial proof. It has already been intimated that the clarification to be hoped for is the relation of science to ethics. Certain of the social sciences (particularly if one includes psychology among them) are more interested in the question of truth. Others, notably anthropology, deal with human institutions as a whole and their learning throws light on the judicial process as an agency of social control. The play of truth against justice, of science versus morality, of proof as a means and the just settlement of disputes as the end of the legal process—all are illustrated in the development of the various branches of the science of man in society.

Let us lift out of its context an example of the right of private retaliation in primitive justice as related by Hogbin in *Law and Order in Polynesia*.

Perhaps the most remarkable case on record is that of a husband who killed, not the adulterer, but his brother. This brother was a notoriously bad lot, while the adulterer himself was a popular man. The relatives took no action, probably being glad to be rid of him.

This is as extreme an instance as one could well imagine of the ethical sense of the community being satisfied without any heed paid to, indeed in obvious defiance of, the "truth" concerning the identity of the wrong-doer. It is not that in primitive communities the truth is not a matter of "judicial" concern. It is. But different cultures rate "truth" differently in their scale of values, and if one wishes to push the inquiry far enough he finds that what is taken to be "true" or what is taken to be "evidence" varies from culture to culture, and presents the social scientist with some

---

[30] *Compare 1* Wigmore, Evidence § *30 (1st ed. 1904) with* Wigmore, Principles of Judicial Proof, 5 *(1913), and with 1* Wigmore, Evidence § *30 (3d ed. 1940).*

[31] Wigmore, Introduction to the Principles of Judicial Proof *(1913).*

of the knottiest problems he has to deal with.[32] Thus it can be said that for the tribe in question, the "true" criminal was the brother of the adulterer, on the theory of familial responsibility and a doctrine which we might label "respondent inferior."

In Hoebel's study of the *Political Organization and Law-Ways of the Comanche Indians,*[33] we find that among these peoples there seems to have been no overt recognition of the problem of evidence, except in sorcery.

The crux of the procedure was bargaining. There was no question of evidence—except in sorcery. In the damage-seeking cases the evidence was obtained before action was brought. In wife-absconding cases the presence of the woman with the absconder was *prima facie* evidence which need go no further. In all our cases but one the bargaining was begun with guilt accepted by both parties. In cases of adultery, beyond *in flagrante delicto,* evidence came from witnesses or by confession of the wife. However it may be, except for cases of sorcery, there was no technique for obtaining evidence from the defendant. Nor was the defendant usually confronted with witnesses. The aggrieved had to ascertain to his own satisfaction who the guilty party might be. After this had been done the defendant could then be confronted.

And what if guilt was denied? Usually it was not. When the defendant refused to own up, the procedure apparently came to an impasse. The aggrieved might be angry enough to take illegal steps (violence), or he might possibly kill some of the accused's horses to satisfy his desire for damages. The latter course would be likely to lead to retaliation, however, for the defendant, in denying guilt, denied cause for damages and such peremptory taking of damages was to him illegal. The reaction of the defendant if the first recourse were taken by his accuser is problematical; it would depend pretty much on his temperament and guilt in fact. Denial of guilt by an accused (except in sorcery) was so uncommon that there are not cases enough to draw sound conclusions.[34]

This does not mean of course that the individual litigant was not confronted with the problem of "proving his case." It means, rather, that unless the matter were one of common repute, the "law" of the community afforded no redress. The question was beyond "the limits of effective legal action," and the individual was left to his own resources without "political" or community help. Of course, if the modern investigator is so

---

[32] SHERIF, PSYCHOLOGY OF SOCIAL NORMS, *Chaps. I–II (1936).*
[33] MEMOIRS OF THE AMERICAN ANTHROPOLOGICAL ASSOCIATION, *No. 54 (1940).*
[34] Id. *at 53–54.*

inclined, and if the materials are available, an inquiry into doubtful cases could be undertaken and the results, perhaps, carefully generalized.

In the always doubtful case of sorcery among the Comanches for example, evidence was an ever present problem, for in sorcery the "act of aggression was secret and the aggressor a dangerous person." The techniques developed for evidencing sorcery were, with these people, either some form of ordeal or torture (to test a wife's fidelity).[35]

We have nothing to learn from the Comanches, or from any other primitive people, respecting the legal use of ordeal or torture and hence these evidentiary techniques in themselves are of no special consequence. What is important, however, is the process by which the investigator is seen to piece together creatively a system of law out of the undifferentiated social behavior of a primitive people. Not only must he look carefully for instances of proof processes, but unless he possesses in advance of his investigation a fairly well developed notion of the function of legal evidence, he is likely to discover nothing on the subject. If, on the other hand, he does possess a conceptual frame-work, results may be forthcoming, but they are as apt as not to require adjustment of the frame-work which often is seen to rest on too restricted a notion of the nature of law and of its constituent elements. Certainly, if the rules of evidence be confined to notions of scientific proof in the modern sense, then the conclusion could easily be forced that primitive peoples could possess no "law of evidence." But if a comparative study of the effect of social norms on what is taken to be proof is desired, then the investigation of the habits of primitive people in settling controversies is invaluable as a way to check against our own cultural biases in the field of the law of evidence.

Moreover, these anthropological studies throw light upon the law of evidence in revealing the fondness of the primitive mind for mechanical solutions in determining disputed matters of fact. Our law of evidence abounds in vestiges of such mechanical solutions. Even where the ends of justice are otherwise sought in refined and sophisticated methods, the evidence rules serve as a hamper on adequate investigation of the truth. Let us take the hearsay rule as one example of this process.

The dispute on the origin and function of the hearsay rule centers first about whether it is a device to safeguard the probative value of testimony (science) or whether on the contrary the rule originates and

---

[35] Id. *at 83* et seq.

persists in a desire to safeguard the fairness of judicial procedure, the *right* of cross-examination (justice). Thayer originally subsumed the hearsay under the Best Evidence rule.

The objection to hearsay, then, goes, fundamentally, to the point that something which should come through an original witness is sought to be put in at second hand, by one to whom it has been told, one who is not a witness properly speaking, who did not perceive it and cannot therefore testify to it, but only to the fact that someone said so.[36]

Thayer, for whom the primary purpose of the judicial process is the just solution of cases (not the ascertainment of truth) regards the hearsay rule as going to the question of probative value.

Wigmore regards the hearsay rule as the result of the operation of a fundamental characteristic of the system of the common law: the right of cross-examination. Ostensibly, for Wigmore, the rule excluding hearsay is a device that safeguards the probative value of testimony, and the right of cross-examination has as its foundation the same fundamental purpose.

Nevertheless, it seems rather evident that the *right* of cross-examination does not have the discovery of truth as its main purpose, nor need truth ever be anything but its incidental result.[37] For, inasmuch as the right of cross-examination is not a *requirement* or a *duty* to cross-examine, but an *opportunity* to cross-examine, it remains as a privilege of the party against whose cause the witness is testifying. Evidently the opportunity to cross-examine goes to the question of fairness to the adversaries. Truth waits on the purposes of the cross-examiners. Indeed the fundamental *caveat* of every cross-examiner is to beware of strengthening his opponent's case by eliciting damaging truths from an adverse witness. In sum, Wigmore, staunch supporter of the science of judicial proof really defends the hearsay rule on the basis of justice and fair procedure. To admit hearsay is to deprive the party (unfairly) of his opportunity to cross-examine.

In the American Law Institute's MODEL CODE OF EVIDENCE (Professor Morgan, Reporter) we have a return to the view which really regards the hearsay rule as a probative device, and since the device does not operate effectively to this end, a virtual though somewhat artificial proposal for its abandonment. The whole of the Introductory Note to Chapter VI on

---

[36] THAYER, A PRELIMINARY TREATISE ON EVIDENCE AT THE COMMON LAW, *501* (*1898*).

[37] *See discussion of* MODEL CODE EVIDENCE (*1942*) infra.

Hearsay Evidence looks at the rule only from the point of view of its probative value.[38] The view there taken is that the hearsay rule arose as a result of change of the common law mode of trial from an investigative to an adversary process. The bulk of the exceptions to the rule can be explained, on this view, only by the adversary method of trial, for there is nothing in their nature to prevent cross-examination. Those who purport to find in the exceptions substitutes for cross-examination are said to be "rationalizing."[39] Without offering the adverse party any substitute for their loss of the opportunity to cross-examine, the writers of the note, we may infer, would have them consoled with the reflection that their loss is rather small in any event and that the real probative value of hearsay would, again we may presume, far outweigh it socially.

We can see in this review of conflicting doctrines the clash and mixture of the two ideals, truth and justice. Yet, the hearsay rule is an intolerably mechanical restriction on the ascertainment of truth and only of very doubtful value in preserving the fairness of the adversary mode of trial. Its primitive character is evident in its rule-of-thumb distinctions between propositions of competing probative value, and in its all-or-nothing nature respecting included or excluded testimony.

The above analysis could be made of other exclusionary rules. The writer ventures the opinion that to the extent that they are designed to guarantee the probative force of certain classes of evidence they are out-moded, and this not because of the jury system nor the adversary nature of the common law mode of trial, but simply because common consciousness of the way to prove things has advanced to the point where the methods of exclusion become gross and mechanical, and refinements and exceptions become mere tinkering. The exclusionary rules are based on an outmoded science and morality, and their results in modern practice are therefore highly "artificial."

## PHILOSOPHY OF LAW

There is one large branch of legal science not heretofore alluded to. I refer to what is often called formal science of law or legal logic. The

---

[38] Id. *at 217* et seq.
[39] Id. *at 222.*

subject is in reality a part of scientific methodology and as such has the closest possible connection with philosophy. And this brings us to the second part of the paper, the *philosophy* of law and its relation to social science.

It is a truism that when a body of knowledge becomes experimental it breaks off from philosophy and becomes an independent domain of inquiry. Thus, physics and chemistry used to be known as natural philosophy; psychology, as mental philosophy; and sociology, social philosophy. The degree of emancipation of any discipline from philosophy is measured by the extent to which its study is put on an experimental basis.

It is not hard to understand, therefore, why law has always had a direct and immediate connection with philosophy and why the history of legal theories in modern times is a record of the rise and fall of philosophical doctrines. Each new philosophic creed finds ready application to law and it is safe to say, I think, that no modern philosophical system exists which does not have as an integral and prominent part of its thought a well-developed philosophy of law.[40]

At the beginning of the modern era,[41] the philosophical system known as rationalism assumed that the basis of knowledge lay in the immediate apprehension of a few fundamental principles, known by the exercise of reason alone, that serve as the postulates from which all detailed knowledge might be deduced. In its wake developed a full fledged rationalistic jurisprudence. The fundamental principles of law were assumed to be known to reason, and the positive enactments of law followed from those by a process of rigid deduction. That these principles turned out to be the common notions inherited from the Roman law simply meant that history confirmed what reason was sure of.

The eighteenth century empiricists evolved a contradictory theory of evidence. Facts alone can be known immediately. Principles follow from them by a process of induction. The application of this theory of evidence to law is immediate. Jurisprudence must collect facts and by a process of analysis extract from them legal principles. Analysis of actually existing legal materials suffices for the development of a science of law. The problems of legal reform, or investigations into the purpose and end of law, are extra-legal pursuits.

---

[40] POUND, OUTLINES OF LECTURES ON JURISPRUDENCE, *197–204* (*1945*).

[41] *See the writer's article on* Legal Pragmatism and Beyond, *in* INTERPRETATIONS OF MODERN LEGAL PHILOSOPHIES, *131* (*1947*).

Kantian philosophy attempted a synthesis of these two views. Some principles can be known *a priori,* the rest by experience. Facts are apprehended immediately, but knowledge can arise from them only in the light of an *a priori* framework of principles. Formal science is separated from empirical science and by the co-operation of each knowledge arises. Kantian legal doctrine found its place in this synthetic philosophy and the present day Kantian legal systems are modifications, whether slight or profound, of the original Kantian philosophy. They are all based on the assumption that a pure science of law can be developed quite apart from experience.

Of all modern philosophical systems, modern theories of law owe most to the Hegelian system of thought. Not only the insight that all facts are social, and with them, therefore, all legal facts, but also the teaching that all facts are fluid and depend for their meaning on their historical conditioning, as well as their present context, are owed to Hegel, and the legal learning of the nineteenth century pays tribute to this huge obligation in specific and numerous borrowings from the Hegelian storehouse.

Positivism contributed largely to the jurisprudence of the last century. Its disdain for completed systems, its insistence on centering attention upon the factual situation to the exclusion of theoretical constructs and its emphasis upon positive law, whether decision, legislation or executive degree, are well-known influences in the law.

Finally, when we come to the present century we see emerging as the dominant philosophical system the doctrine of pragmatism. This theory insists that beyond and beneath legal forms are human interests pressing for recognition. Law comes to be regarded as an agency of social control, one among many. How well law succeeds in its task is the measure of its success. If the purposes which law exists to achieve are effectuated, well and good. If not, law must be moulded and shaped to attain these ends. The idea of law as an abstract system of justice or as a body of commands to be obeyed simply because expressed by a sovereign will is a thing of the past. Legal philosophy becomes a theory of interests[42] and social psychology takes up where law leaves off.[43]

Not alone pragmatism, of course, but the ragtag and bobtail of all other philosophical creeds that enjoy current favor find their counterparts

---

[42] *Pound,* A Survey of Social Interests, 57 HARV. L. REV. *1 (1943).*

[43] STONE, op. cit. supra *note 26, at 673–785.*

in systems of legal philosophy. Transcendental idealism, neo-scholasticism, economic and psychological determinism, all conceivable shades of positivism, logical and otherwise, as well as various eclectic and synthetic systems flourish in the dark waters of modern jurisprudence. The one philosophical system not well represented in jurisprudence is the philosophy of experimentalism,[44] a condition not hard to understand because not until social science becomes truly experimental can law take its proper place as applied science or practical art.[45]

Although the philosophy of experimentalism can be said to have no past so far as law is concerned, since the philosophy has itself had no past, one may be pardoned for looking to the future to see what will or should be the relation of experimentalism to law and the social sciences. Experimentalism views the philosophy of science as methodology. It studies the general conditions under which experiment may most fruitfully be undertaken. It divides methodology into two parts, formal and material, and combines both parts into a system called design of experiment.[46] It believes that only the well-designed experiment can have the most fruitful results, and it attempts to make the experimenter conscious of the difference between the presuppositions he takes with him to his investigations and the data he gets from the subject of the experiment. It is a fundamental assumption of experimentalism (though by no means confined to it alone) that only through experimental methods can a body of learning now advance significantly. When a given area of scientific inquiry fails to make significant advance, this philosophy assumes that its experiments are not well designed and undertakes to discover the methodological causes for the failure.

Experiments in social science are notoriously unsatisfactory. The experimenter in this field is not prepared to assert with any degree of confidence what are even the broadest requirements of a social experiment although he feels intuitively that it differs in some profound way from the laboratory experiments of the physical sciences. He knows that the laboratory is not the proper place for social experiments because it is abundantly

---

[44] *See* SINGER, ON THE CONTENTED LIFE (*1936*); MIND AS BEHAVIOR (*1924*); EXPERIENCE AND REFLECTION (*to appear*); Philosophy of Experiments, THE SYMPOSIUM, *Vol. 1, No. 2 (1930)*; CHURCHMAN, THEORY OF EXPERIMENTAL INFERENCE (*to appear*).

[45] *Cowan*, supra *note 41, at 140–142.*

[46] FISHER, DESIGN OF EXPERIMENTS (*1937*).

clear that laboratory control makes the social situation artificial. And yet, if the laboratory is given up, how can the experiment be controlled? Is it too far-fetched to suggest that the social scientist's "control" is law, or some aspect of law? Law is undoubtedly a mode of social control, the most nearly conscious method by which projected social results are forcibly brought about. I suggest that one aspect of the solution of the social scientist's quest for control lies in law. As was suggested at the outset, legal philosophy should become part of the philosophy of the social sciences.

This thesis can receive no more than mere assertion at this time. Its weaknesses must be apparent to all. Yet I believe it contains a core of truth, that this truth will grow and that with its growth, law and theory of government can take their places as true parts of the body of science, not restricted as they now are, to the "trammels and impediments of expediency," but "liberated from the commercial casuistry of the profession" and free to nourish, and in turn to be fructified by, the beneficent influences of a science of society worthy of the name social science.

# THE ESSENCE
# OF EXPERIMENTAL
# JURISPRUDENCE

*Frederick K. Beutel*

A science of law based on a rigorous application of the scientific method should be devoted to the study of the phenomena of lawmaking, the effect of law upon society and the efficiency of laws in accomplishing the purposes for which they came into existence. It is immaterial whether Experimental Jurisprudence is a branch of sociology, or whether or not all of political science, part of each of sociology, economics, philosophy and many of the other social sciences are included within its ken. The line between the "sciences," like the definition of law, is little more than a quibble which can be left to the pundits, bureaucrats and administrators; to the scientist, the nature of its subject matter, the methods which it uses and the results which it achieves, rather than its definition, are fundamental.

With these preliminary observations in mind, it might be stated that the steps employed in prosecuting a method of Experimental Jurisprudence should be approximately as follows:

1. The nature of the phenomena which law attempts to regulate should be studied. In particular, the social problem to which a specific law is directed should be carefully isolated and examined.

2. The rule of law or other method used to regulate the phenomena or intended to solve the social problem should be accurately stated.

Reprinted by permission of the author from his *Some Potentialities of Experimental Jurisprudence* (Lincoln: University of Nebraska Press, 1957), pp. 18–32. Footnotes have been renumbered to run in sequence throughout the selection.

3. The effect on society of adopting the rule should be observed and measured.

4. There should then be constructed a hypothesis that attempts to explain the reasons for this reaction.

5. This description, when broadened to apply to other analogous situations, might be considered a jural law that describes or predicts results which would occur on application of a similar regulatory law to similar problems.

6. If analysis shows that the law is inefficient, there could then be suggested new methods of accomplishing the originally desired result.

7. The proposed new law could be enacted and the process repeated.

8. A series of such adoptions of new laws and the study of their results might throw important light upon the usefulness of the underlying purposes behind the enactment, thus effecting a possible alteration in or abandonment of this objective, or in the long run, though this now appears doubtful, even induce a revision of our present scale of social and political ethics.

Each of the steps in this process may require the skillful use of complicated machinery and techniques of observation. Some are now in existence, others will have to be developed. The important thing is that scientific jurisprudence is essentially a problem-solving device.

## THE NATURE OF THE PHENOMENA REGULATED

The first step in the methodology of scientific jurisprudence must be a careful isolation of comparatively simple problems. So long as the philosopher-scientists speculated about the nature of the universe or of matter in general, little progress was made; but when Galileo devoted his attention to the swinging pendulum or the speed of falling objects, when Newton sought the reason for a falling apple, or medical sciences began to concentrate upon the cause and cure of a specific disease such as smallpox, the glorious development of natural science was on its way. We may expect similar progress when jurisprudence begins the isolation and study of phenomena that follow simple patterns of behavior. This involves a careful examination of the factual elements of the phenomena toward which a particular law is directed. There are available for such study numerous undesirable conditions with which laws have attempted to deal.

For example, a dangerous intersection of two roads results in traffic snarls and accidents; the youths of a city steal merchandise from the stores and destroy property; a large number of bad checks are being cashed; landlords charge unconscionably high rent; the indigent aged persons in the community do not receive proper care. The solution of these and myriads of other concrete social problems are the tasks which the officers of society have attempted to solve by one or another device. If jurisprudence is to follow the scientific method, it would seem wise and relatively easy for the jurist to isolate such a problem for investigation. Indeed, many such studies have already been completed,[1] and more have been initiated.[2]

When the problem has been thus isolated for study, the determination of its nature as a social phenomenon will often involve the use of other sciences. It is obvious that a traffic study involves mechanical knowledge and some psychology, while a juvenile delinquency problem calls for the help of doctors, psychiatrists and psychologists. Similarly, studies of bad checks and rent control will use economic data. In fact, an adequate analysis of any problem will require aid from many of the modern sciences to expose the implications of its basic facts.

The choice of one particular subject to be studied rather than another . . . will depend upon such factors as convenience, urgency of the problem, resources of finance, personnel available, scientific data, technical tools existing or to be created capable of exposing the pertinent details, time, organization and many other considerations. Each problem will develop its own requirements for solution which will have to follow the experimental design most appropriate to its needs. . . .

## IDENTIFYING THE LAW AND REGULATORY DEVICES

Once the problem is isolated, it may then be easy to discover what legal devices have actually been created for its solution. In the case of a

---

[1] Glueck & Glueck, Five Hundred Criminal Careers (1930), Criminal Careers in Retrospect (1943); Pound & Frankfurter, Criminal Justice in Cleveland (1922); Tappan, Delinquent Girls in Court (1947); Moore & Callahan, Law and Learning Theory: A Study in Legal Control, 53 Yale L.J. 1 (1943).

[2] The Hoover Commission Report on Organization of the Executive Branch of the Government (1949); Fine, Connecticut Studies Schools: Everyone's Opinion Asked, N.Y. Times, Nov. 14, 1949, p. 1, col. 3; cf. Chase, The Proper Study of Mankind 50 (1948).

dangerous corner, many are available. To name only a few, there are city ordinances creating stop lights and stop signs, assigning traffic officers for busy hours, designating one-way streets, prohibiting right or left turns or both, and ordering the construction of overhead crossings and by-passes. To solve the juvenile delinquency problems, laws have been devised punishing particular acts, setting up children's courts, building reformatories and even instituting preventive measures, such as the creation of youth centers.

Sometimes the procedure may profitably be reversed and an attempt made to discover the phenomena toward which a law is directed. There are many laws in connection with which it is difficult to identify the problem or problems attempted to be solved. For example, one investigating enactments against divorce or for the licensing of saloons or public bus lines may find that they exist for multiple purposes. Other laws may remain on the books long after the purposes for which they were created have ceased to exist; for example, the celebrated Louisiana statute limiting the length of ladies' hat pins.[3] The important thing at this stage of the inquiry, however, is to identify the rules of law with the social problems they are supposed to solve. Whether the approach is from the law to the problem or from the problem to the law is immaterial. Although this second step is particularly easy in the case of statutes, it can present an imposing research problem when the so-called common law is involved. Here a rule of law is often identified only after an extended search by expert counsel, as was generally the case with the Restatements of the law promulgated by the American Law Institute, and particularly with many of the rules of torts and property.

Logically there is a third situation where there may be a pressing social problem for the solution of which there is no existing "law." Theoretically, from the point of view of the lawyer, no such condition is possible, since all such cases are supposed to fall into the great residue called the common law. Here when a problem gets to court, or other legal machinery is set in motion, it becomes necessary for the judge or official to improvise a decision. The reason he gives for his results becomes the basis of determining the common law for the future. Actually, as in the case of

---

[3] *La. Laws 1914, No. 64, p. 156; see La. Laws 1896, No. 62, p. 95; (illegal for women to wear hats in theatres); cf. also Palmer, Vestigial Remnants in the Law, 35 A.B.A.J. 905 (1949).*

settling the legal rights of children conceived by the new medical process of artificial insemination, even the legal experts may be faced with so many conflicting analogies and so many possible solutions that for all practical purposes it may be said that there is no rule of "law," or that the legal analogies are in complete confusion.

In such a case it might be argued that facts of this sort fall outside the ken of jurisprudence and into the field of other social sciences; or it could be suggested that in such a situation Steps Three to Five as outlined above should be omitted and the jurist should proceed at once under Step Six to recommend desirable changes in the law to meet the social data which have been collected on the actual facts resulting from the absence of or confusion in the "law." It makes little difference which approach is adopted. In either case it is possible to construct on the basis of knowable facts, either proceeding from the confused "law" or existing in the absence of it, a determination of the desirability for legal change, if any. If such a law were enacted, the process of Experimental Jurisprudence could then proceed as suggested beginning with Step Seven.

Again on critical examination, however, it may appear that a particular law exists for no other social purpose than to provide a rule for settling lawsuits. Whereas laws on negligence may in some instances accomplish social regulation, the "last clear chance" doctrine clearly serves no purpose other than that of reaching a judgment in a litigated case. Nevertheless, even here careful inquiry into the purpose of the law in conjunction with other steps in the methodology of scientific jurisprudence would prove extremely fruitful and might throw great light on its ultimate utility.

On the other hand, the search for the underlying social problem may reveal that the law in its present form was devised to correspond with a theory concerning the nature of the problem toward which it is directed which is entirely at odds with later discoveries regarding the same problem. For example, the current laws governing crime, the treatment of the insane and the weighing of evidence were crystallized long before the scientific method shed new light on the nature of man. Psychiatry and psychology indicate that the tests of *mens rea*, criminal intent and knowledge of right and wrong, presently applied as basic concepts in criminal law, bear no relation to the real state of mind of criminals,[4] while modern

---

[4] *Wertham, The Show of Violence 86, 149, 152 (1949); Zilboorg, Mind, Medicine and Man c. 8 (1943).*

methods of proof of scientific facts have rendered many aspects of the jury system not only obsolete but an actual impediment to fact-finding.[5] In these fields the necessary reconstruction of the problem toward which the law is oriented will require the aid of many other scientists cooperating with the research lawyer. When the reports of such a team are in, many of our present laws will be found to rest upon theories as to the nature of man and the world about him which have been shown by modern science to be inaccurate. Considerations such as these may force the abandonment of many of the basic postulates of criminal law and evidence and will point the way to revisions in the laws themselves.

Just as legal theories on the nature of the problem which the law is attempting to solve may be out of line with scientific discoveries, so also methods or tools sanctioned by the legal system to reach the desired result may not be efficient. . . . [Our] legal system has been woefully slow to adopt the products of physical and social science to modernize its procedures. The discovery and application of current scientific knowledge for the use of legal and government agencies provides one of the most fruitful and neglected fields for current social research. Here again . . . there is a growing demand for cooperative research between jurists and other scientists, both social and physical.

## THE REACTION OF SOCIETY TO A LAW

The third step—the collection of data to gauge the efficiency of the law in accomplishing its purpose—is far more difficult than either of the previous steps. Here the effect of the administration of law on the actions of people in society must be observed. Patterns of mass action and not individual reactions are the important consideration.[6] Such patterns are similar to physical, statistical or mass reactions, such as the molecular action when two colored liquids coalesce in solution, and are made up of the sum total of what appear to be indiscriminate individual reactions. To obtain the information desired here, statistical studies of many individual reactions, both physical and mental, are necessary to make up the picture

---

[5] *See Berry v. Chaplin, 74 Cal. App. 2d 652, 169 P.2d 442 (1946), 34 Corn. L. Q. 78–80 (1948).*

[6] *Cooley, Case Study of Small Institutions as a Method of Research in Personality and the Social Group 182 (Burgess ed. 1929); see also Ohlin, Selection for Parole (1951) and authorities there cited 131 ff.*

of group responses and attitudes.[7] Other sciences must again be called upon to produce data, and experts will have to work in teams and pool their results.

In the case of a single-purpose statute like a traffic law, observation of a particular fact on a particular corner is comparatively easy. The patterns of social action caused by the impact of the legal device on the comparatively simple phenomenon of the movement of vehicular and pedestrian traffic at the corner is readily observable. Here mechanical counters, statistics, moving picture cameras and the like are useful in assembling the pattern of traffic before and after the change in the law.

Where the multiple-purpose statute is involved, the social picture is more complicated. A study might be attempted to determine either the efficiency of the statute in accomplishing only one of its alleged purposes or its success in relation to two or more or all of the postulated purposes. The analyses of sociologists, economists, criminologists, psychiatrists, poll-takers and many other specialists should be employed in assembling the data. To insure accuracy, the elements of the program will have to be isolated and the area selected for study made statistically large enough to eliminate individual variations. Thus the reactions of traffic on one corner will not be enough; behavior patterns at many intersections will have to be observed and compared. So also the study of one juvenile court might be enlightening, but it should be extended to include others over a long period of time in order to eliminate chance factors. This process is similar to the creation of a complicated experimental design in other scientific fields.

On the other hand, the problem of checking a law suspected of obsolescence may be relatively simple. For example, if a preliminary study discloses that ladies have discontinued wearing long hat pins, that there have been no instances of prosecution under the statute regulating them for years, and that the women are neither afraid of the law nor in fact know anything about it, the inference is obvious.[8] Nevertheless, the possibility should not be overlooked that a law which no longer serves the purpose for which it was originally enacted may yet be useful in regulating new phenomena.

---

[7] See for example, Stewart, Empirical Mathematical Rules Concerning the Distribution and Equilibrium of Population, 37 Geographical Rev. 461 (1947).

[8] The Hatpin Act was repealed by La. Crim. Code § 21, No. 43 (1942).

# THE REASONS FOR REACTIONS TO A LAW

Although the discovery, in the absence of well documented legislative sources, of the purposes for which laws are created may cause some speculation and perhaps difficult problems of proof, so far in the process of Experimental Jurisprudence there has been little else suggested than the descriptive scientific technique. In the fourth step, however, scientific imagination, speculation and intuition begin to assert themselves. The formulation of a hypothesis to explain the pattern of group or individual actions revealed by the research may be a simple or complex but not impossible task. Where mere traffic regulations are involved, the results before and after the change in the law are easily and quickly understandable, for when the effect of the law has been identified and described, one can readily infer why congestion has been increased or decreased. If a one-way street or an overhead crossing is established, the results are obvious, and the reaction of society to the rule of law can be explained with little difficulty. On the other hand, where multiple-purpose statutes, such as those creating juvenile courts or probation officers or providing for licensing procedures, are involved, the observation of the effect of the statute on society requires that all of the techniques of descriptive social study be brought to bear on the problem. With their contribution, a hypothesis explaining the effect of the law may be successfully constructed.

# THE PERFECTION OF A JURAL LAW

After a hypothesis concerning the effect of the law on a single situation has been constructed, it may be capable of enlargement into a proper jural law. By examination of similar situations where the same law has been applied, the statement of social reactions in single instances may be generalized. Thus it may be determined that under certain conditions traffic lights eliminate a percentage of accidents on busy crossings, while it is certain that an overhead pass will entirely eliminate traffic accidents caused by collisions at intersections. Again, in the case of the juvenile court, if careful studies of the functioning of a single court are expanded to take like institutions into account, it may be possible to state jural laws regarding the effect of this particular type of organization on juvenile delinquency in general.

Such a comparison is readily available in the United States, where a central government, forty-eight state governments, thousands of county governments, and over one hundred thousand independent governmental units, many of which perform identical functions, exist side by side.[9] By proper statistical study, individual variations can be eliminated, and the jural law governing the institution itself can be clarified. Our uniform commercial statutes, uniform codes of court procedure and almost identical organizations for law enforcement all offer a mine of raw material upon which, after the collection and assimilation of sufficient data, jural laws of social reaction can be constructed. When such studies are made, the results should minimize the basic controversies about the usefulness of the institution or law studied.

A striking illustration of this principle was shown by a recent study of progressive education.[10] Prior to this investigation, emotions ran high among secondary educators as to the value of "tried and true" conservative methods of teaching "the three R's"; progressive education with its haphazard and unorganized methods was roundly denounced all over the country. But when a careful study was made of the success in college of well sampled students from the various progressive and non-progressive institutions under a pattern which eliminated most of the chance variations, the results showed that the students from progressive schools fared slightly better than did those from the orthodox institutions.[11] One striking result of this study which should give pause to any dogmatist in the field of social or legal regulation indicated that students from progressive schools with no previous training in science made better grades in college science courses than did their fellows well drilled in secondary school sciences by the conservative methods.[12] It is clear that success in college is not the sole purpose of secondary education, but it is certainly one. Since this study, much of the heat has gone out of the recurrent controversies in this area, and educators are at least one step further toward finding what is the "best" method of secondary education.

Techniques that are applicable to the study of regulations made by educators are equally applicable to laws passed by legislatures or devised

---

[9] Anderson, The Units of Government in the United States (Pub. Adm. Serv. Monograph 83, 1942).

[10] Aikin, The Story of the Eight-Year Study (1942).

[11] Time, Feb. 16, 1942, p. 53.

[12] Thirty Schools Tell Their Story 668 (1943).

through generalizations upon decisions of judges. The pattern of human reactions in both instances is now within the grasp of our methods of social scrutiny. One leading scientist has summarized the situation as follows:

There is no longer excuse for anyone to ignore the fact that human beings, on the average and at least in certain circumstances, obey mathematical rules resembling in a general way some of the primitive "laws" of physics. "Social physics" lies within the grasp of scholarship that is truly modern. When we have found it, people will wonder at the blind opposition its proponents first encountered.[13]

Up to this point, a scientific jurisprudence has attempted only the descriptive technique of social physics, but, due to variations in the laws of various jurisdictions having similar social structure, jurists can reap many of the benefits of controlled experiments by simply comparing results of studies in existing societies without the necessity of making any changes in the law. Moreover, where societies differ markedly in their legal structure, as is the case when comparing the United States, Spain and Soviet Russia, jural laws can be further verified by comparing the results of social physics as applied to similar phenomena but under totally different legal conditions.

### SUGGESTIONS FOR CHANGE IN THE LAW

When the sixth step in the methods of Experimental Jurisprudence is reached, however, social science or "social physics" may become as truly experimental a science as is physics or chemistry. After observations of the reaction of people to a particular law or class of laws have been collected and formalized, it is possible for the jurist to point out inefficiencies in both the administration of the law and in its technical structure. At this stage most of these defects will appear in terms of failure to accomplish the purposes of the enactment. He can then suggest to statesmen or to other policy-makers changes in the law which might better effectuate the policy for which it was created.

In the past the objection has always been raised at this stage that whether one rule of law or another is adopted poses a question of social values which science alone is unable to answer. Furthermore, it is claimed

---

[13] *Stewart, supra note* [7] *at 485.*

no change in the law should be undertaken without a value judgment, since people do not like to consider themselves experimental guinea pigs. This argument, however, wholly overlooks the fact that an overwhelming majority of the laws now on the books and most current policy judgments are made on an impressionistic basis to solve a specific problem. Often they are the product of impassioned emotions rather than systematic study. Whether we like it or not, therefore, these laws are all in a sense experimental, but they are experiments that have not been subjected to any systematic check as to their results. As a result of this haphazard practice, most current laws are carried along by the force of inertia until they either become obsolete or are repealed due to further pressures based not upon scientific investigation but upon public clamor which often arises from the effectiveness of the law itself. In fact, it is, perhaps, a jural law of our representative democracy that the more effectively a law limits the actions of particular groups, the more it is subject to pressure from these groups for change. It is thus an interesting paradox that governmental agencies created by law to regulate certain "anti-social activity" are often in turn captured by the forces which they are set up to control. The police are occasionally dominated by the underworld,[14] the Interstate Commerce Commission by the railroads,[15] and the labor boards by the unions or the employers, depending upon which is the socially stronger at the moment.[16] This haphazard governmental experimentation might be brought to an end under a regime of scientific jurisprudential study.

In addition, there is no reason to suppose that there would be any immediate necessity for the experimental jurist to make determinations of value. He should study the law to find out its effectiveness in accomplishing the purpose for which the statesmen or judge allegedly created it and be able to advise what changes would further that purpose.

The only value judgments which any properly trained scientist makes about his data are judgments regarding their relevance to his problem, the weight to be assigned to each aspect, and the general interpretation to be made of the observed events. These are problems which no scientist can escape, and they are not at all unique or insuperable in the social sciences.

Have scientists, then, no special function or obligation in determining the

---

[14] *Frank Costello, 54 Time Magazine 15 (Nov. 28, 1949) (cover story).*
[15] *Georgia v. Pennsylvania Ry., 324 U.S. 439, 458 (1945).*
[16] *Cohen & Cohen, The National Labor Relations Board in Retrospect, 1 Indus. & Lab. Rel. Rev. 648 (1948).*

ends for which scientific knowledge is to be used? As scientists, it is their business to determine reliably the immediate and remote costs and consequences of alternate possible courses of action, and to make these known to the public.[17]

It should be the function of the scientific jurist to state these "natural consequences" in the form of jural laws. Thus in the beginning he is necessarily the servant of the lawmaker.

If the experimental jurist will start his work by solving simple problems by an impartial process based upon facts and social reactions while entirely free from preconceived ideas concerning the good or evil of the ultimate results in the same manner in which a medical researcher studies syphilis, it will not be long until he will become the most important colleague of any lawmaker. Thus "the services of real social scientists would be as indispensable to Fascists as to Communists and Democrats, just as are the services of physicists and physicians."[18]

In any event, when the facts of the social reaction to law are known and the jural laws properly determined, much of the argument concerning ultimate values will cease to exist. For example, it was at one time believed that it was a "good" thing to suppress liquor traffic by prohibition laws, but experimentation, haphazard as it was, has shown us that by almost any test the results of prohibition are "worse" than the liquor traffic. If the lawmakers had employed the methods of Experimental Jurisprudence, this jural law would have been known sooner, there would have been less emotionalism, and we would have been far more sophisticated in our attempts to regulate the "evil" in the liquor traffic. In fact, it is not too much to hope that the application of careful scientific methods of study to such problems of social control could lead to means of entirely eliminating many of the "evils" with which we are plagued. . . .

## THE ENACTMENT OF SUGGESTED LAWS

It is apparent that the seventh step, if Experimental Jurisprudence is to reach maximum effectiveness, must consist in the actual enactment of the changes in the law suggested by the jurist after his studies. But in the

---

[17] *Lundberg, Can Science Save Us* 28 (1947).

[18] *Id. 48; cf. Lynd, The Implications of Economic Planning of Sociology, 9 Am. Sociol. Rev. 14, 17 (1944).*

present state of lawmaking, the governmental machinery is an only partially adequate device for this process. Thus the objector can easily point out that legislatures are independent bodies in no way obligated to the jurist, and that he will be lucky indeed if he ever gets his new reforms enacted. This is certainly a difficulty, but in actual practice it should be far from insurmountable.

There are three practical ways of overcoming this legislative lag. (1) The first is delegation by the legislature of rule-making power to officials with authority to change current rules of law. (2) The variation in rules of law now in evidence governing the same or similar phenomena are so great that after a study of the operation of law in a few jurisdictions a little further research may disclose that most of the theoretical legal and administrative variations which an experimental jurist might desire to use as controls to check the working of a law have already been enacted in legal units of similar structure. (3) Third and last, the legislatures, even as now constituted, may themselves be persuaded to change the law.

(1) *Delegation of power* is a current governmental practice in all fields of administrative activity. Its constitutionality with slight checks in the form of standards is recognized in almost every field of legal administration, and . . . it is already beginning to achieve important results in the current development of Experimental Jurisprudence. Where the lawmaking power is thus delegated to an official, he is able to experiment with the subject matter under his jurisdiction in a manner similar to that used by the physical scientist in his laboratory. . . .

(2) *The variation in rules of law* in the various jurisdictions in the United States alone is a phenomenon known to all lawyers and many social scientists. As indicated elsewhere, there are in this country over one hundred fifty thousand units of government with lawmaking power running across the entire hierarchy from the federal government with its various territorial subdivisions through states, counties, school districts, improvement units and various other authorities. Hundreds of these units serve similar functions. Seldom, if ever, do they have identical rules of law or methods of enforcement.

A recent study of the laws and health regulations governing vaccination for smallpox[19] shows that there are at least eight general categories of

---

[19] *Ravenscroft & Solomon, An Experiment in Scientific Jurisprudence, 32 Neb. L. Rev. 547 (1953).*

enforcement in this field scattered among the forty-eight states, varying all the way from compulsory requirement of vaccination for everybody to prohibition of compulsory vaccination in three states. The eight categories in turn can be broken down into numerous variations in the practical rule or method of enforcement. By a careful study of the statistics of the instances of smallpox in the various areas covered by similar regulations, it has been possible to show the effectiveness in general of the eight major categories, and in addition, by comparing variations within categories it has been pointed out that it is now possible to determine the strength and weakness of almost every known type of legal control of smallpox vaccination. Where local laws fail to yield the particular control desired, it is possible to extend the study to foreign nations. Here is a field where existing variations in the type of law and administration supply to the jural scientist, if he is willing to travel a bit through his available governmental laboratory, almost every type of experimental control that the physicist can apply in his laboratory. . . . [Similar] controls are available in hundreds of other fields of legal activity.

(3) *Legislative lawmaking bodies* are not beyond the reach of the experimental scientist. Once a legislature or other rule-making body has initiated a course of action based upon a chosen conclusion of desirability, however derived, experience will show that it is not too difficult to persuade it to adopt changes in the law better calculated to effectuate the original policy. Many of the most fertile fields of initial study for the experimental jurist lie in such areas as traffic control, procedural reform, criminal administration, city government and area planning, where there are few if any violent political prejudices.

Should careful scientific studies indicate a change in direction or policy, they are likely to be the most persuasive argument to all but an emotionally blinded lawmaker. Even where deep-seated emotions that impinge upon individual interests like property ownership, religion or morals are involved, a carefully executed study supporting the suggested changes may be able to win over all but the most prejudiced. Except in cases where these unreasoning positions are held by major political forces, the scientific jurist can expect progress along the lines suggested by his studies. If this result is reached, a new instrument of statesmanship will have been erected which will make possible continued progress in the field of law and government. Legal machinery will be enabled to adopt a technique of orderly social change which will keep abreast of scientific and industrial development. There is no reason why violent revolution must continue to be the chief means of accomplishing permanent social reform.

Where blind prejudiced emotionalism, selfishness or ignorance on the part of the controlling political forces stand in the way of ordered change, the studies of impartial jurists may still be of great aid in shifting the balance of power. Progress temporarily halted may again be resumed, regardless of the means by which the change in political power was accomplished.

Meanwhile let "social planners" beware! Water must be pumped to flow up hill, natural tendencies in human relations cannot be combated and controlled by singing to them. The architect must accept and understand the law of gravity and the limitation of materials. The city or national planner must likewise adapt his studies to natural principles.[20]

It is interesting to note that in the past, whatever may have been the manner in which revolutions have been brought about, whether political or by the force of arms, the leaders of the following reconstruction have often adopted schemes of government already at hand.[21] The transplantation of the theories of Montesquieu into the Constitution of the United States, the adoption of the Civil Code by Napoléon, the use of *Das Kapital* and other works of Marx and Engels by the Russian Politburo and the implementation of *Mein Kampf* by the Nazis all followed revolutions. Historians can offer many other examples of this tendency. Would it not be safer, therefore, when inevitable political upsets occur for the new leaders to have at hand enlightened theories of law and government carefully worked out by rational experimental processes rather than be left to rely on the speculation of cloistered philosophers or the mad dreams of imprisoned fanatics?

Whatever may be the form of government or lack of it, there is strong likelihood that the suggested legal devices built upon carefully studied jural laws will have a chance of enactment. Thus the science of jurisprudence may become fully experimental.

---

[20] *Stewart, supra note* [7] *at 485.*
[21] *Lasswell, Power and Personality 164 (1948).*

# JURIMETRICS:
# THE NEXT STEP
# FORWARD

*Lee Loevinger*

\* \* \* \*

. . . Intuitive concepts and accidental practices seem adequate to primitive man. By repetition, they become habitual, then habit deepens into tradition, and finally tradition becomes unchallengeable truth. One day some skeptical mind suggests that perhaps the current version of truth is only tradition, perhaps tradition is only ossified habit, and, in any event, the adequacy of both beliefs and practices to contemporary situations should be tested by investigation. Immediately all the traditional objections are made: you can't experiment in this field; investigation is old stuff, our ancestors have made all the investigations necessary; since people are involved you can't be objective; this cold-blooded proposal is immoral because it disregards values; and anyway there are no practical methods of making the investigation. Note that exactly the same arguments, with slight changes of phraseology, apply equally whether the subject matter is astronomy (how can you put a star in a test tube?), physics (Democritus knew all about atoms), physiology (you can't study men as though they were animals), psychology (if you don't take account of man's soul you destroy all our values), or, the most recent child of science, cybernetics (don't be silly—how can you make a machine that will think?). Note also that in every case in which we have disregarded these objections, we have been able to formulate meaningful problems, institute effective techniques, gather valid data, and finally not only

Reprinted by permission of the author and of the publishers from 33 *Minnesota Law Review* (1949), 455–493. Footnotes have been renumbered to run in sequence throughout the selection.

enlarge our useful knowledge but increase our control over both the environment and ourselves.

The next step forward in the long path of man's progress must be from jurisprudence (which is mere speculation about law) to *jurimetrics*[1]—which is the scientific investigation of legal problems. In the field of social control (which is law) we must at least begin to use the same approach and the same methods that have enabled us to progress toward greater knowledge and control in every other field. The greatest problem facing mankind at this midpoint of the twentieth century is the inadequacy of socio-legal methods inherited from primitive ancestors to control a society which, in all other aspects, is based upon the powerful techniques of a sophisticated science. The inescapable fact is that jurisprudence bears the same relation to a modern science of jurimetrics as astrology does to astronomy, alchemy to chemistry, or phrenology to psychology. It is based upon speculation, supposition and superstition; it is concerned with meaningless questions; and, after more than two thousand years, jurisprudence has not yet offered a useful answer to any question or a workable technique for attacking any problem.

The utter futility of jurisprudence (as anything more pretentious than classroom or barroom entertainment) can be illustrated by a typical philosophical supposition. Suppose that all the legal scholars and lawyers in the United States (or in the world) were to be gathered in a single great conclave the day after tomorrow and presented with the questions of jurisprudence: What is law? What is the basis of law? What is the end and purpose of law? Define Justice, etcetera etcetera. Now suppose—this is a great feat of imagination—that all these lawyers should agree unanimously on answers to all of these questions. We would, at long last, then have authoritative definitions of concepts like law, justice, and perhaps even of crime, contract, property and tort. (It is too much to suppose that even this imaginary conclave should agree on what constitutes a divorce in the United States.) What would be the result? I venture to suggest it would be nothing at all. If the results of these deliberations were pub-

---

[1] *Of course it is not important what term is used to indicate the scientific discipline suggested. It is important that it have a distinctive name, as well as a general program. The name suggested here seems, to the author, as good as any, since it seems to indicate the nature of the subject matter, and corresponds to other similar terms, such as biometrics and econometrics.*

lished in some Super-Restatement of the Law, they would, no doubt, be cited by judges (together with Coke, Blackstone and appropriate cases) in rendering opinions. But . . . they would not materially influence the result in any particular case, and, most assuredly, would furnish neither better methods nor better answers for any present problems.

Let us continue this supposition one step further. Suppose—what is certainly not impossible—that half a dozen or a dozen competent young lawyers and professors should decide to address themselves seriously to jurimetrics. After a year or so of work in the field, they decide to meet together for the purpose of discussing the problems and results of jurimetrics. A time and place are arranged and an agenda drawn up. What are the questions with which jurimetrics is likely to be concerned? It is certainly impossible to predict, in advance of work in the field, exactly what form the problems will take. Still, the general form and probable subject matter of many of the questions which jurimetrics, at least in its earlier stages, will attempt to investigate can be anticipated. It is reasonable to suppose that the agenda might be something like this:


## THE PROBLEMS OF JURIMETRICS

### A. The Behavior of Witnesses

What is the statistical reliability and validity of present scientific methods of detecting deception?[2]

---

[2] *A substantial amount of work has already been done on the scientific detection of deception. At least fourteen psychometric methods of detecting deception are known: (1) use of scopolamin; (2) use of sodium amytal; (3) hypnotic sleep; (4) measurement of systolic blood pressure; (5) measurement of rate of respiration; (6) measurement of galvanic reflex; (7) word association tests; (8) observation of pupillary reflex; (9) measurement of pulse rate; (10) recording of eye-movements; (11) recording of unconscious muscle-movements; (12) measurement of amplitude and rate of heart beat; (13) analysis of chemical content of blood; (14) change in the brain-wave patterns. These various measures are of various degrees of reliability and many of them are interrelated. There is a substantial body of literature on this subject. Hugo Munsterberg, On the Witness Stand (1908); W. M. Marston, The Lie Detector Test (1938);* Wigmore, Professor Munsterberg and the Psychology of Testimony, 3 Ill. L. Rev. 399 (1909); Use of Psychology Tests to

What is the comparative reliability and validity of cross-examination as a method of testing testimony?[3]

What new or refined techniques will give us better methods of detecting deception by witnesses?

How can the ability of a witness to observe and recollect be most easily measured?

How can the effect of interest or bias upon observation and recollection be measured?

---

Determine Credibility of Witnesses, *33 Yale L. J. 771 (1924)*; *Inbau*, Scientific Evidence in Criminal Trials, *24 J. Crim. L. & Criminology 1140 (1934)*; *Keeler*, Debunking the Lie-Detector, *25 J. Crim. L. & Criminology 153 (1934)*; *Inbau*, "The Lie Detector," *40 Scientific Monthly 81 (1935)*; Detection of Deception Technique Admitted in Evidence, *26 J. Crim. L. & Criminology 262, 431, 499 (1935)*; Bloodhound Evidence, *26 J. Crim. L. & Criminology 926 (1936)*; *Jaycox*, Scientific Detection of Lies, *40 Scientific American 370 (1937)*; *Ruckmick*, The Truth About the Lie-Detector, *22 J. of App. Psych. 50 (1938)*; *Obermann*, Mild Affective States and the Berger Rhythm, *34 J. of Abnormal & Social Psych. 84 (1939)*; Berrien Laboratory Studies of Deception, *24 J. of Exp. Psych. 542 (1939)*; *Tovillo*, History of Lie Detection, *30 J. Crim. L. & Criminology 39 (1939)*; *Forosch*, The Lie Detector and the Courts, *16 N. Y. U. L. Q. 202 (1939)*; *Keeler*, The Lie Detector Proves Its Usefulness, *22 Public Management 163 (1940)*; *Trovillo*, What the Lie Detector Can't Do, *32 J. Crim. L & Criminology 121 (1941)*; *MacNitt*, Electrodermal Response and Cardiac Amplitude as Measures of Deception, *33 J. Crim. L. & Criminology 266 (1942)*; *Trovillo*, Deception Test Criteria, *33 J. Crim. L. & Criminology 338 (1942)*; Pupillary Responses during Deception, *(1943) 32 J. of Exp. Psych. 443 (1943)*, *34 J. Crim. L. & Criminology 135 (1941)*; *Turner*, Crime Detection, *30 Radio News 20 (1943)*; *Johnston*, The Magic Lie Detector, *Saturday Evening Post, Apr. 15, p. 9, Apr. 22, p. 26, Apr. 29, p. 20 (1944)*; *Reid*, Simulated Blood Presure Responses, *36 J. Crim. L. & Criminology 201 (1945)*. *Cases which have considered the legal admissibility of such techniques are:* Frye v. United States, *54 App. D. C. 46, 293 Fed. 1013 (App. D.C. 1923)*; State v. Hudson, *289 S. W. 920 (Mo. 1926)*; State v. Bohner, *210 Wis. 651, 246 N. W. 314 (1933)*; People v. Kenny, *167 Misc. 51 3 N. Y. S. 2d 348 (1938)*; People v. Forte, *279 N. Y. 204, 18 N. E. 2d. 31 (1938)*, rehearing denied, *279 N. Y. 788, 18 N. E. 2d 870 (1939)*; Commonwealth v. Kipple, *333 Pa. 33, 3 A. 2d 353 (1939)*; Commonwealth v. Jones, *341 Pa. 541, 19 A. 2d 389 (1941)*; People v. Becker, *300 Mich. 562, 2 N. W. 2d 503 (1942Q; LaFevre v. State, *242 Wisc. 416, 8 N. W. 2d 288 (1943)*; State v. DeHart, *242 Wisc. 562, 8 N. W. 2d 360 (1943)*; Koonts v. Farmers Mutual Ins. Ass'n, *235 Iowa 87, 16 N. W. 2d 20 (1944)*; Bruner v. People, *113 Colo. 194, 156 P. 2d 111 (1945)*.

[3] *There is a spate of panegyrics on the value of cross-examination, but no body of scientific literature comparable to that on psychometric detection of deception.* See Stern, The Psychology of Testimony, *34 J. of Abnormal & Social Psych. 3 (1939)*.

## B. The Behavior of Judges

What statistical measures will most conveniently summarize the behavior of individual judges in various categories of cases? How can we institute and maintain the basic records for such measures?[4]

How, within the framework of existing rules, can we investigate the behavior of juries, measure their reaction to evidence and instructions, and discover the determinant considerations in reaching verdicts?[5]

On the basis of inquiries relating to the behavior of witnesses, can we construct any objective criteria for weighing testimony?

How can we adapt the generally recognized scientific measures of probability to the problems of legal "proof"?

On the basis of data relating to the behavior of persons engaged in the judging process, are there any observable differences between the behavior of judges-in-court, administrative "judges," and legislators? If we can discover such differences, how can they best be expressed qualitatively and quantitively?

## C. The Behavior of Legislators

What practical measures can be instituted for investigating and recording in summary form the patterns of legislative behavior?

Can reliable patterns of the kind presupposed in the radical-conservative-reactionary terms of popular speech be discovered? If so, are there similar behavior patterns among "judges"? What are the measures of such patterns?

To what extent does the behavior of legislators, in legislature X during period Y, indicate the influence of precedent, evidence, personal interest, and other factors?

---

[4] *Frank reports that an attempt to maintain such records in New York for a few years disclosed results so disconcerting to the judges that the keeping of the records was discontinued. Jerome Frank, Law and the Modern Mind 112-115 (1930).*

[5] *Two promising attempts by individual jurists along this line have been reported recently. See* St. Paul Judge Probes Juror's Mind, 6 *Bench and Bar of Minn.* 17 (1949); *Hartshorne,* Jury Verdicts: A Study of Their Characteristics and Trends, 35 *A. B. A. J.* 113 (1949). *These studies suggest that if some investigators would prepare uniform questionnaire and tabular forms, many judges might be willing to help gather similar data.*

What procedures can be instituted in legislative bodies to secure and present to the members more representative and reliable evidence relating to the subjects under consideration?

To what extent can court and administrative trial procedures be useful in legislative inquiries? What other procedures are available or can be devised to enable legislators to weigh evidence?

### D. Legal Language and Communication

What current legal terms have a core of meaning and which ones become wholly meaningless under semantic analysis?

What operational definitions[6] can be given to the meaningful legal terms?

What semantic devices can be used immediately to make current legal jargon a useful means of communication?

What concepts, and correlative terms, are most useful for communication regarding the data and problems of jurimetrics?

What means can be devised and used to make the legal guides for public action intelligible to the public?

### E. Legal Procedure and Recordation

How can ordinary controversies be presented to a tribunal in the simplest and quickest manner? How can the inordinate delays of current procedure, both in presentation and decision, be eliminated or minimized?

How can business machines and methods be adapted to handle the problems of filing and making available public records of lawsuits, judgments, land titles, births, deaths, marriages, divorces, business liens, and other similar materials? How can public records be made sufficiently available to the public so that "constructive notice" is more than a legal fiction?

### F. Non-aberrant Personal Maladjustments

How can the formation of unstable marriage combinations be prevented or deterred?

---

[6] See P. W. Bridgman, The Logic of Modern Physics (1927). . . .

How can marital maladjustments be separated into those which are capable of being resolved and those which are not?

How can potentially successful marriage combinations be preserved through critical periods of maladjustment in which one or both parties desire divorce?

How can inherently unsatisfactory and unstable marital combinations be quickly and honestly dissolved without encouraging emotionally unstable personalities to seek divorce for reasons of personal whim rather than necessity?

What techniques and institutions can be established to offer normal opportunities for development to children in situations of (a) divorce, (b) unmarried parents, and (c) delinquent homes?

## G. Aberrations of Behavior

How can aberrant tendencies be detected before serious behavior problems occur?

How can the malleable aberrant be separated from the residual intransigent, or the incurable psychotic?

What treatment will cure the tendency to aberrations of behavior of types a, b, c, . . . n, in situations A, B, C, . . . N?

What methods are most likely to deter the normal, or potentially aberrant, person from anti-social, or illegal, behavior?

## H. Unintentional Personal Injury

How effective are present "negligence" laws in deterring conduct likely to cause unintentional injury to others? What laws might be more effective to accomplish this?

How effective are present "negligence" laws in providing for the needs of persons injured by others? What laws might be more effective in providing for such needs?

## I. Macrolegal Techniques of Investigation

What indices will most reliably indicate the social results of laws in categories A, B, C, . . . N?

How can the data to construct these indices be obtained most efficiently?

The contrast between the questions of jurimetrics and the problems of jurisprudence is patent. Perhaps the most striking difference is that the problems of jurisprudence are broad, general, and therefore limited in number, while the questions of jurimetrics are relatively narrow and specific, and so are much more numerous. But this is a superficial distinction. The profound differentiation lies in two facts. First, the problems of jurisprudence are basically meaningless, since they can only be debated but never decided nor even investigated; whereas the questions of jurimetrics are meaningful since they are capable of being investigated, and ultimately answered, even though we may not know the answers now. . . . Second, the problems of jurisprudence are not truly significant problems, since even if they were "solved," in the only sense in which they could be "solved"—by the giving of authoritative definitions, the "solutions" would have no practical consequences in our lives. On the other hand, all of the questions of jurimetrics are genuinely significant, since even a partial or tentative answer to any one is likely to have far-reaching consequences for society and for the individual. In this sense, jurimetrics is eminently "practical" in its approach, as contrasted with the philosophical speculations of jurisprudence.

There are, of course, other differences between the two disciplines, some of which may not be apparent at this time. Certainly one of the most important is that the problems of jurisprudence are formally "static" problems which presuppose the existence of one final authoritative answer, while the questions of jurimetrics are "dynamic" in form in that they allow for changing answers as our knowledge increases. Indeed, in jurimetrics the questions themselves change as the body of knowledge grows, since the problems are constantly reformulated in terms of prior data. Further, it will be noticed that while legal theoreticians, like the traditional economists, have been concerned up to the present time exclusively with microlegal phenomena—theories about the application of law to individuals—jurimetrics takes a broader outlook to include also an inquiry into macrolegal phenomena—the effect of law upon the community. While we can never disregard the problems of the application of law to individuals, experience in many fields indicates that the macrocosmic approach is more likely to be a fruitful one in the early stages of scientific investigation. Even today the science of physics is able to formulate its macroscopic laws with much greater accuracy than its microscopic laws, and—if the Heisenberg principle is correct—there is an absolute limit to the precision of observation and prediction on the submolecular level.

Perhaps the greatest advantage of jurimetrics over jurisprudence, at least from the viewpoint of the public, is that it will establish within the law itself an institutional method for growth and change. It is true that lawyers and jurists are fond of making speeches and writing papers lauding the marvelous vitality of the common law institutions in adapting themselves to social change. It is also true that such praise comes almost exclusively from within the profession and almost always as a defense against the attacks of non-lawyers upon the immobility and inflexibility of the law. Regardless of the forensic facade with which it may be decorated, it is too obvious to admit of controversy that the present method of the law has the effect of making change as slow and as slight as possible, as well as of making law a completely closed system which will admit new knowledge only when it is smuggled in disguised as a "precedent." As in Jhering's juristic heaven, new facts and ideas can gain admission to the house of law today only by smashing their heads through the solid walls. Jurimetrics promises to cut windows in the house of law, so that those inside can see out, and to cut doors, so that those outside can get in. Significantly, jurimetrics is oriented neither to change nor permanence as such. It seeks knowledge, and is prepared to retain, discard or modify principles as the data may, in any case, demand. It seems likely that this approach may at last furnish a satisfactory resolution of the law's eternal paradox that rules which are too inflexible for social growth are still too uncertain for individual security.

It must not be imagined that jurimetrics promises any panaceas. The story of man's progress is full of nostrums, but devoid of panaceas, and there is no reason to think that we may discover one now. Jurimetrics promises no more than an opportunity for law to move forward along the same rocky road that all the other disciplines have already travelled. It is not an easy nor an inviting road (except for those hardy souls who enjoy pioneering), but the grim and inescapable fact is that there is no other road running in the same direction. There are many side-roads, many well advertised cure-alls on the market: appoint all judges; elect all judges; select better judges, however you do it; let juries decide everything; abolish all juries; let panels of experts decide all lawsuits; submit all laws to a popular referendum; call off elections and turn the government over to the engineers. These are just a few of the nostrums; but they all have one thing in common—they all relate to the method of choosing the men who are to exercise power. Once selected, these officials (or the public) would be faced with the same problems confronting the men in power today. There is no reason to think that those in power would behave differently because of a change in the method of their selection.

It is merely tautological to say that if we select better men for judges and legislators we will have better courts and legislatures. There can be no argument about the proposition that we should get the best men we possibly can for public office. But this gives us no hint as to how we may discriminate the well from the poorly qualified. Furthermore, there is not a scintilla of evidence that it would be possible, over any long period of time, to secure public officials of a greater average competence than those we have been getting, or, that if we could, the more competent officials could achieve substantially better results with our present laws and legal system.

As astute an observer as Judge Frank has intimated that the way to improve the administration of law is to have more judges like Justice Holmes.[7] Although based on a brilliant analysis, the suggestion is almost puerile in its naivete. It is equivalent to saying that science would progress faster if there were more scientists of the caliber of Newton and Einstein. Perhaps if all men were truly wise there would be no need for government at all—such speculation is completely idle. Any useful social theory must be predicated on the proposition that all men are limited in wisdom, and most men are *very* limited. Without unduly flattering those now in office, it is submitted that, taken on a broad average, American public officials represent a level of competence and honesty about as much above the common average as we can reasonably hope to maintain over any long period of time within the foreseeable future. It follows that if we are to make any important advance in the business of government we must find new methods and techniques of making and administering law. When our government officials have new tools with which to work we may expect them to achieve some real improvement in results; until then, the cry for better men will remain a pious, but ultimately futile, exhortation.

However, this conclusion is no extenuation of the backwardness of the bar. Lack of tools may be a good defense to a charge of incompetence, but not of indifference. There is a widespread dissatisfaction with our

---

[7] *Judge Frank does not make this conclusion explicit, but it seems to be the obvious inference. Jerome Frank, Law and the Modern Mind 253 et seq. (1930).*

system of laws, and even more, of lawyers. The shortcomings of the legal system can hardly be denied, nor the responsibility of the profession for them escaped. In the face of this, the proposals of the bar associations to raise large sums of money for a program of "public relations" are inane. Advertising is no substitute for research.[8] Whether the lawyers like it or not, knowledge will eventually encroach upon ignorance and research replace speculation as a basis for law. If the legal profession wants to retain its position as the nexus of the social system, it must develop techniques adapted to the modern problems of that system, and it must begin at once. If it does not do this, most surely it will be replaced in function by other more competent groups. In fact, the process has already begun. Those more competent to use the statistical tools of modern economics are beginning to take over the fields of taxation and rate-making; those more competent with the tools of psychology are threatening to take over the fields of delinquency and domestic relations. The large field of industrial risks and workmen's compensation is largely lost to the legal profession because of its refusal to abandon traditional common law ideas. Patent law has become a specialty requiring considerable engineering training in addition to the normal legal education, and therefore is closed to most lawyers. Numerous other divisions of law are beginning to develop in the same way. Neither private nor public wailing will halt this trend. Unless the lawyers acquire new skills they will become mere clerks and scriveners. In history's tomorrow, the possession of merely forensic skill will not even be considered a professional accomplishment. Advertising can no more maintain the prestige of antique abilities and outmoded learning than it can make a basic industry out of buggy-whip manufacturing in an automotive age.

The basic lesson which lawyers must learn, as the scientist William Vogt has recently pointed out, is that *we need to know what we are doing.*[9] There may have been a time when righteousness and good intentions were a sufficient guide to proper conduct. If so, that time is long since past. It requires not only good intentions but a great deal of knowledge for man to orient himself amid the complexities of the modern world. To gain knowledge requires constant inquiry. The price of prog-

---

[8] *Needless to say, the term "research" is here used in its scientific sense, and what is carelessly called "legal research" by the average lawyer has no more relation to it than numerology has to statistics.*

[9] *William Vogt, Road to Survival 141 (1948).*

ress is eternal change; the price of wisdom is eternal doubt. These may seem like high prices, but they are no greater than they have been in the past, and always before there have been those who were willing to pay the price for the privilege of contributing to mankind's knowledge and progress. If the legal profession is willing to abandon the comfortable closed room of jurisprudence and philosophical speculation for the rocky open road of jurimetrics and scientific investigation, then it will deserve and get the respect of all men. If not, then it will deserve, and ultimately get assignment to the same limbo that holds the alchemists and necromancers and other practitioners of man's forgotten superstitions.

More important than the status of any group, however, is the destiny of society. If jurimetrics were no more than a means of maintaining or restoring the position and prestige of the bar, then it would be of only professional interest and parochial importance. But it is much more than that. It is, in sum, the doctrine that the methods of scientific inquiry should be extended to every phase of human activity which is of concern to society. It is based upon the premise that democracy includes the right of citizens to be informed about those matters which they are ultimately supposed to control through their choice of officials, and upon the conclusion that reliable information has been and can be obtained only by free and competitive inquiry with the methods of science. As science itself has contributed to the growth of freedom, and, in turn, requires freedom in order to flourish, so will jurimetrics grow out of democracy yet strengthen and broaden democracy as it grows. Ignorance is the ally of tyranny, for despotisms great and small are authoritarian in that they coerce belief in order to compel obedience. Knowledge and free inquiry are the basis of democracy, since free men can be brought into agreement only by persuasion, and this depends upon demonstrations which satisfy the contemporary tests for truth. Ours is a rational age believing in pragmatic tests; it will not much longer be content to take speculative answers based on ancient authority to its most vital questions.

There will always be those who will scoff at the idea that law can be put on a rational basis as visionary. Let us admit that this proposal is improbable. The most that can be said is that it is just as improbable as the possibility that the weak and stupid creature we call man will survive much longer on an insignificant speck of dust whirling madly about in the finite but unbounded reaches of a vast and expanding universe. It is just exactly as improbable as that, for it is the indispensable condition of such survival.

# THE
# SOCIOLOGY
# OF LAW

*Philip Selznick*

The idea of dealing with legal concepts and doctrine from a sociological point of view has been vaguely familiar to at least two generations of sociologists and legal scholars. In this country, the premises of sociological jurisprudence achieved a rather quick and general victory, helped along by a pragmatic temper, an impatience with abstractions, and a setting of rapid social change. This victory, such as it is, has had but little to do with the actual researches of sociologists; nor does it reflect the particular concepts and funded knowledge of the field. It is a point of view, an approach, a sensitivity that has been accepted.

Of course, the autonomy of legal scholarship still finds considerable support. It could not be otherwise, given the technical character and intricate development of many legal notions, the peculiarities of legal history, the depth of professional pride, and the relative isolation of the law schools. But the overriding fact, it seems to me, is that legal science in America is open to new ideas and influences. Certainly the intellectual foundations for a sociological approach have been laid. There is no need today to argue the general interdependence of law and society or to insist that legal rules be tested by their practical effects. Little will be gained

Reprinted by permission of the author and of the publishers. "The Sociology of Law," by Philip Selznick, Chapter 4, pp. 115–127, of *Sociology Today,* edited by Robert K. Merton, Leonard Broom, and Leonard S Cottrell, Jr., Copyright © 1959 by Basic Books, Inc., Publishers, New York. Footnotes have been renumbered to run in sequence throughout the selection.

from further demonstrations that law serves social interests and that these interests, in turn, reflect the changing structure of society. It may even be that legal realism, legal positivism, and sociological jurisprudence have been accepted altogether too easily and that problems of great moment have received less than their due appreciation and concern. I shall return to that issue presently.

The sociology of law may be regarded as an attempt to marshal what we know about the natural elements of social life and to bring that knowledge to bear on a consciously sustained enterprise, governed by special objectives and ideals. Thus understood, legal sociology follows a pattern similar to that of industrial sociology, political sociology, and educational sociology. With some prophetic license, we can detect in all these efforts three basic stages of development.

The primitive, or missionary, stage is that of communicating a perspective, bringing to a hitherto isolated area an appreciation of basic and quite general sociological truths, such as the significance of group membership for individual behavior. This early phase characteristically includes much theoretical discussion and analysis of everyday experience. There may also be some organized research, but what there is is mostly demonstrative in function, more valuable for its educational effect than for anything else. In law, such demonstrative research has not been particularly important, in part because of the role played by fact-guided judicial decisions and by the writings of men with rich experience in legal affairs. Although most of the theoretical work in this field has been done by European social scientists, the task of communicating an elementary, not-very-sophisticated sociological perspective has been accomplished largely by American legal scholars who were influenced by European thought, and by some of the more articulate appellate judges.

The second stage belongs to the sociological craftsman. It is a muscle-flexing period marked by intellectual self-confidence, a zeal for detail, and an earnest desire to be of service. At this stage the sociologist seeks more than the communication of a general perspective. He wants to explore the area in depth, to help to solve its problems, and to bring to bear quite specific sociological techniques and ideas. There are a number of signs that the sociology of law is about to enter this stage of development.

The third stage, as I envision it, is one of true intellectual autonomy and maturity. This stage is entered when the sociologist goes beyond (without repudiating) the role of technician or engineer and addresses himself to the larger objectives and guiding principles of the particular human enterprise he has elected to study. He reasserts the moral impulse that marked the first stage of sociological interest and influence. But the third stage is of a higher, more sophisticated level than the first because the second stage has provided a sounder basis for critical analysis.

I shall limit myself here to a few remarks concerning the imminent second stage and an even briefer discussion of the ultimate third stage of development in legal sociology. Before going on to these matters, I should like to emphasize one general point. In a broad sense, there is no real problem of articulating sociological inquiry to the needs of legal development. *Sociology can contribute most to law by tending its own garden.* Truly sound knowledge regarding basic human relations and institutions will inevitably find its way into legal doctrine. Truths so well founded that no reasonable, educated man can deny them need no special means of communication beyond the ordinary channels of education. It is well to remember that, although the law is abstract, its decision-making institutions deal with a concrete and practical world. Recognition of basic truths about that world cannot be long denied. Moreover, the legal order is becoming increasingly broad in scope, touching more and more elements of society. This means that sociological research addressed to the important characteristics of society, and to the basic changes in it, will automatically have legal relevance. This relevance, of course, goes beyond bare description. It includes making the law sensitive to the values that are at stake as new circumstances alter our institutions.

If this be true, if sociologists have only to mind their own business, why a special concern for sociology of law? Perhaps the most obvious answer is that two-way communication can bring to legal analysis more rapid and direct benefits from sociological research. But as soon as this communication begins, we see that the real problem and the real opportunity stem from the incomplete and tentative character of our knowledge. There are very few incontrovertible sociological truths. Most of what we know is tentative, not only in the sense that all scientific conclusions are tentative, but also in the sense that our research in many vital areas is still primitive and pioneering. Yet legal scholars are interested in this work, and properly so, because the very least it does is to challenge older images of man and society and offer new guides for the assessment of experience. This kind of knowledge, however, cannot be absorbed directly; it must be tested within the specific areas of legal interest; it must withstand the common-sense critiques of the practical lawyer. Such communication cannot take place effectively unless sociological inquiry is made directly relevant to legal problems.

But the sociology of law has an additional, and more profound, rationale than the communication of specific sociological knowledge regarding nonlegal phenomena. The law is itself a social phenomenon, an important agency of social control. The study of the law for itself, as a part of the natural order, is very much the sociologist's business. From this standpoint the sociology of law can contribute both to the science of society itself and to the self-knowledge of legal practitioners. Since self-knowledge and moral development are so intimately related, it is plain that here lies sociology's most important special contribution. This is the distinctive office of the third, most advanced stage of legal sociology.

## STAGE II AND ITS PROBLEMS

In the second stage of development of legal sociology, as I have suggested, the main effort is to apply sociological analysis to particular problems of legal doctrine and legal institutions.

The present outcropping of interest in law on the part of sociologists has been stimulated by a number of related developments. Probably most important is the rising self-confidence among sociologists—confidence in the ability of the field to cast new light on particular areas and to help in the solution of practical problems. Another stimulus has been the development and refinement of research methods, involving not merely statistical sophistication but the identification of characteristic social factors of proven researchability. This means that at least one brand of empiricism has been available for active service, ready to form the basis of large and quickly organized research operations.

Interest in law has also been encouraged by new work in the sociology of administration. These studies have restated some older problems regarding the interplay of formal systems of social control and the spontaneous behavior of men and groups. Some of us who have worked in that field have discovered that in studying formal organizations we were also studying legal systems. It is clear that what we were learning about the functions of formal rules, the interdependence of authority and consent, and similar matters was not really new from the larger perspective of legal sociology. It is also painfully evident that some sociologists are prone to repeat mistakes of the past by overemphasizing the informal and spontaneous and deprecating the significance and the peculiar problems of a legal order.

Finally, recent years have seen a fresh approach to the relation between custom and law; today we regard the law as a more creative agency than earlier sociologists believed it to be. This new perspective has been largely stimulated and sustained by recent history in the field of race relations, especially by the Supreme Court's extension of the constitutional concept of equal protection of the laws.

These developments promise a new and fruitful period of research and analysis. But we should take a close look at the characteristic avenues by which sociologists will enter the field. Perhaps we should speak of these as temptations, the better to mark out the probable risks and pitfalls.

An obvious temptation (although also an opportunity) is to offer research technique as the peculiar contribution of the sociologist. By technique, of course, I mean the apparatus of survey and experimental research, not the more common-sense historical and reportorial data-gathering that has been the main standby of sociological classics. It seems obvious to me that quantitative research can and must play an important role in legal sociology. Any continuing program of study in that field could easily keep a staff of survey technicians busy on fruitful projects. The subjective meaning of specific rules, such as the lawyer-client privilege, for clients as well as members of the bar; the social composition of the bench and of juror panels; the self-images of lawyers, their career lines and other matters affecting professional integrity; the quasi-legal claims and expectations of various classes of citizens—these and a host of other specific studies depend for their execution on sophisticated survey technique.

But a serious risk is entailed and should not be overlooked. If we emphasize technique, we inevitably design projects that are congenial to the skills at hand. To be sure, such projects often have a market value in that they promise information that seems to be of immediate practical use to a client. Yet we know from experience that technique-stimulated research is seldom effectively guided by significant theoretical concerns or even by matters of the greatest long-run importance to the client himself. Attempts to apply small-group theory to the study of juries may seem an exception, but in fact they are not. The study of small groups, beyond certain first principles, is one of the more weakly developed areas in sociology; if this work is pushed to the forefront in legal sociology, it will be less for the sound knowledge it can offer than for the opportunity it presents to apply sophisticated research technique.

Another approach involves a similar risk, although it also begins from a posture of strength. Here one emphasizes the fund of sociological ideas, rather than the availability of research methods. The plan is to draw upon this sociological armory in order to illuminate particular problems in the legal field, whether of doctrine or of institutional functioning. This is the approach that Leonard Broom and I would take if we were to add a chapter on the sociology of law to the second part of our introductory textbook. The effect upon legal doctrines and institutions of a number of sociological phenomena, including socialization, value systems, stratification, collective behavior, and demographic trends, would be studied. But the main objective of this pedagogical device is to impress upon the student the force of sociological concepts and principles; it is not offered as a substitute for the autonomous, research-oriented organization of a field of inquiry. We cannot indiscriminately apply all our sociological ideas to legal studies; we must have a theoretical ground for supposing that some notions will be more important than others.

An indifferent appreciation of the entire sociological armory encourages intellectually low-level research, for two reasons. On the one hand, there is a natural tendency to choose those sociological concepts or factors that are easiest to handle; since it is all sociology anyway, if no theoretical ground exists for choosing the more difficult problems this solution will seem quite respectable. Yet the net result may be fact-gathering of a quite trivial nature. On the other hand, this same indifference may result in choosing problems of immediate interest to a client, whether or not the studies entail any advance in our general knowledge.

The alternative to these approaches is more painful. It involves a double intellectual commitment, to problems of greatest theoretical concern in sociology and to problems that are truly important to the legal order itself. In sociology, the roughly defined area we call "social organization" remains a challenging frontier. In this field we attempt to identify the essential characteristics of different types of society, to locate the key human relationships that give a social order its distinctive qualities, to discover how major groups interact and what stable arrangements result.

Most of the truly great names in sociology have been identified with broad studies of this sort. At the same time, these problems are the hardest to handle and are most frequently shunned.

From the legal side, the important problems also suggest an emphasis on studies of social organization. For example, what are the limits of law as an instrument of social control? What are the capabilities of courts, as we know them and as they could be? How much does society require of these agencies? How much can legitimately be demanded? Roscoe Pound stated this problem more than a generation ago, and offered some answers.[1] But research has been wanting. This is the kind of problem that can be approached in many ways, but it surely demands both a broad theoretical perspective and an emphasis on societal needs and institutional potentialities. Thus an assessment of demands upon the legal system depends on what is going on within major groups and in the relations among them. Whether modern economic institutions can autonomously safeguard their members against arbitary treatment and undue loss of liberty depends on the nature of participation and the dynamics of internal control. The sociological answer to this question inevitably affects the role of the courts. The potential achievements and vulnerabilities of both legal and nonlegal institutions are a proper and even urgent subject for sociological inquiry.

It is an interesting paradox that theories of social organization include both the best-founded and the most questionable of sociological writings. But this is not really strange. Obviously, any effort to delineate a broad pattern of social change runs the risk of speculative overgeneralization. On the other hand, if a broad theory becomes well established, this is because it finds confirmation on many levels and in a wide variety of contexts. Thus sociology has identified some of the main characteristics of modern industrial society, including the rise and dominance of bureaucratic forms of organization. The outlines of this theory have been well developed, and many specific inferences have been drawn and tested. I am sure that any effort to ground legal doctrine on social-science knowledge must look to these theories of the origins of our social order and the direction in which it is moving. Moreover, such developmental models are

---

[1] *Roscoe Pound, "The Limits of Effective Legal Action,"* Int. J. Ethics, 27 (1917), 150–67.

most likely to have something significant to say about the probable evolution of the law itself.

There is an unfortunate tendency to think of social-science knowledge as equivalent to the conclusions of specific pieces of research. I do not doubt that every generalization must be grounded in specific empirical studies, and there is always the possibility of a logically crucial experiment. But sound general knowledge is a complex result of many diverse pieces of work, analytical and empirical, each indirectly supporting the general theory. This means that we should avoid the temptation to present social-science knowledge as based on the specific results of a limited survey or experiment, for any one of the latter may be vulnerable while the basic generalization remains firm. The general agreement among social scientists regarding the damaging effects of segregation is actually based, not on specific studies of Negroes and whites, but on a theory of personality and on quite diverse, though logically related, empirical work. The very need to defend our own conclusions should recall us to basic theory.

In calling for an emphasis on broader theoretical problems, such as arise in the interpretation of trends in social organization and in the study of cultural systems, I do not mean to say that only the broad-gauged speculative and historical writings of the sociological classics is in order. On the contrary, it is characteristic of this middle stage of development that research must be sharply focused, exploring limited problems in depth. I wish only to emphasize that this work should take its departure from our funded knowledge and carry forward the theoretical concerns that have stimulated the most fruitful and lasting contributions.

\*    \*    \*    \*

## STAGE III AND ITS PROBLEMS

As we approach a more advanced stage of development, all the classic problems of legal philosophy emerge again. For at this point we should be ready to explore the meaning of legality itself, to assess its moral authority, and to clarify the role of social science in creating a society based on justice.

In a consideration of these matters, the central fact is the role of reason in the legal order. Legality as we know it is based on a combination of sovereign will and objective reason. The word *reason* has an old-fashioned ring to it, but its long life is not yet over. Reason is an authoritative ideal, and the bearers of reason have, inevitably, a creative legal role. We see this, not only in the idea and practice of grounded judicial decision-making, but in the vast body of critical literature produced by legal scholars. Whatever the lawyer's commitment to legal positivism, to the belief that law is what the legislatures and the courts enunciate and enforce, there is at least an implicit recognition that not all law is on the same level. Some law is inferior because it contains the wrong mixture of arbitrary sovereign will, including majority will, and right reason. This is especially true of judge-made law, but legislatures can also make inferior laws. An inferior legality is manifested in the disposition of judges to give a narrow construction to statutes that depart from common-law principles, and in the ease with which judicial conclusions are modified or reversed. An inherent legality is doubtless much influenced by the derivation of a rule—whether from immediate political pressures or from a larger evolution consonant with underlying principles of legal order. I think that the quality of legality, and gradations in it, will be a primary preoccupation of the sociology of law in the future, as it has been in the past. In this work, moreover, we shall have to study the relation between reason and social consensus, for we shall not be satisfied with the assumption that community sentiment, as it bears on law, is basically nonrational.

Because reason is legally authoritative, scholarship has a direct significance for law that it does not have for other fields. This is indicated by the special role of law-review articles and legal treatises cited as authority by the courts. This work usually involves a critical restatement of common-law doctrine, but it also can and does locate new rights. The restatement aspect does give this work a special status, but there is no fundamental difference between sociological learning made legally relevant and the kind of analytical writing found in the law reviews. In any case, like any other inquiry, legal reasoning cannot but accept the authority of scientifically validated conclusions regarding the nature of man and his institutions. Therefore, inevitably, sociology and every other social science have a part in the legal order.

The underlying role of reason explains why legal scholarship and the sociology of law are mainly preoccupied with common law, and therefore with judicial behavior, rather than with legislation. It is true that somewhat more emphasis in legal training is now placed on legislation, reflecting the great growth of the legislative process. It is also true that the interpretation of statutes plays a large role in the judicial process. But it is and will undoubtedly remain true that the main access to the law by legal analysts is through the judiciary. More important for legal sociology, legal doctrine is a vital part of common law but of much less importance in legislation.

A concern for the role of reason must bring with it a certain disaffection with what has come to be known as legal realism. The hard-headed effort to base our notion of law on actual behavior is certainly congenial to a sociological orientation. But human behavior is a very subtle mixture of self-restraint and impulse, idealism and self-interest, behavior guided by a long-range end-in-view and behavior compelled by day-to-day pressures. We cannot accept as more than a passing polemical formula the aphorism that the law is what the judges say it is. Taken literally, this settles nothing, for if a consistency is found in judicial behavior, searching out the underlying premises of a normative system and upholding the essential ingredients of legality, then all nonpositivist interpretations of law are still available and the problems they raise are with us still.

The ideal of reason presumes that there are principles of criticism of positive law. It also presumes, as Lon Fuller has pointed out,[2] that there are principles of criticism of "living" law. Little is gained in any ultimate sense by looking beyond positive law to actual normative behavior. We must go on to seek out the foundations in reason for choosing among human norms those that are to be given the sanction of law. This will bring us, I cannot doubt, to an acceptance of some version of a doctrine of natural law, although it may not, and perhaps should not, be called that, given its historical associations. A modern naturalist perspective may be preferable, despite the still-unsettled question of whether an objective basis of normative order can be discovered, and despite the large differences between positivism and pragmatism, affecting the ideal of reason in law, regarding the subjective component of valuation and the role of will in judgment. But whatever the philosophical auspices, the search for principles on criticism based on social naturalism must go on. Law based on reason and nature summons man to his potentialities but sees those

---

[2] *Lon L. Fuller, "American Legal Realism,"* Univ. of Pa. Law Rev., *82 (1934),* 453 ff.

potentialities as something that science can identify; law based on reason and nature locates the weaknesses of the human spirit, such as pride, apathy, and self-abasement, and works to offset them. The natural order, as it concerns man, is compact of potentiality and vulnerability, and it is our long-run task to see how these characteristics of man work themselves out in the structure and dynamics of social institutions.

# POLITICAL
# JURISPRUDENCE

*Martin Shapiro**

A school of jurisprudential thought rarely emerges full blown at a single instant or immediately announces itself as something new and different in the world of legal scholarship. Bentham's *Principles of Morals and Legislation,* one of the most startlingly original and seminal contributions to modern legal thought, might have been greeted by one of today's omniscient and pinch-minded reviewers, transplanted back to 1789, as "a rather interesting application of the thought of several minor continental writers to English conditions." While we can now trace a whole Kantian school of legal theory, it still remains questionable whether Kant himself had a theory of law.[1] Furthermore, the contemporary world does not often find itself blessed with such commanding figures as Bentham and Kant. New intellectual movements are more often the collective work of smaller minds and the products of synthesis, recombination and shifting application of existing ideas. I believe that such a new movement is afoot in legal theory, and I propose to call it political jurisprudence.

This new movement is essentially an extension of certain elements of sociological jurisprudence and judicial realism, combined with the substantive knowledge and methodology of political science. Its foundation is the sociological jurist's premise that law must be understood not as an independent organism but an integral part of the social system. Political

*. . . I wish to thank the office of the Dean of the Graduate School for a supplemental research grant made in connection with this article.

[1] See Brown, Has Kant a Philosophy of Law, 71 *Philosophical Rev.* 33 (1962).

Reprinted by permission of the author and of the publishers from 52 *Kentucky Law Journal* (1964), 294–343. Footnotes have been renumbered to run in sequence throughout the selection.

jurisprudence is in one sense an attempt to advance sociological jurisprudence by greater specialization. It seeks to overcome the rather nebulous and overgeneral propositions of the earlier movement by concentrating on the specifically political aspects of law's interaction with society and describing the concrete impact of legal arrangements on the distribution of power and rewards among the various elements in a given society.

From judicial realism, political jurisprudence derives a peculiar concern for the attitudes and behavior of judges and the environment of judicial decision. Indeed, many of the political jurists have devoted most of their efforts to devising a methodology that will allow them to refine and systematize the impressionistic insights of the realists by isolating and measuring the strength and direction of judicial attitudes and relating them to the actual patterns of decision.

Moreover, the new jurisprudence shares with all modern American thinking about law the premise that judges make rather than simply discover law.[2] Without this premise there could be no political jurisprudence, for one of the central concerns of politics is power and power implies choice. If the judge had no choice between alternatives, if he simply applied the rule supplied him by the tablets and reached the conclusion commanded by an inexorable legal logic, he would be of no more interest politically than the IBM machine that we could soon design to replace him. "Political" can only be linked with "jurisprudence" when it is realized that choice inheres in those phases of human endeavor that have traditionally been the object of jurisprudential study.

Finally, political jurisprudence is fundamentally indebted to political science, and its development is intimately related to the growth of political science as an independent discipline. Political jurisprudence is, among other things, an extension of the findings of other areas of political science into the realm of law and courts, an attempt to rationalize the presence of public law as a field of study within the discipline and an effort to round-out political science by somehow integrating legal and judicial facets into the total picture of political life.

Because political jurisprudence owes so many immediate intellectual debts and because it represents the extension and cross breeding of several lines of continuous intellectual endeavor, it is impossible to say exactly when the movement achieved a distinct identity or for that matter even to

---

[2] *See Cahill, Judicial Legislation* (1952).

argue that it is a movement totally distinct from other contemporaneous developments in law and the social sciences. Moreover, although the total number of political jurists is not very large and a certain amount of leader and discipleship is present, political jurisprudence has not produced any commanding intellectual figure or even set of figures nor an orthodoxy to which all the members can subscribe. Attempting to describe and delimit it is, therefore, something like trying to analyze a literary or artistic movement. We all generally know what and whom we are talking about if the theatre of the absurd or post-abstractionist painting is mentioned. Yet it might be extremely difficult to describe exactly what common characteristics held each of these schools together. Differences indeed direct conflicts, between various works of the same school would be mentioned, and interminable arguments would develop over whether certain marginal figures were to be included or not.

In the end, artistic movements tend to be defined in terms of tone, approach, concern for the same or similar problems, and a shared reaction to past movements rather than by a stylistic and substantive check list. More often than we are willing to admit, movements in the social sciences and philosophy must be described in the same way.[3] Political jurisprudence is such a movement, and basically I shall attempt to describe it here not by a general analysis of a purportedly complete philosophical system but by a survey of the work that has actually been undertaken, a survey that hopefully will suggest a general tone and approach as well as indicating some differences, conflicts and weaknesses.


## COURTS AS POLITICAL AGENCIES

The core of political jurisprudence is a vision of courts as political agencies and judges as political actors. Any given court is thus seen as a part of the institutional structure of American government[4] basically similar to such other agencies as the ICC, the House Rules Committee, the Bureau of the Budget, the city council of Omaha, the Forestry Service

---

[3] See e.g., Eulau, The Behavioral Persuasion in Politics (1963); Dahl, The Behavioral Approach, 55 Am. Pol. Sci. Rev. 763 (1961).

[4] I shall generally treat political jurisprudence as an American movement although it is not entirely confined to this country. See e.g., Torgersen, The Role of the Supreme Court in the Norwegian Political System, Judicial Decision Making (Schubert ed. 1963).

and the Strategic Air Command. Judges take their places with the commissioners, congressmen, bureaucrats, city councilmen, and technicians who make the political decisions of government. In short, the attempt is to intellectually integrate the judicial system into the matrix of government and politics in which it actually operates and to examine courts and judges as participants in the political process, rather than presenting law, with a capital L, as an independent area of substantive knowledge. Quite fundamentally, political jurisprudence subordinates the study of law, in the sense of a concrete and independent system of prescriptive statements, to the study of men, in this instance those men who fulfill their political functions by the creation, application and interpretation of law.

Political jurisprudence is, in a sense, the opposite of Coleridge's "willing suspension of disbelief" as a tool of understanding. The political jurist instead suspends his belief in the whole web and myth of specialty, mystery and tradition that surrounds and supports the judge. Adopting a wide-eyed, and some will grumble too open-mouthed, stance, he sees not the successor of Ulpian and Coke but only one of many government employees, operating in a bureaucratic structure, performing certain governmental services and generally engaging in the same political processes as his fellow public servants. The political jurist simply wishes to know what this fellow does in government, how he does it, why he does it and what his relations are with others in the same government structure and to the citizenry whom the government services. To be sure, in seeking to successfully answer these questions, he may have to reintroduce many of the concepts he has initially ignored if only in the form of objectively incorrect but politically relevant belief systems held by the actors he studies. Again the distinction is one of tone and approach. The political jurist begins with what any fool could plainly see if his eyes were not beclouded by centuries of legal learning, that judges and courts are an integral part of government and politics, would be meaningless and functionless outside of government and politics and are, therefore, first and foremost political actors and agencies. If all this seems obvious, it is amazing how frequently one must touch base with the obvious in order to avoid being caught off by the masses of writing about law and courts which are based on different and often unconsciously held premises.[5]

---

[5] *Kirchheimer, Political Justice (1961) for instance is in some ways a leading work in the new movement, and stresses the use of legal processes for political*

The new jurisprudence is in several ways a natural result of American experience. We are all told very early in life that the Constitution divides our national government into three great branches, and one of these is the Supreme Court. Thus the very Court that has always been preeminent in the American consciousness has always been considered preeminently an agency of government. Moreover, our mutually reenforcing preoccupations with the Supreme Court and the Constitution have made constitutional law a peculiarly important subdivision of American legal studies. And constitutional law is the most openly political of all the areas of law. The Supreme Court and its constitutional decisions have consistently played a significant and often highly controversial role in American political history. *Marbury v. Madison, Dred Scott,* the sick chicken, steel seizure and school desegregation cases are the very stuff of politics. While the notion of an independent judiciary may have been carried further in this country than anywhere else, the central place of the Supreme Court on the American political scene has kept us from equating independence with apoliticism or defining independence in terms of an isolated sphere of competence only peripherally related to public affairs. At least since 1937, it has become an American commonplace that the Supreme Court is either rightly or wrongly a political power holder.[6]

It is hardly surprising then that the Supreme Court has served as the focus for much of the new jurisprudence and indeed for much of the initial opposition to it. To begin with, the whole debate over judicial modesty versus judicial activism has been essentially an attempt to define the political role of the Court and its relations to other facets of American politics. The titles of some of the leading works, *Congress and the Court,*[7]

---

*purposes. Nevertheless, lurking behind nearly every paragraph is an unspoken distinction between political justice which is a perversion of the judicial process and a non-political justice which is normal, as if somewhere at least ideally there were non-political courts.*

[6] *See Mason, The Supreme Court: Vehicle of Revealed Truth or Power Group: 1930–1937 (1953); Mason, Myth and Reality in Supreme Court Decisions, 48 Va. L. Rev. 1385 (1962).*

[7] *Murphy, Congress and the Court (1962). At this point it might be well to explain that the footnotes in this article are dual purpose, designed both to support my statements and provide a basic bibliography of this new field. For this reason I have attempted generally to footnote a given contribution only once. Repetition of citation appears only when necessary for the support or proper illustration of my point. Many works that could and should be consulted in relation to several facets of political jurisprudence are, therefore, not noted in connection with each*

*The People and the Court*[8] and *The Least Dangerous Branch, The Supreme Court at the Bar of Politics*,[9] suggest the nature of the debate, not that all the participants share the viewpoints of political jurisprudence. The most extreme judicial self-deniers, Justice Frankfurter and Learned Hand,[10] seconded by academic commentators,[11] have argued that the Court should not, need not, and cannot engage in politics, that judicial review is essentially a political function, and that the Court should, therefore, cease exercising its power of review or exercise it only very rarely and under the most extreme provocation. Thus, the judicially modest are fundamentally apolitical in their jurisprudence, conceiving of courts as essentially non-political institutions and resenting Justice Marshall's ill-considered institutional foray into American politics. The almost poetic tragedy of the Frankfurter-Hand-Mendelson style of judicial modesty is that, having convinced everyone that judicial review was an essentially political not legal function, they have been unable to convince either a majority of the Justices or the predominant body of professional and academic opinion that the Court ought to give up review. Thus the Court continues to exercise and the legal profession to approve a function that, thanks to the work of the modest themselves, is admittedly political. In this way, the judicially modest have albeit unwillingly made a considerable contribution to political jurisprudence.

This old style of judicial modesty is generally on the wane today and has been replaced by a new style of modesty reflected in the works of such commentators as Robert McCloskey and Alexander Bickel.[12] In the context of our discussion here, it need only be said that the new school of modesty accepts the legitimacy of judicial review and thus of a political

---

*in order to avoid an excessively repetitive bibliography. It should also be added that not all the authors and works cited would identify themselves or wish to be identified with political jurisprudence. Many have been listed which only provide data or analysis useful to political jurisprudence.*

[8] *Black, The People and the Court* (1960).

[9] *Bickel, The Least Dangerous Branch, The Supreme Court at the Bar of Politics* (1962).

[10] *Hand, The Bill of Rights* (1958).

[11] *Wallace Mendelson has been the most prolific academic proponent of judicial modesty and has issued a very long succession of articles and reviews defending and rationalizing Justice Frankfurter's opinions. For a summary of his views see his* Justices Black and Frankfurter Conflict in the Court (1961).

[12] *See Shapiro,* Judicial Modesty: Down With the Old!—Up With the New?, 10 U.C.L.A. L. Rev. 533 (1963).

role for the Supreme Court and concerns itself with precisely what the Court can and cannot do considering its rather limited power. It is modest in the sense of urging the Court not to embark on tasks that are beyond its political capacity to complete or may react negatively on the Court's over-all political position. Thus today the debate over judicial modesty takes place almost entirely within the framework of political jurisprudence since nearly all the parties begin from the premise that the Court, at least in the sphere of judicial review, is a political agency and that the problem of when, where and how it should exercise its review powers is essentially a political problem.

However, the above statement is necessarily a qualified one. Not every participant in the current debate over the Court is per se an active subscriber to the tenets of political jurisprudence. Professor Black for the activists for instance tends to revert to the Hamiltonian and Marshallian argument that the Constitution is law and the Supreme Court is a court of law that must therefore enforce the Constitution when it is violated.[13] Such an argument is of course fundamentally apolitical, equating review with the "normal," "traditional" or routinely legal functions of courts. Judicial review becomes nothing more than a technical exercise in conflict of law jurisdiction. Professor Hyneman, in an attempt to synthesize the whole debate from the standpoint of political science, which is in effect a rather rambling defense of modesty, concludes that the Court is political in the sense of participating in government policy-making, but that a sharp contrast should be drawn between the political and the judicial process. On closer examination, however, this all boils down to the old saw that the Court is not democratic and, therefore, *ought not* to be political.[14]

Nevertheless, the debate over modesty is essentially a debate over the political role of the Court. Moreover, again thanks to the efforts of the modest themselves, particularly Frankfurter, the issue of modesty has become entangled in every substantive area of constitutional law so that constitutional scholarship as a whole has become essentially a political discipline. When every constitutional question must be considered not only on its merits, that is, in terms of traditional legal analysis of the meanings of constitutional provision, statute, precedent, etc., but in terms of whether the Court is the proper governmental agency to provide the

---

[13] *Black,* op. cit. supra *note 8, at 6–7.
[14] *Hyneman, The Court on Trial 237–47 (1963).*

answer, then all the constitutional business of the Supreme Court involves political considerations. While much constitutional commentary is still written in the traditional mode, there has been an increasing tendency to introduce political analysis directly into the discussion of constitutional questions. This tendency is particularly marked in the area of the first amendment.[15] The recent appearance of such titles as *Constitutional Law in the Political Process*,[16] *Constitutional Cases in American Government*,[17] *Constitutional Politics*[18] and *The Supreme Court, Its Politics, Personalities and Procedures*[19] is also indicative of the general tendency to integrate at least the constitutional business of the Supreme Court into the mainstream of thought about American national government.[20]

The principal opposition to political jurisprudence has also arisen in the area of the Supreme Court's constitutional business. The plea for neutral principles of constitutional law voiced by Professor Wechsler and his followers is in reality an attempt to substitute the traditional vision of an apolitical, non-policy-making, law-discovering court for that of a court embedded in the political process and making political decisions. The Supreme Court by process of legal reasoning and communion with the Constitution and the body of Anglo-American law is to divine guiding *legal* principles and, like all mystics, is to do so by divorcing itself from the interests and immediate problems of this everyday world.[21]

The concept of neutral principles has gained such great popularity precisely because it appeals to that still powerful segment of legal thought which resents the attempts of sociological jurisprudence and judicial realism to break law out of its independent sphere and place it in the

---

[15] *See Emerson*, Toward a General Theory of the First Amendment, 72 *Yale L.J.* 877 (1963); *Shapiro*, Judicial Modesty, Political Reality, and Preferred Position, 47 *Cornell L.Q.* 175 (1962).

[16] *Schmidhauser, Constitutional Law in the Political Process* (1963).

[17] *Berns, Constitutional Cases in American Government* (1963).

[18] *Schubert, Constitutional Politics* (1960).

[19] *Schmidhauser, The Supreme Court, Its Politics, Personalities and Procedures* (1960).

[20] *See also Beth, Politics, the Constitution and the Supreme Court* (1962). *Three of the chapters in this book are titled "The Courts as Political Agents." In terms of the sociology of knowledge of the new movement, it is interesting to note that these works are all texts that resulted from attempting to fit constitutional law into the mainstream of undergraduate instruction in political science.*

[21] *Not all of those who desire "principled" constitutional decision are antipolitical. See Bickel*, op. cit. supra *note 9, at 23–28, 49–65, 236–43.*

context of society.[22] The attempt to treat judges as essentially participants in politics, government and policy-making, ineluctably linked to other such participants, represents the extreme of integration of law into real life. The argument that there are neutral principles indwelling in the law itself and discoverable by a specifically judicial or lawyer-like mode of thought, is basically an attempt to return jurisprudence to the position of splendid isolation that it enjoyed in the heyday of analytical jurisprudence. This attempt has been largely inspired by and is a direct challenge to political jurisprudence.

Naturally enough then the rebuttal to the neutral principles concept has formed an important wing of the new jurisprudence by re-emphasizing the law and policy-making roles that are inevitably thrust on the Supreme Court. Since the Court generally deals with the "trouble case," it is typically called upon to decide precisely those questions for which neither the existing body of law nor the other agencies of government have been able to provide a solution. In short, it is asked to make social policy, and to do so it cannot depend on neutral principles but must look to its own assessment of the social and political interests involved and its own vision of the long-range goals of American society. In other words, it is asked to perform the same tasks that every other political decision maker is asked to perform and to do so as a complementary and supplementary segment of the whole complex of American political institutions. Thus runs the message of the anti-neutralists, a message that puts them squarely in the center of political jurisprudence.[23]

So far I have discussed only work that specifically revolves about the judicial review powers of the Supreme Court. If the political treatment of law and courts were confined to this area, it would constitute a special approach to an exceptional problem rather than a jurisprudence of relatively general applicability. But I have begun in this area largely because it serves as one of the channels through which political considerations historically flowed into the study of law not because it is the only or leading area of political jurisprudence. The principal focus of the new jurisprudence has instead been an attempt to integrate courts into the

---

[22] See Levy, Judicial Realism and Prospective Overruling, 109 U. Pa. L. Rev. 1 (1960).

[23] I have attempted to make these points at greather length and with appropriate citation in Shapiro, The Supreme Court and Constitutional Adjudication of Politics and Neutral Principles, 31 Geo. Wash. L. Rev. 587 (1963).

general framework of governmental institutions and the political process quite apart from a rationalization of the power of one court to do one thing, that is, declare statutes unconstitutional.[24] Undoubtedly the leading attempt in this area has been David Truman's *The Governmental Process*.[25] This book presents a general theory of politics built around the notion that political activity is fundamentally interest group activity and that the process of government proceeds through the access of groups to governmental agencies and agency performance in response to group demands. Courts are treated as governmental institutions to whom different groups have varying degrees of access which they employ to enlist the judges in support of their interests. For Truman, politics is group politics and courts are firmly embedded in the group struggle.

Probably because the first general theory of politics into which the courts were fully integrated was group theory, a considerable body of political jurisprudence using the group hypothesis has developed.[26] Particular attention has been paid to groups which have been especially successful in gaining access to the courts[27] and to their methods of access or lobbying.[28] Since the bar as a group has a peculiarly intimate relation to the courts, there has been an increased interest in its political role.[29]

---

[24] *See Jacob*, The Courts As Political Agencies, An Historical Analysis, 8 *Tulane Studies in Political Science 9 (1963)*.

[25] *Truman, The Governmental Process (1958)*.

[26] *See Peltason, Federal Courts in the Federal System (1955)*; *Shapiro*, supra note 15; *Mavrinac*, From Lochner to Brown v. Topeka: The Court and Conflicting Concepts of the Political Process, 52 *Am. Pol. Sci. Rev. 641 (1958)*; *Westin*, The Supreme Court and Group Conflict: Thoughts on Seeing Burke Put Through the Mill, 52 *Am. Pol. Sci. Rev. 665*; *Bachrach*, The Supreme Court, Civil Liberties, and the Balance of Interests Doctrine, 14 *Western Political Q. 391 (1961)*.

[27] *See Vose, Caucasians Only: The Supreme Court, The National Association for the Advancement of Colored People and The Restrictive Covenant Cases (1959)*; *Vose*, The National Consumers League and the Brandeis Brief, 1 *Midwestern J. of Political Science 267 (1957)*.

[28] *Vose*, Litigation As a Form of Pressure Group Activity, 319 *Annals 20 (1958)*; *Newland*, Legal Periodicals and the Supreme Court, 3 *Midwestern J. of Political Science 58 (1959)*; *Comment*, Outside Influences on the Supreme Court of the United States—How Effective Are These?, 39 *Can. B. Rev. 631 (1961)*; *Jacobs, Law Writers and the Courts (1954)*. *The Supreme Court has recently recognized that litigation is a form of political activity. N.A.A.C.P. v. Button, 83 S.Ct. 328, 336 (1963)*. *See also, Krislov*, Constituency v. Constitutionalism: The Desegregation Issue and Tensions and Aspirations of Southern Attorneys General, 3 *Midwestern J. of Political Science 75 (1959)*.

[29] *See Schmidhauser*, op. cit. supra *note 19, at pt. 2*; *Schubert*, Politics and the

However, other theories of politics may provide equally useful insights. For instance, in a critique of group theory, Elmer Schattschneider[30] has argued that politics is not entirely group struggle. When one group sees itself outfought in the initial group arena, it is likely to extend the boundaries of the battlefield by broadening the issues. In other words, whichever group finds itself outnumbered in the initial alignment of groups appeals for outside re-enforcements by recasting the issue in terms that will attract the attention of groups not at first concerned. This process is likely to snowball or escalate until issues have been so broadened that general public sentiment comes into play and the issue is finally settled not by the interplay of special groups but by mass popular opinion. In this context trial court litigation might be conceived as an initial or limited arena and the appellate process as a mode of extending boundaries, or even initial litigation as an attempt to expand an issue beyond the legislative or bureaucratic sphere.[31] For instance Negroes as a group, finding that the immediate alignment of groups in the South disfavored their goals, used Supreme Court litigation to broaden the issues and attention—drawing power of the controversy and eventually overcame their local group disadvantage by enlisting national popular support.

Not necessarily dependent on group or non-group theories of politics has been a general inclination on the part of political scientists to view government in the context of decision or policy-making processes rather than formal structures. The emphasis on process is in effect an emphasis on the interaction and reciprocal influence of governmental agencies in terms of where, when and how each actually participates in decisions. Jack Peltason's *Federal Courts in the Federal System*[32] and Victor Rosenblum's

---

Constitution: The Bricker Amendment During 1953, *16 J. of Politics 257 (1954)*; *Twiss, Lawyers and the Constitution (1942). Legal professional associations present a peculiarly fruitful field for further political (pressure group) analysis. There are, of course, a large number of these associations and subassociations. Many of them are highly specialized and therefore represent particular social and economic interests. Some engage in a considerable amount of statute drafting and direct lobbying of legislatures and nearly all make public or professional pronouncements on policy questions frequently disguised as technical-legal conclusions. All have relatively high direct access to the courts and other adjudicative agencies through the pleadings of their members.*

[30] Schattschneider, *The Semi-Sovereign People (1961)*.

[31] *Of course even the initial trial is a broadening of arenas by introducing the government into a dispute that initially concerned only the two parties.*

[32] Peltason, op. cit. supra *note 26*.

*Law As a Political Instrument*[33] were pioneering efforts to fit courts into this policy-making process framework by showing how they interact with other governmental agencies at all levels. A recent and outstanding text designed to introduce beginning law students to their field suggests its approach in its title, *The Legal Process, An Introduction to Decision-Making by Judicial, Legislative, Executive and Administrative Agencies*,[34] and sets both courts and law firmly within the sphere of public policy-making. Robert Dahl's article "Decision-Making in a Democracy: The Supreme Court as a National Policy-Maker" is an attempt to generally assess the relations of the Supreme Court to other members of "the dominant national alliance," and there have been several attempts to describe the Court's policy-making role and relation to other agencies in specific areas of its jurisdiction.[35]

The case study technique of examining court decisions popularized by Alan Westin[36] is also part of the movement toward examining what courts do in the total political setting of their decisions. It is, to be sure, a bit confusing to talk about case studies of cases. But the case study technique in the social sciences refers to a research design that focuses on a given decision, or set of related decisions, and then develops in the greatest possible detail all the institutional and individual attitudes and behavior that led up to and out of the decision. Such depth studies are designed to

---

[33] *Rosenblum, Law As a Political Instrument (1955). See also Miller*, Policy-Making in a Democracy: The Role of the United States Supreme Court, *6 J. Pub. L. 275 (1957); Schubert*, Policy Without Law: An Extension of the Certiorari Game, *14 Stan. L. Rev. 284 (1962); Sutherland*, Judicial Reticence and Public Policy, *1958 Judicial Rev. 1; Nagel*, Political Parties and Judicial Review in American History, *11 J. Pub. L. 328 (1962).

[34] *Auerbach, Garrison, Hurst, and Mermin, The Legal Process, An Introduction to Decision-Making by Judicial, Legislative, Executive and Administrative Agencies (1961).

[35] *Dahl's article appears in 6 J. Pub. L. 279 (1957). See also Shapiro*, The Warren Court and the Federal Tax Policy, *36 So. Cal. L. Rev. 208 (1962); Barker*, The Supreme Court As Policy Maker: The Tidelands Oil Controversy, *24 J. of Politics, 350 (1962); Ulmer*, Judicial Review As Political Behavior: A Temporary Check on Congress, *4 Ad. Science Q. 426 (1960).

[36] *See Westin, The Anatomy of a Constitutional Case (1958); Pritchett and Westin, The Third Branch of Government, Eight Cases in Constitutional Politics (1963); Westin, Bookies and "Bugs" in California: Judicial Control of Police Practices, The Uses of Power (1962). Another case in the latter work, Hacker*, Pressure Politics in Pennsylvania: The Truckers vs. The Railroads, *provides a peculiarly good illustration of the entanglement of the courts in policy-making and pressure group politics.

validate or suggest the broader hypotheses which it is the goal of the social sciences to formulate. When applied to law, this technique can be used to focus on a given court decision and develop the political matrix in which it occurs, showing that the decision is not an independent or isolated event but an integral part of a political process in which many agencies interact with one another.

While most of the efforts to fit courts into the general pattern of politics have so far occurred at the level of American national government, several recent studies have dealt with the political role of state and foreign courts.[37] Relations between the U.S. Supreme Court, the lower federal courts and the state courts, which have traditionally been handled in the conventional legal categories of jurisdiction, have also begun to receive some attention in more realistic political terms.[38] The most suggestive approach proposes a view of lower courts as essentially bureaucratic structures suggesting that the problems of the highest appellate courts may be basically similar to those of other political leaders vis-à-vis their bureaucratic subordinates.[39]

\* \* \* \*

## CRITICISMS AND PROPOSALS

There has already been and is yet likely to be a great deal of criticism of political jurisprudence. I shall attempt to sketch some of these criticisms and suggest replies. Because political jurisprudence is a relatively new movement, much of the criticism is directed to its incompleteness. Therefore, many of my replies will in fact be proposals for future research.

Probably the principal complaint about political jurisprudence is that it

---

[37] *Jacob and Vines*, The Role of the Judiciary in American State Politics, *Judicial Decision-Making (Schubert ed. 1963)*; *Vines*, Political Functions of a State Supreme Court, *8 Tulane Studies in Political Science 51 (1962)*; *Jacob*, Politics and Criminal Prosecution in New Orleans, Id. *at 77; Schubert, Quantitative Analysis of Judicial Behavior 129–142 (1959)*; *Ulmer*, The Political Party Variable in the Michigan Supreme Court, *11 J. Pub. L. 352 (1962). See also note 4* supra.

[38] *See* e.g., *Murphy and Pritchett, Courts, Judges and Politics 584–617 (1961)*.

[39] *Murphy*, Chief Justice Taft and the Lower Court Bureaucracy: A Study in Judicial Administration, *24 J. of Politics 453 (1962)*; Lower Court Checks on Supreme Court Power, *53 Am. Pol. Sci. Rev. 1017 (1959)*.

obscures the uniqueness of law and legal institutions. In constantly repeating that courts are political agencies and judges political actors, and dealing with courts and judges as an integral part of government, political jurisprudence does tend to emphasize the similarities between courts and judges and other political institutions and politicians. But if all this seems to add up to the statement that judges are just a bunch of politicians, then the mistake is in the eye of the beholder and in the unfavorable connotation frequently attached to the words politics and politician. The study of things political is, to be sure, partially aimed at exposing similarities between various political actors and institutions, but surely it is also aimed at discovering their differences. The State Department, the Cook County democratic machine, the Vatican, the ICC and the Supreme Court are all political agencies and share certain common features. But in saying this, I suppose no one believes that I am saying that the Secretary of State, Jake Arvey, the Pope, the chairman of the ICC and Chief Justice Warren are or should be exactly the same kind of men, thinking the same kind of thoughts and doing exactly the same kinds of things. If I say that Al Capone and F.D.R. were both politicians, I am not saying that the President was just a gangster.

It is true that initially political jurisprudence has probably overemphasized the commonality between courts and other agencies of government. But it is so difficult to eradicate the fundamentally apolitical outlook of both lawyers and laymen, who constantly and almost instinctively backslide into the clichés of the black-robed myth,[40] that it was inevitable and necessary that the point be made by overemphasis. Now that the essentially political role of courts is relatively firmly established, it should be possible for political jurisprudence to turn more of its attention to analyses of the differences in political role between courts and other agencies. The proliferation and complexity of modern government is largely based on the differentiation of function among agencies. If courts and judges were not performing a political function somewhat different from other political agencies and personnel and bringing relatively unique qualities into the political arena, they would not be nearly as politically successful as they are. Political jurisprudence in the future will seek to explore the special qualities of courts and in the light of those qualities determine

---

[40] *See* e.g., *Williamson,* Political Process or Judicial Process: The Bill of Rights and the Framers of the Constitution, *23 J. of Politics 199 (1961).*

what particular governmental chores suit the courts better than their fellow agencies.[41]

* * * *

Probably the most pressing of all the tasks of political jurisprudence is the development of a systematic description and analysis of the relation between lower and higher appellate courts in terms of power, influence and differentiation of function. Let me give just one example to suggest the range of problems. Certain federal circuits build up special expertise in certain fields of public policy, for instance the fifth circuit's oil and gas jurisdiction . . . . The admiralty jurisdiction of the second circuit also comes to mind. We know that in other parts of government specialization and expertise can be powerful forces fostering independent policy views and excessive resistance to supervision and coordination on the part of subordinate agencies. The same specialization often provides the political tools for fulfilling those policy views and making good the resistance. To what extent does specialization and the resultant expertise of certain circuit courts cause them to adopt different views than their more generalized counterparts and resist or seize policy leadership from the Supreme Court in those areas that especially interest them? To what extent have litigants who have a choice of circuits taken advantage of these phenomena to achieve the ends they desire? What methods, if any, have the highest appellate courts used to achieve supervision over and coordination of such specialized lower appellate courts?

In spite of the great prominence of appellate courts in the American judicial structure, generally speaking we as yet know very little about the fundamental problems of interagency relations and coordination posed by our appellate court structure. I have already said that the most promising approach seems to be that of Walter Murphy, who views the lower courts as a form of bureaucracy. However, up to this point little has been done to relate the tools that administrative, organizational and communications theorists have developed for the study of other hierarchically organized bureaucracies to the study of courts.[42] This kind of endeavor should become a core area of political jurisprudence in the future.

---

[41] *See Hyneman,* op. cit. supra *note 14; Bickel,* op. cit. supra *note 9; Shapiro,* op. cit. supra *note 35, at 225–227.*

[42] *The literature of administration and bureaucracy is very large. Pfiffner and Presthus, Public Administration (1960); Pfiffner and Sherwood, Administrative*

Finally political jurisprudence in spite of its close relation to judicial realism has done very little with trial courts, largely, I think, because their role in the policy-making process is least evident and they are most difficult to study. However, in recent years political scientists have considerably developed the technique of direct observation and interrogation of local units of government.[43] We should now begin to send scholars into our local courts to systematically observe their behavior over fairly long periods of time, interview litigants, counsel and subordinate court officers and where possible interrogate the trial judges themselves. We could then begin to build up the body of empirical data necessary to proceed beyond the very vivid but quite haphazard and impressionistic studies of Judge Frank.[44]

*       *       *       *

## THE PERENNIAL QUESTION—IS AND OUGHT

Critical students of jurisprudence who have bothered to follow me this far are likely by now to have two dread words, naive and positivism, ready at hand. It must be confessed that either out of naiveté, or because many of its participants see themselves primarily as political scientists not students of law, political jurisprudence so far has failed to provide itself a theoretical rationale that grapples with the problems of twentieth century legal philosophy. This is a serious flaw in a movement that is so heavily

---

Organization (1961); Blau and Scott, Formal Organization: A Comparative Approach (1962), are recent survey works that note most of the important contributions. Such journals as the Public Administration Review and The Administrative Science Quarterly serve as central clearing houses for new ideas in this area. Some spade work on the relations between various levels and groups of courts has been done. See Snyder, Uncertainty and the Supreme Court's Decisions, 65 American J. Sociology 241 (1959); Nagel, Sociometric Relations Among American Courts, 43 Southwestern Social Science 136 (1962).

[43] See Dahl, Who Governs (1961); Wolfinger, The Politics of Progress (in press).

[44] Frank, Courts on Trial (1949). See Somit, Tanenhaus, Wilke, Aspects of Judicial Sentencing Behavior, 21 U. Pitt. L. Rev. 613 (1960). Curiously enough, recent study has concentrated on juries. See Broeder, The University of Chicago Jury Project, 38 Neb. L.R. 744 (1959); Bevan, Jury Behavior as a Function of the Prestige of the Foreman and the Nature of His Leadership, 7 J. Pub. L. 419 (1958).

dependent on sociological jurisprudence and legal realism both because there have been serious theoretical differences between the two and because each has been challenged by a revived idealism. However, I do not think this flaw is a fatal one because neither the conflict between sociological jurisprudence and realism nor the debate between positivism and idealism has yet been resolved. For the moment at least political jurisprudence can attach itself to the realist and positivist causes and refer its attackers to a set of arguments hallowed by extended if not particularly fruitful development.[45] Nevertheless the strength of the revival of various forms of natural law jurisprudence requires some comment on the particular relation of political jurisprudence to the normative or valuational aspects of legal philosophy.

Political jurisprudence is basically positivistic in the sense of seeking to describe the political-legal process as it is rather than prescribing how it ought to be. But if political jurisprudence is positivism, it is a peculiarly value-laden kind of positivism. The whole attitudinal wing is, of course, attempting to discover what values the participants in law-making hold and how these values affect their law-making activity. The essentially political inquiry into what governmental tasks the courts do efficiently and what services they fail to perform satisfactorily includes a determination of how well the courts function as creators and appliers of moral standards.[46] The general emphasis of political jurisprudence on judge as policy-maker inevitably has made the demand that judges articulate their values and social goals as an integral part of political jurisprudence.[47] For

---

[45] *The positivism v. idealism rubric is, of course, rather bad shorthand since it uses the labels that each side pins on its opponents.* Yntema, American Legal Realism in Retrospect, *14 Vand. L. Rev. 317 (1960), provides a concise outline of the former debate, and Weissman,* An Antitrust Law, Too, Must Be Just, *1962 Wis. L. Rev. 403, of the latter. The parallel debate in political science can be followed in* Book Review Essay, *57 Am. Pol. Sci. Rev. 125 (1963). The close relation between realism and political jurisprudence can be seen in* Llewellyn, Law and the Social Sciences—Especially Sociology, *62 Harv. L. Rev. 1286 (1949). Llewellyn's partial withdrawal from realism in* Deciding Appeals, the Common Law Tradition (1962), *has been attacked from the standpoint of political jurisprudence. See Clark and Trubek,* The Creative Role of the Judge; Restraint and Freedom in the Common Law Tradition, *71 Yale L.J. 255 (1961).*

[46] *See Shapiro,* Morals and the Courts: The Reluctant Crusaders, *45 Minn. L. Rev. 897 (1961).*

[47] *See Miller and Howell,* The Myth of Neutrality in Constitutional Adjudication, *27 U. Chi L. Rev. 661 (1960); Miller,* A Note on Supreme Court Decisions, *10 J. Pub. L. 139 (1961). Professors Lasswell and McDougal have long called for*

policy-making is by its very nature purposive activity implying a choice between alternative means and ends based on some notion of the goods. The judge as policy-maker must, therefore, make moral choices.

I am well aware that many scholars view the reduction of values to psychological data, which then become part of the "is," as the final positivistic rape of moral philosophy. Similarly the emphasis on purposive elements in law-making may be viewed as a false reduction of law to will and appetite, ignoring elements of reason and justice. Finally a jurisprudence which claims that the ought is an essential part of law, while at the same time devoting itself entirely to the is, may well be accused of either insincerity or misdirection. In the face of these arguments, it is not entirely satisfactory to say that political jurisprudence, by emphasizing the political and, therefore, valuation or purposive nature of law, provides a gateway for the passage from empirical to normative study. A gateway is not enough. Someone must go through it and tell us what is beyond.

But if political jurisprudence in the end shows itself incomplete, it at least points to the reasons for its own incompleteness and, indeed, for the unresolved quality of all modern jurisprudence. Since law and law-making are an integral part of politics, legal philosophy is an integral part of political philosophy. The problem of those who wish to create a value-oriented rather than descriptive jurisprudence is that, apart from the Neo-Scholastics, they have been unable to formulate a coherent and generally acceptable statement of the values around which a new jurisprudence could be built. Indeed since the admittedly subphilosophical jural postulates of Roscoe Pound, nearly all the talk has been of the need for and means of finding moral principles rather than the substance of those principles.[48] The reason for this failure is quite obviously the failure of post-Marxian political philosophy to provide any acceptable "truths" about the nature and ends of government,[49] and more particularly the failure of liberal-democratic philosophy, busy defending its threatened procedural axioms, to come to grips with the substantive issues that lie behind the

---

the systematic enunciation of values in law. For the close connection between their call for valuation and a view of courts as political agencies see Lasswell, The Interplay of Economic, Political and Social Criteria in Legal Policy, 14 Vand. L. Rev. 451 (1961).

[48] See e.g., Northrop, The Complexities of Legal and Ethical Experience (1959).
[49] See Shklar, After Utopia (1957).

phrase "public interest."[50] The Neo-Scholastics in fact can appear so self-satisfied and complete only because they deal with law with a capital (or natural) L, or point out the contradictions of other political philosophers, rather than attempting the real and much more difficult task of integrating scholastic theories of law into modern Catholic political philosophy, a philosophy that has yet to prove itself congruent with modern industrial society.

Until political philosophy revives sufficiently to provide us with a set of ultimate truths or a reasonable facsimile thereof, jurisprudence is likely to concern itself with more immediate questions. There is a whole range of intermediate ought problems that we must solve now even though our ultimates are shaky. Ought property owners be forced to sell to Negroes? Ought competitive sectors of the economy be allowed to become oligopolistic? Ought the jurisdiction of juvenile courts be extended? If political jurisprudence provides us with some information on the functions of law-makers in our society, and in the process prods those law-makers into conscious political evaluation of their own governmental roles and the role of government in general, it will have contributed as much and perhaps more to the valuational aspects of jurisprudence as its contemporaries.

---

[50]*See Schubert, The Public Interest (Friedrich ed. 1962).*

# THE
# ANTHROPOLOGICAL
# STUDY OF LAW[1]

*Laura Nader*

## INTRODUCTION

It is my belief that we are just now on the growing edge of an anthropological understanding of law in its various manifestations. Despite the fact that many of our pioneering ancestors were lawyers by training (Morgan, Maine, Bachofen, McLennen, and more lately Redfield), interest in the anthropology of law has, until recently, had a gradual growth. Between the classic monographs of the nineteenth century (Maine 1861, 1871; and Fustel de Coulanges 1864) and the next milestones in the anthropological study of law (Barton 1919; Gutmann 1926; Malinowski 1926; Hogbin 1934; Schapera 1938) several decades

[1] *In conceiving the original outline of this paper I have profited immensely from the papers and discussions at the Winner-Gren Conference on law, April 1964. I am especially indebted to Paul Bohannan, Herma Kay, and Julius Stone for many stimulating interchanges at the Center for Advanced Study in the Behavioral Sciences. For their critical comments and readings of earlier drafts I wish to thank Eugene Hammel, Mel Perlman, Penny Addiss, Carl McCarthy, John Rothenberger, and most of all Norman Milleron. Penny Addiss served as research assistant during the writing of this paper. Anne Brower kindly edited several drafts. My colleagues at Berkeley, especially Elizabeth Colson and C. Lancaster were helpful in directing me to African and Indian materials. The responsibility for the paper in its present form, alas, is solely mine.*

Reprinted by permission of the author and of the publishers from 67 *American Anthropologist* (1965), 3–32. Footnotes have been renumbered to run in sequence throughout the selection.

220

elapsed during which the majority of works on law in preliterate societies were written by colonial administrators, missionaries, and the like rather than by anthropoligists (see Nader, Koch, and Cox 1964). Studies of primitive law developed from collections of normative rules ('laws') to observations on the actual application of such rules; in the 1940's, Richardson (1940), Hoebel (1940), and Lewellyn and Hoebel (1941) (whose work provides the only examples of substantial results from joint research by a law professor and an anthropologist to date) began to publish on the 'trouble case.' Since 1954 a series of monographs have been published (Howell 1954, Smith and Roberts 1954, Hoebel 1954, Gluckman 1955a, Bohannan 1957, Pospisil 1958a, Berndt 1962, Gulliver 1963). It was this intellectual productivity which lead Bohannan to say: "The literature in legal anthropology is small and almost all good—neither claim can be made for very many other branches of the subject" (1964:199).

\* \* \* \*

## PRESENT TRENDS AND NEW DIRECTIONS

During the past two decades the major contributions to the ethnography of law have been descriptive, functional analyses of systems both isolated and in contact situations. The tendency has been to treat the legal system as an institution virtually independent and isolated from other institutions in society, except insofar as 'society' is gleaned from the law materials. This last tendency is especially evident where courts are present, less so where the lack of court institutions virtually forces the anthropologist to elicit the whole life history of the case. Furthermore, we have not been interested in historical developments although the history of our civilization is rich in data (cf. Rheinstein 1963 and H. Kay in this volume [of *American Anthropologist*]). Nor have we pursued to any great extent the examination of hypotheses—either in the manner which Evans-Pritchard (1963) refers to as illustrative (the citing of examples in support of a thesis arrived at deductively), or by cross-cultural statistical studies, or by means of intensive controlled comparison. Our work for the most part has not been comparative.

If we are to develop a true ethnography of law the angle of vision of the ethnographer needs to be broadened in order to include descriptions that would explicate law as part of a many-threaded fabric. Furthermore we should look at both the latent and the manifest functions of the law. We need to understand what the generally agreed upon functions of the law are, as well as to note its other functions which may or may not be recognized in a society. Malinowski observed years ago, "An ethnographer who sets out to study only religion, or only technology, or only social organizations cuts out an artificial field for inquiry, and he will be seriously handicapped in his work" (1922:11). A legal system reflects many facets of a society; because of this an ethnographic study of law is more than a study of judicial institutions. Law and politics are sometimes discussed together in anthropology—what about other aspects of social life that may be relevant to the "law," such as economics, language, ecology, or stratification and rank systems?

As a working frame I would like to reiterate what others have said before—namely that (1) empirical studies of law should be set in the general context of social control (although of course not equated with social control); (2) we should consider the possibility that the range of functions of a legal system may vary cross-culturally; and (3) we should aim at both empirical and explanatory generalizations.

It has often been stated that legal systems constitute only a part of a larger system of social control, and that sometimes the social control functions of law can be understood only when viewed as part of the larger system. Schneider (1957) provides us with one example of the way in which the legal and supernatural systems complement each other in the differential handling of fratricide and patricide on Yap. Nader and Metzger (1963) describe the procedures for handling husband-wife conflict in the court and family systems of two Mexican villages where an important variable is the amount of authority allocated to the court and kinship groups. However, in most of the recent monographs, Gulliver (1963) being a major exception, the law has been treated as isolated from other social control systems, and indeed in some monographs it has been left for the reader to place the law in its socio-cultural context. This is a criticism that Malinowski (1942:1253) leveled at Llewellyn and Hoebel as authors of *The Cheyenne Way*. It is also a criticism that can legitimately be made of most of the law monographs produced since *The Cheyenne Way*.

Furthermore it is not always clear whether the social control functions of law are to "clean up social messes" (Llewellyn and Hoebel 1941), or to maintain order (Malinowski 1942), although how the law handles the breach is usually clearer than how in fact it serves to maintain order. Law may settle conflicts by a variety of means (adjudication, mediation, arbitration, etc.); it may perform solely a punitive function; it may prevent or deter breaches of the law; it may maintain order in the fields of law, politics, and economics—or it may accomplish *all* these tasks. It is not always clear which of these functions the law in a particular society is intent upon performing. Our elaboration of these tasks is not always as precise as we would wish if we are to use ethnographic data for comparative ends, or even if we are to explore the relations between means and ends. In this context I would like to call attention to Aubert's example (1963:19) of the function of legislative formulations. In his discussion of the Norwegian housemaid law he noted that "the language of the law is shaped more profoundly by the function of solving conflicts than by the function of influencing the legally naive"; that is, it was directed at the legal professional rather than at informing the lay citizen of what the law was.

While we have assumed that there was a probable cross-cultural difference in the content and form of a legal system, we have at the same time ignored the variety of different functions a legal system may have. This is in spite of the fact that Riesman (1954:445) credits anthropologists with thinking otherwise:

The anthropologist is not likely to harbor the naive assumption that the law, or any other institution, serves only a single function—say, that of social control—and that any other functions which in fact it serves are excrescences or "contradictions." The concept of ambivalence is part of his equipment; he tends to search for latent functions, transcending the ostensible.

The truth of the matter is, however, that (anecdotal exceptions to one side) the functions of law have generally been assumed to be universally the same,[2] and this is as true of anthropologists as of other social scientists. Aubert (1963:17) states the essence of these functions: "Law seems to have two distinct although interrelated functions: to create conformity with norms, and to settle conflicts."

The oral tradition of the practicing American bar is full of examples which lead us to believe that the law performs many other functions.

---

[2] *Anthropologists have more commonly analyzed other institutions as having legal functions rather than legal institutions as having other than legal functions. See Kaberry 1941 and 1942 for example.*

Every lawyer and perhaps most citizens could cite examples: A business-man may bring a competitor to court with the express purpose of ruining his credit rating. During political campaigns opposing candidates have accused one another of innumerable legal wrongs, usually ending with the filing of a lawsuit for libel, with the object of winning elections. Wives may demand or even initiate divorce actions with little intention of actually obtaining a divorce but rather to frighten the husbands into behavior more acceptable to them. Or an ex-husband may request a change of child custody to harass an ex-wife. Similarly arbitrary enforce-ment of vagrancy laws or Sunday "blue laws" provides an avenue by which "the law" may harass a less than ideal citizen. Selective application of obscenity laws may perform the function of witchcraft hunts in other societies.

Riesman (1954:448–449) brings two interesting novels to our atten-tion: James West's *Plainville U.S.A.* and James Gould Cozzens' *The Just and the Unjust*. These novels provide examples of the trial as both a cohesive and divisive force in small towns, as in West's case of the garagekeeper and the undertaker—a trial that caused a factional split in town. Or, Riesman states, the trial may serve as a divisive point "in terms of a moral turning point, such as . . . the Western world experienced in the trial of Sacco and Vanzetti." A familiar example of the political function of judgeships is also quoted by Riesman (1954:442): "In the big cities . . . judgeships become part of the system of ethnic brokerage by which the party machines keep the urban peace—the rise of the Italian judge is a recent illustration." Riesman also comments on the entertain-ment value of the law as well as its socialization functions.

Thurmond Arnold (1935) adumbrates some of the latent functions of the law. He comments on the drama of the court as partly a socialization or enculturation agency—a place where values are tested, changed, or consoli-dated, and further notes that these may be "legal" values or other such as religious values (Cf. Hoebel's paper in this volume [of *American Anthro-pologist*] as an example.) His observations on the ritual value of the trial should be of interest to anthropologists.

Ethnographic examples from other societies are not easy to locate in the literature athough they are probably well known to most fieldworkers. In this volume [of *American Anthropologist*] Cohn states:

The use of the courts for settlement of local disputes seems in most villages to be almost a minor one. In Senapur, courts were, and are, used as an arena in the competition for social status, political and economic dominance in the village. Cases are brought to court to harass one's opponents, as a punishment, as a form of land speculation and profit making, to satisfy insulted pride, and to maintain local political dominance over one's followers. The litigants do not expect a settlement that will end the dispute to eventuate from recourse to the state courts.

And as Cohn notes these were 'functions' of the court that the British failed to understand; the British system was in many ways at odds with traditional Indian procedures.

Beals (1955:91) reports: "After 1920, a number of individuals in Namhali used the [urban] law courts to acquire land or to bring about the economic ruin of their enemies." The law may function to bring about a more equitable distribution of resources or alternatively it may function to maintain an unequal distribution of power. Berreman (1963:270) gives an example of a typically false legal charge.

A villager's prosperity was envied by his caste-fellows. They had once tried unsuccessfully to get some of his land by bribing the government records officer to testify that he had acquired the land illegally. Failing in this, they obtained revenge by hiding liquor in his house and calling the police to say that he was dealing in illicit liquor.

Along these same lines Bailey (1958:106) mentions various measures taken by the village (i.e. the high castes) to insure that the village servants (i.e. the low castes) do not become too rich:

This particularly applies to the washerman since his eldest son has been working. He has been fined 2 or 3 times for letting his buffaloes stray into other men's gardens, and the fine has been demanded in cash while other offenders are penalized only by admonition or a demand for a small amount of paddy in compensation.

When a village servant shows signs of getting a lot of money, the village seems to resent this and penalizes him. In the dispute that follows, the victory goes always to the village, since the specialist castes are not organized to protect their members against these attacks.

Different sorts of models are brought to our attention by others. In discussing the therapeutic function of Kpelle moots, Gibbs (1963:6) notes: "Moot procedures are therapeutic in that, like psychotherapy, they re-educate the parties through a type of social learning brought about in a specifically structured interpersonal setting." Gluckman (1955a) illustrates the potential socializing effects of the judicial process. Armstrong (1954) considers the case of a Nigerian inquest into the death of a prominent politician. The inquest is shown to serve various functions in Senne Province: it enforces respect for the elders forming the council of the conclave, allows leaders to enhance their social position, serves to place the blame for the death, repair relationships among the living, excite public spectacle, and so on.

Nader (n.d.) illustrates the use of Zapotec courts to increase the revenue of the town treasury.

The court sees itself as an institution which protects community interests at all times and places. Therefore they reason, the court may readily look for redress in situations where a party has not complained. . . . There are also practical considerations which have modeled this court initiative, for in Talea laws governing personal behavior are being redefined with economic gain in mind. During one of my field stays when the Talean treasury needed replenishing for the big fiesta of the year, the president ruled that any individual *echando un grito* would be fined five pesos for each grito. Earlier in this century when the new municipio was still being built the presidente would send a *regidor* out on market day with money especially destined to get visiting Rinconeros drunk. The court would then jail them for drunkenness and the following day would fine them a day or two labor on the municipal building. Although Talean citizens easily discuss the economic motives of the court, the court officials insist that new laws are being created to impress the neighboring towns, as well as the citizens of Talea, with peace and orderliness.

That law courts should be used for purposes other than the maintenance of peace and order is not unique with the Talean Zapotec. Throughout the development of the British common law, the King's court was well known for defining property laws with economic gain in mind.

Colson's materials however, illustrate another way in which the law may be used for economic gain:

They [court councillors] claim that if a man brings his wife to court a third time on an adultery charge they will refuse to grant damages and will instead inform the husband that his only recourse is to divorce his wife and get back his bridewealth, that the woman is now making a business of adultery and is a professional woman of the road [1958:170].

Fathers refuse to listen to a suitor until after an elopement, for they realize that they can then collect both elopement damages and bridewealth. They also disregard the legal limitations on elopement damages, and their demands for damages have steadily increased. The lover, if he wishes, can take the matter to court and refuse to pay more than the legal amount. If he does this, the girl's father will refuse to listen to his suit. He will then have to elope with another girl, and again pay elopement damages before he can hope to pay bridewealth and receive his bride [1960:112].

In terms of conflict theory the function of the breach varies. Disputes may serve to solidify groups or individuals in a society (Beidelman 1959:66, Nader 1965b); they may prevent the formation of political factions (Glasse 1959), or serve to intensify disharmony and cause the development of new factions (Lewis 1958:148, Beidelman 1959:66).

And finally Frake (1963:221) reports on a Philippine group:

Litigation in Lipay, however, cannot be fully understood if we regard it only as a means of maintaining social control. A large share, if not the majority, of legal cases deal with offenses so minor that only the fertile imagination of a Subanum legal authority can magnify them into a serious threat to some person or to society in general. . . . A festivity without litigation is almost as unthinkable as one without drink. If no subject for prosecution immediately presents itself, sooner or later, as the brew relaxes the tongues and actions, someone will make a slip.

In some respects a Lipay trial is more comparable to an American poker game than to our legal proceedings. It is a contest of skill, in this case of verbal skill, accompanied by social merry-making, in which the loser pays a forfeit. He pays for much the same reason we pay a poker debt: so he can play the game again. Even if he does not have the legal authority's ability to deal a verbalized "hand," he can participate as a defendant, plaintiff, kibitzer, singer, and drinker. No one is left out of the range of activities associated with litigation.

Litigation nevertheless has far greater significance in Lipay than this poker-game analogy implies. For it is more than recreation. Litigation, together with the rights and duties it generates, so pervades Lipay life that one could not consistently refuse to pay fines and remain a functioning member of society. Along with drinking, feasting, and ceremonializing, litigation provides patterned means of interaction linking the independent nuclear families of Lipay into a social unit, even though there are no formal group ties of comparable extent. The importance of litigation as a social activity makes understandable its prevalence among the peaceful and, by our standards, "law-abiding" residents of Lipay.

More examples can be found. However, for the most part the inclusion of such extralegal functions in the anthropological literature has been anecdotal. The previous series of examples are not meant to illustrate *the law;* rather they are examples of what should be included in any truly *ethnographic* study of the law.

And finally a word about comparison and generalization. One function of comparative study is to identify uniformities and differences and to explain them. Although it is true that we have a healthy handful of excellent monographs on certain aspects of law, are they indeed comparable? In some respects they are. For example, the mechanisms for dispute settlement (the procedural aspects of law ways) could profitably be compared to isolate answers to questions such as those proposed by Kluckhohn (1960:136): first, "What is apparently incompatible with what else?" Endogamous dual organization villages are found to be incompatible with the development of a court system of judge-made decisions (Nader 1965a); second, "What is extremely likely to be found with what else?" The use of a go-between as an important mechanism of nonfamily dispute settlement will be characteristic of societies which are politically decentralized and bilateral in kin form; finally, "Are some concatenations of cultural features or elements indifferent as far as minimal necessary coherence of the system is concerned and hence found associated or not associated merely as a result of the accidents of the historical process?" Here, we may note that crime rates may or may not be related to any procedural characteristic of law, and some evidence for this is presented by Beatrice Whiting in this volume [of *American Anthropologist*]. Whiting compares the frequencies of assault and homicide in six societies and considers the differences in the light of the concept of "protest masculinity" and the status envy hypothesis of identification.

But there are problems inherent in comparison, even leaving to one side the difficulties of comparing total legal systems, which we believe to be a task not likely to yield much fruit. A major problem, common to all cross-cultural comparative studies, relates to the formulation of concepts or categories which will permit cross-cultural analysis without distortion of the "folk-system" of a particular society. Or phrased in another way, how do we reconcile "the new ethnography" and the importance of generalization in anthropology. Bohannan (1957) is correct in viewing the description of the folk and the analysis of the system as two separate tasks, but his threefold social action model (action, counteraction, correction) is much too general for comparative usefulness. So is Gluckman's (1955a) conceptual model used to describe the judicial process of the Barotse. Yet a comparison of the formal institutions used for settling disputes raises certain problems inherent in Hoebel's volume *The Law of Primitive Man* (1954), that is, the problems of comparing a court system, with a go-between system, with an Eskimo song duel, or even the problems in comparing a grade D court among the Tiv with the *presidente's* and/or the *alcalde's* courts among the Zapotec. We get into further complications by comparing the functions of these formal systems. These problems are similar to those faced in kinship research. For example, we compare a kinship system based on lineage and clan principles with one based on the nuclear family. In kinship we never 'solved' the problem of comparable units and yet comparison was not ignored. Rather we started with certain assumptions about the regularity of kinship forms and with certain questions the answers to which were sought through comparison: Why is it that "marriage" is more brittle in some societies than in others? What aspects of social organization are intimately connected to the marriage pattern? The comparative papers in this volume [of *American Anthropologist*] on law ask such questions. Whiting asks: Why is there more physical aggression resulting in legal wrongs in some societies than in others? Roberts queries: Why do only some societies have oaths and ordeals? Cohn pursues yet another question: What relation is there between coalition formation in villages and frequency of dispute? But if we are going to ask and answer such questions we need good descriptive data, which leads us back to questions of description.

If field studies of law are to result in comparable data what essential materials should be covered by the ethnographer?[3] First, several assumptions should be made clear: 1) there is a limited range of dispute for any particular society; that is, all societies do not fight about all the possible things human beings could fight about; 2) a limited number of formal procedures are used by human societies in the prevention of and/or settlement of grievances (e.g. courts, contests, ordeals, go-betweens, etc.); 3) there will be a choice in the number and modes of settlement (e.g. arbitration, mediation, compromise, adjudication, and so on). How people resolve conflicting interests and how they remedy strife situations is a problem with which all societies have to deal; and usually they find not one but many ways to handle grievances. In any society also there are various remedy agents which may be referred to when a grievance reaches a boiling point, and an understanding of all such agencies is necessary for

---

[3] *The Berkeley project on comparative village law has been concerned with the problem of conducting comparable ethnographic field studies of law. This group met during 1963–64 to work on the formulation of a field guide. In its broadest scope the field guide was intended to cover the social relations and contexts in which breaches of the law tend to develop, the institutions and mechanisms which serve to prevent social conflict, and the systematic collection of dispute cases.*

a comprehensive analysis of social control and for a sophisticated contextual analysis of the court system, should one exist.

Having in mind the range of remedy agents (or agencies) in a society certain empirical questions come to mind: 1) What do people fight and argue about publicly, and how, when, and where do conflicts come about? 2) How do societies handle disputes and what is the outcome for the individual(s) involved as well as for the society? 3) Within what groups are disputes concentrated? 4) How do disputes at one group level (family, kindred, lineage, etc.) affect that at another (village, region, nation, etc.)?

Information on these four areas should enable us to provide answers to such developmental questions as: At what ages (speaking of biological and sociological age) in the life cycle, in what roles, at what rank, and under what conditions do citizens fit into the picture as parties to specific disputes? What is the relation between the composition of the family, the frequency of crime, and the use of the courts? The Gluecks (1950) and B. Whiting in this volume suggest a relation between the composition of the family and delinquent acts. A relation between family structure and the use of the courts is illustrated by the Zapotec situation where the absence of a father and/or brother often forced women to take recourse to formal law agencies as plaintiffs. Why should this be? What are the social and cultural correlates of sex and age-linked offenses? Among the Zapotec for example, women are rarely defendants in dispute cases involving assault and battery, while men on the other hand are rarely defendants in slander cases. These informations should also enable us to answer the question: 5) What are the manifest and latent jobs of the law and how are they related to the social structure?

A quantitative and qualitative sampling of dispute cases from each society could provide key material around which comparison would be made—provided that sampling problems are resolved or indeed that one could guarantee witnessing more than a handful of cases in some populations. The dispute case, unlike any particular form of adjudication or class of disputes or functions, is present in every society. Universally such cases share most of the following components depending on what stage the dispute is in: the dispute or grievance (property, custody, theft, homicide, marital obligations, or however the society may class such disputes); the parties to a grievance (sex, age, rank, status, relation between parties); presentation of the grievance (before a remedy agent such as a judge, go-between, lineage head); procedure or manner of handling a grievance;

the outcome; the termination of the grievance; and the enforcement of a decision. Mapping the component parts of a case so that the sociological aspects of conflict can be systematically discerned has been attempted for the Zapotec material (Nader 1964a). The results are mainly descriptive generalizations which have proved useful as a springboard for comparative work (Nader and Metzger 1963).

In examining monographs that included case materials, certain neglected areas were noted: frequency estimates, sociological data on the parties such as age and status, detailed descriptions of the legal and extralegal factors determining the outcome. The decision-making process is often ignored or barely mentioned. Typically, for example, there might be a statement of a case, then a sentence declaring that "after much wrangling" the case was settled in such and such a manner. We need to know more about the "wrangling." If we are dealing with a society with courts we need to investigate the dispute case in the context of the range of social institutions which adults use in the resolution or prevention of trouble situations, that is, we should sample out-of-court cases as well as court cases. In this way we may reveal the intricate balance between the use patterns of various authority systems. See Schneider 1957, Nader and Metzger 1963, and Gulliver 1963.

But how do we arrive at an understanding of our last question: 6) What jurisprudential ideas are expressed in legal reasoning? If prior to field work we attempt to make a category listing of substantive areas of the law such as family law, tort law, property law, we run into difficulties. Who could say, at this stage of knowledge, what the major categories of family law would be when viewed cross-culturally? The range of possibilities in terms of substantive law are too great to be handled in the same way as procedure, given our present knowledge. Is inheritance, for example, a universal category of law? (Cf. Hoebel 1948 for an example of a comparative treatment of inheritance.) Llewellyn and Hoebel might suggest that we "find" substantive law by noting cases of breach, and this one can do in the field only. But there is another possibility, one which admittedly has its drawbacks. Field workers, both implicitly and explicitly, have described the law ways of preliterate and nonliterate groups usually against a backdrop of Western European law. Hence the familiar chapters of family, property, contract, torts, etc. This has been the subject of much criticism. While I do not believe that we can adopt wholesale Western jurisprudential categories of law for use in non-Western cultures, it is possible that we could explicitly state that we are using an outline of Anglo-American common law, for example, against which or from which we view exotic legal systems. At least we could be clear about what our biases were. Such straightforward comparisons might serve field workers at least as one system against which to contrast their materials. It would also enable us to provide answers to the question, What jurisprudential ideas are expressed in legal reasoning? We could thereby *test* a suggestion made most recently by Gluckman (1965a) that certain jurisprudential ideas found in English and Roman law are universal ideas.

For example, Gluckman (1965a:113) states as a universal legal distinction that

Both developed and underdeveloped legal systems distinguish sharply between immovable and movable property. Basically the distinction is between rights and duties of persons in relation to land, and rights and duties in relation to others with respect to goods, animals and people.

He continues his discussion by accepting a more generalized version of this distinction:

As Maine pointed out, the difference between the two types of property is not absolutely between land and chattels—between immovables and movables. The Roman *res mancipi* included slaves, horses, and oxen besides land. Maine cites Scottish law as ranking a certain class of securities with land, and Hindu law as grouping slaves with land.

And he proposes an interesting hypothesis to explain what contributes to this dichotomy in classifying property:

Immovable property and chattels have different functions in the maintenance, through time, of a social system as an organized pattern of relations. Immovable property provides fixed positions which endure through the passing of generations, through quarrels, and even through invasions and revolutions, and many social relationships are stabilized about these positions (p. 116). . . . Chattels . . . break up the exclusiveness of corporations aggregate by drawing their individual members into other relationships [cross-linkages] (p. 133).

Even disagreement with the universality of the dichotomy that Gluckman poses does not detract from the fact that Gluckman in these recent essays makes a distinctive contribution to an anthropological understanding of both Western and Barotse jurisprudence. His essays also clearly illustrate the stimulus value of Western jurisprudential ideas. However, another approach in the exploration of cognitive categories is illustrated in this volume [of *American Anthropologist*] by Black and

Metzger. Their approach is a contribution to the methodology of description while Gluckman's essays provide an example of anthropological legal interpretation of given descriptive categories. At any rate it remains clear that aspects of law assumed to be universal by eighteenth-century intellectuals remain a matter of search for twentieth-century scholars.

## REFERENCES CITED

ADAM, LEONHARD
  1937  Quellennachweis. *In* Lehrbuch der Völkerkunde. Konrad Theodor Preuss, ed., Stuttgart, F. Enke, pp. 302–306.
ALLOTT, A. N.
  1953  Methods of legal research into customary law. Journal of African Administration 5(4):172–177.
  1960  Essays in African law with special reference to the law of Ghana. London, Butterworths.
  1961  The changing law in a changing Africa. Sociologus, Vol. II, pp. 115–131.
ANDERSON, J. N. D.
  1957  Law as a social force in Islamic culture and history. Bulletin of the School of Oriental and African Studies 20:13–40.
ARMSTRONG, R. G.
  1954  West African inquest. American Anthropologist 56:1051–1069.
ARNOLD, T.
  1935  The symbols of government. New Haven, Yale University Press.
AUBERT, V.
  1963  Researches in the sociology of law. The American Behavioral Scientist 7(4):16–20.
AYOUB, V.
  1961  Review: the judicial process in two African tribes. *In* Community Political Systems, Morris Janowitz, ed., Glencoe, The Free Press.
BACHOFEN, J. J.
  1861  Das Mutterrecht. Stuttgart, Krais and Hoffmann.
BACON, M. K., I. L. CHILD and H. BARRY, III
  1963  A cross-cultural study of correlates of crime. Journal of Abnormal and Social Psychology 66(4):291–300.
BAILEY, F. G.
  1958  Caste and the economic frontier. Bombay and Oxford, Oxford University Press.
BARNES, J. A.
  1961  Law as politically active: an anthropological view. *In* Studies in the

Sociology of Law, G. Sawer, ed., Canberra, Australian National University, pp. 167–196.

BARTON, R. F.

1919 Ifugao law. University of California Publications in American Archaeology and Ethnology 15(1):1–186.

1930 The half way sun: life among the headhunters of the Philippines. New York, Brewer and Warren.

1949 The Kalingas: their institutions and custom law. Introduction by E. Adamson Hoebel. Chicago, the University of Chicago Press.

BEALS, A. R.

1955 Interplay among factors of change in a Mysore village. *In* Village India: Studies in the Little Community, McKim Marriott, ed., Chicago, University of Chicago Press.

1964 Gopalpur: a South Indian village. New York, Holt, Rinehart and Winston.

BEIDELMAN, T. O.

1959 A comparative analysis of the Jajman system. Locust Valley, New York, Published for the Association for Asian Studies by J. J. Augustin.

BERREMAN, G. D.

1963 Hindus of the Himalayas. Berkeley and Los Angeles, University of California Press.

BLACKSTONE, SIR WILLIAM

1765 Commentaries on the laws of England. Oxford, Clarendon Press.

BOHANNAN, P. J.

1957 Justice and judgment among the Tiv. London, Oxford University Press for the International African Institute.

1960 African homicide and suicide. Princeton, New Jersey, Princeton University Press.

1964 Anthropology and the law. *In* Horizons of Anthropology, S. Tax, ed., Chicago, Aldine Publishing Co., pp. 191–199.

BOORSTIN, D. J.

1958 The mysterious science of the law. Boston, Beacon Press. First published 1941.

BERNDT, R. M.

1962 Excess and restraint. Social Control Among a New Guinea Mountain People. Chicago and London, The University of Chicago Press.

BURRIDGE, K. O. L.

1957 Disputing in Tangu. American Anthropologist 59(5):763–780.

BUSIA, K. A.

1951 The position of the chief in the modern political system of Ashanti: a study of the influence of contemporary social changes on Ashanti political institutions. London and New York, Oxford University Press for the International African Institute.

CARLIN, J. E.
  1963 Lawyers on their own. New Brunswick, Rutgers University Press.
CARLIN, J. E. and J. HOWARD
  1965 Legal representation and class justice. UCLA Law Review 12(2):381–437.
COHN, B. S.
  1959 Some notes on law and change in North China. Economic Development and Cultural Change, Vol. 8, pp. 79–93.
COLSON, E.
  1953 Social control and vengeance in plateau Tonga society. Africa 23:199–212.
  1958 Marriage and the family among the plateau Tonga. Manchester, University of Manchester Press.
  1960 Social organization of the Gwembe Tonga. Manchester, Manchester University Press.
DURKHEIM, E.
  1960 The division of labor in society. Glencoe, Illinois, The Free Press. First published 1893.
EVAN, W. M., ed.
  1962 Law and society. New York, The Free Press of Glencoe.
EVANS-PRITCHARD, E. E.
  1963 The comparative method in social anthropology. London, University of London, Athlone Press.
FALLERS, L. A.
  1956 Changing customary law in Busoga district of Uganda. Journal of African Administration 8:139–144.
  1962 Customary law in the new African states. Law and Contemporary Problems 27:605–631.
FRAKE, C. O.
  1963 Litigation in Lipay: a study in Subanun law. In The Proceedings of the Ninth Pacific Science Congress, 1957, Vol. 3, pp. 217–222.
FRAZER, SIR J. G.
  1890 The golden bough; a study on magic and religion. London, New York, The Macmillan Co.
FUSTEL DE COULANGES, N. D.
  1864 The ancient city: a study on the religion, laws, and institutions of Greece and Rome. New York, Doubleday and Co. Inc., 1956. First published 1864.

GIBBS, J. L., JR.
1963 The Kpelle moot: a therapeutic model for the informal settlement of disputes. Africa 33:1–11.

GLASSE, R. M.
1959 Revenge and redress among the Huli: a preliminary account. Mankind (Sydney) 5(7):273–289.

GLUCKMAN, M.
1955a The judicial process among the Barotse of Northern Rhodesia. Manchester University Press, for the Rhodes-Livingstone Institute.
1955b Custom and conflict in Africa. Glencoe, The Free Press.
1959 The technical vocabulary of Barotse jurisprudence. American Anthropologist 61:743–759.
1962 African jurisprudence. The Advancement of Science 75:439–454.
1965a The ideas in Barotse jurisprudence. New Haven and London, Yale University Press.
1965b Politics, law and ritual in tribal society. Chicago, Aldine Publishing Co.

GLUECK, S. and E. GLUECK
1950 Unraveling juvenile delinquency. Cambridge, Harvard University Press.

GULLIVER, P. H.
1963 Social control in an African society: a study of the Arusha, agricultural Masai of Northern Tanganyika. Boston, Boston University Press.

GUTMANN, B.
1926 Das Recht der Dschagga. Mit einem Nachworte des Herausgebers: Zur Entwicklungspsychologie des Rechts. Arbeiten zur Entwicklungspsychologie, F. Krueger, ed., siebentes Stück. Abhandlungen der Sachsischen Staatlichen Forschungsinstitute, Forschungsinstitut für Psychologie, Nr. 7.

HARPER, E. B.
1957 Hoylu: a belief relating justice and the supernatural. American Anthropologist 59:801–816.

HART, H. L. A.
1961 The concept of law. Oxford, Oxford University Press.

HAZARD, J. N.
1962 Furniture arrangement as a symbol of judicial roles. Etcetera 19(2):181–188.

HOBHOUSE, L. T., G. C. WHEELER and M. GINSBERG
1915 The material culture and social institutions of the simpler peoples: an

essay in correlation. The London School of Economics and Political Science, No. 3 of the Monographs on Sociology.

HOEBEL, E. A.
1940    The political organization and law-ways of the Comanche Indians. American Anthropological Association Memoir 54. Contributions from the Santa Fe Laboratory of Anthropology, vol. 4.
1948    The anthropology of inheritance. *In* Conference on Social Meaning of Legal Concepts, E. N. Cahn, ed. New York, New York University.
1954    The law of primitive man: a study in comparative legal dynamics. Cambridge, Mass., Harvard University Press.
1961    Three studies in African law. Stanford Law Review 13: 418–442.

HOGBIN, H. I.
1934    Law and order in Polynesia: a study of primitive legal institutions. Introduction by B. Malinowski. London, Christophers.

HOWELL, P. P.
1954    A manual of Nuer law. Being an account of customary law, its evolution and development in the courts established by the Sudan government. London, New York, and Toronto, Oxford University Press.

JAYAWARDENA, C.
1963    Conflict and solidarity in a Guianese plantation. New York, The Humanities Press.

JONES, JR., EDGAR H.
1964    Power and prudence in the arbitration of labor disputes: a venture in some hypotheses. UCLA Law Review 2(5):675–791.

KABERRY, P. M.
1941, 1942    Law and political organization in the Abelam tribe, New Guinea. Oceania 12(1):79–95; No. 3:209–225; No. 4:331–363.

KANTOROWICZ, H.
1958    The definition of law. Cambridge, Cambridge University Press.

KAPLAN, I.
1965    Courts as catalysts of change: a Chagga case. Southwestern Journal of Anthropology 21(1):79–96.

KEUNING, J.
1963    Customary law and customary courts in Yoruba-land. Read at the Nigerian Institute of Social and Economic Research in Ibadan. (Mimeo.)

KLUCKHOHN, C.
1960    The use of typology in anthropological theory. *In* Selected Papers of the Fifth International Congress of Anthropological and Ethnological

Science, 1956. A. Wallace, ed., Philadelphia, University of Pennsylvania Press, pp. 134–140.

KROEBER, A. L.
1925    Principles of Yurok law. *In* Handbook of the Indians of California. Washington, D.C., Bureau of American Ethnology, Bulletin 78.

LEACH, E. R.
1954    Political systems of highland Burma: a study of Kachin social structure. London, G. Bell and Sons, Ltd.
1959    Letter to the editor: social change and primitive law. American Anthropologist 61(6):1096–1097.
1961    Rethinking anthropology. London, Athlone Press.

LEWIS, O.
1958    Village life in northern India. Urbana, University of Illinois Press.

LLEWELLYN, K. N. and E. A. HOEBEL
1941    The Cheyenne way: conflict and case law in primitive jurisprudence. Norman, University of Oklahoma Press.

McLENNAN, J. F.
1865    Primitive marriage. Edinburgh, A. & C. Black.

MAINE, SIR H. S.
1861    Ancient law: its connection with the early history of society and its relation to modern ideas. London, John Murray. Paperback edition printed by Beacon Press, Boston, 1963.
1871    Village-communities in the East and West. London, John Murray.

MALINOWSKI, B.
1922    Argonauts of the western Pacific. New York, E. P. Dutton and Co., 1961.
1926    Crime and custom in savage society. London, Kegan Paul, Trench, Trubner & Co., Ltd.
1934    Introduction to law and order in Polynesia by H. Ian Hogbin. New York, Christophers.
1942    A new instrument for the interpretation of law—especially primitive. The Yale Law Review 51:1237–1254.

MARCH, J. G.
1956    Sociological jurisprudence revisited, a review (more or less) of Max Gluckman. Stanford Law Review 8:499–534.

MARX, K.
1960    Capital: a critique of political economy. Translated from the third German edition by S. Moore and E. Aveling, F. Engels, ed. Revised and amplified according to the fourth German edition by Ernest Unterman. New York, The Modern Library.

1948 The Communist manifesto. Centenary Edition. London.

MAUSS, M. and M. H. BEUCHAT

1906 Les variations saisonnières des societés esquimaux; étude de morphologie social. Anné Sociologique 9:39–132.

MEAD, M.

1961 Some anthropological considerations concerning natural law. Natural Law Form 6:51–64.

METZGER, D.

1960 Conflict in Chulsanto: a village in Chiapis. Alpha Kappa Deltan 30:35–48.

MONTESQUIEU, C. L.

1750 L'esprit de les lois. London, printed for J. Nourse and P. Vaillant in the Strand.

MOORE, S. F.

1958 Power and property in Inca Peru. New York, Columbia University Press.

MOORE, S.

1960 Marxian law in primitive society. *In* Culture in History: Essays in Honor of Paul Radin, Stanley Diamond, ed., New York, Columbia University Press, pp. 642–662.

NADEL, S. F.

1942 A black Byzantium. London, Oxford University Press.

1947 The Nuba. London, Oxford University Press.

1956 Reason and unreason in African law. Africa 26, No. 2:160–173.

NADER, L.

1964a An analysis of Zapotec law cases. Ethnology 3:404–419.

1964b Talea and Juquila: a comparison of Zapotec social organization. University of California Publications in American Archaeology and Ethnology 48(3):195–296.

1965a Choices in legal procedure: Shia Moslem and Mexican Zapotec. American Anthropologist 67(2):394–399.

1965b Communication between village and city in the modern Middle East. Human Organization, Special Issue: Dimensions of Cultural Change in the Middle East.

n.d. Variations in Zapotec legal procedure. *In* Homenajeal Ingeniero Roberto Weitlaner. Mexico (In press.)

NADER, L., K. F. KOCH and B. COX

1966 The ethnography of law: a bibliographical survey. Stanford: Current Anthropology, special supplement. (In press.)

NADER, L. and D. METZGER
1963   Conflict resolution in two Mexican communities. American Anthropologist 65:584–592.

NAGEL, S. S.
1962   Culture patterns and judicial systems. Vanderbilt Law Review 16:147–157.

NICHOLAS, R. W. and T. MUKHOPADHYAY
n.d.   Politics and law in two West Bengal villages. Bulletin of the Anthropological Survey of India. (In press.)

O'GORMAN, H. J.
1963   Lawyers and matrimonial cases. New York, The Free Press of Glencoe.

POSPISIL, L.
1958a  Kapauku Papuans and their law. Yale University Publications in Anthropology 54.
1958b  Social change and primitive law: consequences of a Papuan legal case. American Anthropologist 60:832–837.

RADCLIFFE-BROWN, A. R.
1933   Primitive law. In Encyclopedia of the Social Sciences, Vol. 9, pp. 202–206. New York, Macmillan. Reprinted in Structure and function in primitive society: essays and addresses by A. R. Radcliffe-Brown, Ch. 12. Glencoe, Illinois, Free Press.

REDFIELD, R.
1950   Maine's ancient law in the light of primitive societies. Western Political Quarterly 3:571–589.

RICHARDSON, J.
1940   Law and status among the Kiowa Indians. American Ethnological Society. Monograph I.

RIESMAN, D.
1954   Individualism reconsidered and other essays. Glencoe, Illinois, The Free Press, pp. 440–466.

RHEINSTEIN, M.
1963   Problems of law in the new nations of Africa. In Old Societies and New States, Clifford Geertz, ed., Free Press of Glencoe.

ROTHENBERGER, J. E.
1963   Judicial process and political organization among the Lozi and Tiv. Ms.

SCHAPERA, I.
1938, 1955   A handbook of Tswana law and custom. London, New York, Cape Town, Oxford University Press for the International African Institute.

1943   Tribal legislation among the Tswana of the Bechuanaland Protectorate. London, Lund, Humphries, for the London School of Economics and Political Science.

Schneider, D. M.

1957   Political organization, supernatural sanctions and the punishment for incest on Yap. American Anthropologist 59, No. 5:791–800.

Schubert, G. A.

1959   Quantitative analysis of judicial behavior. Glencoe, Illinois, The Free Press.

1963   Behavioral research in public law. American Political Science Review 57:433–445.

Schwartz, R. D. and J. C. Miller

1964   Legal evolution and societal complexity. The American Journal of Sociology 70(2):159–169.

Siegel, B. J. and A. R. Beals

1960   Pervasive factionalism. American Anthropologist 62:394–417.

Simmel, G.

1956   Conflict and the web of group affiliations. Glencoe, Illinois, The Free Press.

Simonett, J. E.

1963   The common law of Morrison County. American Bar Association Journal 49:263–265.

Skolnick, J. H.

1965   The sociology of law in America: overview and trends. Social Problems (summer issue), supplemental monograph.

Smigel, E. O.

1964   The Wall Street lawyer. New York, The Free Press of Glencoe.

Smith, W. and J. M. Roberts

1954   Zuni law: a field of values. With an appendix by Stanley Newman. Cambridge, Massachusetts, Peabody Museum Papers 43(1).

Stirling, P.

1957   Land, marriage, and the law in Turkish villages. Part I. The Reception of Foreign Law in Turkey: International Social Science Bulletin 9:21–33. UNESCO.

Strodtbeck, F.

1962   Social process, the law, and jury functioning. In Law and Society, Wm. M. Evan, ed., New York, The Free Press of Glencoe, pp. 152–164.

Tappan, P. W.

1947   Delinquent girls in court. New York, Columbia University Press.

TURNER, V. W.

1957 Schism and continuity in an African society: a study of Ndemby village life. Manchester, England, Manchester University Press.

UCHENDU, V. C.

1964 Livestock tenancy among Lgbo of Southern Nigeria. African Studies Quarterly Journal 23(2):89–94.

WEBER, M.

1954 Max Weber on law in economy and society, M. Rheinstein, ed., Cambridge, Harvard University Press.

WHITING, B. B.

1950 Paiute sorcery. New York, Viking Fund Publications in Anthropology, No. 15.

WHITING, J. W. M., et al.

1953 Field manual for the cross-cultural study of child rearing. Social Science Research Council, New York.

WINANS, E. V. and R. B. EDGERTON

1964 Hehe magical justice. American Anthropologist 66, 1:745–764.

# PART IV | CONTEMPORARY EMPIRICAL RESEARCH

JEROME E. CARLIN · ERWIN O. SMIGEL · JACK
LADINSKY · HARRY KALVEN, JR. · RITA JAMES
SIMON · DALE W. BROEDER · S. SIDNEY ULMER
· MARC A. FRANKLIN, ROBERT H. CHANIN,
AND IRVING MARK · DONALD J. NEWMAN ·
EDWARD J. BARRETT · JOHN P. CLARK ·
WENDELL SHACKELFORD · MANFRED S.
GUTTMACHER · ROBIN M. WILLIAMS, JR.,
AND MARGARET W. RYANS · CHARLES V.
HAMILTON · SAMUEL KRISLOV · ARTHUR
LEWIS WOOD · BERTRAM F. WILLCOX AND
EDWARD J. BLOUSTEIN · JULIUS COHEN,
REGINALD A. H. ROBSON, AND ALAN BATES
· MARTIN MILLSPAUGH · RICHARD D.
SCHWARTZ AND JAMES C. MILLER ·
YEHEZKEL DROR

THE MAJOR CONTRIBUTION WHICH THIS BOOK MAKES TO the sociology of law is its survey of contemporary research. The two main criteria for determining which topics to include in Part IV and how many selections to provide for each topic were (1) the relative importance of the topic to the sociology of law, and (2) the amount of empirical research which has been done on the topic. The variation in number of selections from one section to another is, therefore, a reflection of these criteria.

In some areas—particularly in law and psychiatry, legal ethics, and civil rights—the number of significant publications is large. Unfortunately, however, the number of theoretical publications compared to empirical-research reports is also very large. In contrast, in other areas, such as the legal profession, the publications are predominantly reports of empirical research. Thus, the number of selections on the legal profession is more a reflection of the greater availability of appropriate articles than an indication of the relative importance of that topic vis-à-vis other topics.

The list of topics in Part IV is not exhaustive, the absence of selections on law and the economy being perhaps the most serious omission. This selectivity is due in part to my desire to limit the survey to matters concerned primarily with social-political phenomena and to include problems on which sociologists have done substantial research; and, in part to my greater familiarity with research on the topics included. Within the nine sections there are selections by both behavioral scientists and lawyers, and some of the selections represent the combined efforts of both disciplines.

## THE LEGAL PROFESSION

The section on the legal profession provides a varied perspective. It describes the lawyer as an entrepreneur and as an organization man, as a generalist and as a specialist. The excerpt from *Lawyers on Their Own* by Jerome Carlin is a description of the solo practitioner—the entrepreneurial lawyer whom Carlin places on the lowest rung of the profession's status ladder. Generally, the solo practitioner is from a lower socioeconomic background. He is usually a graduate of a night law school. Becoming a lawyer is a big step up the status ladder. The earning of his LL.B. places him significantly above other, less-educated members of his family and gives him a sense of achievement and prestige.[1] Yet his day-to-day activities, especially during his first few years after law school, are anything but prestigious. He may find himself doing the legwork for an already established entrepreneur or acting

---

[1] *Another study of the legal profession, Hubert O'Gorman,* Lawyers and Matrimonial Cases *(Glencoe, Ill: Free Press, 1963), concentrates on lawyers whose practice is limited almost exclusively to matrimonial cases. O'Gorman reports that his lawyers are usually solo practitioners and that they have the personal and social characteristics described by Carlin.*

as the latter's clerk; he may also be supplementing his income by working as a salesman or fee collector. In building his own practice, he customarily accepts a great variety of cases—petty crime, personal injury, real estate, probate, divorce.

The diffuse responsibilities and activities of the solo practitioner, particularly in the early years of practice, are in sharp contrast to the neophyte period for the recent law-school graduate who enters a large and prestigious firm. The "fresh-out-of-law-school" member of such a firm routinely spends his first few years on specialized and limited matters. He works on one aspect of a complex problem and is responsible to a superior who integrates his contribution into the larger pattern.

In his study of the Wall Street lawyer, Erwin Smigel seems to be describing a different profession from the one Carlin studied. In contrast to the solo practitioner, who has lower-class origins, has attended a state or city college and a night law school, and belongs to a minority religious, ethnic, or racial group, the member of a large firm comes from a high-status white Protestant family and has graduated from a private liberal-arts college and a prestigious law school.

In the final selection in this section, Jack Ladinsky compares the background characteristics and types of law practice of 207 Detroit lawyers. This study explains the effects of self-selection and of organizational recruitment patterns on type of law practice and on the setting in which the practice is conducted. Ladinsky's cross-sectional analysis confirms the findings of Carlin and Smigel as to the distinctive personal, social, and occupational characteristics of lawyers in practice for themselves and in corporations.

By and large, empirical research on the legal profession has been characterized by an absence of comparative research and observational studies. Little is known, therefore, about the prestige of the law relative to other professions and about the patterns of interaction among lawyers within a firm or between firms, except what can be gleaned from the individual interviews reported by Smigel.[2]

---

[2] *Some research has been done on the motivations for studying law and on the professional socialization of young lawyers, but it is not sampled in this section since it is outside the main purview of ths book The interested reader may consult the works of Wagner Thielens, "The Occupational Self Image of the Law Student," (paper read at American Sociological Association meetings, Los Angeles, 1963); Dan Lortie, "The Striving Young Lawyer" (unpublished Ph.D. dissertation, Department of Sociology, University of Chicago, 1958); and Seymour Warkow, "Lawyers in the Making" (National Opinion Research Center, Report No. 96, 1963).*

## LEGAL ETHICS

The section on legal ethics offers another view of the legal profession, with special emphasis on lawyers' reactions to their professional code. The article on the effectiveness of curriculum innovations in law schools evaluates the impact of clinical programs on the attitudes of third-year law students toward issues in which professional ethics are a factor. The purpose of the clinical programs was to sensitize law students, before they begin the practice of law, to the importance of (1) working with other professional persons, especially psychiatrists and social workers, (2) contributing their time and efforts to indigent and unpopular clients, and (3) resolving questionable matters in a professional and ethical manner.

The other selections in the section consider the reactions and behavior of practicing lawyers to ethical dilemmas.[3] The article by Arthur Wood reports the findings from a survey of criminal lawyers (defined as lawyers who devote 10 per cent or more of their practice to criminal law) about their attitudes toward the professional behavior of their colleagues. Wood's conclusions about the "ethical behavior" of the bar support those reported in the section on the legal profession. The tendency to disregard ethical standards is not limited to the field of criminal law; it is a characteristic shared by attorneys who are in practice for themselves and who devote much of their practice to negligence cases and domestic relations as well.

The final selection in the section is an account of a field study on the quality of legal aid available to indigent clients in criminal trials in rural areas —where, admittedly, the problem is less severe than in large metropolitan centers.

## THE JURY SYSTEM

The jury system and the courts are two important legal institutions which have been studied empirically in the past decade and a half. Under the auspices of the University of Chicago Law School, a team of lawyers and sociologists conducted investigations into the American jury system. A wide battery of research techniques was used: observations, surveys, experiments, and analyses of historical documents. The selections included in this section describe some of the findings from the experimental jury studies and from the survey of

---

[3] *Unfortunately, none of the selections describes the relationship between attitude and behavior in matters pertaining to professional ethics. A recent study of the New York City Bar, Jerome Carlin's* Lawyers' Ethics *(New York: Russell Sage, 1966), reports the results of a survey of attitudes toward professional ethics (many of the same items on Carlin's questionnaire are reported in the article on curriculum innovations), but lacks data on the actual behavior of attorneys.*

judicial opinion. "The Dignity of the Civil Jury," by Harry Kalven, compares the verdicts which judges claim they would have reached with verdicts actually reported by jurors in a variety of criminal and civil actions.

The article "Jurors' Evaluation of Expert Psychiatric Testimony" is based on the reactions of real jurors (persons drawn by lot from jury pools in three metropolitan jurisdictions) to recorded trials. The substantive issue is the jurors' evaluation of psychiatric testimony in a criminal case involving a defense of insanity. Other issues reported by the experimental jury study (not included here) are the effects of sex and social status on the jurors' participation and influence, the jurors' reactions to information concerning insurance, the amount of money the plaintiff is suing for, and the jurors' assessments of criminal responsibility.

The second selection by Kalven is based largely on the experimental jury data. It compares the amount of damages juries are willing to award in the same case when all factors are held constant except the amount of money the plaintiff is asking.

The selection by another member of the jury project, Dale Broeder, describes how the plaintiff's family or marital status affects the amount of damages a jury is likely to award.

The final paper in this section, by Sidney Ulmer, analyzes the decision of the Supreme Court on a matter that has long been an obstacle to the securement of fair and just trials: the systematic exclusion of Negroes from jury panels in the South.

## THE COURTS

While the preceding section, on the jury, can make some claim for representativeness, this section, describing research on the courts, completely omits two topics on which there has been a good deal of research: delay and quantitative decision making. These topics are omitted because they are but peripherally related to the sociological aspect of the law. There are also no selections describing research on the specialized courts, such as juvenile, family, and domestic-relations courts. The material on such courts, especially on the juvenile court, bears a certain resemblance to the best of the articles in the area of law and psychiatry. The works are primarily thoughtful, probing criticisms of existing practices. Criticisms, however, which stem not from research findings, but from a legal-philosophical orientation.[4]

---

[4] *Articles and books by Warren Dunham, Joel Handler, Margaret Rosenheim, Paul Tappan, and Francis Allen illustrate this type: Joel Handler, "The Juvenile Court and the Adversary System: Problems of Function and Form,"* 65 Wisconsin Law Review (1965); *H. Warren Dunham, "The Juvenile Court: Contradictory*

This section does, however, describe judicial operations and decisions in many areas. The first selection, which is based on the Civil Justice Project at the Columbia University Law School, discusses personal-injury litigation in New York City. It reports on the following issues: the number of claimants, the proportion of cases which reach trial, the percentage of cases in which damages are recovered, the amount of money that changes hands, the role of the attorney in the recovery process, and the problem of delay.

Donald Newman's article is a critical account of the operations of the criminal courts. It describes the bargains made between defendants in criminal cases and officers of the court in order to persuade the defendants to plead guilty—a faster, cheaper procedure than a public trial.

The concluding selection, by Sidney Ulmer, examines the attitudes of Supreme Court Justices and the Court's decisions in civil-liberties cases. It reports interaction patterns among judges, faction formations, and consistency or lack of consistency in opinions reported by a particular judge.

## LAW, PUBLIC OPINION, AND THE MASS MEDIA

In its review of the Shephard case, the Supreme Court declared that the defendant's right to a fair trial had been violated by the publicity the case had received in the newpapers before and during the trial. In deciding as it did, the Court echoed a growing sense of resentment by members of the bench and the bar toward the role of the mass media. In some cities, the local bar has organized committees to lobby for changes in the law, so that the press and other media would be restricted in their access to victims, defendants, witnesses, and other persons involved in an impending trial.

The first selection describes the result of an experiment in which subjects were exposed to different versions of pretrial newspaper publicity about a forthcoming murder case. The subjects were asked for their opinions about the guilt or innocence of the defendant after reading a series of newspaper stories about the crime. After the subjects listened to a recorded trial, their opinions were solicited again. The findings in the study are clearcut and surprising in their implications.

The second selection compares the public's attitudes toward legal statutes

---

Orientations in Processing Offenders," 23 Law and Contemporary Problems (*Summer, 1958*); *Francis Allen, "The Borderland of the Criminal Law,"* Social Service Review (*June 1958*); *Margaret Rosenheim, ed.,* Justice for the Child (*New York: Free Press of Glencoe, 1962*); *Paul Tappan,* Delinquent Girls in Court (*New York: Columbia University Press, 1947*). *In the past few years, Monrad Paulson, professor at the Columbia University Law School, has been engaged in research on the day-to-day operations of the juvenile courts in New York City; but as yet no reports have been published.*

on a controversial issue in family law: the authority which parents have over adolescent children. The study indicates that there is considerable variance between the moral sense of the community and the formal legal rules.

The last selection, by Martin Millspaugh, is a content analysis of the differential treatment which a Negro defendant in a murder case received in four Baltimore newspapers.

## LAW AND PSYCHIATRY

As mentioned earlier, the section on law and psychiatry is disappointingly thin. The important papers written in this area have been theoretical essays or thoughtful policy statements on commitment procedures, the violations of due process arising out of commitment procedures, the defendant's ability to stand trial, and the quality of psychiatric testimony.[5] Unfortunately, the number of research papers compared to the number of first-rate theoretical articles is regrettably small.

The article by Manfred Guttmacher, psychiatrist and chief medical officer of the Supreme Bench of Baltimore, discusses the attitudes and behavior of judges in the Baltimore courts toward homosexuals who appear as defendants in criminal cases.

The survey of lawyers and psychiatrists by Simon and Shackelford reports the opinions of the two professions on matters relating to the defense of insanity, such as the role of the expert witness, the rights of the accused, who should decide guilt or innocence, and commitment procedure.

## LAW AND THE POLICE

In the past decade sociologists have become increasingly interested in the police as an occupational role and in the police system as a complex organization. Stimulated in part by the thoughtful essays of several law professors[6] and

---

[5] *See for example John Biggs, Jr.*, The Guilty Mind (*New York: Harcourt, Brace, 1955*); *Sheldon Glueck*, Law and Psychiatry (*Baltimore, Md.: Johns Hopkins Press, 1962*); *Joseph Goldstein and Jay Katz, "Abolishing the Insanity Defense— Why Not,"* 72 Yale Law Journal (*1963*); *Winfred Overholser*, The Psychiatrist and the Law (*New York: Harcourt, Brace, 1953*); *Philip Q. Roche*, The Criminal Mind (*New York: Farrar, Straus, and Cadahy, 1958*); *Thomas Szasz*, Law, Liberty and Psychiatry (*New York: Macmillan, 1963*); *Henry Weihofen*, The Urge to Punish (*New York: Farrar, Straus, and Cudahy, 1956*); *Manfred S. Guttmacher and Henry Weihofen*, Psychiatry and the Law (*New York: W. W. Norton, 1952*); *Gregory Zilboorg*, The Psychology of the Criminal Act (*New York: Harcourt, Brace, 1954*).

[6] *Wayne La Fave*, Arrest: The Decision to Take a Suspect into Custody (*Boston: Little, Brown, 1965*); *Sanford Kadish, "Legal Norms and Discretion in the Police and Sentencing Processes,"* 75 Harvard Law Review (*1962*); *Joseph Goldstein,*

in part by a renewed interest in criminology, deviant behavior, and social control, sociologists have studied the operations of metropolitan police departments and the role of police vis-à-vis other social groups.[7]

In this section, the study by Edward Barrett compares the performance of police departments in two cities in California. It examines the process involved in the disposition of persons arrested on felony charges and considers such issues as the number of confessions and convictions and the length of time between arrest and booking, arrest and charge, and arrest and release.

John Clark's selection reports the results of a survey describing some of the forces which contribute to the isolation and integration of the police and police departments in three communities in Illinois. Clark also compares the results of the Illinois study with those of a comparable survey made in Great Britain.

## LAW AND DESEGREGATION

The Supreme Court's decision in *Brown v. Board of Education* (1954) declaring unconstitutional the concept of "separate but equal" stimulated social scientists and lawyers to study the effects of that decision. One of the first and most important of the studies was done by Robin Williams. Williams studied the reactions of 24 communities in different regions of the country. After reporting the varied responses of school administrators, parents (Negro and white), teachers, and other interested parties, he explains why some communities were able to make relatively swift and peaceful transitions from segregated schools, while others reacted with delay and violence.

The second selection deals with discrimination in voting rights. Charles Hamilton, a lawyer and a political scientist, analyzes the responses of three federal courts in communities of the deep South to the civil-rights acts of 1957 and 1960. According to Hamilton, judges in the federal district courts in the South play a key role in expediting or hindering compliance with federal laws.

The final paper uses the desegregation issue as a backdrop for investigating the behavior of Southern attorneys general concerning the enforcement of federal civil-rights laws. Contrasting the differences in behavior between South-

---

"*Police Discretion Not to Invoke the Criminal Process: Law Visibility Decisions in the Administration of Justice,*" 69 Yale Law Journal (*1960*).

[7] *Two monographs describing research on the police and police departments have been published since the completion of this volume. The first, Jerome H. Skolnick,* Justice Without Trial: Law Enforcement in Democratic Society (*New York: Wiley, 1966*) *is a report of the author's observations and participation in the activities of a police department for more than a year. The second is a collection of original research papers: David Bordua, ed.,* The Police: Six Sociological Essays (*New York: Wiley, 1967*).

ern judges on the federal bench and Southern attorneys general, Samuel Krislov observes that the latter have been notable for their lack of activity in enforcement. In line with "reference-group theory," Krislov concludes that Southern attorneys general are responsive to local opinion and local leadership because they aspire to local and state judicial and political offices.

## LAW AND SOCIAL CHANGE

The final section consists of two selections which exemplify two modes of research on law and social change. The first, by sociologists Richard Schwartz and James Miller, traces an evolutionary sequence in the development of legal institutions. It compares 51 societies, ranging from simple to complex, by the presence or absence of three law-related institutions: the use of mediation in the settlement of disputes, the presence of police, and the regular use of counsel. Then it correlates the presence of each of these institutions with other indices of social complexity, such as a symbolic medium of exchange, publishment of crimes through governmental acts, and writing.

The article by Yehezkel Dror represents a more traditional approach to the study of law and social change. Dror demonstrates how legal norms can both anticipate social change and respond to changes which have already occurred in actual behavior. Employing Ogburn's theory of cultural lag—that social change follows slowly on the heels of technological innovation—he describes the situation that exists between the time new laws or changes in laws are instituted and society's adjustment to those changes as manifest by actual behavior and by the practices of social institutions.

# The Legal Profession

# THE ROAD
# TO INDIVIDUAL
# PRACTICE

*Jerome E. Carlin*

The individual practitioner of law in Chicago is a self-made man who came up the hard way from poor, immigrant surroundings. His father, generally an immigrant from Eastern Europe with little or no formal education, was in most cases the proprietor of a small business. The one burning ambition of the son was to escape from the ghetto, to rise above his father, to become a professional man. Again and again, in answer to the question of what led them to become lawyers, respondents revealed this strong drive for professional status:

I never had any visions of glamor or glory, but a profession, honorable, making a living. My uncle [a lawyer] was living comfortably and had standing in the community. I came from poor circumstances, my father was ill many years, and my brother and I had to support the family. We became professional men [his brother is also a lawyer] . . . a tremendous thing, especially during the depression.

I was in a big family of 13 children. When I was 12 I quit school—after two years of high school—to go to work. I was going to make a living for the family. I was doing fairly well, a shipping clerk, $15 a week. I was promised a dollar a week more if I would stay and not go back to school. But I decided to go back to school, in 1923. I decided to have a specific profession, I had no idea of any other profession.

Reprinted by permission of the author and of the publishers from *Lawyers on Their Own* (New Brunswick, N.J.; Rutgers University Press, 1962), pp. 3–19. Copyright 1962 by Rutgers, The State University. Footnotes have been omitted, as have the author's identification of respondents.

I wanted to be a lawyer, and the family wanted me to be one—although since then I've realized that monetarily you can do a lot better in business. Jewish people think it's very important to be a professional, and I was always a big talker.

Principally it was a question of going into some pursuit that involved respect, dignity. Among Jewish people professions are very important. And with my parents, they had little or no education, their children should have professions. There was a certain amount of appeal. Professional men were looked up to then. At one time in former years, the almighty dollar was not as important as it is today.

Well over half the lawyers interviewed claimed they had no specific intention of becoming lawyers. Most of them confessed that they came to the law by default, having abandoned the idea of going into medicine, engineering, or one of a variety of other professional pursuits because they found them to be too expensive, academically too demanding, or because they saw themselves barred by discrimination.

I had been taking all sorts of courses at Crane [Junior College], I didn't know what I was going to be. When I put 'em together I had sufficient for pre-law. That's how I studied law instead of medicine. I wanted to be a doctor but I was too lazy—not that I wasn't a good student, I just didn't get around to it. I'm a pretty fair student.

I decided the day I entered law school. I was thinking of medicine, dentistry, or even pharmacy. Through high school and college I had a narrow education, I couldn't go anywhere on it, except into sales. I didn't get into medical school or dental school. Law was my third choice.

\*     \*     \*     \*

A Negro lawyer said engineering had been his first choice also:

I wanted to be an engineer, but I would have had to go to Argentina to cash in on it, so I went into law as a second choice.

A similar experience was reported by a Jewish lawyer:

I wanted to be a chemical engineer but my college professors said it was no place for a Jew.
*Interviewer:* Why did you decide on the law?
*Respondent:* Family, I guess.
*Interviewer:* Are there any lawyers in your family?
*Respondent:* My brother was a lawyer.

*Interviewer:* Did you want to be a lawyer, or was it something you fell into?

*Respondent:* A combination, both; I gravitated.

The individual practitioner in Chicago has in most cases received his professional training in one of the "proprietary" or Catholic night law schools. Although most of those who went on to a night law school had only a year or two of college credit (if that) from either a downtown night extension school or a local junior college, they encountered little difficulty in gaining admission into the notoriously low-standard night law schools and faced relatively few obstacles in getting through them.

Requirements for admission to the night law school during the twenties and thirties (when two out of three of the respondents entered law school) were practically nonexistent. The general rule in such institutions was to accept any person with a high school diploma or "its equivalent," which frequently meant accepting someone with fewer than four years of high school. The concern of many such schools of that period was not in keeping out the unqualified student but in recruiting as many students as possible regardless of qualifications.

Scholastic standards suffered not only from the absence of any definite rule on exclusions but also from an unwillingness to fail a poor student. Courses of instruction were limited to subjects covered by the state bar examinations, and the instructors, most of whom conducted a full-time law practice during the day, rarely had the time or the inclination to prepare for their classes.

\* \* \* \*

In general, the individual practitioner works for another lawyer as a kind of apprentice during his first few years out of law school. These are usually temporary positions—rarely lasting more than a year or two—paying little or, in the case of the space-for-service arrangement, no salary, the assumption being that the young lawyer will be building up his own practice on the side. The employers—in nearly all cases either individual or small firm lawyers—appear to be primarily interested in getting an inexpensive legman, someone to run their errands in the clerks' offices, to make perfunctory court appearances, to help prepare their routine papers and documents, and occasionally to do some research. The young lawyer, on the other hand, becomes acquainted with the courts and local agencies;

he gets to know his way around—whom to see and how to approach them. In other words, he gets an initiation into the workings of the lower-level judicial and administrative bureaucracies.

As a law clerk I got no particular attention from them [his employers], but I learned from them.
*Interviewer:* You mean your way around the courts?
*Respondent:* Yes, but law too, pleadings and depositions. The big important thing, when you go around and see—at Christmastime it's traditional in Chicago to pass out $25 in envelopes to the clerks of court, the clerks in other offices, the bailiffs. If you don't, you're out of it.

I worked with —— and ——, older men. I followed them around. I did legwork; I was the clerk in the firm. I got experience, contact with the courts. I was helped by coming here. You can't do it by yourself. You must associate yourself with men who have experience. Fifty per cent of your value in Chicago depends on who you know across the street [City Hall and County Buildings]. If you absorb it from someone who knows it, that's 50 per cent of the battle. If you associate yourself you just find out sooner: who to go to, where and how to go. For example, one thing you don't learn [in law school] is what papers you file in lawsuits. You need forms to file, and you have to know where to file them. The same with following return days, books of entry in City Hall, trial dates—the actual, the practical. Here's a summons you get [indicating a form]—what do you do with it? Well, you have to file an appearance. You go across the street and get a form. You have to file in a certain window. Later you have to look and find who is assigned to it, and on what date. It's not difficult but you have to learn it and remember it, and that you get from actual doing.

The relationship between the older lawyer and his "apprentice" is frequently less than harmonious. Many of those who worked for other lawyers reported unpleasant experiences: either that contact with their employer had led to disenchantment or, in most instances, that there had been open conflict with their employer. . . .

\* \* \* \*

While these clerkships do not always end in conflict and mutual recrimination, there seem to be very strong pressures leading in that direction. In large measure these pressures arise from the part-time, temporary character of the position. In most instances the young lawyer will have some practice of his own which he is attempting to expand, and he usually finds it difficult to draw the line between his own time and the time he should give to his employer—and unless he devotes himself wholly to his employer, the situation can only grow less certain, requiring frequent redefinition of the terms of employment. The employer is often more than happy to permit his clerk to develop his own practice (up to a point), since this justifies a low salary. This arrangement, however, soon places the clerk in a potentially competitive relationship with his employer, particularly in view of the fact that whatever gap there may be between older and younger lawyer in terms of competence and business-getting ability is, at this level of the bar, relatively quickly bridged.

For most individual practitioners, getting started on their own was a hard, uphill struggle. Their work in the early years consisted generally of the dregs of legal practice and their income was correspondingly meager. The matters they handled were with few exceptions the least desirable from every point of view: the marginal cases, the cases no one else wanted, the cases involving the least return and the most aggravation.

*Interviewer:* What were the problems of getting started on your own?
*Respondent:* Getting clients that were paying clients. There are enough that float around from lawyer to lawyer who just want to check up on another lawyer—the junk.

The main problem was development of a clientele, and then obtaining lucrative business. A young lawyer is always recommended for small collections, dead judgments, and so on.

There's a lot of business around that it don't pay to handle. After a while you get independent. A lot of people want you to handle their business at your expense.

Collection matters, evictions, rent cases, "dead" judgments, along with some personal injury, criminal, and divorce cases are the kinds of work most frequently handled in the early years in practice. The most distinguishing feature of such cases is their petty character—the small amount of money involved, the tenuousness of the claim (or its nonexistence)—and the inordinate amount of time required to make any headway at all. In short, such practice constitutes the dirty work, the "crap," the "junk" that no one else will handle, but which the younger lawyer will often have to take if he wants any business at all.

The indications are that income in the early years barely reaches a subsistence level. One lawyer reported an average of $2,500 his first two years out of law school; several said that they averaged less than $3,000 over the first four or five years, and many earned less than $100 a month the first six or eight months in practice. In many instances, of course, these lawyers had additional sources of income, but the notion of starving through the first few years is probably not far from the tuth.

The kinds of work most young lawyers get when they first start out, the sources of their business, and the problems they have in making ends meet is well illustrated by the case of a young respondent just going into his second year of practice. Let us call him Ronald.

Ronald was admitted to practice in 1956 and over a period of the next eighteen months he had three jobs working for other lawyers. Before coming to his present position he had an informal arrangement with some friends that he hoped would lead to a partnership, but one of them backed down because he didn't want to share some of his "lucrative matters."

At present Ronald is in a space-for-service arrangement in a downtown office with two other lawyers, one of whom is rarely in the office. About a fifth of his time is devoted to doing legwork for the active lawyer in the office and another six or seven hours a week are given to a lawyer outside the office who pays him on an hourly basis. The rest of his time is his own to build up his own practice.

*Interviewer:* What is the nature of your practice?

*Respondent:* [Looking through his clients' file folders piled on top of his desk and in the drawers] I do all the subrogation work for an insurance company. I have 300 files in the drawer. There's supposed to be $3,000 worth of claims there; a third is mine, but most are uncollectable. It's a lot of work for the income involved.

*Interviewer:* How did you get these cases?

*Respondent:* My brother-in-law's brother knows an attorney who has a half interest in the insurance company. [Continuing through his files:]

Hardware store—collections.

A real estate deal for my milkman.

A will and trust matter for my sister-in-law's neighbor's mother.

My sister-in-law's aunt—personal injury.

This is for my sister-in-law's mother. I will do some estate planning—draw up a will and have some shares of stock transferred.

A case for —— [lawyer for whom he works in the office]. The owner of a trailer claims a faulty installation, a suit for damages.

—— [other lawyer in the office] was in an auto accident.

My brother-in-law was in an auto accident.

I bought a washer and dryer at an appliance store. I asked them if they had any work for me. They gave me a few matters. I hope to get them for a retainer client. If only I had a few small retainers then I'd be okay. Otherwise, it's very sporadic.

Personal injury for my wife's aunt—auto accident.

Personal injury for a friend.

Personal injury for a friend—adulterated food.

Here's my star client—I've thrown her out a hundred times. I'm handling a bunch of things for her. She's not satisfied with a tuck-pointing job in one of her buildings; I called him up and got him to agree to a compromise. Personal property tax for a shoe store she owns. Default judgment against a shoe store; I'll have that vacated. Her son and daughter-in-law got sick from a bad pizza. A precinct captain broke a window in her building; I know him and he'll fix it. I haven't got any fees from her yet. They'll start coming in soon, though.

An immigration matter—I referred it to another attorney and I'm splitting a fee on it.

That's the extent of my practice now.

In his first year out of law school Ronald earned $3,000 from the practice of law. In addition, he made a little over $1,000 as a telephone solicitor for a storm window concern. The first month of the second year he made $50, and in the second, $400. He has a wife and two children, and is having difficulty paying his bills.

It's really touch and go. I don't know whether I'll make it. I may have to give up the practice. . . . I could make a lot more doing something else. I was offered $10,000 at the lumber yard, and I had a $7,500 offer from the Illinois Commerce Commission.

*Interviewer:* Why haven't you taken either of them?

*Respondent:* I don't know. I ask myself that. That's what we talk about—my friends and I—three of my cronies and I—we have coffee every morning and talk about our practice and our problems. If you're a salesman, it doesn't sound so good. It's a matter of pride or ego. I like the law, but it's not a burning thing in my life—I *must* be a lawyer. If I quit now I'd be admitting defeat. I'd be ashamed. . . . It's a nice profession, nice clean work, a respected profession. If I could get some income it would be a good life. You can get away when you want to play golf, and you're your own boss, that appeals to me. And if people ask you what you're doing it's nice to tell them I'm a lawyer, and not a clerk in a store. And my dad gets satisfaction from the fact that I'm a lawyer.

One cannot fully understand the nature of individual practice without first recognizing where and how the individual practitioner fits into the wider structure of the metropolitan bar.

Although half the lawyers in Chicago, as in practically all the other cities of the United States, are individual practitioners, they constitute something like a lower class of the metropolitan bar. The elite of the metropolitan bar is composed of lawyers in the larger firms. These firms have a virtual monopoly of the largest, most lucrative clients—the large corporations whose legal needs they are geared to serve—and of the best qualified lawyers. In hiring lawyers they aspire to the ideal of the giant Wall Street firms of selecting only the top graduates of Harvard, Yale, and Columbia law schools and of bringing them into the firm as soon after they graduate as possible. In Chicago, New York, Boston, Philadelphia, Cleveland, San Francisco, and Los Angeles, for example, at least one out of four lawyers in firms with over 25 lawyers is a Harvard, Yale, or Columbia Law School graduate (principally Harvard), and almost all the others are graduates of the top local university law schools.

The practice of most metropolitan individual practitioners is consequently confined to those residual matters (and clients) that the large firms have not pre-empted: (1) matters not large enough or remunerative enough for the large firms to handle—most general work for small to medium-sized businesses and corporations, the smaller real estate transactions (for individuals or small businesses), and estate matters for middle-income families; (2) the undesirable cases, the dirty work, those areas of practice that have associated with them an aura of influencing and fixing and that involve arrangements with clients and others that are felt by the large firms to be professionally damaging. The latter category includes local tax, municipal, personal injury, divorce, and criminal matters.

Individual practitioners come off second best not only with respect to type of practice but also in terms of quality of training and academic achievement. In Chicago, as we have seen, the majority of individual practitioners have had less than two years of undergraduate training, and two out of three are graduates of night law schools. This pattern seems to prevail in other large cities as well. In New York, Boston, Philadelphia, Cleveland, San Francisco, and Los Angeles 40 to 70 per cent of the individual practitioners are night law school graduates—compared with less than 15 per cent of the lawyers in firms of over 25 lawyers in these same cities.

The rigidity of the class structure of the metropolitan bar is evidenced by the fact that those who start out as individual practitioners rarely become associates or partners in the larger firms. Moreover, most lawyers who are at present individual practitioners entered the profession as such (or as employees of such lawyers) and have remained at that level of practice.

Between the big firm elite and the mass of individual practitioners is a stratum composed of lawyers in small to medium-sized firms. While it is difficult to distinguish the majority of these lawyers from individual practitioners in terms of social background, training, and type of practice, it is likely that the middle-sized firms, at any rate, may constitute something like a middle class of the metropolitan bar.

\*    \*    \*    \*

# WORK
# OF THE WALL STREET
# LAWYER

*Erwin O. Smigel*

Few people know exactly what lawyers do, despite the fact that law is among the professions about which the public has most knowledge. Carlin, studying individual practitioners in Chicago, provides some detailed information about their activities. These, he observed, consisted of the following, roughly in the order of the amounts of time devoted to them: (1) conferring with clients, (2) doing office paper work, (3) doing court work, (4) negotiating, (5) conferring with lawyers, (6) reading legal matter, and (7) doing legal research.

On the surface, at least, the lawyer in the large firm is involved in similar tasks, but despite this the solo practitioner's activities are radically different from that of the lawyers in the law firms. This must be so if only because, in the case of the large law office, the nature of clients and their problems requires (because of their complexity, volume, and stakes) a system of specialization and teamwork. Perhaps the only accurate way to determine the work of the lawyer is through the use of "time and motion" studies. No such method was employed in this investigation. Instead, most lawyers were asked to list what they had done the day before they were interviewed. In answer to this question, which was designed, incidentally, to help us understand the organization of the firm and not primarily to

Reprinted with permission of the author and of The Free Press from *The Wall Street Lawyer* by Erwin Smigel, pp. 141–160. Copyright © 1964 by The Free Press of Glencoe, a division of The Macmillan Company. Footnotes have been omitted.

obtain detailed information about the types of work performed, most lawyers reported their duties as they had listed them in the diaries they are required to keep. Additional information was collected through further questions, by observation, and by analysis of several histories of large law firms. While these techniques give us an over-all picture of the kinds of work involved in a large law office and which of the various types of lawyers within them perform these tasks, they do not provide a great deal of specific detail. For example, what does a man mean when he says, "I worked on a security issue?" Actually a great deal of activity is hidden behind such a seemingly simple statement.

Even physically obtaining a deceased person's will offers complications. Where, for example, does the lawyer get the will—from a vault, from the client, from a bank safe deposit box? If it is in a safe deposit box, the attorney may have to prepare a petition to have the box opened. He has to secure appointments with the safe deposit company and representatives of the tax department. He may have to prepare an estimate of the contents of the box to be checked against the actual contents. He has to obtain a certified copy of the order for the safe deposit company's file. All these steps are, however, relatively minor when compared with the procedure involved in applying for probate of the will. In the latter instance, the lawyer may have to attend to many of the following details: petition for probate of the will, executor's oath and designation, trustee's oath and designation, citations, supplemental citations, waivers of citation, personal service of citations before first publication, proofs of service of citation, adjournment of calendar, depositions of subscribing witnesses, application to dispense the testimony of absent witnesses, giving notice of probate, filings in court, affidavits as to person in military service, decree, obtaining letters testamentary, obtaining short form certificates as to the issuance of such letters, obtaining certified copies of the will.

There is more to the procedure, often with a great many other duties listed under each of the main tasks involved. The will, for example, may have to be recorded in other jurisdictions. Estate assets have to be collected which may call for applications for waivers by taxing authorities on bank accounts, stocks, bonds, etc. There are special proceedings to discover property withheld. A petition for discovery may be needed and this petition also calls for numerous legal steps. Counsel has to take care of claims against the estate. The serious business of income tax returns, local and federal, as well as the estate tax has to be attended to. Again each of these pursuits may entail a variety of additional procedures and a variety of additional legal techniques.

It is not important for our immediate purpose to know the meaning of the legal terms used above. All that is intended here is to point out the difficulty of arriving at an exact picture of the attorney's job. Broad outlines of the kind of law a man practices in the large law firm as he progresses from legal fledgling to senior partner are available, however, from the respondents' own comments.

## TRANSITION FROM LAW SCHOOL TO LAW OFFICE

The neophyte coming to the large law firms quickly learns that what he knows is not the "living law," but an academic version of it. His first job is to find out what the law "really" is and how to practice it. He discovers that he must not only do research, write memoranda and briefs, give advice, learn the "ins and outs" of the courts, but also confer with partners, learn to dictate, gain familiarity with the filing system, and compete with older women stenographers for small power symbols.

### The Beginning Associate

The newcomer does have areas of skill—he can do legal research and does know something about writing briefs. This is especially true of the law review man. The managing partners know this and invariably assign that kind of task to the incoming lawyer.

Walter R. Mansfield, a member of Donavan Leisure Newton & Irvine, when addressing a group of Harvard Law School seniors who were in New York looking for positions, described what they could expect if they worked for his firm:

We have a managing partner whose job it is to keep track of the work load of the entire staff. All requests go to him, frequently in hysterical tones from those with deadlines to meet. The new young lawyer is assigned by him to work with the lawyer requesting help, who is supposed to give a rough estimate of the time the job will take. Perhaps it's a very short job like researching a statute, drafting a subpoena, or the like. Or it may be much longer, such as getting thoroughly familiar with the pleadings and evidence in the case being prepared for trial. This may involve reviewing documents, preparing questionnaires to be used on depositions, researching evidence questions expected to be raised at trial, assisting in writing memoranda of law, and doing the many other jobs needed before trial. In this case the young lawyer will work steadily with the partner in charge, attending hearings and helping out wherever possible. If the case becomes temporarily dormant, he will handle other jobs, usually with other partners, in the meantime. It is the rare instance where one case will absorb all his time for months on end. Most associates have several matters on their lists.

The beginning associates' work involves a wide variety of experience, both in the law and in terms of new human contacts. While they do not often meet the principal clients alone (though they may deal with the client's subordinates on an equal basis), they are occasionally taken by partners to conferences with the clients. Their new social interaction calls on them to develop the ability to get along with the partners, with fellow associates, and with the stenographic staff; later on they may develop techniques for securing and retaining clients.

One associate analyzed his first year and a quarter in a large firm. His experience offers a more comprehensive picture of what the young lawyer does at the beginning of his legal career:

I have been with this office $15\frac{1}{4}$ months. I have been assigned to work under ten partners and about seven associates. My main activities have been as follows:

1. United States v. —— ($46\frac{1}{2}$ working days)

This was a Sherman Act antitrust case. My work consisted of reading and preparing summaries of documents from our client's files, preparing an extensive memorandum of law relating to defenses under the Sherman Act, and preparing a draft of a consent decree.

2. —— (40 working days)

This was a Clayton Act, Section 7 case. My work consisted chiefly of researching and preparing a brief in opposition to defendant's action to enjoin plaintiff's purchase of defendant's stock, preparing a memorandum dealing with the right of a board of directors to dismiss its officers, and researching and preparing a brief in opposition to defendant's motion to hold plaintiff in contempt for alleged violation of a court order.

I also researched various problems in connection with plaintiff's application to the Interstate Commerce Commission for approval of a merger between plaintiff and defendant.

3. —— ($35\frac{1}{2}$ working days)

We are general counsel for these two associations. My work has consisted of reading current correspondence and documents of the association, and preparing a memorandum of manufacturers' products liability and product liability insurance which was printed in booklet form and distributed among the members to assist them in connection with prospective sales of their products to private atomic power plants.

4. ——— (22 working days)

My work consisted of preparing a memorandum on the Government's right to enforce or modify a 1921 Sherman Act consent decree.

5. ——— (18 working days)

We represented plaintiff in an action to recover a commission for the sale of real estate. My work consisted of preparing the evidence for the case and assisting the partner trying the case in court.

6. ABA Moot Court case (17 working days)

My work consisted of researching the law of corporate opportunity and assisting in preparing a brief in connection with a moot court case argued by a partner at the ABA meeting.

7. Merger (13 working days)

My work consisted of preparing a memorandum on Virginia law on appraisal of stock and research on various other matters related to the merger of Virginia corporations.

8. ——— (9 working days)

My work consisted of preparing one memorandum, interpreting a sales contract and analyzing the New Jersey law of fixtures, and another memorandum dealing with the definition of a public utility under New Jersey law.

9. ——— (9 working days)

We were counsel to plaintiff in a trade mark infringement action. I did research in the law of trade marks and assisted in the preparation of plaintiff's brief.

10. ——— (10 working days)

Researched and prepared an opinion letter on the enforceability of a management contract entered into by this Connecticut corporation.

11. ——— v. United States (10 working days)

Prepared various memorandums of law in connection with plaintiff's action against the United States for breach of contract.

12. Diamond Distributors (7 working days)

Research on the law of bankruptcy in connection with our client's claim against an insolvent company.

13. ——— (7 working days)

Researched and wrote opinion letters on validity of our client's fair trade agreements.

14. ——— (6½ working days)

Prepared a memorandum on the applicability of Foreign Agents' Registration Act to our client and this office in connection with our efforts to restore assets seized by the Alien Property Custodian.

15. ——— (6 working days)

Prepared one memorandum on the cost defense under the Robinson Patman Act and another memorandum advising our client on types of contract clauses limiting liability.

16. —— (5 working days)

Researched our client's files in connection with a Sherman Act antitrust charge made against them in a patent infringement action.

In addition to these projects, I have prepared short memoranda of law on various points of law including the law of evidence, the Interstate Commerce Commission's power to regulate passenger railway traffic, contract law, New York divorce law, etc.

I have also spent a total of 4 or 5 days answering calendar calls, making brief motions in court, delivering documents for registration with the SEC, etc.

## What Young Associates Say They Do

Answers to the questions concerning the legal duties of young associates were subjected to a rough content analysis. The results indicate that most of their work consists in researching various fields of the law, writing preliminary briefs, and conferring with partners about what they have discovered. In this process they learn both the law and how to get along. The firms, by design, see to it that they have contact with many aspects of the law . . . and with a great many partners.

Analyzing the information gathered in this study, I was able to prepare a rough list of the jobs done by associates who have been with their respective firms for as long as four years. This record is not complete and no attempt has been made to put it in order of importance or of time spent on each type of work. Despite these shortcomings, the list does add to the picture of the daily legal occupations of the young attorney. The record reveals that they do research, write and revise briefs, confer with partners, fellow associates, and clients, give advice, draft letters, revise corporate charters and bylaws, prepare trial memos, take depositions, work on new issues of securities, engage in general corporation work, banking matters, employee pension plans; they also work up exhibits and continually use the telephone.

\*     \*     \*     \*

## MIDDLE RANGE ASSOCIATES

The middle range associates, those who have been with the firm four to eight years and who follow the average career pattern, take on more and more responsibility and become more and more specialized. One of these associates discusses this development:

I find myself getting more responsibility; I negotiated a contract for sale of residential property, did some drafting on a long-term lease for a block of land in New York, and answered telephone calls on rent law. When I first came into the department I was only allowed to do assignments of mortgages and simple forms of sales situations.

It is difficult to present a true picture of what middle associates do. For while there is overlapping of the kinds of work in which each category of associate is engaged, there is more overlapping for middle associates. This group of men are sometimes treated like novices and at other times treated like experts. Much of this seemingly schizophrenic behavior depends upon the needs of the office. Occasionally it is based on the actual expertise and superior competence of an individual associate.

## SENIOR ASSOCIATES

For most lawyers length of service means greater client contact and with it more independence and responsibility, in addition to some responsibility for supervision of younger associates who are now doing the leg work. By the time a man has been with a law firm for approximately eight years he is engaged in almost the same kind of work as a younger partner, especially if the firm regards him as partnership material. The big difference in what they are allowed to do, besides that of degree, is that the senior associate is not allowed to sign opinion letters and does not attend firm meetings and therefore has less influence than junior partners upon firm policy. Of equal importance is his inability, usually, to command the same status response from his colleagues or from the firm's clients. One senior associate reports his activities in the following fashion:

My day consists and has been progressively consisting more and more of client contact, conferences with clients, assigning research to younger members, reviewing and evaluating their work, corresponding with clients, and advising partners other than tax partners on tax matters. People in the rest of the firm call me or the tax partners, who then call me.

Senior associates listed, as representative of the kind of work in which they were engaged, corporation acquisition, conferring and advising clients, litigation, drafting and briefs and conferring with partners and younger associates.

## PERMANENT ASSOCIATES

The job of the permanent associates has previously been described. Here I only list the type of work in which they say they are engaged. Their work histories indicate that they interview witnesses, draft briefs, draft mortgages, do blue sky work, dictate leases, prepare for closings, work on general banking matters and take care of a great number of odds and ends.

Just before a man is made a partner or is eliminated from the firm, his work noticeably broadens. He now has more contact with clients and their demands call for increased general knowledge. At the same time senior partners, checking for the last time the credentials for partnership of these associates, start assigning them a variety of legal tasks. Suddenly the associate finds himself working again for a number of partners, although on matters of a different and higher level than when he was the new recruit in the legal pool.

## JUNIOR PARTNERS

The young partner goes to the firm meetings and begins to see something more of the over-all picture. He may be given an associate or two to help him with his work. He sees much more of the clients and receives more responsibility from the older partners. The junior partner, however, still remains fairly specialized. A young partner from one large law firm describes one of his days:

I came in and got rid of my correspondence and prepared for a meeting about a hearing. I met with an outside lawyer. We came back to my office and met with another lawyer and spent an hour and a half with him. We then reported to our respective clients and then drafted an answer between us. I'm sitting as a referee and did some preparation for that. I had a hearing which lasted two hours—I had been chosen from a panel. I came back and worked on a letter for the Federal Trade Commission and discussed it with the client who came to the office. Then I went out to supper and worked for three hours last night preparing a deposition.

The diary of a second junior partner from another firm indicates that he was involved in a greater variety of work. This is partially explained by the nature of the business of the firm he is connected with, which has smaller accounts and more clients than the typical Wall Street firm. His diary lists the following items:

1. Phone call—advised client.
2. Called another executive in the same company as (1) about figures which are relevant in the case.
3. A number of calls with another client about a different matter.
4. Reviewed a long memorandum on a tax matter before discussing it with the client.
5. Had a conference on the figures needed in items (1) and (2). It was held in our offices.
6. Analyzed a very complicated plan on reorganization and assigned my two associates to different matters relating to this reorganization.
7. Had a long conference with tax people.
8. A number of phone calls. One about a client tenant who was going bankrupt.
9. Wrote a letter of recommendation.

Young partners are involved more directly with clients and have greater responsibility than associates. Their diaries revealed a larger spread of activities: advising both clients and colleagues, supervising associates, general counsel work, letters and telephone calls, preparation for a trial, analysis of an estate problem, meetings with outside lawyers, preparation for a meeting, contact with the Federal Trade Commission, preparation of a deposition, meeting with an accountant, preparation of questions for arbitration, writing an article.

## MIDDLE PARTNERS

It is difficult to ascribe a separate set of duties to middle partners. Their work, if they are successful, continues to involve greater client contact, including giving a great deal more business advice and increased supervising and responsibility. The following answers offered by two middle partners to the question "What did you do yesterday?" help fill in the picture:

I spent a good deal of time on a memo regarding estate tax apportionment between a large trust and the beneficiaries under a very wealthy lady's will.

The tax amounted to eight or ten million dollars and we are trying to find out how the tax can be reduced.

I spent a long time on the phone with a guy who wants his deceased brother's estate. His father has it now and the father thinks the brother really wanted his brother to have it. I then spent considerable time in preparation for an examination before a trial. A husband, when he died, turned over the management of his business to his second wife. Her step children don't like the way she is managing the business.

I still have a couple of corporate clients that I continue to take care of. I had them before I switched to the tax department. I was also involved in some correspondence concerned with getting Italian securities accepted for trading in this country.

I worked 9 and ¾ hours yesterday. I worked through lunch but that wasn't so bad because we had a business lunch going on at the same time. Only had nine items, which is a fairly small number. I often have as many as fifteen to twenty matters.

I wrote a letter to a client on a new case, on something we had given him an opinion on and on which the Supreme Court had ruled in what to a layman would appear to be similar case and told him his was different. I was trying to allay any fears he might have. Had an extensive telephone conference on the proposed sale of a book to one of our clients.

Received a call from a partner in another law firm. His tax partner was out of town. We have a great deal of stuff which is just a matter of professional courtesy. On another matter I dictated a memo to the files. On still another matter I put the final touches on a petition in a case we lost.

## SENIOR PARTNER

When a man becomes a senior partner he is no longer the narrow specialist, the researcher, the brief writer, but is usually the broad advisor and administrator. As one upward-looking junior partner remarked: "The older partners are the general practitioners and so they need younger people to do the research. Now it is true that we have certain people who do trial work. Some who do tax work. The other areas of business law are done by the other partners." Except then, for the partners who were in the tax department or estates and trusts or other service divisions of a firm, the senior partners become general practitioners of business law. This does not mean that the partners who retain their specialization do not broaden also. They do, but in a different way. They, too, depend more and more on the younger specialist but tend to answer the larger questions in their field themselves. The other senior partners become the managers and coordinate the work of various specialists in their firms—"He must," in Proskauer's words, "direct a legal orchestra." Their job is to put the different segments of a matter together, in a meaningful order, so that they can advise the client. The client expects the senior partners to have the answers. As one partner said, "You can't always say you don't know." He advises the client not only on legal matters but also on business matters. For example, the late Boykin C. Wright, who was then the senior partner in the firm of Shearman & Sterling & Wright, was also a director and counsel for a number of corporations including Corning Glass Works, Georgia-Pacific Plywood, Investors Management, First Railroad and Banking Firm of Georgia, and the Home Insurance Company.

The senior partner's advice-giving role increases as he gets older. Not only does he counsel clients but he advises younger attorneys. He does this because it is expected and is part of the traditional role of the older lawyer. In his position as senior partner he must make recommendations to the younger members of his staff, for in some ways he has final responsibility for the work the firm turns out. In addition to the counseling tasks mentioned above, the senior partner is often called upon by the government, the bar association, and various private philanthropic associations for recommendations. Managing and advice-giving, then, are the main roles of the senior partners.

What we have seen is that legal practice in large law offices means different things for people at different stages of development and for lawyers in various departments. The practice of the law changes for the attorney as he rises in the firm. In terms of scope of work, at least, it can be likened to an hourglass. The practice of the beginning lawyer is broad because he works on a great many matters in a wide variety of fields. If he stays with the firm he becomes more and more specialized, although he now has increasing opportunity to see more of the large picture. If he is made a partner, he begins to broaden again. This time the broadening does not involve research on a number of problems, but advising about these problems. Both advising and responsibility increase as the lawyer grows into a senior partnership. When he arrives at that position he becomes the final interpreter of the law for the firm, its over-all manager, and advisor to colleagues, clients and government, as well as to civic organizations.

\*     \*     \*     \*

# CAREERS OF LAWYERS,
# LAW PRACTICE
# AND LEGAL INSTITUTIONS*

*Jack Ladinsky*

[Headnote omitted.]

The analysis of law as an occupation has traditionally been confined to either sociologists interested in the professions[1] or educators concerned with vocational guidance.[2] This tradition continues today in spite of the pioneering efforts of Karl Llewellyn, who encouraged studies of what lawyers do to increase our understanding of what law is. Llewellyn defined law as the behavior of lawyers and officials involved in

* *Revision of a paper read at the annual meeting of the Midwest Sociological Society, April, 1962. This paper is part of the Labor and Leisure study directed by Harold L. Wilensky of the University of Michigan, a project supported mainly by grants from the National Institute of Mental Health (M-2209), 1958-61. For description and theoretical background of the larger study see Harold L. Wilensky, "Work, Careers, and Social Integration,"* International Social Science Journal, *12 (Fall, 1960), pp. 543-60. For a detailed presentation of the lawyer data used here see the author's unpublished Ph.D. thesis, "Career Development Among Lawyers: A Study of Social Factors in the Allocation of Professional Labor" (University of Michigan, 1962). I am indebted to H. M. Blalock for methodological advice and to Harold L. Wilensky and Morris Janowitz for critical readings of an early draft.*

[1] *See, e.g.,* Everett C. Hughes, Men and Their Work, *Glencoe, Ill.: The Free Press, 1958.*
[2] *See, e.g.,* Donald A. Super, The Psychology of Careers, *New York: Harper & Bros., 1957.*

Reprinted by permission of the author and of the American Sociological Association from 28 *American Sociological Review* (1963), 47–54.

the process of dispute settlement—a definition congenial to sociological perspectives.[3]

Data on who does what and where—analysis of the men who practice law and the settings in which they practice—can illuminate the workings of legal institutions. This paper brings together data on the early socialization milieux of lawyers and the social agencies through which they move in adult life with speculations about how these social contexts affect the legal system. It is an analysis of processes and effects of self-selection and recruitment in the allocation of the lawyer labor supply.

## SOLO AND FIRM WORK SETTINGS

Although the legal profession is composed of a variety of segments,[4] solo (individual) and firm lawyers are the hard core of the profession; they are independent (private) practitioners, i.e., they are not employed within organizations whose ultimate goals are other than the practice of law. Independent practitioners today remain a large majority of all lawyers (about 80 per cent). Among these, solo lawyers are still a majority in the legal profession (about two-thirds of all lawyers).[5] Firm lawyers, as well as solos, think of themselves as free professionals. They compare themselves invidiously with "kept counsel"—salaried lawyers or "house counsel" in industry and elsewhere.[6] Although the large firm associate is

---

[3] *Karl N. Llewellyn*, The Bramble Bush, *New York: Oceana Publications, 1951, p. 12. (In the foreword to the second edition Llewellyn more fully develops this definition to include social control and guidance.) Cf. David Riesman's comment, "Lawyers and how they act interests me . . . . Lawyers bend the system they enter and are bent by it; some stay and others leave, carrying their bent with them. Hopefully, one can begin to understand the law through the men, as well as vice versa." "Law and Sociology: Recruitment, Training and Colleagueship,"* Stanford Law Review, 9 (*July, 1957*), pp. 669–70.

[4] *For descriptions of major segments see A. A. Berle, "Modern Legal Profession," in E. R. A. Seligman (ed.),* Encyclopedia of the Social Sciences, *New York: The Macmillan Co., 1938, Vol. 9, pp. 340–45; and Jerome E. Carlin, "The Lawyer as Individual Practitioner," unpublished Ph.D. thesis (University of Chicago, 1959), Ch. 2.*

[5] *Albert P. Blaustein and Charles O. Porter,* The American Lawyer, *Chicago: University of Chicago Press, 1954, p. 8.*

[6] *Solos also see themselves as more independent than firm men and derisively refer to large firms as "law factories." For studies of house counsel see ibid., pp. 46–51, and Harold L. Wilensky,* Intellectuals in Labor Unions, *Glencoe, Ill.: The Free Press, 1956, Chs. 5 and 11.*

in salaried law practice, he is responsible to other lawyers, and is recruited and molded for advancement to partnership.[7] As a partner he is a participating member of the firm; as an associate he is an apprentice for that position. Neither government lawyers nor house counsel are in comparable positions. In short, individual and firm practitioners are the terminal cases among the free professionals who dominate today's metropolitan legal world. Together they comprise the solid center of the urban bar.

## THE DATA

The analysis is based on a sample of 207 Detroit area lawyers, of which 100 are solo and 107 are medium-to-large firm practitioners, who were interviewed between March and July, 1960.[8] "Solo" includes (1) individual practitioners, (2) "associated" lawyers—those who share office space and secretarial help but maintain their own practices, and (3) two-man family partnerships. No solos employing other lawyers were included in the sample. "Firm" lawyers were selected from among the lawyer members of the 19 law firms in Detroit with ten or more partners and associates. (The largest firm had thirty lawyer members.) Respondents were selected randomly from a consolidated list of the universe derived from the 1959 *Michigan State Bar Roster* and the 1960 *Martindale-Hubbell Law Directory*.

To sift out the specific effects of occupational group and work establishment on leisure style, the design of the larger study applied several controls by selection: Age: 30–55. Race: white. Sex: male. Marital status: married now or in the past. Education: law degree. Family income: more than $8,000 in one of the past five years, and 50 per cent or more of their income from law in the previous year. Initial contact was made by telephone to screen in the eligibles. All respondents meeting selection criteria were interviewed in person. The completion rate was 90 per cent.[9]

---

[7] *See Erwin O. Smigel, "The Impact of Recruitment on the Organization of the Large Law Firm," American Sociological Review, 25 (February, 1960), pp. 56–66.*

[8] *All respondents were in the Detroit metropolitan area as defined by the Detroit Area Study of the University of Michigan. See A Social Profile of Detroit, 1956, Ann Arbor, Michigan: Detroit Area Study, 1957, p. 5.*

[9] *Selection of respondents was stopped just short of the 200-mark to ascertain the religious origin distribution of the sample. Sampling was then continued, as*

# FINDINGS

*Social origins.* Table 1 supports the conclusion that *solo lawyers are "minority lawyers"—they come more often than firm lawyers from working-class and entrepreneurial families of minority religious and ethnic status.* (1) While both solo and firm lawyers come predominantly from homes where fathers held non-manual occupations (70 and 94 per cent, respectively), some 30 per cent of solo and only seven per cent of firm lawyers had manually employed fathers. (2) Fifty-nine per cent of the

TABLE 1. SOCIAL ORIGINS OF SOLO AND FIRM LAWYERS.*

|  | Solo | Firm |
|---|---|---|
| Father's occupation | | |
| Manual | 30.0% | 6.5% |
| Non-manual | 70.0 | 93.5 |
| N | (100) | (107) |
| Entrepreneurial status | | |
| Entrepreneurial | 71.9% | 40.2% |
| Non-entrepreneurial | 28.1 | 59.8 |
| N | (96) | (107) |
| Generation American (father's side) | | |
| First and second | 59.0% | 9.6% |
| Third and over | 41.0 | 90.4 |
| N | (100) | (104) |
| Religious origin (mother's preference) | | |
| Protestant | 31.0% | 68.9% |
| Catholic, Greek Orthodox | 34.0 | 25.5 |
| Jewish | 35.0 | 5.7 |
| N | (100) | (106) |
| Ethnic origin (father's side) | | |
| Northwest Europe | 32.0% | 74.5% |
| Central Europe | 18.0 | 19.8 |
| East and South Europe | 50.0 | 5.7 |
| N | (100) | (106) |

* In this and the following tables N's vary slightly because of "not ascertains" on the comparison variables.

*before, with religion added as a selection criterion. Twelve "oversample" cases were completed. The bias introduced by this procedure does not materially affect the findings.*

solo and only 10 per cent of the firm lawyers are themselves first or second generation Americans. (3) Sixty-nine per cent of all firm lawyers come from Protestant homes, while exactly the same proportion of solos come from Catholic and Jewish homes. While Protestants, as expected, predominate among firm lawyers, they are a distinct minority among the solo lawyers (31 per cent). (4) Solo lawyers come from the Slavic and Mediterranean countries (East and South Europe, 50 per cent); firm lawyers are more often of Northwest European origin (75 per cent).

(5) In the second part of Table 1, the sample is classified by "entrepreneurial" or "non-entrepreneurial" family of origin—an indicator of that portion of early socialization most relevant to integration in the economic order. The following criteria were used to delineate a pure entrepreneurial category: (a) self-other employment, (b) number of levels of authority in work place, and (c) size of work place. Seventy-two per cent of the solo lawyers but only 40 per cent of the firm lawyers come from entrepreneurial families.[10]

*Education.* Table 2 shows that *solo lawyers have quantitatively less and qualitatively inferior educations when compared to firm lawyers.* (1) Eighty-seven per cent of firm lawyers achieved a four year bachelor's degree (B.A., B.S., etc.); only 43 per cent of solos did. (2) About nine in ten firm lawyers attended law school on a full-time basis compared with about four in ten of the solos. The majority of the solos, 57 per cent, took all or part of their legal training on a part-time basis. This means that solo lawyers are more often trained in local Catholic and proprietary law colleges, because most full-time state and national private schools offer neither night classes nor part-time programs. This is reflected in the fact that (3) 73 per cent of firm lawyers and 14 per cent of solos attended top national law schools (Chicago, Columbia, Harvard, Michigan, and Yale).

---

[10] *Generally the entrepreneurial cases were self-employed with fewer than ten employees and two levels of authority. Borderline cases were coded with priority given first to self-other employment, then to levels of authority and size of work place. Cf. Daniel R. Miller and Guy E. Swanson,* The Changing American Parent, *New York: John Wiley & Sons, 1958, Chs. 2 and 3, which labels these "integration settings" as "entrepreneurial" and "welfare-bureaucratic," but includes as entrepreneurial such indicators as foreign and rural origin as well as income from profits, fees, or commissions. For analysis of variations in the organization of work encompassed by "bureaucratic," see Harold L. Wilensky, "Notes on the Relation of Industrial Sociology to General Sociology," unpublished paper presented at the American Sociological Association meetings, Chicago, September 3, 1959.*

TABLE 2. EDUCATION OF SOLO AND FIRM LAWYERS.

|  | Solo | Firm |
|---|---|---|
| Undergraduate education |  |  |
|   Has no bachelor's degree | 57.0% | 13.1% |
|   Has bachelor's degree | 43.0 | 86.9 |
|   N | (100) | (107) |
| Part-time legal education |  |  |
|   Some or all law |  |  |
|     training part-time | 57.0% | 7.5% |
|   No part-time training | 43.0 | 92.5 |
|   N | (100) | (101) |
| Quality of law school |  |  |
|   "National" schools | 14.0% | 72.9% |
|   State and local schools | 50.0 | 25.2 |
|   Proprietary school | 36.0 | 1.9 |
|   N | (100) | (107) |
| Law school affiliation |  |  |
|   Private non-Catholic | 3.0% | 17.8% |
|   State university | 39.0 | 69.2 |
|   Catholic | 22.0 | 11.2 |
|   Proprietary | 36.0 | 1.9 |
|   N | (100) | (107) |

The greatest number of solos, 50 per cent, received their legal educations in state universities (other than Michigan) and Catholic law schools (University of Detroit, Duquesne, etc.). More than a third of solo and only two per cent of firm men attended proprietary law colleges (in almost every instance the Detroit College of Law). (4) When law schools are broken down by affiliation it is seen that the firm men more often attend private non-Catholic institutions (18 per cent—primarily Chicago, Columbia, Harvard, and Yale) and state universities (69 per cent—primarily Michigan), whereas solos attend state (39 per cent—primarily Wayne University in Detroit), Catholic (22 per cent), and proprietary (36 per cent) law schools.

*Work history.* Table 3 reveals that *solo lawyers have been in the labor force longer than firm men and are more likely to have experienced marginal law work, upward mobility, and somewhat disorderly work histories.*

(1) Fifty-five per cent of solo and only 32 per cent of firm lawyers have been in the labor force 20 years or more. This result is in large part

the consequence of selector questions on income used to screen in only the stable lawyers. To achieve economic stability (i.e., to earn more than $8,000 in one of the last five years and also earn at least 50 per cent of his income from his law practice) a solo lawyer apparently has to be in the labor force longer.

(2) Solo lawyers show only a slight tendency to have more jobs than firm men. Twelve per cent of solos have had seven or more jobs, and only four per cent of firm men have had this number; 56 per cent of solos have had one to three jobs, but 64 per cent of firm men have had this number. Is this small difference simply due to the longer period solo lawyers have been in the labor force? When years in the labor force are held constant (not shown in the table), we find that only among those lawyers in the labor force under 20 years do solo men more often hold a larger number of jobs than firm men. Somewhere—around the 20 year mark—firm men must catch up. This would indicate that solo lawyers settle down late in their work-lives, whereas firm men settle early and only begin to move about later, perhaps when job status and income ceilings are reached.

(3) For most people early jobs are significant indicators of later success in the labor market.[11] For the would-be independent practitioner the first job is an important career contingency because it determines, among other things, entrée to the profession and access to clients. Solo and firm lawyers were classified by the jobs they held the year after passing the bar examinations: they were directly in law work or in marginal law—claims adjustor, title or trust examiner, credit manager, broker, etc.—and non-law work. The majority of both solo and firm lawyers held first jobs in law, but the proportion is far larger among firm lawyers (94 per cent) than among solos (72 per cent).

(4) Work-life mobility designates the path in the occupational prestige hierarchy along which a sequence of jobs carries a person—whether up, stable, fluctuating, or down.[12] More solo lawyers than firm lawyers

---

[11] S. M. Lipset and F. T. Malm, "First Jobs and Career Patterns," American Journal of Economics and Sociology, 14 (April, 1955), pp. 247–61.

[12] In coding work-life mobility all jobs were classified by occupational prestige using the following categories: high non-manual, low non-manual, high manual, and low manual. From these categories work histories were coded for direction and distance—much up, some up, stable, some down, and much down—and pattern—stable, fluctuating, or highly fluctuating. Coding was highly reliable; almost all disagreements were within the major code categories used above. For concepts and coding procedures see Harold L. Wilensky, "Orderly Careers and Social Participation:

experienced up-mobility (37 per cent as opposed to 18 per cent), and more firm lawyers than solos were stable (74 per cent and 50 per cent respectively). Thirteen per cent of the solo and eight per cent of the firm lawyers experienced fluctuating work-mobility patterns, i.e., marked rank inconsistency from job to job.

(5) Another perspective for viewing work-life is orderliness of job pattern, or career. A career is a succession of functionally related jobs arranged in a hierarchy of prestige (within or between broad strata), through which persons move in an ordered (more or less predictable) sequence.[13] About 90 per cent of the lawyers enjoyed the orderliness of job patterns that defines careers. However, 17 per cent of solo lawyers and only three per cent of firm lawyers experienced much disorder in their work histories. This means that some 14 per cent more solo than firm lawyers had work histories in which more than a half of the work-life was spent in jobs that are not functionally related.

## INTERPRETATION

The above findings are consistent with other research conclusions.[14] But a major question remains: of the background factors correlated with the solo-firm distinction, which variables are explanatory? Although multivariate correlational analysis is commonly used to answer such questions, the danger of spurious correlation is inherent in this technique.[15] H. A.

*The Impact of Work History on Social Integration in the Middle Mass,*" American Sociological Review, 26 (*August, 1961*), *pp. 524–25.*

[13] *Wilensky, ibid., pp. 523. To be labeled "disorderly" the analysis demanded that more than half the work-life be spent in jobs that are not functionally related.*

[14] *Available studies indicate that the above results on Detroit lawyers do not seriously differ from those on lawyers in other metropolitan centers. Cf. Carlin,* op. cit., *and Dan C. Lortie, "Laymen to Lawmen: Law School, Careers, and Professional Socialization,"* Harvard Educational Review, 29 (*Fall, 1959*), *pp. 352–69, for a picture of Chicago's solo and firm lawyers; Smigel,* op. cit., *on New York's law firms; Arthur L. Wood, "Career Patterns in the Practice of Criminal Law," unpublished paper presented at the American Sociological Society meeting, Atlantic City, September, 1952, on criminal and civil lawyers in three large metropolitan centers (one in the Deep South and two on the East Coast) and two smaller cities (in New England and the Middle West).*

[15] *See, e.g., Patricia Kendall and Paul Lazarsfeld, "Problems of Survey Analysis," in R. K. Merton and P. Lazarsfeld (eds.),* Continuities in Social Research, *Glencoe, Ill.: The Free Press, 1950, pp. 133–96; Herbert Hyman,* Survey Design and Analysis,

TABLE 3. WORK HISTORIES OF SOLO AND FIRM LAWYERS.

| | Solo | Firm |
|---|---|---|
| Years in the labor force | | |
| Under twenty years | 45.0% | 68.2% |
| Twenty years and over | 55.0 | 31.8 |
| N | (100) | (107) |
| Number of jobs | | |
| One to three | 56.0% | 63.6% |
| Four to six | 32.0 | 32.7 |
| Seven and over | 12.0 | 3.7 |
| N | (100) | (107) |
| First job after bar examination | | |
| In law work | 72.0% | 94.4% |
| Marginal or non-law work | 28.0 | 5.6 |
| N | (100) | (107) |
| Work-life mobility | | |
| Up-mobility | 37.0% | 17.9% |
| Stable | 50.0 | 73.8 |
| Fluctuating and highly fluctuating | 13.0 | 8.4 |
| N | (100) | (107) |
| Orderliness of work history | | |
| Orderly* | 83.0% | 97.2% |
| Partial-orderly and disorderly | 17.0 | 2.8 |
| N | (100) | (107) |

* At least half the work-life in functionally related hierarchically ordered jobs.

Simon, however, has introduced a method for making causal inferences from correlational data that obviates the problem of spuriousness; and H. M. Blalock has codified Simon's procedure.[16]

Glencoe, Ill.: The Free Press, 1955, pp. 275–329; Stephan Nowak, "Some Problems of Causal Interpretation of Statistical Relationships," Philosophy of Science, 27 (January, 1960), pp. 23–38.

[16] Herbert A. Simon, "Spurious Correlation: A Causal Interpretation," Journal of the American Statistical Association, 49 (September, 1954), pp. 467–79, reprinted in Herbert A. Simon, Models of Man, New York: John Wiley & Sons, 1957, pp. 37–49; H. M. Blalock, "Correlational Analysis and Causal Inferences," American Anthropologist, 62 (August, 1960), 624–31; "Correlation and Causality: The Multivariate Case," Social Forces, 39 (March, 1961), pp. 246–51; "Evaluating the Relative Importance of Variables," American Sociological Review, 26 (December, 1961), pp. 866–74. The method involves fitting a causal model to a series of temporally-ordered variables like those dealt with above. After choosing a set of

To explore the causal relations between background characteristics of lawyers and type of law practice, the Simon-Blalock technique was applied. Four of the previously considered variables were selected for the causal analysis: religious origin, father's occupational stratum, father's entrepreneurial status, and quality of law school.[17] The selection of these variables is based on the manner in which the labor supply is distributed among occupational positions. Two major forces operate in this social allocation process: (1) *personal self-selection,* which motivates individuals toward certain work positions rather than others, and (2) *organizational recruitment,* which brings about the occupational placement of some and the rejection of others. Personal self-selection is the culmination of early experiences, knowledge, values, and skills cultivated in social groups, such as family, friendship group, church and school. Recruitment criteria are of two classes: universalistic criteria of age, experience, apprenticeship, education, license, etc., which are in varying degrees applied in almost all occupations; and particularistic criteria, such as race, religion, ethnicity and family ancestry, which handicap some would-be candidates while favoring others. Particularistic or ascriptive criteria in many instances may partly replace talent, education, and experience.[18] Many lawyers believe that over-representation of religious and ethnic minorities in solo practice

---

*variables and deriving a series of predicted relationships among correlation co-efficients, one of a number of alternative causal models can be singled out as providing the best fit. The technique yields results similar to those obtained using partial correlation, with the added advantage that spurious relations are eliminated by making blind partialling of all variables unnecessary. Interval scales, linear regression among paired variables, and large sample size are required. Theory and logic must guide the choice of variables and hypothetical relationships. The technique simply provides a means for systematically elucidating and appraising causal inferences.*

[17] *First job after bar examinations was eliminated as spuriously related to quality of law school and present law practice; generation American was eliminated as redundant—it behaved in essentially the same manner as religious origin with respect to the other variables. This latter discovery is consistent with factor analysis of the social characteristics of lawyers, where generation American loaded high with religious origin on the same factor. It would therefore be appropriate to refer to a "religious-ethnic" variable in Figure 1.*

[18] *Although the discussion here is couched in functional terminology it should be stressed that the functionalist's view of the profession is otherwise. Functionalism tends to project an image of professions as operating on universalistic rather than particularistic criteria. Functionalism thus stresses homogeneity and socialization of recruits to a common core of universal values. This view is inconsistent with a variety of research evidence, including the present paper. The ideas of Bucher and Strauss*

issues in large part from the selective recruiting procedures of businesses, industries, and law firms.

But what does the causal analysis reveal? One of the inferred "best fit" models appears in Figure 1, where the arrows represent direction of causality. The model corroborates the existence of direct and indirect causality from background characteristics to type of law practice. Father's occupational stratum has a direct and indirect bearing upon present work setting; the indirect influence is through quality of law school. Likewise religious origin acts both directly and indirectly upon present work setting. The indirect affect of religion comes through entrepreneurial status of the family, on the one hand, and quality of law school on the other. Religious origin and father's occupational stratum are not causally linked ($r_{12} = .030$); neither are father's occupational stratum and entrepreneurial family status ($r_{23} = .153$), nor entrepreneurial family status and quality of law school ($r_{34.1} = .007$).[19]

These findings are consistent with the personal self-selection and organizational recruitment processes discussed above.[20] Religion of mother and occupational stratum of father are independent background characteristics that affect the mature, stable lawyer's "choice" of work setting. Religion acts directly as a career contingency in the form of a tacit recruitment policy to keep Jews and Catholics out of firms. But religion's importance does not cease with discrimination. Religion also acts indirectly, through family entrepreneurial status, as an aspect of early socialization which shapes later choice of type of law practice. Thus, Jews and Catholics are not only passed over by law firms, but are often socialized in an entrepreneurial milieu that predisposes them toward individual law practice. Furthermore, interaction takes place between discrimination and socialization. The desire of minority lawyers for lone practice is in part the consequence of avoiding discriminatory situations. Anticipation of firm rejection comes easily to men with protracted experience in dodging the

---

that professions are "loose amalgamations of segments pursuing different objectives in different manners and more or less delicately held together . . ." seem far more accurate. See Rue Bucher and Anselm Strauss, "Professions in Process," American Journal of Sociology, 66 (January, 1961), pp. 325–34.

[19] The independence of these three variables is also consistent with factor analysis, where each item loaded .5 or higher on single and separate factors.

[20] This particular interpretation is plausible and strongly supported by the arrow sequences. The causal analysis, however, is inferential, and must be taken as tentative.

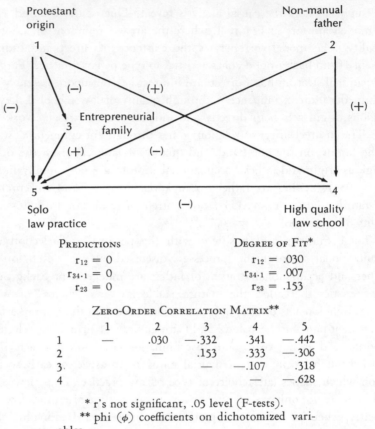

FIGURE 1. A Best Fitting Causal Model between Background and Present Law Practice.

Protestant origin

Non-manual father

Entrepreneurial family

Solo law practice

High quality law school

| PREDICTIONS | DEGREE OF FIT* |
|---|---|
| $r_{12} = 0$ | $r_{12} = .030$ |
| $r_{34 \cdot 1} = 0$ | $r_{34 \cdot 1} = .007$ |
| $r_{23} = 0$ | $r_{23} = .153$ |

ZERO-ORDER CORRELATION MATRIX**

| | 1 | 2 | 3 | 4 | 5 |
|---|---|---|---|---|---|
| 1 | — | .030 | —.332 | .341 | —.442 |
| 2 | | — | .153 | .333 | —.306 |
| 3 | | | — | —.107 | .318 |
| 4 | | | | — | —.628 |

\* r's not significant, .05 level (F-tests).
\*\* phi ($\phi$) coefficients on dichotomized variables.

rebuffs of discriminatory practices. "Being your own boss" provides personal security and self-protection.

Religion also directly influences education. Here it is likely to operate as a motivational mechanism determining, for example, self-selection of Catholics into the Catholic law schools, and hearsay discouragement of Catholics and Jews from attempting to enter the national schools.

What part does father's occupational stratum play? The absence of any links to religion and family entrepreneurial status suggests that occupational stratum of father is significant to lawyers primarily for economic reasons. In the pre-work period, father's occupational stratum would be important as a source of financial support for higher education, especially law school. Most manual fathers could not easily support full-time law school for their sons whereas most non-manual fathers could provide a law school education. After education father's occupational stratum can continue to assist the lawyer in economic ways. Non-manual fathers have business to bring to their lawyer sons, or to the firms which hire their sons knowing that fathers are potential reservoirs for legal trade. Indeed, it is common for large firms to recruit those young men who can bring in family legal business. But if fathers do not offer legal business to their sons then perhaps they can help them financially to establish a practice. It requires a reasonably large investment to set up a law practice; until he has built up a clientele, the lawyer's earnings are small.

A final form of assistance some fathers can offer their sons is contacts. Fathers with the right jobs can help their sons build a clientele or gain admission to a large firm. Manual fathers seldom establish these kinds of contacts.

## SOME IMPLICATIONS FOR LEGAL PRACTICE AND THE LAW

If the above interpretations are correct, the social composition of the recruitment base is apt to impose important constraints upon the operation of legal institutions. Family and school background give rise to career contingencies, i.e., they act as social "filters" impinging upon law practices by differentially screening candidates. Social background prescribes two major career contingencies: level of technical skill and access to clients.

*Impact on practice.* Poorly trained lawyers are likely to be in individual practice. They lack the skills provided by high quality education and specialized work experience to handle the more complex legal problems of modern society. Low quality education is one reason why solo lawyers are rarely invited to join big firms. By default most solo men end up doing the "dirty work" of the bar: personal injury, divorce, criminal work, collections, title searching, etc.

Visibility further limits the kind of work individual lawyers do. The requisite of any profession is availability of clients. The average solo lawyer has no contacts with big business. Neighborhood, ethnic group, family, and perhaps organizational contacts are the relations from which he can build a clientele. Firm men, on the other hand, come more often from high occupational family backgrounds, and are more likely to establish and cultivate relationships which yield business and corporate clienteles. Thus the "good family" and quality law school candidates look attractive to the large firms.

*Impact on legal institutions.* How then do social backgrounds of lawyers influence legal institutions? By shaping the above career contingencies social origins leave their mark on the law in the following ways:

(1) *Partly because legal talent from quality law schools has flowed heavily into the large firms for many years, there has been extensive elaboration of legal procedures to handle the problems of corporate enterprises as opposed to those to care for the problems of private citizens.* The result has been a high development of corporation protection, often at the expense of individual citizens. In addition, areas of law unrelated to the operation of corporate enterprises have not had the same level of creativity devoted to them. Developments in public and private welfare, personal injury, divorce, home finance, etc. have been less dramatic than developments in corporate taxation, mergers, stocks and bonds, etc.

(2) *There has evolved in metropolitan America what can properly be called an ethnic bar.* It is centered around ethnic legal associations, the local courts, and local politics, and is characterized by many mediocre performers competing for the same bread-and-butter cases. The big firms are insulated from this "intellectual slum" as Riesman has called it, where "a largely ethnic bar carries on the Anglo-Saxon rites of trial by jury and 'contaminates' the legal ideal with the demagogic practice."[21] Firm lawyers, if they litigate at all, rarely venture into the local courts. Their briefs carry them before appellate judges or special federal benches.

The existence of this ethnic bar based on *Gemeinschaftliche* relations has colored the local courts and the administration of justice. Llewellyn, some 25 years ago, noted that:

. . . courts are made and shaped more by the character of the bar before them than by any single factor. Courts, over the long haul, tend in their standards and in their performance to fit the character of the bar with whom they deal.[22]

---

[21] *Riesman*, op. cit., *p. 665.*

[22] *Karl N. Llewellyn, "The Bar Specializes—With What Results?"* Annals of The American Academy of Political and Social Science, *167* (*May, 1933*), *pp. 177–92.*

(3) *Finally, with all the talk about "law factories," it is not the large firm lawyer, but the solo whose professional position is most vulnerable to bureaucratization.* Lay organizations in metropolitan areas have successfully taken over the title and abstract, collections, and trust work. Accounting firms have taken over a great deal of tax work; automobile clubs, insurance and real estate companies, banks, and savings and loan associations have, each in their own way, made inroads upon spheres where solo practitioners customarily plied their trade.[23] And would-be individual practitioners have taken salaried positions in these organizations.

The minority lawyer, then, inoculated with the ethic of entrepreneurship, goes solo to remain "free"—only to discover that freedom to practice the rounded kind of law he desires has eluded him.

---

[23] *See James Willard Hurst,* The Growth of American Law, *Boston: Little, Brown & Co., 1950, pp. 319–22.*

# SECTION TWO

---

# The Jury System

# THE DIGNITY
# OF THE
# CIVIL JURY

## Harry Kalven, Jr.

[Headnote omitted.]

A few years ago I had occasion to write a paragraph about the jury which seems so apt for the purpose of introducing the present discussion that, rather than attempt a paraphrase, I risk the gracelessness of opening with a direct quotation from myself.

The judge and jury are two remarkably different institutions for reaching the same objective—fair, impersonal adjudication of controversies. The judge represents tradition, discipline, professional competence and repeated experience with the matter. This is undoubtedly a good formula. But the endless fascination of the jury is to see whether something quite different—the layman amateur drawn from a wide public, disciplined only by the trial process, and by an obligation to reach a group verdict—can somehow work as well or perhaps better.[1]

The passage suggests what I hope is the proper stance for discussing the merits of the jury system. The jury is almost by definition an exciting and gallant experiment in the conduct of serious human affairs; it is not surprising that virtually since its inception it has been embroiled in controversy, attracting at once the most extravagant praise and the harsh-

---

[1] *Kalven*, The Jury, the Law, and the Personal Injury Damage Award, *19* Ohio St. L.J. *158, 178 (1958)*.

Reprinted by permission of the author and of the publishers from 50 *Virginia Law Review* (1964), 1055–1075. Footnotes have been renumbered to run in sequence throughout the selection.

est criticism.[2] Nor is it surprising that the issue cannot be narrowly focussed or definitively put to rest.

\* \* \* \*

# I

Classic debate over the jury went properly to the quality of its performance, to its competence for its task. More recently, however, the debate has tended to go off on other issues. First, there has been the concern with court congestion and the civil jury's contribution to it. Second, there has been the resurgence of interest in auto compensation plans which would effect a major reform of substantive law and, as an incidental by-product, abandon the jury, thus reducing enormously the civil jury's domain.

These are both arresting and complex topics, but I submit that they are largely irrelevant, and should like at the outset to clear them from the path of discussion of the basic issue: the value of the jury as an institution for adjudication.[3]

The point is perhaps clearest with respect to the compensation plan.[4] When one speaks in this context of the merits of the jury trial in personal injury cases, the objection is usually not to the jury trial as a distinctive mode of trial but to the common-law systems of negligence and damages. The reform is aimed not at the jury, but at the substantive criteria for

---

[2] *The basic contemporary American criticism is* FRANK, COURTS ON TRIAL (*1949*); *careful assessments of the argument by English lawyers, who draw somewhat different conclusions, are* DEVLIN, TRIAL BY JURY (*1956*), *and* G. WILLIAMS, THE PROOF OF GUILT *218–304* (*2d ed. 1958*). *Useful bibliographies are found in* JOINER, CIVIL JUSTICE AND THE JURY (*1962*); *Broeder,* The Functions of the Jury— Facts or Fictions? *21* U. CHI. L. REV. *386* (*1945*); *Green,* Juries and Justice—The Jury's Role in Personal Injury Cases, *1962* U. ILL. L.F. *152. The most recent criticism has come from two distinguished New York judges. See Desmond,* Should It Take 34 Months for a Trial?, *N.Y. Times, Dec. 8, 1963,* § *6* (*Magazine*), *p. 29; Peck,* Do Juries Delay Justice?, *18* F.R.D. *455* (*1956*).
*Another distinguished New York jurist, Judge Hart, has recently joined the debate on the side of the jury. See* HART, LONG LIVE THE AMERICAN JURY (*1964*).
[3] *I shall also skip another familiar topic in the modern jury debate—the painless disappearance of the civil jury in England. While this may be high evidence that a civilized people can give up the civil jury and remain civilized, this surrender of the jury is not a strong precedent for the debate because of differences between the English and American jury trial situations.*
[4] *See Blum & Kalven,* Public Law Perspectives on a Private Law Problem— Auto Compensation Plans, *31* U. CHI. L. REV. *641, 714* (*1964*).

determining what compensation, if any, accident victims are to receive. The serious arguments for substantive change would remain the same had the jury never been involved in these cases. The target of reform is the uneven incidence of common-law compensation. Further, the hope of such proposals is not simply to do away with jury trials but to make any trial unnecessary. In varying ways all plans envisage a relatively automatic paying of insurance claims, and so simplify the criteria for recovery as greatly to reduce the likelihood of contested cases. Basically, therefore, such proposals are no more relevant to debate over the merits of the jury system than would be a scheme for reducing or eliminating auto accidents themselves.

There is, however, one noteworthy detail here. Despite the fact that one *could* have a plan which retained jury trial for whatever few controversies were not disposed of by negotiation, all plans appear to transfer such residual controversy into administrative channels. Although the point receives notably little discussion in the various proposals, there are perhaps several reasons for this. But, in any event, if respect for administrative expertise is a reason for thus disposing of residual cases it is worth noting that the case for establishing an administrative agency seems upside down here. Both the liability issue and the damages issue would, under a plan, be substantially simpler than those which are now, at common law, left to the jury. The plans thus appear to be following the curious sequence of first simplifying the issues and then shifting them to an allegedly more expert tribunal. It is possible, however, to take an exactly opposite view of the matter; namely, that the jury with its common sense and feel of the community is the "expert" tribunal for the two great distinctive issues posed by the common law: drawing the profile of negligence and handling the individual pricing of damages. Perhaps the reason compensation plans have so readily surrendered the jury is that the distinctive strengths of the jury are no longer required.

The concern over court congestion is not quite so easily dismissed. It is fashionable today to complain that the time costs of the jury trial have made it a luxury that hard-pressed urban court systems can no longer afford. Here, fortunately, our researches have advanced to the stage of publication, and in our volume, *Delay in the Court*,[5] Hans Zeisel, Bernard

---

[5] ZEISEL, KALVEN & BUCHHOLZ, DELAY IN THE COURT (1959) [*hereinafter cited as* DELAY IN THE COURT].

Buchholz, and I made a careful analysis of the jury's role in causing delay. Our study was confined to a single court system, the Supreme Court of New York County (Manhattan), but the analysis was broad enough to make it relevant to the problem of court delay generally. Several points, more fully developed in the book, may be usefully recapitulated here.

Jury trials can contribute to delay only if it takes longer to try a case to a jury than to try the same case to a judge alone.[6] The point, therefore, must be: If all cases now tried to juries were tried to judges, there would be a sufficient saving of trial time to make a significant contribution to the reduction of backlog and the elimination of delay. Thus, jury trial can be said to "cause" delay only in the special sense that the failure to use a remedy can be said to cause the continuation of a disease. Use of the jury is a cause of delay only in the sense that use of the combined trial of liability and damage issues or the exclusive reliance on adversary medical experts—rather than split trials or impartial medical experts—is a cause of delay.[7]

Confusion about the role of the jury and its effect on delay was deepened in the New York court by the fact that four separate trial calendars were employed:[8] general bench trials, general jury trials, personal injury bench trials, and personal injury jury trials. Further, the New York practice was to grant a wholesale preference to cases on the first three calendars. The result, of course, was that only the personal injury jury calendar was delayed; and this was often taken as evidence that the personal injury jury trial was the cause of the delay. The thirty-nine-month delay figure credited to the personal injury jury trial at the time of our study was simply a consequence of the calendar arrangement; if cases with blond and brunette plaintiffs had been given automatic preferences in the same way, it would have appeared by the same logic that red-headed plaintiffs were the cause of the delay. Indeed, we estimated that had New York given up its preference scheme the average delay would have dropped to ten months.

We return then, to the central point: How much longer is a jury trial than a bench trial? Estimates by experienced judges and lawyers have varied widely; and it is surprisingly difficult to arrive at a satisfactory

---

[6] See id. at 71; Zeisel, The Jury and the Court Delay, Annals, March 1960, p. 46.
[7] See DELAY IN THE COURT ch. 11; Zeisel & Callahan, Split Trials and Time Saving; A Statistical Analysis, 76 HARV. L. REV. 1606 (1963).
[8] DELAY IN THE COURT 7, 29, 200, 271.

answer since we cannot try *the same case* by each method with a stop-watch in hand. Further, since there is good reason to believe that cases tried to a jury are in many respects different and more complex than cases in which a jury is waived, we cannot arrive at an answer simply by comparing a sample of jury trials and a sample of bench trials. We were fairly successful in extricating ourselves from this methodological impasse. By using a series of estimates,[9] we reached the conclusion that on the average a bench trial would be 40 per cent less time consuming than a jury trial of the same case. As far as I know, this 40 per cent figure remains the best estimate of the time savings.[10]

The 40 per cent time cost is, to be sure, not trivial, and it will be weighed differently depending on one's view of the jury otherwise. How-ever, this estimate, standing alone, does little to advance the discussion, regardless of its accuracy. A chief point of our study was to relate the impact on delay of abolishing the jury to the impact on delay of other remedies that were not being urged and thus to attempt to obtain a "price tag" for the civil jury system.

There are four alternative "remedies" to be compared with abolition of the jury:

(1) The New York court at the time of our survey had a total of twenty-six judges, nineteen of whom were sitting in the law division. It was our estimate that abolition of the jury in personal injury cases would have the same impact on court congestion as the appointment of 1.6 judges.[11] The New York court is not in all respects typical, and the savings would be somewhat larger in many other courts. We would suggest, however, that before the jury is sacrificed on behalf of court congestion, a serious estimate be made of how many additional judges would be required to have the same impact on that delay.

(2) The second alternate remedy is more dramatic. In 1956 New

---

[9] *In brief, we controlled the number of witnesses and used, in addition to statistical comparison, estimates derived from two surveys—one of trial judges and one of trial lawyers. See DELAY IN THE COURT 75–78.*

[10] *Judge David Peck in a widely publicized estimate has said that a jury trial takes 2½ times as long as a bench trial. In fairness, however, this is not as different from our 40% estimate as it may seem at first since the base is not the same. In our estimate the length of the jury trial is used as the base and in Judge Peck's estimate the length of the bench trial is used as the base. The parallel statement of our estimate would be that the jury trial is 1½ times as long as the bench trial.*

[11] *See DELAY IN THE COURT 82.*

York had experimented with a summer session as a way of increasing judicial manpower without adding judgeships. In effect the plan required that each judge surrender just two weeks of a three-month summer vacation. This scheme was abandoned after a one-year trial, due as much, perhaps, to the irritation of the trial bar as to that of the trial bench. However, we estimated that had New York continued with the summer session plan, the impact on delay would have been the same as that of 1.5 additional judges—or the same as the savings from abolition of the personal injury jury trial.[12]

(3) A few years ago the Federal District Court for the Northern District of Illinois initiated use of the split trial—that is, separate trials of the liability and the damage issues. My colleagues, Hans Zeisel and Thomas Callahan, have made a careful study of the first two years of experience under the rule and conclude that its full use would save approximately 20 per cent of current trial time—or about half the saving to be expected from abolition of the jury.[13]

These three comparisons make the 40 per cent estimate more meaningful and converge on a conclusion: If the case against the jury is that its abolition is to be considered a remedy for court congestion, then the proper topic is court congestion and what else can be done about it. When the price tag for the jury system is, as in New York, the appointment of 1.6 new judges, or the curtailing of summer vacations by two weeks per judge, or vigorous use of other remedies such as split trials, it seems that the jury is being sold for too low a price. In any event, responsible discussion of the jury's contribution to delay must confront these facts.

(4) There is a fourth set of figures that should be considered. We were able to compare a sample of New Jersey personal injury jury trial cases with a sample of New York personal injury jury trial cases;[14] the two samples were made roughly comparable. Analysis showed that the New Jersey cases, on the average, were being tried 40 per cent faster than the New York cases. Analysis of a sample of trial transcripts, etc., was not very successful in unlocking the secret of New Jersey's speed, but the data strongly suggested that it is feasible to speed up the jury trial. It is arresting, indeed, that the time margin of New Jersey jury trials over New

---

[12] See Id. at 176.
[13] See Zeisel & Callahan, supra note [7].
[14] See DELAY IN THE COURT 94.

York jury trials is about equal to that of the New York bench trials over the New York jury trials, or the amount of time hoped to be saved by abolishing the jury.

The 40 per cent figure does not, to my mind, make out a persuasive case against the jury on grounds of court congestion alone. And there is a further point of some generality. It can well be argued that reduction of delay is a poor *ad hoc* reason for tampering with the jury system in any event.[15] It is important that the pressures generated by the very real and stubborn problems of court congestion not be dealt with in a fashion which might permanently affect the quality of our justice. Delay is not a sufficient reason for altering the jury apart from consideration of the quality of the jury as an adjudicator. At most delay is an additional straw in the calculus of those already dissatisfied with the performance of the jury—and, as the New York study shows, the straw is not a very heavy one.

## II

We are ready, then, for the proper issue about the jury: the quality of its performance.

As we come to the merits of the institution, it may be useful to sketch three main heads under which criticism and defense of the jury have fallen.

First, there is a series of collateral advantages and disadvantages such as the fact that the jury provides an important civic experience for the citizen; that, because of popular participation the jury makes tolerable the stringency of certain decisions; or that because of its transient personnel the jury acts as a lightning rod for animosity and suspicion which might otherwise center on the more exposed judge; or that the jury is a guarantor of integrity since it is said to be more difficult to reach twelve men than one. On the negative side it is urged that jury fees are an added expense to the administration of justice; that jury service often imposes an unfair economic and social burden on those forced to serve; and that exposure to jury service disenchants the citizen and leads him to lose confidence in the administration of justice.

Although many of these considerations loom large in the tradition of jury debate, they are unamenable to research and will not concern us here.

---

[15] See *Zeisel*, supra *note* [6], *at* 52.

We have, however, collected considerable data bearing on the reaction of jurors to service. It will suffice for present purposes simply to state that there is much evidence that most people, once actually serving in a trial, become highly serious and responsible toward their task and toward the joint effort to deliberate through to a verdict. Whether they are good at the job may be open to question, but that they are serious about it and give it a real try is abundantly documentable. Anecdotes about jury frivolity and irresponsibility are almost always false. Further, we can document that jury service does not disenchant, but actually increases the public's preference for trial by jury. A distinction must be made between the attitude of those who have never served and seek to avoid service and the response of the juror once he has been "drafted," so to speak. Finally, the things jurors do not like about the system are quite extrinsic housekeeping defects which can and should be corrected, such as the waiting, the loss of income due to serving, and the often miserable quarters in which they are kept. The heart of the matter, the trial itself and the deliberation, is very often a major and moving experience in the life of the citizen-juror.

The second cluster of issues goes to the competence of the jury. Can it follow and remember the presentation of the facts and weigh the conflicting evidence? Can it follow and remember the law? Can it deliberate effectively?

The third cluster of issues goes to the adherence of the jury to the law, to what its admirers call its sense of equity and what its detractors view as its taste for anarchy.

The latter two issues go to the heart of the debate and have long been the occasion for a heated exchange of proverbs. Further, they may seem so heavily enmeshed in difficult value judgments as to make further discussion unpromising. Yet it is precisely here that our empirical studies can offer some insight, although they too cannot dispose fully of the issues.

When one asserts that jury adjudication is of low quality, he must be asserting that jury decisions vary in some significant degree from those a judge would have made in the same cases. If he denies this and wishes to include the judge, he has lost any baseline, and with it any force, for his criticism. While it is possible to say that even those juries whose decision patterns coincide with those of judges are nevertheless given to caprice, lack of understanding, and sheer anarchic disobedience to law, it is not likely that the critic means to go this far. If he does, he may have an interesting point to make about the legal order as a whole, but he has lost any distinctive point about the jury as a mode of trial. Further, trial by judge is the relevant and obvious alternative to trial by jury. To argue against jury trial is, therefore, to argue for bench trial.

Can one say anything, then, about how often judge and jury decisions agree and how often they differ? We can. One of our major research ventures has been a massive survey of trial judges on a nationwide basis. With their cooperation we were able to obtain reports on actual cases tried to a jury before them, to get the jury's verdict in each case, and to get from the judge a statement of how he would have decided the case had it been tried to him alone. Finally, the trial judge gave us his explanation of any instance of disagreement. We have, in this fashion, collected from some 600 judges, reports on some 8,000 jury trials throughout the United States for each of which we have an actual jury verdict and a hypothetical verdict from the bench. We are just completing a full, book-length, analysis of the picture thus obtained for criminal cases and plan in the ensuing year to complete the companion book reporting on the civil cases. . . . The methodological details about the sample, about the reality and accuracy of the judges' responses, and about the logic by which we infer explanations for the disagreements must be left to the book presentation.[16] We are satisfied that the methods were sound and that we have developed an effective tool for studying the nature of the jury's performance.

While there are rich nuances in the patterns of jury disagreement that cannot be detailed here, we can report the main findings and place the jury system against the baseline of the bench trial system, thus giving an empirical measure of the quality of the jury performance. We shall do so first for criminal cases and then for civil cases; the contrast may help to put the performance of the civil jury in perspective.

It is evident that the matching of verdicts in criminal cases yields four possible combinations: cases where judge and jury agree to convict, where they agree to acquit, where the judge would acquit and the jury convict, and where the jury would acquit and the judge convict. Hence, the quantitative results can be readily summarized in a fourfold table. Table 1 gives the data on the criminal cases.

The table contains two main conclusions. First, the jury and judge agree in the large majority of cases; to be exact in 13 per cent plus 67 per

---

[16] *Some preliminary remarks about the methodological problems involved are found in Zeisel,* Social Research on the Law: The Ideal and The Practical, *in* LAW AND SOCIOLOGY *124 (Evan ed. 1962).*

| Judge Would Have Found: | Jury Found: | | |
|---|---|---|---|
| | For Defendant | Against Defendant | Total Judge |
| For Defendant | 13 | 2 | 15 |
| Against Defendant | 18 | 67 | 85 |
| Total Jury | 31 | 69 | 100 |

cent or 80 per cent in all. Second, in the remaining 20 per cent of the cases, in which they disagree, the disagreement is generally due to the jury's being more lenient toward the criminal defendant. In summary, the overall performance of the jury is such as to produce a high degree of conformity to that of the judge, but with elbow room left for the jury to perform a distinctive function. Or, as we have put it on other occasions, the jury agrees with the judge often enough to be reassuring, yet disagrees often enough to keep it interesting.

Table 2 gives the companion figures for personal injury cases.

TABLE 2. JUDGE AND JURY AGREEMENT ON
LIABILITY IN PERSONAL INJURY CASES.[17]

| Judge Would Have Found: | Jury Found: | | |
|---|---|---|---|
| | For Plaintiff | For Defendant | Total Judge |
| For Plaintiff | 44 | 10 | 54 |
| For Defendant | 11 | 35 | 46 |
| Total Jury | 55 | 45 | 100 |

Again we see that there is massive agreement; in the personal injury cases it runs 44 per cent plus 35 per cent or 79 per cent, almost exactly the same as for the criminal cases. Here, however, the pattern of disagreement is much more evenly balanced. The judge disagrees with the jury because he is more pro-plaintiff about as often as the jury disagrees with him because it is more pro-plaintiff. Whereas the greater leniency of the jury toward the criminal defendant is congruent with popular expectations, the equality of pro-plaintiff response between judge and jury in civil cases is in sharp contrast to popular expectations.

[17] *Tables 1 and 2 have been simplified by the omission of hung juries.*

It must be added that Table 2 does not present quite the whole picture. If we look for the moment simply at the 44 per cent of the cases where both decide for the plaintiff, we find considerable disagreement on the level of damages. In roughly 23 per cent the jury gives the higher award, in 17 per cent the judge gives the higher award and in the remaining 4 per cent they are in approximate agreement. More important, however, is the fact that the jury awards average 20 per cent higher than those of the judge.

The two tables considered together imply that the jury's disagreement with the judge is not a random matter; they indicate something more interesting about the nature both of judge and jury as decision makers. The precise quality of that something cannot be properly sketched here. We have had considerable success in finding explanations for the instances of disagreement and thus in reconstructing a full and rounded rationale. Our thesis is that it is the jury's sense of equity, and not its relative competence, that is producing most of the disagreement. Thus, debate over the merits of the jury system is in the end debate over the jury as a means of introducing flexibility and equity into the legal process.

There are, however, some further observations about the issue of jury competence. We have been told often enough that the jury trial is a process whereby twelve inexperienced laymen, who are probably strangers to each other, are invited to apply law which they will not understand to facts which they will not get straight and by secret deliberation arrive at a group decision. We are told also that heroic feats of learning law, remembering facts, and running an orderly discussion as a group are called for in every jury trial.[18] In the forum of armchair speculation, a forum which on this topic has enrolled some of the most able and distinguished names in law, the jury often loses the day.

The two basic tables giving the architectural statistics of the jury's performance vis-à-vis the judge's performance have already indicated that the armchair indictment of the jury must go awry somewhere. We can, however, in a variety of ways document more securely our assertion that intellectual incompetence or sheer misunderstanding of the case is not a problem with the jury.

---

[18] *For varying expressions of this view see* Frank, Courts on Trial (*1949*); *Green,* Juries and Justice—The Jury's Role in Personal Injury Cases, *1962* U. Ill. L.F. *152; Sunderland,* Verdicts, General and Special, *29* Yale L.J. *253* (*1920*).

In the judge-jury survey the trial judge, among other things, classified each case as to whether it was "difficult to understand" or "easy." We can therefore spell out the following hypothesis to test against the judge-jury data. If the jury has a propensity not to understand, that propensity should be more evident in the cases rated by the judges as difficult than in those rated as easy.[19] Further, disagreement should be higher in cases which the jury does not understand than in cases which they do understand since, where the jury misunderstands the case, it must be deciding on a different basis than the judge. We reach, then, the decisive hypothesis to test, namely, that the jury should disagree more often with the judge in difficult cases than in easy ones. However, when we compare the decision patterns in easy cases with those in difficult cases we find that the level of disagreement remains the same.[20]

This rather intricate proof is corroborated by the fact that although the trial judges polled gave a wide variety of explanations for the cases in which there was disagreement, they virtually never offered the jury's inability to understand the case as a reason.

Any mystery as to why the plausible *a priori* surmises of jury incompetence should prove so wrong is considerably reduced when we take a closer look at the dynamics of the jury process, a look we have been able to take as a result of intensive and extensive post-trial juror interviews in actual cases and as a result of complete observation of jury deliberations in mock experimental cases, a technique used widely in the project.[21] We observed that the trial had structured the communication to the jury far more than the usual comment recognizes and had made certain points quite salient. A more important point is that the jury can operate by *collective* recall. Different jurors remember, and make available to all, different items of the trial so that the jury as a group remembers far more than most of its members could as individuals. It tends, in this connection,

---

[19] *It might be noted that some 85% of the cases were rated by the judges as falling in the "easy" category.*

[20] *The data here discussed come from the study of criminal cases; there is no reason to believe the point will not hold for civil trials as well.*

[21] *The experimental jury technique was developed for the project by Fred L. Strodtbeck and some aspects of the method are discussed in Strodtbeck,* Social Process, the Law and Jury Functioning, in LAW AND SOCIOLOGY *144 (Evan ed. 1962). The forthcoming volume,* SIMON, THE JURY AND THE DEFENSE OF INSANITY *. . . will be the first full length publication of the results of a jury experimental sequence.*

to be as strong as its strongest link. The conclusion, therefore, is that the jury understands well enough for its purposes and that its intellectual incompetence has been vastly exaggerated.

Often in the debate over the jury the capacity of *one* layman is compared to the capacity of one judge, as though this were the issue. The distinctive strength and safeguard of the jury system is that the jury operates as a group. Whether twelve lay heads are better than one judicial head is still open to argument, but it should be recognized that twelve lay heads are very probably better than one.

It has been a major characteristic of debate over the jury that its critics are quick to announce at the outset that they are talking only of civil juries—their argument is not meant to impeach juries in criminal cases. The view I have been developing in this paper sees the jury as an adjudicating institution with certain basic characteristics and qualities which would be relatively constant as its business moves from civil to criminal cases. The question I wish to explore for a moment is the logic by which one would abolish the civil jury and cherish the criminal jury.[22] I recognize, of course, that as a practical matter there are great differences here in terms of both constitutional requirements and popular reaction. I wish, however, to look theoretically at this matter. If the jury operates in a civil case as its critics say, can one justify retaining such an archaic and incompetent institution in criminal cases?

Dean Griswold, for example, has recently observed:

But jury trial, at best, is the apotheosis of the amateur. Why should

---

[22] *Consider, for example, the conclusion of the careful essay on the civil jury by Milton Green:*

*(T)he defects appear to be nonremediable. To be a jury, within constitutional definitions, it must be a fair cross-section of the community. As such it will never be a competent fact-finder, and it will never be able to make an intelligent application of the law to the facts. The inescapable conclusion is that, in the interest of dispatch and justice, the jury should be abolished.*

*It may be argued that this is all very well in theory, but the public will never stand for it. It would take a constitutional amendment to eliminate the jury and the people will not give it up. I would readily agree if we were talking about eliminating the jury in criminal cases, and the people would be right. It is quite another matter to ask the public to give up the jury in civil cases, to ask people to give up an irksome chore which they frequently seek to avoid. . . . Average citizens may be inept as fact-finders and law-appliers, but they generally have good common sense and are able to recognize an important public need created by the changing pace of our time.*

Green supra *note [18], at 166–67.*

anyone think that twelve persons brought in from the street, selected in various ways, for their lack of general ability, should have any special capacity for deciding controversies between persons?[23]

Dean Griswold was arguing for the abolition of the jury in civil cases. Is there not an obligation to try this biting premise on the criminal jury as well? For these grave and important controversies the jury should not be any abler; it must still be "the apotheosis of the amateur" and the twelve men must still be "selected in various ways for their lack of general ability."

The answer to all this, of course, is likely to be that we favor the jury in criminal cases as a safeguard for the accused, and that we need no corresponding safeguard in the civil case. There are two things to note about this line of reasoning, however. First, it would seem to be waiving any objections about the jury's incompetence and resting the case on the jury's sense of equity. Second, since it recognizes that introducing equity into the legal scheme is a characteristic of the jury, is there sufficient basis for applauding the jury's brand of equity in criminal cases while being critical of it in civil cases?

## III

The discussion thus far has been regrettably general and colorless and removed from the particular issue or the particular case. I should like to try to compensate a bit for this abstractness by pausing to explore one pocket of "jury law" as an example of the human flavor of the jury process and of the ambivalence of the legal system toward the jury's precise function. The topic is the jury's handling of counsel fees in the personal injury case.[24]

I begin with an anecdote that comes, not from our study, but from a bar meeting I attended a few years ago. It seems a lawyer chanced to overhear a jury deliberating in a personal injury case. They had agreed on liability and were moving to the issue of damages. Their first step was to agree on a fee for the plaintiff's lawyer. They then proceeded to multiply it by three to get the damages!

What do the materials from our study do to the picture of the jury

---

[23] *1962–63* HARVARD LAW SCHOOL DEAN'S REP. *5–6.*

[24] *See generally Kalven,* The Jury, the Law, and the Personal Injury Damage Award, *19,* OHIO ST. L.J. *158, 163, 176, (1958).*

suggested by this story? To begin with we might note some points about the law within this area. Under American law counsel fees are not to be awarded as part of the plaintiff's damages. This rule, although clear, embodies a controversial policy which is not uniformly followed in other legal systems.[25] Second, the jury normally is not instructed about fees; that is, they are not told they are not to award them. The theory is that it is enough to explain the heads under which damages are to be awarded and that it would be dangerous to mention the fee problem for fear that the negative instruction might boomerang. Fees along with taxes and interest are therefore instances of what may be called "silent" instructions.[26]

What then does the jury do about fees? It is curiously difficult to come to a firm conclusion, but the data run about as follows. The jurors often discuss fees in the course of deliberations and see no impropriety in so doing. They are frequently but not invariably well informed about the one-third contingent fee contract. Do they then add the fee? We are inclined to conclude not. It is more that fees provide a useful talking point in the deliberations over damages, functioning as a device in argument to facilitate agreement. And the salience of fees in the discussion appears to vary inversely with the clarity of the damage measurement. Thus, in a series of property damage cases where the damages had objective referents, the jury did not discuss fees. Furthermore, we never found a jury determining the damage total and then as a group deciding on the fee and adding it.

I shall conclude this brief sketch with an anecdote that does come from our own files. In one of the experimental jury deliberations there was a sharp split in the jury over the damages. The majority faction favored 35,000 dollars and the minority 25,000 dollars and after considerable discussion the impasse seemed firm. Finally, one of the majority raised the fee issue for the first time and reminded the holdouts that the plaintiff would have to pay his lawyer. The holdouts agreed that this was a point they had not previously considered and yielded rather rapidly. An overly logical member of the majority then raised the point that in reaching their figure of 35,000 dollars they had not considered fees either. He was summarily silenced by the other majority jurors, and a verdict of 35,000 dollars was unanimously agreed upon!

---

[25] See McCormick, Damages § 71 (1935); Delay in the Court 290.

[26] See Gregory & Kalven, Cases and Materials on Torts 464–76 (1959).

The anecdote has echoes at the appellate court level. In *Renuart Lumber Yards, Inc. v. Levine*,[27] a relatively recent Florida case, the court found an award of 75,000 dollars excessive, estimated that some 30,000 dollars must have been for pain and suffering, and ordered a remittitur. Judge Hobson in dissent argued that for this purpose the court should consider the facts of life as to fees. He said:

> Moreover, although there is no legal basis for the inclusion of an attorney's fee in the judgment it is a matter of common knowledge that in personal injury actions lawyers do not customarily perform services for the plaintiff gratuitously. As a practical proposition it is indeed probable that after paying for the services of his attorney appellee would have little, if any, of the $30,000 left. . . . Such circumstance cannot be ignored by the writer in performing his part of this Appellate Court's duty to determine whether the judgment is so grossly excessive as to shock the judicial conscience.[28]

Presumably Judge Hobson would have held it error for the jury to be instructed to consider fees. Yet he feels it appropriate to consider them himself for the special purpose of resolving the issue before him. We are tempted to say that the jury, insofar as we can tell, treats fees much the same as the judge did—not as simply additive but as an acceptable reason for not rejecting a given award as excessive.

Finally, I suspect the law likes the fee rule the way it is. The fee question as an explicit issue of policy is difficult to resolve. Since we cannot decide what we want to do about fees as damages, we are happy to let the whole troublesome issue go to the jury. The jury's performance with respect to counsel fees can be read as furnishing both an argument for the civil jury and an argument against it. My immediate point in reviewing it was not so much to sharpen the debate as to give some indication of how complex jury decision-making behavior is.[29]

It has been a traditional point of argument against the jury that it ameliorated the harsh rules of law just enough to dampen any enthusiasm or momentum toward proper reform. And the fee example may support

---

[27] *49 So. 2d 97 (Fla. 1950).*

[28] Id. *at 102.*

[29] *The difference between the two anecdotes about fees can be taken as the difference between the lore of the bench and bar and the systematic empirical study of the behavior. In a sense the systematic study of the jury simply rediscovers truths that the bar has long known; but I would hasten to add that when so rediscovered the bar's "truths" appear to be half-truths.*

this. It is easy to say that a rule of law is either sound or unsound. If it is sound it should be enforced as written; if it is unsound it should be changed by proper process. This logical scheme, however, seems to me too rigid. Reform of private law is notoriously hard to effectuate, and in the long interim there is room for the jury's touch. Further, there is not inconsiderable evidence that jury resistance to a rule is often a catalyst of change.[30] Finally, and perhaps most important, we have a sense that many of the jury's most interesting deviations would be exceedingly hard to codify and incorporate by rule.

The content of jury equity in civil cases is obviously a topic of high interest, and we have not yet documented it fully in our studies. There are, however, three or four major points to be at least noted here. First, as has been long recognized,[31] in certain areas of law jury equity is fully legitimated by the system. Here, it is not what we suspect the jury may do in bending the law; it is what the jury is instructed to do according to the official view. For example, in defamation it is the jury's official task to define the content of the defamatory standard, and in negligence cases its task is to define negligence for the particular conduct involved.[32] Although I realize that history and comparative law are against the notion, I cannot but wonder whether a negligence criterion would have developed without the jury—and whether it can make any real sense without a jury.

Second, there are three big points of jury equity on which our research may alter the popular view. The jury does not simply ignore the contributory negligence rule and apply a comparative negligence formula of its own; this view, popular among torts professors, is at most a half-truth, and the less interesting half at that.

Again, it is perhaps evident from Table 2 that the jury has not, in

---

[30] *See, e.g., Vascoe v. Ford, 212 Miss. 370, 54 So. 2d 541 (1951), where the court, in explicitly changing its rule as to the allowance of damages for humiliation from scars, recognized the jury's refusal to follow the old rule.*

[31] *See* HOLMES, THE COMMON LAW 98–103 *(Howe ed. 1963).*

[32] *This familiar point as to negligence is made fully explicit in the new standard jury instructions made mandatory in Illinois by* ILL. SUP. CT. R. 25–1:

*When I use the word negligence in these instructions, I mean the failure to do something which a reasonably careful person would do or the doing of something which a reasonably careful person would not do under the circumstances similar to those shown by the evidence.* The law does not say how a reasonably careful person would act under these circumstances; that is for you to decide.
ILLINOIS PATTERN JURY INSTRUCTIONS *10.1 (1961). (Emphasis added.)*

keeping with the mood of the day, silently revolutionized the basis of liability so that today we have in effect a strict liability system.[33]

Finally, the jury in personal injury cases has perhaps radically altered the official doctrine on computing damages; it tends to price the injury as a whole in a fashion analogous to the use of general damages in defamation.[34]

And as a final teaser it should be recalled that the jury, as Table 2 warns, is not monolithically pro-plaintiff in personal injury cases. The thesis here is complex and centers on the distribution of the equities vis-à-vis the existing legal rules. The jury tends to follow the equities, in a very loose and rough sense, and the law has not uniformly deprived the plaintiff of them. The jury's response to collateral benefits, to imputed negligence, and, on occasion, to the use of criminal statutes to establish negligence may be quickly cited as instances of what we have in mind here.

In the end, then, debate about the merits of the jury system should center far more on the value and propriety of the jury's sense of equity, of its modest war with the law, than on its sheer competence. Criticism of the jury raises a deep, durable, and perplexing jurisprudential issue, and not a simple one of the professional engineer versus the amateur.

## IV

On most issues of policy one may question the relevance of an opinion poll as an aid to forming his own opinion. In the case of the jury, however, an opinion poll may have extra force. In any event, the final item of data I wish to report is a survey we conducted among a national sample of trial judges as to their opinions of, and attitudes toward, the jury system. The trial judge's views as to the value of the jury are especially entitled to respectful hearing: he is the daily observer of the jury system in action, its daily partner in the administration of justice, and the one who would be most affected if the civil jury were abolished.

The questionnaire was elaborate and reflected a series of specific points about which we had become concerned during the life of the project. When reported in full, it should yield a rounded profile of

---

[33] See Blum & Kalven, Public Law Perspectives on a Private Law Problem— Auto Compensation Plans, 31 U. Chi. L. Rev. 641, 648 (1964).

[34] See Kalven, supra note [24].

contemporary judicial attitudes toward the jury and toward specific reforms that might increase its usefulness. At the moment we shall rest with reporting two basic tables. The judges were asked to choose among three positions on the jury for criminal, and then for civil trials:

(1) On balance the jury system is thoroughly satisfactory.

(2) The jury system has serious disadvantages which could be corrected and should be corrected if the system is to remain useful.

(3) The disadvantages of the jury system outweigh its advantages so much that its use should be sharply curtailed.

There were some 1,060 trial judges in the national sample. Table 3 gives the results for criminal cases and Table 4 for civil cases.

TABLE 3. TRIAL JUDGES' OPINIONS OF JURY—CRIMINAL CASES.

|  | Number | Per Cent |
|---|---|---|
| (1) Thoroughly Satisfactory | 791 | 77 |
| (2) Satisfactory if Certain Changes | 210 | 20 |
| (3) Unsatisfactory | 29 | 3 |
|  | 1,030 | 100 |

TABLE 4. TRIAL JUDGES' OPINIONS OF JURY—CIVIL CASES.

|  | Number | Per Cent |
|---|---|---|
| (1) Thoroughly Satisfactory | 661 | 64 |
| (2) Satisfactory if Certain Changes | 280 | 27 |
| (3) Unsatisfactory | 97 | 9 |
|  | 1,038 | 100 |

The tables require little comment. It is evident that the trial judges are overwhelmingly against sharp curtailment of the jury; that a substantial majority find the jury thoroughly satisfactory; and that this support for the jury does not decline appreciably as we shift from criminal to civil cases.[35]

## V

As the second alternative offered the judges in our opinion poll suggests, it has been a strong tradition in the jury debate for one group of

---

[35] *Another poll of judges on their attitudes toward the jury system which also finds widespread support for the jury system is reported in* HART, *op. cit. supra note 2, at 4–32.*

its supporters to specify certain reforms of the jury which would then make it a satisfactory institution. I have said nothing thus far about reforms and deliberately elect not to do so. It is not that the jury system could not conceivably be improved; nor is it that all of the specific reforms suggested are unsound. It is, rather, that the debate is over the basic architecture of a jury trial system and the basic architecture of a bench trial system.[36]

I am therefore not discussing such matters as: improving the administration of jury selection systems; having the judge do the *voir dire* questioning; standardizing jury instructions; summation of the evidence by the judge; comment on the evidence by the judge; use of vigorous pretrial procedures to narrow issues; whether the jury is instructed before or after the closing arguments; written versus oral instructions; special verdicts; impartial medical experts; reducing the size of the jury; eliminating the unanimity requirement; or permitting the jurors to take notes. These measures have a considerable literature in their own right and appear to constitute a good part of what is currently called judicial administration.[37] In varying degrees our studies have given us data and views on virtually all of these measures. Some of the measures are ill-advised, in my view, some are trivial, and some would be definite improvements. But the case for the civil jury does not, I think, stand or fall on the adoption of any one or any combination of them.

Sometimes I suspect that the jury issue will go to whichever side does not have the burden of proof. And in the forum of policy debate the assignment of the burden of proof tends to be a debater's strategy rather than an accepted convention. Does the argument stand differently if, on the one hand, the issue is put in terms of introducing the civil jury into a system that does not have it or perhaps extending it to areas where we do not have it today, such as the Federal Tort Claims Act, than it does if, on the other hand, the issue is whether we should abolish the jury in areas where we do now have it? I think it does, and I incline toward the view that old institutions should not be changed lightly.[38] We lack, I feel, fresh

---

[36] *Milton Green would appear to agree that the issue is basic and not conditional upon specific reforms of the jury; he would therefore resolve it against the jury. See Green,* supra *note [18].*

[37] Elliott, Improving Our Courts *passim (1959).*

[38] *Compare T. B. Smith,* Civil Jury Trial in Scotland, *50 Va. L. Rev. 1076, 1095 (1964).*

arguments against the civil jury, apart perhaps from delay. I cannot resist observing that we need to hear a fresher point than that the civil jury consists of twelve laymen.

Inevitably, debate over an institution as complex and long standing as the jury will continue to be inviting and will continue to be inconclusive. It should be stressed that it was not the primary purpose of our project to appraise the jury, but simply to study it. In the course of the many years of that study it should be clear that I, personally, have become increasingly impressed with the humanity, strength, sanity, and responsibility of the jury. I suspect that that is not a proper argument for it, and I profoundly agree that it would be far better to have our careful studies ready to speak for themselves and give the rounded picture.

# JURORS' EVALUATION
# OF EXPERT PSYCHIATRIC
# TESTIMONY

*Rita James Simon*

The specific concern of this paper is to describe jurors' reactions to expert psychiatric testimony in a criminal trial involving a charge of incest and a plea of insanity. Placing the question in its broadest context, the practice of experts appearing in the court has given rise to two widely recognized problems: How much authority should be delegated to the experts; and, how much should the trial procedures be changed so as to make more professionally responsible the courtrooms' utilization of the expert testimony. In this article we shall address ourselves to a less well recognized question, but one which we believe has a logical priority over the two indicated above, so long as one assumes continuation of existing court procedures. Namely, we need to know how jurors interpret and act upon the psychiatric testimony they receive before we can reasonably recommend modifications of current practice. . . .

I

\*    \*    \*    \*

. . . Perhaps the chief complaints of the psychiatrists lie in the adversary nature of the proceedings. They assert that the atmosphere of the courtroom is incompatible in both aims and procedure with the usual

Reprinted by permission of the author and of the publishers from 21 *Ohio State Law Journal* (1960), 75–95. Footnotes have been renumbered to run in sequence throughout the selection.

surroundings and expectations associated with the role of the physician. The courtroom resembles neither the examining room nor the laboratory. The expectations involved in the patient-doctor relationship are such that the doctor rarely hears either his authority or his technical skill questioned. It is also a relationship in which both participants believe that the doctor will act responsibly.[1] However, as Guttmacher and Weihofen have indicated,

A trial is not a scientific investigation, it is not a search for objective truth. The doctor who undertakes to go into court to testify as an expert witness must bear in mind that he is stepping squarely into the middle of a fight.[2]

In addition the psychiatrists note that in the courtroom the expert is subject to cross-examination; that he may be asked to give categorical replies on matters that he believes are heavily shaded by special circumstances or unique events. He may hear his own opinions compared with those of a colleague, whom he knows to be less competent in the area in which he is testifying.

The expert may be asked to state his opinion on hypothetical questions which he believes have no bearing on the particular proceeding, or indeed which may illustrate a point that is contradictory to the case at hand. He may find that his attempts to present a full clinical account of the nature of the defendant's symptoms are objected to as irrelevant; and instead he may be asked to state his views on matters that he believes are non-related both to his own area of expertise and to the nature of the case. Questions concerning the defendant's sense of responsibility, and his understanding of right from wrong are usually directed to the medical expert. As Dr. Guttmacher stated in a special issue of the University of Chicago Law Review commemorating the *Durham* decision,

So much for the psychiatrists' side of the story; how do lawyers view

Most psychiatrists who have had courtroom experience feel that they have been as greatly hampered from giving honest and effective assistance to the court by the methods and rules of legal procedure as they have been by working in the M'Naghten strait jacket.[3]

the problem? Even before the expert takes the stand, the lawyer may be

---

[1] For a fuller discussion of the patient-doctor relationship, see Parsons, *The Social System* 428–479 *(1951)*.

[2] *Guttmacher & Weihofen, [Psychiatry and the Law (1952)], at 205.*

[3] *Guttmacher, "The Psychiatrist as an Expert Witness," 22 U. Chi. L. Rev. 329 (1955).*

fearful that the psychiatrist's orientation, his view of human nature, of the origins of conforming behavior in contrast to criminal behavior, may be so far removed from the legal orientation that his opinion can have no relevance for the ongoing trial.

A frequently cited source of concern for the lawyer is the belief that, unless the function of the expert is carefully delineated, he could, by the combined effects of his general prestige and his detailed technical knowledge, virtually dictate to the jury the outcome of the case. While the lawyer may be fearful of the potential influence of the psychiatrist, he may be also somewhat skeptical of the "scienticity" of the discipline he represents. The lawyer may be dismayed by the open, and at times bitter, conflicts that have been waged in the courtroom between proponents of "different schools of psychiatry." He has witnessed what in the past, especially in major criminal trials, was not an infrequent occurrence, that of heated intra-professional controversies between psychiatrists called by the opposing sides.[4]

For many members of the bar, the problem becomes one of a control of power, even when it is in the hand of a benevolent representative. The expert, as many lawyers have indicated, should be available when needed, but in a situation in which he clearly performs as a witness whose credibility is subject to the usual scrutiny of the jury.

This brief review of the attitudes of practicing lawyers and psychiatrists to the expert's performance in the courtroom has served as an introduction to the major concern of this paper. The comments of the experts are directed primarily to one audience, the jury. How does this body of judges evaluate the performance they have heard? . . .

## II

The research reported here is part of a much larger study of the American jury system that has been in progress at the Law School of the University of Chicago since 1953. In carrying out this study a variety of

---

[4] *At the present time at least twenty states have statutes which authorize the court to appoint experts and report. The same provision is also found in the Federal Rules of Criminal Procedure. As the practice of court-appointed experts becomes more general, perhaps one of the sources of difficulty, that of partisanship among the experts, will be substantially reduced. For a full discussion of this see Wigmore, A Students' Textbook of the Law of Evidence (1935) and Guttmacher & Weihofen, Psychiatry and the Law (1952).*

methods have been employed from the analysis of historical documents concerning the origins of the jury system to the carrying out of intensive interviews in the homes of each of the twelve jurors who had recently deliberated together on a case to the presentation of recorded trials based on real cases for the consideration of jurors who are serving on their regular period of jury duty. These recorded trials then are replicated before a number of different juries. . . .

\*　\*　\*　\*

The transcript used for this experiment was adapted from the case of *United States v. Claison King*,[5] heard originally in the District Court of the District of Columbia in 1956. The recorded trial, renamed *The People v. Jason Lunt* was played before sixty-eight juries in three jurisdictions, Chicago, St. Louis and Minneapolis. As of this time, fifteen of these deliberations have been transcribed and their content analyzed.[6] These fifteen deliberations, along with the questionnaire responses of the entire sample of 816 jurors ($68 \times 12$) form the basis of this paper.

\*　\*　\*　\*

In the full research design two experimental variables were included: one was concerned with the rule of law and the other with expert psychiatric testimony. The rules of law that the jurors received from the judge were systematically varied so that one-third of the jurors were instructed along the lines of the traditional *M'Naghten*, or right from wrong version, one-third along the lines of the more recent *Durham*, or product of mental disease formula, and one-third received "no instructions," or no specific criterion concerning the insanity pleas. In addition, two versions of the psychiatric testimony were presented. Half the juries heard what we have labeled "model" expert testimony. In this version an attempt was made to present a detailed clinical history of the defendant's illness from infancy until the time of his indictment. Along with the detailed account we sought to present testimony which was as free of technical jargon as ideally could be expected from a medical diagnosis. In the second version, heard by the remaining half of the juries, more "typical" psychiatric testimony was prepared, in which little attempt was

---

[5] *United States v. Claison King, Docket Number 665–55 (D.C. 1956).*
[6] *The deliberations transcribed thus far were randomly selected from the three jurisdictions.*

made either to present a developmental picture of the defendant's illness or to delete the rather rich sprinkling of technical vocabulary usually heard in such accounts.

*　*　*　*

## III

The first cluster of data comes from the questionnaires distributed after the deliberation. Jurors were asked to respond to a series of items concerning the expert psychiatric testimony. The first group of questions sought reactions on the following points:

A—Did the jurors find helpful the testimony of the two psychiatrists called by the defense?

B—Did they want more information from the experts?

C—Did they believe that the language the experts used in testifying was too technical?

It was anticipated that the reactions of the jurors might be related to one or both of the following factors: The version of the psychiatric testimony they had heard; and their disposition to believe the defendant was guilty or not guilty by reason of insanity. Concerning the first factor, it was expected that jurors who heard the psychiatrists present the longer, more detailed, and relatively straightforward description of the defendant's symptoms would be more likely to find the expert testimony helpful; would have less need for further information; and would be less likely to believe that the language employed by the experts was too technical.

On the relationship between verdicts and the above questions, it was thought that the jurors who found the defendant not guilty by reason of insanity generally would be more appreciative and, perhaps, less critical of the experts' testimony. They might be less likely to believe that additional information was needed or that the language employed by the experts was too technical.

Let us now examine the data. Concerning item A, about three quarters, or 74 per cent, of the jurors indicated that they found the testimony helpful. No differences were observed between jurors who heard the "model" as compared with those who heard the "typical" testimony; or between jurors who found guilty and those who found not guilty by reason of insanity.

The responses to item B had much the same flavor as those given to item A. On this question, two thirds of the jurors indicated no expressed need for further information. Jurors who heard the "typical" version of the psychiatric testimony expressed no greater need for more information than those who heard the longer and more detailed "model" version.

As indicated in Table 1, shown below, of the one-third minority who did want more information, the need was significantly greater among jurors who believed the defendant was not guilty by reason of insanity; 44 per cent in contrast to 29 per cent for the guilty-prone jurors.

TABLE 1. PER CENT OF JURORS INDICATING THAT THEY WANTED MORE INFORMATION FROM THE TWO DEFENSE PSYCHIATRISTS, BY EDUCATION AND VERDICTS.*

| Verdict | Grade | High | College | Combined |
|---------|-------|------|---------|----------|
| NGI | 35 | 46 | 48 | 44 |
|  | (62)** | (139) | (58) | (259) |
| Guilty | 26 | 29 | 30 | 29 |
|  | (112) | (276) | (164) | (552) |
| Combined | 29 | 35 | 35 | 33 |
|  | (174) | (415) | (222) | (811) |

* $[X_2^2 \text{ df } (.99) = 9.2, X^2 = 16.97 \text{ P} < .01.]$
** Frequencies are in parentheses.

When the jurors were divided into different educational categories, it may be noted that this relationship between a verdict of not guilty by reason of insanity and a desire for more information was distributed relatively evenly across each of the educational groupings.

Jurors' responses to item C followed much the same pattern in that slightly more than two thirds, or 69 per cent, of the responses expressed no dissatisfaction with the language employed by the experts. Jurors who heard the "model" version were only slightly less critical than those who heard the "typical" testimony. Of the former, 71 per cent did not believe that the language was too technical, white of the latter 65 per cent indicated that they did not find the language too technical. These differences are not statistically significant.

As shown in Table 2, listed below, the belief of the jurors concerning the guilt or insanity of the defendant was not a significant factor. Of the 31 per cent who found the language too technical, 34 per cent were jurors who believed the defendant not guilty by reason of insanity and 29

TABLE 2. PER CENT OF JURORS INDICATING THAT THE LANGUAGE OF THE DEFENSE PSYCHIATRISTS WAS TOO TECHNICAL, BY EDUCATION* AND VERDICTS.

| Verdict | Grade | High | College | Combined |
|---------|-------|------|---------|----------|
| NGI | 39 | 35 | 28 | 34 |
| | (62)** | (139) | (58) | (259) |
| Guilty | 37 | 32 | 20 | 29 |
| | (112) | (276) | (164) | (552) |
| Combined | 38 | 33 | 22 | 31 |
| | (174) | (415) | (222) | (811) |

* [$X_2^2$ df (.95) = 6.0, $X^2$ = 8.97 P < .05.]
** Frequencies are in parentheses.

per cent were jurors who believed the defendant guilty. It may be noted that of this 31 per cent, a significantly high contribution was made by jurors with a grade school education: 38 per cent in contrast to only 22 per cent for the college educated jurors.

In summary, the responses of at least two thirds of the jurors to these rather general questions indicated that they had a favorable, if somewhat uncritical reaction to the experts' performance. The responses did not indicate that there was a systematic tendency to view the model testimony any more favorably or less critically than the typical testimony. It is interesting that, in contrast to our expectations, the jurors who found the defendant not guilty by reason of insanity were no more appreciative of the experts' performance and they did indicate a greater desire for more information than the guilty-prone jurors. It would almost seem that, having gone along with the psychiatrists' views on the matter, they would have liked even more information in order to further substantiate their own beliefs. As we move to an examination of more specific questions, we shall see if the trends reported here are substantiated.

The next series of items sought to compare jurors' evaluation of expert, in contrast to lay, testimony as the testimony might have influenced their decision in the case. The total number of witnesses appearing for both sides was eight: four lay and one expert witness were called by the prosecution, and two expert witnesses were called by the defense. The defendant did not take the stand but the statement he gave immediately after he was picked up by the police was read into the record by the prosecuting attorney.

Concerning the order and length of testimony, the prosecution opened his case by calling the two complaining witnesses; the testimony of Henrietta, the younger daughter, preceded that of Roberta, the older one. They in turn were followed by a family friend and former colleague in the fire department, and finally by Detective McKay, the arresting officer. For the defense, Dr. Weinstein preceded Dr. Fairchild. On rebuttal, the prosecution recalled the family friend, then the detective, and for the first time he called the deputy fire chief who was also the defendant's immediate superior in the municipal fire department, and finally, also for the first time, an expert witness, a psychiatrist, Dr. Grant. In both the "model" and "typical" versions, the combined testimony of the two defense psychiatrists was the longest, with Dr. Weinstein's taking slightly longer than Dr. Fairchild's. Next in order of length of time on the witness stand was the deputy fire chief, followed by the arresting officer, the younger daughter, the family friend, the older daughter, and finally the government psychiatrist.

On the questionnaire, next to the names of each of the witnesses, the jurors were asked: How important was this testimony in causing you to hold the opinion you have? In response, the jurors were to check one of the following:

> — very important
> — fairly important
> — not important.

In Table 3, shown below, jurors were divided into three groups: those who rated the testimony of all, or from five to seven of the witnesses[7] very important; those who rated three or four very important; and those who rated two or less of the witnesses' testimony very important. The reason for this division was to differentiate into relatively homogeneous groups those jurors who were likely to have a restrained or critical reaction to all the testimony they heard, those who were intermediate in their critical assessment, and those who found importance in everything they heard.

We note, from Table 3, that jurors in each of the groups found the testimony of the daughters, that is, the prosecution's principal witnesses, equally or more important than they found the testimony of the psychiatrists. However, only among the jurors in the "0–2 category" are the differences in favor of the daughters of a significant magnitude.

---

[7] *The jurors were asked to make one rating for the testimony of both daughters. In total, then, there were seven witnesses to be rated.*

| Number of Witnesses Juror Rated Very Important | Expert | | | Lay | | | | |
|---|---|---|---|---|---|---|---|---|
| | 1st Def Psych | 2nd Def Psych | Govt Psych | Two Dau's | Friend | Arrest Officer | Deputy Fire Chief | Combined |
| 5–7 | 91 | 92 | 89 | 91 | 80 | 76 | 73 | 85 (271)* |
| 3–4 | 66 | 60 | 45 | 70 | 46 | 28 | 37 | 54 (326) |
| 0–2 | 20 | 17 | 10 | 44 | 19 | 7 | 14 | 25 (215) |
| Combined | 62 | 60 | 50 | 70 | 50 | 39 | 43 | 57 (812) |

* Frequencies are in parentheses.

It might be of interest to compare the importance ratings received by the witnesses with the length of their appearance on the stand. In the preparation of the experimental transcript an attempt was made to delete as much of the repetitious material as possible without, of course, seriously jeopardizing the realism of the experience. It may be assumed that all of the testimony that was retained was considered relevant to some degree.

| Length of Time on Stand | Witness | Importance Rating |
|---|---|---|
| 3 | Both daughters[8] | 1 |
| 1 | First Defense Psychiatrist | 2 |
| 2 | Second Defense Psychiatrist | 3 |
| 6, 7 | Friend-Government Psychiatrist | $4\frac{1}{2}$, $4\frac{1}{2}$ |
| 4 | Deputy Fire Chief | 6 |
| 5 | Arresting Officer | 7 |

The testimony of the two defense psychiatrists was rated second and third in importance; it was exceeded only by that of the complaining witnesses.[9] The expert testimony, however, was rated no more important

---

[8] This ranking represents the combined testimony of both daughters.
[9] It should be noted that the two daughters were the first two witnesses to appear in the trial; and it may be that a primacy factor is operative, thereby causing

than might be anticipated if one were estimating the importance of the psychiatrists' influence from the amount of time that the jurors were exposed to their views. Also, if the percentage of very important ratings received by the defense psychiatrists were compared with the combined row per cents that appear in the final column (85, 54, 25) in each of the three juror categories, the difference between the psychiatrists and the combined per cents is only slightly in favor of the experts.

*　*　*　*

[Table 4 omitted.]

## IV

The main brunt of the jurors' discussion of the expert psychiatric testimony consisted of a detailed examination of what the doctors included or failed to include in their testimony, and the implications of this testimony for the plea of insanity offered by the defense. That is, did the testimony provide adequate guidance to a body of laymen delegated the responsibility of determining whether or not the defendant should be declared legally insane? The following are quotations selected from the fifteen typed protocols of the deliberations presently available. The first excerpt may serve to establish the general tone of the jurors' comments. It was taken from a jury that heard the "typical" expert testimony, and the comment was made after the discussion had been going on for about half an hour.

Here you have two psychologists, psychiatrists, who knew and worked with the man, say that he is insane. I don't just have to sit here and say that the man isn't when two medical men, of course you don't have to believe in doctors; some people don't. Secondly there are people who do not believe in psychiatrists, but I personally do and I wouldn't ever put a man in prison, when psychiatrists get up and say that the man is emotionally disturbed, when he is sick. Is there anybody in this room that doesn't believe in psychiatry? That's the whole thing in my estimation. It's whether or not you are going to take the word of these two men, who are well known and are admired in the field, and have excellent jobs. They are impartial. They're working for the county hospital. Are you going to take their word, or are you going to sit there and say that we know? We don't even know this man. They worked with him, they both say that he is mentally disturbed. If you don't take that as proof, I don't

---

*the jurors to remember the testimony more clearly than they remember the testimony of the other, later witnesses.*

know what you are going to do. I mean to me, in other words, if you don't find him not guilty by reason of insanity, you're sitting here disregarding the two psychiatrists in the case.

A few minutes later, in the same deliberation, another juror responded.

What I'm trying to say is just because these two people are educated and they are way up over our heads that we have to accept what they say as truth and that's it. In other words, they would be deciding for us, then we are not deciding for ourselves what is right in this particular case.

A third juror interrupted to agree:

If that's the case, this case shouldn't ever have gone to a jury. I mean that we should have to depend upon men specialized in the field of psychiatry to judge this man.

\* \* \* \*

During the trial, in cross-examination both defense psychiatrists had insisted that insanity was a judicial term and involved a determination which they "did not feel qualified to make." This statement was the source of considerable puzzlement in practically every deliberation. One juror expressed it this way:

What I don't clearly understand is are we talking in terms of legal insanity; or technical insanity; or medical insanity, the jargon of the psychiatrists? In the jargon of the psychiatrists, they do not declare him insane; they do not associate this man with the term that they generally associate with insanity, people who do not have control over their actions. The word psychosis came up, but they do not identify this man with having a psychosis, he had a mental disorder.

Later in the deliberation the same juror commented:

My argument is that the experts do not associate a mental illness to this man that has significance in terms of insanity. He had a mental disorder but was it such that the man was not responsible for his actions?

For some jurors the fact that the psychiatrists could not state whether or not the defendant was insane, was a reflection of their own competence and perhaps of the competence of the entire field. One juror expressed it this way:

Don't you think doctors with such high standards as they should have would have been able to tell you a little more surely, whether they thought he was insane or not?

Or, as several jurors observed in another deliberation:

As far as I can see, the defense psychiatrists didn't come right out and say that they thought the man was insane. They wouldn't say that.
No, they did—didn't. They didn't state it right out. They were only giving ideas of their own which are never always correct.
Now when it comes to mental sickness, everyone has their own.
Mental sickness isn't insanity.

Perhaps the main point of discussion stimulated by the expert testimony was the meaning of the distinction between neuroses and psychoses. During the trial, each expert had testified that in his opinion the defendant was not psychotic, but that he was suffering from a psychoneurosis. What implications did the negative finding *re* psychoses have on the jurors' determination of the sanity or insanity of the defendant? One juror put it this way:

Didn't that one doctor testify that he had an outside practice and that his whole practice practically was of people who had a neurosis. They're jumpy, nervous, maybe they do funny kinds of things. But you don't see his patients locked up in some institution do you? Well this fellow has a neurosis, or say, he has a mental illness. These other people they have a mental illness and they go to their psychiatrist and get treatment. But you don't see them doing irrational acts and maybe breaking windows or robbing stores.

\*     \*     \*     \*

Or, still another juror made the following analysis:

Part of the thing that bothers me about this is that everyone of us to some degree has a mental disorder. Anybody that likes the Cardinals but doesn't like the Browns has a mental disorder because I like the Browns, you follow me? So in our different beliefs, and I, oh, I raise my children differently than my neighbor raises his, so there's something wrong with my neighbor. My only point is that in the realm of the mind there is lots of room for differences of thinking and behavior and patterns of organization. Technically, none of the experts crossed the line and said that this man is insane, is definitely insane. They said he had a mental disorder.

A problem especially interesting to trial lawyers is how jurors assimilate conflicting expert opinion; and how in turn this reflects on the status of the expert witness. That is, can one still depend upon the testimony that has been "tinged by partisanship" to reflect the accumulated knowledge represented by the particular discipline? While the present trial does not provide the best opportunity for examining jurors' reactions on this problem, in that although both sides called "experts," the psychiatrist for the prosecution made almost a perfunctory appearance, having neither seen nor examined the defendant before his testimony in the courtroom. It may still be of some interest to observe jurors' reactions to the differences in conclusions expressed by the experts. . . . [One] juror distinguished the testimony of each side in the following way:

The big factor in my mind was that the two psychiatrists who testified that he was mentally deranged really examined the defendant. The other one I think the other man was a brilliant man, probably, but the other man definitely had *not* examined this particular gentleman. I would have thought a lot more of his testimony, I mean, I see no reason for disbelieving him, but I would have thought a lot more of his testimony if he had examined him. The other two doctors had examined him and that's an important difference in my opinion.

For some jurors, the testimony of the psychiatrist called by the prosecution was shown to be inadequate under cross-examination and therefore need not be given serious consideration in their deliberation. The following is one such instance:

As I remember part of the testimony [the testimony of Dr. Grant], the defense attorney was questioning the doctor and that doctor said that sexual perversion is not necessarily insanity; but he said it was disturbed emotions. Then the defense attorney asked what the difference was and the doctor couldn't say.

Before concluding, we might discuss one other aspect of this problem of jurors' evaluation of expert testimony. For those cases in which expert knowledge has been introduced, to whom shall the responsibility be delegated for deciding the issues in the case? In this period of increased expertise and specialization, many criticisms have been raised against the practice of laymen deciding matters about which their knowledge can at best be only on the level of an intelligent amateur. . . . The procedure, as it is commonly practiced today, is for each side to call the experts of his choice, who then testify for the enlightenment of the jury. How do jurors, as representatives of the general public, react to the idea of relinquishing their responsibility for deciding such cases? In this instance, the specific question posed to the jurors was:

Which to you, is the best way of deciding what should be done with a person who has committed a crime and pleads that he is insane?
——He should be tried before a jury, just like anyone else.
——He should be tried before a judge.

————He should be turned over by the court to psychiatrists and they should determine what is to be done with him.

Only 7 per cent of the jurors selected the judge. The choice then was between a jury of laymen or a group of medical experts, and between those two the jury was favored almost two to one. Of the one third who were willing to delegate authority to the psychiatrists, the jurors who found the defendant not guilty by reason of insanity exceeded the guilty-prone jurors to a significant extent. The strongest support for the psychiatrists came from those jurors who found the defendant not guilty by reason of insanity after listening to the "model" psychiatric testimony.

TABLE 5. PER CENT FAVORING PSYCHIATRIST BY PSYCHI-
ATRIC VERSION AND JURORS' VERDICTS.*

| Verdict | Model | Typical | Combined |
|---------|-------|---------|----------|
| NGI | 45 | 36 | 41 |
| | (124)** | (116) | (240) |
| G | 29 | 30 | 30 |
| | (242) | (271) | (513) |
| Combined | 34 | 32 | 33 |
| | (366) | (387) | (753) |

* $[X_1^2 \, df \, (.99) = 6.6, \, X^2 = 8.59 \, P < .01.]$
** The frequencies (figures in parentheses) do not include the 57 jurors who selected the judge.

But, perhaps the point to be emphasized is that two thirds of the jurors were not ready to relinquish their responsibilities to an expert body. . . .

### V

\*   \*   \*   \*

In their reactions and evaluations of the expert testimony, the jurors made several points. They distinguished the contributions made by the defense and government psychiatrists. That is, they acknowledged that a doctor's testimony not based on first hand knowledge of the subject may not be worth as much as testimony which was derived from direct contact. Generally speaking, most jurors granted to the experts the recognition appropriate to their specialized training and greater knowledge. Jurors did not, so far as can be judged at this time, indicate any differences in their evaluation of the "model" in contrast to the "typical" version of psychiatric testimony. The longer, more detailed, straightforward account was not perceived as being significantly more helpful or more influential than the shorter and more technical "typical" version. Generally, jurors indicated that they were impressed with the full scope of the experts' performance on the stand. About three quarters of the jurors indicated that the testimony was helpful, and two thirds did not believe the language they employed was too technical or that more information was needed. But as to the experts influencing the jurors insofar as the verdict was concerned, this was another matter.

It was almost because the jurors recognized that these men were experts, that they were members of a profession, that it gave the jurors license to grant them a certain degree of deference which did not also oblige them to accept the witnesses' statements as directives for their own action. As experts, these witnesses had a position and a view to represent, just as a member of the Chamber of Commerce might present the businessman's view, or a union leader, the working man's perspective. These witnesses represented the views of psychiatry about criminals. It is suggested that for many of the jurors they appeared as extreme and perhaps impractical views which, in the final assessment, most jurors did not choose to accept. This interpretation, concerning the failure of the experts to influence the jurors in their ultimate decisions, that of finding the defendant guilty or insane, is strongly supported by one statistic which we have deliberately delayed reporting: of the sixty-eight juries who heard and deliberated the case, only nine, or 13 per cent, found the defendant not guilty by reason of insanity. In brief, 71 per cent of the juries in finding the defendant guilty voted against the experts, and 16 per cent were unable to arrive at a unanimous verdict.

# THE JURY,
# THE LAW
# AND THE PERSONAL INJURY
# DAMAGE AWARD*

## *Harry Kalven, Jr.*

A few years ago Professor Jaffe in one of his customarily wise and urbane articles[1] observed: "I suggest that the crucial controversy in personal injury torts today is not in the area of liability but of damages." I think he is right on several counts. First, the criticism of personal injury awards today is at least as much concerned with their level as with their frequency. Second, it is my impression that on the bar's view the difference between lawyers—at least plaintiff lawyers—is measured more in terms of what they would get in a given case than it is in terms of winning or losing. Again, as a matter of simple arithmetic there is of course a greater difference between a $30,000 and a $10,000 verdict than there is between a $10,000 one and a verdict for the defendant. And finally to pick up the point Professor Jaffe was most concerned with—it is

* This article owes a major debt to the work of several colleagues on the jury project; in particular, to Fred Strodtbeck, Hans Zeisel, Dale Broeder, and to Allen Barton, Saul Mendlovitz, Rita James, and Phillip Ennis. Their work will in the reasonably near future be published in its own right. The debt is to the stimulus of innumerable discussions as well as to their data.

[1] Jaffe, Damages for Personal Injury: The Impact of Insurance, 18 LAW & CONTEMP. PROB. 219, 221 (1953).

Reprinted by permission of the author and of the publishers from 19 Ohio State Law Journal (1958), 158–178. Footnotes have been renumbered to run in sequence throughout the selection.

selecting the appropriate award level that is the most troublesome issue in proposals to shift areas of tort to strict liability compensation schemes.[2]

Professor Jaffe went on in the passage quoted to wonder why damages received so little attention in law school study and in the secondary literature on tort.[3] "Questions of liability," he continued, "have great doctrinal fascination. Questions of damage—and particularly their magnitude—do not lend themselves so easily to discourse. Professors dismiss them airily as matters of trial administration. Judges consign them uneasily to juries with a minimum of guidance, occasionally observing loosely that there are no rules for assessing damages in personal injury cases. There is analogy for this situation in Jerome Frank's complaint that fact finding, though of paramount importance, is neglected by teachers who devote themselves too exclusively to appellate law. This may reflect not so much their judgment of relative importance (as Judge Frank supposes) as the relative adaptability of the subjects to conceptualization. And so it probably is with the subject of damages."

Once again I think he is right. And I would add only this—the reason the law of damages escapes ready conceptualization is because it is so pre-eminently jury law. Damages even more than negligence itself is law written by the jury. I would suggest therefore that it is the absence of data as to jury behavior on damage issues which places an important topic generally beyond our reach.

The purpose of this comment is not to supply the necessary data. The Jury Project at the University of Chicago Law School has for several years now been studying the jury empirically.[4] It has progressed far enough to

---

[2] *Professor Jaffe's principal point is that there is a serious tension today between the drive on the one hand to extend liability coverage and the drive on the other to make damages increasingly comprehensive and "civilized." This tension is vividly illustrated in the current controversies over FELA [Federal Employers' Liability Act]. Here it is recognized on both sides that the employees have for the moment the best of two possible worlds—a de facto strict liability system combined with common law jury damages. It is also the point of Professor Morris' shrewd remark that if an auto compensation plan finally comes it will be as a result of its sponsorship by defendants.* MORRIS, TORTS 374 (1953). *See also the handling of the award level in* EHRENZWEIG, FULL AID INSURANCE FOR THE TRAFFIC VICTIM *(1954) and Kalven, Book Review, 33 Texas L. Rev. 778 (1955).*

[3] *The point is perhaps no longer quite so true as it once was. The Shulman-James and Smith-Prosser casebooks do have sections on damages. The recent Harper and James treatise on torts devotes a full chapter to it.*

[4] *For a brief report, see* KALVEN, REPORT ON THE JURY PROJECT, CONFERENCE

reaffirm that the jury's handling of damages is an extraordinarily interesting topic. It has also progressed far enough to realize that it would take a full life time of empirical research to document the many nuances in this corner of jury "law". . . .

*  *  *  *

The first general point is what we might call the variance in jury verdicts. The experimental jury technique has made an important contribution here by making it possible to try the same case several times and compare the results. This is an opportunity the legal system can very rarely provide and even when it does it is always a somewhat different case on retrial. The key point then is that if we run say ten trials of the same personal injury damage case we are very likely to get ten different results. And the experimental jury results provide therefore direct experience with the range of possible verdicts in a given case and also some sense of their relative probability.[5] This underscores the familiar point that jury law is unstable and uncertain, and more important it provides the proper intellectual model for thinking about jury decision making. A jury verdict is simply one of a series of possible verdicts for the single case.[6] And this in turn means that at most we should talk of *averages* when we talk about jury tendencies. The first point then is simply that this is the way it really

ON AIMS AND METHODS OF LEGAL RESEARCH 155 (*University of Michigan Law School 1957*). *By use of post-trial juror interviews, survey, and experimental jury techniques the project has been studying various aspects of the American jury system, with special emphasis on jury decision making behavior. The results will be reported out over the next two years or so in a series of volumes. It is important to emphasize that our research methods can give only an approximation of actual jury behavior. The post-trial interview with jurors is subject to inaccurate and incomplete recall; the experimental jury technique involves behavior on mock cases. There is therefore a margin of error on what is reported here as jury reaction. But we are persuaded that the evidence from these indirect approaches is plausible enough to warrant discussing it seriously as indications of actual jury behavior.*

[5] *It is probable that the experimental jury tends to exaggerate the variances somewhat for two reasons. First, our experimental cases may be more ambiguous on their facts than many actual jury cases; second, our experimental juries, although drawn from actual jury pools, have not been subjected to voir dire and include therefore relatively more jurors with extreme views.*

[6] *The project has less direct evidence on the variance of bench trial decisions, but it would appear that the model is equally correct for the individual judicial decision.*

is and that this variance is somewhat concealed from our normal view of the jury by the fact that we try the case only once.

But from a slightly different standpoint this averaging process is quite familiar to the trial lawyer. It makes explicit what he must in part be considering when he evaluates a case for settlement.[7] If he says a case is worth $20,000 he means not that a jury will invariably give $20,000 and, if he is very thoughtful about it, not that any jury will give $20,000. He means rather that the average of a series of verdicts in this case will be around $20,000 and that therefore he runs the smallest risk of error in settling as against trial if he sticks to his $20,000 figure. Our first experimental case supplied a vivid example of this. We had taken our script from an actual case which was settled just before verdict for $42,000. We ran ten experimental trials of the case; the verdicts ranged from $17,500 to $60,000 with only one $42,000 verdict and only one $40,000 verdict. Yet the average for the ten cases was $41,000.[8]

The settlement process in personal injury cases is an integral part of the total decision making institution; the vast majority of cases are disposed of by the settlement mechanism; and jury law controls not only the small minority of cases finally tried to verdict but those settled as well since the yardstick for settlement is the expectation of jury decision. And in weighing such expectations the bar more or less explicitly recognizes that they are dealing with the average verdict in the individual case.

The source of this variability in verdict is two-fold. It results from the ambiguity of the facts and the law, which makes for difference in viewpoint, and from the enormously wide public from which the jury is recruited, which makes it likely that those different viewpoints will be differentially represented on different juries. In brief, particularly on issues of personal injury damage, the jury system puts to the public precisely the kind of question on which differences in background, temperament and experience are likely to produce differences in opinion. Or to put this another way, it is still regarded as a somewhat refreshing point to observe

---

[7] *Variance also provides the key rationale for the doctrine of res judicata; see* Currie, Mutuality of Collateral Estoppel, 9 STAN. L. REV. 281 (1957).

[8] *This raises the amusing point that a lawyer who refuses to settle say, for $20,000 and is hit by a $40,000 verdict may in fact have been more right than his opponent. It may however be small comfort to him, or to his client, to realize that had the case been tried over and over to eternity the average of all verdicts would approximate $20,000.*

that changes in the personnel of the United States Supreme Court may have something to do with changes in its decisions. But with the jury we take for granted that personnel as well as rule and tradition make a difference.

From the viewpoint of the social scientist the jury offers a rich possibility for exploring further the correlations between background and opinion, a topic of wide general interest to him. We have talked thus far of the jury's sense of equity as though it were a single uniform sentiment interestingly different from the legal norm. But the truth of course is that so heterogeneous a population as the American jury has a great variety of sentiments on any given issue. And it is therefore pertinent to see what can be learned about what kinds of people have what kinds of views. Roughly we can break our inquiry into two stages. First, what kind of background and experience will dispose the individual juror to a given view at the end of the trial and before the deliberation begins; and second what kind of jurors will be influential in the deliberation process where the view must weigh if it is ever to matter to the result.

This is not the place to detail the results of our inquiry. But this much might be emphasized. First, we find repeated correlations between some background factors such as ethnicity and the jury's viewpoint on damages in the particular case. Second, as with the social sciences in general at this stage of their development,[9] the factors which correlate best are the demographic variables like ethnicity, occupation, income, etc. But these are relatively crude indices and do not contain on their face the explanation for the correlation. Our quest for deeper factors such as personality traits or basic sentiments which would both explain more and correlate more tightly has been only modestly successful. Third, we are again speaking only of averages; there is great variation within any general category of individuals. Thus on the average, business men of Scandinavian origin tend to be conservative on damages, but this or that individual Scandinavian business man might be enthusiastically pro-plaintiff. Fourth, some juror types who are most strongly pro-plaintiff or pro-defendant are most easily influenced to change their views in the deliberation process. But again the tracing of juror influence in the deliberation is a subtle and

---

[9] See STOUFFER, COMMUNISM, CONFORMITY AND CIVIL LIBERTIES (1955); Blum and Kalven, The Art of Opinion Research: A Lawyer's Appraisal of an Emerging Science, 24 U. CHI. L. REV. 1 (1956).

difficult matter. Fifth, we have made a special study of the regional variations in awards which permits us to make a fair map of the award "temperature" in the United States. But once again the explanation as to why different regions differ so much is hard to come by.

It should be abundantly clear by now that what we talk of as correlations between demographic variables and juror pre-deliberation bias is altogether familiar to the trial bar however alien the vocabulary. The institution of voir dire examination is the lawyer's version of the same point. In his exercise of peremptory challenges he is practicing the art of the social scientist. One phase of our study is therefore concerned with finding out what rules and hunches the lawyer plays in actual practice and how closely these check out with our own results. Suffice it here to note that the lawyer has observed well and it is somewhat a matter for mutual congratulation that our results are so close to his; similarly our study of regional variation has its obvious counterpart in the migratory tort suit and here again the bar and we are largely in agreement.

Men differ as jurors not only because of the differences in their backgrounds but also because of the differences in their experience. One of the most interesting chapters of the jury study concerns the juror's use of extra-record information in the deliberation. Whatever the law's interest in keeping the trial record aseptic, it cannot in fact prevent the juror from augmenting it out of his own experience. Thus the record is enlarged in the jury room by juror testimony. And the documenting and inventorying of this addition to the record is a fascinating business indeed. One recurring instance of this has special relevance for the damage issue. It concerns the juror's reactions to medical testimony and to illness in general. It may be as simple as the juror's identification with the injured plaintiff where he himself or a close friend or relative has experienced a comparable injury. The bar has recognized this in its aphorism that the risk of having the aged and infirm on the jury is that the defendant will have to pay for their ills as well as those of the plaintiff. It may take the form of grave suspicion of ills less obvious than the broken leg, on the general view that no one feels altogether healthy anyway, or more con-cretely as in the case of a railroad man plaintiff where several jurors knew railroad men intimately that no real railroad man would complain about such minor ills. Or the very vagueness of the ailment may turn in the jury's eyes into a guarantee of authenticity as in the case of a back ailment where all the medical testimony tended to show that the doctors could find nothing organically wrong. In one such case which we studied through post-trial interview a juror indicated that his mother had complained of such an ailment for thirty years, that no doctor had been able to find anything wrong, *and* that he was certain his mother was not a hypochondriac. The jury faced with the delicate choice of believing the plaintiff or charging the juror's mother as a hypochondriac sided in the end with the plaintiff.

There remains then the pooling of individual juror views in the deliberation process to yield the group verdict. Here again the jury involves an important area of research in contemporary social science—the study of small group behavior. And here the blending of the lawyer's perspective with its emphasis on the logic of argument with the social scientist's perspective with its emphasis on the social process of the group has proved a considerable but a rewarding job. The lawyer is likely to view the deliberation as simply a formal debate; the social scientist is likely to view it as group problem solving where everything but the content of the problem is of interest.

The dynamics of group behavior in the jury room is too complex a story to attempt here. The great point is that a jury verdict is a group product; that the jury is not simply an atomistic electorate, but must work to a solution which is at least tolerable to all twelve. One result is that the filtering of individual eccentricity through the group process furnishes a major safeguard in the jury system. It is not merely that twelve heads may be better than one but that a verdict hammered out as a group product is likely to have important strengths.

We have anticipated in the prior discussion several of the most important points about the jury's behavior when it turns to the damage issue as a group. The cardinal point is that the quest is more for the appropriate sum than for the summation of the specific components. The impression, as already noted, is one of considerable fluidity in argument—the sum is more important than the arguments advanced on its behalf. If this argument is disallowed, another will take its place. And one important reason the jury can reach agreement is that it does not try for agreement on all the subordinate premises. Juror A may rate pain and suffering more important than Juror B, and Juror B may take disability as more substantial than Juror A. They will air these differences, to be sure, in the deliberation but they will not insist on their resolution so long as by whatever route they can agree on the overall sum.

One illustration of this will have to suffice. We touched earlier on their view as to lawyer's fees as damages. Do they actually award fees? The answer is not simple. They frequently discuss them in the deliberation; they see no impropriety in so doing. They are frequently well informed, although not always, about the level of contingent fees today. Does this then mean that awards are higher by the amount of the fee? We seriously doubt it.[10] First we virtually never have a jury which after agreeing on the proper damage figure then decides on the fee as a group and adds it. We have some property damage cases where the damage is more objectively set and in these the jury does not consider the fee. And we have a variety of suggestions that the fee point is used simply as a device in argument to facilitate agreement. Perhaps the most vivid illustration occurs in an experimental jury deliberation where a majority of jurors finally reach agreement on a sum which does not reflect fees. In an effort to persuade one of the hold-out low award jurors the point is made for the first time. The hold-out agrees he has overlooked fees and raises his figure accordingly. An over-logical member of the majority then asks about the majority adding fees to their award and is quickly and decisively rebuffed.

The miracle of the jury is that it is somehow able to reach agreement despite the divergent views with which it enters the deliberation. This is the result of many pressures including a great reluctance to fail to do their job and have the jury hang. In part it is the result of a decent respect for the opinions of others on matters where certainty is hard to come by. In

---

[10] *To balance the impressions here I should report a jury anecdote I recently heard from a lawyer. The particular jury is said to have begun its deliberation by deciding first on the lawyer's fee and then multiplying it by three to get the damages.*

*Occasionally an appellate judge will himself be explicit about lawyers' fees when he is appraising whether a verdict is excessive or not. In Renuart Lumber Yard, Inc. v. Levine, 49 So. 2d 97 (Fla. 1950) where the court entered a remittitur of $15,000 on a verdict of $75,000, Judge Hobson dissenting, said in part: "Moreover, although there is no legal basis for the inclusion of an attorney's fee in the judgment it is a matter of common knowledge that in personal injury actions lawyers do not customarily perform services for the plaintiff gratuitously. As a practical proposition it is indeed probable that after paying for the services of his attorney appellee would have little, if any, of the $30,000 left. . . . Such circumstances cannot be ignored by the writer in performing his part of this appellate court's duty to determine whether the judgment is so grossly excessive as to shock the judicial conscience."*

part it is the result of a subtle shift in their own perception of the facts as the deliberation continues. We find with high frequency that a genuine consensus has been reached at the end with the jurors now preferring the jury verdict to their original position. And finally in part it is the result of negotiated compromise when argument can go no further.

We come then to the quotient verdict. Is the damage award simply the quotient of the twelve individual answers? Here again the answer is complicated. The final awards will not infrequently come close to the original pre-deliberation averages for the group. But this will often be the result even though a quotient is never taken. There is a natural tendency for the extremes to come toward the middle as the range of positions is disclosed. The jury often takes a quotient early as a guide but then goes on with its deliberation. And in the cases where the quotient is the final answer the compromise usually comes late after a serious effort to bridge difficulties by other means. The merit of a compromise verdict is thus difficult to assess without knowing the full context of the deliberation.

In general we have concealed from ourselves the difficult position in which the formal law may place the jury. Surely there is nothing about the damage issue in many personal injury cases which makes it likely that twelve men acting seriously and in good faith can reach full agreement on it. What do we then want the jury to do? There are only two alternatives left: negotiated compromise or a hung jury. The practical jury always prefers the former with the interesting result that the function of the jury in the end may be not to adjudicate the case, but, as it were, to settle it vicariously.

In any event, the nature of the damage question permits the jury to behave differently than do the yes/no issues of guilt and liability. It permits the small adjustment, the slight shift, and if necessary, the full compromise which makes the verdict possible. The damage verdict therefore is especially likely to reflect the composite view of the jury as a group and not to be the product of the single strong juror or the strong faction. Perhaps the legal system should seek some way to avoid having questions of such flexibility and indeterminacy arise, but so long as it continues to furnish them the jury would seem to provide a remarkably congenial mechanism for the official resolution.

We have left to a brief postscript the consideration of the parallel performance in comparable cases of the judge. Logically perhaps, this is the first question to ask about the jury—how differently do judge and jury decide the same case. We are by no means clear on how much like the judge and how different from him we wish the jury to be. If it is too much like the judge, the jury may lose all claim to a distinctive function. If it is too little like him we are disturbed by how easily jury equity elides into jury anarchy.

The question is specially pertinent for the personal injury case where the jury is so widely thought, as jury waiver ratios indicate, to favor the plaintiff. A major segment of the jury project is devoted to a survey in which trial judges have reported on a case by case basis how they would have decided on bench trial actual cases tried before them with a jury.[11] Once again the results indicate considerably more complexity than the popular view supposes. I shall not report the data here except to note two points. First, the difference is not monolithic. While jury awards on the average are higher than judge awards, there are a surprising proportion of cases in which the judge would have given more than the jury in fact did. Second, the detailed profile of judge-jury differences obtained from the survey gives us another perspective on the jury's sense of equity and the law's success in controlling it.

The judge and jury are two remarkably different institutions for reaching the same objective—fair impersonal adjudication of controversies. The judge represents tradition, discipline, professional competence and repeated experience with the matter. This is undoubtedly a good formula. But the endless fascination of the jury is to see whether something quite different—the layman amateur drawn from a wide public, disciplined only by the trial process and by the obligation to reach a group verdict—can somehow work as well or perhaps better. And in any event in its persistent struggle to dispose of the difficult issues our legal system gives it—among which measuring personal injury damages occupies a prominent place—the jury throws much light on the ultimate issues of justice involved.

---

[11] *The survey is based on a nationwide sample of some 700 trial judges and includes some 5000 actual jury trials. Roughly 1400 of these are personal injury cases. The results will be reported out in detail in the publications of the Project.*

# PLAINTIFF'S FAMILY STATUS AS AFFECTING JUROR BEHAVIOR: SOME TENTATIVE INSIGHTS

*Dale W. Broeder**

## INTRODUCTION

This is one of a series of jury strategy pieces. The data which follow are based on the observation of a series of twenty-three consecutively tried jury trials in a single federal district court in the Midwest. The trials in question (16 civil and 7 criminal) were observed from beginning to end, all lawyers involved therein were interviewed at length and, with the permission of the Court, 225 jurors serving in such cases were personally interviewed at their homes. The average interview lasted two and a half hours, some of the interviews running in excess of four hours.

Much more would be stated by way of introduction except that the "much more" has been repeatedly stated elsewhere. Suffice it to say that what appears here is a very small portion of the data garnered by the University of Chicago Jury Project.[1]

---

*. . . The author is deeply indebted to Professor Harry Kalven, Jr., of the University of Chicago Law School without whose support and encouragement this article would not have been possible.*

[1] *For* Jury Project *data generally, see* KALVEN, REPORT ON THE JURY PROJECT OF THE UNIVERSITY OF CHICAGO LAW SCHOOL *(1955)*; *Kalven,* A Report on the Jury Project of the University of Chicago Law School, 24 INS. COUNSEL J. *368 (1957). See*

---

Reprinted by permission of the author and of the publishers from 14 *Journal of Public Law* (1965), 131–141.

Plaintiff's family and/or marital status affected the thinking of one or more jurors in all five of the personal injury cases studied where plaintiff prevailed and where the question was investigated in the course of personal interviews with the jurors. And, because family relationship is by definition part of a wrongful death action, it also was necessarily involved in *Field* where a moderately attractive twenty-two year old widow and her two baby girls were awarded $52,500 for the husband-father's death. "Widowhood" and "fatherlessness," however, were there considered in ways which the legal system does not recognize. *Field* has several surprises in this regard.

Family status was also a factor in *Ford #1*, a personal injury action, where the jurors hung on the question of liability necessitating a retrial and again in *Rose*, a wrongful death action, where the verdict was for defendant. It would also undoubtedly have had its impact in *White*, another personal injury case, had that case not been settled by the parties just after the judge instructed the jury. In sum, we deal here with no marginal item. Plaintiff's family and/or marital status was materially involved in nine of the sixteen civil cases studied.[2]

---

*also, Meltzer,* A Projected Study of the Jury as a Working Institution, 287 ANNALS 97 *(1953).*

*With regard to the author's own published* Jury Project *work see Broeder,* The University of Chicago Jury Project, *38* NEB. L. REV. *744 (1959); Broeder,* The Jury Project, *26* S.D.B.J. *133 (1957). See also Broeder,* The Functions of the Jury: Facts or Fictions?, *21* U. CHI. L. REV. *386 (1954).*

*For other* Project *publications see,* ZEISEL, KALVEN & BUCHHOLZ, DELAY IN THE COURTS *(1959); Zeisel,* Split Trials and Timesaving: A Statistical Analysis, *76* HARV. L. REV. *1606 (1963); Kalven,* General Analysis of and Introduction to the Problem of Court Congestion and Delay, SECTION OF INSURANCE, NEGLIGENCE AND COMPENSATION LAW: PROCEEDINGS ABA *322 (1963); Zeisel,* Splitting a Liability and Damage Issue Saves 20% of the Court's Time, SECTION OF INSURANCE, NEGLIGENCE AND COMPENSATION LAW: PROCEEDINGS ABA *328 (1963); Zeisel, Kalven and Buchholz,* Is the Trial Bar a Cause of Delay? *43* J. AM. JUD. SOC'Y. *17 (1959); Kalven,* The Jury, The Law, and the Personal Injury Damage Award, *19* OHIO ST. L.J. *158 (1958), reprinted in 7* U. CHI. L.S. REC. *6 (1958).*

*For those readers who may have read all of the writer's published* Jury Project *articles and noticed a discrepancy regarding the number of jury trials actually reported as studied, it should be noted that there were 23 jury trials (16 personal injury cases and 7 criminal cases) actually studied, not including cases settled before the verdict's rendition. In the case of certain articles, however, cases not studied in detail and/or which were settled prior to verdict yielded data important enough to include them as "a case studied."*

[2] *Necessarily, all names and places referred to in this article have been changed.*

Let us first take the four personal injury cases involving married male plaintiffs with dependent wives and minor children—*Phillips #2*,[3] *Thomas* and the two *Ford*[4] cases.

*Phillips #2* perhaps most clearly illustrates the situation involved. Plaintiff, a forty-three year old truck driver, was married and had one child, a boy of sixteen, in high school. The major damage claim was for impairment of future earning capacity. Unfortunately, the six jurors who, with one exception, either originally voted against liability or favored low damages, were neither asked about nor volunteered comment on the question of plaintiff's family responsibilities. Their six colleagues, however, all of whom favored high damages, volunteered that they were led to do so in part out of sympathy for the situation in which plaintiff's wife and child might find themselves if plaintiff could no longer work. And, indeed, the query, "what would happen to them, (i.e., plaintiff's family), if . . . (plaintiff) lost his job because he was too sick or if he had to have an operation on his back," it seems certain, was a persistent and unchallenged theme of the deliberations. It was obvious that family life, family solidarity, and security ranked high in the values of all these jurors. Their families came first, before themselves, and it was perhaps only natural that they should think about plaintiff's family, too. Juror Scott felt very strongly, as his young nephew had only recently been hospitalized on account of complications resulting from an apparently minor injury sustained years before: nephew's wife and young child had suffered serious economic privation and Scott was unwilling to expose plaintiff's family to a similar risk. "I guess, when you come right down to it, that's why I favored higher damages than any other juror." The question, "What would you have done if plaintiff was a bachelor without family responsibilities?" would undoubtedly have produced some interesting responses. But even without them, it seems safe to state that the award would have been materially lower. Especially is this true as the data bearing upon the problem were volunteered by the jurors themselves and not elicited by questions specifically addressed to it.

---

It goes without saying that this is likewise true of the Negro in Court piece, 1965 DUKE L.J. 19. For the reader's convenience, the various name changes are kept constant in all of this writer's published Jury Project work.

[3] The Phillips case was tried twice. Hence the reference to "#2."

[4] Ford was likewise tried twice and . . . the first trial resulted in a hung jury.

*Thomas,* a Federal Employers' Liability Act case, while slightly more complicated, clearly carries forward the pattern reflected in *Phillips* #2. Plaintiff was a forty-four year old locomotive engineer, was married and had one child, a boy of eighteen, just starting college; and, again, as in *Phillips* #2, the major damage claim was for impairment of future earning capacity. And here, too, several of the jurors—at least five and probably more—were in part influenced to increase damages on account of sympathy for "what his family would do" if plaintiff's injuries later forced him to quit work and/or if plaintiff were discharged by defendant for having brought his lawsuit. Plaintiff's family rather than plaintiff and/or his income was the focal point of the jurors' discussion of impairment of future earning capacity. The jurors drew heavily on their own personal experience in this regard, mentioning several of these experiences during the deliberations.

But at least four of the *Thomas* jurors are known not to have increased damages on account of plaintiff's family responsibilities. Refusal to do so, however, was not prompted by a feeling that the question was irrelevant. To the contrary, it was probably more important to them than to the five jurors previously considered. The difference between the two groups was simply that the former did not find plaintiff's family responsibilities onerous enough to merit increasing damages or even to find in plaintiff's favor on the question of liability. As one of these jurors succinctly phrased the notion during his personal interview: "If he (plaintiff) had little bits of kids and as time went on he would have trouble, that would be a different story. But his family was raised, he had a boy in . . . college."

The point was repeatedly advanced during the *Thomas* deliberations, both as a reason for voting against liability and, later, for keeping the award at a minimum. Indeed, the deliberations began with a discussion of plaintiff's family responsibilities. The foreman, having read of the $52,500 verdict rendered in *Field,* attempted at the outset to employ it as a standard by which to fix plaintiff's damages in *Thomas.* The attempt, however, was met with a violent objection from one of the jurors favoring defendant: "We can't use that verdict here because that case involved a *penniless young widow and two children.* Mr. Thomas can still work, makes a good salary, has his own home, his *children are grown,* and he has a cabin where he goes fishing in . . . (Michigan) The cases are altogether different." (emphasis added.)

The *Thomas* jurors' knowledge of plaintiff's family responsibilities had still another impact. The four jurors favoring defendant—while of the opinion that such responsibilites were not large—nevertheless used them as a partial basis for concluding, and for arguing during the deliberations, that plaintiff's contributory negligence was the sole cause of the accident. This was on the theory that plaintiff, in not carrying accident insurance, displayed a callous disregard for his family's welfare and hence was the kind of man "very likely to be negligent." The importance of "the family" in *Thomas* seems clearly to be established.

The *Ford* cases, while providing data similar to that elicited in *Phillips #2* and *Thomas,* add other dimensions to the effect on the verdict of a married male plaintiff's family responsibilities. Plaintiff, a forty year old truck driver, was married and had seven children. Unsymmetrically, however, with reference to the cases previously considered, his personal injuries were conceded to be minor; the only major claim was for the destruction of a recently acquired tractor the value of which was stipulated to be $5,000. As we have seen, the first *Ford* trial resulted in a hung jury on the question of liability; the second brought a verdict for $8,000. Ford's wife and large family had perhaps their greatest (and certainly their least legitimate) impact in the jurors' determination of the crucial and only question of liability, viz., whether it was plaintiff or defendant's employee who had negligently driven across the center line. Thus at least fourteen jurors, five in *Ford #1* and nine in *Ford #2,* reasoned that defendant's employee was at fault in part on account of plaintiff's large family: "A man with such heavy responsibilities and so many mouths to feed simply has to be careful. If anyone was at fault, it must have been . . . (defendant's employee)." The point was frequently made without objection in the deliberations of both juries.

But the pattern of sympathy for the family evident in *Phillips #2* and *Thomas* likewise played an important role. This was true even in *Ford #1,* where four of the jurors felt—and one strongly urged during the deliberations—that plaintiff should recover simply because of his large family: "He's a family man; he needs the money to pay off the finance company. How would you like it if you had your means of livelihood (i.e., plaintiff's tractor) destroyed and you had eight mouths to feed?" While the argument was not criticized during the deliberations, several of the jurors strongly regarded it as improper, three of whom likewise expressed irritation with plaintiff's frequent testimonial references to his wife and seven children. "He was just trying to play on our sympathy; it worked, too, so far as some of the jurors were concerned." It also worked in *Ford #2* where, though plaintiff did not so often refer to his family, three of the four jurors favoring high damages admitted having done so in part on account of their sympathy for plaintiff's heavy family responsibilities. The argument that damages should be increased out of sympathy, while vigorously objected to as improper, was several times advanced during the deliberations. Sympathy for the family likewise appeared during the fight over liability where Juror McGee, who felt very strongly on the point, argued loudly that "this is a case where the plaintiff is a family man and the defendant is insured. If you (referring to the two jurors favoring defendant) can't see that, you can't see anything." The intensity of McGee's feeling is perhaps even better illustrated by his interview response when asked "what . . . (he) liked least about the trial?" "That some of the jurors couldn't get the two real issues into their heads—that Ford was a family man and that it was merely a suit between two insurance companies to see which one would pay him."

If the four cases considered present any criterion, there seems to be little doubt that a male plaintiff's family responsibilities must often be a factor tipping the scales in his favor on the question of liability and in increasing the level of his award and that the greater the responsibility (i.e., the larger the family), the higher the verdict and the greater the likelihood of recovery in the first place. In this latter regard the division of opinion among the jurors in *Thomas* is especially enlightening. If the hypothesis suggested by the data is correct, one cannot help viewing with some irony the concern expressed in many quarters over the general refusal of the courts to allow recovery by wives and children whose economic interests have adversely been affected by third-party negligence towards the husband. Our juries, it would appear, have often set the courts' decisions on end. The only major blot on this otherwise rosy picture for plaintiff-husband-provider is the danger—illustrated in *Ford #1*—of irritating the jurors by laying too heavy stress on the existence of his responsibilities.

However, the hypothesis suggested is based on the assumption that plaintiff-provider is a "good one," that is, a husband who does the best he can. None of the four cases thus far presented actually involved a derelict provider, though at least one example of what might happen in such a situation was afforded by *Thomas,* where four of the jurors voted against liability partly on the theory that plaintiff's failure to possess accident insurance showed him to be callous towards his family and thus the kind of man very likely to have been negligent. The implication from *Thomas,* however, is supported by certain data from *Rose,* a wrongful death action decided for defendant and the only "derelict provider" case studied. Four of the jurors there voted for defendant in part on account of deceased husband's excessive drinking and failure adequately to support plaintiff-widow. Their marriage had been a rocky one—for which plaintiff, as well as deceased, these jurors reasoned, was in part to blame—and, all things considered, plaintiff was "better off now that he (deceased) was dead." There was, therefore, no reason to grant recovery. The expression of this theory during the deliberations, however, touched off a violent protest from several of the jurors favoring recovery and doubtless materially contributed to such jurors' unwillingness to change their votes. But the proponents of the theory held fast and reaffirmed faith in its validity during their personal interviews. Derelict providing, it seems probable, like good providing, must also sometimes illicitly be taken into account by our juries.

## II

A sixty-eight or seventy year old laborer whose marital and parental status was not disclosed during the trial, and eighty-five year old widow with several grown children, a forty year old divorcee without children and a fairly attractive twenty-two year old widow with two baby girls— these persons respectively, were the plaintiffs in the remaining cases where the impact either of plaintiff's family and/or marital status or the jurors' assumptions in this regard were studied. How, then, did the jurors deal with such questions and what, if any, theories of behavior are suggested by the data?

*Drake* was the case involving the elderly laborer never questioned as to his marital or parental status. The major claim was for total and permanent destruction of earning capacity, the evidence establishing that plaintiff had not worked since the accident. Defendant's liability was readily agreed upon during the deliberations and one of the first questions discussed in determining the damages was whether plaintiff had a wife dependent upon him for support and "whether there were any children to take care of him and help him along in a financial way." Reasoning that such persons, if they existed, would certainly have been referred to during the trial, both questions were answered in the negative. A general consensus was reached that while "a wife did not have to be considered" plaintiff's lack of children to rely upon was material and therefore on balance damages had to be increased. The word increase, of course, is misleading; what is meant is that the damages were higher than they would have been had the jurors concluded that plaintiff had children. In this sense, seven jurors stated that the absence of children to care for plaintiff caused them to increase damages; the remaining five, while failing to challenge the propriety of the increase during the deliberations, at least privately refused to take the absence of children into account.

The former group of jurors, it will be noted, were assuming that the children, if there were any, would be grown and in a position such that they would and should be obligated morally to provide plaintiff with help; plaintiff, after all, was between sixty-eight and seventy years of age. The moral obligation of a grown child to provide for an injured aged parent, in other words, was viewed as in the nature of accident insurance, the existence of which would require a reduction in aged parents' damages. Of course, if the children were dependent minors, as in *Phillips #2, Thomas,* and the two *Ford* cases, damages would be increased. Drake's wife, on the other hand, had her existence been assumed rather than the contrary, would clearly have been regarded as within the minor children dependent category as were the wives in the cases just mentioned.

*White,* involving the eighty-five year old widow, illustrates even more clearly than *Drake* the "accident insurance" role played by an aged plaintiff's grown children. Plaintiff had broken her leg and the claim was for pain and suffering, medical expenses, and the cost of hiring a practical nurse for 5.9 years, plaintiff's remaining life expectancy. It was uncontradicted that plaintiff would remain bedridden for the rest of her life whereas she had been normally active for her age prior to the accident. However, it was equally clear that she would never hire a practical nurse but would, as before, continue to be gratuitously cared for by her two grown daughters and their families, with whom she had lived for nearly all of the past ten years. The jury were fully instructed on the collateral benefits rule[5] and specifically that plaintiff was entitled to recover the reasonable cost of hiring the nurse. Plaintiff's counsel likewise explained

---

[5] *See generally,* GREGORY AND KALVEN, CASES AND MATERIALS ON TORTS 476–83 (1959).

this, particularly emphasizing that recovery should be granted notwithstanding that the jurors might be of the opinion that his client would probably not hire a nurse. Unfortunately for jury research, the case was settled immediately after the judge gave his instructions and there was consequently no deliberation. However, seven of the eight jurors returning a mailed questionnaire, distributed to the panel within a few days of the trial, expressly indicated that they would personally have opposed any compensation for the practical nurse. Plaintiff had her children to rely upon, just as before. The children's tendency to reduce damages for the eighty-five year old widow White would seem to be well-established. Lucky, indeed, was Drake that he possessed none. The lone *White* juror in favor of granting recovery for the nurse apparently did so on account of his recollection of and willingness to abide by the court's instruction. None of his colleagues returning their questionnaires recalled the instruction. Taken together, *Drake* and *White*—the only two cases studied in which the problem of grown children of aged parent plaintiffs was involved—strongly suggest that such children are far from a blessing in parent's action for personal injuries. Plaintiff's counsel in *White,* it is submitted, might just as well have told the jury that his client was insured.

*Grey,* involving the forty year old divorcee without children, like *White,* is also related to *Drake.* A semiskilled factory worker, plaintiff [Grey's] major claims were for loss of wages, pain and suffering, and future medical expenses attendant upon an alleged traumatic neurosis. There was also the suggestion, not vigorously pressed, that her earning capacity had been impaired. While the personal interviews unfortunately did not focus to any extent upon whether the jurors or any of them considered or discussed plaintiff's lack of children, data were elicited with regard to the effect of plaintiff's lack of a husband-provider to depend upon, the thought being that the lack of a husband, like aged plaintiff Drake's apparent lack of grown children or the benefit Mrs. White would presumably have derived from having had no children, might conceivably have benefited plaintiff. And this, in fact, seems to have been the case. All eleven of the *Grey* jurors personally interviewed stated that plaintiff's marital status was a factor causing them to increase damages. Plaintiff was not merely an energetic housewife taking on an additional job in order to help with the mortgage or to buy a new TV set or a new car. Having no husband-provider to fall back on, she was all alone and would be in dire straits should the damages awarded later prove insufficient to cover the medical expenses allegedly necessary to cure her nervousness and enable her to continue working as before. The point was firmly urged without objection during the deliberations and there was a general consensus to this effect. The standard or comparison, it will be noted, was not the forty year old widower or the forty year old bachelor, but the forty year old housewife working outside the home to augment her husband's income. It was in this sense, and this sense only, that plaintiff's damages were increased and that plaintiff seems to have benefited. Her lack of a husband, in other words, was like Drake's lack of grown children upon which to rely; both being like the absence of accident insurance protection, which, with reference to persons possessing it—as Mrs. White did in the form of her two grown children—meant that damages had to be increased. So far as the cases studied are concerned, then, a working divorcee is in the same category as aged widows and widowers without grown children.

One final point remains: there seems to have been a complete absence of any juror prejudice against Mrs. Grey on account of her marital status. Indeed, such prejudice as existed on this score was in her favor. One of the jurors, herself a forty year old divorcee, greatly sympathized with plaintiff on this account.

*Field,* the wrongful death action, the last of the cases to be considered, is for present purposes the most illuminating. The action, as we have seen, was for the benefit of a fairly attractive, twenty-two year old widow and two baby girls, aged one and two and a half years. Deceased (husband-father) was a twenty-three year old truck driver. Pecuniary losses only were recoverable, but there was no statutory limit on the amount which could be recovered. The uncontradicted evidence as to damages showed that deceased was in excellent health at the time of the accident, that he earned approximately $4,500 per year, most of which was spent on his family, that his income was gradually rising and that he had a life expectancy of forty-four years. Properly figured, of course, the damages would represent the present value of the sum deceased would probably have spent on his wife and children during their respective lifetimes. The jury, in other words, were required to say what the situation would have been had deceased not been killed. What in fact happened, (i.e., the wife's "widowhood" and the children's "fatherlessness") was legally irrelevant. The verdict, as previously noted, was for $52,500.

As the lengthy prelude implies, the jurors were almost exclusively concerned with the situation as it turned out. Most significant for present purposes perhaps was their preoccupation with the fairly attractive widow's remarriage prospects. In contrast to the trial—where the question was never once referred to—such prospects were exhaustively reviewed without objection during the deliberations and a consensus reached that widow would almost certainly remarry within two years and that her failure to do so would be something for which defendant could not, in justice, be held responsible. Damages, therefore, had to be materially reduced.[6]

All twelve jurors, only one of whom had any doubt as to the propriety of such a reduction, and he only because of the lack of evidence on the question, stated that they made substantial reductions on account of such consideration. Widow's ability to remarry, in other words, apparently as measured by her degree of attractiveness, was regarded as an economic asset stemming from or freed by her husband's death and thus requiring a reduction of damages in the same sense, for example, as the right to receive the proceeds of an insurance policy carried for her benefit on deceased husband's life.

As in *Drake, White,* and *Grey,* the collateral benefits rule[7] and/or the policy considerations prompting it did not occur to the *Field* jurors. The life insurance analogy, it will be noted, is especially apt in view of the jurors' position that widow had an affirmative duty to mitigate damages by promptly securing a new husband. For the right to receive such proceeds, like the securing of another husband, can ordinarily only be realized through prompt affirmative action on the part of the beneficiary. Getting off this analogical plane, the practical point suggested by the data is simply that widow's damages in *Field* were less on account of her moderate good looks and correspondingly good prospects for remarriage and that an ugly and/or incapacitated young widow would presumably have recovered more. A beautiful and charming young widow, on the other hand, would presumably have fared worse.

Widowhood was again considered from the point of view of giving

---

[6] *It is also possible that such reductions might reflect the notion that young widowhood is an unnatural state and that the young widow should be forced into the marriage market either for her own good or for the good of the children. The jurors were unfortunately not questioned regarding such possibility.*

[7] Gregory and Kalven, op cit. supra *note 5.*

plaintiff an increased opportunity to take an outside job. Having no husband to look after, she could now work part time and later, when the children were older, full time; assuming, of course, that she did not remarry. The point was repeatedly urged without objection during the deliberations and eleven jurors stated that it caused them to reduce damages. There was, in addition, a strong feeling on the part of these jurors that a capable young widow should work, as should her children, and damages also were reduced due to the children's ability to help out later on. The earning ability, actual or potential, of beneficiaries in death actions, it would seem, must often perform an accident insurance role like that of the two grown daughters in *White*. One *Field* juror, however, refused to reduce damages: being a mother to the children was a full time job and Mr. Field was not the kind of man to permit his wife and children to work.

But the widowhood[8] and fatherlessness of the beneficiaries also enlisted the jurors' sympathy, five jurors admittedly having awarded damages for the widow's pain and suffering and for the children's loss of their father's love, guidance, and affection. Nonpecuniary losses, it seems certain, were also frequently referred to in the jury room. And, notwithstanding that several jurors realized the impropriety involved in awarding them, no objection appears to have been raised. Indeed, one of these jurors, herself a widow, was especially sympathetic. Psychologically unable to follow the court's instruction, she obviously felt that the emotional losses were entitled to as much as or more than the consideration given pecuniary losses.

Acutally, however, neither the aforementioned juror nor most of her colleagues were in the least concerned with compensating the beneficiaries for their pecuniary losses. So far as the jurors as a whole were concerned, the measure of damages was not the amount of the beneficiaries' losses as measured by their probable shares of deceased's income, but the cost of supporting the beneficiaries now that the husband-father was dead. Cost of support was the touchstone both of the deliberations as to damages and of the jurors' private reflections on the subject. Indeed, only three jurors so much as considered deceased's income and beneficiaries' probable lifetime shares therein and even these jurors were materially influenced by reflections as to the sum sufficient for support. Their nine colleagues, though

---

[8] *See Moss v. Associated Transport, Inc.*, 344 1.2d 23 (6th Cir. 1965).

differing widely as to the sum required and as to the support costs to be considered (*e.g.,* a college education for the children), exclusively relied upon their cost of support notions. There is, accordingly, little doubt that the damages awarded were substantially higher than they would have been if only one child or if no children had been involved; if only the children (and no widow) had been involved; or if both had been involved but the children had been older. The obvious analogy, of course, is to the damage-increasing effect of the dependent wives and minor children in *Phillips #2, Thomas,* and the two *Ford* cases where plaintiff was a husband-provider. But there is also an analogy to *Drake* and *Grey,* involving plaintiffs with no one to depend on, and to *White,* where there were grown children to provide help.

The point, of course, is the simple one, implicit in most of what has gone before, that the major impact of plaintiff's family and/or marital status in the cases studied (viz., in increasing or decreasing damages according to whether the injured party is required to support or is instead entitled to be supported by his spouse and/or children) involves a repudiation by the jurors of the fundamental tort concept that a negligent defendant's duty is to pay strictly according to the pecuniary value of the interests he directly injures (plaintiff's earning capacity, for example, in a personal injury action or the pecuniary value of deceased's life to the beneficiaries in a wrongful death action). Defendant instead pays, to an important degree, according to the existence and/or size of injured party's (or deceased's) marital and family responsibilities and/or injured party's moral right to help from his spouse or family. Cost of supporting plaintiff and his family—so dramatically illustrated in *Field*—and/or the moral right of plaintiff to be supported is the touchstone throughout. Viewed from this standpoint, of course, it would certainly have been surprising had the *Field* jurors, after deciding to award damages on a cost of support basis, then ignored factors as relevant and important on such a basis as widow Field's prospects for remarriage and her and the children's present and probable future earning capacity. Indeed, in terms of the jurors' premise, the exclusion of such items would have been indefensible.

## CONCLUSION

It remains only to caution the reader about the limited number of cases upon which the suggestions advanced herein are predicated and of the great variety of factors affecting the outcome of any case. The vast situational gaps in the data should also be appreciated. There was, for example, no case involving a housewife or a professional woman or a young bachelor. Indeed, one could go on this way ad infinitum. Yet with all these limitations and with the further and, from the standpoint of many academic disciplines, even more serious limitation that a lawyer was doing the work, it is hoped that something of value can legitimately be drawn from the presentation as is.

# SUPREME COURT BEHAVIOR IN RACIAL EXCLUSION CASES: 1935–1960

*S. Sidney Ulmer*

The United States Supreme Court is often guided by rules of law which make the disposition of cases depend upon singular combinations of circumstances. It is a relatively simple procedure to go through the cases in a subject matter area and compile a list of the facts the justices seem to have considered material to their solution of the issue at hand. But the identification of the peculiar combinations of events which push the decisions in one direction or the other is more difficult. The number of possible combinations is almost endless: with as few as twenty specified circumstances there are more than one million possible combinations. And the weight of a particular circumstance may depend on the combination of factors in which it appears.

Fred Kort has pointed to the "concrete differentiation of factual elements" which seem decisive in cases involving such procedural civil rights as protection against unreasonable searches and seizures, coerced confessions, and unfair trial procedures.[1]

This paper does not employ the methods developed by Kort, but its point of departure is also a recognition of the fundamental importance of

[1] Fred Kort, "Predicting Supreme Court Decisions Mathematically: A Quantitative Analysis of the Right to Counsel Cases," this REVIEW, Vol. 51 (March, 1957), pp. 1–12.

Reprinted by permission of the author and of the publishers from 56 *American Political Science Review* (1962), 325–330.

factual elements in certain kinds of cases. The subject area here is the type of unfair trial procedure at issue in cases involving the exclusion of Negroes from jury service in state courts. Supreme Court decisions on this issue are well known and the general topic has been well plowed by students of constitutional law. My purpose is to see whether inferences about Supreme Court behavior in racial exclusion cases can be sharpened by a shift from the traditional method of analysis. The shift in method involves no change in focus since my investigation will use the same facts chosen as material by those employing other workways. But my aim is quantitative generalization.

## I

Racial exclusion in the Federal courts has been barred by a congressional statute for many years and since 1875 state officials discriminating against Negroes in determining jury service in state courts have been subject to a fine of not more than $5,000.[2] But the vindication of Negro rights in this area has depended not on prosecutions under this statute but primarily on appeals to the Supreme Court invoking the Fourteenth Amendment against convictions in state courts obtained from juries from which Negroes are said to have been systematically excluded. In deciding these appeals the Court has developed the concept of a "representative" jury that is "an impartial jury drawn from a cross section of the community."

As Black put it in *Smith v. Texas:*

It is part of the established tradition in the use of juries as instruments of public justice that the jury be a body truly representative of the community. For racial discrimination to result in the exclusion from jury service of otherwise qualified groups not only violates our Constitution . . . but is at war with our basic concepts of a democratic society and a representative government.[3]

The Court has held that this principle entitles the Negro to a jury system in which Negroes are not intentionally and systematically excluded solely on account of race or color. But whether exclusion is intentional and

---

[2] *18 USC at 243.*
[3] *311 U.S. 128, 130 (1940).*

systematic and solely on the basis of race or color must be determined on the facts.[4] If the facts suggest a *prima facie* case of discrimination, the burden is on the state to rebut the presumption. In deciding whether a *prima facie* case has been made out the Court has chosen to focus on a particular type of fact, *i.e.,*—as David Fellman has expressed it—"Usually it is a matter of numbers."[5] The crucial facts, in short, seem to be qualitative variables, the variations in which may be represented numerically. A judgment as to discrimination is a rebuttable inference from a particular combination of numerically expressed facts or factual relationships. The lawyer, by necessity, must be interested in identifying the criteria which guide the formulation of such a judgment. The political scientist specializing in public law may equally have an interest if he would explain the Court's actions. The test which the Court has used to distinguish the combinations of circumstances which show unconstitutional exclusion seems to have been clearly stated on several occasions by several different justices.

In *Smith v. Texas,* for instance, Justice Black declared that "Chance and accident alone could hardly have brought about the listing for grand jury service of so few negroes from among the thousands shown by the undisputed evidence to possess the legal qualifications for jury service."[6] Stone remarked in *Hill v. Texas* that " . . . chance or accident could hardly have accounted for the continuous omission of negroes from the grand jury lists for so long a period as sixteen years or more."[7] And as late as 1958, Black, speaking for a unanimous Court in *Eubanks v. Louisiana* said, " . . . the uniform and long-continued exclusion of Negroes from grand juries shown by this record cannot be attributed to chance [or] to accident . . ."[8]

These statements, and others like them, suggest that while the Court sees the event of exclusion as a juncture of innumerable forces, a distinction is made between determinative and chance factors. When convictions

---

[4] *As Black expressed it in Patton v. Mississippi: "Whether there has been systematic racial discrimination . . . in the selection of jurors is a question to be determined from the facts in each particular case." 332 U.S. 463 at 466.*

[5] *David Fellman,* The Defendant's Rights (1958), p. 103.

[6] Loc cit., p. 131.

[7] *316 U.S. 400, 404.*

[8] *356 U.S. 584, 587.*

have been upset in exclusion cases, the Court has found that intentional and purposeful racial discrimination has determined the exclusion. It seems perfectly clear at the same time that exclusion resulting from chance factors constitutes no violation of the Fourteenth Amendment. In deciding whether a particular exclusion of Negroes from some part of the jury system is a chance occurrence, the Court has been careful to note two types of statistics. One is the ratio of qualified Negroes to qualified whites in the jurisdiction involved. In determining this ratio the Court has utilized such measures as the percentage of Negro taxpayers, the percentage literate, the percentage of Negro males 21 years and older, and the percentage of Negroes in the total population of the county. It has not, however, considered all these factors in every case. In fact, the only statistic running through all cases is the raw population figure.

The second type of statistic the Court has looked at is the ratio of Negroes to whites in the area of service from which exclusion is charged. The ratio chosen for emphasis usually depends on the nature of the claim, since exclusion from petit juries, grand juries, or jury lists may be involved.

Evidently, we have here an application of the statistical concept of sampling, and it suggests a testable hypothesis, namely, that the outcome in racial exclusion cases depends upon the relationship of a sample to a population on a particular attribute—racial heterogeneity (RH). The population consists of the Negroes and whites from which the sample (read jury or jury list) is drawn. The play in the joints of the judicial machine is of great importance here. For whether the racial heterogeneity of a sample is representative of a population is a meaningful question only if the population and sample are relevant for each other.

The racial heterogeneity of a population or a sample may be measured by an index of qualitative variation. This method essentially counts differences. The greater the number of differences among a set of items, the more heterogeneous the aggregate and hence the greater the variation in it. By counting the differences between each item and every other item in a set, we get a total number of differences in the aggregate. This becomes meaningful when we relate the observed differences to the maximum number of differences possible. The index of qualitative variation is the ratio of total observed differences to maximum possible differences, a ratio that can vary between zero and 100 per cent.

## II

An idea of what the court has been doing in exclusion cases can be gained by comparing the racial heterogeneity of the populations and samples to which the court has paid attention. RH values for populations and samples are presented in Table I for the 13 cases decided in the period 1935–1960. The table shows that the court has often used the racial composition of a total county population as a basis for comparison with the racial composition of juries and jury lists. Yet, it is safe to say that in no county or state is the total population the relevant base for determining jury service. Total population always needs refining by the elimination of those who lack the requisite qualities and characteristics specified by the statutes. There is some tension between the notion of a representative cross-section of the community and the long lists of requirements and exemptions which characterize jury selection procedures in many states.[9] But as long as the Supreme Court has not seen fit to prohibit such disqualifications, the representative jury should be interpreted as one which represents fairly the population of qualified prospects. And indeed, the justices have at times used a refined rather than a raw population count as a basis for their computations, though they have not been as careful to distinguish the one from the other as might be wished.[10]

In five of the 16 relationships examined, the court used total population statistics. In four of these racial heterogeneity of the sample popula-

---

[9] *For example, Alabama excludes those who are under age, habitual drunkards, permanently diseased or unfit because of physical weakness, illiterates (except property holders), and those convicted of any offense involving moral turpitude. Alabama exempts from jury service judges, attorneys, officers of the United States, officers of the Executive Department of the state, sheriffs, deputies, clerks of court, county commissioners, physicians, dentists, pharmacists, optometrists, teachers, actuaries, boat engineers, bus drivers, truck drivers (under jurisdiction of the Public Service Commission), railroad engineers, firemen, conductors, train dispatchers, bus dispatchers, railroad station agents, telegraph operators, reporters, embalmers, radio-broadcasting engineers and announcers, superintendents, doctors and regular employees of Bryce and Searcy Hospitals, officers and enlisted men of the National Guard and Naval Militia, convicts and prison guards. See Anderson v. Alabama, pending before the U.S. Supreme Court, 1961 Term, Docket No. 326.*

[10] *It is only fair to say that the necessary distinction with supporting statistical data has not often been presented in the parties' briefs. On several occasions, the court has apparently found it necessary to take judicial notice of census data in order to reach a determination.*

| Case | Year | Out-come | RHP % | RHS % | P | Vote |
|---|---|---|---|---|---|---|
| Norris v. Alabama | 1935 | + | 29.8(M) | 0 | | 8–0 |
| Hale v. Kentucky | 1938 | + | 41(Tx) | 0 | | 8–0 |
| Pierre v. Louisiana | 1939 | + | 88.8(R) | 0 | | 8–0 |
| Smith v. Texas | 1940 | + | 36(PT) | 13.4(JL) | < .001 | 9–0 |
| Smith v. Texas | 1940 | + | 13.4(JL) | 4.5(GJ) | < .05 | |
| Hill v. Texas | 1942 | + | 52.3(R) | 0 | | 9–0 |
| Akins v. Texas | 1945 | − | 52.3(R) | 23(JL) | < .05 | 6–3 |
| Patton v. Mississippi | 1947 | + | 92.1(R) | 0 | | 9–0 |
| Brunson v. N. Carolina | 1948 | + | 9.3(JP) | 3.1(JL) | < .001 | 9–0 |
| Cassell v. Texas | 1950 | + | 24.3(PT) | 25(GJ) | > .7 | 7–1 |
| Cassell v. Texas | 1950 | + | 24.3(PT) | 24(GJ) | $P_{21}$ < .01 | |
| Brown v. Allen | 1953 | − | 53.7(Tx) | 53.3(JL) | > .8 | 6–3 |
| Brown v. Allen | 1953 | − | 53.7(Tx) | 34.4(JL) | > .16 | |
| Speller v. Allen | 1953 | − | 94.2(Tx) | 26(JB) | < .001 | 6–3 |
| Reece v. Georgia | 1955 | + | 37.5(M) | 4.3(JL) | < .001 | 9–0 |
| Eubanks v. Louisiana | 1958 | + | 88.8(R) | .07(GJ) | < .001 | 9–0 |

* Distinguishing Negroes and Whites only.

Legend:    + = decision for the Negro claimant
          − = decision against the Negro claimant
      RHP = racial heterogeneity of the relevant population
      RHS = racial heterogeneity of the relevant sample
        M = males, 21 and over
       Tx = total tax paying population
        R = raw population
       PT = poll tax paying population
       GJ = grand jury
       JL = jury list
       JP = jury pool
       JB = jury box
        P = probability of the difference between RHP and RHS occurring by chance

tion over extended periods of 16 years or more was zero. In the fifth case, the court used the county tax list to identify the qualified population, but here again exclusion was total over a period of 30 years. Since all five cases were decided against the state, it seems fair to conclude that where the Negro population is substantial (7.2 per cent or more), and exclusion from the sample absolute, the court has required no further test. Indeed, the language in the opinions occasionally suggests that proof of total exclusion alone may be sufficient for showing racial discrimination, assuming there were some qualified Negroes in the county. Typical of this view is the comment of Black in *Patton v. Mississippi* that

. . . whatever the precise number of qualified colored electors in the county, there were some. . . . We hold that the state wholly failed to meet the very strong evidence of purposeful racial discrimination made out by the petitioner upon the uncontradicted showing that for thirty years or more no Negro had served as a juror in the criminal courts of Lauderdale County.[11]

Total exclusion cases, therefore, appear to require no further analysis, though problems could arise if the period of exclusion is sufficiently shortened. For the court has often asserted that exclusion of a race from a small enough sample is not sufficient for showing intentional and purposeful discrimination on a racial basis.[12]

The remaining cases raised problems of the type likely to plague the court in the future. In these cases the sample was racially heterogeneous as was also the population with which it was compared. The question the court has been asking is whether the differences in degree of heterogeneity are due to chance or intentional racial policy. As Frankfurter put it in *Cassell v. Texas*, the question is whether there was "a purposeful non-inclusion of Negroes because of race or a merely symbolic representation, not the operation of an honest exercise of relevant judgment or the uncontrolled caprices of chance."[13] While the court has not publicly used statistical tests of significance for the differences observed, nothing prevents us from doing so in our search for a standard. Associated probabili-

---

[11] *332 U.S. 463, 468–469. This comment was in response to an attempt by the Mississippi Supreme Court to play the role of statistician. "Of the 25 qualified Negro male electors there would be left, therefore, as those not exempt, 12 or 13 available male negro electors as compared with 5,500 to 6,000 male white electors as to whom, after deducting 500 to 1,000 exempt, would leave a proportion of 5,000 non-exempt white jurors to 12 or 13 non exempt negro jurors, or about one fourth of one per cent negro jurors,—400 to 1. . . . For the reasons already heretofore stated there was only a chance of 1 in 400 that a Negro would appear on such a venire and as this venire was of 100 jurors, the sheriff, had he brought in a negro, would have had to discriminate against white jurors, not against negroes—he could not be expected to bring in one fourth of one Negro." (p. 467).*

[12] E. g., *Cassell v. Texas, 339 U.S. 282, 286; Akins v. Texas, 325 U.S. 403.*

[13] Loc. cit., *p. 291.*

ties have been calculated for each of the bi-racial distributions in Table I.[14] In *Smith v. Texas,* the grand jury list was rated 13.4 per cent on the RH factor as compared to 36 per cent for the relevant population, composed of those paying poll taxes in the county. The chance expectation of such a difference is much less than 1 in 1,000. But when the grand jury list and the grand jury are compared on the same factor, the former exceeds the latter by a three-to-one-ratio—a difference expected by chance less than five times in a hundred. In *Brunson v. North Carolina,*[15] *Reece v. Georgia*[16] and *Eubanks v. Louisiana,*[17] the differences observed have associated probabilities of considerably less than .001. In *Brown v. Allen*[18] on the other hand, the observed differences in drawing grand jury and petit jury lists would be expected by chance about nine times in ten for the latter and approximately 17 times in 100 for the former. Social scientists analyzing these data would be likely to reject chance as an explanation in the first three cases but not in the *Brown* case since .05 is the usual cutting point. In these cases, the Supreme Court consciously or unconsciously has chosen to use a region of rejection consistent with established statistical procedures. And in *Brown,* the decision is for the state, racial discrimination not having been proved.

The remaining three cases do not fit the same pattern. In *Cassell v. Texas,* the difference between the racial heterogeneity of the poll tax

---

[14] *Unless otherwise indicated, all probability statistics used in this paper are two-tailed and were computed with the binomial expansion if N was small and with the binomial test and the Yates correction for continuity if N was large. The formula for the binomial expansion is*

$$P(x) = \binom{N}{x} P^x Q^{N-x}$$

*where P = proportion of cases expected in one category,*

$$Q = 1 - P \text{ and } \binom{N}{X} = \frac{N!}{x!(N-x)!}.$$

*For large samples*

$$(N > 25)Z = \frac{(x \pm .5) - NP}{\sqrt{NPQ}}$$

[15] *333 U.S. 851 (1948).*
[16] *350 U.S. 85 (1955).*
[17] *356 U.S. 584 (1958).*
[18] *344 U.S. 443 (1953).*

population and that of the grand jury is so minimal that its associated probability of occurrence is about eight times in ten. On that basis, we might expect a decision for Texas. In *Akins v. Texas*,[19] the disparity between the RH of the poll tax population and the jury list would be expected by chance less than five times in a hundred. We should therefore anticipate a decision for the Negro claimant. Contrary to these expectations, Texas won the decision in *Akins* but lost it in *Cassell*. The difficulties of squaring the two cases in terms of legal doctrine have been recognized. Herman Pritchett says that "the authority of the *Akins* ruling was subsequently impaired by the somewhat confused decision in *Cassell v. Texas*."[20] And it is true that the seven members of the majority in *Cassell* split 4–3 in choosing a rationale for their decision. The behavior of this majority, however, is entirely consistent with the statistical considerations previously introduced. For Reed, speaking for the court, was no more impressed by the differences in the racial heterogeneity of the poll tax population and that of the grand jury population than we are. And he declared, "Without more it cannot be said that Negroes had been left off grand-jury panels to such a degree as to establish a *prima facie* case of discrimination."[21]

The decision in the case turned, therefore, on the second charge that "the Dallas County grand-jury commissioners for 21 consecutive lists had consistently limited Negroes selected for grand-jury service to not more than one on each grand jury."[22] While the justices split 4–3 in agreeing with this charge, the decision for the Negro can be explained statistically since the associated probability of no more than one Negro on 21 consecutive grand juries is less than .01. This explanation eliminates the confusion in Reed's opinion and makes the outcome in *Cassell* consistent with the outcome in the other cases. In *Akins*, on the other hand, the Negro claimant failed because his sample was too small, not because the observed differences between sample and population were insignificant. As Reed pointed out for the court, the only complaint was said "to consist of an arbitrary and purposeful limitation by the Grand Jury Commissioners of the number of Negroes to one who was to be placed upon the grand jury

---

[19] *325 U.S. 398 (1945)*.
[20] *C. Herman Pritchett*, The American Constitution *(1959)*, *p. 546*.
[21] Loc. cit., *pp. 285–286*.
[22] Ibid., *p. 286*.

panel of sixteen for the term of court at which the indictment against petitioner was found. This is petitioner's only complaint as to racial discrimination." [23] If this is viewed as a claim for proportional representation, it would have no standing. If it is viewed as a claim of intentional racial discrimination, a sample of 16 persons containing one Negro was not sufficient to prove racial discrimination where Negroes constituted 15.5 per cent of the population sampled. The court, indeed, seems to have found the sample inadequate even when doubled to 32 persons including two Negroes. It may be surmised that had no more than one Negro name appeared on 21 consecutive lists, the sample would have been sufficiently large to support an inference consistent with that drawn in *Cassell*.

While the court has not been prone to use such terms as "sample size," an inference that such a factor is important in exclusion cases is entirely consonant with the data we have examined. The sample size in the 13 cases studied varied from 16 in *Akins* to 2,126 in *Speller*. And the sample in *Akins* was only about one-fourth the size of the next smallest sample. This alone is sufficient to put *Akins* in a class by itself. But even more striking is the fact that the court has decided no case in favor of a Negro claimant where the sample available numbered less than 252 names. It is also worth noting that a total of 25 different justices have compiled, over a period of 24 terms, a record of remarkable consistency in racial exclusion cases. For, as Table I shows, the 25 justices cast a total of 113 votes; all but 10 of these were cast consistently with the statistical explanations here advanced. This record shows that the liberal-conservative dichotomy which often characterizes the Supreme Court has not been operative in this area of litigation. It also shows that the court did not wait for Earl Warren to bring unanimity to one area of decision making of vital importance to those subjected to racial discrimination.

The final case, *Speller v. Allen*, is the only one not decided consistently with the statistical formulations we have advanced. In *Speller* no Negro had served on a Vance County, North Carolina jury in "recent" years. In examining the jury box, it was found that of 2,126 names, only 145 were those of Negroes. The majority of six justices (Vinson, Reed, Jackson, Burton, Clark and Minton) failed to find racial discrimination. Yet the probability of such an observed difference in the racial composition of the tax list and the jury box would be less than .001. *Speller,*

---

[23] Loc. cit., *p. 400.*

therefore, is a deviant case not explained by our formulations. In terms of the standards seemingly used by the court before and after that decision it would appear, as Black and Frankfurter agreed, that there was "unconstitutional discrimination" in the makeup of the jury box in *Speller*.

III

What may be concluded from all this? Basically, that it is now possible to formulate a set of explanatory hypotheses as follows:

(1) The total absence of Negroes from a state jury system or a part thereof is a violation of the Fourteenth Amendment given two conditions:

(a) The proportion of Negroes in the qualified population is substantial (*i.e.,* 7.2 per cent or more).
(b) The period of exclusion is long (*i.e.,* 16 years or more).

(2) Partial absence of Negroes from a state jury system or a part thereof is a violation of the Fourteenth Amendment given two conditions:

(a) The racial heterogeneity of a sample population (read jury or jury list) differs from that of a qualified population to an extent expected by chance less than five times in one hundred.
(b) The sample is sufficiently large (60 or more cases).

These hypotheses are not offered as final explanations or as complete explanations or as the only explanations for the Supreme Court's decisions in racial exclusion cases. They are submitted as explanations consonant with the data examined and are stated with sufficient precision to make empirical testing possible.

# The Courts

# ACCIDENTS, MONEY, AND THE LAW: A STUDY OF THE ECONOMICS OF PERSONAL INJURY LITIGATION

*Marc A. Franklin, Robert H. Chanin, and Irving Mark*\*

## I. INTRODUCTION

### A. The Accident Problem

For its increasing mobility, spreading cities, and booming technology,

\* *We are deeply indebted to Professor Maurice Rosenberg, Director of the Project, for his assistance in the preparation of the study. We are particularly grateful for his critical reading of the manuscript and his many helpful suggestions.*

*Several other members of the Project staff have contributed to the work reported here, and we regret that space does not permit us to thank them individually. We owe a special debt to the Columbia University Bureau of Applied Social Research for its help with the statistical aspects of this report. Bureau sociologists and statisticians have supervised the methods of analysis and projection which are such an essential part of this study.*

*We are also indebted to the members of the Project's Advisory Committee for their invaluable guidance. The views expressed here, however, do not necessarily reflect those of the Committee or particular members thereof.*

*The funds for the Project's work have been supplied primarily by grants from the Walter E. Meyer Institute of Law, Inc., and the New York Foundation, Inc.*

Reprinted by permission of the authors, the publishers, and the Columbia University Project for Effective Justice, at the Columbia Law School, from 61 *Columbia Law Review* (1961), 1–39. Footnotes have been renumbered to run in sequence throughout the selection.

modern society pays a fearful price in accidental injuries.[1] Each year accidents claim 10,000,000 victims, of whom 100,000 are fatalities.[2] In a nation of 180,000,000 people[3] this means that over 5 per cent of the population annually become accident statistics.

Pale before the human cost, but staggering in its own right, is the economic price of accidents. Evidence for recent years suggests that lost wages and medical expenses alone amount to almost $5,000,000,000 annually.[4] In addition, there are other, more indirect consequences,[5] and the total economic cost of accidents may well exceed $15,000,000,000.[6]

Countermeasures proceed on two principal fronts: reduction of the number of accidents and alleviation of the dislocating effects of those that do happen. Better understanding of human behavior, better designing of human products, and safer habits have helped to check the accident rate and to hold it below the rate of population increase.[7] But as long as man,

---

[1] *The technical meaning of "accidental" contemplates harm that is not caused by any tortious act of the person whose conduct is in question.* RESTATEMENT, TORTS § 8 (1934). *In its more common usage, however, the term includes all harm except that intentionally inflicted. Thus, accidents may be caused by negligent conduct, by conduct subjecting the actor to strict liability, or by conduct for which the defendant will not be held liable in tort. It is in this more common and broader meaning that the term is used in this article.*

[2] NATIONAL SAFETY COUNCIL, ACCIDENT FACTS 3 (1958 ed.); id. at 3 (1959 ed.); id. at 3 (1960 ed.).

[3] *According to the United States Department of Commerce, Bureau of the Census, on April 1, 1960, the official Census Date, the population of the United States was 179,323,175.* N.Y. Times, Nov. 16, 1960, p. 1, col. 4.

[4] NATIONAL SAFETY COUNCIL, op. cit. supra *note* 2, at 4 (1958 ed.); id. at 4 (1959 ed.); id. at 4 (1960 ed.). *This total includes approximately $4,000,000,000 resulting from wage loss due to temporary inability to work, lower wages after returning to work due to permanent impairment, and present value of future earnings of those totally incapacitated or killed. Medical fees and hospital expenses account for slightly less than $1,000,000,000.*

[5] *These include such things as the cost of investigating accidents, time lost by others in assisting and caring for victims, inefficiency and partial shutdowns caused by work absences, and the collapse of small enterprises that depend for their existence on one or a few skilled persons.*

[6] *It has been estimated that the indirect costs of accidents are more than twice the direct costs.* 2 HARPER & JAMES, TORTS § 11.1, at 729 (1956).

*Other evidence tends to suggest an even higher ratio. In the field of industrial accidents, for example, the relationship between indirect and direct costs has been estimated at four to one.* Heinrich, Management's Part in Safety, 40 Best's Insurance News (Fire & Cas. ed.), Feb. 1940, p. 37, at p. 39.

[7] *Between 1950 and 1959 the annual number of accidental injuries increased by*

his machines and his materials are fallible, accidents can be expected, and society must be prepared to grapple with their consequences.

\*     \*     \*     \*

[Section B omitted.]

## C. Scope of the Present Study

Because of the unique local differences that would complicate a national study of the accident compensation problem, it was decided to undertake a study of the situation in a particular geographical area and, if possible, to generalize from the findings. We have focused on personal injury litigation in New York City.[8] This city was selected for several reasons: it is a large metropolitan area with a high accident rate;[9] personal injury cases comprise a substantial part of the business in its courts,[10] and it is the site of an unusual collection of highly informative records on personal injury cases.[11]

---

*approximately 2%.* Compare NATIONAL SAFETY COUNCIL, ACCIDENT FACTS 3 (*1951 ed.*) with id. *at 3 (1960 ed.). During the same period, the population increased by 19%.* Compare *N.Y. Times, Nov. 3, 1950, p. 1, cols. 2–3* with id., *Nov. 16, 1960, p. 1, col. 4.*

[8] *Because what is true of New York City need not be true for other parts of the country, an attempt was made to find out something of the situation existing elsewhere so that we could determine the extent to which our findings might be generalized and our conclusions extended. The results of this effort reveal that many of the New York City features are characteristic of the situation in other large metropolitan areas throughout the nation. These results are reported in Appendix A.*

[9] *According to the National Safety Council, the accident rate in New York City is higher than that of any other city in the United States. N.Y. Times, Mar. 28, 1960, p. 31, col. 1. There were over 2,250,000 injuries, 2,600 of which resulted in death, in 1959.* Ibid.

[10] *In the New York State Supreme Court, for example, personal injury actions comprised 61.8% of the new issues filed in the judicial year ending June 30, 1959.* 4 N.Y. JUDICIAL CONFERENCE ANN. REP. 163 (1960). *When only the 12,905 law issues are considered, personal injury cases constituted 85.1% of the workload.* Ibid. *The latter percentage is probably a more revealing indication of the relative contribution to the court's total workload made by these cases, since the 16,192 equity cases include numerous uncontested matrimonial actions that are disposed of by referees with minimal burden to the courts.*

[11] *The following description of the sources of data is substantially derived from an earlier Project study, which drew upon much of the same material. See Rosenberg & Sovern,* Delay and the Dynamics of Personal Injury Litigation, 59 COLUM. L. REV. *1115, 1118–20 (1959).*

Since January 1, 1957, a rule of the New York State Supreme Court's Appellate Division, First Department, has required attorneys to file "closing statements" in certain personal injury and wrongful death cases.[12] The requirement applies to cases in which counsel (1) is retained on a contingent fee basis;[13] (2) succeeds in recovering damages for personal injury or wrongful death;[14] and (3) either has his office in Manhattan or the Bronx or brings suit in a court located in one of those boroughs. Despite this geographical limitation, a large majority of the personal injury cases arising throughout New York City are subject to the closing statement rule.[15] It should be stressed that the rule applies not only to suits but also to the thousands of cases in which a First Department attorney obtains a recovery for his client without bringing a lawsuit. Each statement shows, among other things, whether the case was closed with or without suit;

---

[12] N.Y. SUP. CT., APP. DIV., FIRST DEP'T R., Special Rules Regulating Conduct of Attorneys, *Rule 4.* . . .

*On July 1, 1960, the Appellate Divisions of the First and Second Departments put into effect a uniform rule requiring the filing of closing statements.* N.Y. SUP. CT., APP. DIV. FIRST DEP'T R., Special Rules Regulating Conduct of Attorneys, *Rule 4. Elsewhere in the state the filing of closing statements has been required in Monroe and Erie Counties in the Fourth Department since January 1 and March 1, 1957, respectively.* N.Y. SUP. CT., APP. DIV., FOURTH DEP'T R., *Rules Relating to Attorneys, Rule III–B.*

[13] *Under this arrangement, the attorney agrees to prosecute the case, including taking it into a trial or appellate courtroom if necessary, usually with little more than a nominal outlay by the client. The attorney's compensation is an agreed percentage of the recovery. If there is no recovery he receives no compensation.*

[14] *The uniform rule recently adopted in the First and Second Departments, see note [12] supra, requires the filing of closing statements even if there has been no recovery.* N.Y. SUP. CT., APP. DIV., FIRST DEP'T RULE:, Special Rules Regulating Conduct of Attorneys, *R. 4(2)*; N.Y. SUP. CT., APP. DIV., SECOND DEP'T RULES, Special Rules Regulating Conduct of Attorneys, *R. 4(2)*.

[15] *Although we are unable to specify exactly what portion of the New York City attorneys who handle personal injury cases have their offices in Manhattan or the Bronx, we do know that approximately five-sixths of all the attorneys admitted to practice in New York City have their offices in these two boroughs, See* AMERICAN BAR FOUNDATION, THE 1958 DISTRIBUTION OF LAWYERS IN THE UNITED STATES 48–49 (1959). *In addition, First Department lawyers institute approximately four-fifths of all personal injury suits begun in the city. This estimate is derived from an analysis of a random sample of 233 cases obtained from an agency to which most of the self-insurers and insurance companies underwriting in New York City report their personal injury cases. (This source will hereinafter be referred to as the Insurance Group.) Of the 100 suits in this sample, 78 were brought by First Department attorneys.*

whether it was closed before, during, or after trial;[16] whether it terminated in settlement or judgment; how much was recovered; and how the proceeds were distributed. About 44,000 such statements were filed during 1957.[17] By 1959 the annual rate had risen to 66,000, and during the first six months of 1960, over 40,000 statements were filed.[18]

With court authorization the Project analyzed and compiled data from a random sample of 3,000 statements filed during 1957.[19] In order to determine whether any significant changes had occurred since then, we conducted a spot check among closing statements filed in 1959.[20] The results of this check tend to corroborate the basic findings.[21]

---

[16] In determining the point at which suits were closed, three stages were distinguished: "before trial," which means before the first witness was sworn; "during trial," which means after the first witness was sworn, but before the return of a verdict or award; and "after trial," which means after return of a verdict or award. Although some lawyers may have employed different meanings when filing closing statements, interviews conducted with a random sample of attorneys practicing in New York City have convinced us that the above definitions are generally employed by members of the profession.

[17] This has been reported to the Project by the Clerk of the Supreme Court, Appellate Division, First Department.

[18] This was also reported to the Project by the Clerk of the Supreme Court, Appellate Division, First Department. As of July 1, 1960, statements are no longer to be filed with the clerk, but are filed with the New York State Judicial Conference.

[19] Court permission was necessary to obtain access to the closing statements because they are not public records. An order made on March 7, 1957, by Presiding Justice David W. Peck of the Appellate Division, First Department, authorized the Project to analyze the closing statements filed during the first six months of 1957. A random 2,000-case sample was then drawn by selecting every fourth statement filed between February 4 and April 17, 1957. Detailed analysis of these statements suggested a number of hypotheses that warranted further investigation. Accordingly, upon the Project's application a second court order was made on February 3, 1958, by Presiding Justice Bernard Botein, who had succeeded Justice Peck, authorizing the Project to examine additional closing statements on file. A further random sample of 1,000 closing statements was then collected by extracting 1 out of every 35 statements filed between April 17 and December 31, 1957.

[20] The spot check sample consisted of 150 closing statements. To avoid possible differences due to seasonal variations, these were taken for the same periods of the year as those of the 3,000-case sample.

[21] This statement requires some qualification. A discrepancy exists between the two samples in the ratio of sued to unsued cases: in the 3,000-case sample 56% of the cases were sued and 44% unsued; in the spot check sample the figures are 63% and 37%, respectively. It is highly unlikely that this difference reflects a basic change since 1957 in the percentage of cases that reach suit, and the most likely explanation is that it results from a statistical insufficiency in the spot check sample.

Then, to check further on a number of findings and to determine whether the data thus obtained comprised a cross section of New York City personal injury business, we gathered information from the confidential records of several insurance companies cooperating with the Project[22] and from numerous other sources, both official and private.[23]

## II. HOW THE PRESENT SYSTEM OPERATES

Each year in New York City some 193,000 accident victims seek to recover damages for injuries ascribed to someone else's fault.[24] For about 154,000 of these claimants the first step is retaining an attorney,[25] while 39,000 proceed without the aid of counsel. Theoretically, a claim is but the first step on the road to the courthouse, but in fact very few of the 193,000 claims ever get that far. Approximately 116,000 are closed without suit,[26] leaving 77,000 that are actually sued. Almost all claimants who have been unable to recover without suit, and who wish to continue, retain an attorney.[27]

The next step in the process is the filing of a note of issue by which

---

*Since the status of a case as sued or unsued is related to certain other factors, this divergence affects several of the other comparisons between the samples. However, the important point is that most of the significant discrepancies are explainable by the greater predominance of suits; e.g., the fact that a smaller percentage of the spot check cases close within one year as compared to the cases in the basic sample is consistent with our finding that suits generally take longer to close than do unsued cases. See text accompanying note [74] infra.*

*A discrepancy that is not explained by the disproportionate number of suits, and one which may be important, concerns the attorney's fee in small cases. . . .*

[22] *The cooperating insurance companies have requested that their names be withheld.*

[23] *These sources are referred to at appropriate points* infra. *For a full discussion of these materials, see Rosenberg & Sovern,* supra *note [11], at 1120 n.24.*

[24] *This estimate is based upon computations reported in Rosenberg & Sovern,* supra *note [11], at 1160, app. C. It is important to emphasize that we do not claim that figures derived by these or similar computations are precise. We do believe, however, that they are reasonably close approximations of recent experience in New York City and fairly accurate forecasts of the short run future as well.*

[25] Ibid.

[26] Ibid.

[27] *This conclusion is based upon an analysis of the Insurance Group sample, see note [15],* supra. *Of the 100 suits contained in the sample, all were handled by attorneys. It is also supported by the experience of the M Insurance Co. over a period of many years.*

the parties signify that they are ready for trial.[28] Of the 193,000 original claimants only 48,000 reach this stage.[29] By the time of trial, only 7,000 suits remain.[30] Of these, 4,500 close during trial,[31] leaving only 2,500 cases that reach verdict.[32] The attrition rate for the 193,000 claims made each year is pictured in Chart I.

CHART I. PERCENTAGE OF CASES THAT REACH SUIT, NOTE OF ISSUE, TRIAL AND VERDICT.

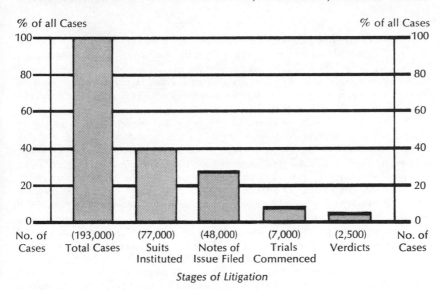

This chart indicates the marginal role that the courts play in the personal injury field. Less than 2 per cent of the claims made each year in New York City are directly controlled by court adjudication and, to

---

[28] N.Y. CIV. PRAC. ACT § 433.

[29] *For the computations on which this figure is based, see Rosenberg & Sovern, supra note [11], 1124 n.36.*

[30] Ibid.

*Since the publication of the earlier Project study, certain data have become available from the New York State Judicial Conference which suggest that this figure may be high because of an overestimation of the number of cases reaching trial in the Supreme Court. We expect that the new statistical recording system instituted by the Conference will make it possible to ascertain the precise figure in the near future.*

[31] *Rosenberg & Sovern, supra note [11], at 1124.*

[32] *No distinctions are drawn in this article between jury verdicts and bench awards. "Verdict" is used to signify the completion of trial without regard to whether the trier of fact was judge or jury.*

anticipate a later finding, these adjudications account for only 3 per cent of the money that changes hands.[33] The other 98 per cent of the claims are disposed of, and the money moved, by a bargaining process in which victims, defendants,[34] lawyers, and insurance companies' representatives are the chief participants.

Since most defendants are insured,[35] the cases are defended by a limited number of insurance company attorneys. These attorneys gener-

---

[33] *We estimate that personal injury cases in New York City result in the transfer of some $220,000,000 each year. See note* [47] *infra. Fully-tried cases account for approximately $7,300,000, or a little over 3% of the total. This latter figure is derived by multiplying the number of recoveries after trial, 1,500, by the average amount recovered in these cases, $4,859. See text accompanying note* [46] *infra; text following note* [65] *infra. See also note* [45] *infra.*

[34] *Although it is extremely unusual for an individual defendant to appear in these negotiations unrepresented, there are a considerable number of self-insurers in the City, and it is not uncommon for these groups to have their own representatives, who may or may not be lawyers. These include the City itself, most public utilities, and some commercial companies. Although we do not know the precise extent to which commercial companies self-insure in New York City, judging from nation-wide experience, it is probably not very great. A survey of the balance sheets of 600 of the largest corporations in the nation, including public utilities, showed only 139 with reserves for insurance, and of these, only 46 were specifically designated "self-insurance."* AMERICAN INSTITUTE OF ACCOUNTANTS, ACCOUNTING TRENDS AND TECHNIQUES IN PUBLISHED CORPORATE ANNUAL REPORTS *130 (7th ed. 1953).*

*We do not have any figures on the amount of money paid by defendant self-insurers in New York City each year in relation to that paid by insurance companies. However, in 1957, insurance companies throughout the nation paid $1,658,320,000 for personal injury and wrongful death claims, Gallagher,* Compensation for Injuries Without Regard to Fault, *in* A.B.A. SECTION ON INSURANCE, NEGLIGENCE, AND COMPENSATION LAW *46, 47 (1958), and it is estimated that self-insurers paid an additional sum equal to 1/3 of that paid by insurance companies. Ibid.*

[35] *Although we do not know precisely what proportion of all defendants are insured, we can estimate the answer by reference to a survey of New York City personal injury cases conducted by the All-Industry Committee Representing Insurance Companies. Most of the liability insurers underwriting in New York City participated. Their report, which is unpublished, was submitted in 1952 to the Court's Committee on Calendar Congestion, appointed by David W. Peck, then Presiding Justice of the Appellate Division of the Supreme Court, First Department, with Justice William C. Hecht as chairman. A similar survey was conducted for the month of June, 1957. [The two studies will hereinafter be referred to as the* PECK-HECHT *studies.] The 1957 study reveals that about 24,000 claims are filed each month with the liability insurers underwriting in New York City, or an annual total of about 288,000 claims. Unfortunately, we do not know how many of these cases involve only property damage. We do know, however, that approximately half of the notes of issue filed in the New York City Courts are for personal injury cases.*

ally specialize in personal injury cases and are quite experienced in their handling. The situation on the plaintiff's side is somewhat different. Our 3,000-case sample involved the services of 1,775 attorneys and law firms—the great majority of which handled only a few cases each. But there are also some "professionals" on the plaintiff's side. For analytical purposes, we have considered any attorney or firm gaining recoveries in nine or more cases in the sample as a "specialist." By this standard each specialist would average more than 100 recoveries each year.[36] Thirty-three or approximately 2 per cent of the 1,775 attorneys involved in the sample were specialists, and they handled slightly less than 13 per cent of the cases. This suggests that of the approximately 15,000 plaintiffs' lawyers

---

*This ratio is derived as follows. There were 16,712 law notes of issue filed in the Supreme Court in 1959, of which 14,205 were for personal injury cases. 5 N.Y. JUDICIAL CONFERENCE ANN. REP. 164 (1960). In the City Court in 1959 there were 29,765 notes filed in law cases. Id. at 184–85. Of these, 97% were for negligence cases. Ibid. Allowing for the small percentage of cases involving only property damage, we concluded that approximately 95% or 28,297 were for personal injury cases. In the Municipal Court there were 57,234 notes filed, id. at 76 (1960), of which 20% or 11,442 were for personal injury cases. Rosenberg & Sovern, supra note [11], at 1160, app. C n.4. This equals a total of 104,711 notes of issue filed, of which 53,924 or about 50% were for personal injury cases. Assuming that the proportion of personal injury cases remains roughly constant between the time the claim is made and the time the note of issue is filed, we conclude that there are about 144,000 personal injury claims made against defendants represented by insurance companies each year. Since there are an estimated 193,000 claims made, it would seem that at least 75% of the time the defendant is insured. However, this figure is clearly too low in view of the fact that the PECK-HECHT figures do not take account of the claims made against the City or other self-insurers. Since we do not know the number of cases brought against self-insured defendants each year, we can only conclude that defendants are insured in at least 75% of the cases, and probably in a substantially larger percentage. . . .*

[36] *On a simple projection, an attorney who handled 9 out of 3,000 cases would have handled 132 out of the 44,000 closing statements filed during 1957. However, a special check of the busiest attorneys found in the original sample of 2,000 closing statements examined under the order of March 7, 1957, see note [19] supra, suggested that a simple projection tends to overestimate the volume of cases handled by specialists. In that original sample of 2,000 closing statements there were 22 attorneys whose annual projected case load equalled 100 cases or more. All of the closing statements filed by these 22 attorneys during the first half of 1957 were culled and counted, and it was discovered that they had filed an average of 44 closing statements apiece; in other words, they had filed at an average annual rate of 88 per man. Taking both the simple projection and the special check into account, we think it safe to conclude that a 9-case man in the 3,000-case sample recovers in about 100 cases per year.*

who handle these cases each year,[37] about 300 are specialists, and that these 300 handle some 20,000 personal injury cases annually.

Another indentifiable group of plaintiffs' attorneys enters the personal injury picture when the attorney retained by the plaintiff does not wish to handle the case himself. While remaining attorney of record he may call in another or "extra" attorney to collaborate with him or to assume direct control of the case. This occurred in 16 per cent of the 3,000 cases, suggesting that "extra" attorneys are retained in 24,000 personal injury cases annually.[38] It is commonly thought that "extras" are trial specialists brought in when the case is destined for trial. But this cannot explain more than a few instances since our figures show that only 9 per cent of the cases involving "extras" reached trial. Of course, a case destined for trial may settle when an "extra" attorney enters the picture—and, indeed, his entrance may be an important factor in inducing the settlement. But the finding that almost 35 per cent of the "extra" cases do not even proceed to the point of commencing suit suggests that at times a firm may accept a personal injury case from a regular client and "farm it out," either because it does not handle such cases or is too busy to do justice to this particular one.

## A. How Many Recover

Approximately 162,000 or 84 per cent of all those who make claims each year ultimately achieve some recovery.[39] When we look further into this recovery figure we find that it is the weighted average of two disparate recovery rates. In those cases in which the claimant is repre-

---

[37] *This figure was reported to the Project by the Clerk of the Supreme Court, Appellate Division, First Department. All the* retainer *statements filed in the First Department were examined. It was discovered that 15,000 different attorneys had filed statements. In applying percentages obtained from the closing statement sample to this figure and deriving the figures reported in the text, it must not be forgotten that the closing statement percentages are based on cases in which the plaintiff was successful. If specialists were to have a rate of recovery significantly different from other attorneys, our estimates would be wrong to that extent. We have no empiric data on the point.*

[38] *As with our estimates concerning specialist attorneys, see note [37] supra, the accuracy of this figure depends on the validity of the assumption that "extra" attorney cases do not show a markedly different rate of recovery than other cases.*

[39] *Data obtained from Insurance Company M, the Insurance Group, the New York City Corporation Counsel, and the New York City Transit Authority indicate that defendants win approximately 16% of all personal injury cases. Applying*

sented by an attorney the frequency of recovery is 90 per cent, while in those cases in which the claimant acts for himself the rate of recovery is only 65 per cent.[40] The data thus point to the presence of the attorney as a factor that is associated with greater plaintiff success, and the question arises whether this disparity is due to the presence of the attorney, or whether there is some other explanation. It is, of course, *theoretically* possible that a victim will retain an attorney when he has a strong case and will handle a weak one himself. But several factors militate against such self-selection. First, how likely is a claimant to know enough about the rules of liability to decide the strength of his case? Even if a victim could distinguish a strong liability case from a weak one, and acted differently in each instance, the expectation would be that he would handle the strong case himself and try to improve his chances of recovery on the weak one by retaining counsel. Certainly, such a knowledgeable layman would also know about the contingent fee arrangement and would not hesitate to take a weak case to an attorney. In addition to these theoretical considerations, we do have independent evidence, from a study of accident compensation in Philadelphia, which suggests that the plaintiff who retains an attorney improves his chances of recovery.[41]

Several considerations may explain why an attorney increases the likelihood of recovery. First, he may be able to assemble the facts and articulate the legal grounds much more clearly than the victim, and in this way convince the defendant to make a payment when none would otherwise have been offered. This explanation is consistent with the expected function of legal assistance. But there is another possible explanation, in which the intrinsic value of the case is not controlling. Attorneys who do any significant amount of plaintiffs' personal injury work become acquainted with the representatives and attorneys who handle the other

---

this figure to the 193,000 claimants who seek compensation each year we obtained the figure reported in the text.

[40] *These figures are based on the random sample of 233 cases obtained from the Insurance Group. See note [15] supra. Of the cases in this sample, 155 were handled by attorneys and 78 were handled by the claimant. The experience of M Insurance Company suggests that these percentages are substantially correct.*

[41] *[Temple University Bureau of Economic & Business Research,* A Survey of the Economic-Financial Consequences of Personal Injuries Resulting from Automobile Accidents in the City of Philadelphia, 1953, *Economic & Bus. Bull., March 1955. (hereinafter referred to as The Temple Study)]* 47–51.

side of these cases. In order to maintain a good working relationship, defendants may make small payments in some weak cases to give the plaintiff's attorney a fee.[42]

The frequency of recovery is not the same at all stages of the litigation process: as cases proceed, the rate of recovery decreases. While defendants prevail in slightly less than 15 per cent of the claims[43] and suits that close before trial,[44] they are successful in about 20 per cent of the cases that close during trial,[45] and in some 40 per cent of the cases that go to verdict.[46]

## B. How Much Money Changes Hands

In gross terms about $220,000,000 change hands each year as a result of accidents.[47] However, most recoveries are small. Although recoveries in the 3,000-case sample ran as high as $132,500, in 70 per cent of the cases, recoveries were $1,000 or less, and 91 per cent of the cases resulted in recoveries of $3,000 or less. Nearly half of the recoveries, 47 per cent, were $600 or lower, while 25 per cent were $300 or below. The general breakdown is shown in Chart II.

Because of the previously noted limitations in the applicability of the closing statement rule, figures derived from the 3,000-case sample cannot

[42] *Although we can cite no formal empiric evidence in support of this proposition, informal conversations with members of both the insurance industry and the bar have indicated that this may at least partially account for the observed correlation.*

[43] *The term "claim" is hereinafter used to mean an "unsued case."*

[44] *This figure is based upon information obtained from the* M *Insurance Company, the New York City Transit Authority, and the New York City Corporation Counsel.*

[45] *This figure is based upon data obtained from the sources cited in note* [44] supra. *It is attributable in large measure to directed verdicts and other judicial determinations during trial, and does not indicate that plaintiffs abandon 20% of the cases that they have prosecuted to the point of trial.*

[46] *This figure is based upon data obtained from* M *Insurance Company, the New York City Transit Authority, the New York City Corporation Counsel, and a sample of 206 fully tried 1957 cases drawn by the Project staff from the files of the New York County Supreme Court. . . .*

[47] *This figure is derived as follows. There are approximately 162,000 recoveries each year: 137,000 with attorneys and 25,000 without attorneys. The closing statements show that the average recovery in attorney-handled cases is $1,553. In a sample of 78 no-attorney recoveries obtained from the Insurance Group, see note* [40] supra *and accompanying text, the average recovery was $285. On a simple projection, attorney cases recover $212,761,000 and pro se cases $7,125,000, or a total of $219,886,000, which we have rounded to the figure reported in the text.*

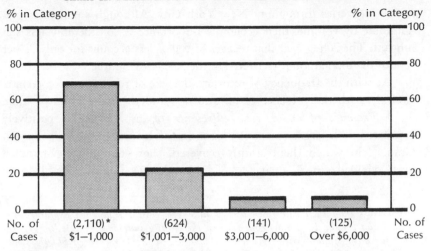

CHART II. PERCENTAGE OF CASES IN EACH SIZE CATEGORY.

| No. of Cases | (2,110)* $1–1,000 | (624) $1,001–3,000 | (141) $3,001–6,000 | (125) Over $6,000 | No. of Cases |

Size Categories

\* *In this and in the following chart, this figure represents the total number of cases in the size category and not merely the portion depicted in the bar.*

be accepted a priori as representative of personal injury recoveries throughout New York City. Accordingly, other and independent sources have been checked. They reveal a similar pattern.[48] We conclude, there-

---

[48] *In a random sample of 190 New York City cases obtained from the Insurance Group in which there was a recovery, 77% recovered $1,000 or less; 16% recovered $1,001-$3,000; 4% recovered $3,001-$6,000; and 3% recovered over $6,000. The large proportion of $1,000-or-less recoveries, as compared to the closing statement sample, is due to the presence of pro se cases in this sample, which tend to recover substantially less than attorney-handled cases. See text following note [51] infra. If we omit the pro se cases, we find that of the 139 attorney-handled cases, 95, or 68%, recovered $1,000 or less. A large random sample of 3,242 First Department cases closed by M Insurance Company in 1957 was distributed as follows: 88% in the $1,000 or under category; 8% in the $1,001-$3,000 category; 2% in the $3,001-$6,000 category; and 1% in the $6,001-$10,000 group. The concentration of $1,000-and-under cases is apparently again due to the presence of a large number of pro se cases.*

*An extensive study of 2,133 New York City personal injury suits closed during June 1952 contained 63% in the $1-$1,000 category; 23% in the $1,001-$3,000 category; 9% in the $3,001-$6,000 category; and 5% in the $6,001-$10,000 group. This sample was taken from the* PECK-HECHT *study, see note [35] supra. The somewhat lower proportion of cases recovering $1,000 or under as compared to the 3,000-case sample is accounted for by the absence of unsued cases in this sample, which generally*

fore, that the sample figures fairly reflect the general size of personal injury recoveries throughout New York City. Although small cases predominate by volume, their economic importance is considerably less significant. The 70 per cent that recover $1,000 or less account for only 22 per cent of the total amount recovered in the 3,000-case sample.[49]

As with the frequency of recovery, the size of recovery also correlates strongly with the presence of an attorney and the stage of disposition.

1. *Presence of an Attorney.* Presence of an attorney is positively correlated with larger recoveries. Cases in the Insurance Group's random sample[50] in which the plaintiff recovered, show that attorney-handled cases[51] yielded a median payment of $313 and an average of $676.[52] In cases

---

*recover less than sued cases. See text at note [58] infra. When we examined the breakdown for the 1,681 suits contained in the closing statement sample, the figures were far more similar: 65% recovered $1,000 or less; 22% recovered $1,001-$3,000; 7% recovered $3,001-$6,000; 3% recovered $6,001-$10,000; and 3% recovered over $10,000.*

[49] *Of a total $4,662,426 recovered, the $1,000-and-under cases accounted for $1,044,145. This economic imbalance is further illustrated by the fact that the average recovery for all cases in the sample was $1,553, although the median was only $647. The percentage of the total damages taken by cases in each of the size categories is shown in the following table.*

PERCENTAGE OF TOTAL DAMAGES TAKEN BY CASES IN EACH SIZE CATEGORY.

| Amount Recovered | Percentage of Total Damages | Percentage of All Cases | Number of Cases in Size Category |
|---|---|---|---|
| $    1-$  1,000 | 22% | 70% | (2,110) |
| $1,001-$  3,000 | 24 | 21 | (  624) |
| $3,001-$25,000 | 40 | 8 | (  251) |
| Over $25,000 | 14 | .5 | (   15) |

[50] *See note [15] supra.*

[51] *This sample contained 139 attorney-handled cases in which there was a recovery.*

[52] *The average recovery in attorney-handled cases in this sample is considerably below that in the 3,000-case sample, $676 to $1,553. This disparity is due primarily to the absence of any very large recoveries in the Insurance Group sample, while there were some such recoveries in the closing statement sample. In spite of this divergence, however, the attorney-handled cases in this sample distribute among*

settled without an attorney[53] the median recovery was $100 and the average was $285.

Here again, the probabilities are strongly arrayed against self-selection. Since most of the *pro se* claims are small in amount,[54] we limit our consideration to those cases recovering $1,000 or less.[55] The average attorney-handled recovery in this size bracket was $407—more than two and one half times as large as the average *pro se* recovery of $158. Is it likely that within this group the victim was able to determine at an early stage the potential worth of his case and that he handled it himself if small and took the larger case to an attorney? We doubt the ability of the layman to estimate the value of his case so accurately. That not *all* small cases are handled by the victims themselves is evident from the fact that 47 per cent of the cases in the 3,000-case sample, all of which were handled by attorneys, recovery was $600 or less, and in 25 per cent recovery was $300 or less. Another factor that decreases the likelihood of self-selection is that some victims may automatically retain attorneys, unaware that they might prosecute cases by themselves, while others may not be acquainted with any attorneys and act for themselves in all cases. The aforementioned study of accident compensation in Philadelphia also suggests that the presence of an attorney increases the amount of recovery.[56]

The most likely explanations for the attorney's link with large cases are those offered earlier to explain his impact on frequency: his ability to assemble the facts and articulate the legal grounds more clearly than the victim, and the desire of defendant's representative to maintain good professonal relations with the "plaintiffs' bar."[57]

2. *Stage of Disposition.* The correlation between size of recovery and stage of disposition is introduced by the observation that suit recoveries are

---

the size categories quite similarly to the closing statement cases. For the comparative figures, see note [48] supra and text accompanying note [47] supra.

[53] *The sample contained 51 pro se cases in which there was a recovery.*

[54] *Of the 51 pro se recoveries in the sample 56% recovered $100 or less, 88% recovered $500 or below, 92% recovered $1000 or less.*

[55] *This gives us a working sample of 47 pro se cases, see note [54] supra, and 95 attorney-handled cases, see note [52] supra.*

[56] *The Temple Study 48. In a sample of 38 attorney-handled cases in which the victim was successful, the amount recovered was in excess of expenses in 28 or 74% of the cases. On the other hand, in a sample of 40 pro se recoveries, the amount received exceeded expenses in only 13 or 33% of the cases. Id. at 50.*

[57] *See text following note [40] supra.*

generally larger than those in unsued cases. For the 1,681 suits in the 3,000-case sample, the median recovery was $725, and the average was $2,058. For the 1,319 cases in which suit was not brought, the median recovery was $575, and the average $912.[58] Although suits account for only 56 per cent of the cases, they account for 75 per cent of the money that changes hands.[59]

This relationship can be seen from another vantage point. If the sample cases are arranged in categories according to the amount recovered, we find that as the recovery size increases, the proportion of suits also increases.[60] Phrased differently, the greater the recovery, the more likely it is that there was a suit. Table 1 pictures this pattern in detail.

TABLE 1. PERCENTAGE OF CASES SUED AND UNSUED, ACCORDING TO AMOUNT RECOVERED.

| | | | Total | |
| Amount Recovered | Suits | Claims | Per Cent | Number |
|---|---|---|---|---|
| $ 1–$ 1,000 | 52% | 48 | 100% | (2,110) |
| $1,001–$ 3,000 | 60% | 40 | 100% | ( 624) |
| $3,001–$ 6,000 | 77% | 23 | 100% | ( 141) |
| $6,001–$10,000 | 88% | 12 | 100% | ( 61) |
| Over $10,000 | 94% | 6 | 100% | ( 64) |
| All cases | 56% | 44 | 100% | (3,000)[61] |

Recovery is greater in suits that reach trial than in suits that are settled before trial. The average recovery for the 1,546 suits that were settled before trial was $1,750, the average recovery in the 135 that reached trial was $5,502. Only 1 in 20 of the $3,000 or under recoveries reached trial,

---

[58] *This pattern of larger recoveries for suits than for claims is repeated in the random sample of 155 attorney-handled cases obtained from the Insurance Group. See note [40] supra. Of the 139 recoveries in the sample, the median suit recovery was $550; the median claim recovery was $312. The average suit recovered $1,464; the average claim recovered $675.*

[59] *Of the total $4,662,426 recovered, suits accounted for $3,459,498.*

[60] *One qualification must be noted. Size does not affect the claim or suit status of cases falling in the group recovering $1,000 or less. For example, a case recovering $600 is no more likely to be sued than one recovering $300.*

[61] *In the random sample of 139 recoveries obtained from the Insurance Group, see note [58] supra, 62% of the cases recovering $1-$1,000 were sued, as compared with 83% in the over-$3,000 bracket.*

while 1 in 5 of the over $3,000 recoveries did so. This size-durability relation is shown in detail in the following table.[62]

TABLE 2.[63] PERCENTAGE OF SUITS THAT REACHED TRIAL ACCORDING TO AMOUNT RECOVERED.

| Amount Recovered | Percentage of Suits That Reached Trial | Number of Suits in Sample |
|---|---|---|
| $    1–$ 1,000 | 6% | (1,087) |
| $1,001–$ 3,000 | 8% | (  371) |
| $3,001–$ 6,000 | 12% | (  109) |
| $6,001–$10,000 | 20% | (   54) |
| Over $10,000 | 33% | (   60) |
| All suits | 8% | (1,681) |

[62] *The strong relationship between trials and size can be expressed in other terms. The following table shows what proportion of the total damages recovered in each size category was taken by the suits that reached trial. It can be seen that the higher the recovery bracket, the greater the proportion recovered after trial was commenced.*

PERCENTAGE OF TOTAL DAMAGES IN EACH SIZE CATEGORY RECOVERED AFTER TRIAL WAS REACHED.

| Amount Recovered | Percentage of Total Damages Recovered After Trial Was Reached |
|---|---|
| $    1–$ 1,000 | 6% |
| $1,001–$ 3,000 | 9% |
| $3,001–$25,000 | 23% |
| Over $25,000 | 46% |
| All cases | 21% |

[63] *Because of the relatively small number of large recovery cases in the 3,000-case sample, the Project gathered a random sample of 500 closing statements confined to cases recovering more than $3,000. This sample was drawn under the authority of Justice Botein's order, see note [19] supra, from closing statements filed during the periods of April 29 to May 27, and December 4 to December 17, 1957. Merging the 375 suits in this special sample with the 223 over-$3,000 suits contained in the 3,000-case sample, we obtained a group of 302 cases recovering $3,001–$6,000; 168 cases recovering $6,001–$10,000; and 128 cases recovering over $10,000. The trial-reaching percentages in these larger samples are almost identical to those in the 3,000-case sample alone: 14%, 20% and 32%, respectively.*

A similar pattern appeared in the 961 First Department suits that the *M* Insurance Company closed in 1957 with a payment to the plaintiff. Only 7 per cent of the suits resulting in recovery of $3,000 or less reached trial. Of those resulting in recovery of between $3,001 and $25,000, 25 per cent reached trial, as did 6 of the 13 cases resulting in recovery of over $25,000. That this size-durability correlation exists throughout New York City, and is not confined to Manhattan and the Bronx, is made clear by additional data received from *M*.[64]

We have concluded, on the basis of extensive earlier research, that the value of a case will not be substantially increased solely by the act of suing or going to trial. The observed relationship is probably due to the fact that potentially larger cases are more resistant to settlement, that is, more likely to go to suit and trial.[65]

When we compared the average settlement during trial with the average verdict we found that the correlation disappeared. In fact, recovery in cases that went to verdict averaged 16 per cent less than in cases settled during trial. The comparable figures were $4,859 and $5,763.

Initially, this observation seemed to suggest that defendants paid more in settlement than they would have had to pay if the case had gone to verdict. Upon closer analysis it appeared, however, that this relationship was attributable to the fact that the settled-during-trial group contained a larger proportion of cases in the courts with large jurisdictional limits than did the fully-tried group.[66] We therefore divided the group of trial-

---

[64] *Analysis of a 197-suit random sample taken from all New York City personal injury suits in which a plaintiff recovered yielded the following results: of the 109 suits recovering $3,000 or less only 9% reached trial; of the 88 suits recovering more than $3,000, 26% reached trial. Only 8 of the cases in the sample recovered more than $25,000, but that 4 of them reached trial is suggestive.*

[65] *For a detailed discussion of this hypothesis, see Rosenberg & Sovern,* supra note [11] *at 1127–36.*

[66] *Of the 135 cases in our sample that reached trial, 30 were brought in the Municipal Court, which has a monetary jurisdictional ceiling of $3,000,* N.Y. CITY MUNICIPAL CT. CODE *tit. 1, § 6; 31 in the City Court, with a ceiling of $6,000,* N.Y. CITY CT. ACT *§ 16; and 59 in the Supreme Court, which has an unlimited ceiling,* N.Y. CIV. PRAC. ACT *§ 64. The remaining 15 were primarily cases in which the forum could not be ascertained from the closing statement, with a few brought in the Federal District Court and in other state courts. Since we are unable to break these latter 15 down according to court, we concentrated on the 120 cases that reached trial in the three state courts mentioned above.*

*Of the 89 cases in this group that settled during trial, 51% were in the Supreme Court; 24% were in the City Court; and 25% were in the Municipal Court.*

reaching cases according to the court in which the case was brought, comparing settlements during trial witth verdicts in each court.

In City Court, verdicts averaged substantially more than settlements during trial, the comparable figures were $1,340 and $837. A contrary result was observed, however, in Municipal Court and Supreme Court cases.

The average fully-tried Supreme Court case recovered $9,717, while the average settlement during trial was $10,816. This relationship changes radically, however, if one atypically high during-trial settlement is eliminated from the average.[67] Using 44 during-trial settlements, instead of the actual 45, the average drops to $9,244, 5 per cent less than the fully-tried average.

In Municipal Court we find that settlements during trial averaged $369, while fully-tried cases averaged $326. This anomaly may merely reflect a statistical insufficiency in the sample, for it included only 23 settlements and seven complete trials.[68]

And, finally, even if defendants *are* paying out slightly more in settlement than might be awarded by the trier of fact, this does not

---

*For the 31 fully-tried cases the breakdown was Supreme Court, 45%; City Court, 32%; and Municipal Court, 23%. The importance of the 6% drop in the proportion of Supreme Court cases is evident when we see that the average recovery in Supreme Court cases that reach trial is so much larger than that of cases in either the City or Municipal Court—$10,553, as against $999 and $359, respectively.*

[67] *This case recovered $80,000. The next highest recovery in this Supreme Court sample was $50,000.*

[68] *Beyond these statistical modifications, the significance of these observations is weakened by another consideration: we must be sure that the two groups of cases are identical in all respects other than the stage of disposition. The objective criteria apparent from the closing statements do not distinguish them. We have thus far seen that size does not serve to distinguish the trial-finishing cases from those that settle during trial. Three other factors available from the data are (1) the presence of an extra attorney; (2) whether the case was handled by a specialist in personal injury work; and (3) the presence or absence of a lien.*

*Of the 96 cases that settled during trial 31% had extra attorneys, 7% were handled by specialists, and 39% had liens. For the fully-tried group the corresponding figures were 28%, 8%, and 33%, respectively. The two sets of figures are sufficiently similar to indicate that none of these factors distinguishes the two groups of cases.*

*However, there may be other, less readily observable, characteristics that distinguish the "settlers" from the "finishers." Defendants may settle when the plaintiff's case has been unexpectedly impressive; when they feel that their own case has not been as impressive as had been anticipated; or at any other indication that the tide is turning against them.*

necessarily indicate that they would be better advised to await the verdict. Many of these cases may well be settled early in the trial, thus sparing the defendants the time and expense of trying them to completion. In addition, settlements also eliminate the risk of atypically high verdicts. These considerations may more than outweigh the small sums defendants might possibly save in most cases by not settling.

*     *     *     *

[Section C omitted.]

## D. Delay

[A] major consideration that is important to an understanding of how the present system operates is the problem of how long it takes the victim who does recover to get his money. Extended delay may vitiate the relief finally obtained, especially if money is urgently needed and the prospective recovery is virtually the victim's sole financial asset. Another, and related, aspect of delay is its possible coercive effect that encourages victims to settle early for less than the full value of their claim, rather than to wait indefinitely for trial in the hope of getting a larger amount.

Although delay is an essential ingredient of any discussion of the economics of personal injury litigation, this subject has been extensively explored in an earlier Project study.[69] We shall therefore only summarize some of the more important findings here.

It turned out that 64 per cent of the 3,000 sample cases closed within one year, and 82 per cent within two years.[70] These, of course, were exclusively attorney-handled cases. If the quickly closing no-attorney cases

---

[69] *Rosenberg & Sovern*, Delay and The Dynamics of Personal Injury Litigation, 59 COLUM. L. REV. *1115 (1959)*.

[70] *The victim views delay as the period from the injury until the day he receives whatever payment is forthcoming. Although the closing statements do not disclose these dates, they do contain two other relevant dates, those of filing the retainer statement and the closing statement.*

*Attorneys must file a statement of retainer within 30 days after being retained on a contingent basis.* N.Y. SUP. CT., APP. DIV., FIRST DEP'T R., Special Rules Regulating the Conduct of Attorneys, *Rule 4-A. It seems likely that if brought in at all, the attorney is retained shortly after the accident. The closing statements themselves must be filed within 15 days after the counsel receives compensation.* N.Y. SUP. CT., APP. DIV., FIRST DEP'T R., Special Rules Regulating the Conduct of Attorneys, *Rule 4(e). We have taken the period between these two dates as a measure of delay. Prior research has confirmed the accuracy of this measure. See Rosenberg & Sovern, supra note* [69], *at 1121 n.28.*

are included in the computation, 71 per cent of all the cases would close within one year, and 86 per cent within two years.[71] The volume of cases is so large, however, that this means that about 23,000 victims wait more than two years for payments they will ultimately receive.[72]

Delay correlated closely with several other factors. Perhaps the most striking was the correlation between delay and the amount recovered. An analysis of the sample cases showed that of those recovering $1,000 or less, 68 per cent closed within one year and 85 per cent within two years. On the other hand, of those cases recovering more than $3,000, only 20 per cent closed within one year and 40 per cent within two years.[73]

There was also a strong correlation between delay and the stage of disposition. As might be expected, suits closed more slowly than claims; after one year 90 per cent of the claims, but only 43 per cent of the suits, had closed. While suits generally recovered more than claims, this is not a complete explanation since the relation held true even when like-sized claims and suits were compared.[74] If it is true that bringing suit does not

[71] *For the derivation of these percentages, see Rosenberg & Sovern,* supra *note* [69], *at 1121–22 nn.28 & 29.*

[72] *This figure was obtained by applying the finding that approximately 14% of all recoveries occur after two years, see text at note* [71] supra, *to the annual total of 162,000 successful claimants.*

[73] *There is ample evidence to indicate that delay does not increase the size of recovery, but that large size causes delay. See Rosenberg & Sovern,* supra *note* [69], *at 1139. The reasons for greater delay in large cases are not hard to explain. Such cases usually involve extensive injuries, and medical experts need time to determine their full extent and implications. When large sums are involved both sides can afford to hold their ground even though fees and other expenses mount, while the small case can not bear added expense or justify extended medical scrutiny.*

[74] *The following table shows the age at closing of suits and claims within each of the various size categories within various recovery brackets.*

AGE AT CLOSING—CLAIMS AND SUITS, ACCORDING TO AMOUNT RECOVERED.

| | Percentage Closed Within: | | | | No. of Cases in Sample | |
| | One Year | | Two Years | | | |
| *Amount Recovered* | *Claims* | *Suits* | *Claims* | *Suits* | *Claims* | *Suits* |
|---|---|---|---|---|---|---|
| $    1–$ 1,000 | 91% | 46% | 98% | 74% | (1023) | (1087) |
| $1,001–$ 3,000 | 89% | 43% | 96% | 72% | ( 253) | ( 371) |
| $3,001–$10,000 | 90% | 28% | 100% | 58% | ( 39) | ( 163) |
| Over    $10,000 | 50% | 13% | 75% | 42% | ( 4) | ( 60) |
| All cases | 90% | 43% | 97% | 71% | (1319) | (1681) |

increase the amount of recovery,[75] suing may at times be to the victim's disadvantage by promoting delay.[76]

Another strong correlation was between delay and the presence of "extra" attorneys.[77] This may have been due to two factors. First, "extra" attorneys are often called in on cases that have already proven settlement-resistant. Second, it takes time for the new attorney to become familiar with the case and for him to confer with the original attorney.

It was found, however, that the presence of a specialist did not increase delay. Indeed, the figures suggest that delay is slightly less when a specialist is involved than when a nonspecialist handles the case.[78]

### III. SUMMARY AND CONCLUSIONS

This survey sought to obtain some of the basic empiric data essential to understanding the operation of today's tort law. From intensive analysis of thousands of closing statements filed in court, and by drawing on the experience of insurance companies and studies by others, a considerable mass of knowledge about the economic aspects of New York City per-

---

[75] *See text following note [64] supra.*

[76] *Similarly, as the cases reached trial, delay increased. Of those suits in the 3,000-case sample that settled before trial, 45% closed within one year and 73% within two years. But for cases that reached trial, the figures are only 19% within one year and 43% within two years. This is to be expected, since cases that resist settlement must wait for trial and their average age will be greater than that of suits settled before trial.*

[77] *Comparing cases in the same size brackets, we found that in those recovering $1,000 or under, 39% of the "extra" cases closed within one year, while 49% of single-attorney cases closed within that time. In the $1,001–$3,000 group, 34% of the "extra" cases closed within one year against 48% in the single-attorney cases. This disparity persisted in the over-$3,000 cases.*

[78] *In the $1,000-and-under group, 69% of the specialist cases closed within one year and 87% within two years, as against 68% and 84% for the nonspecialist cases. In the $1,001–$3,000 bracket, 67% closed within one year and 85% within two years when brought by specialists, compared with 61% and 69% when a nonspecialist was involved. Cases in the higher recovery brackets presented essentially the same pattern.*

*These figures are consistent with our findings that the specialist sued only 52% of his cases, while the nonspecialist average was 58%, and the specialist trial rate was 5% as compared with 8% for nonspecialists.*

sonal injury cases has emerged. For convenience, we might at this point bring together some of our major findings.[79]

The first observation is that personal injury litigation in New York City is big business. Each year there is an estimated total of 193,000 claimants and $220,000,000 in payments.

Over three-quarters of the claimants retain attorneys, while the others proceed by themselves. Virtually all cases that reach suit, however, are handled by attorneys.

The court's direct role in personal injury litigation is a marginal one limited to a small fraction of the cases and the money involved. The process that resolves more than 98 per cent of the cases, and disposes of 97 per cent of the money, is not adjudication but negotiation—a process of bargaining and settlement between the parties and their representatives without direct judicial intervention.

The frequency of recovery is high, with some payment made in 84 per cent of the cases. For cases in which the victim retains an attorney the rate of recovery is 90 per cent. The recovery rate varies with the stage of disposition; while defendants make no payment in only 15 per cent of the cases that close before trial, they are successful in 40 per cent of the cases that go to verdict.

Recoveries are typically small—about 70 per cent of the cases recover $1,000 or less. Lawyer-handled cases show higher average recoveries than *pro se* cases. About half of the lawyer-handled cases are sued, and these recoveries are generally larger than those in unsued cases. Cases that reach trial recover more than those that settle before trial. But no correlation has been found between the stage of trial at which the case closed and the amount recovered.

Lawyers' fees take 36 per cent of the sums recovered—a total of about $77,000,000 annually. There is strong evidence, however, that despite this cost, plaintiffs do better with a lawyer than they would have done had they handled the cases themselves.

The almost universal method of compensating plaintiffs' attorneys in these cases is the contingent fee. In New York City this fee is subject to court-imposed ceilings. The rule permits lawyers a choice of method, and

---

[79] *Our findings on delay were summarized above, see text accompanying notes [69–78] supra.*

in 80 per cent of the cases they choose the sliding scale, which is consistent with their financial interests.

In more than half the cases lawyers' fees do not reach the permissible ceiling. Though the rule allows a 50 per cent charge in the cases resulting in recovery of $1,000 or less, lawyers' fees average only 41 per cent in this size bracket. Strangely, if the case closes at a later stage of disposition, lawyers seem to get a lower percentage fee even though the same amount is recovered. Specialists' fees are higher than those of lawyers who handle negligence cases only occasionally. Similarly, bringing in an "extra" attorney increases the fee.

\*　　\*　　\*　　\*

## APPENDIX A. HOW PERSONAL INJURY CASES BEHAVE IN METROPOLITAN AREAS OTHER THAN NEW YORK CITY

This appendix presents the results of a survey undertaken to determine whether personal injury cases in other metropolitan areas throughout the nation behave in a comparable fashion to those in New York City. Although we were unable to obtain sufficient data to make direct comparisons for both suits and claims, we were able to compare the following four basic characteristics for sued cases: the stage of disposition; the percentage of defendant wins; the size of recovery; and the age at closing. The data used for these comparisons consist of a group of 3,630 suits obtained from the *M* Insurance Company, and represent all the personal injury suits closed by *M* in 1957 in Baltimore, Boston, Chicago, Los Angeles, Philadelphia, Pittsburgh, and San Francisco. In the following tables, which summarize the results of these comparisons, N.Y.C. represents the New York City cases and O.N.Y.C. signifies the *M* Insurance Company cases.

It will be seen that in no instances did the comparisons yield identical figures, and only rarely were they what might be termed "very close." However, the tables show that many of the trends that were observed in New York City suits appear to exist outside of New York City as well: the courts play a minor direct role in the disposition of these suits (Table A–1); the rate of recovery is relatively high, with a decrease as the suit proceeds further into litigation (Table A–2); most recoveries are small

#### TABLE A-1. STAGE OF DISPOSITION—SUITS.

|  | N.Y.C. | O.N.Y.C. |
|---|---|---|
| Percentage: |  |  |
| Reaching trial | 9% | 14% |
| Completing trial | 3% | 9% |

#### TABLE A-2. DEFENDANT WINS—SUITS.

|  | N.Y.C. | O.N.Y.C. |
|---|---|---|
| Percentage of cases won by defendant: |  |  |
| Before trial | 15% | 11% |
| During trial | 20% | 39% |
| After trial | 40% | 55% |
| All cases | 16% | 17% |

#### TABLE A-3. RECOVERY SIZE—SUITS.

|  | N.Y.C. | O.N.Y.C. |
|---|---|---|
| Percentage recovering: |  |  |
| $1,000 or Under | 65% | 61% |
| Over $1,000 | 35% | 39% |

#### TABLE A-4. AGE OF CLOSING—SUITS.

|  | N.Y.C. | O.N.Y.C. |
|---|---|---|
| Percentage closed: |  |  |
| Within one year | 43% | 25% |
| Within two years | 71% | 53% |

(Table A–3); and a majority of the suits close within two years (Table A–4). Accordingly, we conclude that, although absolute numbers and precise percentages probably reflect unique local conditions, in broad outline there are many similarities in the way these suits behave in large metropolitan areas throughout the nation.

\* \* \* \*

[Appendix B omitted.]

# PLEADING GUILTY
# FOR CONSIDERATIONS:
# A STUDY OF
# BARGAIN JUSTICE

*Donald J. Newman*

[Headnote omitted.]

One of the major problems faced by social scientists interested in studying criminal behavior involves obtaining samples of offenders to be used as units of research. Ordinarily such samples are drawn from prisons or probation files because the study of unapprehended criminals is extremely difficult. Conviction by a court or authorized agency is, therefore, the usual basis of sample selection.[1] Virtually all sociologists admit the inadequacy of such a technique and qualify their samples as non-representative of any kind of a criminal universe. At the same time, the conviction record of the offenders who are selected for study from prisons and courts is used as the basis for typing the offenders and for various statistical computations. In general, the man's conviction record is assumed to be a quasi-automatic legal stamp which defines those activities which make him a criminal.

Of course very few researchers would treat a person such as Al Capone as merely an income tax violator, but this is because they would

---

[1] *See* Paul Tappan, Who is the Criminal? *in:* Amer. Sociol. Rev., *Vol. 12, no. 1 pp. 96–102 and* Donald R. Cressey Criminological Research and the Definitions of Crimes, Amer. Jour. of Sociol. (*Vol. 57, May 1951*) *pp. 546–551.*

Reprinted by permission of the author and of the copyright owner, The Williams & Wilkins Co., from 46 *Journal of Criminal Law, Criminology and Police Science* (1956), 780–790.

know, or think that they know that such an individual had committed other offenses or had different patterns of criminal behavior than those for which he was sentenced. In less notorious cases, however, the type of offense and the severity of the sentence, remain the pivotal points around which research is pursued and prison classification systems are built.

This does not mean that sociologists naively accept conviction on a specific charge as definitive nor that they have little interest in the mechanics of justice. The reverse, of course, is more accurate. But the emphasis of both sociological exposition and research has been on the *gross* misuse of justice, on methods used by criminals, political officials and the business elite to avoid conviction. It is also true that some sociological interest has been shown in procedural variation, particularly brutal, and in many cases, illegal, arrest and interrogation methods. The police particularly have come under sociological scrutiny.[2] Nevertheless, apart from the "fix" and the "third degree", the conviction process has generally been neglected in research as of minor importance in the complicated process of defining "criminal" as the basic unit of research.

## METHODS OF STUDYING THE CONVICTION PROCESS

In order to bring to light some of the less apparent factors influencing the procedural steps by which society labels the criminal, a sample of men, all convicted of "conventional" felonies in one court district was interviewed in regard to the processes involved in their own convictions. Men from a single county were selected in order to keep formal legal procedures and court and prosecuting officials constant for each case. The lawyers and judges of this district had been interviewed previously by the author,[3] so that information was available about conviction processes from the legal participants' viewpoints. The county was located in the mid-west (Wisconsin) and was of "medium" size, neither rural nor metropolitan. The county seat had a population of approximately 100,000 persons. Furthermore, the district was politically clean, having no widespread organized crime or vice nor a tradition of "fixing" criminal cases by

---

[2] WILLIAM WESTLEY, Violence and the Police (*in:* AMER. JOUR. OF SOCIOL., *July, 1953*) *pp. 34–41 and* ERNEST J. HOPKINS, OUR LAWLESS POLICE (*New York: Viking Press, 1931*).

[3] *This study took place in 1951 and 1952 as part of the American Bar Association's study entitled* Criminal Law and Litigation.

bribery or intimidation. Supposedly in such a setting, felony convictions would follow a quasi-automatic, "combat" theory of criminal justice, involving a jury trial or at least an unconditional plea of guilty.

## MOST CONVICTIONS THE RESULT OF GUILTY PLEAS

The felons who were interviewed, a group of ninety-seven representing all men from the district under active sentence, had all been convicted of felonies ranging from non-support to murder. There were no white-collar criminals in the group, except for three clerks serving sentence for embezzlements, nor were there any racketeers or professional criminals such as confidence men, and no individuals sentenced from Juvenile Court were included. The men were serving sentences under the following conditions:

| | |
|---|---|
| State prison | 34 |
| State reformatory | 6 |
| Parole | 9 |
| Probation | 48 |
| Total | 97 |

Most of the convictions (93.8 percent) were not convictions in a combative, trial-by-jury sense, but merely involved sentencing after a plea of guilty had been entered. On the surface this might lend support to the contention that most convictions are mere rubber stamps of the court applied to the particular illegal behavior involved in each case.

On closer analysis, however, it was seen that over a third (38.1 percent) of the men had originally entered a not guilty plea, changing to guilty only at a later procedural stage short of an actual trial. The question immediately arose; why did these men change their minds? Was it because of a promise of leniency or some such bargain as suggested by the Wickersham report, Moley and other writers of a decade ago?[4] A second

---

[4] NATIONAL COMMISSION ON LAW OBSERVANCE AND ENFORCEMENT, Report on Prosecution, *Bulletin 4 (Washington, D. C.: Government Printing Office, 1931)*; *and* RAYMOND MOLEY, OUR CRIMINAL COURTS (*New York: Minton, Balch Co., 1930*) *and* POLITICS AND CRIMINAL PROSECUTION (*New York: Minton, Balch Co., 1929*). *See also* NEWMAN F. BAKER *and* EARL H. DeLONG, The Prosecuting Attorney: Powers and Duties in Criminal Prosecution (*in:* JOUR. OF CRIM. L. AND CRIMINOL., *Vol. 24, No. 6, March–April 1934*) and NEWMAN F. BAKER, The Prosecutor—Initiation of Prosecution (*in:* JOUR. OF CRIM. L. AND CRIMINOL. *Vol. 23, No. 5, September, 1933*).

TABLE I. TYPE OF PLEA BY RETENTION OF COUNSEL.

| | Type of Plea | | |
| --- | --- | --- | --- |
| Retention of Counsel | Guilty | Changed Not Guilty to Guilty | Total |
| Offenders with lawyers | 21 | 24 | 45 |
| | (23.2) | (26.3) | (49.5) |
| Offenders without lawyers | 39 | 7 | 46 |
| | (42.7) | (7.8) | (50.5) |
| Total | 60 | 31 | 91* |
| Percent | (65.9) | (34.1) | (100.0) |

\* Offenders pleading not guilty and retaining this plea through a jury trial were eliminated. All, however, had counsel.

$x^2 = 14.713$, d.f. $= 1$, significant at the 5 percent level. Yules Q $= -.728$ indicating a negative correlation between initial admission of guilt and the retention of counsel.

question followed. Did the men who pleaded guilty immediately do so unconditionally to the charge as contained in the complaint or was there any evidence of informal "arranging" of the sentence so widely alleged in criminology texts?

Pursuing these lines of inquiry, an interesting difference between the two groups of men was seen. Men entering an initial plea of not guilty were significantly more often represented by defense attorneys than the men pleading guilty immediately. On all other demographic characteristics, age, gross type of offense for which sentenced (personal, property, sex, and miscellaneous violations such as carrying a concealed weapon), education, occupation, residence and so on, the groups showed no significant differences. Furthermore, on the eventual disposition of the cases, e.g., whether sent to prison or placed on probation, the groups did not differ. In fact, only one other difference besides the retention of counsel was noted. It was found that the men who initially pleaded guilty and who more often than not did not hire or request counsel were recidivist, whereas the men with lawyers, who at first pleaded innocent, were more often experiencing their first conviction.

This phenomenon is rather curious when it is recalled that the groups showed no differences in the frequency of being placed on probation. It might logically be expected, in the light of current sentencing practices, that first offenders would more likely receive probation than men with previous convictions, particularly if, as was the case, there was no significant variation in the types of crimes for which they were sentenced. The implication of this lack of difference in sentences for the role of the lawyer in the conviction process was so great that the men were further analyzed by dividing them into two groups, one characterized by the retention of counsel, the other comprising men who pleaded without an attorney.

The outcome of the conviction process from the point of view of the offender is satisfactory or unsatisfactory depending upon the actual sentence he receives compared to his expectations of punishment at the time

TABLE II. EXPECTED PUNISHMENT BY RETENTION OF COUNSEL.

| Punishment Expected at Time of Arrest | Retention of Counsel | | Total |
| | Offenders with Lawyers | Offenders without Lawyers | |
| --- | --- | --- | --- |
| Expected same as actual or didn't know what to expect | 3 | 10 | 13 |
| | (3.2) | (10.3) | (13.5) |
| Expected less severe than actual | 11 | 11 | 22 |
| | (11.3) | (11.3) | (22.6) |
| Expected more severe than actual | 37 | 25 | 62 |
| | (38.1) | (25.8) | (63.9) |
| Total | 51 | 46 | 97 |
| Percent | (52.6) | (47.4) | (100.0) |

$x^2 = 5.827$, d.f. $= 2$, not significant at five percent level.

TABLE III. NON-REPRESENTED OFFENDERS' REASONS FOR NOT RETAINING COUNSEL.

| | Percent |
| --- | --- |
| Obviously guilty, hoped for mercy from the court | 19.5 |
| Made deal for concurrent sentence or had charges dropped | 30.4 |
| Made deal for lesser charge or a light sentence | 23.9 |
| Don't trust lawyers | 4.4 |
| Had no money, didn't know about court-assigned lawyers | 13.0 |
| Other* | 4.4 |
| Not ascertained | 4.4 |
| Total | 100.0 |

*These cases claimed that they were subjected to long and arduous questioning and "confessed" to "get it over with" and thus had neither the time nor the inclination to get a lawyer.

he is arrested. It might be supposed that a violator who expected a severe sentence would seek legal advice. However, an analysis of the responses of the men showed that their expectations were not the determining factor in their decisions to retain counsel or to plead without counsel.

## REASONS FOR PLEADING GUILTY WITHOUT A LAWYER

The reasons given for claiming or for disdaining counsel varied from confessions of "obvious" guilt and a hope for mercy from the court to poverty coupled with ignorance of provisions for state-paid defense attorneys. The chief reason, however, appeared to be an expedient one, related to the factor of past experience in going through the conviction process. The recidivists were both conviction wise and conviction susceptible in the dual sense that they knew of the possibility of bargaining a guilty plea for a light sentence and at the same time were vulnerable, because of their records, to threats of the prosecutor to "throw the book" at them unless they confessed. Over half (54.3 percent) of the men claimed that they had bargained for their sentences, and 84 percent of these men had been convicted previously. A number of factors, all interrelated, seem to account for this. First, a general fear expressed by multiple offenders of facing a jury or of antagonizing sentencing officials was revealed in most cases. Some felt that their records would be held against them by a jury (actually the admission in court of the offender's previous criminal record is closely regulated by law to assure a fair trial on the current charge). They felt conviction would be more certain because in the public mind they were "ex-cons". A more general fear, however, was that the judge would be especially severe in sentencing if they did decide to fight and then lost. They felt that pleading not guilty and hiring a lawyer would only irritate the various officials, particularly the prosecutor, whose recommendation at the time of sentencing is an important consideration of the court. One of the men said:

When the day comes to go and the D.A. stands up and says you're a dirty rat and a menace to society and should be locked up and have the key thrown away—then look out! You're going away for a few years.

These fears, whether justified or not, undoubtedly made these men more amenable to an informal "settling" of their cases.

A second factor making for bargaining and the rejection of counsel was the experience of these men gained in previous convictions. Many of the recidivists, particularly those with two or more convictions, knew the sentencing judges and some of the prosecutors quite well and all of the offenders knew most of the police. They were on a first name basis with many of these men and could bargain in a friendly or even a jocular manner. One man (on probation) said:

Old —— told me he was going to throw the book at me. I told him he didn't have a damn thing on me. He said I'd get five to ten. I told him he couldn't even book me, that's how little he had. I knew he was riding me; he didn't mean a thing by it. I've known him for years. He just likes to act tough.

Men who had been convicted in other states or in other counties but never before in this district were quite conscious of this "friendship" factor in the bargaining processes. Each of them expressed the belief that had he been a "local" he would have fared better.

Previous sentences served in institutions also seemed to be relevant to bargaining without a lawyer. Former inmates were more legal-wise; their conceptions of their offenses were not primarily in terms of guilt or innocence but contained more references to evidence and its relation to the outcome of the conviction process. They referred to how much the prosecutor "had on me" and the ability of the prosecution to make a charge stick. One of the men expressed it this way:

The D.A. needed my help. His evidence was all circumstances (*sic*). He knew I done it but he couldn't ever prove it. But I couldn't go to court and take a chance with my record. When I saw he was going to stick me with something, I was willing to make the best deal.

Not only does a quasi-legal knowledge evidently develop in incarceration (most of these men knew the statute numbers of their offenses and all knew such terms as "preliminary hearing", "arraignment" and "presentence investigation") but those men seemed better able to recognize a good bargain when they saw one. Although all offenders recognized probation as the best break, of course, and many knew the possible length of sentence for their particular crime, recidivists knew customary sentences (and court district variations) for their offenses. In short, they recognized a "good-as-compared-to-other-guys-I-know" sentence when they faced it.

# OFFENDERS WHO RETAIN COUNSEL

Over half (52.6%) of the men in the total sample retained lawyers and proceeded through more of the formal stages of the conviction process (preliminary hearing, arraignment) than those men who pleaded without attorneys. As anticipated from the analysis of the group of non-represented offenders, the factor of recidivism with its accompanying implication of bargaining skills learned from past experience was almost completely absent from this group. As one of these men expressed it:

I'd never been in trouble before. I didn't know which end was up. I thought sure I was going to prison. It seemed as if they had a million laws I'd broken. The only thing I could think of was calling my wife to get me a lawyer.

These men with their lawyers, either privately hired or court assigned, significantly more often pleaded not guilty when first apprehended, changing their pleas only later in the process. On the surface, this observation might lead to one of two conflicting conclusions. The fact that the retention of counsel correlated with a change of plea to guilty might mean that the lawyers, having a better grasp of the legal worth of the evidence against their clients, advised them to plead guilty and that the clients followed their advice. Or, it could with equal validity indicate that perhaps the lawyers, through informal bargaining skills similar to the non-represented recidivists, had arranged satisfactory charges or more lenient sentences than originally expected by their clients. The latter would seem to be the most convincing in view of the offenders' responses. When asked their lawyer's advice in regard to pleading, 75 percent of those first pleading not guilty and then guilty, responded that their counsel's advice was to maintain a not guilty plea "until something can be arranged." This they did. The remainder were advised to plead guilty without promise of any arrangement, although bargaining is not thus ruled out.

Only fifteen of the represented offenders said that their convictions were the result of unconditional pleas of guilty. The remainder, including not only the offenders whose lawyers' advice was to hold off pleading guilty until settlement was made, but twelve of the men who entered initial guilty pleas as well, claimed to have received some consideration in the nature of the charge or type and length of sentence in exchange for their admissions of guilt.

# TYPES OF BARGAINING WHERE ATTORNEY HAS BEEN RETAINED

While the frequency of claimed bargaining does not differ significantly between the groups of offenders without lawyers and with lawyers, there is some difference in the frequencies of the various types

TABLE IV. OFFENDERS PLEADING GUILTY AFTER BARGAINING OVER CHARGE OR SENTENCE.

| | Offenders Pleading Guilty | | |
| Retention of Counsel | Pleaded Guilty for Consideration | Pleaded Guilty Without Bargaining | Total |
|---|---|---|---|
| Offenders with lawyers | 30 | 15 | 45 |
| | (33.0) | (16.5) | (49.5) |
| Offenders without lawyers | 25 | 21 | 46 |
| | (27.4) | (23.1) | (50.5) |
| Total | 55 | 36 | 91 |
| Percent | (60.4) | (39.6) | (100.0) |

$x^2 = 1.443$, d.f. $= 1$, not significant at 5 percent level.

TABLE V. FREQUENCY OF TYPES OF BARGAINING BY RETENTION OF COUNSEL.*

| | Offenders With Lawyers | Offenders Without Lawyers | Total |
|---|---|---|---|
| 1. Pleading to a lesser charge | 8 | 3 | 11 |
| | (14.5) | (5.5) | (20.0) |
| 2. Pleading for a light sentence | 17 | 8 | 25 |
| | (30.9) | (14.6) | (45.5) |
| 3. Pleading for concurrent sentences | 3 | 9 | 12 |
| | (5.5) | (16.3) | (21.8) |
| 4. Pleading for the dismissal of charges | 2 | 5 | 7 |
| | (3.6) | (9.1) | (12.7) |
| Total | 30 | 25 | 55 |
| Percent | (54.5) | (45.5) | (100.0) |

* Combining the first two types (lesser charge, light sentence) and comparing them with the last two (concurrent sentence, charge dismissed) a significant difference between types of bargaining and retention of counsel is seen. $x^2 = 23.72$, d.f. $= 1$, significant at 5 percent level. Yules Q $= -.732$ indicating a negative correlation between retention of lawyer and pleading guilty for considerations of concurrent sentences or dismissed charges.

reported. Men without attorneys significantly more often mentioned as the consideration they received in exchange for a guilty plea either the reduction of the charge or the promise of a suitable, fixed sentence.

It would seem from this that lawyers are more likely to be retained by offenders who fear a severe punishment or in cases involving a disputable charge whereas violators with many charges against them "cop a plea" directly from the prosecution or the court without a lawyer as intermediary. This would also seem to substantiate the evidence from the unrepresented defendants that the function of the lawyer in bargaining is not essential for all offenders, and that men experienced in the conviction process can informally and successfully arrange their own legal fate.

## TYPES OF INFORMAL CONVICTION AGREEMENTS

The considerations received by the offenders in exchange for their guilty pleas were of four general types:

1. *Bargain concerning the charge.* A plea of guilty was entered by the offenders in exchange for a reduction of the charge from the one alleged in the complaint. This ordinarily occurred in cases where the offence in question carried statutory degrees of severity such as homicide, assault, and sex offenses. This type was mentioned as a major issue in twenty percent of the cases in which bargaining occurred. The majority of offenders in these instances were represented by lawyers.

2. *Bargain concerning the sentence.* A plea of guilty was entered by the offenders in exchange for a promise of leniency in sentencing. The most commonly accepted consideration was a promise that the offender would be placed on probation, although a less-than-maximum prison term was the basis in certain instances. All offenses except murder, serious assault, and robbery were represented in this type of bargaining process. This was by far the most frequent consideration given in exchange for guilty pleas, occurring in almost half (45.5 percent) of the cases in which any bargaining occurred. Again, most of these offenders were represented by attorneys.

3. *Bargain for concurrent charges.* This type of informal process occurred chiefly among offenders pleading without counsel. These men exchanged guilty pleas for the concurrent pressing of multiple charges, generally numerous counts of the same offense or related violations such

as breaking and entering and larceny. This method, of course, has much the same effect as pleading for consideration in the sentence. The offender with concurrent convictions, however, may not be serving a reduced sentence; he is merely serving one sentence for many crimes. Altogether, concurrent convictions were reported by 21.8 percent of the men who were convicted by informal methods.

4. *Bargain for dropped charges.* This variation occurred in about an eighth of the cases who reported bargaining. It involved an agreement on the part of the prosecution not to press formally one or more charges against the offender if he in turn pleaded guilty to (usually) the major offense. The offenses dropped were extraneous law violations contained in, or accompanying, the offense alleged in the complaint such as auto theft accompanying armed robbery and violation of probation where a new crime had been committed. This informal method, like bargaining for concurrent charges, was reported chiefly by offenders without lawyers. It occurred in 12.6 percent of cases in which bargaining was claimed.

The various types of informal conviction agreements were described in the majority of the cases and, as mentioned, only six members of the sample went to jury trial. The remainder of the sample (37.1 percent) pleaded guilty, they said, without any considerations. It is possible, however, that in those 15 instances where the men had counsel, the attorney had bargained, or had attempted to bargain, without the knowledge of the offender.

In instances where informal methods were used, the roles of the various participants were cooperative rather than combative. Central to the entire process were the roles of offender and prosecutor; the defense attorney played a significant part chiefly in cases of first offenders and in instances where the nature of the charge was in dispute. The judge sometimes played an informal role in cases involving a fixed sentence, but even here the prosecutor's role dominated because of the common practice in the court whereby the judge asks for, and generally follows, the prosecutor's recommendation as to sentence in cases pleading guilty.

## THE BARGAIN THEORY OF CRIMINAL JUSTICE

The most significant general finding of the study was that the majority of the felony convictions in the district studied were not the result of the formal, combative theory of criminal law involving in effect a legal battle between prosecution and defense, but were compromise convictions, the result of bargaining between defense and prosecution. Such informal conviction processes were observed in over half of the cases studied.

In the informal process the accused, directly or through his attorney, offered to plead guilty to the offense for which he was arrested, providing it was reduced in kind or degree, or in exchange for a given type of length of sentence. The prosecutor benefitted from such a bargain in that he was assured of a conviction, yet did not have to spend the time and effort to prepare a trial case. He also avoided the ever-present risk of losing even a clear-cut case should the accused have gone before a jury. The court, too, benefitted. Court calendars were, and are, crowded and the entire court system would be admittedly inadequate to cope with criminal trials should all, or even a fraction of the felony arrests decide to go to trial. This, coupled with a generally favorable attitude toward bargaining processes on the part of the lawyers, civil and criminal, in the local bar, made informal methods of conviction almost inevitable.

Instead of proceeding through all the formal stages of conviction such as hearing before a magistrate, preliminary hearing, arraignment, etc., the majority of the offenders waived most of these procedures and because of informal promises of leniency or threats of long sentences, entered guilty pleas and were sentenced. About half (50.5 percent) of the sample went to preliminary hearings of their cases but only 6.2 percent proceeded through a jury trial.

## CONCLUSIONS: SIGNIFICANCE OF INFORMAL CONVICTION PROCESSES TO CRIMINOLOGY

Criminological research has generally ignored methods of conviction in conventional felony cases except the illegal "fix" and brutal "third-degree" as primarily legal steps automatically defining the unit to be studied. The automatism of conviction has here been challenged, and within the limits of the present research, interaction processes of sociological interest in themselves, have been outlined.

It was felt in conducting this research that, if informal methods of convictions were discovered, they would be of a nature to negate the use of conviction records in many types of research and correctional administration. In the typology of criminals, in prison classification, and in other applied fields such as parole prediction, bargaining techniques would rule out the accuracy of the "paper" conviction as an index of the offender's actual patterns of criminality. In spite of the high incidence (56.7 percent) of admitted bargaining in the sample, however, only a very small proportion of cases admitted guilt to offenses grossly different from those alleged in the complaint, and only a small proportion had offenses dismissed so that they did not appear at all on the offenders' records. In other words, the informal conviction processes tended to result in guilty pleas to the same or very similar offenses, so that the offenses for which convicted did not usually deviate greatly from the crime actually committed. The greater proportion of the bargaining was concerned with directly gaining a lighter sentence regardless of the offense, rather than indirectly by pleading to a lesser charge.

One of the most important implications of the informal methods is the effect of these processes on selection for probation. A promise of the prosecutor's recommendation for probation was one of the most common values given in exchange for a guilty plea. This occurred in 34.5 percent of the cases reporting bargaining. With such informal tactics, selection for placement on probation is determined by the skill of the offender or his lawyer in bargaining, rather than on factors of the case which would have more relevance to successful rehabilitation by field rather than institutional placement.

The existence of informal methods also has broader significance to law and law enforcement as well as to criminology and related areas. The use of such methods involves a differential implementation of the law comparable to the discrepancies noted by Reckless in his "categoric risk" of conviction and Sutherland in his conceptions of white collar crime.[5] An analysis of the sample of offenders showed no clear cut categories separating bargained from non-bargained convictions, yet the fact that some offenders, without going to trial, pleaded guilty without any considerations in the charge or in sentencing while others "settled" their cases informally, raises again the sociological, and presumably the moral, problems of criminal justice.

---

[5] *See* WALTER RECKLESS, THE CRIME PROBLEM, *2nd edition,* (*New York: Appleton-Century-Crofts, Inc., 1955*) *pp 26–42; and* EDWIN H. SUTHERLAND, WHITE COLLAR CRIME (*New York: Dryden Press, 1949*) *pp 3–14.*

Evidently the criminal law is not only differentially enforced in general, but as far as this study shows, this also occurs within groups of offenders convicted of the ordinary (or conventional) felonies of robbery, homicide, burglary, larceny and sex offenses. Certain proportions of these violators (56.7 percent in this sample), without resorting to bribery or other methods of the professional "fix", can modify the nature of the charge against them or the length or type of their sentences in much the same manner as the white collar offender.

Whether bargaining is legal, that is, whether men convicted as the result of bargaining are convicted by due process of law, is a difficult question to answer without referring the decision to a specific case. Likewise, whether bargaining is ethical cannot be summarily answered. Certainly in cases where bargaining is misused, where the accused is exploited or the community subjected to danger, the issue is clear. Under these conditions bargaining is not only unethical but would probably be held unconstitutional, as a violation of the "due process" clauses of the Constitution.

When compromise is used, however, to gain a certain conviction of a surely guilty offender, the question is not so clear. Defense lawyers, prosecutors, and criminal court judges interviewed in an earlier study overwhelmingly favored bargain-justice where judiciously used. They felt it to be the most expedient way of gaining justice. Likewise the offenders who bargained successfully were well satisfied with this process. It was the men who went to trial or who failed to bargain successfully who more often claimed injustice in their cases.

As the lawyers said, bargaining appears to be an expedient method of answering numerous problems of the administration of justice. Our criminal procedure is cumbersome. Legal defense is expensive both for the state and the accused. Court calendars are crowded and would not be able to cope with the number of trials which would ensue if all arrestees pleaded not guilty. Furthermore, no conviction is ever a sure thing, no matter how overwhelming the evidence, if the case goes before a jury. Prosecutors, who need convictions to be successful, know this. For these reasons "bargain-justice" appears the natural answer to lawyers and court officials and, of course, to offenders who are guilty. For these reasons, too, the problem of bargaining cannot easily be corrected, if it should be corrected at all. Bargain-justice appears as a natural, expedient outgrowth of deficiencies in the administration of our "trial-by-combat" theory of justice. It is supported by both the attitudes of offenders who see justice as a purely personal thing, how well they fare in sentencing, and by the attitudes of lawyers and court officials who can only "get things done" in this way.

While bargain-justice may thus be an expedient and at present even a necessary and legitimate legal phenomenon in certain cases, some broader implications of bargaining should be mentioned. Cases of conventional felonies that are "settled" may well result in strengthening attitudes which favor a general disregard for law and for justice, in much the same way as does the differential legal treatment of business and political violators. If conviction on a charge is to be determined in great part by skill of the offender in bargaining with the court or in hiring a lawyer to bargain for him, then our concept of impartial justice based upon facts and rules of evidence becomes meaningless. Furthermore, the fact that opportunities and techniques for bargaining exist in our system can have an adverse effect upon attempts to rehabilitate offenders and generally to decrease crime rates. What happens, for example, when one man, merely because he is unsophisticated, does not know of bargaining techniques nor of the right lawyer to contact, is sentenced to prison while another more sophisticated offender, a recidivist who commits the same offense, arranges a sentence to be served on probation? Certainly the rationalizations of the man sentenced to prison to the effect that he is a "fall guy", and his conception of himself gained from serving prison time, make rehabilitation far more complex if not impossible. The way bargaining now works, the more experienced criminals can manipulate legal processes to obtain light sentences and better official records while the less experienced, occasional offenders receive more harsh treatment. Under these conditions the effectiveness of law as a means of social control is seriously jeopardized and any long range attempts to build respect for the law and law abiding attitudes will prove extremely difficult.

# THE ANALYSIS
# OF BEHAVIOR PATTERNS
# ON THE UNITED STATES
# SUPREME COURT

## S. Sidney Ulmer

In an era of speed and mass production it is anachronistic to find the justices of the Supreme Court assembling each Decision-Monday for a public reading of their printed opinions. The desirability of continuing this tradition is sometimes questioned in view of the fact that it is occasionally responsible for calling public attention to interpersonal conflict among the justices. A recent example of this occurred on December 14, 1959, in an exchange between Whittaker and Douglas in which the latter charged his colleague with writing a "smart-alecky" opinion.[1]

While exchanges of this type may not enhance the confidence of the public in the olympian qualities of the judicial process, they are neither uncommon nor unexpected. Supreme Court justices are neither anointed priests, removed from knowledge of the stress of life, nor impersonal vehicles of revealed truth. They are men with vigorous minds and diversified backgrounds who interpret the Constitution in terms of their experience, their judgment about practical matters and their ideal pictures of the social order.[2] The differences which men inevitably have about these

---

[1] *Reported in the* New York Times, *December 15, 1959.*

[2] *See generally, Benjamin Cardozo,* The Nature of the Judicial Process (*New Haven, 1921*); *Fred V. Cahill,* Judicial Legislation (*New York, 1952*); *Robert H. Jackson,* The Supreme Court in the American System of Government (*Cambridge,*

---

Reprinted by permission of the author and of the publishers from 22 *Journal of Politics* (1960), 629–653.

matters is an important factor in the development of the law. But the classical theory of American jurisprudence does not recognize the legitimacy of such considerations in judicial decision-making.

The antagonism between the mechanistic view of the judicial process and human limitations is one of the factors contributing to tension among judges faced with the continuous responsibility of reconciling fact and theory. Since verbal presentation of opinions (and the side remarks which accompany them) serves as a tension-releasing device, the continuation of the practice may have a functional justification.

It is both pertinent and instructive to study the interpersonal relationships and behavior patterns of the members of a collegial court. By doing so, we recognize what legal analysis ignores, namely, that the law, the courts and the judges are something more than mere abstractions. The nature of the endowments, outlooks and attitudes which judges bring to the discharge of their duties may be revealed in the identification of individual behavior patterns. The discrepancies among these patterns, in turn, reflect the differences among the actors.

This paper attempts to illustrate some of the methods by which the behavior patterns of Supreme Court justices may be identified and analyzed. It is in one sense, therefore, methodological in character. But it is not designed solely as an essay on methodology since substantive relationships of importance are revealed through the application of new methods as well as through the use of previously developed techniques. The cases used are those raising questions of civil liberty in the 1958 term, a choice of

---

*1957*); *Alpheus T. Mason,* The Supreme Court: Vehicle of Revealed Truth or Power Group, 1930–1937 (*Boston, 1953*); *John P. Frank,* Marble Palace (*New York, 1958*). *For a recent analysis of lawmaking on the Court, see S. Sidney Ulmer, "An Empirical Analysis of Selected Aspects of Law-Making on the United States Supreme Court,"* Journal of Public Law, *VIII (Fall, 1959), 414–436. Cf. Felix Frankfurter, "Twenty Years of Mr. Justice Holmes' Constitutional Opinions,"* Harvard Law Review, *XXXVI (June, 1923), 909, 916, 918. For quantitative applications in this area see, especially, Glendon A. Schubert,* Quantitative Analysis of Judicial Behavior (*Glencoe, Ill., 1960*) *and "The Study of Judicial Decision-Making as an Aspect of Political Behavior,"* The American Political Science Review, *LII (1958), 1007–1025; also see Eloise Snyder, "The Supreme Court as a Small Group,"* Social Forces, *XXXVIII (1958), 232–238, and "Uncertainty and the Supreme Court's Decisions,"* American Journal of Sociology, *LXV (1959), 241–245. A recent study of interest on the background of judges is John R. Schmidhauser, "The Justices of the Supreme Court: A Collective Portrait,"* Midwest Journal of Political Science, *III (1959), 1–57.*

subject matter which reflects the view that the attitude of the judge is of above average significance in such cases.[3]

The article is divided into five parts. Part I is a general statistical summary of civil liberty cases for the 1958 term, and includes a brief comparison to several previous Court terms. The remainder of the paper is devoted to an analysis of interpersonal relations and behavior patterns in three selected areas. Part II is an investigation of cohesion tendencies among the justices. A modified method of factor analysis is introduced and its usefulness illustrated. The number of blocs on the Supreme Court is determined and the composition and nature of each is discussed. Attention is given to interpersonal support rates among the justices as measured by a Solidarity Index and to leadership or power within blocs and within the Court as measured by the Shapely-Shubik Power Index. An analysis of a neglected area of study, opinion behavior, is undertaken in Part III. The authority to assign the writing of opinions is conceptualized as an aspect of power. It is shown that the assigning judges discriminate among their colleagues and that the choices are related to interpersonal factors. The nexus between cohesion tendencies and opinion behavior is observed. It is suggested that the discriminatory decisions have significant consequences for the development of the law. Part IV is concerned with the role of attitude and attitude consistency in Court treatment of civil liberty cases. A scalogram analysis of all such non-unanimous cases in the 1958 term is presented. The results are compared to those derived from analyses in two previous terms, and they reveal a high degree of consistency among the justices. The stability of cohesion tendencies in civil liberty cases is noted. Finally, in Part V we attempt to reach some tentative conclusions about the relationships studied in this paper.

I

In its 1956 term the protection given civil liberties was adroitly expanded by the Supreme Court through restrictive statutory interpretation and deft manipulation of key constitutional provisions. One measure

---

[3] *A civil liberty case is defined for the purposes of this paper as any case which raises a question concerning the type of non-economic personal right covered by the first eight and the Civil War Amendments to the Constitution. On this definition it makes no difference whether the case concerns a statutory or constitutional provision since the focus is on the substance rather than the form of the right claimed.*

of the expansion was the rejection of only 26 per cent of all civil liberty claims during the term. The rejection rate increased to 41 per cent in the following term and, in the 1958 session, to 48.8 per cent.

The Court decided 43 civil liberty cases in the 1958 term as compared to 46 in the previous session.[4] Federal participation as a litigant increased from 43 to 46.5 per cent while state participation moved from 50 to 51.2 per cent. Only one case involved private parties. Of those cases in which the civil liberty claim was upheld, approximately half were decided against the federal government and half against state governments. This suggests a slight discrimination against the federal government which carried over from the 1957 term. Overall, the Court seems to have been more permissive toward governmental activity in the civil liberty field in the 1958 term than in the two terms preceding.

Classification of the substantive rights in contention in the 1958 term is complicated by the presence of several unusual questions before the Court during the term. An attempt at classification is made in Table 1.[5] One of the novel problems getting increasing attention from the Court is that of multiple punishment for single offenses. This area of contention is related in general to that of former jeopardy, but it also has certain unique aspects. Table 1 lists four multiple-punishment cases during the term, three of which were decided for the defendant. While two of these were decided unanimously, the third found the Court split 8–1 for the defendant, with Clark in dissent. One of the four cases went against the defendant, with Douglas and Black in dissent.

A second sub-area of civil liberties which got inordinate attention in the 1958 term was that of the right to withhold information. The claim made by defendants in these cases covered legislative as well as judicial institutions, with four of the six decisions going against the defendant. On balance, the Court moved to curb the scope of the rights claimed in this general area. Other rights in contention were more traditional, involving such things as race relations, free speech and the right to counsel. Cases in which Negroes were involved were more prevalent in the 1958 term than has generally been the case in the post-1954 period. One outstanding

---

[4] S. Sidney Ulmer, "The Supreme Court and Civil Liberties," The Western Political Quarterly, XIII (June, 1960), 288–311.
[5] Compilation of similar data for the 1957 term may be found in ibid.

TABLE 1. SUBSTANTIVE RIGHTS IN CONTENTION IN CIVIL LIBERTY CASES, 1958 TERM.

| Subject Matter | Number of Cases |
|---|---|
| Racial Discrimination | 6 |
| Right to Withhold Information* | 6 |
| Free Speech | 4 |
| Multiple Punishment for Single Offense | 4 |
| Former Jeopardy | 3 |
| Jury Trial | 2 |
| Right to Counsel | 2 |
| Search and Seizure | 2 |
| Other "Fair Trial" Rights** | 9 |
| Miscellaneous*** | 5 |
| Total | 43 |

\* Includes claims under both the First and Fifth Amendments.

\*\* Consisting of: right to indictment (1); improper exposure of jury to news articles during trial (1); coerced confession (1); perjury of prosecution witness with knowledge of prosecutor (1); habeas corpus (1); rights of indigent defendants (1); rights of criminal defendants under the Jenck's rule (3).

\*\*\* Consisting of: right to travel (1); right against arbitrary dismissal from federal service (2); right against defamation of character by governmental action (2).

difference between the rights in contention in 1957 and in 1958 is that, in the former period, five different cases revolved around claimed rights of citizenship while the Court decided no cases on this point in the latter period.

## II

Those who write about the United States Supreme Court often find it convenient to speak of "blocs" on the Court and, since Herman Pritchett's work on the Roosevelt and Vinson Courts, the existence of such blocs has been common knowledge.[6] Yet we cannot assume that the number, size, composition and cohesion tendencies of blocs of justices are constant. We can identify and speak more meaningfully about change in such characteristics if we first devise adequate methods of measurement. Moreover, the

[6] *C. Herman Pritchett*, The Roosevelt Court (*New York, 1948*); Civil Liberties and the Vinson Court (*Chicago, 1954*).

term "bloc" in its general sense is one of those words which has many shades of meaning. A prime requisite to the maturing of any social science is the development of precision in definition and communication.

Appropriate to these goals is the modified form of factor analysis developed by McQuitty.[7] The method seeks to identify a "typal structure" which is a structure in which "every member of a type is more like some other member of that type (with respect to the data analyzed) than he is like any member of any other type." When the members of a type have been isolated, a prototype may be defined. The prototype is a composite of the characteristics possessed by members of the type and represents the characteristics which the members possess in common. It is, in short, the centroid of the characteristics common to the typal members. The relevancy which each member of the type has to the centroid or prototype may be computed by the method used to extract first factor loadings in factor analysis. The loadings are extracted, however, from sub-matrices rather than from the entire matrix.

The first step is to construct a matrix of correlation coefficients expressing the relations of the variables being analyzed. Table 2 is such a matrix. The coefficients reflect the tendency of pairs of justices to agree or disagree in responding to civil liberty cases. A linkage analysis of this matrix establishes the existence of types or sub-matrices. The analysis

---

[7] McQuitty has developed a number of techniques for dealing with social science data. Among the more useful ones are Hierarchical Syndrome Analysis, Pattern Analysis, and Agreement Analysis. The method used in this paper is known as Linkage Analysis. For a reference, see Louis L. McQuitty, "Elementary Linkage Analysis For Isolating Orthogonal and Oblique Types and Typal Relevancies," Educational and Psychological Measurement, XVII (1957), 207–229. Also see, for general reference, Raymond Cattell, "A Note on Correlation Clusters and Cluster Search Methods," Psychometrika, IX (September, 1944), 169. A simplified treatment of factor analysis is B. A. Fruchter, Introduction to Factor Analysis (New York, 1954). There is some question among statisticians as to the required size of the expected frequencies when using Phi. For evidence of the disparity of views, see Allan L. Edwards, Statistical Methods for the Behavioral Sciences (New York, 1954), p. 384; Sidney Siegal, Nonparametric Statistics for the Behavioral Sciences (New York, 1956), p. 46; and cf. Morris Zelditch, A Basic Course in Sociological Statistics (New York, 1959), pp. 169–171. The assumptions necessary for the use of Phi with judicial voting statistics have been made by L. L. Thurstone and J. W. Degan, A Factorial Study of the Supreme Court (Chicago, 1951); a related study using tetrachoric coefficients with judicial data is Fred Kort, "Quantitative Content Analysis of Judicial Opinions" (mimeographed, 1959).

| | DO | BL | WA | BR | WH | FR | HA | ST | CL |
|---|---|---|---|---|---|---|---|---|---|
| DO | | 708 | 843 | 706 | −232 | −296 | −313 | −172 | −313 |
| BL | 708 | | 713 | 593 | −155 | −259 | −223 | −223 | −223 |
| WA | 843 | 713 | | 882 | −203 | −183 | −183 | −151 | −238 |
| BR | 706 | 593 | 882 | | −116 | −180 | −183 | −064 | −183 |
| WH | −232 | −155 | −203 | −116 | | 795 | 670 | 180 | 263 |
| FR | −296 | −259 | −183 | −179 | 795 | | 1000 | 448 | 480 |
| HA | −313 | −223 | −183 | −183 | 670 | 1000 | | 414 | 392 |
| ST | −172 | −223 | −151 | −064 | 180 | 448 | 414 | | 053 |
| CL | −313 | −223 | −238 | −183 | 263 | 480 | 392 | 053 | |

DO—Douglas    WA—Warren    WH—Whittaker    HA—Harlan    CL—Clark
BL—Black       BR—Brennan    FR—Frankfurter   ST—Stewart

* Using the Phi coefficient with a range of −1 to +1. For a methodological note on the use of Phi, see Fn. 7. Decimals have been omitted.
** One case is omitted due to a (4–4) split.

consists of the following steps. First, the highest coefficient in each column of the primary matrix is underlined. The highest coefficient for the entire matrix is then determined and the two variables involved constitute the core of the first type. The underlined coefficients in the row of each of the two variables are then used to link additional variables to the type. These are called "first cousin" variables. The same procedure is repeated for the rows of the "first cousin" variables and if additional linkage results the additions to the type are called "second cousin" variables. This procedure is continued until all the variables of one type have been determined. When one type has been established the procedure is applied to the remaining variables and so on until all variables have been classified. In the present case two types are identified. The first is composed of Frankfurter, Harlan, Whittaker, Stewart and Clark. The second consists of Warren, Douglas, Brennan and Black. The relationships within the typal structures are portrayed in Figure 1.

Figure 1 shows that each member of a bloc correlated at a higher rate with each member of his own bloc than with any justice not a member of the bloc. It also indicates that the highest correlation within the two blocs was respectively between Harlan and Frankfurter and between Warren and Brennan. Speculation concerning leadership within the blocs is promoted by the fact that each member of a type correlated at a higher rate

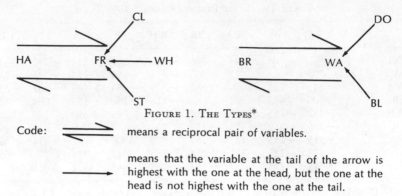

FIGURE 1. THE TYPES*

Code: ⇌ means a reciprocal pair of variables.

⟶ means that the variable at the tail of the arrow is highest with the one at the head, but the one at the head is not highest with the one at the tail.

\* *(Key to abbreviations may be found in Table 2.)*

with either Frankfurter or Warren, as the case may be, than with any other member of his respective type. This facet of the typal relationships may be measured by the extraction of typal relevancies using the method previously mentioned. The results reported in Table 3 indicate that Warren and Frankfurter have more of the characteristics common to the members of the type than other justices in the respective blocs. These two

TABLE 3. TYPAL RELEVANCIES.*

|     | Type I | Type II |
| --- | --- | --- |
| DO | .887 | |
| BL | .780 | |
| WA | .950 | |
| BR | .876 | |
| WH | | .749 |
| FR | | 1.000 |
| HA | | .956 |
| ST | | .424 |
| CL | | .464 |

(Key to abbreviations used in left-hand column may be found in Table 2.)
\* Possible numerical range for the matrix in Table 3 is 0 to 1.

justices closely approximate the prototype. If a positive relationship between possession of characteristics common to a group and influence within the group may be assumed, Warren and Frankfurter may be suspected of being "leaders" of their respective blocs. This inference would not violate prevailing conceptions, for the Court is generally considered to have Warren and Frankfurter wings.

In the Warren group, Black, Douglas and Brennan all have a high loading on the prototype. In the Frankfurter group, however, we note that Stewart and Clark have relatively low loadings on the prototype. The inference is that if a third bloc were to form on the Court, its most likely nucleus would be Stewart and Clark. We should not imply necessarily from these data that Frankfurter and Warren dominated their two reciprocating justices, Harlan and Brennan. The influence or status relationship between any pair of justices must be analyzed in a different manner because a correlation of the behavior of two justices may show that they tend to act together, but it does not indicate who is leading and who is following. We shall return to this problem shortly.

At this point we are concerned with leadership within a bloc. The suggestion is that where a justice more closely approximates the prototype than any other member of his own group, leadership ability on his part may be suspected. This may very well be, however, what is known as second-order leadership. For example, Frankfurter and Harlan have the highest reciprocating correlation in civil liberty cases in the 1958 term. Whittaker, Clark and Stewart correlate highest with Frankfurter, suggesting that he has influence within the group. If Frankfurter, however, tends to be influenced by Harlan, then a tendency on the part of Whittaker, Clark and Stewart to follow Frankfurter would, in effect, result in leadership for Harlan. In other words, it is important to establish, if possible, the status relationship between the two highest reciprocating justices in each bloc. This obviously is not simple to achieve in view of the inability to secure general agreement on the meaning of such concepts as "leadership" or "status." Yet, some insight may be gained by examining the interpersonal relationships and, at the same time, varying the angles of observation.

One approach is through Solidarity Analysis. This furnishes us with an index based upon the ratio of supportive and non-supportive behavior directed by each justice to each other member of the Court. Support or non-support is conceptualized respectively as the agreement or disagreement of one judge with the written opinions of another. In a given case a justice has a number of choices about such things. He may, of course, be asked to write the opinion for the Court. If he does not write for the

Court his area of choice is much larger. Possible behavior would include the following:

(1) He may concur in the result.

(2) He may write a concurring opinion.

(3) He may dissent.

(4) He may write a dissenting opinion.

(5) He may concur with a concurring opinion, with a dissenting opinion or with the opinion of the Court.

It is surmised that the way in which he makes this choice furnishes one *crude* indication of his relationship to his colleagues. This, of course, becomes even more significant if consistent patterns of behavior can be observed through time.

Table 4 contains data which bear upon the relationships between the two justices in each group who correlate at the highest level. The Solidarity Index[8] shows that Brennan received almost twice the ratio of suppor-

TABLE 4. INTER-INDIVIDUAL SOLIDARITY INDEX*: CIVIL LIBERTY CASES, 1958 TERM.

| Justices as Targets | Justices as Initiators | | | | | | | | |
|---|---|---|---|---|---|---|---|---|---|
| | DO | BL | WA | BR | CL | ST | WH | FR | HA |
| Douglas | | .73 | .53 | .53 | .20 | .20 | .20 | .14 | .13 |
| Black | .58 | | .58 | .42 | .25 | .08 | .08 | .09 | .08 |
| Warren | .88 | .67 | | .56 | .33 | .25 | .44 | .33 | .22 |
| Brennan | .64 | .88 | 1.00 | | .11 | .15 | .22 | .22 | .22 |
| Clark | .00 | .00 | .00 | .11 | | .44 | .44 | .44 | .56 |
| Stewart | .22 | .11 | .22 | .33 | .22 | | .44 | .33 | .44 |
| Whittaker | .25 | .75 | .67 | .75 | .75 | .75 | | .67 | .75 |
| Frankfurter | .00 | .00 | .09 | .09 | .67 | .67 | .67 | | .78 |
| Harlan | .11 | .22 | .11 | .11 | .78 | .44 | .78 | .78 | |

(Key to abbreviations used in column headings may be found in Table 2.)

* $\text{ISI} = \dfrac{\text{aij}}{\text{aij} + \text{dij}} \times 100$ where aij = the number of supportive acts originated by the ith individual and directed toward the jth individual; dij = the number of non-supportive or negative acts originated by the ith individual and directed toward the jth individual. Supportive and non-supportive acts in this case are represented by agreement or disagreement by the ith individual with an opinion written by the jth individual.

[8] *For a general reference, see Robert F. Bales,* Interaction Process Analysis: A Method for the Study of Small Groups (*Cambridge, 1951*).

tive acts from Warren that Warren received from Brennan. We infer that Brennan exerted strong influence upon the Chief Justice in the 1958 civil liberty cases. We note further that Brennan had the highest mean excess of support in his bloc. In comparing Frankfurter and Harlan we encounter a tie. It is notable, however, that Frankfurter's mean excess of support is more than double that of Harlan.

A third way of looking at the relationships on the Court is in terms of the relative exercise of power in civil liberty cases. For this purpose we may utilize the Shapely-Shubik Index,[9] which defines power as the probability of being pivotal in a majority decision. The index is a function, therefore, of both the frequency of participation in the majority and the size of the majority. Table 5 gives the relative rankings for forty-three

TABLE 5. RELATIVE RANKING OF SUPREME COURT JUSTICES ON SHAPELY-SHUBIK POWER INDEX, 1958 TERM.

| Justice* | All Cases** | | Civil Liberty Cases Only | |
|---|---|---|---|---|
| | Mean Coefficient | Rank | Mean Coefficient | Rank |
| Douglas | .0908 | 9 | .0803 | 9 |
| Black | .1012 | 8 | .1004 | 7 |
| Warren | .1084 | 7 | .0898 | 8 |
| Brennan | .1218 | 2 | .1014 | 6 |
| Clark | .1249 | 1 | .1273 | 2 |
| Stewart | .1122 | 6 | .1227 | 4 |
| Whittaker | .1135 | 5 | .1316 | 1 |
| Frankfurter | .1153 | 3 | .1200 | 5 |
| Harlan | .1148 | 4 | .1246 | 3 |

* Burton is omitted because he participated in too few cases.
** 121 opinion cases only.

civil liberty cases (unanimous and non-unanimous) as well as for 121 cases accompanied by written opinions. If only the civil liberty cases are used, Brennan turns up as the most powerful member of his bloc while Warren ranks third within the bloc. Frankfurter ranks a poor fifth in his own bloc. The failure of Frankfurter and Warren to reflect in this index the roles indicated by the correlation analysis reveals the fact that much of the support they received came in cases decided by large rather than small

[9] *The method is explained in detail in L. S. Shapely and Martin Shubik, "A Method for Evaluating the Distribution of Power in a Committee System," The American Political Science Review, XLVIII (September, 1954), 787–792.*

majorities. The Shapely-Shubik Power Index places a premium on participation in marginal majorities.

In comparing the rank order of all cases with that of civil liberty cases only, we find a correlation that is statistically significant at the .02 level.[10] But the coefficient (.64) does not obscure the fact that, as far as the full Court is concerned, Whittaker's role is more crucial and Brennan's less crucial in civil liberty decisions than in decision-making in general. In sum, it would seem that firm conclusions about leadership on the Court must await more conclusive evidence, although Warren, Brennan, Frankfurter and Harlan seem more likely candidates for this mantle than do other members of the Court.

## III

A related area of choice for the justices of the Supreme Court is that of opinion writing. With the exception of opinions for the Court, the judge may determine for himself the type, nature and number of opinions which he writes in a given term. Table 6 records the appropriate data for the 1958 term.[11]

The table shows that Douglas, Brennan and Black wrote the largest number of opinions in civil liberty cases. The overall totals, however, are not particularly significant since judges vary in total opinion production. Douglas, for example, wrote thirty-six opinions in the 1958 term as compared to seventeen for Whittaker and fourteen for Warren. The statistics from Table 6 may be used, however, to examine for civil liberty opinions the quantity and directions of deviation from the expected frequency. In the 1958 term, opinions in civil liberty cases constituted 40.4 per cent of the total opinions. If substantive civil liberty issues concerned all justices equally, each would be expected to devote approximately 40 per cent of his total opinion production to such cases. The extent that the production of a justice falls on either side of this ratio is a *crude* measure of the concern or intensity of feeling with which the judge views civil liberty questions. This is borne out by the fact, derived from the data of Table 6, that those who expressed themselves in an "excessive" number of

---

[10] *The Kendall Rank Coefficient is used here. A general reference is Sidney Siegal,* Nonparametric Statistics for the Behavioral Sciences (*New York, 1956*), *pp. 213–223.*

[11] *Compilation of similar data for the 1957 term may be found in Ulmer, "The Supreme Court and Civil Liberties,"* op. cit.

| Justice | OC | C | D | T | CL Op. as % of Total Opinions | Deviation* From Expected | Previous** Deviation |
|---|---|---|---|---|---|---|---|
| Douglas | 4 | 2 | 9 | 15 | 41.6 | + .2 | +3.2 |
| Black | 3 | 4 | 5 | 12 | 48 | + 7.6 | + .8 |
| Warren | 5 | 0 | 4 | 9 | 64.2 | +23.8 | +9 |
| Brennan | 5 | 2 | 7 | 14 | 42.4 | + 2 | +9 |
| Whittaker | 3 | 1 | 0 | 4 | 23.5 | −16.9 | −7.5 |
| Frankfurter | 5 | 1 | 5 | 11 | 39.2 | − 1.2 | +3.3 |
| Harlan | 6 | 2 | 2 | 10 | 31.2 | − 9.2 | −8.8 |
| Stewart | 3 | 4 | 2 | 9 | 39.1 | − 1.3 | *** |
| Clark | 3 | 2 | 4 | 9 | 40.8 | + .4 | +19 |

* Expected frequency is 40.4% (the ratio of civil liberty opinions to total opinions).
** Deviation from the expected frequency in the 1957 term.
*** Not sitting in the 1957 term.
Code: OC—Opinion for the Court
     C—Concurring opinion
     D—Dissenting opinion (includes opinions dissenting and concurring in part).
     T—Total opinions written in CL cases in the 1958 term.
Note: The presentation of the statistics in this table does not imply statistical significance. The size of the opinion frequencies suggest caution in generalizations for which accumulated data from subsequent terms will furnish more meaningful tests.

civil liberty cases were the four "libertarians" and Clark. Douglas, Black, Warren and Brennan have been identified as "soft" on civil liberty questions since the 1956 term. Clark on the other hand usually takes an extreme position in a contrary direction. The other four justices showed less involvement, with Whittaker and Harlan, in particular, appearing relatively disinterested in such matters. The most striking performance was that of Warren, who wrote 64 per cent of his opinions in civil liberty cases. This simply substantiates what is known to be Warren's consuming preoccupation with civil liberty problems.

A second area of choice in respect to Court opinions is more limited than that just discussed. The choice here is restricted to the judge who assigns the opinion to be written for the Court in each case decided. The assigning judge is the Chief Justice if he is in the majority; otherwise the privilege goes to the senior justice in the majority. It has been suggested that the assignment of opinions represents a meaningful exercise of power.[12] That it is viewed as such by those on the receiving end is evident in a letter from Justice Harlan to Chief Justice Fuller in 1898 which contained the following complaint: "Two Saturdays in succession you have not assigned to me any case but have assigned cases and important cases to Justice Gray. I was in the majority in each case assigned to him."[13] The assignment of opinion writing is clearly the most important duty of the Chief Justice in relation to his associates. In discharging this duty he must, of course, attempt to spread the work load to maximize the chances of clearing the docket by term's end. But an assigning judge may have other ends in view. Among the purposes which have been identified[14] are (1) public relations (as when a liberal opinion is assigned to a conservative judge to promote an image of objectivity for the Court) and (2) reward (as when "choice" opinions are assigned to particular justices and "chore" opinions to newcomers or those in whom the assigning judge has little confidence). Other possibilities are suggested in the discussion which follows.

Table 7 shows that Chief Justice Warren assigned twenty-four civil liberty opinions during the 1958 term, personally assuming the responsibility for writing five of these. Brennan was next in line with four assignments; Harlan and Clark were given one opinion each, thereby making them the least popular of all the justices for this particular function. The more significant statistics, however, are those expressing the opinion assignments as a ratio of the times available for assignment. The availability of the justices for assignment from Warren varied from sixteen to twenty-four times, the variance depending on the extent to which each justice agreed with the Chief Justice in the majority. The percentage figures suggest discrimination against Harlan and Clark while Whittaker, who is not normally associated with the Warren wing of the Court, fared slightly better than other members of the Warren bloc.

In exercising the power of assignment the judge may be expected to discriminate in his choices depending upon the factors operative in a given situation. For example, opinion assignment in a marginal case (5–4)

---

[12] Cf. Frank, op. cit., pp. 76–79.

[13] Willard L. King, Melville Weston Fuller (New York, 1950), p. 245. For comments from an assigning judge, see Bruce R. Trimble, Chief Justice Waite (Princeton, 1938), pp. 259ff.

[14] Frank, op. cit.

TABLE 7. WARREN OPINION ASSIGNMENTS IN CIVIL LIBERTY CASES, 1958 TERM.

| Justices | Times Available | Opinions Assigned to | Marginal (5-4)* | Unan. | Assignments as % of Times Available |
|---|---|---|---|---|---|
| Douglas | 21 | 3 | 0 | 2 | 14.2 |
| Black | 22 | 3 | 1 | 1 | 13.6 |
| Warren | 24 | 5 | 0 | 2 | 20.8 |
| Brennan | 24 | 4 | 3 | 0 | 16.2 |
| Whittaker | 18 | 3 | 0 | 2 | 16.6 |
| Frankfurter | 16 | 2 | 0 | 1 | 12.4 |
| Harlan | 16 | 1 | 1 | 0 | 6.2 |
| Stewart | 18 | 2 | 0 | 2 | 12.4 |
| Clark | 16 | 1 | 0 | 0 | 6.2 |
| Totals | 175 | 24 | 5 | 10 | |

\* Includes one case decided (4-4).

is a different matter from assignment in a unanimous case (9-0). The marginal opinion must be written in such a way as to hold every member of the 5-vote group.[15] Otherwise, the majority may become the minority, a possibility not to be risked unnecessarily. Table 7 shows that Warren assigned opinions in five marginal cases and in ten cases decided unanimously. Since Brennan was given three of the five marginal assignments, it is not unreasonable to surmise that there were factors associated with the Brennan assignments which tended to maximize the coherence of the majority bloc. There are a number of reasons why a particular justice may be favored for opinion assignments in marginal cases. Some of the general considerations have been mentioned; the following are additional possibilities:

(1) The justice is pivotal in the case, and the assignment is a "pay off" or reward designed to hold him in the majority.

(2) The justice is closest in view to that of the assigning judge.

---

[15] *This obviously does not apply with the same force to situations in which the thinking of a justice is so divergent from that of his colleagues as to warrant a separate concurrence. Such instances are clearly exceptions to the general rule, having occurred only twice in the 1958 term. Even in such cases the actual vote of the pivotal justice may have been influenced by the cogency and logic of the opinion for the Court. The concurring opinion, therefore, often serves merely to clarify, embellish or modify one or more points of the Court's opinion.*

(3) The justice has some unusual attraction for one or more members of the opposition group.

(4) The justice represents what is common to the bloc to which he belongs rather than some extreme position.

Close analysis at this point produces interesting results. One of the three Brennan assignments was in *Raley* v. *Ohio*,[16] decided by a 4–4 split. A possible explanation for this assignment is the close relationship between Brennan and Warren. Of the four justices voting together in *Raley* (Douglas, Black, Warren and Brennan), the overall agreement rate in civil liberty cases was highest between Warren and Brennan, as expressed by a correlation coefficient of .882.[17] The other two assignments may be explained on the same grounds but additional factors of interest are present. In both of these cases we find that the "four horsemen" (Douglas, Black, Warren and Brennan) picked up a fifth vote from that side of the Court not normally associated with the group. The fifth vote in both cases was that of Stewart. This leads us to suspect some unique relationship between Brennan and Stewart. Investigation shows that in terms of agreement in civil liberty cases Brennan and Stewart correlated at —.064. This means that the tendency was to disagree. But all members of the Warren bloc tended to disagree with the remaining members of the Court since all four correlated negatively with the other five justices. The tendency toward disagreement was lower between Brennan and Stewart than between any other pair of inter-typal justices. Thus an assigning judge wishing to maximize the probability of holding a five-man majority together would, where Stewart is pivotal, assign the opinion to Brennan. The assignments in *Irvin* v. *Dowd*[18] and *In re Sawyer*,[19] therefore, may be explained by reasons (2) and (3) stated above.

In *Vitarelli* v. *Seaton*[20] we find the Warren bloc picking up Harlan. Since Harlan was obviously pivotal, the opinion assignment may be viewed as a "pay off" per (1) above. Finally, in *Farmer's Cooperative Union* v. *WDAY*[21] Black was given the opinion and Clark was pivotal. In this case it seems that Brennan would have been the better choice, but

---

[16] Raley v. Ohio, 79 S. Ct. 1257 (1959).
[17] *The Phi coefficient is used unless otherwise specified.*
[18] 79 S. Ct. 825 (1959).
[19] 79 S. Ct. 1376 (1959).
[20] 79 S. Ct. 968 (1959).
[21] 79 S. Ct. 1302 (1959).

Black had the second highest rate of agreement with Clark. Moreover, the fact that Stewart wrote concurring opinions in *Irvin* and *Sawyer* suggests that his alignment with the Warren bloc in these cases was more tenuous than that of Clark in *Farmer's Cooperative Union*.

The remaining opinion assignments were made by Black and Frankfurter. The former justice made one assignment to Whittaker and two assignments to Harlan, one of which was a 5–4 decision. In this case, *Barr v. Matteo*,[22] Black shifted to the Frankfurter side of the Court while Stewart sided with Warren, Douglas and Brennan. In assigning the opinion Black chose a member of the Frankfurter bloc. But while this led to an opinion to which the other bloc members subscribed it did not satisfy Black himself. Thus we observe the assigning justice writing a concurring opinion expressing his own views because as Black writes: "they are not altogether the same as those stated in the opinion of Mr. Justice Harlan."[23] The opinion assignment, possibly, was designed to accomplish other purposes.

Table 8 records the data on the remaining assignments during the term, all of which were made by Frankfurter. Several aspects of the table invite comment. Black and Warren were never available for opinion assignment from Frankfurter by virtue of the mechanics of the system, but this did not apply to Douglas. Yet Table 8 indicates that Douglas was never in the majority with Frankfurter unless joined by either Warren or Black or both. In only two instances was Brennan pulled into a majority from which Warren and Black were absent and in both cases (decided by identical 6–3 votes) he won the opinion assignment. One might speculate that this was reward for deviation from the Warren bloc. Whittaker, though available in every possible instance, received no Frankfurter assignments during the term. This could mean that Whittaker's reliability as a member of the Frankfurter bloc is unshakable. It does not appear explainable on the "share the work" theory since Brennan was assigned more opinions by Warren than Whittaker was, yet Brennan received two additional assignments from Frankfurter.

Frankfurter made assignments in eight marginal cases as compared to

---

[22] *79 S. Ct. 1335 (1959)*.

[23] Ibid., *p. 1342. This is not the only remarkable behavior in opinion writing during the term. Equally notable was the fact that in* Abbate *v.* United States, *79 S. Ct. 666 (1959),* Brennan wrote the opinion for the Court as well as a concurring opinion.

| Justices | Times Available | Opinions Assigned to | Marginal (5–4) | Unani- mous | Assignments as % of Times Available |
|---|---|---|---|---|---|
| Douglas | 0 | 0 | 0 | 0 | 0 |
| Black | 0 | 0 | 0 | 0 | 0 |
| Warren | 0 | 0 | 0 | 0 | 0 |
| Brennan | 2 | 2 | 0 | 0 | 100 |
| Whittaker | 11 | 0 | 0 | 0 | 0 |
| Frankfurter | 11 | 3 | 3 | 0 | 27.2 |
| Harlan | 11 | 3 | 2 | 0 | 27.2 |
| Stewart | 11 | 1 | 1 | 0 | 9 |
| Clark | 11 | 2 | 2 | 0 | 18.1 |
| Totals | 57 | 11 | 8 | 0 | |

five by Warren. Contrary to Warren's practice, Frankfurter wrote all three of his opinions in marginal cases reflecting, perhaps, confidence in his ability to hold his majority. Warren, of course, was generally faced with the problem of attracting and holding a member of the Frankfurter bloc in order to make a majority. In contrast, in *all eight* of the marginal cases in which Frankfurter made the assignment the five members of the majority were all members of the Frankfurter bloc. The Frankfurter bloc, therefore, merely had to hold its own members in the marginal splits. Finally, it should be noted that all eleven of the Frankfurter assignments were made in cases deciding against the civil liberty claim, while six of Warren's twenty-four assignments were in cases deciding against the claim. All six were assigned to Whittaker, Frankfurter or Clark.

## IV

At this point a major question remains unanswered. We have suggested that decision-making in civil liberty cases is impinged upon by such factors as judicial philosophy, endowments and attitudes. These attributes are not easily changed and all experience shows that they are the sturdiest of human reliances. If such factors actually governed decision-making in civil liberty cases, we should expect a consistency of behavior which is not significantly affected by such things as the legal classification of the case, or the law or constitutional provision which seems called into play by the facts. Here we adopt a hypothesis that has already been affirmed in both the 1956 and 1957 terms of Court, to wit: the responses of the justices in civil liberty cases are functions of one dominant variable.[24] Guttman Scalogram analysis can tell us whether the response pattern of the judges in those cases can be satisfactorily accounted for by one variable.[25] The nature of that variable must be separately derived.[26]

Scale analysis is now common enough in political science to justify omission of the details of the operation. In general, a one-variable solution is established if a scale exists. A perfect scale is said to exist if the questions and responses to a series of questions can be arranged in such a way that "persons who answer a given question favorably all have higher ranks than persons who answer the same question unfavorably."[27] Since perfect scales are not expected, Guttman has developed a measure of the difference between a perfect scale and a given scale pattern. This measure is known as the Coefficient of Reproducibility. Any pattern with a CR of less that .90 is classified as a non-scale type. The nature of the variable involved must be inferred. The confidence with which one can draw the inference that variable i has the nature j depends upon the extent to which the questions posed are true attributes of a universe j. The cases selected for the instant study were those involving, in varying degrees, the deprivation of a claimed civil liberty. If the responses to these cases scale, we may infer the existence of one dominant variable, to wit: the attitudes of the respondents toward civil liberty deprivations.

Table 9 presents the scalogram of the twenty-nine non-unanimous civil liberty cases decided in the 1958 term. This scale is well within the requirements of scale theory. The judges are ranked along an attitude continuum with Douglas at the pole most favorable to civil liberty claims and Clark occupying the least favorable position. The scale thus enables us to infer something about the attitudes of the two blocs we have observed operating in civil liberty cases. Moreover, it identifies the relative position

---

[24] See Ulmer, "The Supreme Court and Civil Liberties," op. cit. For the application of scalogram analysis to a different area of judicial behavior, see Ulmer, "Judicial Review as Political Behavior: A Temporary Check on Congress," Administrative Science Quarterly, IV (1960), 426–445.

[25] See S. A. Stouffer (ed.), Measurement and Prediction (Princeton, 1950).

[26] For a treatment of some of the problems associated with determination of the nature of the dominant variable, see Ernest Q. Campbell and Alan C. Kerckhoff, "A Critique of the Concept 'Universe of Attributes'," Public Opinion Quarterly, XXI (Summer, 1957), 295. Cf. Warren S. Torgerson, Theory and Methods of Scaling (New York, 1958), pp. 307ff.

[27] Stouffer, op. cit., p. 5.

TABLE 9. SCALOGRAM ANALYSIS: CIVIL LIBERTY CASES, U.S. SUPREME COURT, 1958 TERM.

| Scale Score** | Douglas | Black | Warren | Brennan | Whittaker | Frankfurter | Harlan | Stewart | Clark | Votes |
|---|---|---|---|---|---|---|---|---|---|---|
| | 29 | 27 | 25 | 23 | 6 | 4 | 3 | 3 | 1 | |
| Cases* | | | | | | | | | | |
| Marshall v. United States, 1171 | + | − | + | + | + | + | + | + | + | 8–1 |
| Greene v. McElroy, 1400 | + | + | + | + | + | + | + | + | − | 8–1 |
| Ladner v. United States, 209 | + | + | + | + | + | + | + | + | − | 8–1 |
| Smith v. United States, 991 | + | + | + | + | + | + | − | − | − | 6–3 |
| Lee v. Madigan, 276 | + | + | + | + | + | − | − | + | − | 6–3 |
| Burns v. Ohio, 1164 | + | + | + | + | + | − | − | NP | + | 6–2 |
| In re Sawyer, 1376 | + | + | + | + | − | − | − | + | − | 5–4 |
| Farmer's Union v. WDAY, 1302 | + | + | + | + | − | − | − | − | + | 5–4 |
| Barr v. Matteo, 1335 | + | − | + | + | − | − | − | + | − | 4–5 |
| Howard v. Lyons, 1331 | + | − | + | + | − | − | − | − | − | 3–6 |
| Brown v. United States, 539 | + | + | + | + | − | − | − | − | − | 4–5 |
| Bartkus v. Illinois, 676 | + | + | + | + | − | − | − | − | − | 4–5 |
| Frank v. Maryland, 804 | + | + | + | + | − | − | − | − | − | 4–5 |
| Irvin v. Dowd, 825 | + | + | + | + | − | − | − | + | − | 5–4 |
| Beacon Theatres v. Westover, 948 | + | + | + | + | − | NP | − | − | + | 5–3 |
| Vitarelli v. Seaton, 968 | + | + | + | + | − | − | + | − | − | 5–4 |
| Uphaus v. Wyman, 1040 | + | + | + | + | − | − | − | − | − | 4–5 |
| Barenblatt v. United States, 1081 | + | + | + | + | − | − | − | − | − | 4–5 |
| Harrison v. N.A.A.C.P., 1025 | + | − | + | + | − | − | − | − | − | 3–6 |
| Raley v. Ohio, 1257 | + | + | + | + | − | − | − | NP | − | 4–4 |
| Pittsburgh Glass v. U.S., 1237 | + | + | + | + | − | − | − | − | − | 4–5 |
| Rosenberg v. United States, 1231 | + | + | + | + | − | − | − | − | − | 4–5 |
| Anon. 6 & 7 v. Baker, 1157 | + | + | + | + | − | − | − | − | − | 4–5 |
| Mills v. Louisiana, 980 | + | + | + | − | − | − | − | − | − | 3–6 |
| Abbate v. United States, 666 | + | + | + | − | − | − | − | − | − | 3–6 |
| New York v. O'Neill, 564 | + | + | − | − | − | − | − | − | − | 2–7 |
| Harris v. United States, 560 | + | + | − | − | − | − | − | − | − | 2–7 |
| Draper v. United States, 329 | + | − | NP | − | − | NP | − | − | − | 1–6 |
| Williams v. Oklahoma, 421 | + | − | − | − | − | − | − | − | − | 1–8 |
| Total Participations: | 29 | 29 | 28 | 29 | 29 | 27 | 29 | 27 | 29 | 256 |
| Inconsistent votes: | 0 | 4 | 0 | 0 | 0 | 0 | 1 | 4 | 3 | 12 |

Legend:  +—For the civil liberty claim     Coefficient of Reproducibility: .953***
         −—Against the claim
         NP—Non-participation

    * The figures following case titles represent the beginning page of the case in the Supreme Court Reporter, volume 79.

    ** But for his non-participations Stewart could have been ranked 5th instead of 7th. This fact emphasizes the need for caution in interpreting the significance of the rank order within blocs when the S.S. differences are as narrow as in the 1958 term.

    *** Tests for chance occurrence indicate this scale pattern is highly significant.

of each individual in his bloc as well as on the Court as a whole. Since consistency of response is measured by a CR of .953,[28] we may say that 95.3% of the overall response can be accounted for by one operating variable: attitude toward claimed civil liberty deprivations. Our hypothesis is therefore affirmed.

We may assume that where individuals are concerned basic attitudes change slowly, if at all. Furthermore, attitude changes may affect decision-making groups in such a way that the relative positions of group members remain unchanged. Thus we find that scale patterns can be used successfully as the basis for certain types of predictions. For example, relative constancy has been observed in the rank orders which occur from year to year. It is reasonably safe to assume that as long as the same justices sit and the same types of questions are presented the rank order derived from the response patterns will remain constant or near constant. The rank order of the justices in terms of favorableness toward civil liberty claims was identical in the 1956 and 1957 terms. A tentative prediction could be made from these data that the 1958 ranking (given the necessary assumptions) would not differ from that of the preceding terms. A qualifying factor was the appointment of Stewart in October, 1958. No prediction could be made about Stewart, and accurate predicting concerning the remaining justices was subject to the impact which Stewart would have on his colleagues. Scale analysis of the 1958 term indicates that the relative rank order remained the same for all but one of the eight justices who sat through the three terms. The exception was Whittaker, who was constant in 1956 and 1957, but in the 1958 term moved from seventh to fifth. It may be surmised that the change in the composition of the Court had something to do with this shift, but firm conclusions must wait for the data of subsequent terms.

Douglas, Warren, Brennan, Whittaker and Frankfurter had perfectly consistent voting patterns in civil liberty cases during the 1958 term, a finding which suggests well-structured attitude continua for those justices. Warren and Douglas were also perfectly consistent in the 1957 term. Douglas, clearly, exercises virtually no discrimination in deciding civil

---

[28] *The 1958 CR may be compared with those of the two previous terms:*

1956 CR = .950
1957 CR = .953
1958 CR = .953

liberty cases. In the 1956 term he voted against the claim one time out of a possible thirty-nine, in 1957 once in forty-one non-unanimous cases, and in the 1958 term he is for the civil liberty claim in every one of twenty-nine non-unanimous cases. This performance is so striking that one could predict, with a high probability of success, the Douglas vote in any *single case* raising a civil liberty question. With a slightly lower probability of success one could do the same for Black, Warren and Brennan, as well as for the members of the Frankfurter bloc.

The basic difference in attitude toward civil liberty claims is revealed by the break which occurs between Brennan and Whittaker. This is a breakpoint line between the two blocs and is represented by the difference in the scale scores of Brennan and Whittaker respectively. While we expect differences concerning the interpretation of statute and constitutional provisions, we also expect the degree of disparity to have some reasonable limitations. The magnitude of the discrepancy in behavior of the two blocs in the 1958 civil liberty cases suggests that something more basic than mere problems of interpretation were involved.

The degree to which the two blocs have moved apart can be observed in a comparison of the scale scores of the fourth and fifth ranks on the scale in 1957 and 1958. In the 1957 term the respective scores were 31 and 16. In 1958 the difference becomes 23 and 6 respectively. In 1957 the justice in the fifth position compiled a scale score equal to 40 per cent of that compiled by the justice most favorable to civil liberty claims. In 1958 the ratio becomes 21 per cent. Here we have in part a possible explanation for the Whittaker shift. Whittaker's scale score in 1957 was 27.5 per cent that of Douglas, the justice at the most favorable pole. In 1958 Whittaker's ratio was 21 per cent. Since Douglas was equally extreme in both terms it is clear that Whittaker was slightly less favorable toward civil liberty claims in 1958 than in 1957. The mean shift for the remaining justices in the Frankfurter bloc, however, is from 24 to 9.5 per cent. Thus while Whittaker moved in the same direction as his bloc, his movement was of considerably less magnitude. This explains in part his shift from seventh to fifth position on the attitude continuum. Within the Warren bloc the mean shift of the bloc members relative to the Douglas polar position was almost nil (amounting to a positive mean shift of 1 per cent).[29]

---

[29] *The performance of the Warren bloc in civil liberty cases has caused considerable consternation in some quarters, particularly in respect to decisions in-*

The inconsistent votes reflected by the scale were cast by Stewart (4), Black (4), Clark (3), and Harlan (1). Only one case received more than one inconsistent vote. It is informative to examine this case (*Barr* v. *Matteo*) in which Black and Stewart were inconsistent. Barr was an Acting Director of the Office of Rent Stabilization who, intending to release Matteo and others from governmental employ, issued a press release specifying the reasons for the planned dismissal. Matteo brought suit for libel but the Supreme Court, per Harlan, held that Barr had absolute privilege. Warren and Douglas thought the majority gave not even "the slightest consideration to the interest of the individual who is defamed."[30] They saw the decision as a "complete annihilation" of the individual's rights. Stewart, dissenting separately, agreed with Harlan's principle that governmental officers must be enabled to act within the "line of duty" without unnecessary harassment. But he made his decision on what he took to be a "personally motivated effort on the petitioner's part to disassociate himself from the alleged chicanery with which the agency had been charged."[31] Stewart's inconsistency may be explained by his judgment of the motivation behind an act outside the "line of duty." Black, on the other hand, reached a conclusion contrary to that of Warren and Douglas with whom he is usually associated, but he apparently did so out of the same concern for personal liberty which motivated the Warren-Douglas dissent. Recognizing the "freedom people have to applaud or to criticize the way public employees do their job,"[32] Black evinced concern for the freedom of speech which governmental officers must have in order to keep the public properly informed. This freedom may be restrained, he noted, only by the Congress, and any such restraint would have to run the gauntlet of the First Amendment. This case is, therefore, an excellent example of the fact that the Court is sometimes asked to choose between promoting the civil liberty of one party and that of the other.

## V

This study has suggested that the heterogeneous outlooks, attitudes, philosophies and general backgrounds which justices of the Supreme

---

volving communism. See Ulmer, "*The Supreme Court, the Bar and Free Speech*," The American Bar Association Journal (*forthcoming*).

[30] Barr *v.* Matteo, 79 S. Ct. 1335, 1343.

[31] Ibid., p. 1347.

[32] Ibid., p. 1342.

Court bring to their work manifest themselves in diverse patterns of reaction to the stimuli presented by the judicial process. On the premise that these pattern variables have important consequences for judicial decision-making, some appropriate methods for their study have been presented.

On balance, the Court seems to have been less favorable toward civil liberty claims in the 1958 term than in the preceding term, continuing a trend evident in 1957. The attitude shift occurring in 1958 was brought about primarily by members of the Frankfurter wing of the Court. Two cohesive blocs of justices operated on the Court in civil liberty cases during the 1958 term. The membership of these blocs has been determined. The leaders of the blocs have been *tentatively* identified as Warren and Frankfurter, with Brennan pinpointed as exerting strong influence on the Chief Justice. The Warren bloc has been shown in general to be highly favorable to civil liberty claims. The Frankfurter bloc has been, on the whole, negative toward such claims. Bloc membership seems to have been of some consequence in the assignment of opinions. There are cogent indications that such assignments are not made arbitrarily.

The responses of the justices in civil liberty cases have been used to affirm the hypothesis that the civil liberty decisions may be explained by one dominant operating variable: attitude toward claimed civil liberty deprivations. The possibilities of successful prediction of Court behavior on the basis of socio-psychological considerations have been discussed. The outlook here is encouraging, particularly in respect to subject matter areas in which attitude plays an important role. We have suggested that the field of civil liberties is one such area. Finally, it should be said that no attempt has been made to suggest or imply that judicial behavior can be understood or explained solely by consideration of the types of factors we have examined or by the methods we have used. The focus of this paper has been motivated by the belief that while all facets of social phenomena which promote better understanding should be studied, somewhat greater emphasis upon empirical analysis of the judicial process seems justified by the promising results.

# Law
# and the
# Police

# POLICE PRACTICES
# AND THE LAW—
# FROM ARREST TO RELEASE
# OR CHARGE

*Edward J. Barrett**

Within modern urban nations the trend has been in the direction of reliance on the law, particularly the criminal law, as the means of governing wider and wider aspects of human behavior. The days of self-help and vigilance committees have gone; each of us has no choice but to rely on the law and the official mechanisms for its enforcement to make life tolerable in our urban society. Progress in creating legal controls has only begun in the international field, but there is a widespread feeling that the science of destruction has so far preceded the science of international law that the nations of the world now must choose between mutual annihilation and law. Current headlines indicate both that the time for choice may be short and that the process of creating a viable international legal order will be incredibly complex and difficult—perhaps calling for a revolution in international political technology even greater and more complex than the revolution in scientific technology that brought us from gunpowder to hydrogen bombs.

Legal controls—both the existing ones within nations and the poten-

*. . . I am indebted to the Walter E. Meyer Research Institute of Law for a grant that assisted in this inquiry.

Reprinted by permission of the author and of the publishers from 50 *California Law Review* (1962), 11–45. Copyright 1962, California Law Review, Inc. Footnotes have been renumbered to run in sequence throughout the selection.

tial ones between nations—depend for their effectiveness upon widespread respect for and obedience to the law. And this respect and obedience depend in large part on the adequacy of the mechanisms for enforcement of the law. Where enforcement mechanisms are inadequate, respect wanes and legal controls become impotent.[1] The basic problem is the same at every level.

Because of the necessity of maintaining respect for the law, Western societies have shown an increasing concern with the fairness and legality of the methods by which the law is enforced. In our country police procedures and methods evolved over a long period of time during which legal controls over police conduct were in practice, if not in theory, minimal.[2] Furthermore, they evolved and continue to exist in a completely fragmented system with thousands of autonomous units subject to no overall administrative supervision or control.[3] In default of any other general controlling authority, the courts are attempting to fill this vacuum by asserting controls over police conduct.[4] Judicial control, which did not begin to be a significant factor until the 1920's, is now expanding rapidly.[5]

---

[1] *See generally* REITH, THE BLIND EYE OF HISTORY *(1952).*

[2] *See* HOPKINS, OUR LAWLESS POLICE 26–27 *(1931). For the English experience in the gradual development of informal controls, see* DEVLIN, THE CRIMINAL PROSE-CUTION IN ENGLAND *(1958) [hereinafter cited as* DEVLIN]; *Williams,* Questioning by the Police: Some Further Points—2 *[1960]* CRIM. L. REV. *(Eng.) 352, 353.*

[3] SMITH, POLICE SYSTEMS IN THE UNITED STATES 20–23 *(2d rev. ed. 1960).*

[4] *See Mapp v. Ohio, 367 U.S. 643, 660 (1961): "[W]e can no longer permit it [the right to privacy embodied in the fourth amendment] to be revocable at the whim of any police officer who, in the name of law enforcement itself, chooses to suspend its enjoyment."; People v. Cahan, 44 Cal. 2d 434, 445, 282 P.2d 905, 911 (1955): "We have been compelled to reach that conclusion [that evidence obtained in violation of constitutional guarantees is inadmissible] because other remedies have completely failed to secure compliance with the constitutional provisions on the part of police officers with the attendant result that the courts under the old rule have been constantly required to participate in, and in effect condone, the lawless activities of law enforcement officers."*

[5] *During its 1960 Term alone the Supreme Court of the United States wrote opinions in ten cases dealing with the legality of activities of state and federal police. Marcus v. Search Warrant, 367 U.S. 717 (1961); Mapp v. Ohio, 367 U.S. 643 (1961); Culombe v. Connecticut, 367 U.S. 568 (1961); Reck v. Pate, 367 U.S. 433 (1961); Coppola v. United States, 365 U.S. 762 (1961); Chapman v. United States, 365 U.S. 610 (1961); Rogers v. Richmond, 365 U.S. 534 (1961); Silverman v. United States, 365 U.S. 505 (1961); Wilson v. Schnettler, 365 U.S. 381 (1961); Monroe v. Pape, 365 U.S. 167 (1961). On the Supreme Court history see generally Allen,* Federalism and the Fourth Amendment: A Requiem for Wolf, *1961* SUP. CT. REV. *1, 2–3.*

Initial concern was with search and seizure[6] and with brutality that led to confessions.[7] Increasing attention is now being given to arrest policy and the handling of persons arrested.[8] More generally, the courts are concerned with the dangers to respect for the law if official lawbreaking is countenanced. What was said by Mr. Justice Brandeis in dissent in 1928 has become the central theme of modern judicial policy:

Decency, security and liberty alike demand that government officials shall be subjected to the same rules of conduct that are commands to the citizen. In a government of laws, existence of the government will be imperilled if it fails to observe the law scrupulously. Our Government is the potent, the omnipresent teacher. For good or for ill, it teaches the whole people by its example. Crime is contagious. If the Government becomes a lawbreaker, it breeds contempt for law; it invites every man to become a law himself; it invites anarchy. To

---

*Since the decision in People v. Cahan, supra note 4, the appellate courts in California have decided hundreds of cases involving the legality of police practices. For a list of those cases relating to searches and seizures and probable cause to arrest that were decided up to January 1, 1960, see* MARTIN, PROBABLE CAUSE TO ARREST AND ADMISSIBILITY OF EVIDENCE *(rev. ed. 1960).*

[6] *Substantial judicial attention to the problem began with Weeks v. United States, 232 U.S. 383 (1914), holding that evidence obtained by federal officers by illegal searches should be excluded from use in the trial of the defendant. For a discussion of the early cases see Fraenkel,* Concerning Searches and Seizures, *34* HARV. L. REV. *361 (1921). State courts gradually followed suit until by 1960 the federal practice was followed in 26 states. See Elkins v. United States, 364 U.S. 206, 224–32 (1960). In 1961 the United States Supreme Court held that all states were compelled by the fourteenth amendment to follow the federal rules of exclusion. Mapp v. Ohio, 367 U.S. 643 (1961). See generally* MAGUIRE, EVIDENCE OF GUILT *167–240 (1959);* McCORMICK, EVIDENCE *291–301 (1954); Allen,* Federalism and the Fourth Amendment: A Requiem for Wolf, *1961* SUP. CT. REV. *1.*

[7] *For a discussion of the early cases dealing with the problem as a matter of common-law evidence doctrine, see Annot., 24 A.L.R. 703 (1923). The doctrine that the due process clause prohibits the use of confessions obtained by force began with Brown v. Mississippi, 297 U.S. 278 (1936). See generally* MAGUIRE, EVIDENCE OF GUILT *107–54 (1959).*

[8] *See Culombe v. Connecticut, 367 U.S. 568 (1961); Coppola v. United States, 365 U.S. 762 (1961); Spano v. New York, 360 U.S. 315 (1960); Crooker v. California, 357 U.S. 433 (1958); Mallory v. United States, 354 U.S. 449 (1957); People v. Garner, 57 A.C. 151, 367 P.2d 680, 18 Cal. Rptr. 40 (1961); People v. Hamilton, 359 Mich. 410, 102 N.W.2d 738 (1960); People v. Noble, 9 N.Y.2d 571, 175 N.E.2d 451, 216 N.Y.S.2d 79 (1961); People v. Waterman, 9 N.Y.2d 561, 175 N.E.2d 445, 216 N.Y.S.2d 70 (1961);* MAGUIRE, EVIDENCE OF GUILT *155–66 (1959); Coakley,* Restrictions in the Law of Arrest, *52* Nw. U.L. REV. *2 (1957); Foote,* Safeguards in the Law of Arrest, *52* Nw. U.L. REV. *16 ( 1957); Kamisar,* Illegal Searches or Seizures and Contemporaneous Incriminating Statements: A Dialogue on a Neglected Area of Criminal Procedure, *1961* U. ILL. L.F. *78.*

declare that in the administration of the criminal law the end justifies the means—to declare that the Government may commit crimes in order to secure the conviction of a private criminal—would bring terrible retribution. Against that pernicious doctrine this Court should resolutely set its face.[9]

But this substantial increase in judicial pressures to compel police to adjust their practices to conform with law has created new problems and tensions. No one disputes the simple proposition that the police must obey the law.[10] The difficulty arises because in many areas there is wide disagreement about what the law is that the police must obey—and even wider disagreement about what rules governing police are consistent with adequate law enforcement under modern conditions.[11] Of course, it is agreed on all sides that police brutality and police corruption should not be tolerated.[12] Disagreement in this area is primarily about the extent to which such abuses exist;[13] their elimination is a principal objective of the leaders in law enforcement today.[14] But when the question shifts to determining the legality of the methods used by policemen honestly attempting to enforce the law, disputes rage.[15]

---

[9] Olmstead v. United States, 277 U.S. 438, 485 (1928). See also Mapp v. Ohio, 367 U.S. 643, 659 (1961); Elkins v. United States, 364 U.S. 206, 222–23 (1960); People v. Cahan, 44 Cal. 2d 434, 446, 282 P.2d 905 (1955); Paulsen, The Exclusionary Rule and Misconduct by the Police, 52 J. CRIM. L., C. & P.S. 255 (1961).

[10] See, e.g., WILSON, PARKER ON POLICE 125 (1957). But cf. SMITH, POLICE SYSTEMS IN THE UNITED STATES 323–28 (2d rev. ed. 1960).

[11] Compare Wilson, Police Arrest Privileges in a Free Society: A Plea for Modernization, 51 J. CRIM. L., C. & P.S. 395 (1960), with Foote, The Fourth Amendment: Obstacle or Necessity in the Law of Arrest?, 51 J. CRIM. L., C. & P. S. 402 (1960). See also Symposium—Are the Courts Handcuffing the Police?, 52 Nw. U.L. REV. 1–89 (1957).

[12] See ARTHUR & CAPUTO, INTERROGATION FOR INVESTIGATORS 199-207 (1959); Inbau, "Fair Play" in Criminal Investigations and Prosecutions, Northwestern University Tri-Quarterly (Winter, 1961), p. 3, at 6; Roberts, Paradoxes in Law Enforcement, 52 J. CRIM. L., C. & P. S. 224 (1961); Scott, The Mallory Decision and The Vanishing Rights of Crime Victims, 4 POLICE 61, 62-63 (May–June 1960). Of course, individuals in police service may take a different view. See McALLISTER, THE KIND OF A GUY I AM (1957); SMITH, POLICE SYSTEMS IN THE UNITED STATES 9–13, 324–28 (2d rev. ed. 1960).

[13] For a current appraisal see U.S. COMM'N ON CIVIL RIGHTS, JUSTICE 5–28 (1961); cf. SMITH, POLICE SYSTEMS IN THE UNITED STATES 324–28 (2d rev. ed. 1960).

[14] See the statement by J. Edgar Hoover quoted in Elkins v. United States, 364 U.S. 206, 218 n.8 (1960).

[15] See the authorities cited note 11 supra. See also Coakley, Law and Legislative Committee, Cal. Peace Officer, July–Aug. 1957, C–6, at C–8:

*    *    *    *

In this article attention will be focused on one area where the gap between law and practice appears to be very great. The main question to be discussed is that of the role played by the police and prosecuting officials in determining which persons arrested for serious offenses shall be brought before courts and formally charged with commission of offenses. Is the screening function primarily for the courts? Is post-arrest police investigation to determine whether to charge or release the arrested person a legal procedure? A necessary procedure? What are the roles actually performed by police and prosecutors, on the one hand, and courts, on the other hand, in the screening process? Subsidiary questions will also be considered in less detailed fashion: Assuming that post-arrest police investigation is necessary, what restrictions does the law place on such investigation? What are presently accepted practices in such investigations? To what extent should such practices be legalized?

*    *    *    *

The chiefs of police in two California cities (City *A* in the 250,-000-500,000 bracket and City *B* in the 100,000-250,000 bracket) conducted surveys in 1960 to discover in detail the performance of their own forces in the processing and disposition of persons arrested on felony charges. Special report forms (substantially identical in each city) were devised and the members of the detective division in each city were required to complete a form for each arrested person processed by them during a three month period (January-March 1960 in City *A* and February-April in City *B*). The original forms completed during this survey and statistical analyses of them were made available to the author by each police department for use in preparing this article.

---

*They say that we want the right to knock doors down to obtain evidence. That is a lot of bunk, and pure poppycock. We don't want any such things. I am sure that no right thinking peace officer, or district attorney wants to, or would condone or approve the knocking down of doors, and the illegal obtaining of evidence, but there are times in the course of our work, when in hot pursuit of the criminal, or in the hot pursuit of the crime—a murder, a kidnapping, a robbery, that the policeman follows from one clue to another, and in good faith, because he is doing his job as he sees it, an honest conscientious job.*

# A. LIMITATIONS OF THE DATA

Before examining the results of these unique surveys, it is important to examine the limitations of the data procured. They may be summarized as follows:

(1) In each city records were completed only for adults who were arrested and booked and then processed by the detective divisions. In City *A* arrests for narcotics, gambling, and other vice offenses were not included in the survey because they were processed by a special unit separate from the detective division. In City *B*, however, vice arrests were included. Neither city included juvenile arrests. An undetermined number of felony arrests handled without the intervention of the detective divisions were not included. However (aside from vice arrests in City *A*) it seems probable that substantially all adult felony arrests of a type that resulted in delay between arrest and charge for purposes of investigation were included. It is assumed (but not known) that in each city the detective divisions in fact completed records on all arrests processed by them.

(2) The records were completed by the detectives themselves with knowledge that they were to be part of a special survey of their practices. It is not known to what extent the fact that the records had to be completed resulted in changing the actual practices of the detectives. However, it seems fair to assume that the completed forms accurately represented the police practices during the reporting period. Each form was signed by a detective and reviewed by a superior officer. They were also examined and checked for discrepancies within the departments in the process of completing the statistical analyses.

(3) The samples were too small to permit valid generalizations from the data received. In particular, the samples did not permit an appraisal of the performance of the police departments concerned when faced with serious crimes of violence and public pressures for their quick solution.

(4) The data are of only the most limited utility in comparing City *A* with City *B*, or either of these cities with other cities. Policing problems are determined in large measure by the individual characteristics of the area involved. Here there were marked differences between City *A* and City *B*. City *A*, for example, had substantial areas of high crime incidence—skid row and slum housing areas. City *B* was more residential in character with very little area that could be described as skid row or slum.

These differences were reflected in the 1960 figures for felony crime reports of the seven major offenses plus forgery and check offenses: City *A* had reports of about 2,317 per 100,000 population, while City *B* had only 1,863 per 100,000. Similarly, during 1960 City *A* had a felony arrest rate of about 721 per 100,000 population, while City *B* had a rate of only 325.

## B. RESULTS OF THE SURVEY

### 1. Arrests

The survey was not designed to and did not give any information about the circumstances under which arrests were made or the incidence of legal and illegal arrests. It did disclose, however, some information about the extent to which warrants were used for felony arrests. In City *A*, 17 out of the 399 arrests reported (4.3 per cent) were made on warrants. In City *B*, 9 out of 59 (15.3 per cent) were on warrant. In each city the largest group of warrant arrests were made for forgery and bad check offenses—6 out of 17 in City *A* and 6 out of 9 in City *B*.

### 2. Processing of Arrested Persons

The practices of the two police departments involved must be evaluated against the background of the California law with respect to bail in cases where arrests are made without warrants. A person arrested on a misdemeanor charge is entitled to be admitted to bail by the officer in charge of any jail in which he is held according to a fixed schedule.[16] He can post cash or a surety bond and obtain his release without the need for a court appearance, usually at any time during the day or night after he has been booked into the jail. The statute provides, however, that a person arrested on a felony charge cannot be admitted to bail until bail has been set by a judge.[17] In the normal routine in City *A*, bail in felony cases is not set until the prosecutor files a complaint in court and a warrant fixing bail is issued and served on the defendant in jail. For bail to be fixed at an

---

[16] CAL. PEN. CODE § *1269b*.

[17] CAL. PEN. CODE §§ *1269b, 1276; see 32* OPS. CAL. ATT'Y GEN. *84 (1958). For the law prior to the adoption of §1276 in 1957, see Gustafson,* Bail in California, *44* CALIF. L. REV. *815 (1956).*

earlier period the defendant may be able to get an attorney or friend to take the initiative for him and go before a judge for a special setting of bail prior to the filing of a complaint. In City *B,* as a matter of local practice, a bail schedule has been established for felony cases and bail is taken at the jail without going to the judge for each case. This means that a person arrested on a felony charge in City *B* may secure his release on bail shortly after he is booked.

Against this background the surveys disclose some variations in the procedures of the two police departments. In City *A* it appears that whenever a person is arrested without warrant on a felony charge, he is taken to the city jail and booked for "investigation" of the particular felony. This booking charge appears to be standard practice—at least for all cases assigned to the detective division for processing—and bears no relationship to the extent of the evidence against the defendant. If it is decided to file a complaint against the defendant, then a "final charge" will be made on the records to conform with the complaint. In City *B* the practice appears to be somewhat different, with most initial bookings being made "on the nose" for the offense suspected. In this department a booking for "investigation" appears to be reserved for those cases where the evidence against the defendant is considered inconclusive at the time of booking.

The original report forms also disclose the existence (but not the extent) of another practice in City *A.* The booking sheet of a person arrested and booked for a misdemeanor may have added to it a "hold" for investigation of a specified felony. For the purposes of the felony charge he is treated as though arrested on such charge and a decision is made either to release the hold or to file a felony complaint. Even though the felony hold is released, the defendant normally will be proceeded against on the misdemeanor charge. The principal reason for this practice appears to relate to bail procedures. The effect of the "hold" is to prevent the defendant from being released on bail under the misdemeanor schedule and to require judicial setting of the bail—thus prolonging in the normal case the period of time in which in-custody investigation may be carried on. The report forms did not disclose a similar practice in City *B.*

This study was not designed to disclose data on the number of cases in which defendants arrested on felony charges were able to secure their release on bail prior to the filing of the complaint. Neither this study nor any other study known to the author gives significant statistical detail regarding the administration of bail in California. However, the original report forms tend to substantiate the general impression gained from interviews with knowledgeable persons that very few defendants in either city obtain their release on bail prior to the filing of the felony complaint. The reason usually is that no bail has been set, or the necessary money is unavailable.

The surveys do give helpful data about police practices in the following areas: Release rate; time between arrest and booking; for those released, time between arrest and release; for those charged, time between arrest and charge.

### a. Release Rate

*City A*. 137 (34.4 per cent) of the 399 arrests included in the survey resulted in releases. The raw data contained in the forms are not adequate for a statistical survey of the reasons leading to the releases. A subjective impression is that about 75 per cent of the releases were because of insufficiency of the evidence to justify charging the defendants.[18] In a surprisingly large number of release cases—perhaps as high as 20 per cent—the defendant made either a confession or an admission connecting him with the offense. Most of these involved stolen autos or bad checks and the complaining witnesses refused to prosecute on learning the identity of the offender or upon restitution of the property.

*City B*. 11 (18.5 per cent) of the 59 arrests included in the survey resulted in releases. Inspection of the original forms suggests that 7 of the 11 releases resulted from insufficient evidence to charge the defendant with an offense committed within City *B*. In the other 4 cases the defendants confessed. Two of these 4 were released because the victim refused to prosecute, two because the prosecuting attorney refused a complaint "in the interests of justice."

### b. Time from Arrest to Booking

*City A*. Despite the large area of the city and the necessity of booking all arrested persons into a single jail, delay between arrest and booking

---

[18] *It is not meant to imply that in such cases the original arrests were necessarily unwarranted—only that after investigation it was thought there was insufficient evidence to meet the high degree of probability of conviction required by the prosecutor for the issuance of a complaint.*

was minimal. 115 (28.8 per cent) were booked within an hour of arrest. 346 (86.7 per cent) were booked within 4 hours of arrest. In only 4 cases did the time exceed 7 hours, and these were cases where the arrests took place in other cities or other special circumstances explained the delay.[19]

*City B.* Delay in this city was also minimal. The reduction in delay relative to City *A* is probably attributable to the smaller area covered by City *B*. 29 (49.0 per cent) were booked within an hour of arrest. 52 (88.1 per cent) were booked within 4 hours of arrest. In only 3 cases did the time exceed 7 hours, and in each of these cases the delay resulted from the arrest being made in another city.[20]

### c. Time from Arrest to Release[21]

*City A.* Of the 137 persons who were released, the survey showed the following time intervals between arrest and release:

---

[19] *In 21 cases the times involved were not specified on the report form. Information concerning the time periods between arrest and booking is generally available in police department files, since arrest reports commonly show both times. However, such forms may not disclose total detention times. E.g., a suspect may be interviewed at the police station for a period of time before the officer decides to "arrest" him.*

[20] *The excellent record of these two police departments in holding to a minimum custody prior to booking should be compared with practices shown in Chicago before the 1960 scandals and the new administration of the police department there.* AMERICAN CIVIL LIBERTIES UNION, SECRET DETENTION BY THE CHICAGO POLICE (1959).

[21] *Compare Los Angeles Police Department, Special Order No. 50 (Dec. 23, 1958) setting forth the following rules governing investigation and release of prisoners:*

  *I. When a person is arrested by an officer of this Department, the investigating officer assigned to the case shall begin the investigation as soon as possible, and continue, or cause the investigation to be continued, until a final disposition is made of the case.*

  *II. The prisoner shall be arraigned or released by the investigating officer without unnecessary delay.*
  *\* If the assigned investigator is not available at the time a prisoner is due to be arraigned or released, it shall be the responsibility of the watch commander of the investigating division to effect the arraignment or release.*
  *\* If no investigator is assigned it shall be the responsibility of the custodial jailer to insure arraignment or effect release of the prisoner.*

  *III. In no event shall the prisoner be held in custody of this Department longer than forty-eight hours from the time of arrest without having been arraigned, excluding Sundays and holidays.*

(a) 66 (48.2 per cent) were released within 24 hours after arrest.

(b) 56 (40.8 per cent) were held from 24 to 48 hours before release.

(c) 15 (10.9 per cent) were held in excess of 48 hours, the longest period reported being 66 hours. 11 of the 15 cases included in the period of detention one or more week-end days or holidays. These periods of long detention appeared to be primarily the result of skeleton staffs working over week-ends. A person arrested late Friday or early Saturday might be checked briefly on Saturday. But unless this checking resulted in a definite clearance, he would usually be held for investigation on Monday by the regular detectives assigned to the particular type of offense. These detectives would interrogate the defendant to check his story or look for other evidence, and clear with the prosecuting attorney before deciding whether to charge or release.

*City B.* Of the 11 persons who were released, the survey showed the following time intervals between arrest and release:

(a) 5 (45.4 per cent) were released within 24 hours after arrest.

(b) 3 (27.2 per cent) were held from 24 to 48 hours before release.

(c) 3 (27.2 per cent) were held in excess of 48 hours with the longest period reported being 49 hours. Two of these three cases involved persons arrested in another city, the period of custody being about 48 hours after they were brought to City *B*.

### d. Time from Arrest to Charge

*City A.* 246 were arrested without warrants and later charged. (14 arrests on warrants and 2 charges by federal authorities account for the remainder of the group charged.) The survey did not make clear whether the time of charge was the time the complaint was signed in the prosecuting attorney's office or the time the complaint was filed with the clerk of the court.[22] It apparently did not mean the time at which the defendant actually appeared in court to answer to the charge. The following time intervals between arrest and charge were shown:

(a) 119 (48.4 per cent) were charged within 24 hours of arrest.

---

[22] *The practice is to have a warrant with bail fixed in it issued at this point and served on the defendant in the jail, thus making him eligible for immediate release on bail without waiting for the court appearance.*

(b) 63 (25.6 per cent) were charged between 24 and 48 hours after arrest.

(c) 64 (26.0 per cent) were charged after being held in excess of 48 hours. 56 of these 64 cases involved week-end or holiday periods.

*City B.* 39 were arrested without warrants and later charged. (9 were arrested on warrants.) In this department it was made clear that the time of charge was the time the complaint was filed in the prosecuting attorney's office. In addition, the time at which the defendant actually appeared in court was usually given. In 31 out of the 39 cases the complaint was signed in the morning and the defendant appeared in court on the 2 p.m. calendar the same day. In 4 cases the complaint was signed in the late morning or afternoon and the defendant appeared in court on the 2 p.m. calendar the next day. In the remaining 4 cases the information on court appearance was not given. The time intervals between arrest and signing of the complaint were shown as follows:

(a) 21 (53.8 per cent) were charged within 24 hours of arrest.

(b) 14 (35.9 per cent) were charged between 24 and 48 hours after arrest.

(c) 4 (10.3 per cent) were charged after being held in excess of 48 hours. 2 of these 4 were cases in which the police took custody of the defendant several hundred miles from City *B*. The other 2 involved arrests made on week-ends. In fact, in 13 out of the 18 cases in which more than 24 hours elapsed between the arrest and the signing of the complaint, the arrests were made on Friday, Saturday, or Sunday.

### 3. Interrogation and Confessions

The survey in the two cities was also designed to elicit information about the extent to which persons arrested were subjected to interrogation and the results of such interrogation. In City *A* only interrogation by members of the detective division was recorded. Initial interrogation on the street by patrol officers making arrests was not shown. In City *B* all interrogation, including that of arresting officers, was shown.

### a. Amount of Interrogation

*City A.* Interrogation solely by detectives resulted in the following figures for the entire sample of 399 cases surveyed:

| | |
|---|---|
| (a) 30 minutes or less | 197 (49.4%) |
| (b) 30 minutes to 1 hour | 99 (24.8%) |
| (c) 1 hour to 2 hours | 62 (15.5%) |
| (d) 2 hours to 3 hours | 20 ( 5.0%) |
| (e) 3 hours to 4 hours | 10 ( 2.5%) |
| (f) 4 hours to 6 hours | 3 ( 0.8%) |
| (g) Not interrogated | 8 ( 2.0%) |

This sample included only 6 arrests for investigation of homicide. In 4 of these cases complaints were filed charging murder; the interrogation time ranged from 30 to 40 minutes in each case. In 1 of the other 2 cases there was 30 minutes of interrogation followed by the filing of a misdemeanor charge. In the other the defendant was interrogated for 4 hours and then charged with falsely reporting a crime.

Also of interest are the data concerning the time of day when interrogation took place. In City *A* the detective division works primarily during the day and only detective division interrogation was recorded. As a result, out of the 399 cases only 22 persons were interrogated by the detective division between 7 p.m. and 6 a.m. and of these only 9 persons between 9 p.m. and 6 a.m.

*City B.* The data presented below cannot be compared directly with that for City *A*, since in City *B* the interrogation by arresting officers was included as well as that by members of the detective division. Hence the following table includes all interrogation by police of the entire sample of 59 cases:

| | |
|---|---|
| (a) 30 minutes or less | 16 (27.1%) |
| (b) 30 minutes to 1 hour | 13 (22.0%) |
| (c) 1 hour to 2 hours | 21 (35.6%) |
| (d) 2 hours to 3 hours | 3 ( 5.1%) |
| (e) 3 hours to 4 hours | 3 ( 5.1%) |
| (f) 4 hours to 6 hours | 1 ( 1.7%) |
| (g) 6 hours to 8 hours | 2 ( 3.4%) |

No homicides were included in the sample. As might be expected from the inclusion of interrogation by arresting officers, there was a higher incidence of interrogation during night hours than was recorded for City *A*. 16 persons were interrogated between 7 p.m. and 6 a.m.—11 of these between 9 p.m. and 6 a.m.

Of some interest in disclosing the kind of problem that often gives rise both to delay in charging and to extensive interrogation are the police notes made in conjunction with the case in City *B* that involved the longest delay between arrest and charge (78 hours) and the greatest amount of interrogation (7 hours, 55 minutes). With reference to the delay in charging the police note read:

The defendant was apprehended in a house at 4:13 A.M., Saturday, February 13th. A man using an identical modus operandi had previously committed several early morning burglaries, and a special plan to apprehend the latter was actually in operation at the time this offense was committed. The subject was extensively interrogated but denied any burglarious intent. He was interviewed by our psychiatrist on Monday. After 78 hours in custody, a complaint charging vagrancy-trespassing was signed on Tuesday morning. (Our string of early morning burglaries stopped.)

With reference to the interrogation the police note read:

The defendant was arrested during the commission of a burglary at 4:13 A.M., February 13th. He was questioned for 3 hours 40 minutes immediately thereafter. Later in the day he was questioned by detectives for 2½ hours because he was believed responsible for a string of other burglaries. On February 15th he was questioned for 1¼ hours, and on February 16th, for one-half hour. He admitted responsibility only for the offense in which he was apprehended. The string of early morning burglaries stopped and we are morally certain, without evidence, that he was responsible for them.

### b. Results of the Interrogations

*City A.* The data received from this city were adequate to show the numbers of cases in which confessions or admissions were received and the amount of custody that preceded such confessions or admissions. The data do not show the extent to which the confessions or admissions were essential to ultimate conviction of the persons who made them. The following useful information was developed:

(a) Of the 399 persons arrested, 115 (28.8 per cent) gave confessions and 232 (58.1 per cent) gave either confessions or admissions.[23] Of the 262 persons who were charged, 106 (40.5 per cent) gave confessions and 198

---

[23] *One limitation on this data for both cities should be emphasized: The individual reporting officers characterized the responses of the defendants as confessions, admissions, or negative. There is no way of knowing what criteria they used for classification, or even if the various officers used similar criteria.*

(75.6 per cent) gave either confessions or admissions. Of the 137 who were released, 9 gave confessions and 34 gave either confessions or admissions.

(b) Of the 232 defendants who made either confessions or admissions, 38 (16.4 per cent) made them when they had been in custody for 1 hour or less; 100 (43.0 per cent) when they had been in custody 8 hours or less; 183 (79.0 per cent) when they had been in custody 24 hours or less.

*City B.* The survey in this city showed the following with respect to the numbers of cases in which confessions or admissions were received and the amount of custody that preceded such confessions or admissions:

(a) Of the 59 persons arrested, 36 (61.0 per cent) gave confessions and 52 (88.1 per cent) gave either confessions or admissions. Of the 48 persons who were charged, 30 (62.5 per cent) gave confessions and 43 (89.6 per cent) gave either confessions or admissions. Of the 11 who were released, 6 gave confessions and 9 gave either confessions or admissions.

(b) Of the 52 persons who made either confessions or admissions, 39 (75.0 per cent) made them when they had been in custody 1 hour or less; 42 (80.8 per cent) when they had been in custody 8 hours or less; 48 (92.3 per cent) when they had been in custody 24 hours or less.

### 4. Dispositions

Prior to the fall of 1961 there was no requirement in California for the courts to make reports to police concerning the disposition of criminal cases.[24] As a result, a police department that wished to get such information usually had to bear the expense of securing it from court records or, perhaps, from records in the prosecutor's office. City *A* did not at the time of this survey routinely obtain disposition information. City *B* did collect such information and it was included in the survey for that city.

*City B.* Of the 48 persons who were charged, 31 (64.6 per cent) pleaded guilty, and in 1 case the complaint was dismissed. Of the 16 who pleaded not guilty, 13 were convicted, and 1 was acquitted. In 2 cases dismissals were entered based on search and seizure rulings.

### 5. Conclusions: Two-City Survey

What conclusions can be drawn from this admittedly inadequate sampling? The principal one, perhaps, is that there is a great need for

---

[24] *Such reporting is now required.* CAL. PEN. CODE § *11116.*

more research and for broader statistical analysis in this area. Police departments, prosecutors, and courts should be encouraged to provide the information necessary to measure performance in the handling of arrested persons. Time and money can be usefully employed immediately in extracting and analyzing information already present in police department files. For example, arrest reports and jail records typically contain such information as time of arrest, time of booking, initial booking charge, final charge, and time of release.

The sample presented here suggests that a full scale survey covering a large number of police departments over a substantial period of time might put police practice problems in a substantially different perspective from that given by reading newspaper accounts and appellate opinions. The data on detention time suggest that police performance in good police departments is considerably better than has been generally assumed by police critics. The data also suggest that with the application of enough money and manpower, permitting more investigations to be conducted on nights and week-ends, detention times could be substantially reduced even below those shown in the survey.

Perhaps the most interesting aspect of the survey relates to interrogation and confessions. It is useful to know that in the overwhelming percentage of cases interrogation times in these departments were both surprisingly short and surprisingly productive of confessions and admissions. More data of this kind are essential to a realistic determination of the desirability of any proposals to restrict the authority of police to engage in such interrogation. Our system for the trial of criminal cases would be burdened to the verge of collapse if the percentage of guilty pleas were substantially reduced. This survey suggests that a substantial percentage of these pleas results from confessions or admissions given as a result of minimal police interrogation. Of even greater interest would be a survey on a scale broad enough to permit an analysis of interrogation practices and confessions in homicide cases and other cases that, because of public pressure or other reasons, are given more than the routine investigative treatment.

\*　　\*　　\*　　\*

# A STUDY
# OF POLICE
# ISOLATION

*John P. Clark*

\*    \*    \*    \*

. . . In the research reported here data were collected on the following indicators of isolation:

1. The social isolation of police officers and their families.\*
2. The quality and quantity of police interaction with other agencies of social control.
3. The consensus among the public, police, and other social control agency personnel on certain moral attitudes.
4. The consensus among the public, police, and other social control agency personnel on the conception of proper police action in "police situations."

Data regarding these indicators were gathered during 1963–64 as part of a larger study of the role of the police in social control.[1] Data were collected in three Illinois cities of 80,000 to 130,000 population from three

---

\* *Data on this indicator are not included in this excerpt.*—R.J.S.

---

[1] *Essentially the larger study is focused upon the image the public and police have of policing, the attitudes social control agency personnel (including the police) have toward related agency personnel and the behavioral consequences of these attitudes.*

---

Reprinted by permission of the author and of the copyright owner, The Williams & Wilkins Co., from "Isolation of the Police: A Comparison of the British and American Situations," 56 *Journal of Criminal Law, Criminology and Police Science* (1965), 307–319. Footnotes have been renumbered to run in sequence throughout the selection.

sources: (1) the total universe of municipal police, (2) a random sample of the public age 15 and over (approximately 200 from each city), and (3) the total universe of those in other social control agencies who were likely to have direct interaction with the police through the normal pursuit of their occupation. . . .

*     *     *     *

[Table 1 omitted.]

## POLICE ISOLATION FROM OTHER SOCIAL CONTROL AGENCIES

If we conceive social control to be a *system* of relationships which pervade a community,[2] and if we agree that part of the policing function is to effect social control, then we might logically expect police personnel to interact with other organizations who also play social control roles. Both formal regulations and informal understandings require interaction between the municipal police and other control agencies under certain circumstances although the great majority of such contacts are left to the discretion of the agencies involved. The failure of the police to initiate interaction with another control agency when situations dictate they should, or for the other agency not to establish contact with the police in similar situations, would indicate something of the quality and quantity of police isolation in a given community.

Members of both the police department and the other social control agencies were asked to indicate the frequency with which they failed to interact with the other on official matters because the personnel of the other agency's not being "what they should be." Failure to interact was operationally defined to mean (1) avoiding or ignoring a situation which might result in the need for interaction, or (2) turning to somebody else for assistance, or (3) handling the matter themselves without the assistance of others.

The data in Table 2 demonstrate that a significant portion of the

---

[2] *We stress again that the social control activities of police, although few in number when compared to total social control efforts, are important to the total efforts and must be integrated into them for greater efficiency. See* CLINARD, SO-CIOLOGY OF DEVIANT BEHAVIOR [*Rev. ed., New York: Holt, Rinehart and Winston*] *148–152 (1963).*

TABLE 2. PER CENT OF AVOIDANCE OF INTERACTION BETWEEN POLICE AND OTHER
SOCIAL CONTROL AGENCIES.*

| | Avoided or Ignored the Situation | | Turned to Somebody Else | | Took Care of Things Personally | |
|---|---|---|---|---|---|---|
| | Agency Avoidance of Police | Police Avoidance of Agency | Agency Avoidance of Police | Police Avoidance of Agency | Agency Avoidance of Police | Police Avoidance of Agency |
| Prosecutors | 63 | 27 | 50 | 30 | 87 | 31 |
| School Officials | 25 | 23 | 24 | 34 | 31 | 32 |
| Court Personnel | 21 | 26 | 26 | 39 | 22 | 30 |
| Clergymen | 33 | 20 | 39 | 26 | 45 | 26 |
| Public Social Workers | 42 | 37 | 47 | 50 | 50 | 47 |
| Private Help Agencies | 33 | 27 | 40 | 39 | 30 | 40 |

* Percentages are those who failed to interact "sometimes," "often," or "almost always."

police *and* other agency personnel manage to curtail indicated interaction in official matters, and therefore, mutually isolate each other within the social control system. This phenomenon is particularly noticeable between the police and public social workers,[3] which may reflect the presence of conflicting operating ideologies, lack of professional respect, and ignorance of the other's operations.

One may only speculate on the relative isolation of the police from other control agencies in Great Britain. The greater overall integration of the British society and the commonly accepted notion of greater respect for police and their operations in Britain suggest that isolation of the police might not be as great there.

---

[3] *The author was impressed, as others have been, with the institutionalized hostility between those in police work and those in social work. The nature of "inter-institutional conflict" will be examined in a later article. See Miller,* Inter-institutional Conflict as a Major Impediment to Delinquency Prevention, HUMAN ORGANIZATION 20–23 (1958). *A paper,* The Control of Delinquent Behavior by Police and Probation Officers *by Peter G. Garabedian and read at the 1964 annual meeting of the Society for the Study of Social Problems, reports an extremely interesting study of the differential commitment these two categories of officials have to punitive reactions toward legal offenders which may have direct relevance here.*

## ISOLATION OF THE POLICE ON MORAL ATTITUDES

Banton suggests that the isolation of the British police has resulted in their espousing a value system somewhat different (more traditional) than that held by the general public.[4] To the extent that the American police are also isolated, one might expect to discover similar differences between the police and public in this country, although of smaller magnitude if it is assumed that American police are more socially integrated than their British counterparts. Unfortunately there are no comparable British data to compare with those gathered in our research on this aspect of police isolation. However, data are available in this study to measure divergence in moral value orientations between the police and those in other social control agencies and the general public in the three Illinois communities.

All respondents were presented with six hypothetical situations which might involve police action. These situations were constructed so as to be brief, free of direct involvement of juveniles, and ranging from instances where it was thought most would agree that no police action was required to those where most would agree that police action was appropriate. These six situations were:

1. A police officer finds a grocery store illegally open for business on Sunday.

2. A Negro meets a police officer on a street and tells him that he has just been refused service in a nearby restaurant. He says that he is willing to do whatever is necessary to take action against the owner of the restaurant.

3. A police officer learns of card games being played for large amounts of money in a private home. The card games are being run by professional gamblers although the games are not crooked. No juveniles are involved.

4. A police officer discovers a couple of bums who had been drinking in the alley and are pretty drunk. The officer knows both because he has found them many times before in the same condition.

5. A police officer finds out about a woman who is charging men to sleep with her. No juveniles are involved.

---

[4] [MICHAEL BANTON, THE POLICEMAN IN THE COMMUNITY (New York: Basic Books, 1965)], at Chapters 7 and 8.

6. A police officer learns that a person is in town selling obscene magazines. These magazines are written and have pictures for the purpose of being sexually exciting. As far as the officer can tell, no juveniles are involved.

All respondents were asked to reply to several questions about each of the six hypothetical situations. One such question was, "Do you believe this kind of thing is morally wrong?". As demonstrated in Table 3, there is great similarity between the distribution of the public and police

TABLE 3. PERCENTAGE OF RESPONDENTS WHO BELIEVED THE CONTENT OF HYPOTHETICAL POLICE SITUATIONS TO BE MORALLY WRONG.

| Situations | Police | Public | Prosecutors | School Officials | Court Officials | Clergymen | Public Social Workers | Private Help Personnel |
|---|---|---|---|---|---|---|---|---|
| 1. Sunday Blue laws | 13 | 28 | 0 | 19 | 11 | 58 | 20 | 25 |
| 2. Racial Prejudice | 62 | 71 | 25 | 81 | 96 | 87 | 82 | 92 |
| 3. Gambling | 68 | 72 | 25 | 69 | 85 | 91 | 55 | 60 |
| 4. Drunken Bums | 85 | 86 | 38 | 78 | 93 | 93 | 69 | 68 |
| 5. Prostitution | 90 | 94 | 63 | 100 | 96 | 99 | 89 | 92 |
| 6. Obscene Literature | 94 | 96 | 63 | 97 | 100 | 97 | 88 | 89 |

responses, indicating the absence of a unique moral orientation of policemen and suggesting no significant isolation in this regard. However, there are some interesting differences between the distributions of responses among the municipal police and certain other social control agencies. The police were more likely than any other category of respondents measured to indicate that the case of racial prejudice was not morally wrong. However, a higher proportion of police officers interpreted gambling and being a drunken bum to be moral transgressions than did the public social workers and private help agency personnel. To some extent then, the police appear to be isolated, although cultural integration of all agencies is the predominant indication from this comparison.

# POLICE ISOLATION ON CONCEPTION OF POLICE WORK

One of the most direct indicators of the isolation of policing is the dissensus existing between the police and others on the conceptions of proper police activity. It is not realistic to expect the public to exhibit expertness on the allocation of police resources. Yet, however misinformed it may be, public opinion provides the foundation for actions concerning the police. Isolation of the police is keenly felt when considerable discrepancy exists between police and public expectations of policing, although the magnitude of this discrepancy is at best an imperfect indicator of the magnitude of the reaction by the police and the public to this difference.

The Illinois public was asked if there are any areas in which the police should spend more of their time or less of it. A significant portion indicated they did not know (20 and 35 per cent, respectively), which may in itself suggest a lack of sufficient police integration to prompt minimal knowledge or concern on the part of the public. Nearly one-half of the public sample stated that there were areas where the police should spend more time, while only 15 per cent responded that the police should spend less of their time on certain matters. Obviously more persons see circumstances in which additional police activity is thought appropriate than where it should be diminished or eliminated—a provocative finding! This phenomenon is not as evident in the British data where about 38 and 28 per cent of the public note areas where police should spend, respectively, more and less time.[5] These data suggest that there is considerable discrepancy between the conception of proper police operations and the perception of actual police operations in the mind of the public.

As would be expected, policemen gave more specific responses to the above two questions as revealed in Table 4. Eighty-two per cent of the Illinois officers believed that there were areas where more of their time should be spent, although somewhat similar to the Illinois public, a much smaller proportion identified areas in which police effort should be curtailed. These data suggest that in any police officer's opinion there are discrepancies between the conception of the ideal police role and the real one. The situation in Great Britain appears to be similar.

In the sense that the police and public *agree* in principle that the roles of the police on the desired and real levels are far from being identical,

---

[5] ROYAL COMMISSION [ON POLICE, *Minutes of Evidence (1962)*], *at 19.*

| Question and Response | Public | | Police | |
|---|---|---|---|---|
| | U.S. | G.B. | U.S. | G.B. |
| | % | % | % | % |
| 1. Are there any things you think the police should spend *more* time on than they do now? (YES responses) | 47 | 38 | 82 | 73 |
| 2. Are there any things you think the police should spend *less* time on than they do now? (YES responses) | 15 | 28 | 52 | 75 |
| 3. Do you think there is anything the public should do to help the police more to prevent crime or enforce the law? (YES responses) | 76 | 73 | 88 | 97 |
| 4. Do you think that in general the public helps as much as they should when they see a policeman in trouble, for example in dealing with violent drunks or gangs? (NO responses) | 60 | 75 | 87 | 87 |
| 5. Have you ever been asked by the police to testify as a witness in a case? (OF THOSE THAT RESPONDED YES) Did you agree to be a witness? (NO responses) | 24 | 10 | | |

* Data on public and police respondents gleaned from Royal Commission on the Police, Appendix IV to the *Minutes of Evidence*, "Relations between the Police and the Public," by R. Morton-Williams, London: H.M.S.O., 1962.

one could say that the police and public conceptions are integrated. However, to the extent that the character of this discrepancy is different for the police and public, then isolation exists. After noting the difference in proportion of police and public respondents who indicated that the allocation of police effort should be modified, it is interesting to discover that there is basic agreement between the public and police *within each country* on the areas wherein police efforts should be altered. The Illinois police officers agreed with members of the public that the police should spend more time on "crime prevention and detection" and "improving relations with the public," and less time on "being on duty at public affairs," and "office work."[6] The British public and police agreed that the

[6] *The Illinois public also indicated the police should spend more time on "traffic control and supervision" and the police suggested less time should be spent on "checking buildings to see if they are locked." To this extent the public and police conceptions of the ideal police role are different.*

A Study of Police Isolation/Clark | 455

officers should devote additional time to "foot patrols" and less to "enforcement of licensing regulations," "office work," and "traffic control and supervision."[7] Again, these crude data reveal basic integration of public and police disposition on desired police operations. It would appear that portions of the police role, as they are now being performed, are somewhat isolated from the preferred role content as viewed by large segments of both the public and police.

The role of policing society has traditionally included public assistance to law enforcement agencies under certain circumstances. As mentioned previously, there is recurrent concern about a seeming decrease in the willingness of the public to perform this role. Banton concludes that police officers in the United States are more likely than their British counterparts to have "to go it alone."[8] In both the British and American surveys respondents were asked if the public should assist the police more in prevention of crime and enforcing the law. Table 4 demonstrates that the large majority of both the police and public answered affirmatively. Although a slightly smaller majority answered negatively, the public and the police in both this country and Great Britain went so far as to declare that the public does not help as much as they should to assist policemen in difficulties, e.g., in dealing with violent drunks or gangs. An extremely high proportion of the British respondents (especially the police) felt the public was not responsive enough to police needs. Although it might be concluded that there is limited cooperation between the public and police, these findings might also reflect deep concern on the part of both parties of some slight change in what traditionally has been a very close relationship. The responses to a further question tend to support the latter conclusion. In response to an inquiry of those who had been asked at some time by the police to serve as a witness, a relatively small number of the British respondents had refused to do so compared to about one-fourth of those asked in Illinois. Although other forces than commitment to police assistance probably affect these decisions, it would appear that the British police receive more assistance from the public than is the case in Illinois, although Britishers tend to be more concerned about the lack of public-police cooperation.

In summary, there is a consistent response pattern of both the public

---

[7] ROYAL COMMISSION, op. cit. supra *note* [5] *at 35–36.*
[8] BANTON, op. cit. supra *note* [4] *at 100–101; 110–114.*

and police in both countries regarding the desirable character of the policing role. To this extent the police do not appear to be isolated. However, since such high proportions of the public and, particularly, the police, would suggest changes in actual policing activities, there is an overpowering suggestion that the police are isolated by the manner in which they perform their operations.

Further data pertaining to this tentative conclusion were gathered through the use of the six hypothetical situations mentioned previously. With each situation all respondents were asked several questions concerning the nature of police action dictated and usually received in their local community. Great divergence between the orientations of the police and others toward the role of the police in these circumstances would indicate police isolation from the larger society.

As the data in Table 5 demonstrate, the proportions of the public,

TABLE 5. PERCENTAGE OF RESPONDENTS WHO INDICATED THE POLICE SHOULD TAKE ACTION IN THE HYPOTHETICAL SITUATIONS.

| Situations | Police | Public | Prose-cutors | School Offi-cials | Court Offi-cials | Clergy-men | Public Social Workers | Private Help Per-sonnel |
|---|---|---|---|---|---|---|---|---|
| 1. Blue Laws | 2 | 6 | 0 | 9 | 4 | 7 | 0 | 7 |
| 2. Racial Prejudice | 58 | 55 | 75 | 48 | 48 | 54 | 54 | 63 |
| 3. Gambling | 91 | 71 | 0 | 83 | 85 | 87 | 78 | 76 |
| 4. Drunken Bums | 99 | 94 | 100 | 97 | 96 | 96 | 94 | 100 |
| 5. Prostitution | 95 | 89 | 100 | 98 | 93 | 98 | 83 | 93 |
| 6. Obscene Literature | 95 | 92 | 100 | 94 | 100 | 93 | 88 | 92 |

police, and those in other social control agencies who would have the police take action in each situation is rather uniform. Almost all would have the police take no action in the Sunday blue-law case. Conversely, almost all would have the police take some sort of action in the situations concerning drunken bums, prostitution, and obscene literature. Nearly all categories of respondents were equally divided on the issue of police intervention in the instance of racial prejudice, and a significantly greater proportion of the police (91 per cent) than the public (71 per cent) believe the police should take action in the gambling situation. Once again, the data reveal the public and other control agencies in essential agreement about the desired role of the police in these hypothetical situations. Obviously, this measure is not sensitive to the intensity of police-public or police-other control agency conflict that might occur between those of conflicting persuasions.

Knowing that the ecological distributions of the police, public, and control agencies are similar on whether action should be taken does not assure us that there is commensurate integration of orientation on the nature of the action to be taken. Cries for action do not necessarily provide useful guides to the exact police performance expected. Police officers were asked what they believed the people in the community wanted them to do, and the public was asked what they really would like the police to do in each of the situations. Although the possible responses were somewhat tailored to each situation, in each case a response was available which focused upon (1) doing nothing, (2) mediating, (3) harassing, (4) warning, (5) arresting, or doing "something else."[9] Evidence of significant discrepancies between the distribution of responses across these possible answers is submitted as evidence of a type of police isolation. Table 6 summarizes the results.

Again, the percentage distributions are somewhat similar in many cases, which signifies certain similarity between public desires of policing and the police perception of these desires. However, there is the noticeable tendency for the police to misperceive public desires between the warning and arresting of offenders. In almost all cases a significantly larger proportion of the public wished to have the police warn the offenders than was judged to be the case by the police, and in four of the six hypothetical situations a significantly smaller portion of the public would like to see arrests made than was perceived by the police. As mentioned previously, these data are not extremely helpful in predicting the outcome of encounters between those of different persuasions, but there is clear evidence that

---

[9] *For example, in Situation No. 1, the possible responses were:*

1. *Do nothing at all.*
2. *Keep them off the streets.*
3. *Keep the pressure on people like this until they move on.*
4. *Warn them that if they keep doing this they will be arrested.*
5. *Arrest them and book them for legal action.*
6. *Something else (what?)* ————.

| Situations | Do Nothing | Mediate | Harass | Warn | Arrest | Something Else |
|---|---|---|---|---|---|---|
| 1. *Blue Laws* | | | | | | |
| Police perceive public | 75 | 17 | 1 | 0 | 0 | 7 |
| Public desires | 67 | 23 | 3 | 2 | 1 | 4 |
| Police performance | 93 | 3 | 0 | 0 | 1 | 3 |
| 2. *Racial Prejudice* | | | | | | |
| Police perceive public | 24 | 46 | 1 | 7 | 4 | 18 |
| Public desires | 17 | 52 | 9 | 10 | 4 | 8 |
| Police performance | 24 | 41 | 1 | 10 | 8 | 16 |
| 3. *Gambling* | | | | | | |
| Police perceive public | 10 | 5 | 14 | 4 | 61 | 6 |
| Public desires | 9 | 13 | 12 | 23 | 41 | 2 |
| Police performance | 10 | 2 | 7 | 3 | 74 | 4 |
| 4. *Drunken Bums* | | | | | | |
| Police perceive public | 1 | 42 | 6 | 3 | 43 | 5 |
| Public desires | 2 | 15 | 7 | 31 | 33 | 12 |
| Police performance | 1 | 12 | 4 | 5 | 77 | 1 |
| 5. *Prostitution* | | | | | | |
| Police perceive public | 2 | 10 | 6 | 2 | 76 | 4 |
| Public desires | 4 | 5 | 7 | 24 | 57 | 3 |
| Police performance | 3 | 1 | 3 | 1 | 89 | 3 |
| 6. *Obscene Literature* | | | | | | |
| Police perceive public | 2 | 8 | 4 | 5 | 79 | 2 |
| Public desires | 2 | 8 | 11 | 18 | 59 | 2 |
| Police performance | 5 | 2 | 3 | 5 | 83 | 2 |

a greater proportion of the public than of the police is likely to wish police effort which stops short of formal arrest, however untenable this position may appear to police officials. Police officers are more likely to be aware of a series of events which precede their making an arrest, while the knowledge of the private citizen is more likely limited to the immediate incident. Based only upon the single incident the judgment that a warning is sufficient may seem to be the most appropriate action. Whatever the reason for the difference in orientation, the police can be said to be isolated in their perception of public desires regarding the arrest of certain offenders.

The final evidence regarding conceptions of the policing role as an indicator of police isolation from other aspects of society is the discrepancy between the police action desired by the public and that which the police actually perform. With each of the six situations, all police officers were asked to disclose the action usually taken by their department in such circumstances. These responses were compared to the public's declared desires for police action (see Table 6). In most situations the actual police performance is noticeably different than the desires of the public for it. In all cases except the racial segregation issue, reported police action becomes much more unified into a single response. Apparently police action is much more likely to be an actual arrest than public desires would dictate, and even more likely than the police perception of community desires would suggest. The blue-law situation is an exception, but even here, there is much greater consensus among the police on their taking no action in such cases than is warranted by expressed public desires or of the police perception of them.

When it comes to actual behavior, then, the police tend to act in a unitary manner and somewhat differently from what a large segment of the public desires in these situations. The findings are clear enough to suggest the strong influence of separate organizational (and perhaps professional) standards to guide police operations. As was hinted in the comparison just prior to this, the closer one's measures approach actual police operations, the greater the isolation of the police from the larger society.

*　　*　　*　　*

# Law and Psychiatry

# THE DEFENSE OF INSANITY:
# A SURVEY OF LEGAL
# AND PSYCHIATRIC OPINION

*Rita James Simon*
*and Wendell Shackelford*

[Headnote omitted.]

The assassination of John F. Kennedy touched off a series of political and social consequences, one of which bears direct relationship to this paper. Jack Ruby, having committed murder before millions of television witnesses as he shot Lee Oswald, entered a plea of not guilty by reason of insanity. This act served as a dramatic reminder not only to the legal profession but also to the general public of one of the most disputed issues in legal history—the question of legal *responsibility* for a crime.

Our legal system traditionally has admitted the possibility of various defenses against punishment for committing a crime. One relatively un-controversial example is the plea of self-defense. Just as we have generally accepted the idea that a person who has killed in order not to be killed should not be held responsible, we also have held that a person who is mentally ill or mentally defective is not punishable. One of the elements which must be proved in order to establish criminal guilt is *mens rea,* the willful *intention* to commit the crime, the active choice, and the "guilty mind" where the crime is concerned. It is *mens rea* which is challenged by the defense of insanity.

The decision as to the defendant's responsibility or lack of it rests

Reprinted by permission of the publishers from 29 *Public Opinion Quarterly* (1965), 411–424.

with a jury. If the jury believes the defendant was responsible for his behavior at the time he committed the acts, it will find him guilty. If it believes he was not, it will acquit him on grounds of insanity.

Many people, among them judges, lawyers, psychiatrists, question the jury's ability to solve so complex and technical a problem as the determination of a defendant's mental state at the time he commits an unlawful act. Critics of the jury system argue that such decisions can be more intelligently made by a body of legal or medical experts or both.

Closely related to the issue of "who decides" is the problem of what should be done with a defendant if he is found not guilty by reason of insanity. Some jurisdictions have an automatic commitment procedure; others require a separate hearing before a judge, or a jury, or a group of medical experts. As a result of the hearing the defendant can be released or placed on "psychiatric probation," among other alternatives.

If the defendant is committed to a mental hospital, the problem does not end there. The length of the defendant's stay in the institution and the criteria for determining his release are frequently areas of controversy. In some states, the decision rests completely in the hands of the staff physicians. In other states, responsibility is shared between medical experts and the court. In still other states, a formal hearing is conducted and the decision is made by the judge.

What standards should govern the defendant's release? Some argue that the defendant should remain institutionalized until he is cured. Others believe this standard is too rigorous and urge that the criterion be whether the defendant is no longer dangerous to himself and to others.

Each of these problems—the appropriate criteria for criminal responsibility, commitment, and release, and who should determine responsibility, commitment, and release—are important practical issues about which most trial lawyers and psychiatrists are expected to have opinions.

## PURPOSE OF STUDY

This study was designed to poll the opinions of lawyers and psychiatrists on topics about which they are believed to disagree, but where they must interact either as a team or as members of opposing teams. Specifically, it measures the amount of agreement and disagreement between the two professions on the following topics: the role of the psychiatrist as an expert witness in criminal cases involving a defense of insanity; the relationship between mental illness and criminality, with special emphasis on the defense of insanity; the Ruby trial.

We say that lawyers and psychiatrists are *believed* to disagree on these matters. But we know relatively little about the extent of the disagreement, the specific topics on which disagreement is sharpest, or the topics on which opinions may converge. We recommend that the psychiatrists' and lawyers' responses to this study serve as indicators of their desire for changes in public policy and courtroom procedure, or as indicators of their support for existing procedure.

## SOURCES OF DATA

Respondents were obtained from two sources: psychiatrists from the *Biographical Directory of the American Psychiatric Association,* and lawyers from the Martindale and Hubbell directory of lawyers. The psychiatrists were selected by choosing every fourth listing in the American Psychiatric Association Directory in seven cities across the country: Baltimore, Chicago, Cleveland, Dallas, Denver, Fort Worth, and San Francisco. For each city, the number of lawyers was made to equal the number of psychiatrists by selecting every "$n^{th}$" name from Martindale and Hubbell. The sample consisted of 251 psychiatrists and 251 lawyers.

Each respondent was sent a twenty-item multiple-choice questionnaire with a letter explaining the purpose of the study and requesting cooperation. A stamped, self-addressed return envelope was provided. The rate of return was better among psychiatrists than it was among lawyers. One hundred thirty-nine (55 per cent) of the psychiatrists returned their questionnaires, compared with 79 (31 per cent) of the lawyers. Considering that no follow-ups were made, the rate of return was good for a mail survey.

## PROFILE OF THE RESPONDENTS

Forty-six per cent of the lawyers were partners in firms that range from two to more than fifteen people; 34 per cent were in small firms that had between two and five people. Thirty-two per cent were solo practitioners, and the remaining 22 per cent worked for local, state, or Federal agencies. The lawyers were distributed almost evenly across four age categories, ranging from twenty-five years to over fifty-five. Only 35 per cent had any experience with criminal cases involving a defense of insanity (almost all as defense attorneys) and 49 per cent with civil cases involving an insanity issue.

Half the psychiatrists were in private practice exclusively, 30 per cent combined teaching and private practice, and the remaining 20 per cent were attached to private, veteran, or state hospitals. Fifty-two per cent were between thirty-five and forty-five years old, 22 per cent were between forty-five and fifty-five, and the rest were divided evenly between the youngest (twenty-five to thirty-five) and the oldest (over fifty-five) categories. Fifty per cent had more than fifteen years of experience; 49 per cent had appeared as witnesses in criminal trials involving a plea of insanity (mostly for the defense); and 43 per cent had appeared in civil actions.

## THE FINDINGS

*The psychiatrist as an expert witness.* The procedure commonly used today in criminal cases involving the defense of insanity is for the defense to call one or more experts to testify as to the mental state of the defendant at the time of the crime. The state may or may not summon experts of its own. The practice of the courts has been to permit almost any person holding a medical degree to testify on any specialty, psychiatric or otherwise, in the field of medicine. When we asked lawyers and psychiatrists for their opinions concerning the qualifications of an expert psychiatric witness, we found that the majority opinion in both groups opposed the existing practice (question 1).

|  | Per Cent of Psychiatrists | Lawyers |
|---|---|---|
| 1. A psychiatric expert witness should be at least: | | |
| a. A Ph.D. holder in clinical psychology | 4.3 | 20.3 |
| b. A medical doctor | | 13.9 |
| c. A psychiatrist | 77.0 | 44.5 |
| d. A psychiatrist specializing in legal problems | 18.0 | 17.7 |
| e. No answer | .7 | 3.6 |

Ninety-five per cent of the psychiatrists believe that only psychiatrists should qualify as expert witnesses, and 18 per cent would restrict the qualifications to psychiatrists who specialize in legal problems. The 62 per cent of lawyers who believe that only psychiatrists should qualify is considerably less than the 95 per cent reported for psychiatrists,[1] but the significant finding is that 62 per cent oppose and only 34 per cent favor the prevailing practice of the courts. Thus most lawyers and psychiatrists recommend the adoption of more stringent qualifications than those presently applied.

Another assumed point of disagreement centers around the adversary system now in use in our courts. Most psychiatrists are believed to be strongly opposed to it, claiming that it produces such tension between their usual role expectations and those expected of them in court that they seek to avoid all courtroom appearances. Most lawyers are believed to be strongly in favor of the adversary system, profoundly distrusting anything that cannot be exposed to adverse scrutiny. The lawyer is fearful that the psychiatrist's orientation, his view of human nature, and his beliefs concerning the origins of conforming behavior in contrast to deviant or criminal behavior will be so far removed from the legal orientation that his opinion would have no relevance for the trial. Lawyers also fear that, unless the function of the expert is carefully delineated, the combined effects of the latter's general prestige and his detailed technical knowledge can virtually dictate to the jury the outcome of the case. They want to have the expert available, but as a witness whose credibility is subjected to the usual scrutiny of the jury. Our findings confirm this difference of opinion and show that it is a powerful one (see question 2).

|  | Per Cent of | |
| --- | --- | --- |
|  | Psychiatrists | Lawyers |
| 2. I prefer the following system of calling experts: | | |
| a. Only the defense should be allowed to call them | | 5.0 |
| b. Both defense and prosecution should be allowed to call them | 30.9 | 72.2 |
| c. Both attorneys should agree on which experts are called | 10.8 | 7.6 |
| d. Only the court should be allowed to call experts | 56.8 | 12.6 |
| e. No answer | 1.5 | 2.6 |

Two-thirds of the psychiatrists favor doing away with the adversary system and replacing it with a system where the court appoints the experts

---

[1] *Lawyers v. psychiatrists favor psychiatrists:* $\chi^2_{tat}$ $(.95) = 3.8;$ $\chi^2 = 36.2$ $p <$ .001.

or the two attorneys agree on which experts will testify, presumably as impartial investigators.[2] Over three-quarters of the lawyers support their great invention, the adversary system.[3] When lawyers' and psychiatrists' responses were divided on the basis of prior experience with criminal cases involving the defense of insanity, lawyers with experience were more likely to endorse the adversary system than lawyers with no experience (85 to 73 per cent), and psychiatrists with experience were more likely to endorse the court-appointed system than psychiatrists with no experience (63 to 54 per cent). We see that on this matter the impressionistic accounts reflect accurately a true cleavage of opinion between the two professions. The lawyers favor the existing procedure; the psychiatrists recommend change.

Certain members of both professions have deplored the quality of psychiatric testimony that is obtained under the adversary system. Both Dr. Guttmacher and Judge Niles believed that the present system attracts the least able members of the profession and alienates psychiatrists who enjoy the highest prestige among their colleagues.[4] The responses to question 3 show that only a minority of the lawyers and psychiatrists in this study share Judge Niles's and Dr. Guttmacher's views.

| | Per Cent of | |
| | Psychiatrists | Lawyers |
|---|---|---|
| 3. Psychiatrists who most often act as expert witness generally have the following status within their profession: | | |
| a. They tend to be held in low esteem | 20.9 | 15.2 |
| b. They are in neither the lowest nor the highest status group | 26.6 | 32.9 |
| c. They tend to be the most highly esteemed | 2.9 | 1.2 |
| d. Participation in court cases and professional status are unrelated | 48.2 | 39.2 |
| e. No answer | 1.4 | 11.5 |

---

[2] *Lawyers v. psychiatrists favor nonpartisan experts:* $\chi^2_{1df}$ *(.95) = 3.8;* $\chi^2 =$ *48.92* $\rho < .001$.

[3] *Baltimore is the only city in our study in which the adversary system has been replaced by court-appointed experts. We examined the responses of lawyers and psychiatrists from that city separately and found that the distribution was roughly the same as for the entire sample.*

[4] *Manfred Guttmacher,* The Mind of the Murderer, *New York, Farrar, Strauss, and Cudahy, 1959, p. 119; Emory H. Niles, "Impartial Medical Testimony," address before Section of Judicial Administration, American Bar Association, 1956, published in* Illinois Bar Journal, *Vol. 45, 1957, p. 282.*

Over 70 per cent of both the lawyers and psychiatrists believe that professional status and courtroom activity are unrelated, or that persons who perform as expert witnesses are found in neither the highest nor the lowest statuses. We note, however, that 21 per cent of the psychiatrists and 15 per cent of the lawyers believe that psychiatrists who tend to make a career of appearing as expert witnesses are held in low esteem. By contrast, only 3 per cent of the psychiatrists and 1 per cent of the lawyers believe these experts enjoy the highest prestige.

A crucial issue in the defense of insanity trial is how the jury reacts to the expert's testimony. Do the jurors understand the testimony? Are they persuaded by it? Or do they ignore and reject it? The popular impression is that lawyers are fearful, on the one hand, that the jury will be overwhelmed by the expert's knowledge and prestige and will follow him blindly, and, on the other, that the jury will be so confused by the expert's erudition that it will ignore his testimony completely.

The typical procedure in trials involving expert testimony, psychiatric or otherwise, is for the judge to instruct the jury along these lines:

You are not bound as jurors to accept the testimony of expert witnesses. You should certainly consider carefully the qualifications of the witnesses, their experiences. . . . You are to give to their testimony as experts such weight as in your judgment it is fairly entitled to receive. . . .

We asked the lawyers and psychiatrists the following question:

|  | *Per Cent of* | |
| --- | --- | --- |
|  | *Psychiatrists* | *Lawyers* |
| 4. Which best describes the usual effect of psychiatric testimony on a jury? | | |
| a. Jurors are so impressed that they conform their verdicts to the expert's opinion | 4.3 | 3.7 |
| b. Jurors listen carefully to the expert but base their verdicts on all factors in the case | 37.7 | 54.6 |
| c. Jurors ignore expert testimony because they don't understand it | 17.2 | 13.9 |
| d. Jurors treat psychiatric testimony like any other testimony | 30.0 | 21.5 |
| e. No answer | 10.8 | 6.3 |

Most lawyers and psychiatrists believe the jury follows the court's instructions. Fewer than 5 per cent in each group believe that the jury becomes a rubber stamp to the expert and less than 20 per cent believe that the jury ignores expert testimony. The great majority believe that the jury listens carefully to the expert and gives as much weight to his testimony as it believes it deserves.

*The defense of insanity*. We stated earlier that the lawyer is anxious to expose the psychiatrist's testimony to the adversary system because he is fearful that the psychiatrist's orientation, his view of human nature, and his beliefs about the origins of criminal behavior will differ radically from the legal orientation. The popular impression is that psychiatrists believe that all or most criminals are emotionally disturbed. But the responses to question 5 demonstrate that psychiatrists' opinions are far from unanimous on this matter.

|  | *Per Cent of* | |
|---|---|---|
|  | *Psychiatrists* | *Lawyers* |
| 5. Which best states the relationship between serious criminal activity and mental illness? | | |
| a. Anyone who commits a serious crime is mentally ill | 8.0 | 3.7 |
| b. Most people who commit serious crimes are mentally ill | 41.8 | 29.2 |
| c. Most people who commit serious crimes are *not* mentally ill | 25.1 | 20.3 |
| d. There is no relationship between mental illness and serious crime | 15.1 | 34.2 |
| e. No answer | 10.0 | 12.6 |

Half the psychiatrists and a third of the lawyers believe that most or all people who commit serious crimes are mentally ill. These figures are surprising on two counts: the 50 per cent figure for psychiatrists is lower and the 33 per cent figure for lawyers is higher than expected. Lawyers and psychiatrists do not differ on this matter nearly so much as writers have warned.

Two other comparisons are worth making. A greater percentage of lawyers than psychiatrists believe there is no relationship between mental illness and serious crime; and respondents in both groups are unhappy with the choice of alternatives that the question provided. This is shown by the high proportion of "no answers" among both lawyers and psychiatrists.

In recent years the system of trial by jury has been the subject of considerable controversy and criticism. In the last three decades, the jury has been used less and less frequently. In England, jury trials have been virtually abandoned for civil actions and are used primarily in major criminal cases.

At the core of the criticism is the belief that the jury does not determine its verdict on the basis of the evidence and that the members of the jury do not have the special skills and training needed to make a rational decision about the kinds of disputes with which they are confronted. Many critics of the jury urge its replacement by a body of men selected on the basis of their expert knowledge of the particular issues raised by a given case, or by a bench trial in which the judge would be free to seek the advice and guidance of experts.

The substitute for trial by jury most frequently offered in trials that involve a defense of insanity is decision by a body of experts—medical, legal, or both. When the lawyers and psychiatrists were asked in question 6 who should make the final decision, the jury failed to receive majority support from either group, although they fared somewhat better among the lawyers.[5] Prior experience had no effect on preferences among either lawyers or psychiatrists. Both groups, the psychiatrists more strongly than the lawyers, favored decision by medical and legal experts over decision by the jury.

|  | Per Cent of | |
|---|---|---|
|  | Psychiatrists | Lawyers |
| 6. The final verdict in a plea of insanity trial should rest with: | | |
| a. A jury of laymen | 27.3 | 39.2 |
| b. A group of medical experts | 12.2 | 11.3 |
| c. A judge | 5.0 | 7.6 |
| d. A combined group of medical and legal experts | 53.2 | 38.0 |
| e. No answer | 2.3 | 3.9 |

When we compared the responses of lawyers and psychiatrists to questions 4 (effect of psychiatric testimony on the jury) and 6 (decision as to final verdict), we found that respondents in both groups who believe that jurors listen carefully to the expert's testimony are much more likely to favor decision by a jury than are respondents who select other alternatives to question 4 (58 compared with 29 per cent among psychiatrists and 65 compared with 49 per cent among lawyers).

Psychiatrists who believe that there is a relationship between mental

---

[5] *Lawyers v. psychiatrists favor trial by jury:* $\chi^2_{1df}$ $(.95) = 3.8;$ $\chi^2 = 2.8$ $p <$ .10.

illness and criminal behavior are less likely to favor decision by jury than are psychiatrists who see no relationship or who believe that most persons who commit serious crimes are not mentally ill (22 per cent compared with 36 per cent). Among the lawyers, there is no relation between responses on the two items.

In almost all jurisdictions, if a defendant is found not guilty by reason of insanity, he is committed to a mental institution. The commitment procedure, however, is not uniform. In some states it is automatic; in others, a separate hearing is held in front of a judge, a jury, or a group of medical experts.

In the figures in response to question 7 we note that there is relatively little disagreement between lawyers and psychiatrists as to which is the best system. Fifty-five per cent of the psychiatrists in contrast to 42 per cent of the lawyers believe that the decision concerning commitment should be made by medical experts.[6] Most of the lawyers favor automatic commitment or leaving the decision in the hands of a lay body.[7]

|  | Per Cent of | |
|  | Psychiatrists | Lawyers |
| 7. I think the following is the most sensible system regarding institutional commitment when the defendant is acquitted on grounds of insanity: | | |
| a. Commitment should be automatic in every case | 23.7 | 29.1 |
| b. Commitment should be at the discretion of the person or groups rendering the verdict | 10.8 | 7.6 |
| c. A separate hearing before a jury should be held to determine the question of commitment | 6.5 | 17.6 |
| d. Medical experts should determine | 55.4 | 41.8 |
| e. No answer | 3.5 | 3.9 |

We found that both lawyers and psychiatrists who wish to see the jury retain power of decision in the original trial (question 6) are more likely to favor automatic commitment or a hearing before a jury than they are decision by medical experts—among psychiatrists, 63 compared with 41 per cent, and among lawyers, 71 compared with 40 per cent.

Two related problems that are frequently raised in connection with commitment procedures are (1) the criteria that should govern the de-

---

[6] *Lawyers v. psychiatrists favor decision by medical experts:* $\chi^2_{1df}$ *(.95)* $= 3.8$; $\chi^2 = 3.2$ $p < .10$.

[7] *In almost all instances, alternatives a, b, and c would involve decision by a jury.*

fendant's commitment and (2) the length of his commitment. We dealt with the first problem in question 8. Half of the lawyers and 62 per cent of the psychiatrists believe that the current mental state of the defendant should be the most important criterion in determining his commitment. Respondents in both groups offer little support to the "dangerous in the past" criterion or to the "punishment for the sake of justice" standard.

| | Per Cent of | |
| | Psychiatrists | Lawyers |
|---|---|---|
| 8. The following is the *most important* criterion to be considered in deciding whether the defendant is to be committed: | | |
| a. He needs restraint because he is now dangerous to himself and others | 26.6 | 27.8 |
| b. He has been dangerous and needs to be deterred from becoming so again | 9.3 | 16.5 |
| c. Justice requires some form of penalty | | 2.5 |
| d. He is mentally ill and in need of treatment | 62.0 | 50.7 |
| e. No answer | 2.1 | 2.5 |

Question 9 compares the lawyers' and psychiatrists' reactions to the problem of release. Over three-quarters of the respondents in both groups agree that medical men rather than the court should make the decision about the defendant's release from a mental hospital. But lawyers and psychiatrists disagree about the standard that should be employed. Psychiatrists are more likely to favor the more realistic criterion of "no longer dangerous," while lawyers are more likely to recommend the more rigorous standard of "cure."[8] We are surprised that as many as 21 per cent of the psychiatrists selected that alternative, because psychiatrists traditionally are extremely reluctant to describe a patient as cured.

| | Per Cent of | |
| | Psychiatrists | Lawyers |
|---|---|---|
| 9. A defendant who has been committed should be released from the hospital when: | | |
| a. He has stayed for a predetermined period of time | | 1.3 |
| b. In the judgment of the *court*, he is no longer dangerous | 15.8 | 20.3 |
| c. In the judgment of *doctors* at the hospital, he is no longer dangerous | 61.1 | 40.5 |

---

[8] *Lawyers v. psychiatrists favor "cured" standard:* $\chi^2_{1df}\ (.95) = 3.8;\ \chi^2 = 4.8$ $p < .05$.

| | | |
|---|---|---|
| d. In the judgment of doctors, he is cured | 20.9 | 35.4 |
| e. No answer | 2.2 | 2.5 |

In the responses to each of the items in this section, the lawyers were more willing to delegate responsibility and power of decision to medical experts than our review of the literature would have led us to expect. On specific issues the lawyers seem to have more faith in the psychiatrists' expertise than either the psychiatrists or the lawyers who write on these problems believe.

*The Ruby trial.* The trial of Jack Ruby was the most dramatic courtroom event of the last thirty years. We started our research only a couple of days after the verdict in the Ruby trial was announced. The fact that the defendant entered a defense of insanity made it particularly convenient and pertinent for us to include items about the trial in our questionnaire. The responses to question 10 show that the decision in the Ruby case that he was legally sane was a popular one. Among lawyers and psychiatrists who had an opinion, the ratio was almost 2 to 1 in favor of the jury's decision. A quarter of the psychiatrists and a third of the lawyers claimed they had no opinion, and many of them wrote in that they felt they "could not have an opinion" without examining the record.

| | Per Cent of | |
|---|---|---|
| | Psychiatrists | Lawyers |
| 10. In Dallas, Jack Ruby was found legally sane and responsible. How do you feel about the decision? | | |
| a. I agree with the verdict | 41.0 | 41.7 |
| b. I disagree with the verdict | 27.3 | 17.6 |
| c. I have no opinion about the verdict | 25.1 | 34.2 |
| d. No answer | 6.5 | 6.3 |

We compared the lawyers' and psychiatrists' opinions on the Ruby verdict with their beliefs about the relation between mental illness and criminal behavior in general (question 5). Respondents in both groups who believe that all or most persons who have committed serious crimes are mentally ill are more likely to disagree with the verdict in the Ruby case than are respondents who see no relationship between crime and mental illness or who believe most criminals are not mentally ill—among the psychiatrists, 35 compared with 16 per cent, and among the lawyers, 39 compared with 9 per cent.

We asked three additional items about the Ruby trial, questions 11, 12, and 13. About 15 per cent of the respondents refused to answer (most of them on grounds that they had insufficient information about the trial). Among those who did respond, the modal category for both groups is that the defense's case on the whole was less impressive. We were surprised to find that the psychiatrists gave more weight than the lawyers to the impression the defense attorney made on the jury.[9] Only a small proportion of respondents in both groups feel that the jury acted out of anger and a desire to retaliate against Ruby for bringing additional bad publicity to their community.

|  | Per Cent of Psychiatrists | Lawyers |
|---|---|---|
| 11. Which was probably the most important factor in determining that verdict? | | |
| a. The defense's case as a whole was less impressive to an impartial jury | 37.4 | 43.3 |
| b. Regardless of other factors, jurors were angry at Ruby for bringing bad publicity to Dallas | 10.8 | 8.9 |
| c. The tactics of defense attorney Melvin Belli alienated the jury | 26.6 | 12.6 |
| d. The battle of psychiatrists under the M'Naghten test confused the jury about the meaning of insanity | 11.5 | 17.6 |
| e. No answer | 13.7 | 17.6 |

The remaining two items pertained to the expert testimony. Half the psychiatrists are divided almost equally in their evaluation of the effectiveness of the defense's expert testimony. Lawyers are less critical of the experts. Half of them believe that the defense's expert testimony affected the defendant's case, and by a ratio of almost 4 to 1 they believe that the influence was in the direction of increased effectiveness. The remaining half in both groups said that it was not an important factor, or refused to answer.

|  | Per Cent of Psychiatrists | Lawyers |
|---|---|---|
| 12. The effect of the psychiatric testimony brought by the *defense* was: | | |
| a. To reduce the effectiveness of the defense's case | 25.2 | 11.3 |
| b. To increase the effectiveness of the defense's case | 27.3 | 40.6 |

---

[9] *Lawyers v. psychiatrists believe the tactics of the defense attorney alienated the jury:* $\chi^2_{1df}$ $(.95) = 3.8$; $\chi^2 = 5.1$ $p < .05$.

c. Not an important factor in the defense's case 31.0 25.4
d. No answer 16.5 22.7

A similar question was asked about the government's expert witnesses. Hardly anyone feels that the expert testimony detracted from the government's case, and about half the respondents believe that it increased the government's case. This is hardly surprising, since the jury brought in a verdict of guilty. About the same proportion as in the previous item felt that the expert testimony was not an important factor, or refused to answer.

|  | Per Cent of Psychiatrists | Lawyers |
|---|---|---|
| 13. The effect of the psychiatrists' testimony brought by the prosecution was: | | |
| a. To reduce the effectiveness of the prosecution's case | 3.7 | 6.3 |
| b. To increase the effectiveness of the prosecution's case | 49.6 | 48.1 |
| c. Not an important factor in the prosecution's case | 29.5 | 24.0 |
| d. No answer | 17.2 | 21.5 |

## SUMMARY AND CONCLUDING REMARKS

This study surveyed the opinions of lawyers and psychiatrists on three issues: (1) the role of the psychiatrist as an expert witness in defense of insanity trials; (2) the relationship between mental illness and criminality, with special emphasis on the defense of insanity; and (3) the Ruby trial.

The topic on which disagreement was greatest pertained to the system of calling expert witnesses. Two-thirds of the psychiatrists advocated doing away with the adversary system in favor of a system of court-appointed or impartial experts. Over 75 per cent of the lawyers supported the adversary system. Lawyers and psychiatrists with experience in defense of insanity trials disagreed even more sharply than respondents in each group who lacked experience.

This difference of opinion is more than a disagreement about procedure. It reflects the lawyer's doubts and fears about the quality of the expert opinion and of the psychiatrists' potential influence on the jury. On the part of the psychiatrist, it reflects his dislike for the role which he is forced to play in the proceedings and for the limitations which he believes are placed on the information that he can give to the court.

But on two related topics we found more agreement between lawyers and psychiatrists than we would have expected: (1) Most of the lawyers and almost all the psychiatrists advocated the adoption of more stringent qualifications by the court for the accreditation of psychiatric experts than exists presently. (2) Neither the lawyers nor the psychiatrists were as critical of the psychiatrists who testify under the present system as a review of the literature had led us to believe.

In general, the lawyers were somewhat more favorably disposed toward retaining the jury in defense of insanity trials than were the psychiatrists. To a slight extent, the lawyers were also more likely to believe that the jury listens carefully to the expert's testimony. They were also more willing to allow a jury of laymen to decide not only the responsibility question but the commitment issue as well. But the differences between lawyers and psychiatrists on these issues were not as great as we had expected. They did not, for example, attain statistical significance.

This study represents a relatively unusual attempt at collecting systematically the opinions of lawyers and psychiatrists on practical, professional issues that influence the day-to-day operations of the courts and the administration of justice. Our most important finding is that lawyers and psychiatrists agree much more on specific substantive issues pertaining to criminal responsibility, commitment, and release than the impressionistic literature would lead one to believe.

So much has been made of the differences in points of view that exist between the two professions that it is important to publicize the areas on which there is relative agreement. The points of agreement should serve as a stimulus for lawyers and psychiatrists to work together in bringing about those changes in courtroom procedure and atmosphere which would permit the fullest exploitation of psychiatric knowledge about mental illness and deviant behavior.

# THE

# HOMOSEXUAL

# IN COURT[1]

### Manfred S. Guttmacher

   This is an extremely difficult subject for valid generalizations. Since most statutes on homosexuality provide a rather broad range of discretion on the part of the sentencing judge, and since judges, even on their own admission, are human beings, we can expect a marked disparity in severity of sentences. Penal sanctions naturally reflect the basic attitudes of the sentencing judge. These are dependent upon his convictions and his prejudices, born of his early training, his life experiences, his religious beliefs, and, perhaps above all in this area, upon his psychosexual make-up.

In the preparation of this paper I made inquiry in regard to the attitudes toward homosexuality displayed by the judges in the Court of General Sessions of New York, probably the most important criminal court in America. A daily observer of the court's activities and an individual, in my opinion, of great reliability wrote:

There is no general attitude of the General Sessions Judges toward homosexuality. Each one of the 9 General Sessions Judges has his own personal, individual attitude toward homosexuality. These attitudes run from the most

---

[1] *Read in the Section on the Legal Aspects of Psychiatry at the 111th annual meeting of The American Psychiatric Association, Atlantic City, N.J., May 9–13, 1955.*

---

Reprinted by permission of the author and of the *American Journal of Psychiatry* from 107 *American Journal of Psychiatry* (1956), 591–598.

punitive to the most realistic. Some of the judges feel that it is a crime more abhorrent than armed robbery. Other judges feel that so long as no general nuisance is created that it should not be considered a crime at all. There is no agreement among judges on this subject.

In further effort to discern current attitudes toward sexual crimes and, particularly, to measure the effect of Kinsey's work, I asked Professor Kinsey for his view of present trends. He replied:

In general, sex laws throughout the United States have continued to increase the penalties and to include a wider variety of sexual acts as crimes.

Why there exists in this country this trend toward the use of harsher penal sanctions against homosexuality and other sexual offenses, while there is in general an ameliorating trend in most countries, is a baffling problem.

In a memorandum on "Present Trends in European Sex Crime Legislation," prepared by Gerhard Mueller for the Illinois Commission on Sex Offenses, he points out that mutually desired homosexual relations between adults is not today considered to be a civil crime in most Catholic countries and was not so considered under the Code Napoleon. He states that the new Danish code has made sex offenses primarily a medical problem and has given the medical authorities almost complete control of the disposition in such cases. Bestiality is no longer a crime in East Germany. West Germany has recently given up the death penalty for rape. And so it goes, nowhere does he report a stiffening of penalties abroad.

A recent privately circulated report on the problem of homosexuality prepared by the Moral Welfare Council of the Church of England recommends that sodomy, unless force or age disparity is involved, should not be considered a crime. In this report, the Church does not condone the offense, which it notes had been declared under an act of Henry VIII, "the abominable crime not to be mentioned among Christians," but it considers it a religious rather than a civil issue. In speaking of the homosexual it states that the Church "may expect him by the grace of God to resist the temptation to which his condition gives rise."

Professor Louis B. Schwartz of the University of Pennsylvania Law School has prepared an excellent report on Sexual Offenses for the Criminal Law Advisory Group of the American Law Institute, which is now in process of writing a Model Code of Criminal Law. In it, he proposed to exclude from the criminal law all sexual practices not involving force, adult corruption of minors or public offense. This recommendation has been accepted by the Council of the Institute.

One of the great problems in dealing with homosexuality, in fact with all paraphilias, is that such offenses are not always committed by paraphiliacs. Strictly speaking, this is more the concern of psychiatrists than of the courts. In the eyes of the Law, the offense is paramount and the offender is of secondary importance. But, we are all aware that there has been a general shift in emphasis. With the growing use of probation and parole and the advent of such legislation as the sex-psychopath statutes, the focus is now upon the offender as well as upon the offense. In this area, psychiatry must be of the very greatest assistance to the courts. The psychiatrist is better equipped than anyone else to measure the meaningfulness of behavior—was the act a chance occurrence or was it the expression of an inveterate need that is poorly controlled? This should prove to be a vital datum in the disposition of any case, particularly in cases of sex offenders.

Since the tendency toward paraphilias, and particularly toward homosexuality, is so general, necessarily many problems of degree arise. I recall that on practically every visit that I made as a consultant to Fort Lee, Virginia, the Commandant of the WAC Training Center would discuss with me the virtual witch hunts, carried out by the Inspector General's Office, because a couple of the trainees had been seen walking hand in hand or kissing each other.

All of us, I am sure, have seen adolescent youths, rigidly suppressing their need for heterosexual expression and suddenly overwhelmed by the force of their sexual drive, become involved in a homosexual act. Then, there are the individuals who have on a few occasions become involved in homosexual relations only when their superegos have been sedated by effective doses of alcohol. These individuals are not true homosexuals and are often treated with leniency by the courts. However, if the sexual objects are boys or if any force is involved in the offense, the attitude of the court is likely to be far more punitive, unless competent psychiatric study is available to the court and the psychiatrist's recommendation is favorable, based on his belief that the crime is essentially alien to the defendant's ego or that the defendant is a good prospect for psychotherapy.

Five years ago the Court referred to our clinic a 40-year-old white man for examination. This man had approached a colored policewoman, who was not in uniform, while she was talking with two uniformed police officers. He called her aside and offered her the 92 cents that he had in his pocket to perform fellatio with him, partially disrobing during the proposal. On examination, the patient professed an amnesia for the episode, which was only partially dispelled under pentothal. The electroencephalogram was negative.

The patient's history indicated that he was a profound neurotic, subject to severe anxiety attacks since his only brother had committed suicide by shooting himself in the head, shortly after discharge from a state hospital, 10 years before.

He suffered severely from claustrophobia. He had not been to a movie in 7 years. To avoid crowds, he attended 6 o'clock mass and stood in the back of the church, next to an exit. He walked the 6 miles back and forth to work daily, because he generally became panicky on buses.

On the day of his offense his wife coerced him into going downtown to pay a bill to a finance company for her. Since they lived in a remote section, this necessitated using buses. He suffered acutely on the trip into town. On the return trip, things became unbearable. He said, "The walls seemed to be pressing in on me, so I got out and started walking. I went into a store to get a cold drink, but it was crowded, so I got out. I remember leaning against an iron railing. I put my head down, everybody was looking at me, so I went on. I saw a nigger woman. I thought she was a pick-up. I figured she was queer and might suck me off. It was the first thing that came to my mind, somehow. I figured I was having a nervous breakdown—like I was going crazy like my brother. I felt she'd take my mind off myself."

The psychiatric report recommended probation and psychotherapy. The patient's very interested employer made it possible for him to get treatment. During the 5 years that have elapsed, the patient has got into no further difficulties and his psychiatric condition has greatly improved.

This case, it seems to me, illustrates clearly that a paraphiliac offense does not necessarily indicate that the offender is a true paraphiliac.

On the other hand, we are all aware of the fact that sexual pathology can be the basis for many crimes that are not overtly sexual in nature. To illustrate, I shall present the case of a 21-year-old white man convicted of assault with intent to kill.

The patient had been recently discharged from the army. While serving on Okinawa and in Korea, he had 2 gonorrheal infections. He had been a patient on a locked psychiatric ward in Korea after threatening suicide, because of a frustrated love affair with a prostitute. The girl's profession would seem to have particular significance in view of his mother's sexual activities.

The patient was an attractive, extremely neat, little man, 5 feet 3½ inches tall, weighing 120 pounds. He was a very bright fellow, and had graduated from a good preparatory school at 16. His mother's lover, a wealthy man, had paid the tuition. This man had since married the patient's maternal grandmother. At 17 he enlisted in the Air Force.

He said of his mother, "Of course, I love her very much. She has always done what she thought right for me but she has impulses and whims that get the best of her. She has been more like a sister, in fact most people take us for brother and sister. She likes that. She used to be very beautiful. She is a very frivolous person and I don't approve of that, but we do understand each other."

The patient stated that from about the age of 13 to 15, he had a number of homosexual experiences with boys at school. He said that he had been approached by many homosexuals while he was in the army but rejected them, commenting, "I can not stand them, it disgusts me."

After his return to Baltimore from the army, he became involved with a girl in nurses' training. She was a virgin. They began having frequent sex relations. On a couple of occasions he was impotent. On the afternoon of December 31, he and his mother began drinking whiskey together in early celebration of the New Year. Toward evening his girl joined them and the three drank together. His mother left about eight to go to work in a night club. He then attempted to have sex relations with his girl several times but could not achieve an erection. At 1 o'clock he took her back to the hospital and started for the night club where his mother worked. En route he stopped at a bar where he was immediately approached by a man who offered him money if he would spend the night with him at a hotel. In speaking of the shooting, the patient said, "I was sitting in a booth with him, he was across from me. He had been paying for the drinks. He offered me quite a bit of money. I had had plenty to drink—I am not sure just what did happen. I remember the fellow tried to put his hand on my leg, under the table. I got to thinking about the money he had on him. I really did not need money, but I figured since he was so anxious to give it to me, I might as well take it from him. I pointed the gun at him. I did not mean it to go off. It struck him in the abdomen. It was just as if I had been watching the whole thing. It seemed like a play." When it was suggested that he might have felt some homosexual response toward this man and was resisting it, he considered the idea quite preposterous. The patient's projective tests also indicated a great deal of sexual conflict.

To me, there is little doubt that we are dealing in this case with a man with strong unconscious homosexual impulses and that his crime was in reality a sexual one. It was an expression of his effort to defend himself against his homosexuality.

The topic that was assigned to me was the Homosexual in Court. I take it that your interest is not so much in theoretical discussion, as in the presentation of data—what are the present-day attitudes of the Courts toward the various types of homosexuality and how does the homosexual fare in the Criminal Court. I do not have the means for securing and scrutinizing such data in any courts other than those of Baltimore, where I have directed the court clinic for almost 25 years. After surveying the problem, I concluded that we could obtain a broader and yet more accurate perspective, if we did not confine ourselves to an analysis of homosexual cases alone, but considered them along with, and in comparison to, the cases of individuals charged with all other types of sexual offenses. We must also bear in mind that Karpman in his recent and very valuable book on sex offenses says, "Virtually all paraphilias relate to unconscious, unresolved homosexuality."

I have taken from our files for study, the last 100 cases of sex offenders that I have personally examined. These are cases referred during 1954, 1953, and the latter half of 1952. My co-workers, Drs. Boslow and Styrt, have seen approximately the same number, but I have not included their cases. I shall not attempt to present any of these cases in detail, nor speculate about their dynamics. The emphasis shall be upon the disposition of the offenders by the courts (see Table 1).

Sex offenders now form about 20% of the cases referred to the Baltimore Court Clinic for psychiatric study. This is in contrast to the 3% to 5% of the total that the sex offenders represented 20 to 25 years ago. This marked increase in incidence of sex offenders referred is not due to any significant increase in sex offenses tried in our courts, because this has been very small, but rather to the fact that the judges have come to recognize sexual criminality as an area of social pathology to which psychiatrists can contribute understanding and counsel of value.

In line with this, it is a matter of interest and satisfaction, that none of these 100 recent sex offenders had been examined in our clinic previously. Several of them had been before the criminal court but none had been referred for examination. Since the clinic's recommendation is followed in more than 90% of the cases of sex offenders, it would suggest that our recommendations do not, at any rate, promote recidivism.

An analysis of the sentences given by more than a half dozen judges to homosexual and heterosexual offenders in the Baltimore Criminal Courts fails to present the picture of gross discordance that is reported to exist in some courts. There seems to be an unexpected degree of unanimity in regard to the types of cases in which probation should be used and in those to which long prison sentences should be given. One cannot in

TABLE 1. ANALYSIS OF HOMOSEXUAL OFFENSES.

| Case | Age | Race | Judge | Plea | Charge | Crime | Diag. & Recom. | Dispo. | Prev. Adult Rec. | Remarks |
|---|---|---|---|---|---|---|---|---|---|---|
| WM | 41 | W | 1 | NG | Assault | Touching genitals of boy in movie | Personality disorder. Prob. with psychother. | Prob. with psychother. | Police court for fighting | |
| JS | 23 | W | 1 | G | Assault | Gave 10 yr. boy whiskey. Masturbated boy in park. Inserted finger in anus of boy 8 | Severe character disorder. Poor prob. material | 3 yrs. | 2 conv. larceny of auto | Drunk at time of offense with boy 10 yrs. |
| UP | 42 | W | 1 | NG | Perv. Pract. | Fellatio with son 13 | Not psychotic. Very guarded in examination | 10 yrs. (41-yr. total) | None | Conv. of incest with 2 daughters same time |
| ER | 54 | W | 1 | NG | Assault | Forcing 4 yr. boy to ground, handling girl 10 | Severe character disorder with alcoholism. Sentence | 7 yrs. | Conv. in Police Courts 1949-1950 for assaults on small girls | |
| EW | 28 | W | 1 | NG | Sodomy | Anal intercourse boy 14 | Borderline intel. Severe char. disorder. Sentence | 18 mos. | Larceny auto | |
| MO | 60 | W | 1 | G | Perv. Pract. | Fellatio with 2 boys 13 | Chr. alc.—possible early senile changes. Prob. | Prob. | 1 arrest for drunkenness | |
| RT | 35 | N | 2 | G | Sodomy | Forced anal interc. with boys and men | Confirmed homosex. Aggressive pedophile. Sent. | 8 yrs. | 2 sent. contrib. delinq. minors. Other conv.—1 for larceny | At time of offen. on escape from sent. contr. to del. of minors |
| TB | 28 | N | 2 | G | Sodomy | Anal intercourse boy 11 | Imbecile. Recom. Commit. State Hospital | Com. to State Hospital. | In State Hospital 1937-1947 | While in St. Hosp. involved fellatio |

| | | | | | | | | | | |
|---|---|---|---|---|---|---|---|---|---|---|
| AS | 48 | N | 2 | G | Perv. Pract. | Fellatio with 2 small Negro boys | Chron. alchol. Sentence | 1 yr. | Sev. Pol. Court conv. drunkenness | |
| WD | 74 | W | 3 | NG | Perv. Pract. | Fellatio with boys 11, 13, 14 | Senile deterioration. State Hospital | Prob. | None | |
| AS | 49 | W | 3 | NG | Perv. Pract. | Fellatio with Negro 12 | Chr. alcoholism. Sentence | 9 mos. | Com. to St. Hosp. 6 wks. 4 yrs. earlier alc. psychosis | Last job: Santa Claus |
| TG | 51 | N | 3 | NG | Assault | Having 6 yr. boy suck his tongue | Personal. disor. No recommend. | 3 mos. | One Pol. Court conv. fighting | |
| JS | 29 | N | 4 | NG | Sodomy | Anal intercourse with boy 15 | Severe mental defective. Comm. State Hospital | Com. to State Hosp. | Pol. Court convict. indec. Assaults 1948 & 51 Indec. Exp. 1951 | Psychotic after arrest. Tried after psy. cleared |
| DB | 16 | W | 5 | G | Perv. Pract. | Fellatio with boys 13 & 14. Force? | Adolescent immaturity. Prob. | Prob. | None | |
| AG | 19 | W | 5 | G | Perv. Pract. | Fellatio with boys 13 & 14. Force | Chr. homo. Poor prob. or psychotherapy | 12 mos. | None | |
| JJ | 16 | N | 5 | G | Sodomy | Anal intercourse boys of varying ages | Confirmed homo. prostitute. No recommendation | 5 yrs. | Police Court deadly weapon | Patient's house hideout for truants, etc. |
| JR | 16 | N | 6 | NG | Sodomy | Anal intercourse with boy 13 | Severe charac. disor. Penal incarcer. during adolescence | 3 yrs. | | Juv. Court twice for aggres. behavior with boys & girls |

TABLE 1. ANALYSIS OF HOMOSEXUAL OFFENSES. (*Continued*)

| Case | Age | Race | Judge | Plea | Charge | Crime | Diag. & Recom. | Dispo. | Prev. Adult Rec. | Remarks |
|---|---|---|---|---|---|---|---|---|---|---|
| SG | 40 | W | 1 | NG | Perv. Pract. | Fellatio in toilet railroad station with man | Homo. Prob. & psychotherapy | Prob. & psychotherapy | Same offense 6 mos. earlier | Drunk on both occasions |
| BJ | 41 | N | 1 | NG | Sodomy | Living as man & wife with youth 20 | Confirmed homo. very unreliable individual | 3 mos. | Prev. conv. for contrib. delin. of minor | In prev. offense masturb. before 3 small boys |
| RP | 20 | N | 1 | G | Sodomy | Living with man as wife. Man 41 | Confirmed homo. no reason to punish | Prob. | None | |
| EB | 41 | N | 2 | G | Dist. Peace | Anal intercourse with adults | Confirmed homo. prostitute. Sentence | 3 mos. | 30 conv. in 14 yrs., including perv. pract., prostitution & robbery | Made up as female when arrested |
| CB | 22 | W | 3 | G | Perv. Pract. | Fellatio in car | Personal. disord. Prob. without verd. | Prob. without verdict | None | In Army subs.; hon. discharge |
| LG | 29 | W | 3 | G | Perv. Pract. | Fellatio in car | Neurotic char. Prob. without verdict | Prob. without verdict | None | Law student, now having psychoth. |
| WF | 37 | N | 4 | NG | Perv. Pract. | Being masturbated in public park | No psychiat. condition. No recommendation | 6 mos. | None | Claims was asleep |
| KJ | 43 | N | 4 | G | Perv. Pract. | Masturbating man in public park | Chronic alc. with deterioration. Com. to state hospital | Com. to State Hosp. | 2 police court conv., minor, nonsexual offense | |
| BM | 23 | W | 7 | G | Perv. Pract. | Fellatio with adult Negro in car | Borderline intel. Prob. to return to wife in Tenn. | Prob. | None | Patient drunk. Negro suicided after arrest |

fairness say of any one of these sentencing judges that he showed an unreasonable attitude toward sexual offenders as a group nor in any particular type of sexual offense. It should be noted that there were representatives of the Protestant, Catholic, and Jewish religions among these judges.

Despite the fact that there are only 26 homosexual offenders in this study, certain conclusions can be made as to the attitude of the courts toward them. These conclusions are also supported by the author's experience with a very much larger number of homosexual offenders.

Homosexual offenses involving only adults are treated with leniency except where one of the individuals is an inveterate professional prostitute or where the acts have been carried out publicly. For example a 6 months' sentence was given to a 48-year-old Negro who was masturbated in a public park in daylight. His partner, a deteriorated chronic alcoholic, was committed to a state hospital. In the case of a soldier and a law student, apprehended while having homosexual relations in a parked automobile, the court followed the clinic's recommendations that probation without verdict be granted, so that the law student would not be disbarred from the practice of law and so that the soldier could receive an honorable discharge from the Army.

Homosexual relations by adults with children showed a marked variation in disposition depending upon several circumstances. In our series only 2 elderly men were involved in this offense. Neither had had previous convictions, both were given probation. This is in line with the disposition in cases of elderly men involved in sexual offenses with girls.

In the homosexual offenses, penal sentences of more than 1 year were given to a Negro boy, 16, who was already an inveterate prostitute and was seducing small boys; a 35-year-old Negro who had forced men and boys to submit to anal relations; a 23-year-old white man who made a 10-year-old boy drunk and then indulged in homosexual relations with him in a park; a 42-year-old white man who involved his son in fellatio; a 28-year-old white man who had anal intercourse with a boy of 14; and a 16-year-old Negro boy found guilty of anal intercourse with a boy 13. In the next-to-last case, a prison sentence was recommended by the clinic because the man's complete lack of frankness and borderline intelligence made him a poor prospect for both psychotherapy and probation. In the last case, that of the 16-year-old Negro boy, a prison sentence was recommended in our report, largely, on the basis of his aggressive sexual behavior toward boys and girls which had brought him before the juvenile court twice previously. We recommended that he be isolated from society until the thrust of adolescent sexual pressure had somewhat expended itself.

Of course, this series of cases is too small to permit statistical evaluation. However, it is of interest to note that probation was given to about one-third of the homosexual offenders and to nearly half of the heterosexual offenders. In both groups nearly a seventh were committed to a state hospital or to an institution for mental defectives. The new Maryland institution, the Patuxent Institution, to which dangerous intellectual defectives and dangerous emotional defectives can be committed on an indeterminate basis, had not begun to function by the end of 1954. No doubt, in the future, certain of the more malignant sex offenders will be committed to this new institution, which is psychiatrically oriented, in hope that some of them can be effectively treated.

Now let us consider briefly the attitudes of the Baltimore courts toward heterosexual offenders, as they are reflected in the sentences given by the criminal court judges during the past 2½ years. Of the 12 exhibitionists, one was given a prison sentence. He was a severe chronic alcoholic, previously convicted of a nonsexual crime. Three were committed to mental hospitals, the others were given probation. Sexual assaults on female children not involving coitus, or attempted coitus, were treated quite differently in the aged and in young offenders. Of the 9 cases involving men over 55 years of age, 5 were committed to a state hospital and 4 were placed on probation. Of the 12 cases in the younger age group, 6 were given probation, 1 was committed to an institution as intellectually defective, and 5 were given penal sentences ranging from 6 months to 8 years. There is in the author's opinion a good basis for such a distinction. The rate of recidivism is very high in young pedophiles and those offering poor material for psychotherapy should be isolated from the community, preferably for a considerable time. On the other hand, recidivism in the older group of pedophiles is extremely rare.

In the 6 rape cases, none was given probation. One was committed as irresponsible, 2 were sentenced to be hanged, in both cases the sentence was commuted by the Governor to life imprisonment, and 3 were given prison sentences. Of the 4 attempted rape cases, 1 was given a life sentence, 2 were sentenced to 10 years, and 1, in accordance with the clinic's recommendation, was given probation. The man given a life sentence was a 32-year-old white man, who had been referred to the Louisville Child Guidance Clinic for juvenile sexual offenses. As an adult he had served a 10- and a 5-year sentence in Kentucky for sexual offenses. Our report to the court said, "In this examiner's opinion, this man is a serious risk to society and will remain so for an indefinite period."

Of the 5 statutory rape cases, 2 were given probation, 1 was committed to a state hospital, and 2 were given prison sentences. One of these two cases was guilty of regular coitus over a prolonged period with a 13-year-old stepdaughter. The other had impregnated 2 girls, 14 and 15, and had been previously convicted of statutory rape.

Of the 3 carnal knowledge cases, 2 were given probation, the third, a white man who was guilty of coitus with several young Negresses, was given a sentence of 1 year. In Baltimore, which is after all south of the Mason Dixon Line, there appears to be a tendency, on the part of courts, to deal somewhat more harshly with those sexual offenses in which both Negroes and whites are involved.

There were 8 cases of incest. One 16-year-old white boy, involved with an 8-year-old half-sister, was returned to the school for defectives. Six were given prison sentences, 4 for 10 or more years. These 4 were all very aggravated cases. One man had incestuous relations with 2 daughters and practiced fellatio with a 13-year-old son. Another man had incestuous relations with 3 daughters, 11, 14, and 15, and impregnated a 13-year-old stepdaughter. The third man practiced cunnilingus and had incestuous relations with 2 stepdaughters for a period of more than 5 years. The fourth case of incest that resulted in a long sentence was that of a 27-year-old Negro who gave his 9-year-old daughter a sleeping pill and then brutally raped her. Although all these 4 men gave evidence on psychiatric examination and on projective testing, of having seriously warped characters, none of them, in our opinion, could be considered truly psychotic.

The one case of incest given probation represents the very great difficulty that is often involved in making psychiatric recommendations in the cases of sexual offenders. In this case a white man, 31 years of age, had sexual intercourse with his 9-year-old daughter, although there was no actual penetration. The child, a bright and extremely attractive little girl, was obviously in great conflict over her role in the case. She accused her father, then she denied his guilt, later she reaffirmed it. The man and his family had come from the Kentucky coal mining region 6 months before.

He, his father, his mother, and his wife all had jobs at the Bethlehem Steel Works near Baltimore. He had at times been heavily alcoholic but had not been drinking since coming to Baltimore, except on the night of the offense. On that night, the patient's wife had a violent quarrel with him over his drinking, before she left for her job on the night shift as a sorter in the tin mills. The following is an abstract from the report of my interview with the little girl:

She said her father was earning about 86 dollars a week at Sparrows Point. In fact, some weeks he earned 90 dollars. Her mother, on the other hand, only makes 30 dollars from her work as a sorter.

When asked whether her original story was true, she said, "It really happened." She was then asked why she had denied the truth of the story and she said, "There is some things I don't get while daddy is away, clothes and shoes and ribbons and stuff to fix your hair with. Sometimes I cannot even get paper but the teacher does give it to me sometimes. I want daddy out so he can come home and live with us. I know he won't do it anymore. It was the first time in a year that he drank. He makes a lot of money and can support us good. By the time my mother pays rent and the baby-sitter, there is no money for food. She had to borrow money from Mrs. D. to buy shoes to come down here with. She don't get her pay until Friday."

Billie Jean was then asked whose idea it was to retract her story of her father's sex relations with her. She said, "It was my idea because I want daddy back." She was then asked what made her change her story again to the original account, and she said, "That was my idea too. I'm glad I got it off my chest, I would be in misery the rest of my life." She then asked the examiner, "Will daddy get hung?" Asked how she got such a notion, she said, "My mother told me that to get me to lie to get him out."

The impression and recommendation to the Court in this case concluded as follows:

What disposition of this offender would be best for this promising little girl, who certainly must have been adversely affected by the whole experience, it is very difficult to say. Taking the child away from her parents and sending her to a foster home would seem, to this examiner, hazardous, since she has strong attachments to her family. Incarceration of the patient will probably make her dependence on him even greater because of her own feelings of guilt in the situation and her acute consciousness of economic factors.

The judge considered the disposition in this case for some time. He went over the psychiatric report with great care, and discussed it and various phases of the problem with the psychiatrist. He finally decided to put the man on probation. The probation period has now expired without any violations.


## CONCLUSIONS

I believe that we are justified in making certain deductions as to the attitudes of the judges of the criminal courts of Baltimore in the cases of homosexual and heterosexual offenders. For the most part, the same general trends can be seen in regard to both types of offense.

1. During the past 25 years, the courts have come to consider sex offenders as individuals who should be referred to the medical office for a psychiatric report.

2. There appears to be little variation in the attitudes of the 7 judges, who have been in the Baltimore Criminal Courts during the past 3 years, toward the various sex offenses.

3. Sexual offenses entered into willingly by 2 adults are viewed benignly, unless public affront is involved or unless one of the individuals is an aggressive prostitute.

4. Sexual offenses by adults with children are viewed rather benignly if the adults are beyond 55; they are treated much more harshly if the offender is in the younger age group.

5. Sexual crimes of violence, whether they involve children or adults, are treated as very serious offenses.

6. Incest is considered one of the more grievous sex offenses.

7. Exhibitionism is considered an offense of very minor importance.

8. The disposition of sexual offenders is in agreement with the recommendations in the medical office's psychiatric reports in well over 90% of the cases.

9. There appears to be no real difference in the attitudes of the Judges of the Criminal Courts of Baltimore toward homosexual and heterosexual offenders.

# Law and Desegregation

# SCHOOLS

# IN TRANSITION

---

*Robin M. Williams, Jr.,*
*and Margaret W. Ryan*

In reviewing the experiences of the twenty-four commu-
nities reported on [in preceding chapters of *Schools in Transition*], the
following questions arise: What clues do they offer to other communities
that soon may need to prepare plans concerning desegregation? Do they
give any indication of the types of problems involved or the most acceptable solutions found to them?

A most striking immediate impression of an enormous range of
different solutions and experiences is created by the examination of these
communities from New Jersey to Arizona. Variety seems to be the
keynote; local responsibility and control in the public schools are again
vividly illustrated. The complexity of forces at work in each community is
impressive, as is the delicate balance of factors making for stability and for
change.

Yet there seem to be underlying similarities and uniformities in the
experiences of community after community in the processes of desegregation and of resistance to it. Each situation is unique in some ways—but
never in all ways. For this reason, the lessons of experience in any one
community never can be applied in detail to another community; but at
the same time, there are always some common principles that apply to

---

Reprinted by permission of the author and of the publishers from Robin M. Williams, Jr.,
and Margaret W. Ryan, eds., *Schools in Transition* (Chapel Hill: University of North
Carolina Press, 1954), Chap. 12, "In Summary: Review and Prelude," pp. 233–248. Footnotes have been renumbered to run in sequence throughout the selection.

many situations, if the local decision makers can look deeply enough to discern them.[1]

## RESPONSE TO LEGAL DECISION

Initial reactions within the United States to the decision of the Supreme Court were generally rather matter-of-fact. Those who approved were restrained in their praise of the decision, recognizing that many years might elapse before desegregation became integration; many of those who opposed desegregation accepted the decision as a fact that had to be recognized, while warning that in many communities implementation would be a long process.

A week after the decision was announced the *New York Times* was able to report that the keynote speaker at the North Carolina State Democratic Convention was applauded when he said, "As good citizens we have no other course except to obey the law as laid down by the Court."[2]

After the initial reaction, there were various rumblings. It appeared entirely possible that Southern reaction at the state level might resist the implementation of the ruling. As in the individual communities studied in the preceding chapters of [*Schools in Transition*], both opposition and some measure of cooperation could be expected in the time to come.

How the net balance of such varying reactions will come out in the long run is by no means clear. It does seem certain that further desegregation will occur, and that many of the experiences reviewed in this book will be repeated in other communities, both in the South and elsewhere.

The process may seem slow or fast, depending on whether it is resisted or welcomed. Divided reactions are to be expected among both whites and Negroes. Resistance or welcome does not, contrary to popular belief, precisely follow the color line. Some Negro parents as well as teachers have been inclined, in the past, to feel that unless the rest of the community's public facilities were also non-segregated, the child's exposure to desegregated education could create personal problems for him in the larger segregated environment and at the same time expose him to

---

[1] *For a compilation of propositions on intergroup behavior, see Robin M. Williams, Jr.*, The Reduction of Intergroup Tensions, *Social Science Research Council, Bulletin 57, New York, 1947.*

[2] The New York Times, *Sunday, May 23, 1954, p. 1.*

damaging experiences in the school. Not every parent wanted his child to be a pioneer.

Many white parents and teachers who react from long established custom are expected to exhibit reluctance, even though an increasingly large number of white people have come to feel that some change is due in public education for Negroes.

The community cases show, however, that desegregation is an uneven, shifting process, not a sudden massive change. It has been pointed out repeatedly that even though desegregation has been ordered by the Supreme Court, it probably will be a number of years before the segregated school will be ancient history in many communities. For years to come, communities here and there across the United States will be dealing with complexities of segregation and desegregation resulting from contingent factors over which the school administration has little or no control. And when desegregation has been accomplished, the development of truly integrated school activities is a continuing process.

Again, it must be emphasized that each community has its own special blend of factors that are at work to produce integration or resistance to it. In some aspects, every community going through the process in the future will meet the detailed problems in its own individual way. But the central interest here is to find regularities that may be applicable to many communities. What, then, are the uniformities? What are the conclusions to be drawn from them?

*   *   *   *

## FOR THE SCHOOLS

Where the white community is not strongly opposed or where attitudes are unstructured, confused, and in flux, decisive importance attaches to the policies and actions of school boards and school officials. In such instances these gatekeepers can tip the balance one way or the other in the degree of ease with which the transition is made. Outstanding examples from the studies are Tucson, where the superintendent had his plan ready to put into action at the earliest possible moment; Douglas, Arizona, where the superintendent was willing to wait a year until he had unanimous support of his board before announcing a change; Elkhart, where a school board was convinced by a reasoned appeal; and Cairo, where resistance was tinged with bitterness and the transition fraught with tension.

A tendency frequently observed in communities where desegregation initially aroused opposition was a lack of communication between white and Negro leaders and a tendency on the part of the whites to attribute the local call for desegregation to "outsiders." Sometimes responsibility was imputed to national organizations having a local branch or chapter. Sometimes the reaction took the form of "our own Negro people are satisfied with things as they are—it is only those outsiders who want change." Where definite information was available, however, it usually showed that among the local Negro people there were proponents of integration and that the white members of the community did not always have the full knowledge of the hopes and feelings of their Negro co-residents.

Both the removal of legal and customary arrangements for separation (desegregation) and the establishment of mutually acceptable shared participation (integration) are best thought of as processes rather than suddenly achieved end-conditions. One does not "push a button" and effect an over-night change. Desegregation is only a preliminary step; integration is the continuous process of achieving and maintaining cooperative association in which people share *compatible* values and goals.

The unevenness with which desegregation and integration have proceeded in the communities studied is shown by the fact that what happens in the school does not necessarily lead to important immediate changes outside the school. In most of the towns observed, educational integration has not yet had time to show whether it will affect other aspects of community life. Undoubtedly the changes in the schools are related to the general trend which has increased the participation of Negroes on school boards and in integrated PTA's, as well as in some other community activities.

Transition from segregation to non-segregation—and to some measure of true integration—took place in most of the twenty-four communities with a smoothness and lack of open friction which typically surprised officials and teachers. In this the public schools shared the same reaction found in Southern universities. In nearly all instances, the amount of difficulty and tension actually experienced was less than had been anticipated and predicted. Only in one town—Cairo, Illinois—was there any violence, and even in this instance no blood was shed. There was some evidence also that the violence in this case resulted partly from a configuration of *other* community tensions which were focused temporarily on an unpopular move.

The "medicine of nature" which operates in such instances should not be underestimated. Few communities of the kinds described here can sustain, over protracted periods of time, intense bitterness and tension involving only one of the functions of the community. The natural processes of spontaneous control and social adjustment absorbed the impact of change rather quickly. What was news one day, and news of a kind to stir heated comments, both official and informal, soon became another back-page item in the newspaper. Active resistance gave way to passive resistance, and that in turn became relative indifference or positive acceptance.

The implications of this point in respect to the entire nation are worth attention. Because the recent cases decided by the Supreme Court had been discussed publicly, in articles, forums, and in free discussions on a more informal level for two years before the decision was announced, individuals had time to adjust their thoughts and attitudes to the possibility of desegregation. That more time will elapse, and with it more discussion and opportunity for planning, before implementation of decrees governing the forms desegregation may take in the Southern states will mean that in some cases the impact of the idea of impending change will have been absorbed before desegregation actually occurs. It is also true, as some of the communities here studied attest, that this time span gives opportunity for opposition to crystalize and for community cleavages to develop. Instances of both outcomes are to be expected. Which will occur in particular communities depends upon factors already discussed at various points in preceding chapters. There is no substitute for careful local diagnosis.

Among the significant factors to consider in making an initial diagnosis of a particular community are:

1. Number and proportion of Negroes.
2. Presence of other "minority" racial or cultural groups.
3. Extent and nature of segregation and discrimination in public facilities and activities other than the schools.
4. Activity of organizations dealing with intergroup relations, local and non-local.

5. Organization and financing of the school system.

6. Amount and kind of communication between school board and administration and other citizens, and between Negroes and whites.

7. Employment status, tenure, and qualifications of white and Negro teachers.

8. Local attitudes toward the schools and their leadership.

9. Policies and practices of state agencies concerned with public education.

10. Role of local groups such as churches, service clubs, and civic organizations.

For example, as these studies repeatedly have shown, segregation in the school system is powerfully supported by the larger patterns of segregation of Negroes and whites, especially by residential segregation. Succinctly stated by Harry Ashmore, "residential segregation creates a slum atmosphere, which reinforces the race prejudice of the community at large, which in turn is translated into the public attitudes which insist upon residential segregation."[3]

For most of the communities analyzed here, a much more specific point is also apparent. Residential segregation necessarily results in fringe areas in which some whites and Negroes live in close proximity. Typically also, portions of these areas contain intermingled residences of whites and Negroes, resulting either from the settlement of whites around an area of Negroes' dwellings or from the extension of Negro occupancy outward from a crowded area of concentration. If, then, districts for elementary schools are drawn on a purely geographic basis, the consequence usually is that either Negroes or whites will be in the great majority for any given district. Therefore, the families *directly* affected by desegregation in such situations will be the relatively small number living in "border" or "transitional" zones. Although there are, of course, exceptions to this pattern, it does seem to be a very common situation and one with important implications for the whole process of desegregation.

Another significant general finding is that public school desegregation or integration is only loosely correlated with the attitudes or prejudices of the population. Successful public school desegregation has been carried out in places where supposedly the prevailing attitudes favored segrega-

---

[3] [*Harry Ashmore,* The Negro and the Schools (*Chapel Hill: University of North Carolina Press, 1954*)], *p. 77.*

tion and where other institutions continued to be segregated such as Indianapolis; Mount Holly, New Jersey; and Gary, Indiana. Segregation has persisted for years in other instances where attitudes were *relatively* favorable for integration, such as Cincinnati, Camden, or Atlantic City. In some instances, as in Douglas, Arizona, school desegregation was successful in a completely segregated environment. Without a careful local diagnosis it is impossible to predict whether the school or some other local institution will move first toward integrated activity.

In those communities in which there was a tradition of activity in intergroup relations, and in which during the past decade such organizations as a mayor's friendly relations committee or human relations committee was active, the transition from segregation to desegregation seemed to have been made with relative ease. Such organizations were favored by a permissive community setting. Once active, they were able to lead in the discussion of the problem, furnish speakers for forum and other discussion groups, and in other ways help create the necessary favorable climate of opinion and leadership during the transition. Some communities made more direct use of such agencies than did others, depending on the tradition of cooperation between them and the schools. In some of the smaller communities where such interracial groups were inactive, the human relations aspects of desegregation were handled directly by the school administration.

A variety of procedures used in some of the communities results in retarding or minimizing desegregation even when the public policy seems to favor it. The most critical of these concerns districting. For example, "school of choice" under conditions of residential segregation, tends to retain segregation and to put the psychological "burden of proof" upon Negro parents and children. It also leaves the way open for the white children of higher socioeconomic level (those who can afford the extra expense involved in extra travel) to retreat to more remote schools as the near-by schools increase in Negro enrollment.

At the other pole a clear policy of geographic districting, with minimal allowance for "hardship" transfers, gives decisive force to the integration of schools. In some of the communities, an initially flexible policy was changed to a stricter one as it became too much of a burden to arrange transfers to pacify small dissident groups on the margins of school districts.

This last point has a wider application. In general a clear-cut policy, administered with understanding but also with resolution, seems to have been most effective in accomplishing desegregation with a minimum of difficulty. Long-drawn-out efforts and fluctuating policies appear to have maximized confusion and resistance. Even in those states which allowed either segregation or non-segregation, as in Indiana where the law permitted gradual change, interpretations of the legal position varied widely and application of the law apparently was subject to more criticism than where no alternatives were left open.

Some school administrations attempted to avoid all publicity; others cooperated fully with news agencies. The deciding factor in each case seemed to be the customary procedures within the school administration in regard to publicity in other aspects of school life. Publicity seemed to be a complex, rather than a simple variable. In some instances the school administrations shared their decision-making powers with a citizens' committee or with the general public through open meetings or forums. These seemed to have been successful where the administration and the board kept control of the situation, but where the citizens' committees were organized independently, without an invitation from the administration, there was indication of community resistance to desegregation. Once the board reached a decision, open meetings to explain the nature of the change in the school system usually resulted in its acceptance. News releases through press and radio were uniformly favorable to school administrations, except during periods of initial hesitation. Editorial comment on desegregation was uniformly favorable.

Statistics on the number and proportion of Negro children who were desegregated in each of the communities and on the extent to which they were really integrated into the school activities must, perforce, be educated guesses, since records of this kind vary from place to place or are not kept at all. From the evidence at hand it seems that the majority of Negro children in the states included in this study still live and go to school in segregated environments, but the last decade has seen this begin to change rather rapidly. Where desegregation has been in operation a number of years and where community attitudes have come to accept it as natural and normal, integrated extra-curricular participation has increased.

If desegregation does take place and there are white parents who object, they will be alert to any aspect of the assignment of white children to schools or classes with Negro pupils that can be interpreted as "favoritism." As Gary and Indianapolis show, partial desegregation that affects only one or a few schools in a community opens the door to charges that "we are being asked to do this, but the others aren't." This is one of the consequences of gradual desegregation that may not always be foreseen. A similar process can occur *within* a particular school, where some classes or rooms contain Negroes and others do not, unless an obviously impartial and objective procedure of selection was used. It was apparently to forestall charges of favoritism in such a situation that Salem, New Jersey, used a random method of assignment.

Many Negro pupils feel especially high motivation to prove their ability and good behavior in the integrated situation. In a number of the communities it was apparent that the Negro students were taking the initiative, with the help of interested Negro adults, in easing the transition. Most reports indicated that they tended to keep themselves apart unless sought out for the more informal activities connected with school or for social occasions. Some—probably fewer—Negroes reacted by initial sensitivity and overcompensating behavior. Aggressive behavior on the part of Negro youth was reported only from those schools in which the initial transfers were not handled in a sympathetic manner or where the extra-curricular activities continued to be segregated.

Pupil-to-pupil friction between whites and Negroes generally has been slight. A reiterated comment from nearly all communities was that if the parents did not interfere, the children got along all right. What evidence there is points to an impersonal friendliness in school and school-related activities, along with some withdrawal to like-groups after school. Again, only in the communities in which there was overt resistance to desegregation were there initial reports of friction, and these apparently resolved into the live-and-let-live attitudes described above.

In a sizeable but unknown proportion of instances Negro pupils have been hurt or embarrassed by deliberate remarks or unwitting "slips" on the part of white teachers. Unless the channels of communication are open in both directions (from the student to the administration and the reverse) these instances do not come to the attention of the school authorities. Sometimes an increase in "incidents" in a school can be traced to such lack of communication. Where the channels are blocked, the administration has no direct way of knowing if work in human relations is or is not needed in the schools among staff and students.

The use of Negro and white teachers with bi-racial classes in an integrated system tends to pose complex questions, and a great variety of patterns have been tried. Some communities like Las Cruces, dismissed the Negro teachers rather than use them in the integrated schools. Others have kept the Negro staff in the segregated schools, using only white teachers in the desegregated ones. Still others, like Cincinnati, have used both races in the elementary schools only. And finally, places like Tucson, Atlantic City, Elkhart, and a few others have placed the teaching staff according to ability and training without regard to race. In some of the smaller communities, where they were only a few Negro teachers in the first place, they have been rotated from school to school with special assignments to give all children an opportunity to participate in a bi-racial situation or for other reasons. This is true for some of the smaller communities in southern New Jersey and also in some of the Indiana communities.

The studies show that in the actual situation of faculty integration, where it has been tried, professional standards soon take precedence over previous racial attitudes. Teacher-to-teacher relations, over a period of time, come to be carried out in the normal professional way according to the usual customs among teachers. Interpersonal relationships develop according to shared interests and personal choice.

Where public school desegregation was made in communities in which residential segregation was prominent, immediate assignment of white and Negro teachers to schools or classes predominantly of the other race provided the initial step toward full integration by giving the students some experience in interracial communication and participation. The experience in southern New Jersey was that this was possible without delay when the public schools adopted such a program with tact and firmness. Such communities as Burlington, Camden, Atlantic City, Salem, and others have begun this process successfully.[4]

If there is no early discussion of the position or retention of the Negro staff under a proposed desegregation program, the Negro professional often fears for his job and promotion opportunities. In some instances these fears have been justified by later events, effectively limiting the expectation of professional security under the new system. Where these fears were well grounded, there often was resistance to the change among Negro teachers as strong as that put up by the whites. There is some

---

[4] *John Hope II, Some Case Studies of Public School Desegregation in New Jersey (unpublished manuscript), p. 156.*

inconclusive evidence that Negro teachers and principals fared better in the larger cities and in those with a higher proportion of Negro students. Where the proportion of Negro students was small as was the Negro staff, no new Negro teachers were hired as vacancies occurred.

At the teacher-student level, the children become not so many Negroes and whites as children who are to be taught. There is some evidence that Negro students, especially at the high school level, perform better in classes and are involved in fewer incidents either in class or on the school grounds when the faculties are at least partially integrated. These students understand more clearly than younger children the implications of a segregated faculty even when the student body is bi-racial.

Teacher-student relations show in the main that Negro teachers who are professionally well-qualified tend to be accepted by their white pupils, both in elementary and high schools, and that white teachers who can master whatever prejudices they have usually gain the acceptance of the Negro pupils. In many of the communities trying integrated faculties, the best qualified teachers from both races were put in the bi-racial schools to ease the transition period. That this policy was successful is indicated by the comments of students and parents interviewed in the course of the studies.

\*      \*      \*      \*

Important social changes generally do not occur without some resistance and friction. School desegregation is no exception. The change involves established interests, operating customs, cherished beliefs, and deep sentiment. It also poses a number of technical, economic, and administrative problems, even from a purely educational point of view. As the South begins what undoubtedly will be a gradual and uneven movement toward integration, there will be some incidents of personal conflict and name-calling—even instances of disturbances such as those in Cairo. There will be hurt feelings among children, Negro and white. There will be hectic days for school officials and parents. All these things have been seen in some of the communities reviewed in this book.

\*      \*      \*      \*

# SOUTHERN JUDGES
# AND NEGRO VOTING RIGHTS:
# THE JUDICIAL APPROACH
# TO THE SOLUTION
# OF CONTROVERSIAL
# SOCIAL PROBLEMS†

*Charles V. Hamilton*

[Headnote omitted.]

Many Negroes—because they are Negroes—have been denied the right to vote in some Southern States. The Civil Rights Acts of 1957[1] and 1960[2] gave the federal district courts the task of insuring that Negroes would be able to register and to vote uninhibited by restrictions based upon race. Thus the federal district courts have become one of the main instruments for implementing change in that aspect of southern race

† This article is a revision of a paper delivered at the 22d annual meeting of the Midwest Conference of Political Science at Madison, Wisconsin, April 30–May 2, 1964. I wish to thank Professors David Fellman and Donald R. Reich for their constructive criticisms and comments. In addition, I am grateful to the United States Department of Justice both for granting me candid interviews and allowing me access to the trial records in their files.

[1] 71 Stat. 634 (1957) (codified in scattered sections of 5, 28, 42 U.S.C.).
[2] 74 Stat. 86 (1960) (codified in scattered sections of 18, 20, 42 U.S.C. [Supp. V, 1964]).

Reprinted by permission of the author and of the publishers from 1965 *Wisconsin Law Review*, 1–31 (Winter). Footnotes have been renumbered to run in sequence throughout the selection.

relations relating to voter registration. However, the efficacy of using a judicial approach for this purpose has been severely criticized by some observers.[3] This study will first outline and then attempt to determine the validity of these criticisms.

## OBJECTIONS TO UTILIZING THE FEDERAL COURTS

The major arguments against using the federal courts, that is, the judicial approach, to enforce voting rights fall into three general categories. Each of these three criticisms must be viewed, in turn, against the background of the realities of the judicial process. That process has been characterized as slow, reactive, passive, negative and cumbersome:

The Supreme Court . . . is limited because its process is essentially reactive. The Federal judiciary [in general] cannot initiate cases or seek out violations of liberty but must choose from those cases appealed by others. It cannot take immediate action upon observing a violation of constitutional rights. Moreover, once it does act, in the carefully prescribed realm of "case or controversy," it cannot, except by implication, suggest alternatives. Its role is largely negative—reconciling, cautioning, and retarding the policies of the other branches and other levels of government. The Federal courts, in a word, possess "no self-starter," and by definition, leadership cannot exist under circumstances of counteraction alone.[4]

Similarly, former Governor G. Mennen Williams in 1960 expressed the view that the judiciary did not have the ability to get out "in the backwoods" and get people "who perhaps don't even know what it means to register."[5] And Professor Paul A. Freund, in a 1960 memo to then

---

[3] *The basis of these criticisms is the character of certain southern judges' performances. Although certain federal judges in the South have been very unsympathetic toward the rights of Negroes, as a general rule it must be conceded that most of the southern district judges have done a good job of enforcing the rights of Negroes.*

*There is validity in the criticisms with which the Article deals, however, because the notorious civil rights records made by several of the southern district judges have resulted in serious setbacks for the expectations of Negroes seeking to assert their rights. This reflects on the efficacy of the judicial approach to the solution of civil rights issues.*

[4] LONGAKER, THE PRESIDENCY AND INDIVIDUAL LIBERTIES 13 (1961).

[5] *106 Cong. Rec. A1719 (daily ed. Feb. 29, 1960) (Notre Dame University Conference on Civil Rights).*

Senator John F. Kennedy, assumed that the use of judicial approach would necessitate appeals from lower court rulings which would result not only in delays, but also would be cloaked with the "uncertainties inherent in the bringing of law suits by the Attorney General."[6] Because of the nature of the judicial process, therefore, it is possible that suits asserting the voting rights of Negroes will be subject to long delays and will possibly not result in a significant number of Negroes being able to register.

Given the nature of the judicial process, judicial enforcement of voting rights cannot be at all effective unless the individual judge is willing to push the process to its ultimate limits of efficiency. The objections to the use of judiciary in voting rights cases, however, rest on the conclusion that many federal judges, for one reason or another, approach voting cases in such a way that the inherently slow process is made even slower and thus ineffective.

The first objection deals generally with the influence of community pressures and local attitudes on the southern district courts. "All policy-makers in a free society are the focus of contending pressures. Judges are no exception. . . . And just as the laws enacted by the legislature reflect the dominance of certain values in the community, so do the decisions of judges."[7] Thus it is argued that southern district judges are not well-suited to enforce Negro voting rights because of their susceptibility to the influence of strong community opinion against enforcement of these rights. The fact of hostile local opinion, coupled with, in some instances, a judge's personal segregationist bias, likely contributes to making the inherently slow and cumbersome judicial process even more slow and therefore even less effective in the enforcement of Negro voting rights.

There is impressive evidence that the operation of the judiciary in the field of Negro rights has not been effective at the local level. Against the background of the record of southern district courts with respect to the school desegregation problem, Professor Peltason drew these conclusions about the prospects of effective enforcement of Negro voting rights:

Southern federal judges have shown no greater desire to protect the Negroes' right to vote than they have to desegregate the schools. In Georgia, Judge T. Hoyt Davis even went so far as to declare the 1957 Act unconstitutional. Other

---

[6] Id. *at A1728.*
[7] PELTASON, FIFTY-EIGHT LONELY MEN *247 (1961).*

judges discovered technical reasons for refusing to enjoin voting officials from discriminating against Negroes. Only Judge J. Skelly Wright has so far used the Act of 1957 to protect Negro voters. But in 1960 the Supreme Court reversed the judges who were dismissing the complaints filed by the Department of Justice. Henceforth though litigation is inherently slow, southern judges will have to find other reasons to refuse to act.[8]

Peltason also pointed to District Judge Benjamin C. Dawkins, Jr. of Louisiana, whom he described as "among the more ardent segregationists serving on the federal bench." Dawkins held court in Shreveport in northern Louisiana, in the center of the strongest segregation area of the State. He was the judge who not only refused to interfere when the White Citizens' Council manipulated the law with the help of Monroe city officials to "purge" 2500 Negro voters from the registration rolls, but also accused the Negro plaintiff of "bad faith [and] sheer stubborn vindictiveness." It was Judge Dawkins who made the statement, "It is all a part of the game," when he enjoined the United States Commission on Civil Rights from holding hearings in Shreveport.

While the first objection to using the federal courts to enforce Negro voting rights is based upon the fear that the courts might not produce the results intended by the Civil Rights Acts, the second objection focuses on what might happen to the prestige and effectiveness of those courts and judges that do enforce the law. Of concern here is the anticipated community reaction to those judges who, unlike Judges Dawkins and Davis, consistently see to it that Negro voting rights are enforced. The basis of this objection is the feeling that courts are most vulnerable when dealing with politically controversial matters:

If [judges] are given the task of forcing many unpopular reforms on their local communities, they may cease to be effective instruments for the administration of justice. Judges function best when they are handling issues of little political explosiveness. If large numbers of southerners, for reasons just or unjust, come to consider federal judges to be nothing but "yankee agents," even civil rights advocates may lose more than they may gain from immediate legal victories. These men will not only be lonely, but ostracized.[9]

The third objection is based upon apprehensions about the inability of the judicial system to deal effectively with what many feel to be the major deterrent to Negro voting in the South—economic reprisals and other

---

[8] Id. *at 133.*
[9] Id. *at 252–53.*

forms of intimidation. Interestingly enough, this criticism is most prevalent among southern Negro leaders who make their point by emphasizing
their special knowledge of these problems resulting from their "working
everyday in this business of trying to get our people registered."

## FACTORS TO BE CONSIDERED IN ANALYZING THE VALIDITY OF THE OBJECTIONS

To a large degree, the validity of these objections depends upon the
character of performance of the judge enforcing the law. There are,
however, external factors that reflect upon the usefulness of the judicial
approach as a device for enforcing Negro voting rights. Thus, both actual
judicial performance and the external factors bearing on that performance
will be discussed. In the context of the resultant data, the validity of the
objections to the use of the judicial approach will be explored.

### Judicial Enforcement

The character of performance in the voting rights field varies greatly
between judges. We will examine illustrative cases tried before four
judges sitting in three different southern states: Alabama, Mississippi, and
Louisiana.[10] The study of these judges reveals essentially three types or
characters of performance: judicial aggressiveness, judicial resistance, and
judicial gradualism.

#### JUDICIAL AGGRESSIVENESS

The State of Alabama is generally referred to in civil rights parlance
as a "hard core" southern state. Resistance on the part of public officials
and white citizens to changes in race relations is exhibited in a most
extreme form. And yet it is in Alabama, in the United States District
Court for the Middle District, that one finds the best example of an
"aggressive" federal judge in voting cases— Judge Frank M. Johnson, Jr.
Judge Johnson has dealt with cases coming out of three black-belt counties: Macon, Bullock and Montgomery. Resistance to Negro voting in
these counties over the years has been most intense. All three counties are

---

[10] *These cases were chosen because, for the most part, they were completed at
the time the major research was conducted in 1963 and early 1964.*

characterized by a large Negro population—predominantly Negro in Macon and Bullock—and a small number of registered Negroes, substantially lower in each county than the white population. In each county different methods were used to restrict the registration of Negro voters. Judge Johnson was both aggressive and versatile in dealing with each unique situation. This will be clear from the following description of an illustrative case from each county.

THE MACON COUNTY CASE[11]

Although in 1960 there were approximately 11,900 Negroes of voting age in Macon County, less than ten per cent (approximately 1,100) were registered to vote. Judge Johnson found this to be largely the result of the discriminatory administration of the registration tests:

The evidence in this case is overwhelmingly to the effect that the State of Alabama, acting through its agents, including former members of the Board of Registrars of Macon county, has deliberately engaged in acts and practices designed to discriminate against qualified Negroes in their efforts to register to vote. Such acts and practices have brought about and perpetuated the disparity between the relative percentages of Negroes and whites registered to vote.[12]

Essentially, the registrars relied on three tactics: resignations, a double standard in receiving and approving applications for registration from Negro and white applicants, and slowdown. The court found these practices to have existed for at least five years. Operationally these tactics resulted in white applicants being given assistance by the registrars. Frequently whites were not required to write out a section of the United States Constitution, and if they were, they were given a section much shorter than that required of all Negro applicants. Only Negro applicants were rejected for errors of a formal, technical or inconsequential nature. Whites committing the same errors were passed.

With these and many other tactics operating in 1960, only fifty persons were able to complete applications over a seven month period—thirty-two whites and eighteen Negroes. Of these fifty, all thirty-two whites passed, while only ten Negroes were successful. The Board of Registrars would process only one Negro applicant at a time. In 1960, the largest number of applicants received by the Board in one day was five.

---

[11] *United States v. Alabama, 192 F. Supp. 677 (M.D. Ala. 1961).*
[12] Id. *at 679.*

There was no doubt in Judge Johnson's mind that the motive behind these tactics was to preserve discriminatory voting patterns.

The Court, in an effort to understand fully the attitude of the present members of the Board of Registrars in Macon county, called Johnson and Dyson [the two current registrars] as witnesses of the Court. Their lack of concern and their failure to take any action toward changing the pattern and practice of racial discrimination was fully evident from their testimony.[13]

### THE BULLOCK COUNTY CASE[14]

The facts in the Bullock County case also dealt with the activity of the registrars. But here the focus was narrowed to two specific practices: requiring a "voucher," and requiring applications to be completed "with technical precision." Since 1951, the Bullock County Board of Registrars followed the practice of requiring each applicant to have a registered voter of the county, that is, a "voucher," appear before the Board and swear to the bona fide residence and good character of the applicant. The rules established by the Board limited each "voucher" to two applicants per year. The evidence in the Bullock County case showed that no white citizen had ever vouched for a Negro. At the trial, one Negro witness was asked by Judge Johnson if Negro applicants "made an effort [to secure] people of your own race . . . to vouch for you." The witness stated that this effort had been made several times without success. He gave an example of such an attempt: "Oh yes. Mr. Russell [a registered Negro] said his wife was teaching school and someone had passed the word to her that if he comes [sic] back up there vouching for anyone else they would fire her from her job."[15]

The Government argued that the particular racial conditions and the minimal number of registered Negroes[16] made the voucher rule constitutionally impermissible. Bullock County was a racially segregated community. Negroes and whites neither interacted socially, nor did they attend the same public or private schools or the same churches. The voucher rule

---

[13] Id. at 681.

[14] United States v. Alabama, Civil No. 1677-N, M.D. Ala., Sept. 13, 1961.

[15] Brief for Plaintiff, p. 6, United States v. Alabama, Civil No. 1677-N, M.D. Ala., Sept. 13, 1961.

[16] Bullock County had in 1960 a total population of 13,462 of which 9,681, or 71%, were Negroes. At that time there were 2,200 whites registered to vote (95% of those of voting age), while only five Negroes were registered (0.1% of those of voting age).

meant that Negro applicants in reality had to "attain not only the consent but the active cooperation of members of the white community as a prerequisite to voting and thus whites hold the key to the registration door."[17] Because of the small number of registered Negroes and the two voucher per year rule, Negroes would have to approach in most instances only white voters to secure vouchers.

While the registars in Macon County had been found to apply double standards, the evidence in the Bullock case revealed that after March 1960, the registrars in that county had proceeded to apply a "single standard." Yet the Government attacked this as an unconstitutional "freezing device." The Board had adopted very strict standards which it applied to white and Negro applicants alike. This was another sophisticated way of avoiding the fifteenth amendment. The Government argued:

Although a State may set registration standards, in a community like Bullock county, to require future applicants, white and Negro, to complete their applications with technical precision is constitutionally suspect. . . . This amounts to a freezing of the status quo. And the effect is the practical disfranchisement of almost ninety-nine per cent of the unregistered Negroes, while only about five per cent of the whites remain unregistered.[18]

THE MONTGOMERY COUNTY CASE[19]

The activity of the registrars in Montgomery County came under scrutiny in the third case handled by Judge Johnson. The evidence taken in that case dated back to January 1, 1956, and consisted of the oral testimony of 175 witnesses and 13,000 exhibits. During the five year period from January 1, 1956, to November 14, 1961, according to the testimony of one Board member, the Board consistently gave assistance to white applicants in the completion of the application form, but such aid was never given to Negroes. The court concluded that the registration questionnaire was used as a "tricky examination or test" when applied to Negroes, but merely as a method for obtaining substantive information when applied to whites. In the five years from 1956 to 1961, ninety-six per cent of the whites applying were registered (1,070 of these had applications which contained the same kinds of technical errors used to reject Negroes),

---

[17] Brief for Plaintiff, p. 7, United States v. Alabama, Civil No. 1677-N, M.D. Ala., Sept. 13, 1961.

[18] Id. at 14.

[19] United States v. Penton, 212 F. Supp. 193 (M.D. Ala. 1962).

while seventy-five per cent of the Negroes applying were rejected. Approximately 4,522 Negro applications had been made. Of those rejected, 710 had twelve years or more of formal education, six had Master's degrees, 152 had four years of college training, 222 had some college training, and 108 were public school teachers.

After February 1961, the Board raised the standards to require a perfect application. Very strict requirements were put on white and Negro applicants. This was, of course, similar to the Bullock County freezing tactic. Approximately 600 Negroes were rejected because they failed to sign the oath on page three of the four-page questionnaire. The omission was not called to their attention, although the oath was administered orally by the registrar. Exhibits presented on trial showed that hundreds of white applications had x's, check marks, dots and dashes on the oath line of the application form. Judge Johnson concluded from this:

This Court would be naive to the point of absurdity if this evidence (such as the marks themselves, the contrasting shades of ink used in making them, the places where they occur, the fact that no marks appear on applications of Negroes and the oral testimony concerning the marks) did not compel the conclusion that they were made by the registrars and made for the purpose of showing the white applicants where to sign.

The only witness offered by the defendants in an attempt to explain these marks was a clerk in the office of the Judge of Probate. Her explanation—which is totally inadequate—was that some marks were placed on the applications when they were processed by the office of the Judge of Probate. The marks which this witness demonstrated that she used are totally different from those made to indicate where the oath is to be signed. This is aside from the fact that applications of Negroes are processed at the same place and no such marks appear on them—only on applications of whites.[20]

Judge Johnson was not impressed that several whites were rejected after 1961. The fact that certain white applications were rejected "approached the ridiculous when the Board rejected the law partner of one of the defense attorneys (in the instant case); a retired general, a graduate of West Point; and the college graduate son of one of the State's attorneys general. Such evidence has little or no probative value."[21] Johnson's further comment on this was as follows: "The rejection of whites subsequent

---

[20] Id. *at 199.*
[21] Id. *at 198.*

to June 1960 (and particularly since June 1961, when it became apparent this case was to be filed) impresses this Court as being nothing more than a sham and an attempt on the part of the Board to disguise their past discriminatory practices."[22]

THE TECHNIQUES OF JUDICIAL AGGRESSIVENESS

Judge Johnson first demonstrated his "aggressive" approach to these problems by ordering sixty-four specific Negroes registered immediately in Macon County—without reexamination or voter referees. The local registrars were ordered to do this within ten days and to so notify the Negroes. While Johnson made a finding of a pattern and practice of racial discrimination, he declined to appoint voter referees in order to give the registrars time to register all applicants fairly themselves. He said:

Such a declination is made with the idea that the defendants can act fairly if the directions spelled out in this Court's decree are followed in good faith. If the defendants so act, they will have regained for Macon county and for the State of Alabama the integrity that the evidence in this case makes abundantly clear has been lost in this field of voting rights.[23]

In Bullock County, the Board of Registrars was ordered by Judge Johnson on March 30, 1961, to report to him each month on the progress of registration in the county. He discontinued the "voucher" system, but again he did not appoint voter referees, saying, "this Court is impressed by the declarations of good faith by these members of the Board of Registrars."

Early in September 1961, the United States filed a motion to have the Bullock County Board expedite the registration process. The court heard the motion and issued its finding and order on September 13, 1961. In that order Johnson set forth very specific "operational standards" to guide the Board. At first, he summarized the Board's practices since his first order in March 1961. Over 700 Negroes had signed the priority list as a first step in the registration process. Only 250 Negroes on that list, however, had been able to make application, and one-half of those were rejected by the Board. Four hundred Negroes were still waiting to apply. At that time (September 1961), there were approximately 4,400 Negroes of voting age in Bullock County and only 130 were registered. The court found that the

---

[22] Id. *at 198.*
[23] *United States v. Alabama, 192 F. Supp. 677, 683 (M.D. Ala. 1961).*

Board was receiving applications at the rate of twenty-four per day. The Judge noted that on March 7, 1960, a day when all applicants were white, the Board handled forty-five applications. On July 4, 1961, the Board advised Negroes that the Board would not be open for business, and yet it did work on that day and received application from white citizens—one of whom testified to that fact. Negro applicants were handled in groups of eight, and the proceeding group had to wait until the slowest one of the previous group had finished.

This evidence, according to Judge Johnson, indicated that his faith in the Board had not been vindicated:

The defendants have been practicing token registration in the face of a large backlog of large groups of Negroes waiting to apply. The Court can do no less than conclude that the registrars have failed to live up to their sworn statements that they were ready and willing to register all qualified Negro citizens in Bullock county and would do so if given the opportunity.[24]

As a consequence of this failure of the Board to perform without further prompting by the court, Johnson entered a finding of a pattern and practice of racial discrimination and issued very specific orders in the form of a mandatory decree spelling out how the Board was to operate in the future. He concluded that where the percentage of one race already registered was very large and that of the other race very small, the Board could not maintain the existing imbalance by arbitrarily adopting stricter standards and procedures. In addition, the Board was given a certain number of days within which to process all of the waiting applicants.

It would be difficult to conclude that Judge Johnson had acted hastily in laying down specific operational standards for the Bullock County registrars. He issued his first ruling on March 30, 1961. Four months intervened before his next order. Then in January 1962, he called an informal conference in his chambers which was attended by the Bullock County registrars, the attorneys for the Department of Justice and attorneys for the State of Alabama. The purpose of the conference was to discuss the activity of the Board during December 1961. Johnson was disturbed by the large number of rejections of Negro applications on the basis merely of minor, formal or inconsequential errors. An attorney for the Department of Justice made the following observation: "This business of chamber-ruling is very important. Take Judge Johnson, for instance, in

---

[24] *United States v. Alabama, Civil No. 1677-N, M.D. Ala., Sept. 13, 1961.*

the Bullock case. That was one of the strongest sessions [the January 1962, informal conference] I had ever heard. It showed just what a judge can do if he wants to."[25]

\*　　\*　　\*　　\*

In Montgomery County, Johnson issued a decree on November 20, 1962, whereby he personally registered 1,076 Negroes, and set forth very definite standards for registering future Negro applicants: "In determining whether such applicants are qualified the Court must apply the standards used by the Board of Registrars in qualifying white applicants during the period in which the pattern of discrimination is found to exist."[26]

In all three cases, Johnson retained jurisdiction for purposes of enforcing, modifying or extending his orders. He ordered that the United States, acting through the Department of Justice, be given the opportunity at all reasonable times to inspect voting records in the respective counties. The Department was also to submit monthly reports containing the same information covered in the reports required from the county Boards. In addition, the Department of Justice was to furnish information to the court periodically to assist the court in determining if the decree was being fully complied with and to determine if contempt proceedings should be instituted. Likewise, if vacancies occurred on the Boards, the Department of Justice was to ascertain and report to the court if such vacancies could be filled by the State Appointing Board within a reasonable time. Finally, the Department was to assist the court in determining if a resignation was made in good faith or was an effort to frustrate the orders of the court.

Judge Johnson's orders erased many of the obstacles besetting many Negroes attempting to conduct voter registration drives in the three black-belt counties. In addition to overcoming frustrations connected with resignation of board members, Negro civil rights groups no longer had to worry about instructing prospective applicants in the "art" of completing letter-perfect applications. Voting clinics were prolific in the three counties in the late 1950's and early 1960's. Much of the time spent in these classes

---

[25] *Interview with Attorneys, Civil Rights Division, United States Department of Justice, in Washington, D.C., Jan. 22, 1963.*

[26] *United States v. Penton, 212 F. Supp. 193, 199 (M.D. Ala. 1962).*

was devoted to checking and rechecking to make sure the applicants had dotted all "i's," crossed all "t's" and placed periods at the end of each sentence. Before Judge Johnson issued his orders, the application form filled out by Negroes was a "test" that they would pass or fail as one passes or fails an examination in school.[27] As a result of the cases, it was no longer necessary for civil rights groups to check on the work of the Boards. One such group in Macon County had established the practice of stationing a person at the courthouse to note the times the Board met, the number of applicants appearing, the length of time the Board remained in session, and the results of the attempted registration. This time-consuming and tedious police work was now assumed by the Board members themselves and by the Department of Justice. Whatever other effects the Civil Rights Acts of 1957 and 1960 have had, it is important not to overlook these factors.

The data do not reveal at this time the existence of many judges like Johnson hearing these right-to-vote cases. Circuit Judge Rives is the only other southern federal judge who has adopted the federal government's theory against the "freezing tactic," but this was in a dissenting opinion.[28]

JUDICIAL RESISTANCE

A study of the work of the federal judiciary in Mississippi presents a stark contrast to the work of Judge Johnson. The performance of three judges in Mississippi—Harold Cox, Claude Clayton, and the late Ben Cameron[29]—is sufficient to vindicate in large measure those who objected to using the federal courts to enforce Negro voting rights on the ground that the southern federal courts would not be able to successfully resist local opinion committed to continuing patterns of discrimination. The Mississippi judges have presented innumerable obstacles to the federal

---

[27] *The manner of conducting voter clinics was described by one Negro civil rights leader in Macon County: "[W]e have continued to conduct voter registration clinics. It has been our position all along that we should not be satisfied by having Negroes meet the minimum requirement necessary in filling out the questionnaire. . . . Judge Johnson's rulings have been for the most part adhered to by the Board." Letter from Mr. William P. Mitchell, Chairman, Voter Franchise Committee, Tuskeegee Civic Association, to Charles V. Hamilton, March 26, 1964.*

[28] *United States v. Ramsey, 331 F.2d 824, 833 (5th Cir. 1964).*

[29] *Judge Cameron died in April 1964.*

government's efforts to prosecute discriminatory practices by voting registrars.[30] From the outset the Government was faced by a variety of barriers
aimed at keeping it not only from obtaining inspection of local voting
records and speedy hearings on its complaints, but also at keeping it from
receiving final court rulings on the complaints it was able to bring into
court.

Notwithstanding the fact that the Court of Appeals for the Fifth
Circuit had reiterated several times the "routine" right of the Department
of Justice to inspect voting records, it was more than once denied this
right. In an effort to inspect voting records of Bolivar County, Mississippi,
the Department of Justice filed its initial request on the registrar on
August 22, 1960. Twenty-eight months later Judge Clayton issued a
limited order permitting the inspection. The frustrations resulting from
endless delays were so great in that case that the Justice Department had
to petition for a writ of mandamus in the Fifth Circuit in an effort to
force Clayton to act in the case.

The Department of Justice also has been required to plead very
specific facts in its complaints on the ground that a suit under the Civil
Rights Acts of 1957 and 1960 is an action alleging fraud and thus should
state very specifically the particular basis for the actions.

At no time has a judge in Mississippi found a registrar guilty of
engaging in a "pattern or practice" of discrimination. And, of course, one
finds none of the specific instructions to registrars that are found in Judge
Johnson's orders.

The attitude of the "resistor" judge toward the various witnesses is
quite different from Johnson's. In a protracted case arising in Forrest
County, Mississippi, the registrar stated that he did not permit his female
deputies to register Negroes—they could register white citizens. The
explanation given was that this procedure was followed for "political"
reasons in that the lady deputy registrars had become apprehensive about
processing Negro applicants. The only testimony as to the cause of the
apprehension, however, was that on one unspecified occasion an unidenti-

---

[30] *It is not necessary to recount detailed fact situations in the several cases arising
in Mississippi. For purposes of this Article, it is sufficient to note that the registrars
in several counties in Mississippi were proceeded against by the Department of
Justice for engaging in the same kind of racially discriminatory practices as occurred
in Alabama.*

fied Negro man had asked the lady deputy a "personal question,"[31] and that on another occasion a Negro woman fumbled in her handbag while waiting for the registrar, left the office, and returned with a Negro man. When the Government asked Judge Cox to end the practice of requiring Negroes to seek out the registrar himself, the judge refused:

I think the colored people brought that on themselves. I am thoroughly familiar with some of the conduct of some of our colored gentry, and I am not surprised at Mr. Lynd's [the registrar's] reaction to what he stated into the record. I think that is a clear justification of what he did. You people up north don't understand what he was talking about and I think he did just exactly right in taking those things on himself. He said he couldn't afford any male help and he used girls in there and those girls didn't want to be subjected to that kind of influence and that is understandable. Otherwise I think that he certainly did need a good explanation.[32]

Another point of comparison between Cox and Johnson is the evidence each considered relevant. Johnson felt that the Government's evidence was "overwhelming" in the Macon and Montgomery cases, and that the court would be "absurd" and "naive" to overlook some obvious discriminatory practices by the registrars as well as the results of those practices. Cox, on the other hand, took judicial notice of the high illiteracy rate among Negroes. The Government produced statistics showing that there were approximately 7,495 Negroes and 22,431 white persons of voting age in Forrest County, and of these, about twenty-five Negroes and a substantial majority of the whites were registered to vote. The Government's intent, of course, was to offer evidence tending to prove that the great disproportion was due in large measure to the discriminatory practices of the registrar.[33] Judge Cox, however, chose to listen to different facts:

I think that the Court could take judicial notice of the illiteracy that is prevalent among the colored people, and I do know that of my own knowledge, and the intelligence of the colored people don't [sic] compare ratio-wise to white people. I mean, that is just a matter of common sense and common

---

[31] *The deputy registrar testified that the Negro man had asked her "how long [she] had been there and didn't he know [her] and didn't [she] remember him and one thing and another."*

[32] *Record, p. 10, United States v. Lynd, Civil No. 1646, S.D. Miss., Feb. 15, 1962.*

[33] *The Fifth Circuit declared in Alabama v. United States, 304 F.2d 583, 586 (5th Cir. 1962): "In the problem of racial discrimination, statistics often tell much, and Courts listen."*

knowledge. . . . [M]entioning figures like that to me wouldn't mean a thing in the world without something to go along with it.[34]

In one instance, Judge Cox refused to permit the Department of Justice to present evidence against the State of Mississippi as a co-defendant with the registrar. Notwithstanding the fact that the Civil Rights Act of 1960 provides for joining the State as a party defendant,[35] and such provision has been held constitutional,[36] the following colloquy took place in court:

By the Court: The bad part about that is that the State don't [*sic*] have a thing in the world to do with registration.

By Mr. Doar: [Department of Justice attorney]: Yes, but the State is made a defendant under the provision of Congress.

By the Court: I know, but you might as well have made me a defendant in there. I don't have anything to do with it and the State don't [*sic*] either. I know from many, many years of experience and familiarity with the situation that it's a very troublesome question.[37]

Only a verbatim reproduction of the above could attest to the almost incredible position taken by Judge Cox. His views were directly contradictory to a host of authorities, including the fourteenth and fifteenth amendments, as well as Supreme Court opinions.[38] It is impossible, by any stretch of the concepts of judicial review or judicial policy-making, to defend him in this ruling.

---

[34] *Record, p. 405, United States v. Lynd, Civil No. 1646, S.D. Miss., Feb. 15, 1962.*

[35] *74 Stat. 92, 42 U.S.C. § 1971(c) (Supp. V, 1964).*

[36] *United States v. Fox, 211 F. Supp. 25 (E.D. La. 1962); cf., United States v. Raines, 362 U.S. 17 (1960).*

[37] *Brief for Appellant, p. 37, United States v. Lynd, 301 F.2d 818 (5th Cir. 1962).*

[38] Cf., *Cooper v. Aaron, 358 U.S. 1, 16–17 (1958), where the Supreme Court quoted Ex parte Virginia, 100 U.S. (10 Otto) 339, 347 (1879): " 'A State acts by its legislative, its executive, or its judicial authorities. It can act in no other way.' "*

*This idea was developed fully in Ex parte Virginia, supra at 347:*

*"The constitutional provision of the 14th Amendment, therefore, must mean that no agency of the State, or of the officers or agents by whom its powers are exerted, shall deny to any person within its jurisdiction the equal protection of the laws. Whoever, by virtue of public position under a State government . . . takes away the equal protection of the laws, violates the constitutional inhibition; and as he acts in the name and for the State, and is clothed with the State's power, his act is that of the State."*

Another important point of comparison between Judges Johnson and Cox is the way in which the two judges issued their orders. In the Bullock County case, Johnson issued his ruling in open court immediately after the trial and before a courtroom filled with Negroes. Both judges expressed faith in the local registrars, but Johnson employed a method more likely to produce results. One United States attorney made the following observation on the effect of an open court ruling:

What Johnson was really doing . . . was talking . . . directly to the Negroes in the audience—looking straight at them. He was telling them in so many words, "O.K., now you've heard the registrars. I've heard them. They've said they would do the right thing. Now let's see. Go out there and register." And those guys went out and got a lot of people to register. This was Johnson's way of trying to let the local authorities do it rather than himself.[39]

In a case coming out of Jefferson Davis County, Mississippi, Judge Cox made a similar statement of faith in the registrar, but he waited until three months after the trial and issued it in written form which few Negroes would see.

## Judicial Gradualism

Frequently, one talking to Department of Justice attorneys would be told that many southern federal judges were segregationists. But in the same breath these lawyers would add that these judges, nonetheless, had a profound respect for the law. This has had important meaning for those Government lawyers who have argued voting rights cases before these judges. Most of the attorneys were not as candid as the one who singled out Judge Ben C. Dawkins, Jr. of Louisiana for comment when he described that judge as a segregationist, but one highly sensitive to the "injustices" and "gross inequalities we present to him."[40] This means that despite Dawkins' strong pro-segregation views, it is still possible to obtain favorable decrees from him. The Department of Justice presented its first case under the Civil Rights Acts before Judge Dawkins in a case arising out of Bienville Parish. "We knew we didn't have a [Judge] Skelly Wright or [Judge] Frank Johnson," one attorney stated. "But we also felt that Dawkins was what you might say, torn—a segregationist with respect

---

[39] *Interview with Attorneys, Civil Rights Division, United States Department of Justice, in Washington, D.C., Jan. 23, 1963.*

[40] Ibid.

for the law."[41] With these factors at work the Government set out to prove that some 570 Negro voters were unconstitutionally "purged" from the rolls, that the registrar was engaging in a pattern and practice of discrimination, that a voter referee should be appointed, and that those Negroes should be immediately restored to the registration books.[42]

Judge Dawkins was impressed by the thorough preparation of the Government's case to the extent that he found virtually no dispute as to the facts. Dawkins noted that in elections prior to October 1956, Negroes "had engaged in the reprehensible practice of 'bloc voting,'" and concluded that this undoubtedly was a major motivation behind the purge. But Dawkins stated that he could not let this "alter one whit our duty under the fifteenth amendment to see to it, wherever we are called upon to do so, that there is no discrimination in voting registration because of race or color."[43] He added: "It is to be earnestly hoped that in the future those Negroes who are qualified to vote will achieve a degree of political maturity so as to vote according to the best interests of their State and Nation rather than for their own selfish or venal purposes."[44] Dawkins concluded that a pattern and practice of discrimination existed, but that the appointment of a voting referee was not then necessary. The names of the illegally purged Negroes were ordered restored to the rolls, and the registrar was enjoined from future discrimination. Dawkins' decree did not go as far as Johnson's decree registering the Negroes with the stroke of the pen, nor was the registrar required to make detailed monthly reports; but the case did not result in the countless delays and the weak decrees characteristic of the cases in Mississippi.

In the same month that the decree was entered in the Bienville Parish case, the Government tried its second suit before Judge Dawkins in a case arising out of East Carroll Parish.[45] The case had been filed seven months earlier in April 1961. The Government alleged the denial to Negroes of the right to vote on account of race. This denial was accomplished by the registrar, Cecil Manning, who required Negroes to undergo virtually impossible conditions to establish their identities to the satisfaction of the

---

[41] Ibid.
[42] *United States v. Association of Citizens' Councils of La., Inc.*, 196 F. Supp. 908 (*W.D. La. 1961*).
[43] Id. *at 911.*
[44] Id. *at 911.*
[45] *United States v. Manning*, 205 F. Supp. 172 (*W.D. La. 1962*).

registrar. If the registrar had a reason to question the identity of the person, the registrar could require him to produce two credible persons registered to vote in his ward and precinct to identify him under oath.

There were approximately 4,183 Negroes and 2,990 white persons of voting age in the parish. A new registration period began in the parish on January 1, 1961. From that time until November 1961 about 500 white persons and no Negroes were registered. In fact, no Negro had been registered in the parish since 1922.

The Department of Justice had four major theories to counter both the activity of registrars and the State registration requirements. First, a system of "vouching" or identification used in parishes with few registered Negroes, should be declared constitutionally impermissible because of the extreme hardship it worked on Negroes. In effect, it required Negroes to solicit help from whites in order to register. Secondly, whenever a registrar proceeds to require very stringent standards for whites and Negroes alike in areas where very few, if any, Negroes are registered, the practice should be declared an unconstitutional "freezing" of the status quo operating to the detriment particularly of Negroes. Thirdly, the standards by which the registrars should be guided in registering future Negro applicants should be those standards used to register the least qualified white persons during the period of racial discrimination. Fourthly, where it was shown that none or a very small percentage of the voting age Negroes had attempted to register, and a substantial majority of the white persons of voting age were registered, this evidence alone should state a claim for relief under the fourteenth and fifteenth amendments and under the Civil Rights Acts of 1957 and 1960.

Judge Dawkins accepted at least the first and fourth theories in the East Carroll Parish case. He made a finding of a pattern and practice of discrimination based on race. The particular ways by which the registrar manipulated the identification requirement amounted to discrimination per se. Consequently, he enjoined any acts of racial discrimination and specifically the identification requirements the registrar had been using. The registrar had "to make reasonable inquiry as to the identity of Negroes seeking to apply for registration." Negroes were to be permitted to establish their identity, Dawkins said, by use of driving, hunting or fishing licenses, library cards or automobile registrations, as well as by military papers, records of property ownership, rent receipts and the like.

Then Dawkins assumed the role of overseer. He ordered the registrar to file monthly progress reports to include the following: a list of new registrants; a list of persons "scratched from the rolls"; a list of transfers; a list of names, race and addresses of all applicants rejected on the ground of lack of identification, the kinds of identification each offered, and the reasons for unacceptability on the ground of identification. Finally, the monthly report was to contain a list of the names, race and addresses of all persons whose applications for registration were rejected and the reasons therefor. Likewise, the Government was given the right to inspect the voting records at any and all reasonable times.

Some lawyers for the Department of Justice expressed the belief that Judge Dawkins was annoyed with the blatant fact that no Negro had been registered in the parish in forty years. His sympathies were with the registrars, because he abhorred the thought of a black bloc-vote. But he sincerely believed that all qualified persons—black or white—should be able to vote. One Justice Department attorney made the following observation:

I believe, also in terms of the effect of a suit, that Dawkins [in the East Carroll Parish case] called the District Attorney [counsel for the registrar] in[to] his chambers and said something like: "Now listen, I want to save you as much embarrassment as possible; so [,] you all get on over there and register those Negroes. I am not going to have those people running in and out of here. I'll order a referee if I have to, but I would rather you folks handled this yourself."

Of course, I do [not] know what he said to them, but I do know he called the D.A. into his chambers. And this is perfectly legal. He can call in the defendants and their lawyers [alone]. I suspect this happened.[46]

### Reprisals and Intimidation

Up to this point we have examined the character of judicial performance with respect to the enforcement of the Civil Rights Acts of 1957 and 1960. To a great degree the nature of judicial enforcement will determine the validity of the objections set out at the beginning of this Article to the use of the judiciary to enforce Negro voting rights. However, as we noted at the outset, factors external to judicial performance, in the form of reprisals and intimidation against Negro complainants, are also important to the analysis of the efficacy of the judiciary in the voting rights field.

---

[46] *Interview with Attorneys, Civil Rights Division, United States Department of Justice, in Washington, D.C., Jan. 24, 1963.*

There have been many instances of intimidation of activist Negroes. For example, Negro sharecroppers were evicted from their land in Tennessee for participation in a voter registration drive,[47] and a Negro in Louisiana found he could not get his cotton ginned after he testified before the Civil Rights Commission.[48] Thus Negroes have found that vindication of their rights in court is possible only at great cost. Even when court actions have been instituted in spite of the threat of reprisal, the pressure brought to bear during the usually long proceedings often has been so unbearable as to produce settlements out of court.[49] To those complainants who have been able to withstand the threat of reprisal before an action, as well as the continuous pressure during the course of the proceedings, community reprisals after the action have often been applied. Furthermore, to make matters worse, further court action to bring to account those who have been responsible for such intimidation has usually been unsuccessful.[50]

The significant effect that these forces of reprisal external to the judicial process have had on the efficacy of judicial enforcement of voting rights can be seen in the detailed study of one case.[51] Mrs. Ernestine Denham Talbert was a resident of George County, Mississippi. She was a teacher of ten years' experience. In 1961, she signed a one-year contract to teach and serve as part-time librarian at the Vocational High School in neighboring Greene County. Her contract was to run until the close of school in June 1962.

On the morning of January 6, 1962, Mrs. Talbert went with her husband to the registrar's office in George County to make application for a voter certificate. There were several other Negroes in the office filling out registration forms at the time. They were told to return after lunch,

---

[47] *United States v. Atkesion, Civil No. 4131, 6 Race Rel. L. Rep. 200, W.D. Tenn., Dec. 30, 1960; United States v. Barcroft, Civil No. 4121, 6 Race Rel. L. Rep. 201, W.D. Tenn., Dec. 23, 1960; United States v. Beaty, Civil No. 4065, 6 Race Rel. L. Rep. 201, W.D. Tenn., Dec. 16, 1960.*

[48] *United States v. Deal, Civil No. 8132, 6 Race Rel. L. Rep. 474, W.D. La., Feb. 3, 1961.*

[49] E.g., *cases cited notes [47] & [48] supra.*

[50] *See United States v. City of Greenwood, Civil No. GC-638, N.D. Miss., 1964; United States v. LeFlore County, Civil No. 20839, N.D. Miss., 1964. Contra, United States v. Wood, 295 F.2d 772 (5th Cir. 1961),* cert. denied 369 U.S. 850 (1962).

[51] *United States v. Board of Educ. of Greene County, Civil No. 1729, S.D. Miss., Aug. 29, 1962,* aff'd 332 F.2d 40 (5th Cir. 1964) *(Rives, J. concurring specially).*

which they did. The registrar, Mr. Green, gave them the application forms and the oath, and he asked Mrs. Talbert to read and interpret section 50 of the Mississippi constitution.[52] She gave her interpretation of the provision. Mr. Green then asked the Talberts if they knew their county officials. Mr. Talbert began to name them. The registrar then asked if they knew the fifteen members of the Election Commission, the group that determined the eligibility of applicants for registration. They did not know those officials. Mr. Green then asked several questions connected with the Election Commission, the answers to which the Talberts did not have for the most part. Green then advised them that there was "a lot to voting that people don't realize."[53] At that point, he told them that the Election Commission, after its meeting in March 1962, would inform them if they were qualified to vote.

The Talberts waited until April 2, 1962, and returned to the George County registrar's office to inquire about the status of their application. There was another Negro couple present for the same purpose. The registrar informed them that he had given their applications to the Election Commission, but that the Commission wanted to talk to them personally. Mr. Green indicated that he could register persons whom he knew personally, but otherwise the applicants had to meet with the Commission. Mrs. Talbert asked him if this was the normal procedure. The registrar replied: "If you want me to disprove [sic] of your application I guarantee you I can do that. But I thought you were interested in becoming a registered voter."[54] He then advised them that the Commission would be in session again in August. The Talberts stated that they wanted to vote in the State primaries in June. The other Negro woman applicant then noticed a notation in a ledger on the counter that the Commission would meet again on June 4, 1962.

On April 16, 1962, the United States filed a suit against the registrar of George County and the State of Mississippi under the Civil Rights Act[55]

---

[52] MISS. CONST., art. IV, § 50 provides: "The governor and all other civil officers of this state, shall be liable to impeachment for treason, bribery, or any high crime or misdemeanor in office."

[53] Record, p. 14, United States v. Board of Educ. of Greene County, Civil No. 1729, S.D. Miss., Aug. 29, 1962.

[54] Id. at 16.

[55] Rev. Stat. § 2004 (1875), as amended 71 Stat. 637 (1957), as amended 78 Stat. 241, 42 U.S.C.A. § 1971(a) (1) (1964).

alleging denial of voting rights to Negroes on account of their race.[56] The complaint charged racial discrimination in the registration process. Mrs. Talbert and five other Negroes gave affidavits in that case attesting to their inability to become registered. On April 17, 1962, wide publicity was given to the suit in Mississippi newspapers and in the press of Mobile, Alabama. The names, addresses and educational levels of the six Negro complainants were published with the news stories. One week later, the press again published the identity of the Negroes in connection with the news of a temporary restraining order issued by the United States District Court.[57]

About the time that this suit was filed, the Greene County Board of Education was making its decision with respect to which teachers would be retained for the next school year. Mrs. Talbert was recommended by her principal for rehiring. The recommendation, however, was not binding upon the county school superintendent. For an unspecified reason the superintendent recommended to the Board that Mrs. Talbert not be rehired and the Board acted affirmatively on that recommendation.

On April 28, 1962, after she had learned that her teacher's contract would not be renewed, Mrs. Talbert returned to the registrar's office in George County and was successfully registered.

On June 16, 1962, the United States filed a suit against the Board of Education of Greene County, the Board members individually, and the county school superintendent under the Civil Rights Act of 1957.[58] The case was filed in Judge Cox's court at Hattiesburg, Mississippi. The complaint alleged that the refusal to reappoint Mrs. Talbert as a teacher for the 1962–63 school year was directly connected with her activities relating to the voter registration effort and law suit in George County. Such refusal, the Government urged, was an attempt to intimidate, threaten and coerce her and other Negroes in their attempts to become registered and to vote. The refusal to rehire her was not based on any consideration of her ability or performance as a teacher. Furthermore, the

---

[56] *United States v. Green, Civil No. 2540, S.D. Miss., April 23, 1962.* At the time this suit was filed there were 580 Negroes of voting age in George County only ten of whom were registered to vote. Substantially all of the 5,276 whites of voting age were registered.

[57] *Record, p. 20, United States v. Board of Educ. of Greene County, Civil No. 1729, S.D. Miss., Aug. 29, 1962.*

[58] *71 Stat. 637 (1957), 42 U.S.C. § 1971(b) (1958).*

United States contended, the refusal served as an obstruction of the work of the Department of Justice in the performance of its duties of prosecuting voting denials, inasmuch as the failure to rehire Mrs. Talbert would effectively deter other Negroes from coming forth to attest to racial discrimination. The fear of losing their jobs or suffering some other form of economic retaliation would be too great. The Government asked for a preliminary and permanent injunction against the defendants, and requested the court to require the Board of Education of Greene County to offer Mrs. Talbert a contract of re-employment for the ensuing 1962–63 school year.

The trial on the merits was held on July 25, 1962. At the outset, the defendants objected to the introduction of any documents relating to the George County case, but the court overruled the objections and permitted the Government to offer the complaint in the George County case, Mrs. Talbert's affidavit in that case, and various other motions and orders in evidence.

*    *    *    *

At the close of all the testimony, a colloquy developed between Judge Cox and Mr. Doar [the attorney for the Government] which highlighted the fundamental difference between their respective approaches to the case. The Government, according to Cox, was in essence asking the court to require the Board of Education to enter into a contract with Mrs. Talbert. This theory, Cox indicated, was contrary to that rule, applied for centuries, which forbids courts to make contracts for parties. As a rule, courts do not make contracts, they only interpret contract rights arising out of an agreement the parties have made with each other. There may have been "indirect implications, involvements or coincidental things" that resulted in the refusal to contract, Cox said, but these were not sufficient to require the court to rule otherwise than against the Government. It was clear to Judge Cox that this was a matter of private contract rights "where the situation simply incidentally affects the civil rights area." Moreover, by asking that the court compel the defendants to make a contract with the teacher, the United States was seeking mandatory relief. Cox understood the Civil Rights Acts to provide only preventive relief. Mrs. Talbert had a one-year contract; she fully performed, and was fully compensated. She had no vested right to a new contract. "Now what right," Cox stated, "does somebody else have to come in here—the United States or anybody else—and assert some vested right when there is no existence of any such vested right even on her part if she were suing. That's the question that's in my mind."[59]

Attorney John Doar argued that the interest of the United States was not solely that Mrs. Talbert be given a job for the next year, but that all citizens be guaranteed the right to vote. Not giving her a new contract, the Government contended, was an act of intimidation and retaliation on the part of the Board for her registration activities.

The court reminded Government's counsel that Mrs. Talbert's position had been filled by a new appointment for the coming year. This would make preventive relief difficult. And then the court talked about the connection between Mrs. Talbert's involvement in the voter registration suit in George County and the Board's subsequent refusal to renew her contract. Judge Cox said:

Now you say that there's some question in evidence here about whether these defendants were to some extent influenced. And I say at least to some extent. But they probably were influenced by the fact that she was participating in some litigation which had some effects which were not regarded as too wholesome[,] particularly when this school board looked unfavorably on all kinds of litigation, even debt litigation[,] and had gone so far as not to renew contracts[,] I believe[,] of two teachers in a prior year who were involved or would be involved in some litigation. And they didn't consider that in the interest of the school.[60]

So, although the defendants swore under oath during the trial that they were not influenced by the George County suit, Judge Cox concluded otherwise, but offered grounds of justification for the defendants.

Doar argued that preventive relief meant to put a stop to further acts of intimidation, and that it seemed unfair for the court to contend that it could do nothing since she had been discharged and someone else had been hired in her place. For all practical purposes, the colloquy and the case ended when Judge Cox interrupted Doar and admonished:

Mr. Doar, you don't seem to get the impact of what I'm saying. You keep using the word "discharge." If she were discharged, you'd have a very much stronger case here. She wasn't discharged. She filled her contract. She simply wasn't rehired and you're just trying to get the Court to rehire her.[61]

---

[59] Id. *at 545.*
[60] Id. *at 551.*
[61] Id. *at 552–53.*

The court entered its final order dismissing the complaint August 29, 1962, on the grounds that the plaintiff had failed to show a connection between the Board's refusal to rehire Mrs. Talbert and her voter registration activities.

*     *     *     *

## CONCLUSION

The role of the judge in dealing with the discriminatory acts of the registrars is a crucial one. The aggressive judge in these voting rights cases sees his role as that of an enforcer, an overseer. It will not take much to convince him that registrars are discriminating on the basis of race, and he will be concerned largely with prodding the registrar to mend his ways. The resistant judge, on the other hand, approaches these cases more as a judge would hear a criminal case. The defendant is clearly innocent until proven guilty beyond a doubt. The process thus should be slow, deliberate. The resistant judge weighs, sifts through the facts—and then the penalty is light.

The judicial aggressor emphasizes the comparative qualifications of particular Negroes and certain whites, that is, those Negroes rejected and those whites accepted. If the evidence shows the former equal to the latter, then the Negroes must be registered. The judicial resistor talks about his knowledge of the fact that most Negroes are inferior to most whites and this generalization, along with other stereotypes, influences his judgment when disposing of the particular Negro applicants before him in a specific case.[62]

The judicial aggressor does not talk about the political consequences of wholesale Negro voting, while this factor is obviously uppermost in the mind of the judicial resistor. The latter fears that Negroes will bloc-vote and that this will result in an uninformed, unsophisticated vote; so the resistor applies as many tactics as possible to forestall this event, or to mitigate it by issuing "weak" decrees.

The judicial gradualist presents different combinations of characteris-

---

[62] *Professor David Fellman has suggested that—all evidence considered—a more appropriate title for this category of performance would be "judicial lawlessness."*

tics. He has the fears of and feelings toward Negro bloc voting possessed by the resistor, but he orders the Negroes registered and hopes for the best. In short, he seems to share the social and political opinions of the resistor, but he tends to reach the results of the aggressor. Like the aggressive judge, the gradualist is impressed with voluminous evidence pointing toward racial discrimination, and he tends to become more and more impatient with efforts of local registrars to perpetuate discriminatory tactics. He does not like the statute, but he abides by it because he respects the law. He does not engage in the various delaying tactics of the resistor. In all likelihood, if the cases coming before the gradualist constantly involve blatant examples of racial discrimination, there is great possibility of this type of judge becoming an aggressor. He will do so not so much to protect Negroes, but to maintain and protect the integrity of the law he is called upon to apply.

The character of judicial performance in the voter registration cases discussed in this Article provides a tool to analyze the validity of the objections to using the judicial process for the enforcement of civil rights. At the outset, it is important to note that although the judicial process is inherently slow, there are still certain important indirect benefits to be derived from its use. For example, the educational and motivational effects of statements made by local registrars in open court before Negro observers ought not be underestimated.

The validity of the first and second objections can be considered together. Those advocating the first objection say, it will be recalled, that the judicial process is deficient because judges cannot escape the influences of community pressure, and even use such pressure to buttress any segregationist predilections they may have. The second objection was to the effect that enforcement of politically controversial legislation in the local area of controversy is not good for the prestige of the courts.

While it may be true that community pressures buttress some judges' segregationist attitudes, it is not true that community pressures will control the result of the litigation. The judicial aggressor, and to a lesser degree the judicial gradualist, are examples of the invalidity of this objection. The fact is that community pressure has not proven to be an insurmountable obstacle.

The character of performance of the judge also demonstrates that the second objection is invalid. There is some evidence that the prestige of the courts does not suffer even though the judge decides against the segregationist attitudes of the community. For example, Judge Johnson, who was classified as a judicial aggressor, has received public support from leading pro-segregationist newspapers. The following editorial from the *Birmingham News,* appearing three days after Johnson issued his decree in the Montgomery County case, is significant enough in this regard to be reproduced fully here:

Judge Frank M. Johnson, Jr., has ordered the Montgomery county Board of Registrars to enroll 1,100 Negroes. He had been considering evidence on the case for months.

The ruling is not surprising. Judge Johnson's position as a jurist consistently has been clear on this issue, when evidence was substantial. Through his court it previously had been determined that the federal bench may direct such registration. This had been done in Macon county.

Judge Johnson also asked the Justice Department to provide him with a list of three qualified persons to serve as federal voter registration referees should Montgomery county registrars refuse to obey his instructions—or should they resign. Courts have power to enforce Negro registration. Naturally many in Montgomery county, and in much of the rest of Alabama, will resent such direct federal action. Common consensus in the state is that voter registration is a state matter.

But as the *News* has said ever since this issue first came up in Alabama, it is not realistic to assume that the federal government, under either a G.O.P. or Democratic administration, will fail to act to guarantee Negroes' right to vote in federal elections.

Whether one likes federal intervention or not, the record is clear that, in some such cases at least, obviously qualified citizens have been denied the vote. In the Montgomery case, evidence as reported indicated that vastly more Negroes proportionately than whites had been refused registration. Among those refused: six holders of master's degrees obtained through advanced college work beyond a normal four years; 152 persons with four years of undergraduate work in college; 222 with some college work; 710 applicants with at least a high school educational equivalent, and 108 Negroes teaching public school in the county.

There is no logic in any argument that such citizens, regardless of their color, could be denied the vote.

Apparently it still needs saying in this state that it is the opposite of wisdom to invite federal intervention through wholesale failures to grant the privilege of voting to qualified persons. Negroes are citizens. If any whites turn their backs on that hard fact, then the federal government will certainly intervene.[63]

---

[63] *Birmingham News, Nov. 23, 1960, editorial page.*

It would be difficult to conclude that Judge Johnson or the federal court system suffered from that type of editorial comment coming from such an influential pro-segregation daily in the State. One should not, of course, generalize from one or even a few editorials in newspapers, but it is significant that so important an issue as Negro voting should receive such treatment in the local southern press.[64]

This brings us to the third and most important objection: intimidation and reprisal as obstacles to voter registration. It is clear that notwithstanding the effectiveness of the judicial approach in some districts in overcoming barriers to Negro voting, there remains the problem of protecting Negro complainants from harm if and when they attempt to assert their right to register or vote. It may well be that as long as the threat of intimidation or reprisal persists, *ad hoc,* out-of-court settlements can be expected. Moreover, the very existence of that threat robs the judicial process of its effectiveness, even when there is an aggressive judge on the bench.

The problem of intimidation and reprisal is two-fold: the fact that countless numbers of southern Negroes are at the economic mercy of people who do not share the Negroes' ambition to exercise a free franchise is made worse by the extreme difficulty of proving that acts of intimida-

---

[64] *Editorials from other southern newspapers have expressed a similar attitude. Occasionally, editorials have appeared similar to the one in the* Lee County [Alabama] Bulletin *of February 2, 1960, on the proposal to provide federal registrars:*

"[I]t is simply a bill drawn by the attorney general and approved by the President which rescues thousands of colored voter applicants from a hopeless situation. Nothing is to be gained by crying foul. It is true that this matter ought to be handled by the states. But the states have failed to act fairly and honorably. Alabama, along with several others, has asked for what it is getting. At the time of the Civil Rights Commission hearings in Alabama last year this paper pleaded that Alabama officials ought to act in good faith in this matter of registering voter applicants regardless of race or color. . . ."

*In an editorial on May 17, 1960, the* Montgomery Advertiser *made a distinction between voting and school desegregation. The bad constitutional law of the editor aside, the following comment illustrates an attitude not unfavorable to the activity of the judiciary in voting rights litigation:*

"Negro voters and Negroes butting their way into white schools where they are not wanted are organically different matters. It's not a federal dispensation, but the law of Alabama enacted by Alabamians that qualified Negroes are entitled to vote. Qualified Negroes are entitled legally and morally to vote. . . ." (*Emphasis added.*)

tion are based on race and are connected with voting rights. Thus the fact remains that in many places in the South, many Negroes will not attempt to register because they will be subjected to severe reprisals in the form of physical or economic harm. The courts will continue to try to deal with these cases as the Department of Justice laboriously tries to build sound cases. In many cases, the evidence necessary will be almost impossible to obtain—as in cases where a single employer tells his Negro handyman not to register or the Negro woman domestic is warned in casual conversation by her employer's wife.

It is virtually impossible to estimate how many Negroes stay away from the registrar's office because of this factor, but a hard fact is that many southern Negroes do not dare attempt to register to vote because they simply cannot afford to run the economic risk. The Negroes cannot see any effective protection being provided by the federal courts. Negroes in Macon County, Alabama, for example, can make application for voter certificates knowing that Judge Johnson will not tolerate arbitrary action by the registrars, but there is no sure protection for these Negroes against the subtle reprisals that are very likely to occur.

To continue to treat this problem as one solely for judicial solution is insufficient. The procedures of the judiciary are too rigorous, and the results too tenuous for the solution of such a major, but subtle problem. Combined with this is the high degree of economic vulnerability of southern Negroes. Perhaps the latter situation could be overcome somewhat if there were some signs that the federal government was able to act decisively. But such decisiveness under the judicial approach is not possible because of the difficulty of legal proof. The Civil Rights Act of 1964[65] does not deal with this aspect of the voting problem. It concentrates on methods to overcome the obstructions of resistant judges: providing for a three-judge court;[66] stipulating that right-to-vote cases must be given early consideration;[67] making a sixth grade education a rebuttable presumption of literacy.[68] All these innovations buttress the judicial approach, and in a limited way will be useful, as indeed the previous laws have been helpful, in registering some Negroes—significant numbers in some places,

---

[65] 78 Stat. 241 (1964) (codified in scattered sections of 5, 28, 42 U.S.C.A.)
[66] 78 Stat. 243, 42 U.S.C.A. § 1971(h) (1964).
[67] 78 Stat. 243, 42 U.S.C.A. § 1971(h) (1964).
[68] 78 Stat. 242, 42 U.S.C.A. § 1971(c) (1964).

an inconsequential number in others. Strengthening the existing laws to provide for speedier trials and the like, however, is only a partial solution to the problem of Negro voting rights, because there remain the problem of proof within the judicial system and the problem of subtle intimidation external to, but bearing on, the judicial system.

# CONSTITUENCY VERSUS CONSTITUTIONALISM: THE DESEGREGATION ISSUE AND TENSIONS AND ASPIRATIONS OF SOUTHERN ATTORNEYS GENERAL*

*Samuel Krislov*

## I

Some issues so cry out for immediate attention that longer-range research seems almost trivial and tends to be pushed aside. Such an issue is desegregation. It would be unfortunate if the zeal and moralistic energy which impel us toward a new solution in the field of race relations were to result in wasted opportunities. For in the desegregation process there is rich material in the field of basic social science research, for the student of

* A revision of a paper presented at the American Political Science Association Convention, New York City, September 5–7, 1957. Research was aided by a grant from the Faculty Research Fund of the University of Oklahoma. Muzafer Sherif, University of Oklahoma, and Clement Vose, Wesleyan University, were kind enough to offer detailed critiques of the original paper.

politics as well as the sociologist or social psychologist.[1] In this vein, the attorney general seems a natural subject of scrutiny. The potentialities of the office are many. The struggle on desegregation has been couched primarily in legalistic terms and the strategic importance of the post is quickly and almost intuitively grasped. Governor Coleman's youthful triumph in Mississippi, for example, was credited to public appreciation of the advantages of a legal officer in the current situation.[2] The attorney general represents the force of both national and local law within his state. He could act as a creatively legalistic interpreter of existing decisions and conditions within the state. But the southern attorney general has by and large been interesting for what he has not done as much as for his accomplishments.

*The Southern School News* some time ago listed 168 important developments in the desegregation process.[3] It is remarkable that such a list could be compiled without a single mention of an attorney general. Nor by and large can one quarrel with the implicit evaluation. For the attorneys general of the various states have not led in the field of desegregation. Rather they have represented a very close and sensitive evaluation of political forces within the state, following the leadership of the locality and the dominant trend of public opinion.

This conduct of the attorney general is explicable and predictable rather than haphazard or indigenous to the current situation. An analysis of the office in terms of its demands and of holders of the office in terms of their commitments suggests the patterns of behavior of the attorneys general. An examination of the actual conduct of the southern attorney general on desegregation thus becomes a useful prelude to an analysis of the motive source of that conduct. This in turn has itself broader implications. The problem is a relevant one not just for the pointing of fingers or assessing praise or blame, but for deepening our understanding of the methods and operations of our democratic government. One of the great lacunae of political science is that it has not adequately explored the problem of how public opinion is conveyed to public officials and translated into public action. Dennis Brogan has aptly epitomized this by

---

[1] *For a digest of recent research, see Melvin Tumin,* Segregation and Desegregation (*New York: Anti-Defamation League, 1957*).

[2] Current Biography, *1956.*

[3] Southern School News, *May 1957, p. 1.*

calling for more mapping of the "conduit or sluice by which the waters of social thought and discussion are brought to the wheels of political machinery and set to turn those wheels."[4]

## II

\* \* \* \*

Why is it that the southern attorney general has reflected the prejudices, if you will, or the wishes, if you prefer, of his area? Of course he is a southerner, and a southern public official. Still this conduct contrasts very sharply with the conduct of others similarly situated. A specific instance seems in order. In June of 1955 a federal district court of three issued an opinion on implementation of the Supreme Court decision that Thurgood Marshall found generally satisfactory.[5] One of the judges was the father of a governor of South Carolina; as a private individual he has denounced the Supreme Court decision and helped force out his pastor for too "broad" an attitude on the race question. Another, during the course of the discussion, sneered at "a foreign Communistic anthropologist," an undoubted reference to Gunnar Myrdal, and one reflecting current southern propaganda.[6] The third judge, whose personal opinions (in all fairness) we don't know too much about, was refused confirmation to the Supreme Court in part due to objections of the NAACP, since in running for office he had once expressed views derogatory of Negroes.[7] The ability of southern judges on the federal level at least in part to set aside their personal opinions and reflect the law as interpreted by the Supreme Court is borne out most clearly by the southern opposition to the civil rights legislation without jury trial provisions and more positively, by the stand of civil rights adherents in favor of that same provision.

Why is it that on the one hand we have federal judges who can and do put aside their own opinions and ignore the immediate local pressures

---

[4] *Of course the works of Gabriel Almond, Richard Snyder, and Lewis Dexter, among others, must be recognized as important efforts to deal with precisely this problem.*

[5] Race Relations Law Reporter, *I (1955)*, 73.

[6] New York Times, *July 26, 1957, p. 7;* Southern School News, *August 1955, pp. 6–9, December 1955, p. 6.*

[7] *Some definite indications of his views, though, can be found in John J. Parker, "Chief Justice Fred M. Vinson: Meeting the Challenge to Law and Order,"* American Bar Association Journal, *XLI (April, 1955),* 324, *especially p.* 325.

of public opinion, and on the other hand the southern attorney general who has reflected his own evaluations of the mores and demands of his area? What is the mechanism that compels the one to be subservient and allows the other to be independent, that makes one responsive to local opinion and the other responsive to national opinion?

It is certainly not enough to speak of the electoral process, for no southern attorney general has been defeated because of his stand on desegregation. Indeed, none has taken to the hustings in defense of either segregation or desegregation in areas where either course was unpopular. The niceties and irregularities of our democratic government, the evasions that characterize our American system of politics, have prevented the problem of desegregation from being an issue in any but the meagrest number of elections in the United States. We will have to go deeper by looking in more detail at the office of the attorney general.

The position is an historic one dating back to the British sergeant-at-arms. It is certainly a responsible and important office, and it is one that on first sight is fairly obvious in its obligations and duties. The apparent simplicity and obviousness of its responsibilities has in fact made the office largely unknown to observers because there exists virtually no body of investigation or study of what the position entails beyond simple statutory listings or descriptions of statutory requirements in the various states.

But it is a surprisingly complex office. It is curious to see how much of the annual conferences of the attorneys general is devoted to self-conscious discussion of the true nature of the position.[8]

In one sense the attorney general is subservient to federal law. Yet he is at the same time the expounder and defender of state law. Since he is called upon to give legal opinions to the various departments the attorney general basically exercises judicial power. Yet he is not merely a judicial official. More than the independent regulatory commissions he combines the executive, legislative, and judicial functions.

The attorney general is also the chief law enforcement officer for his state, and in the words of a former president of the National Association of Attorneys General, "in many states their powers literally exceed those

---

[8] *This extends even to the title of the office. A perennial question is what the plural of "attorney general" should be and how to refer to one another. They resolve it by addressing each other as "General" and retaining the older form for the plural.*

of the governor in the law enforcement field."[9] Arthur Bromage's description of the attorney general as law enforcer as the head of a "continuous chain of irresponsibility" is no doubt accurate;[10] but his position remains more difficult precisely because of the lack of power given to him to enforce his obligations.

In addition, the attorney general is a policy-making official; as a leading elective official he is called upon and must make decisions beyond the domain of legal processes. At the same time, the attorney general is the trial lawyer—always the appellate trial lawyer and often the lower court trial attorney—for his state. He both advises and represents the administrative units and in many states rules on legal questions expounded by the legislature.

He is also, at least in theory, legal advisor to the governor. But at the same time that he is advisor he is also too often the governor's rival. Both are elective officials and both therefore have a standing with the public largely independent of each other, and often they choose or wish to compete in the future.

The conflicting pressures that are so evident and that bear so strongly upon the attorney general have been rendered particularly irreconcilable by the process of popular election. The anomalies implicit in this arrangement are already reflected in an institutional change—probably the most precise and definite measure of a contradictory governmental arrangement. In practice it is common for the governor to have a legal advisor other than the attorney general, and in many states this is a recognized position with the title of legal advisor or legal counsel to the governor.[11]

Political scientists have usually studied the process of parcelling out the executive power to a number of officials on the state level solely in terms of efficiency. It is also interesting and would be worthwhile to study these officials in terms of irreconcilable and unrealistic multiple pulls and

---

[9] Louis C. Wyman, Attorney General of New Hampshire, communication to writer, May 15, 1957.

[10] Bromage, State Government and Administration in the United States (New York: Harper & Bros., 1936), p. 255. For some treatments of the office see John A. Farlie and Donald F. Simpson, "Law Departments and Law Officers in the States," State Government, XIV (1941), 237, and G. W. Keeton, "The Office of Attorney General," Juridical Review, LVIII (1946), 107, 217.

[11] Coleman B. Ransone, Jr., The Office of Governor in the United States (University of Alabama: University of Alabama Press, 1956), pp. 332–333.

loyalties that are imposed upon the office holder and that make successful carrying out of his office almost impossible. In this process of illogical demands and loyalties no office can hold a candle to the attorney general, for no other office is within the framework of the federal and state law, yet responsible for the enforcement of local law. No other office is elective and yet advisory, policy-making and yet administrative, legal and yet political, creating institutional rivalry with the man he is supposed to work with and advise.

The attorney general, then, is faced with a definite potential in the office. In one sense it would be theoretically possible for him to utilize his position as an important force in the advancement of a particular program or idea. Yet it is inherent in the multiple stresses and his alternative roles that the attorney general will rather seek to placate all forces and will therefore accommodate himself to these stresses and become a vector rather than a directional force. It is also inherent in the ambiguity of his position, suspended between the importance of the governor and the obscurity of the other state executive officials, that the attorney general will seek to assert some importance and yet will not move decisively and powerfully.

## III

But in his choice between the various roles and in his choice between following the push and pull of particular power relationships or power formations, which will the attorney general choose? In further exploring this problem one suggestion seems appropriate. Interpretive studies have been made of office holders and political pulls and affiliations both in terms of the past and of the present. But students of politics have neglected the future.

Studies of the origins of office holders are common to many schools of thought in political science—Laswellian elite analysis, for example, or Marxist analysis for another. There has also been investigation of present pulls and present affiliations—that is, the study of pressure groups and pressure group activities as well as decision-making generally. In doing so political scientists have in part anticipated and in part followed the findings of sociology and social psychology that indicate strongly the extent to which group affiliations and group identifications influence human beings. These findings are summarized under the rubric of "reference group theory" by many sociologists and social psychologists and indicate that people conceive of themselves primarily in terms of identifications and affiliations with some group or groups. Thus faced with pencil and paper and a question, "Who am I?" individuals quickly answer in terms of some objective characteristics which identify them with some external group. Thus "I am a man, a teacher, an American, an Ohioan." All of this would indicate very sharply that individuals, particularly in our society, conceive of themselves in terms of those groups. It is only after exhausting the telling of those external groups that we come to such internal characteristics as "I am happy, I am kind," and the like.

Now in a mobile society, and this is a mobile society, there exists a special type of group which plays a part in our lives. This encompasses those groups that we are not actually members of but that we wish to belong to, not only in a sense of actually knowing and being conscious of our wish, but also in an unconscious sense. "I look up into the hills from whence cometh my promotion." For these groups an appropriate term might be "aspiration groups."[12] From the standpoint of opinion formation, their importance is that they tend to shape and form an individual's opinion often before he is conscious of the fact that he is striving for a change of his group position.

Ultimately the importance of the aspiration group from the viewpoint of the social scientist is that it could provide an additional tool for analysis.

---

[12] *Reference group theory is summarized in the essay by Robert Merton and Alice Kitt Rossi in* Studies in the Scope and Method of the American Soldier *(Glencoe, Illinois: The Free Press, 1954), and reprinted in the revision of Merton's* Social Theory and Social Structure *(Glencoe, Illinois: The Free Press, 1956). Muzafer Sherif has advanced the theory in a number of important statements, particularly in Sherif and Wilson,* Social Psychology at the Crossroads *(Norman, Oklahoma: University of Oklahoma Press, 1953), and Sherif and Sherif,* An Outline of Social Psychology *(New York: Harper & Bros., 1956). Other important sources include Ralph Turner, "Role Taking, Role Standpoint, and Reference-group Behavior,"* American Journal of Sociology, *LXI (1956), 316, and Shibutani, "Reference Groups as Perspectives,"* American Journal of Sociology, *LX (1955), 562.*

*"Groups" as used here are shared-attitude groups, not concrete organizations, complex psychological manifestations rather than simple membership units. So far as I know, the use of the term "aspiration group" is a neologism, and linkage with career patterns an innovation. Turner's argument for rejecting the importance of such groups seems an over-zealous application of scientific parsimony, particularly in view of the unconscious element involved in their influence. The present suggestion would allow use of the generic term "reference group" and the sub-species "membership group" and "aspiration group." This is independent of the value versus orientation controversy.*

Origin analysis and group pressures tell us what is happening or what has happened, but they do not tell us to any great degree how the individual experiences or interprets either his past experiences or his present pressures. By studying the aspiration group we get in a flash an individual's interpretation of both his past and present, as well as his future. Ideally the aspiration group will provide us with evidence on all of these factors; in practice it will be somewhat less useful as a tool. It is necessary to make the somewhat dangerous assumption that by studying the regular career patterns of a group of individuals we can get a clue as to what these individuals regard as a desirable future and therefore their psychic affiliations for the present. There are many difficulties involved in this approach, as with any other in social science, but perhaps the suggestions here will justify some claims and prove useful.[13]

Career patterns of a group constitute relevant evidence of current thinking in that they are overt manifestations of deeper affiliations not otherwise easily studied. There are several distinguishable patterns of influence that can be assumed to be operative.

An individual in any on-going system will find certain actions generally lead to personal enhancement while other types of activity lead to a loss of effectuality. Thus any system tends to perpetuate within limits a "modal character" (or perhaps several types of personality structures) as a by-product of its own operations. Another force tending toward perpetuation of personality structure and self-identification in any group is to be found in the recruitment pattern. Considerable evidence suggests that social systems recruit individuals who already share attitudes typical of members of the system. Above all, there is a tendency for individuals to adjust their behavior to conform with that of highly esteemed and prestigious groups and individuals.[14]

---

[13] *Difficulties include: (1) the fact that career patterns can shift; (2) we are reduced to interpreting individual motivation in terms of mass activity, which of course is not always reliable in the individual case; (3) there may be a striking divergence between aspiration and achievement.*

[14] *See the essay by Alex Inkeles and Daniel Levinson on modal character in Gardner Lindzey,* Handbook of Social Psychology *(Cambridge: Addison-Wesley Pub. Co., 1954) and, inter alia, T. M. Newcomb,* Personality and Social Change *(New York: The Dryden Press, 1957), and Elihu Katz and Paul Lazarsfeld,* Personal Influence *(Glencoe, Illinois: The Free Press, 1955). A recent study of the suburban voter seems to indicate that the change in voting behavior precedes the change in residence. This would be in accordance with the position presented here.*

So, for example, in *The American Soldier* it was found that enlisted men with attitudes resembling those of officers had a statistically significant greater likelihood of having been promoted when restudied at a later date.[15] It is, of course, difficult to distinguish cause and effect here; the most significant aspect is the recurrence of this type of social behavior rather than the disentanglement of these forces which so often interact. An individual is shaped by what he would like to be; a system tends to recruit and reward individuals who meet important requisites from the standpoint of the system, not only in talents and equipment, but in general outlook and orientation as well.

In line with this reasoning one can consistently assemble data on the career patterns of the attorney general and derive conclusions therefrom. The general pattern that emerges from such data is that primarily the attorney general has been and is a locally oriented official. His aspiration groups are local and his affiliations are local. Those individuals who depart from this pattern tend also to depart from the pattern of politics in their states and thus help confirm the treatment given here.

The data can briefly be set off as follows. First of all, attorneys general do not generally go to Congress. The 1957 Congressional Directory lists only one representative and four senators with previous experience as attorneys general. This compares with two members of the House and 21 members of the Senate who have been governors. It also compares unfavorably with previous state legislator experience. 28 members of the Senate and 147 members of the House have had such state legislative experience. The attorney general's position is inferior as a stepping stone to the lieutenant governor's position—5 members of the House and 5 members of the Senate have had such experience—and is roughly comparable to that of state treasurers or highway commissioners.

We may also say, somewhat surprisingly, that the attorney general does not often move on to federal judiciary, in spite of the rather conspicuous exception at the apex of the federal judiciary. Only one Court of Appeals judge and three district court judges list previous experience as an attorney general in the only authoritative compilation of judicial office holders. Again the governorship was a more likely stepping stone to these posi-

---

See *John Millet and David Pittman*, *"The New Suburban Voter: A Case Study in Electoral Behavior,"* Southwestern Social Science Quarterly, *XXXIX* (1958), 33.

[15] *Samuel Stouffer*, et al., The American Soldier (*Princeton: Princeton University Press, 1949*), *1, 260–264.*

TABLE 1. PREVIOUS GOVERNMENTAL SERVICE LISTED BY MEMBERS OF CONGRESS.

| List Previous Service as: | House | Senate |
|---|---|---|
| Attorney General | 1 | 4 |
| Governor | 2 | 21 |
| Lieutenant Governor | 5 | 5 |
| Assistant Attorney General | 9 | 1 |
| Highway Commissioner | 2 | 1 |
| State Treasurer | 2 | 2 |
| State Legislature | 147 | 28 |

Source: *Congressional Directory*, 1957

In the compilation of this and the ensuing data I was aided by Donna Krislov and Donald Slater, now a Fellow, Department of Politics, Princeton University.

tions, while the lieutenant governorship and such other state executive offices as those of the legal counsel to the governor and the state highway commissioner rivaled the attorney general as positions leading to the judicial chair.

What, then, does happen to the attorney general? The answer is that for many his is a terminal position. Particularly in the South the attorney general will often stay on for many years of service. The attorney general's position may also be terminal in the sense that it is his departure from politics.

TABLE 2. PREVIOUS GOVERNMENTAL SERVICE LISTED BY MEMBERS OF FEDERAL JUDICIARY.

| List Previous Service as: | Court of Appeals | District Court |
|---|---|---|
| Attorney General | 1 | 3 |
| Governor | 1 | 6 |
| Governor's Counsel | 0 | 3 |
| Lieutenant Governor | 0 | 1 |
| State or County Judiciary | 17 | 60 |
| House or Senate | 4 | 16 |
| Federal Judicial Experience | 20 | 2 |

Source: Charles Liebman, ed., *Directory of American Judges*

Many then return to private practice. Another resting place is the state supreme court. Here we have large numbers of former attorneys general. In one-third of the states there is at least one such individual on the bench.

Above all, many aspire and some succeed in obtaining the gubernato-

TABLE 3. SUBSEQUENT ACTIVITIES OF OCCUPANTS OF THE ATTORNEYS GENERAL POSITION.

| | Occupied Office in: | |
| --- | --- | --- |
| | 1927 | 1937 |
| Candidate for Governor (defeated) | 3 | 4 |
| Served as Governor | 1 | 3 |
| Died in office | 1 | 1 |
| Remained in office ten years or more | 3 | 4 |
| State Supreme Court | 7 | 6 |
| Other State Judiciary | 2 | 3 |
| Private practice, corporation law, business | 9 | 5 |
| Federal Legislature | 0 | 3 |

Source: *Who's Who in America*, various years

rial position. And those individuals who go on either to federal legislative or judicial positions are those who have succeeded in reaching the governor's chair. This is reflected in the extraordinary attention paid to the fortunes of those who aspire to the governor's post at annual conferences of the attorneys general, and the perennial bad jokes about "demotion" to the executive mansion.[16]

In summary, then, the attorney general normally looks for promotion on the local level. He therefore identifies himself with local groups and derives his opinions from them. This is reinforced by the fact that his contact with the federal government is normally in the position of defender of the state against the national government. The Association, for example, has reflected a surprisingly local point of view. It has opposed the federal government's actions with regard to invalidation of state subversion laws and labor regulations. It has endorsed the general outline of the Bricker Amendment and was opposed to the Tidelands Oil Decision. It even formally disapproved the action of several states in suing to prevent return of the Tidelands to the states. The most revealing stand was during the war. The Association called for passage of a "Uniform Law to Oppose Federal Encroachments" authorizing the attorneys general to review fed-

[16] *Annual Conference of the National Association of Attorneys General, 1952, pp. 5-6; 1956, p. 60; 1956, p. 25. The National Association of Attorneys General, it should be noted, was organized in 1907, and the Council of State Governments was designated in 1940 as the Secretariat for the Association. It is composed of all Attorneys General of states and territories, as well as the Attorney General of the United States. Annual meetings are held, and the proceedings published. A weekly digest of opinions of the Attorneys General is another major publication.*

TABLE 4. PREVIOUS GOVERNMENTAL EXPERIENCE LISTED BY
MEMBERS OF HIGHEST STATE TRIBUNALS.

| List Previous Service as: | Number |
|---|---|
| Attorney General | 20 |
| Governor | 3 |
| Lieutenant Governor | 3 |
| State or County Judiciary | 57 |
| State Legislative Experience | 54 |
| U.S. House or Senate | 8 |

Source: As in Table 2

TABLE 5. PREVIOUS GOVERNMENTAL EXPERIENCE OF GOVERNORS,
AUGUST 1957.

| | Number |
|---|---|
| Attorney General | 5 |
| Lieutenant Governor | 10 |
| State Treasurer | 2 |
| U.S. House of Representatives | 6 |
| U.S. Senate | 3 |
| State Legislature | 23 |

Sources: *Who's Who in America*, 1956–57; *Current Biography*,
1956; *New York Times*, November 8, 1956, p. 29.

eral legislation and memorialize both state and federal officials when they
found legislation exceeding constitutional bounds. At least one resolution
has been reactivated in the current controversy.[17]

The attorney general tends to see himself as a local popular official.
This is borne out by the frequent recurrence of the term "politician" in
their self-descriptions at the annual conferences. John Ben Sheppard, in
his presidential address in 1956, got great applause with his observation
that "an attorney general has to have the eye of an Indian scout so he can
follow the trail of public opinion, avoid being ambushed along the way,

---

[17] Ibid., *1953, pp. 5 and esp. 34–35; 1954, p. 87; 1955, p. 22; 1956, pp. 4, 5 and
76. See also Abram P. Staples, "The Attorneys General and the Preservation of
Our System of Government," State Government, XVI (1943), 29. Civil Rights,
Hearings before Subcommittee No. 5 of the Committee on the Judiciary, House
of Representatives, 85th Cong., 1st Sess. pp. 1170–77, contains a copy of the remarkable "uniform law." On the perennially defensive attitude of attorneys general
see Walter White, How Far the Promised Land? (New York: Viking Press, 1955),
pp. 38–40.*

and cover his tracks."[18] Supporting this, in response to a questionnaire, the small number who were willing to commit themselves espoused this view of the office. Of eleven, five thought of themselves as elected policy-making officials, three as executive policy-implementing officials, only one preferred the judicial label, and one insisted upon a combination of the elective judicial tag. On the question of federal versus local orientation, the number who committed themselves to a straight-out preference for state law when in conflict with federal law (which seems an extreme legal doctrine) was about equal to the number that were willing to espouse a balance of authority with federal predominance. . . .

Here, then, is the situation in a nutshell. The attorney general lives in a universe of local groups and local opinions. The federal judge looks to national groups and the higher judiciary for approval and promotion. It is no coincidence that those who aspire beyond their state borders are to a greater or lesser degree resistant to local opinion. Neither is it coincidence, but necessity, that forces the attorney general with his local attitudes and aspirations to follow the maxim "vox populi vox Dei." It is, in short, in the light of objective sociological data that we can predict and explain some of the social-psychological influences that lie behind overt political actions.

---

[18] *Annual Conference of the National Association of Attorneys General, 1956,* p. 131.

# SECTION SEVEN

## Legal Ethics

# PROFESSIONAL ETHICS AMONG CRIMINAL LAWYERS*

*Arthur Lewis Wood*

A profession is particularly appropriate for sociological investigation because it manifests a degree of closure from the remainder of society, its purpose is relatively specific, and because there are comparable groups to study within the same cultural area. It is consequently not surprising that the professions are being studied by contemporary sociologists.

What aspects of a profession are of interest to the sociologist? Among topics for investigation are the *careers* of its members, including the relationship between types of training, requirements for admission, paths to advancement and aspirations of participants. Under *organization* the researcher may consider types of membership, leadership, its authoritarian or democratic structure, and the system of rules. Regarding *relationship to society*, its authority and functions, quality of relation to clients, its control

*This report is part of a larger study of the criminal lawyer, "Survey of Criminal Law and Litigation," directed by the writer under the sponsorship of the Survey of the Legal Profession of the American Bar Association. The present article is a revision of a paper given before the seminars on Sociology and the Law, Rutgers University School of Law, Spring, 1956.*

Reprinted by permission of the author and of the publishers from 7 *Social Problems* (1959), 70–83. Footnotes have been numbered to run in sequence throughout the selection.

and encouragement by government, and its position vis-a-vis changing social conditions may be selected for study.[1]

The quality of professional orientation to a calling is the general framework for sociological analysis. This social behavior takes place in a particular kind of system of social relations and norms. The system exists in the public's expectations for conduct, and it is internalized by members of the profession. Its structure includes provision for general and specialized training, admission requirements and standards of competence, as well as norms regulating relations with other members, clients and the public.[2]

These characteristics of a profession may be thought of as a *constructed typology* in the sense that they logically define an extreme theoretical system as an absolute standard with which empirical reality may be compared. Knowing in advance that all professions deviate from the standard, no invidious comparison is intended by the analysis. Ultimate evaluation of deviations must refer to disciplines other than science; the function of social science is to explain deviations.

## THE SIGNIFICANCE OF PROFESSIONAL ETHICS

Notwithstanding a tendency for lay definitions of a profession to emphasize the "learned" nature or special knowledge requirements of a profession, all of the occupations which have aspired to professional status have stressed the importance of *public service* or what is implicit in this term—an ethical code. The practice of law is no exception; in fact its rise from a low level of respectability in American society a century ago is closely associated with the Bar's commitment to such standards (8, Ch. VIII, IX). Although the enunciation of these professional norms comes largely from lawyers in academic positions and in the higher courts of the land—as is inevitable and desirable—by now the *Canons of Professional*

---

[1] *No attempt is made to exhaust possible subjects for investigation. For an outline of topics to be considered in analyzing a profession running to 63 mimeographed pages, see (6).*

[2] *In the "Introduction" to their monumental work A. M. Carr-Saunders and P. A. Wilson state they have no interest in drawing a line between professions and other vocations (3, p. 3). One cannot follow their analysis, however, without arriving at a fairly clear conception of what these authors consider a profession.*

*Ethics* of the American Bar Association (revised from their adoption at the Bar's first meeting in 1908) have been followed in the codes of about 25 state bar associations and more generally function as a "common law" basis for enforcement procedures in courts and grievance committees.[3]

It is hardly an accident of history that the leading professions have directed attention to the subject of ethics. Far from being a matter limited to self-interest and public relations or to unattainable ideals, an ethical code is a functional necessity to the very existence of a profession in contemporary society. This development is clearly related to the growing dependence of the layman on the expert's advice—the former's relative ignorance in regard to an increasing number of fields of rational knowledge in which he is incompetent to judge the quality of service. Not only the fact of the expert's superior knowledge, but the general rationalization of society to the point where the specialist is less often accepted on the authority of charisma than on expectations for practical results constitutes a social pressure for normative standards in professional conduct.

A second reason for professional ethics pertains to the governmental delegation of monopoly status to the practitioners that lends public protection from outside competition and allows for considerable self-regulation of recruitment and conduct standards. A third factor in this connection follows from the non-material nature of professional service and often its confidential character that lessen the effectiveness of a public or market evaluation of the "product." Finally, the fact that so much may be at stake—health, reputation, career or life-long savings—is a matter that requires assurance of integrity among those who practice in these areas.

With reference to the lawyer in particular, his normative obligations are to his client, the court, his colleagues and to the public at large. Conflicts of interest among those loyalties are potentially the rule rather than the exception in his roles as advocate, attorney or counselor, and his own self-interest is presumed to be secondary to any of these obligations. Public confidence in professional conduct is virtually required for the organization of these services.[4]

Despite the fact that the general character of the conflicts in interest are much the same for the criminal and civil law practices, it is widely

---

[3] *For a selection of representative affirmations in regard to the importance of legal ethics, see (4, Ch. III).*

[4] *For an excellent summary of lawyers' obligations see (1, Ch. 2). See also (5).*

held in the profession that the problems of ethics are qualitatively differ-ent. The former's clients, for instance, come largely from low socio-economic strata; fees from those accused of crime are difficult to collect and these clients are less trustworthy. Consequently, a retainer fee is more often demanded. The conflicts of interest in this field of practice are clear: the practitioner's desire for clients versus a taboo on solicitation; right to refuse a case versus obligation of Bar to provide service to all—even to those believed guilty of crime; the client's and his attorney's desire to win a case versus obligation of the latter to aid the court in support of "justice." These same dilemmas are nevertheless quite in evidence throughout the profession: solicitation, refusal of undesirable clients, and pressure to use questionable practices are hardly limited to the criminal field.

## DESIGN OF PROJECT

With a constructed typology of a profession as reference, the plan of this study was to investigate the practice of criminal law in a number of cities using questionnaire and interview techniques. During the summer of 1951 lawyers were interviewed in five different areas of the United States: three large metropolitan cities (one in the deep South and two on the Eastern seaboard) and two smaller cities (in New England and the Middle West). For purposes of research a criminal lawyer was defined as an attorney who devotes ten per cent or more of his practice to criminal law. In two of the larger cities a sample of over 40 per cent was randomly selected from lists of their total populations and virtually all criminal lawyers were included in the three other cities—making a total sample of 101 attorneys in criminal law. From the same cities random samples of civil lawyers (defined as all other practicing lawyers) were interviewed for purposes of comparison—a total of 104.

An interview schedule of some 50 questions, pretested in the field by the research staff and criticized by several legal consultants,[5] covered the

---

[5] *Judge Alexander Holtzoff and Professor Sheldon Glueck were official con-sultants to the project. Professor Willard Hurst also made helpful suggestions for the design of the questionnaire. The research staff included David Caplovitz, Harold R. Katner, Sol Levine, Donald J. Newman and H. Carl Whitman. The author is indebted to these persons for their effort and insights, although the former must take the responsibility for the design of the project and its administration.*

social background characteristics of the respondent, career and nature of his legal practice, community and political activities, relations with clients, and attitudes toward the profession and some of its problems.[6] Each lawyer selected for interviewing received a letter describing the purpose of the study and its sponsorship and one from an officer of the local bar or judge of the county court, followed by a telephone request for an appointment.[7]

The method of analyzing the data is primarily statistical, and includes classification with straight enumeration of responses and a cross-classification of answers. An attempt has been made to avoid reporting mere random occurrences in the comparative analyses by using standard tests for statistical significance.[8] For purposes of classification the following operational definitions have been used: *specialists* in criminal law have 40 per cent or more of their practice in this field; others are *general practitioners*. Also, lawyers with *low incomes* receive less than $10,000 and with *high* incomes receive $10,000 or more net income annually; *nongraduates of college* includes those with no undergraduate experience and those who went to college some years without graduating; and lawyers in the category of *minority religion* includes Catholics and Jews.

The empirical findings and their interpretations reported here relate to one topic of the project: professionalization as it concerns attitudes and activities regarding ethics—matters which constitute the *sine qua non* of professional behavior.

## OPINIONS ON VIOLATIONS OF ETHICAL CODES

For the legal practitioner ethical norms are formally prescribed by the American Bar Association, state and local bar association, legislative statutes and court precedents. To discover the extent to which lawyers violate these regulations would be a difficult if not impossible task for there are

---

[6] *A copy of the questionnaire is available upon request from the author.*

[7] *Each member of the research staff was largely responsible for interviewing in one of the five cities. Approximately five per cent of the original samples of lawyers were not interviewed. The interview took from one to three hours.*

[8] *The five per cent level of significance has been assumed. Chi square, used for this test of statistical significance, must be* at least *3.84 in a 2 × 2 table, or 5.99 in a 2 × 3 table. "Correction for continuity" was used in all 2 × 2 tables.*

problems of including and excluding conduct as unethical and of extensive investigations to determine the validity of accusations. Moreover, the extent of misconduct does not answer the question of its seriousness.

What is perhaps of greater significance, and at the same time easier to obtain by way of interview techniques, are the conceptions which lawyers themselves have of the standards maintained in the profession. While these conceptions are only a crude indication of the frequency of violations, they may have a bearing on the quality of professional morals in regard to these standards. Psychology has demonstrated the importance of one's self-conception in individual behavior; important also are the images of one's group. Conceptions of the standards of conduct are likely to bend the quality of the practitioner's behavior in the direction of these conceptions.

*Most Common Unethical Practices.* Attorneys in criminal law were asked, "Will you describe the most common unethical behavior you know of in the practice of criminal law?" Other attorneys responded to a similar query in regard to civil law. The answers are presented in Table 1.

TABLE 1. OPINIONS ON THE MOST COMMON UNETHICAL BEHAVIOR IN THE PRACTICE OF CIVIL AND CRIMINAL LAW (PERCENTAGES OF RESPONDENTS).*

| Types of Unethical Behavior Mentioned Total respondents | Criminal Lawyers (99) | Civil Lawyers (97) |
|---|---|---|
| Can think of nothing: mentions only trivial matters | 24% | 23% |
| Soliciting clients | 28 | 28 |
| Exploiting clients | 28 | 34 |
| Suborning witnesses | 23 | 18 |
| Unethical re other attorneys | 4 | 10 |
| Activities re bondsmen | 23 | 0 |
| Other matters | 15 | 8 |

* Percentages total more than 100 because some lawyers mention more than one type of unethical behavior (lawyers in first category are not included again).

Keeping in mind that the proportions in this table do not indicate the amount of unethical activity, it is perhaps significant that the responses of the two groups of lawyers parallel one another so closely and that over half of each group mention relatively serious matters of misconduct. Although "soliciting clients" may not be so considered, from 18 to 34 per cent of each group list "exploiting clients" and "suborning witnesses" as the "most common unethical behavior." The latter practices are serious in terms of the public interest, and civil lawyers mention a little more frequently "exploiting clients" than do criminal lawyers in regard to their respective field.

*Surprise on Entering Practice.* A test of the norms maintained by a profession may be had from the experiences of those starting a practice. Law school tends to inculcate ideal norms. How far must these be compromised in adjusting to the realities of the practice? Hence the query: "Were you at all surprised, upon entrance in practice, at seeing how casually professional ethics are sometimes regarded by members of the legal profession?" Appropriate probes distinguished those who were not surprised because there was little unethical behavior from the lawyers who felt they knew what to expect.

Replies to this question, in Table 2, indicate that those in the criminal

TABLE 2. REACTIONS TO ATTITUDES FOUND TOWARD MATTERS OF PROFESSIONAL ETHICS ON ENTERING PRACTICE (PERCENTAGES OF RESPONDENTS).

| Reactions<br>Total respondents | Criminal<br>Lawyers<br>(98) | Civil<br>Lawyers<br>(101) |
|---|---|---|
| Surprise at casual regard for matters of ethics, or "I knew what to expect" | 60% | 44% |
| No surprise, unqualified | 22 | 19 |
| No surprise: "Lawyers not unethical," "Didn't see much of it," or resents implication of question | 18 | 37 |
| Total | 100% | 100% |

Chi square is 8.51.

field more often than lawyers in civil practice are struck by the extent of casual regard for unethical conduct they find when starting the practice of law; or ignoring this difference, approximately half of all lawyers are surprised. Respondents who give affirmative answers to this question were further asked, "What things particularly surprised you?" "Exploiting clients" was definitely the most common reply for both groups of lawyers: 33 per cent of the criminal lawyers and 24 per cent of the civil lawyers among those who admitted surprise.[9] A final probe for these attorneys was used: "How do you feel about such things today?" Here again criminal

---

[9] *Total respondents here were only 52 and 37, respectively.*

lawyers admit somewhat more frequently concern for the problem of ethical conduct (Table 3).

*Conditions Leading to Unethical Conduct.* To the social scientist, behavior is something to be explained. This includes normal, expected behavior and that which deviates from prescribed norms. The attitude that *conditions* of action do affect behavior and some awareness of these factors are probably important prerequisites to effective social control in such a professional group. With this in mind, lawyers were further queried to discover their conceptions of the genesis of unethical behavior: "What is there in the set-up of the court system and the practice of criminal law which makes for whatever unethical behavior may exist?"

TABLE 3. "How Do You Feel About Unethical Behavior Today?"*
(Percentages of respondents).

| Type of Response<br>Total respondents | Criminal<br>Lawyers<br>(64) | Civil<br>Lawyers<br>(61) |
|---|---|---|
| Admits surprise or concern for amount of unethical behavior today | 39% | 31% |
| Denies surprise or concern for amount of unethical behavior today, but admits that some exists | 36 | 28 |
| Denies unethical behavior today; "Lawyers basically honest" | 25 | 41 |
| Total | 100% | 100% |

* Not a statistically significant comparison.

Responses to this were also obtained from civil lawyers with the expectation that they might reflect a different point of view (Table 4).

Of course civil lawyers are less familiar with the practice of criminal law, and consequently more often disclaim any knowledge of these conditions. The most striking fact revealed by these figures is that from one-half to three-fourths of all respondents could think of nothing in particular regarding the practice or the criminal court which could help to explain unethical conduct. It may also be significant that criminal lawyers more often than other attorneys are prone to point out conditions of the criminal court rather than the conditions of the practice as leading to misconduct. Civil lawyers, on the other hand, reverse these proportions to a slight extent by finding the difficulties in the practice of criminal law itself. In contrast with the number of attorneys who admit the existence of

TABLE 4. OPINIONS ON CONDITIONS WHICH LEAD TO UNETHICAL BEHAVIOR
(PERCENTAGES OF RESPONDENTS).

| Opinions on Conditions Re: | Criminal Lawyers | Civil Lawyers |
|---|---|---|
| *Practice of Criminal Law** | | |
| Total respondents** | (86) | (56) |
| "Can think of nothing," "human nature," etc. | 64% | 68% |
| Pressure of client; type of client | 13 | 4 |
| Fees uncertain, inadequate | 8 | 0 |
| Insufficient vigilance by bar | 7 | 13 |
| *Criminal Court*** | | |
| Total respondents** | (86) | (56) |
| "Can think of nothing," "human nature," etc. | 50% | 75% |
| Incompetent personnel | 17 | 13 |
| "Conviction psychology" of D. A. | 8 | 0 |
| Party politics | 7 | 5 |
| Activities of bondsmen | 7 | 2 |

* Other conditions mentioned 1 to 3 times: excessive competition, contacts with police or D. A., inability to counsel client immediately, inadequate training or incompetence, and public officials in practice of law.

** Lawyers insistent that no unethical behavior exists, and in addition many *civil* lawyers of two cities, were not asked this question. Included in percentages are lawyers who mention more than one condition.

*** Other conditions mentioned 1 to 4 times: corruption of personnel, variation in attitudes of judges toward prosecution, collaboration of judge and D. A., jury incompetence, and desire of police to convict.

unethical conduct, the data of this table suggest that relatively few of them have seriously considered the reasons for it; many are apparently indifferent; or there is a tendency to project the blame onto others such as the type of client or the criminal court.

*What Types of Lawyers Hold These Views?* Of particular interest for a sociological analysis are the categories of lawyers who hold these conceptions in regard to unethical conduct. Consequently, the sample of criminal lawyers was divided into categories by degree of specialization, income, amount of college education, and religious background. The most obvious conclusion here is that the attitudes classified in the foregoing tables are widely distributed among criminal lawyers such that there are few statistically significant differences between categories of lawyers, although significant distinctions would no doubt emerge should larger samples be available. Some tentative conclusions can be reported.

Comparing criminal lawyers who did not graduate from college with those who obtained a college degree, there are a number of consistent findings. Thus, the nongraduates mention more unethical practices per respondent and more frequently refer to the serious matter of subornation of witnesses; they more often say that they were surprised on entering practice,[10] say they are concerned for the amount of unethical behavior today, and in this connection mention the serious matter of exploiting clients; and they more often refer to party politics in the court organization as a cause of low ethical standards. By contrast, the college graduates among the criminal lawyers tend to deny that lawyers are unethical; and they find the reasons for nonprofessional behavior in the incompetence of the criminal court personnel.

In part, the above relationships may be based on the higher ethical standards observed by the group of college graduates and possibly their ignorance of the real extent of deviation from professional codes. The author would tend to put more emphasis on an explanation which points to the tendency of certain members of the bar, in this case college graduates, to discount the seriousness of unethical conduct, to identify with the public relations interest of the Bar and therefore to deny in the interview situation as well as to themselves the existence of deviant behavior. Elsewhere in this survey, there is shown to be a category of criminal lawyers who are idealistic, interested in reform, humanitarian, and oriented toward helping the underdog. These lawyers are more often found among the nongraduates of college. The interpretation here is that these attorneys are frank to admit low ethical standards, whereas the experience of a college education is functionally associated with stronger career interests of lawyers who are more likely to overlook lower ethical standards.

The latter explanation finds some support in the fact that the attitudes which admit of unethical behavior are duplicated with about the same frequency among the lawyers with minority religious backgrounds in which group there are fewer college graduates and in which the humanitarian orientation is particularly strong. Moreover, since the degree of specialization in criminal law and income manifest virtually no correlation with the amount of college training, it is not surprising that the former two categories apparently have no consistent relationship with

---

[10] *A statistically significant relationship when categories are reclassified from Table 2.*

attitudes toward matters of ethics. General practitioners and low income attorneys in the criminal practice are extremely ambivalent toward admitting the existence of misconduct—on the one hand insisting lawyers are ethical, but admitting certain serious violations—and the general practitioner is particularly prone to project the blame for any misconduct on weaknesses in the criminal court.

## A CASUAL REGARD FOR PROBLEM OF PROFESSIONAL CONDUCT

In this section we draw from more qualitative information evidence of a tendency to avoid responsibility for unethical behavior.

*The Grievance Committees.* Perhaps indicative of a low esteem for the work of grievance committees is the fact that the chairman of one had had no college training and attended no law school. In any case, descriptive material bearing on the work of two committees is presented below.

In one of the areas we were told that the Bar took rigorous action against open solicitation of clients a few years before this study was made. However, in the presence of the interviewer, a "runner" asked an attorney for more business cards and many comments refer to this problem, for example, referring to "the most common unethical practice":

Hustling cases in jail . . . attorneys blank and blank—see them there all the time. I used to do it myself. Never knew there was anything wrong with it. . . . C78*

*Numbers refer to cases in the sample; "C" to criminal lawyer and "N" to noncriminal lawyer.

Well truthfully I think there's less of it now (solicitation). Now it's undercover. When I first began everyone was using runners, even I. Later they tried to stop it and the majority of us cut it out, but there are still a few who continue to do it. N62

A member of the grievance committee in this jurisdiction admits that soliciting clients is now the most common complaint. The chairman of this committee adds, ". . . . clients feel that the lawyer has overcharged them, but we've never been able to find such a case." Nevertheless, 12 other respondents mention exploiting clients, including excessive fees, unnecessary litigation, or splitting fees, as that which surprised them upon entering practice; and eight attorneys mention this as the most common unethical practice.

A large proportion of interviewees in another jurisdiction insist that they have a "very clean bar" and all of our information indicates that higher standards prevail than in other areas. The following quotations, however, are all from members of this bar, the first from an attorney active in the local organization:

(What surprised you?) General attitude of the Bar. Could be on a much higher level. Lack of interest in Bar itself.

(How do you feel about it today?) Bar should be strong. Lawyers should stick together and keep the standards up. (Describe the most common unethical behavior. . . .) Deplorable grievance system here. Whole Bar system here is weak. (1) Measuring your fee—undercutting the standard—have done this myself; (2) Accepting two fees on a divorce charge—one initially and one from the settlement. N110.

To be really successful, make a lot of money, any lawyer has to cut corners. If you're strictly unethical you'll starve to death. C111

Yes (I was surprised). I was very naive but soon discovered that there were shady deals in law just as in other professions. C88

*Projection of Unethical Conduct.* Criminal and civil lawyers are likely to hold the opposite field of practice responsible for violations of professional ethics. These and other targets are selected for blame in the following excerpts. "What do you think of the practice of criminal law?" Answer from a civil lawyer:

It is the finest profession there is, but you cannot be successful there unless you feed the bondsmen—but law and criminal law much more ethical than medicine. N43

From a criminal lawyer:

Never wanted to be anything but a criminal lawyer. Love trial work. Have a lot of sympathy for my clients. Actually they're a lot more honest than most judges. C85

Projections onto the corporation lawyer, and the corporation lawyer onto the corporations.

(Admits nothing unethical.) Actually I think the criminal lawyer does more for the profession than other types in that it is he who spends so much of his time and energy handling "free" cases which other lawyers feel no responsibility for. It is the criminal lawyer who comes to the aid of those who are being persecuted for political reasons—not the corporation lawyer. C174

About the only thing I can think of is falsifying grounds for divorce. You see in our type of practice—corporate—if there is anything unethical it is the business itself, i.e., the business practices of the corporations the firm represents rather than in the behavior of the lawyers. I think you find that sort of thing (unethical behavior) is more prevalent in courtroom work—the trial lawyer. N169

The partial truth that lies in these accusations also projects blame on others while detracting attention from the shortcomings of one's own group.

*Courtesy Among Lawyers.* Honesty and courtesy of lawyer vis-a-vis lawyer is essential to efficient legal service, nevertheless one is struck by the extent to which respondents tend to interpret questions on professional ethics as exclusively a matter of courtesy among colleagues, better known as professional etiquette. These illustrative comments are replies to the query on surprise concerning a casual regard for ethics.

No, because I haven't witnessed any breach of ethics, they have been damn nice about that. Several times I have made mistakes in court and the other lawyers will later call me up and tell me what I'm doing wrong. . . . C46

I was surprised at the great degree of camaraderie among attorneys. Even though their respective clients are on opposite sides of the issue—are not even talking to each other—they (the lawyers) will get together and try to work out a settlement. Frankly I was amazed at the amiability of lawyers. . . . N162

Some respondents confuse matters of ethics with the problem of unauthorized practice by non-lawyers; and, furthermore, action by grievance committees is often predicated on probable public relations effects rather than protection of the public interests.

### ARE CRIMINAL LAWYERS MORE UNETHICAL?

When civil lawyers are asked whether they ever considered going into criminal law, 26 per cent refer to the low ethical standards of the practice. This opinion is supported by the comparative frequencies with which attorneys in the two fields admit surprise at the casual regard for matters of ethics. Yet respondents in the two branches in approximately equal numbers acknowledge "most common unethical practices" in their respective fields, specify equally serious types of misconduct, and know of cases they believe were not properly handled by grievance committees. Moreover, the greater frequency with which criminal lawyers admit surprise or concern for the problem of ethics may be a function of a less reticent personality type. This interpretation finds some support in the fact that nongraduates of college are most often among those concerned with ethical standards and that criminal lawyers predominate in the category of nongraduates.

In replying to the query on "the most common unethical behavior in the civil practice" there are respondents in this field who question the association of low standards with the criminal practice:

Subornation of perjury, especially in negligence work. You will find as much bad stuff in negligence work as you will find in the field of criminal law. N41

From an attorney who formerly was an inferior court judge:

By and large criminal lawyers are as ethical as any other lawyers. They may be tricky, but they have to be. People don't understand that all the tricks they use are perfectly legitimate. N122

An attorney who used to do some criminal work:

More fraud in civil; on the whole the criminal lawyer is very ethical. N1

"What do you think of the practice of criminal law?":

Necessary, is not more evil than other branches of law. Does not deserve as bad a reputation as it has. N39

With the data at hand one cannot disprove the assumption that the criminal practice has more than its share of violations of professional norms. It would appear reasonable to suspect, however, that the tendency to disregard ethical standards is not so much limited to this field as it is more generally characteristic of some attorneys in certain segments of the bar: the lower status fields of negligence, domestic relations as well as criminal law. The assertion is made with two qualifications: (1) responsibility for the condition must also be shared by other segments of the Bar, including the grievance committees, for their indifference to the condition; and (2) it is largely a matter of personal opinion whether the amount of misconduct which exists is more than should be expected among members of any profession.

# DISCIPLINING MEMBERS OF THE BAR

Compliance with the canons of professional ethics is difficult to maintain in the face of complexities of conflicting interests. Otherwise, it appears that unethical behavior in the legal profession is largely a manifestation of pressures from the commercial world which from example of income level and amoral behavior as well as requests for professional assistance in dishonest activities plague the practitioners in business law. To this observation it should be added that relatively low standards of recruitment in the field of law—including nonaccredited schools, the preceptorial system, etc.—have made the practice not only extremely competitive but also one allowing for many to enter the bar with insufficient financial means to establish a practice. Spokesmen for legal education and admission requirements have put emphasis on law school courses in professional ethics and more rigorous character investigation (1, pp. 241-244; 7, Ch. 3; 2, Ch. 6), though the writer shares the opinion of some of these authorities that experience with what actually takes place in law practice tends to outweigh formal indoctrination. In regard to the criminal lawyer in particular, his close association with the personnel of the criminal court—a court that is usually politically oriented—does not contribute to a professional orientation (9).

The professional organization itself, including its special activities regarding ethical conduct, is also a factor in the discipline of members. We report below on the integration of this aspect of professionalism with various segments of the Bar.

*Activities of Grievance Committees.* Each of the five local bars of this study had within its organization a grievance committee with which complaints against lawyers are filed, investigations of cases are made and action, if any, is initiated. Although lawyers may be sued and prosecuted through ordinary legal channels and judges may possess authority to disbar, the grievance committee is the agency of primary jurisdiction in the enforcement of professional ethics and lawyers themselves are responsible for applying sanctions in cases of misconduct. There are excellent reasons for this common procedure among the various professions. For one thing, it may aid greatly the psychological internalization of professional norms—the most effective means of social control in any group—and for technical reasons lawyers are obviously better qualified to judge cases in their own profession. To carry out the former function, however, the grievance committee must play an active role in all segments of the bar.

We are mainly interested in the extent to which various categories of lawyers participate in the work of these committees. The first of four questions in this area merely asked the respondent whether the local bar has a grievance committee. Four criminal lawyers and two civil lawyers said their bar did not have a grievance committee or they were not sure whether one existed. Table 5 shows the relative degree of participation on grievance committees by each field of practice.

We find the civil lawyers have served on grievance committees over twice as often as criminal lawyers (18 as compared with 7 per cent:

TABLE 5. MEMBERSHIP ON GRIEVANCE COMMITTEES
(PERCENTAGES OF RESPONDENTS).

| Participation<br>Total respondents | Criminal<br>Lawyers<br>(98) | Civil<br>Lawyers<br>(104) |
|---|---|---|
| Served on grievance committees | 7% | 18% |
| Never has served | 93 | 82 |
| Totals | 100% | 100% |

$X^2 = 4.62$). Only seven or eight per cent of the members of either branch of the profession have ever preferred charges on anyone. This proportion appears to be relatively low in terms of the last in this series of questions: "Do you know of any cases where grounds existed for preferring charges, but they were not preferred, or were not pressed, *or* they were not in your judgment properly handled?" About 40 per cent of the lawyers of each field answer this in the affirmative.

Further analysis of the types of lawyers who participate in the activities of grievance committees suggests to us how they function in the organization of the local bar. It may be significant, for instance, that of the six attorneys who were not aware of their grievance committee, all received low incomes and four had not graduated from college. Of greater statistical significance are the characteristics of lawyers who have been members of these committees. Civil lawyers serve more often whatever their income, which discounts the income differential between the groups as the only factor disqualifying criminal lawyers.[11] In both groups, how-

---

[11] *In most cities the average income of criminal lawyers is lower.*

ever, there is a greater preponderance of high income lawyers among the members of grievance committees.[12] In regard to the questions of having preferred charges and knowing of cases not properly handled, income of the lawyer, however, is not related. In fact the only significant variable is religion of the lawyer; Protestant lawyers more often lodge complaints against colleagues.[13]

Participation on grievance committees—serving, preferring charges. or knowing of improper handling—it is interesting to note, is totally unrelated to the attorney's graduation from college. Positively, the committees are dominated by high income civil lawyers, while Protestants, regardless of income or education, seek more action. These latter attorneys are apparently projecting their standards on criminal lawyers and other lower status fields of practice that are more dominated by members of minority religions.

*Participation in Professional Organizations.* Unlike physicians, all lawyers are not members of local societies that are integrated in a national association, and although local bars may nominally include all practitioners, they are often loosely organized activities. Consequently, participation in the special purpose professional associations in legal work is indicative of a lawyer's professional commitment.

Membership of criminal lawyers in the American Bar Association shows that they belong to this group less than half as often as other lawyers, with percentages of 14 and 31, respectively,[14] and further analysis reveals that specialists in criminal law belong to the association even less frequently than other criminal lawyers. There is no relationship between membership and extent of college education, but income is highly associated with belonging to the ABA among both criminal and civil lawyers.[15] That criminal lawyers in general enjoy more modest incomes than

---

[12] *Twenty-three per cent of high income as opposed to only four per cent of low income lawyers participate on grievance committees: statistically significant with a chi square value of 12.21. Controlling for age demonstrates that this factor does not account for the relationship.*

[13] *"Has preferred charges," Protestants 13 per cent against 3 per cent; significant with a chi square value of 5.30. "Knows of cases not properly handled," Protestants 48 per cent against 31 per cent; significant with a chi square of 5.40.*

[14] *A significant relationship; chi square is 7.47.*

[15] *High income, 37 per cent as opposed to low income lawyers, 10 per cent; a significant relation with a chi square value of 16.77. This relationship cannot be accounted for by age.*

their colleagues is only a partial explanation for respondents' comments suggest a more meaningful correlate of nonparticipation. The ABA is accused of discrimination against the Negro or of being a politically conservative group. More generally, however, it is probably the lower status position of criminal lawyers and that the ABA is a high status group which explains their nonparticipation. Criminal lawyers feel they are outsiders and that the ABA has little to offer them professionally.

There are numerous other professional and semiprofessional, local and national, organizations to which lawyers belong: legal fraternities and honorary societies; the American Judicature Society, the American Law Institute and similar national organizations; and all associations in any way related to legal work such as real estate, claims, accounting, insurance, maintenance of law and police work, trial law and legal aid. Respondents from the two branches of the profession were compared on a composite index of professional participation in all types of societies related to law, excluding local bar associations to which lawyers nominally belong.[16]

This comparison shows that attorneys in the criminal practice are likely to remain outside these professional organizations: a majority of 60 per cent compared with 44 per cent of other lawyers belong to none of them; and as we go from inactive to active status as measured by our index, the proportion of civil lawyers becomes greater.[17] Regardless of the subcategory of criminal lawyers a disinterest is shown in professional associations, but among their colleagues in other fields participation is most characteristic of those in higher income brackets.


CONCLUSIONS


Comparative data on professionalism in the practice of criminal law have been presented. In a series of responses to questions concerning

---

[16] *The index differentiated between inactive and active membership and whether the respondent was an officer of the group during the years 1949 to 1951, allowing one point for an inactive membership, two points for an active membership (attends meetings two or more times a year), and three points for holding an office. Each respondent was given a total score based on all memberships in these professional and semiprofessional organizations.*

[17] *In a 2 × 2 table the relation is statistically significant; chi square is 4.74.*

unethical conduct, the conceptions of many lawyers portray the legal profession as exhibiting relatively serious deviations from professional norms. Lawyer-opinions do not limit violations to one segment of the bar, but compromises with standards may be concentrated in the negligence, domestic relations as well as the criminal practice, and indifference to these standards is exhibited by all sections of the bar. Self-images among practitioners are not always flattering, nor are they conducive to maintaining professional standards.

Whether violations of ethical codes are viewed as serious or inconsequential, a meaningful sociological contribution lies in their analysis as manifestations of behavior in a structure of social relations, i.e., the professional institution. Here we have analyzed only one aspect of this system: namely, ineffective integration of certain segments of the bar (primarily practitioners in criminal law and all lawyers having low incomes) with enforcement procedures for maintaining standards and with professional organizations. Whether the better educated lawyers are themselves more strongly committed to professional ethics, we are unable to say. They are, however, apparently more indifferent to unethical practices as they exist and they are not more active either in joining professional organizations or on the grievance committees of the Bar.

Not discussed here are other characteristics of the professional system related to this problem such as the unintegrated role of the solo practitioner and compelling career aspirations which focus on community and political rather than professional activities for advancement. The import of these is a matter of judgment, but they are correlates of deviations from professionalism as seen in a tendency to identify with the interests of clients, toward differential treatment of clients, and toward substituting contacts for technical knowledge in servicing clients.

Shortcomings of the legal practice as a professional system must also be explained in terms of the *conditions* within which it operates. Thus, it has tried to cope with large numbers of upwardly mobile persons and overcrowding; with practitioners unable to achieve reasonable success by diligence and technical knowledge alone. Work for these practitioners neither constitutes a regular clientele able to pay reasonable fees nor even a service which is always technically legal. Moreover, these lawyers practice before lower courts often lacking in professional competence, and in communities where career aspirations are invidiously tied to a stereotype of successful businessmen.

# REFERENCES

1. Blaustein, Albert P., and Charles O. Porter, *The American Lawyer, A Summary of the Survey of the Legal Profession* (Chicago: University of Chicago Press, 1954).
2. Brenner, James E., *Reports of Consultant and the Advisory and Editorial Committee on Bar Examinations and Requirements for Admission to the Bar* (New York: Shepard's Citations, 1952).
3. Carr-Saunders, A. M., and P. A. Wilson, *The Professions* (Oxford: Clarendon Press, 1933).
4. Cheatham, Elliott E., *Cases and Materials on the Legal Profession,* second edition (Brooklyn: The Foundation Press, Inc., 1955).
5. Drinker, Henry S., "Legal Ethics," *The Annals of the American Academy of Political and Social Science,* 297 (January, 1955), 37–45.
6. Merton, Robert K., and William J. Goode, *Professions in Modern Society, The First Cumulative Summary of Seminar Discussion* (Columbia University, February, 1951), Mimeographed.
7. Phillips, Orie L., and Philbrick McCoy, *Conduct of Judges and Lawyers, A Study of Professional Ethics, Discipline and Disbarment* (Los Angeles: Parker and Co., 1952).
8. Pound, Roscoe, *The Lawyer From Antiquity to Modern Times, With Particular Reference to the Development of Bar Associations in the United States* (St. Paul: West Publishing Co., 1953).
9. Wood, Arthur Lewis, "Informal Relations in the Practice of Criminal Law," *The American Journal of Sociology,* LXII (July, 1956), 48–55.

# AN EVALUATION
# OF THE EFFECTIVENESS
# OF SOME CURRICULUM
# INNOVATIONS
# IN LAW SCHOOLS

*Rita James Simon*

[Headnote omitted.]

One important quality which distinguishes the professions from other occupations is that members of a profession are governed by and are expected to internalize a code of values and behavior. The code of a profession defines the ethical standards and prescribes the norms that should govern the professional's relations with clients, colleagues, members of other professions, and other groups in the society. From time to time, under the impetus of internal dissatisfaction or because of complaints from other groups in the society, a profession reevaluates the relevance and intrinsic value of its code and the manner in which neophytes are educated to the principles of the code.

Such a reevaluation occurred about six years ago in the legal profession. A National Council of Legal Clinics was formed through collaboration among the American Bar Association, the Association of American Law Schools, and the National Legal Aid and Defender Association. The

Reprinted by permission of the publishers from 2 *Journal of Applied Behavioral Science* (1966), 219–237. Footnotes have been renumbered to run in sequence throughout the selection.

collaborating agencies decided to reevaluate the extent and quality of the training that law students were receiving on matters relating to professional responsibility. . . .

* * * *

In a report by the Chairman and Executive Director of the National Council of Legal Clinics (Marden & Sacks, 1962), they described their objectives as follows:

Our basic theory is simple. The great virtue of student experience in a legal clinic, working with live clients on live problems, is that it is real. No matter how challenging the words on a page, the voices on a tape, or the images on a screen, they cannot compare with reality. Likewise, participation in a practice trial, moot court argument, or counseling exercise simply is not the same as being in a real courtroom or law office. Whatever may be the deficiencies of the legal clinic, no one will deny its principal virtue—giving students a sense of reality. And, if an experience seems real, the beneficial effects on students are likely to be several.

Students have more interest in the subject matter and are better motivated to learn. They work harder and pay closer attention to what is happening. They tend to learn things at a deeper level and thus to remember them longer. Their prejudices and stereotypes are subject to more intensive attack, and their feelings of concern about perceived injustice and misery are more easily aroused.

If these results can flow from the traditional legal clinic experience, why not attempt to broaden and deepen this teacher device and put it to work in the service of education for professional responsibility? If students "learn by doing," why not let them learn about ethical issues by giving them experience with a prosecutor, public defender, private law office, or bar association grievance committee? If prejudices suffer when they bump up against reality, why not have students encounter social workers and psychiatrists in welfare agencies and mental hospitals where they can work out differences and disagreements which frequently originate in ignorance? If encountering injustice and misery fires the soul of some who see it, why not expose students— many of them from sheltered backgrounds—to slums, prisons, and divorce courts?

Of course, it may not be enough to let students see these things. Mere exposure may breed cynicism, despair, or disgust. Thus, it is often necessary to give students perspective on what they see: the causes of the problem, what is being done about it, the special responsibilities of the legal profession in the area. Hence, a strong classroom element ought to accompany the fieldwork experience.

In 1960, the Council obtained financial support for its proposal and invited law schools to submit applications. . . . Between the fall of 1961 and the spring of 1964 at least ten law schools received grants from the National Council of Legal Clinics to conduct clinical programs in professional responsibility.[1]

Each school that instituted a program in professional responsibility included a plan for evaluating the effectiveness of its program. Since there were wide variations in the particular programs adopted by the different schools, the kinds of evaluations that each school would make independently could not be generalized across schools. The Council, however, was interested in having a general evaluation of the effectiveness of the clinical programs. Consequently, I was asked to devise a scheme for evaluating the effectiveness of the clinical programs in general, irrespective of their particular problem emphasis.

The basic proposition that would be tested by the evaluation was that students who were exposed to a clinical program for an academic year would change their attitudes toward professional responsibility more than students who had no exposure. The *implicit* assumption underlying this proposition was that changes in attitudes would be reliable predictors of future professional behavior. In other words, students who were exposed to programs would behave more responsibly once they were in practice than students who were not exposed.

Much of the research on the effectiveness of inducing change as a result of exposure to experimental stimuli has been limited to changes in subjects' verbal responses. The work of Carl Hovland, Irving Janis, and Harold Kelley (1953) at the Yale Communication Research Program exemplifies this tradition. Our evaluation was modeled after the experiments of Hovland et al. But like the research at Yale, our design had a basic limitation. From the point of view of their impact on the legal profession and on society's image of the legal profession, the clinical programs' success or failure would be determined by how the law students behaved once they were in practice. But the Council could not afford to wait until the students were graduated from law school and had practiced for a couple of years before deciding whether they should continue

---

[1] *At least three other schools also instituted professional responsibility programs but on much smaller scales. These schools will not be included in this report because they were not subject to a uniform evaluation program.*

subsidizing the clinic programs. Thus, practical considerations dictated that the dependent variable in the evaluation must be the attitudes of the law students before and after exposure to the programs.

The first, and possibly the only, problem to be discussed in this paper is: Did the students who were exposed to the programs alter their attitudes toward matters of professional responsibility more than students who were not exposed? If the evaluation shows that they did, then we shall consider a second problem: What assurances can we offer that the changes in attitudes are reliable predictors of future behavior? If we answer the first question negatively, we shall not even speculate about the second.


## RESEARCH DESIGN


For three years, between the fall of 1961 and the spring of 1964, schools of comparable quality and reputation that had not instituted clinical programs in professional responsibility were asked to cooperate in a survey of law students' attitudes toward their profession. The nonprogram schools were matched against schools that had instituted clinical programs by law professors who had no attachment to the program but who had extensive knowledge about the calibre and curricula of different schools. These matched schools became the "control schools" for the evaluation of the effectiveness of the clinical programs.

Questionnaires[2] were distributed to third-year students in "program" and "control" schools at the beginning and again at the end of the school year. . . .

Specifically, the questionnaire was designed to test whether students who were exposed to clinical programs—

---

[2] *Most of the items in the questionnaire were taken from an earlier questionnaire constructed by Jerome Carlin (Center for Law and Society, University of California, Berkeley), Allen Barton (Bureau of Applied Social Research, Columbia University), and Saul Mendlovitz (Rutgers University). The questionnaire was designed to test the sense of justice of law students and practicing lawyers. Carlin, Barton, and Mendlovitz distributed their instrument to third-year law students at Rutgers Law School. Carlin and Barton also used a very similar instrument in their study of The Metropolitan Law Office. Professor Carlin reports the results of these efforts in* [Lawyers' Ethics (*New York: Russell Sage, 1966*)].

1. Learn more about professional responsibility than students who are exposed to the usual methods of teaching professional responsibility.
2. Experience a greater change in attitudes toward professional responsibility.
3. Plan to engage in activities once they go into practice that would demonstrate their concern for professional responsibility.

The chart below describes the overall design.

| PROGRAM SCHOOLS | | | | CONTROL SCHOOLS | | | |
|---|---|---|---|---|---|---|---|
| *1961–1962* | | | | | | | |
| Ohio State* (59) | | | | Wisconsin* (44) | | | |
| *1962–1963* | | | | | | | |
| Ohio State (53) | Illinois (33) | Willamette** (15) | | Wisconsin (46) | Vanderbilt (39) | Willamette (16) | Kansa City (14) |
| *1963–1964* | | | | | | | |
| Ohio State (64) | Illinois (45) | Willamette (24) | Louisville (17) | Wisconsin (45) | Vanderbilt (45) | Willamette (24) | Kansas City (15) |

* The numbers in parentheses represent the number of respondents.
** Half the Willamette third-year class was involved in a clinical program; the other half was not. Students volunteered for the program.

## THE FINDINGS

### Legal Ethics

The questionnaire contained 11 hypothetical problem situations in which matters involving legal ethics had to be decided. The problems focused on the lawyer's relations with clients, with other lawyers, with government agencies, and with other professions. Each respondent was asked to select, from among three or four alternatives, the course of action he would be most likely to follow if he were the attorney in the situation.[3]

---

[3] *The following is one of the problems included in the questionnaire. It is typical of the others.*

*Assume that you are a practicing lawyer, with considerable experience in criminal*

Although the professional responsibility program at one law school might focus on the problem of the relations between lawyers and other professions such as psychiatrists or social workers and the program at another law school might emphasize the lawyer's obligation to his clients, the hypothetical situations were general enough so that students exposed to any kind of professional responsibility program should have become sensitized to the ethical choice.

Each student received a score based on his responses to all 11 items. The highest possible score was 33, the lowest 11. The lower the score, the more ethical the decision. Table 1 describes the mean scores for each law school on the first and second surveys.

Two facts should be noted about the data in Table 1. In each of the years represented, the scores on the first survey among students at program and control schools were very similar. In any one year, the range in scores was never greater than 2.8. The two schools involved were both control schools: Vanderbilt (1962) had a mean score of 19.0, and Kansas City (1962) had a mean score of 21.8. In other words, students at both program and control schools began their third year of law school with about the same amount of ethical concern.

The second fact is that students exposed to a program showed a slight but not significant increase in ethical concern over students who were not exposed to a program. An increase in ethical concern is operationally defined by *lower* scores on the second survey. In 1961–62, the difference in scores on the first and second surveys in the program school was —1.6, and in the control school it was —.8. In 1962–63, the combined mean difference in scores for all the program schools was —1.2, and for all the control schools it was —.3. In 1963–64, the combined mean difference in

---

*law. An admitted Communist asks you to represent him in a case in which he has been charged with advocating the forcible overthrow of your government. He is able to pay you your normal fee. The case is likely to result in considerable newspaper publicity.*

*Which of these actions comes closest to what you would do under these circumstances?*

*1. I would take the case.* ⎯⎯

*2. I would take the case, if I thought the resultant publicity would not harm my career.* ⎯⎯

*3. I would not take the case.* ⎯⎯

*With some modifications, eight of the legal ethics items were adopted from the Sense-of-Justice questionnaire described in footnote [2].*

## Table 1. Mean Score on Legal Ethics Problems by Law School.

| Time of Survey | Program Schools | | | | Control Schools | | | |
|---|---|---|---|---|---|---|---|---|
| | | | | *1961–1962* | | | | |
| | Ohio State | | | | Wisconsin | | | |
| First Survey | 20.9 | | | | 21.0 | | | |
| Second Survey | 19.3 | | | | 20.2 | | | |
| | | | | *1962–1963* | | | | |
| | Ohio State | Illinois | Willamette | | Wisconsin | Vanderbilt | Willamette | Kansas City |
| First Survey | 21.3 | 21.4 | 20.3 | | 20.9 | 19.0 | 20.5 | 21.8 |
| Second Survey | 20.2 | 19.8 | 19.9 | | 20.0 | 19.4 | 20.3 | 22.2 |
| | | | | *1963–1964* | | | | |
| | Ohio State | Illinois | Willamette | Louisville | Wisconsin | Vanderbilt | Willamette | Kansas City |
| First Survey | 20.3 | 19.8 | 18.9 | 20.7 | 20.9 | 19.8 | 19.0 | 19.8 |
| Second Survey | 19.5 | 20.1 | 18.2 | 20.1 | 20.8 | 20.1 | 19.0 | 19.8 |

scores for all program schools was —.4, and for control schools it was +.1. In sum, over a three-year period, there was a consistent but not significant difference in the scores on legal ethics between the program and control students.

### Expected Activity in Community Affairs

The first few years of practice are usually crucial. The young attorney must work hard if he is to build a reputation, obtain clients, perhaps develop a specialty, and find a place in the professional and community hierarchy. The amount of time he plans to devote to public affairs and community problems during this early period should be an important clue as to how successful the professional responsibility program was in socializing his goals.

Every professional responsibility program placed some emphasis on the lawyer's obligation toward deprived groups in the society such as the indigent, the mentally ill, and the politically unpopular. The evaluation tried to determine how successful the programs were in making the law student aware of his obligations and in motivating him toward working with other professions, community agencies, and deprived clients in need of legal services.

This was done by asking the students to anticipate how active they expected to be in the first few years of practice in the following activities:[4]

1. Working with community agencies concerned with hospitals, social work, helping young people, and the like
2. Working for law reform and improvement of legal institutions
3. Handling cases for unpopular clients
4. Working for improvement of local and state governments
5. Handling cases of indigents and mentally ill persons who can pay only nominal fees
6. Working to improve the legal profession's standards of service to the public
7. Trying to influence or participate in making federal policy on economic and social issues
8. Working in defense of civil liberties, civil rights, and rights of workers.

Table 2 describes the responses for each activity by year, time of survey, and school.

TABLE 2. PER CENT OF LAW STUDENTS WHO EXPECT TO BE VERY ACTIVE.

| Items and Program Schools | 1961–62 Survey 1 | 2 | 1962–63 Survey 1 | 2 | 1963–64 Survey 1 | 2 | Items and Control Schools | 1961–62 Survey 1 | 2 | 1962–63 Survey 1 | 2 | 1963–64 Survey 1 | 2 |
|---|---|---|---|---|---|---|---|---|---|---|---|---|---|
| *Working with Community Agencies Concerned with Hospitals, Social Work, and the Like* | | | | | | | | | | | | | |
| Ohio State | 10.3 | 13.6 | 10.6 | 9.4 | 4.7 | 9.3 | Wisconsin | 9.5 | 7.5 | 4.3 | 19.6 | 2.2 | 8.8 |
| Illinois | | | 11.4 | 9.1 | 14.1 | 8.8 | Vanderbilt | | | 23.7 | 12.8 | 15.6 | 8.8 |
| Willamette | | | 12.5 | 6.7 | 13.0 | 16.7 | Willamette | | | 6.3 | 12.5 | 13.0 | 16.7 |
| Louisville | | | | | 29.4 | 5.8 | Kansas City | | | 6.3 | 7.1 | 11.1 | 19.9 |
| *Working for Law Reform and Improvement of Legal Institutions* | | | | | | | | | | | | | |
| Ohio State | 15.5 | 3.4 | 8.5 | 3.8 | 6.3 | 12.5 | Wisconsin | 9.5 | 10.0 | — | 6.5 | 6.5 | 11.1 |
| Illinois | | | 5.7 | 6.1 | 6.3 | 4.4 | Vanderbilt | | | 28.9 | 12.8 | 8.9 | 6.6 |
| Willamette | | | 12.5 | 13.3 | 13.0 | 20.8 | Willamette | | | 6.3 | 12.5 | 13.0 | 4.1 |
| Louisville | | | | | 17.7 | 17.6 | Kansas City | | | 18.8 | — | — | 66.6 |

[4] *All but one of these items were taken from the Sense-of-Justice questionnaire. See footnote* [2].

*Handling Cases for Unpopular Clients*

| Ohio State | 3.5 | 5.1 | 10.6 | 7.5 | 12.5 | 6.2 | Wisconsin | 20.9 | 15.0 | 6.4 | 8.7 | 4.4 | 4.4 |
|---|---|---|---|---|---|---|---|---|---|---|---|---|---|
| Illinois | | | 8.6 | 9.1 | 7.8 | 6.6 | Vanderbilt | 18.4 | 20.5 | | | 6.7 | 4.4 |
| Willamette | | | 12.5 | 13.3 | 13.0 | 12.5 | Willamette | | | 6.3 | 6.3 | 13.0 | 34.1 |
| Louisville | | | | | 23.5 | 5.8 | Kansas City | 12.5 | — | | — | | 6.6 |

*Working for Improvement of Local and State Governments*

| Ohio State | 24.5 | 15.4 | 19.1 | 15.1 | 12.5 | 15.5 | Wisconsin | 34.8 | 25.0 | 14.9 | 17.4 | 21.7 | 15.5 |
|---|---|---|---|---|---|---|---|---|---|---|---|---|---|
| Illinois | | | 17.1 | 21.2 | 18.8 | 13.3 | Vanderbilt | 31.6 | 23.1 | | | 15.6 | 17.7 |
| Willamette | | | 6.3 | 13.3 | 26.1 | 20.8 | Willamette | | | 6.3 | 6.3 | 8.7 | 4.1 |
| Louisville | | | | | 11.8 | 11.7 | Kansas City | 18.8 | — | | | 16.7 | 13.2 |

*Handling Cases of Indigents and Mentally Ill Persons Who Can Pay Only Nominal Fees*

| Ohio State | 17.2 | 5.1 | 10.6 | 11.3 | 17.2 | 9.2 | Wisconsin | 28.5 | 17.5 | 10.6 | 13.0 | 6.5 | 8.8 |
|---|---|---|---|---|---|---|---|---|---|---|---|---|---|
| Illinois | | | 5.7 | 12.1 | 12.5 | 2.2 | Vanderbilt | 28.9 | 17.9 | | | 11.1 | 6.6 |
| Willamette | | | 6.3 | 12.3 | 21.7 | 20.8 | Willamette | | | 18.8 | 12.5 | 13.0 | 8.4 |
| Louisville | | | | | 23.5 | 23.4 | Kansas City | 12.5 | — | | | 16.7 | 19.9 |

*Working To Improve the Legal Profession's Standards of Service to the Public*

| Ohio State | 6.8 | 8.5 | 10.6 | 7.5 | 15.1 | 15.0 | Wisconsin | 23.8 | 12.5 | 14.9 | 20.9 | 8.7 | 17.7 |
|---|---|---|---|---|---|---|---|---|---|---|---|---|---|
| Illinois | | | 5.7 | 6.1 | 6.3 | 8.8 | Vanderbilt | 28.9 | 20.5 | | | 15.6 | 8.8 |
| Willamette | | | 18.8 | 20.0 | 8.7 | 16.7 | Willamette | | | 31.3 | 12.5 | 27.7 | 4.1 |
| Louisville | | | | | 5.9 | 5.8 | Kansas City | 12.5 | — | | | 11.1 | — |

*Trying To Influence or Participate in Making Federal Policy on Economic and Social Issues*

| Ohio State | 24.1 | 15.3 | 12.8 | 15.1 | 17.2 | 10.9 | Wisconsin | 30.9 | 7.5 | 25.5 | 19.6 | 15.2 | 13.3 |
|---|---|---|---|---|---|---|---|---|---|---|---|---|---|
| Illinois | | | 14.3 | 12.1 | 9.4 | 6.6 | Vanderbilt | 18.4 | 10.3 | | | 17.8 | 11.1 |
| Willamette | | | 12.5 | — | 8.7 | 8.5 | Willamette | | | 6.3 | 6.3 | 13.0 | — |
| Louisville | | | | | 29.4 | 5.8 | Kansas City | 6.3 | — | | | 5.6 | — |

*Working in Defense of Civil Liberties, Civil Rights, and Rights of Workers*

| Ohio State | 17.2 | 10.2 | 10.6 | 5.7 | 12.5 | 10.9 | Wisconsin | 21.4 | 12.5 | 8.5 | 8.7 | 4.4 | 4.4 |
|---|---|---|---|---|---|---|---|---|---|---|---|---|---|
| Illinois | | | 14.3 | 12.1 | 14.1 | 11.1 | Vanderbilt | 13.2 | 7.7 | | | 8.9 | 6.6 |
| Willamette | | | 25.0 | 6.7 | 8.7 | 8.5 | Willamette | | | 6.3 | 6.3 | 13.0 | 4.1 |
| Louisville | | | | | 5.9 | 5.8 | Kansas City | 12.5 | — | | | 11.1 | — |

The figures in Table 2 demonstrate that the students who were exposed to the professional responsibility programs did not expect to be any more active in any of the activities than the students who were not exposed. Even in those activities that the programs stressed most (handling cases for unpopular clients, working in defense of civil liberties, representing indigents and mentally ill persons who can pay only nominal fees, and working to improve the legal profession's standards of service to the public), the program students responded no differently from the control students.

The summary figures in Table 3 confirm the detailed results described in Table 2.

The percentages in Table 3 also show that in 13 out of 17 comparisons, the students expect to be less active at the end of their third year than at the beginning of it. This finding indicates that the closer the students

TABLE 3. COMBINED PER CENT VERY ACTIVE.

| Time of Survey | Program Schools | | | | Control Schools | | | |
|---|---|---|---|---|---|---|---|---|
| | | | *1961–1962* | | | | | |
| | Ohio State | | | | Wisconsin | | | |
| First Survey | 14.6 | | | | 22.0 | | | |
| Second Survey | 9.4 | | | | 13.9 | | | |
| | | | *1962–1963* | | | | | |
| | Ohio State | Illinois | Willamette | | Wisconsin | Vanderbilt | Willamette | Kansas City |
| First Survey | 11.7 | 10.4 | 13.3 | | 10.6 | 24.0 | 10.9 | 13.3 |
| Second Survey | 9.4 | 11.0 | 10.8 | | 13.0 | 15.7 | 9.4 | 1.8 |
| | | | *1963–1964* | | | | | |
| | Ohio State | Illinois | Willamette | Louisville | Wisconsin | Vanderbilt | Willamette | Kansas City |
| First Survey | 12.1 | 11.2 | 14.1 | 20.6 | 8.7 | 12.5 | 14.3 | 9.0 |
| Second Survey | 11.1 | 7.7 | 15.7 | 12.4 | 10.5 | 8.8 | 5.7 | 8.3 |

are to leaving law school and entering practice, the less willing they are to devote their time to matters not directly related to building a practice and earning a living. Exposure to programs in professional responsibility had no effect on moderating those goals.

In two basic areas, then, legal ethics and allocation of professional time, there were no significant differences between students who were exposed to programs especially designed toward changing behavior in these areas and students who were exposed to the usual third-year curriculum. In response to the legal ethics problems, there were slight differences in the expected direction between program and control students. On the expected activity items not only were there no observable differences between program and control students, but only a small proportion (no more than 15 per cent) of all the students stated that they expected to be very active in these matters. Among both categories of students, the percentages decreased on the second survey.

### Handling Cases for Special Clients

A primary ingredient in the concept of professionalism is the ability to relate to clients according to universalistic criteria, and not according to personal or particularistic criteria. In other words, the professional is expected to learn that his reactions to a client's mannerisms, dress, speech, or color, his feelings about the problem or act that motivated a client to seek legal advice, his nonprofessional ties or contacts with a client, should not interfere with his ability to serve that client. An admittedly crude measure of the program's success in educating students in this area, but a measure that could be applied to students in different programs, was obtained by comparing program and control students' responses to the following situation.[5]

A client comes to your office with a request to draw up a complicated document of a type involving both careful preliminary research and precise working on its execution. You know that to do a good job in preparing this kind of document you need a careful, impartial analysis, requiring your most clear and dispassionate thought. Assuming all are able to pay your fee, for which of the following might you have some trouble handling the matter well? The clients are:
1. Your mother
2. An individual for whom you have a strong personal dislike
3. A member of a small religious cult of whose beliefs you disapprove
4. A local politician who you know lives mainly on graft
5. A Communist.

---

[5] *This problem was taken from a questionnaire constructed by Wagner Thielens, Research Associate, Bureau of Applied Social Research, Columbia University. Mr. Thielens used his questionnaire to study law students' attitudes toward various aspects of law training and practice. The study was sponsored jointly by Columbia Law School and the Bureau of Applied Social Research.*

We expected that on the second survey students who were exposed to professional responsibility programs would foresee *less* trouble in relating to these clients than students who were not so exposed. Table 4 lists the responses for each client by year, time of survey, and school.

TABLE 4. PER CENT OF LAW STUDENTS WHO ANTICIPATE TROUBLE.

| Items and Program Schools | 1961–62 Survey | | 1962–63 Survey | | 1963–64 Survey | | Items and Control Schools | 1961–62 Survey | | 1962–63 Survey | | 1963–64 Survey | |
|---|---|---|---|---|---|---|---|---|---|---|---|---|---|
| | 1 | 2 | 1 | 2 | 1 | 2 | | 1 | 2 | 1 | 2 | 1 | 2 |
| *Your Mother* | | | | | | | | | | | | | |
| Ohio State | 27.1 | 32.2 | 33.4 | 37.7 | 35.9 | 25.0 | Wisconsin | 25.6 | 27.5 | 50.5 | 50.0 | 34.8 | 40.0 |
| Illinois | | | 42.9 | 33.3 | 42.2 | 44.5 | Vanderbilt | | | 50.0 | 56.4 | 48.9 | 43.4 |
| Willamette | | | 31.2 | 33.3 | 30.4 | 41.7 | Willamette | | | 37.5 | 50.0 | 43.5 | 62.5 |
| Louisville | | | | | 64.7 | 64.8 | Kansas City | | | 68.7 | 50.0 | 50.0 | 46.7 |
| *An Individual for Whom You Have a Strong Personal Dislike* | | | | | | | | | | | | | |
| Ohio State | 56.6 | 64.4 | 61.7 | 62.3 | 64.1 | 64.1 | Wisconsin | 56.0 | 57.5 | 72.3 | 72.0 | 63.0 | 62.3 |
| Illinois | | | 57.1 | 60.6 | 60.9 | 60.0 | Vanderbilt | | | 60.5 | 66.7 | 55.6 | 64.5 |
| Willamette | | | 50.0 | 40.0 | 69.6 | 54.2 | Willamette | | | 56.2 | 68.7 | 73.9 | 54.2 |
| Louisville | | | | | 76.5 | 64.8 | Kansas City | | | 62.5 | 78.6 | 38.9 | 53.4 |
| *A Member of a Small Religious Cult of Whose Beliefs You Disapprove* | | | | | | | | | | | | | |
| Ohio State | 27.5 | 22.0 | 23.4 | 20.8 | 12.5 | 17.2 | Wisconsin | 10.2 | 17.5 | 14.9 | 21.7 | 23.9 | 26.7 |
| Illinois | | | 31.4 | 18.2 | 17.2 | 22.3 | Vanderbilt | | | 23.7 | 25.6 | 28.9 | 20.0 |
| Willamette | | | 31.2 | 26.7 | 17.4 | 20.8 | Willamette | | | 31.2 | 31.2 | 13.6 | 16.7 |
| Louisville | | | | | 35.3 | 23.6 | Kansas City | | | 12.5 | 7.1 | 27.8 | 13.4 |
| *A Local Politician Who You Know Lives Mainly on Graft* | | | | | | | | | | | | | |
| Ohio State | 67.7 | 59.3 | 70.2 | 67.9 | 66.7 | 70.4 | Wisconsin | 53.1 | 57.5 | 70.2 | 71.7 | 68.9 | 71.7 |
| Illinois | | | 62.9 | 63.6 | 64.1 | 68.9 | Vanderbilt | | | 57.9 | 76.9 | 77.8 | 68.9 |
| Willamette | | | 56.2 | 60.0 | 73.9 | 70.8 | Willamette | | | 75.0 | 75.0 | 77.3 | 66.7 |
| Louisville | | | | | 64.7 | 76.5 | Kansas City | | | 50.0 | 64.3 | 55.6 | 46.7 |
| *A Communist* | | | | | | | | | | | | | |
| Ohio State | 67.7 | 50.8 | 51.1 | 54.7 | 50.8 | 50.0 | Wisconsin | 46.3 | 42.5 | 61.7 | 56.5 | 46.7 | 46.7 |
| Illinois | | | 60.0 | 54.5 | 50.0 | 48.9 | Vanderbilt | | | 65.8 | 54.3 | 62.2 | 55.6 |
| Willamette | | | 25.0 | 26.7 | 56.5 | 41.6 | Willamette | | | 56.2 | 62.5 | 45.4 | 54.2 |
| Louisville | | | | | 76.5 | 70.6 | Kansas City | | | 62.5 | 71.4 | 38.9 | 33.4 |

Three findings emerge from the mass of figures in Table 4: (1) There are no significant differences between the responses of the program students and those of the control students. (2) There are only slight shifts in responses between the first and second surveys, and they form no

TABLE 5. COMBINED PER CENT ANTICIPATE TROUBLE BY LAW SCHOOLS.

| Time of Survey | Program Schools | | | | Control Schools | | | |
|---|---|---|---|---|---|---|---|---|
| | | | *1961–1962* | | | | | |
| | Ohio State | | | | Wisconsin | | | |
| First Survey | 49.4 | | | | 34.0 | | | |
| Second Survey | 45.5 | | | | 40.0 | | | |
| | | | *1962–1963* | | | | | |
| | Ohio State | Illinois | Willamette | | Wisconsin | Vanderbilt | Willamette | Kansas City |
| First Survey | 43.5 | 46.7 | 34.4 | | 46.5 | 47.8 | 46.9 | 46.9 |
| Second Survey | 43.5 | 42.4 | 32.2 | | 48.9 | 51.7 | 44.2 | 48.8 |
| | | | *1963–1964* | | | | | |
| | Ohio State | Illinois | Willamette | Louisville | Wisconsin | Vanderbilt | Willamette | Kansas City |
| First Survey | 42.0 | 43.4 | 46.3 | 56.9 | 43.3 | 48.9 | 47.3 | 41.7 |
| Second Survey | 39.6 | 46.0 | 44.4 | 52.0 | 46.0 | 46.7 | 50.0 | 38.9 |

consistent pattern. (3) Among both program and control students the ordering of clients from "most to least troublesome" is identical:

1. A politician who is accused of taking graft
2. An individual for whom one has a strong personal dislike
3. A Communist
4. Your mother
5. A member of a religious cult of which you disapprove.

The ranking, which remained stable for all three years, has a curious order. We find it curious because the categories of people that are first, third, and fifth on the list describe clients toward whom one would be more likely to have an impersonal reaction than the clients who appear second and fourth on the list. The students' responses show that a personal-impersonal distinction was not the criterion they applied. Another criterion which they could have used, but did not, was the degree of controversy that the client would be liable to arouse in the community. Frankly, we do not understand the basis for the rankings and, fortunately, it was not crucial to the evaluation.

When we combined the responses to each client to form a mean per cent, the students in the program schools showed a slightly greater tendency to change their responses in the expected direction (less trouble on the second survey) than did the control students. But the differences between the program and control students were not significant.

The results thus far show that in three important areas of professional responsibility, legal ethics, expected involvement in community and professional activities, and reactions to certain types of clients, the responses of students who participated in clinical programs were not significantly different from the responses of students who simply completed their third year of law school.

### Personality Assessment Scales

Having found no significant differences between program and control students on items directly concerned with legal practice, it would have surprised us if the programs had succeeded in changing students' responses on matters less pertinent to professional practice. For example, the questionnaire contained three personality assessment scales that presumed to measure:[6]

1. Cynicism—a contemptuous belief in man's sincerity of motives or rectitude of conduct, characterized by the conviction that human conduct is suggested or directed by self-interest or self-indulgence
2. Humanitarianism—a regard for the interests of mankind, benevolence, philanthropy
3. Machiavellianism[7]—a conception of human nature as fallible and weak, a lack of affect (i.e., the value of detachment in dealing with people), and the use of expedient procedures in social relations.

---

[6] *Each of these scales was used in studies of other professional groups such as medical students, social workers, and nurses and was found to correlate with attitudes on professional ethics. The studies were called to the author's attention by Allen Barton. See Eron (1955a, 1955b); Eron & Redmount (1957); Christie & Merton (1958).*

[7] *This definition expresses the meaning of the items included in the "Machiavellian" scale. It was not expected that this definition would coincide with the traditional meaning of Machiavellianism.*

Table 6 describes the program and control students' scores on each scale.

The results were not surprising. The students exposed to clinical programs did not become less cynical, less machiavellian, or more humanitarian. As anticipated, in most schools, the responses to the personality measures changed even less than did the responses to the items pertaining to legal practice. We can at least take comfort in the consistency of the results.

TABLE 6. SCORES ON PERSONALITY MEASURES BY LAW SCHOOLS.

| Personality Scales and Program Schools | 1961–62 Survey | | 1962–63 Survey | | 1963–64 Survey | | Personality Scales and Control Schools | 1961–62 Survey | | 1962–63 Survey | | 1963–64 Survey | |
|---|---|---|---|---|---|---|---|---|---|---|---|---|---|
| | 1 | 2 | 1 | 2 | 1 | 2 | | 1 | 2 | 1 | 2 | 1 | 2 |
| Cynicism | | | | | | | | | | | | | |
| Ohio State | 9.1 | 8.6 | 9.5 | 9.0 | 8.4 | 8.6 | Wisconsin | 8.9 | 9.5 | 8.1 | 8.8 | 9.1 | 9.8 |
| Illinois | | | 9.5 | 9.5 | 8.4 | 6.8 | Vanderbilt | | | 10.0 | 9.7 | 9.6 | 9.9 |
| Willamette | | | 7.7 | 6.5 | 8.9 | 9.3 | Willamette | | | 9.6 | 6.9 | 8.5 | 8.8 |
| Louisville | | | | | 10 6 | 10.1 | Kansas City | | | 8.1 | 8.3 | 8.3 | 9.3 |
| Humanitarianism | | | | | | | | | | | | | |
| Ohio State | 4.7 | 4.8 | 4.9 | 4.6 | 5.0 | 4.7 | Wisconsin | 4.4 | 4.5 | 4.7 | 5.0 | 4.8 | 4.4 |
| Illinois | | | 5.1 | 4.3 | 4.4 | 4.6 | Vanderbilt | | | 4.2 | 4.7 | 5.2 | 5.4 |
| Willamette | | | 4.6 | 5.3 | 4.9 | 4.8 | Willamette | | | 4.7 | 4.7 | 4.9 | 4.8 |
| Louisville | | | | | 6.1 | 5.7 | Kansas City | | | 5.1 | 5.9 | 5.1 | 5.6 |
| Machiavellianism | | | | | | | | | | | | | |
| Ohio State | 4.9 | 4.6 | 4.9 | 4.7 | 4.8 | 4.4 | Wisconsin | 5.0 | 4.2 | 4.5 | 5.3 | 5.0 | 5.1 |
| Illinois | | | 4.8 | 4.5 | 4.0 | 4.6 | Vanderbilt | | | 4.1 | 4.2 | 5.1 | 5.9 |
| Willamette | | | 4.4 | 3.8 | 4.3 | 4.2 | Willamette | | | 4.3 | 4.1 | 4.0 | 5.7 |
| Louisville | | | | | 4.8 | 4.4 | Kansas City | | | 4.2 | 4.0 | 4.9 | 4.4 |

## DISCUSSION

There are two possible explanations for the lack of significant differences between the students exposed to clinical programs and the students in the control schools. One possibility is that the questionnaire failed to pick up differences that in fact occurred in the attitudes of the students exposed to the clinical programs. The other is that the programs did not produce significant effects. Neither explanation can be answered conclusively by looking at the data. At best, after examining the data we can only speculate as to why there were no differences.

In defense of the instrument, we emphasize again that every item pertaining to legal practice—the hypothetical problem situations, the areas of expected activity, the relations with special types of clients—was written or reviewed by law-trained persons who were closely connected with the objectives of the clinical programs.[8] The personality assessment items were adopted, with only slight modifications, from other evaluations studies of students in professional schools. For these reasons, primarily, we doubt that the lack of differences can be attributed to weaknesses in the questionnaire.

The second possibility is that the programs did not succeed in changing students' attitudes toward professional responsibility. If true, this is a much more discomfiting explanation than the first. Obviously, it is more important that the programs in fact produce change than that the evaluation measure the change. As educators, we place great value on our ability to teach and to induce change, or alterations, in students' outlooks, values, and behaviors. But, here we find an instance in which basic innovations were introduced into a curriculum, innovations that lasted an entire academic year and involved students in a variety of out-of-classroom activities. Yet, measured by the students' verbal responses, these innovations had little effect. Why?

Writing now, even with the knowledge of hindsight, we are puzzled about the lack of significant results. We offer a possible explanation, but before doing so we emphasize that it does not fully satisfy us. The likelihood of innovations in law schools producing significant effects on the students' sense of professional responsibility would be enhanced if comparable changes were also instituted simultaneously in the real world, namely, among the profession's practitioners. As long as the distribution of rewards (financial, honorific, and meritorious) in the profession is not directly related to the objectives of the clinical programs, students will have little motivation to adapt their attitude or their behavior to the goals advocated by the clinical programs. After all, the time they are students in

---

[8] *That is, they were persons connected with the general objectives of the clinical programs. None of our consultants was involved in planning any of the specific programs. Thus, none of the items was tailor-made to anticipate the results of a specific program.*

a professional school is relatively brief compared with the time they will practice as professionals. When the behavior of the profession's practitioners is at odds with the values advocated in the law schools, the likelihood that a student will succeed in the real world is greater if he adheres to the behavior of the practitioners. If the student observes that the goals of the clinical programs are incompatible with the distribution of power, prestige, and financial rewards in the profession, the more realistic and the more profession-oriented he is, the more likely he is to cast his lot with the practices of the profession.

This argument assumes that students have knowledge about the workings of their profession. It assumes that students know the kinds of practice that are most lucrative, the law firms that are most prestigeful, and the activities that are most likely to gain them professional recognition. When one considers the market knowledge of the average Ph.D. student in the social sciences, I think one generally finds that he can name the universities that have the best department in his field; that he can estimate with fairly high accuracy the going salary for different professorial ranks; and that he can indicate the activities that are the most rewarded by his profession. By analogy, we assume that students in the professional schools have comparable knowledge about their professional marketplace. It is this knowledge that makes them reluctant to internalize the goals advocated by the clinical program.[9]

We conclude by suggesting that innovations in the curricula of professional schools, no matter how radical, are not likely to seriously alter students' outlooks unless comparable innovations are going on in the profession. Students must be able to see that they will be rewarded in the real world for adopting the behaviors advocated in the programs.

## REFERENCES

Christie, R., & Merton, R. K. Procedure for the sociological study of the values climate of medical school. *J. med. Educ.,* October 1958, *33,* 125–153.

---

[9] *We are not suggesting that the students' experiences in legal clinics increase their adherence to the norms of professional practice. We are saying that by the time the students are in their third year of law school, there is little likelihood that their values and attitudes toward their profession can be significantly changed.*

Eron, L. D. Effect of medical education on medical students' attitudes, *J. med. Educ.*, 1955, *30*, 459–466. (a)

Eron, L. D. Effect of nursing education on attitudes. *Nurs. Res.*, 1955, *4*, 24–27. (b)

Eron, L. D., & Redmount, R. S. Effect of legal education on attitudes, *J. leg. Educ.*, 1957, *9*, 431–443.

Hovland, C. I., Janis, I. L., & Kelley, H. H. *Communication and persuasion.* New Haven, Conn.: Yale Univer. Press, 1953.

Marden, O. S., & Sacks, H. R. *Education for professional responsibility in the law school.* Chicago, Ill.: The National Council of Legal Clinics, American Bar Ass., 1962. P. 2.

# ACCOUNT OF A FIELD STUDY
# IN A RURAL AREA
# OF THE REPRESENTATION
# OF INDIGENTS
# ACCUSED OF CRIME

*Bertram F. Willcox*
*and Edward J. Bloustein*

The effective defense of poor persons accused of crime is a major social problem. Most of the discussion of it has been focused upon the great metropolitan areas, with their crowded courts and overworked officials. In the present article, by contrast, we report on the same problem in a more rural setting: Tompkins County, a farm community of central New York, and Ithaca, the small city which is the seat of Tompkins County.

For awareness of the problem today, much is owed to a case decided in the United States Supreme Court seventeen years ago, *Powell v. Alabama*.[1] Nine teen-age negro youths had been brought to trial in Alabama for the rape of two white women. The youths stood before a community explosive with rage and vengeance to plead not guilty. The court's solicitude for justice had been expressed by making a half-hearted

---

[1] *287 U.S. 45 (1932)*.

Reprinted by permission of the authors and of the publishers from 56 *Columbia Law Review* (1959), 551–574. Footnotes have been renumbered to run in sequence throughout the selection. The authors' appendixes have been omitted, as have references to them.

appointment of all the members of the local bar to act in their behalf on the arraignment. This appointment had been so casual that no lawyer felt himself responsible for preparing the case for trial after arraignment; and no one did prepare it. On the morning of the trial, a lawyer from Tennessee, interested but not retained, agreed to assist any local counsel the court might assign. But the judge said he was reluctant to assign counsel if the Tennessee lawyer was to appear. After a confused colloquy, one local lawyer agreed to help the Tennessee lawyer. It is not surprising that the defense was perfunctory and that eight of the nine youths were quickly found guilty and sentenced to death.

The United States Supreme Court reversed the convictions. The Court's holding, under the due process clause of the fourteenth amendment, was explicitly narrow:

[I]n a capital case, where the defendant is unable to employ counsel, and is incapable adequately of making his own defense because of ignorance, feeble mindedness, illiteracy, or the like, it is the duty of the court, whether requested or not, to assign counsel for him as a necessary requisite of due process of law; and that duty is not discharged by an assignment at such a time or under such circumstances as to preclude the giving of effective aid in the preparation and trial of the case.[2]

But the effects of the decision, like those of many other germinal cases, have reached out far beyond the confines of this holding; the case has served not merely as a precedent on its own facts but also, to some extent, as a moral inspiration and touchstone.

In speaking for the Court, Mr. Justice Sutherland gave this classic emphasis to the importance of counsel for the defense:

The right to be heard would be, in many cases, of little avail if it did not comprehend the right to be heard by counsel. Even the intelligent and educated layman has small and sometimes no skill in the science of law. If charged with crime, he is incapable, generally, of determining for himself whether the indictment is good or bad. He is unfamiliar with the rules of evidence. Left without the aid of counsel he may be put on trial without a proper charge, and convicted upon incompetent evidence, or evidence irrelevant to the issue or otherwise inadmissible. He lacks both the skill and knowledge adequately to prepare his defense, even though he have a perfect one. He requires the guiding hand of counsel at every step in the proceedings against him. Without it, though he be not guilty, he faces the danger of conviction because he does not know how to establish his innocence. If that be

---

[2] Id. *at 71.*

true of men of intelligence, how much more true is it of the ignorant and illiterate, or those of feeble intellect.[3]

These sentences have often been quoted, but they cannot be quoted too often. This vivid and succinct statement, spoken in the context of a holding that due process was violated where Alabama made an ineffectual assignment of defense counsel, is now a part of the enlightened judicial conscience. Again and again courts test provisions for the defense of indigent defendants against the moral of *Powell v. Alabama:* that effective defense counsel are indispensable to justice. In morals, if not always in law, *Powell v. Alabama* clothes a defendant's bare right to counsel with the requirement that if the defendant is poor, counsel must be provided for him, and that such provision must be effective.

Of course, the usual case of injustice where an indigent person is ineffectively represented, or is not represented at all, has none of the drama of *Powell v. Alabama.* And, unfortunately—human emotion being what it is—run of the mill injustice arouses less sense of outrage than does dramatic injustice. But no serious concern for our democratic faith can neglect the routine case in favor of the dramatic one. If day by day "little

---

[3] Id. *at 68–69. It is interesting to contrast Mr. Justice Sutherland's remarks with those of an eighteenth century writer, 2* HAWKINS, PLEAS OF THE CROWN *554– 55 (8th ed. 1824):*

> . . . *if it be considered, that generally every one of common understanding may as properly speak to a matter of fact, as if he were the best lawyer; and that it requires no manner of skill to make a plain and honest defence, which in cases of this kind is always the best; the simplicity, the innocence, the artless and the ingenuous behavior of one whose conscience acquits him, having something in it more moving and convincing than the highest eloquence of persons speaking in a cause not their own. And if it be further considered that it is the duty of the court to be indifferent between the king and prisoner, and to see that the indictment be good in law, and the proceedings regular, and the evidence legal, and such as fully proves the point in issue, there seems no great reason to fear but that generally speaking, the innocent, for whose safety alone the law is concerned, have rather an advantage than a prejudice in having the court their only counsel. Whereas, on the other side, the very speech, gesture, countenance, and manner of defence of those who are guilty, when they speak for themselves, may often help to disclose the truth, which probably would not so well be discovered from the artificial defence of others speaking for them.*

*For the reader likely to be lulled by this language into a comforting belief that innocence will always triumph, good antidotes, a quarter century apart, are the classic* BORCHARD, CONVICTING THE INNOCENT *(1932) and* FRANK & FRANK, NOT GUILTY *(1957).*

men," men whose circumstances of life and character—whose very violations of the law—are ordinary, are sentenced to prison for a few months or a few years without effective help from counsel, can we pretend to respect individual liberty? That is what our study and this article are about.

In the United States, at present, the availability of counsel to an indigent criminal defendant tends to vary with the court he is in and the crime with which he is charged.[4] Some jurisdictions do not go beyond the precise holding in *Powell v. Alabama;* these make assignment of counsel mandatory only when a death penalty is at issue. Other jurisdictions provide for counsel in prosecutions for a felony only. Still others provide for them in prosecutions for a misdemeanor or for even a lesser criminal offense.

*Powell v. Alabama* makes it clear that a merely formal appointment of counsel must be distinguished from effective representation by counsel. Due process is not satisfied by a bare legal right to retain counsel if exercise of the right is impossible because of poverty.[5] Similarly, due process is not satisfied by any formal appearance of counsel who are unable or unwilling, for any reason, to conduct an effective defense. It is the legal reality, not the legal appearance, that counts.

Thus, it is not enough in evaluating the defense of indigents to say, for example, that a jurisdiction makes the appearance of counsel mandatory in felony cases. The realistic test, and in some cases the legal test, is whether the appearance is effective. Was counsel able and willing to fulfill the minimum requirements of representation of a criminal defendant?

---

[4] *For tabulations of the existing statutory provisions regarding the provision of council to indigents, see* BEANEY, THE RIGHT TO COUNSEL IN AMERICAN COURTS *237–39 (1955);* E. BROWNELL, LEGAL AID IN THE UNITED STATES *300–06 (1951);* SPECIAL COMM. TO STUDY DEFENDER SYSTEMS, EQUAL JUSTICE FOR THE ACCUSED *app. (1959). A bibliography on defense of indigents, prepared in the early stages of this study, and later supplemented by some additional items supplied by the courtesy of The Institute of Judicial Administration, is on file in the libraries of Columbia and Cornell law schools.*

[5] *This seems to have been the position of both the majority and the minority in* Powell v. Alabama; *at least the minority did not take issue with the majority's tacit assumption of this position. More recently the Court has divided on a similar issue, the majority holding that when the right to appeal has been provided by a state, the fourteenth amendment is not satisfied if the appeal is impossible because of poverty.* Griffin v. Illinois, 351 U.S. 12 (1956); *see Willcox & Bloustein,* The Griffin Case— Poverty and the Fourteenth Amendment, *43* CORNELL L.Q. *1 (1957).*

The answer depends to a large extent on the system by which counsel is provided.

In American courts poor persons charged with crime may be represented by attorneys in private practice or by attorneys who are paid a salary for such representation. The latter are called defenders, public defenders when their salary is paid by a governmental body, private defenders when it comes from some private source such as a legal aid society. The attorneys in private practice who serve occasionally are assigned by the courts, either haphazardly or from a rotating roster. In some jurisdictions their services will in the ordinary case be compensated out of public funds; in most jurisdictions, however, they will be so compensated only in an unusually serious case.

The assigned counsel system is used in all but a few jurisdictions.[6] The system varies somewhat from state to state on such matters as whether the assignment is mandatory or discretionary, at whose instance it is made, the type of case in which it will be made, the time at which it will be made, the use of a rotating roster of attorneys, and the compensation and expenses provided.[7] One major similarity in the various methods of assignment, however, enables us to make some generalizations about the system of assignment as a whole. This similarity lies in the nature of the basic relation between the indigent defendant, his counsel, and the court. The assigned counsel serves his client as an officer of the court at the court's request, and usually without adequate remuneration. He is motivated by a sense of obligation to the court, to the indigent client, and to society in general. The adequacy of the assignment system must therefore depend, fundamentally, on the strength of the assigned lawyer's sense of

---

[6] For lists of the limited number of defender offices in the United States, see E. BROWNELL, op. cit. supra note 4, at 130–31; SPECIAL COMM. TO STUDY DEFENDER SYSTEMS, op. cit. supra note 4, passim and app.

[7] E. BROWNELL, op. cit. supra note 4, at 300–06, and SPECIAL COMM. TO STUDY DEFENDER SYSTEMS, op. cit. supra note 4, app., categorize the assignment provisions of all the states on the basis of the types of crime for which an assignment is made, whether it is mandatory or discretionary, at whose instance it is made, when it is made, and what compensation is provided. For extended discussion of the use of rotating assignments see Hartshorne, "Equal Justice for All": The Bar and the Indigent Criminal Defendant, 37 A.B.A.J. 104 (1951) (in Essex County, New Jersey); Trebach, The Indigent Defendant, 11 RUTGERS L. REV. 625, 636 (1957) (New Jersey); Webster, Defense of the Indigent in the Erie Bar Plan, 24 N.Y.B.A. BULL. 84 (1952) (Erie County, New York).

social responsibility as measured against the demands on his time and effort which the assignment makes.

A number of students of legal aid have evaluated the system of assigned counsel. From the classic treatment of Reginald Heber Smith[8] to the recent study of Emery A. Brownell,[9] the uncontradicted judgment is that the system, on the whole, usually fails in several ways to do what it is intended to do.[10] And yet the system of assigned counsel persists, and there seems to be little impetus for drastic change.

It is hard to understand this persistence of a legal procedure which has been disapproved over so long a time by so many competent critics. It will hardly do to cite social inertia as the reason, for social inertia does not always succeed in blocking change. The question always is why such inertia is or is not effective in the given instance.

We suggest that an important reason why the system of assigned counsel has not been improved is that most of the adverse criticism focuses on its failures in metropolitan areas. The accepted view is that it works well in rural areas.[11] This statement has, in fact, come to be taken as a

---

[8] SMITH, JUSTICE AND THE POOR (3d ed. 1924).

[9] E. BROWNELL, op. cit. supra note 4.

[10] One of the strongest arguments against the assignment system was made by Judge Augustus N. Hand to the Judicial Conference of the United States in 1944. Judge Hand said:

It is clear that when cases of poor persons needing defense become numerous and occur repeatedly, the voluntary and uncompensated services of counsel are not an adequate means of providing representation. To call on lawyers constantly for unpaid service is unfair to them and any attempt to do so is almost bound to break down after a time. To distribute such assignments among a large number of attorneys in order to reduce the burden upon anyone, is to entrust the representation of the defendant to attorneys who in many cases are not proficient in criminal trials, whatever their general ability, and who for one reason or another cannot be depended upon for an adequate defense. Too often under such circumstances the representation becomes little more than a form.

COMM. TO CONSIDER THE ADEQUACY OF EXISTING PROVISIONS FOR THE PROTECTION OF THE RIGHTS OF INDIGENT LITIGANTS IN THE FEDERAL COURTS, REPORT, quoted in E. BROWNELL, op. cit. supra note 4, at 138-39.

Some other authorities who regard the assignment system as a failure are Hearings on H.R. 398 and H.R. 2091 Before Subcommittee No. 4 of the House Committee on the Judiciary, 83d Cong., 2d Sess., ser. 13, at 19-25 ( 1954) (testimony of H. Brownell), and Callagy, Legal Aid in Criminal Cases, 42 J. CRIM. L., C. & P.S. 589 (1952). See also SPECIAL COMM. TO STUDY DEFENDER SYSTEMS, op. cit. supra note 4, at 63-68.

[11] For instance, E. BROWNELL, op. cit. supra note 4, at 136 says:

truism. And when it is coupled with the tendency of many Americans, even well educated ones, to think of the United States as still mainly rural, it may help to explain the lack of general concern over the system of assigned counsel and the feeling that its failure is essentially a problem for a few metropolitan areas rather than for the nation as a whole. If this diagnosis is correct, a study of the operation of the assignment system in a rural area should serve as a critical test, since all agree that rural areas see the system at its best. If it works poorly there, it must work poorly everywhere.

A study of the assignment system in a rural area also serves another purpose. It directs attention to that segment of American society to which Americans are traditionally responsive. Our cities are rather new arrivals, as contrasted with our towns. When something is wrong with the cities "somebody ought to do something about it," but when something goes wrong in the towns "something has to be done."

## I. THE STUDY

Our survey was designed, as we have said, to describe and evaluate the system of assigned counsel as it operates in Tompkins County and in Ithaca, the county seat.[12]

---

*In the period of our history when cities were much smaller and more isolated, the system of assigned counsel functioned well. The relative stability of most communities was conducive to wider personal relationships and personal responsibilities. More often than not the defendant was known to the counsel assigned him.*

*And* BEANEY, *op. cit. supra note 4, at 213, states that*

*. . . in rural or small-town communities the concern of the bar and the people has been more evident, and a real effort to provide counsel has been the rule. This has resulted either from the volunteering by attorneys, the creation of an informal "system of appointment" by the small local bar, or the actions of judges whose contacts with the bar are more intimate and whose powers are in many ways more persuasive than those of their city colleagues.*

[12] *Tompkins County is a rough square lying in the central part of New York State. It is about twenty miles on a side. Its nine towns are also rough squares, arranged like the central part of a shuffleboard. Ithaca, the only city in the county, lies in the town that forms the central square. It has some 30,000 people; the whole county has some 60,000. In addition to the city, Tompkins County contains five incorporated villages.*

*The county court house, where the supreme court, the county court, and the*

Our investigation was carried out by means of conferences, observation, study of court records, and questionnaires. It was conducted mostly in the last three months of 1956 and the first three months of 1957. We talked with judges and justices, lawyers, prosecutors, and other officials whose work had given them knowledge of how the system of assigned counsel actually functioned. (These persons will sometimes be referred to as "our consultants.") We did not talk with police officers, either state or local. The statements about the role of police officers in criminal enforcement, therefore, like other evidence coming from our consultants, are set forth as our consultants' opinions and not as established fact. They are relevant because they bear upon what the local practicing lawyers deem to be the difficulties confronting an indigent accused of crime. From time to time we observed the proceedings of the city court.

After we thought we had learned what questions to ask, we sent out our questionnaire to 57 members of the local bar. We asked for anonymous answers. Many of our consultants, of course, were members of this group of 57, although the judges, the probation officer, and some other officials were not.

Of the 57 lawyers, 44, or 77 per cent, responded. These responses were received and tabulated in April and May 1957. The following fall we decided to send similar questionnaires to the bars of two nearby counties, where the conditions might be expected to be similar, to try to get some light on whether Tompkins County was fairly typical. These counties were Cortland County, adjoining Tompkins on the east, and Tioga County, adjoining it on the south. Of 30 lawyers in Tioga County to whom questionnaires were sent, 21, or 70 per cent, sent answers. Of 34 lawyers in Cortland County receiving questionnaires, 22, or 65 per cent, sent answers. Thus, of all 121 questionnaires sent out, 87, or 72 per cent,

_children's court sit, is located near the center of Ithaca. The city court is in a nearby building. Within a block, too, are buildings housing the city and county jails._

_Elsewhere the county is generally rural in character, consisting of rolling farm lands and some woodlands. A spider's web of roads centering in Ithaca makes it possible to reach most parts of the county by car from any other part within a couple of hours. Buses furnish an additional means of transportation. The times required for all kinds of travel may be increased in the spring by potholes in the roads, and may approach infinity during and after winter storms. But in ordinary times the county seat and its courts and officials are easily accessible to the whole county._

were answered.[13] While the numbers are not large, because these are small communities, the percentage of answers returned and the interest thus shown in the problem were gratifying. We owe much to the lawyers and bar associations of these three counties.

There is no record, in the courts or elsewhere, of the number or proportion of the persons accused of crime in Tompkins County who cannot afford to pay for counsel. Estimates vary from 50 per cent to 80 per cent. The highest estimate was given by the County Probation Officer, who has recently retired after many years of service. These estimates, or guesses, refer to the persons appearing before all the courts in the county. Considering all of them, we believe that it is reasonable to assume that more than half of the persons accused of crime are too poor to hire a lawyer.[14] If so, the importance of the problem needs no underscoring.

## A. The "Lower Courts"

"Lower courts" is the term usually applied to the Ithaca City Court and to the justice courts presided over by the justices of the peace of the towns and by the police justices of the villages. The judge of one of these lower courts is normally the first judicial officer to see a person accused of a crime. (For brevity the justices of the peace and the police justices will be called "justices.")

If the charge is of an indictable offense, the function of the city judge, or the justice, before whom the accused is first brought, is to decide whether there is enough evidence to hold him for the grand jury. For the making of this decision the city judge or the justice must hold a preliminary hearing on the People's case, unless that hearing is waived by the accused. If it is decided—as it is in most cases—that there is enough

---

[13] *For the form of questionnaire used and a tabulation of the results in each of the three counties, see appendix I [not included here].*

[14] *For estimates which have been drawn mainly from metropolitan areas, see 1951* LEGAL AID SOC'Y OF N.Y. ANN. REP. *10 (in 1951 the criminal courts branch of the Society handled 62.6% of the cases in the court of general sessions; 45.4% of those in the court of special sessions, exclusive of gambling cases; 41.2% in the felony part of the magistrates' courts; 76.6% in the youth term part of the magistrates' courts; and 9.8% in the women's court);* Hearings on H.R. 398 and H.R. 2091, supra *note 10, at 23;* SPECIAL COMM. TO STUDY DEFENDER SYSTEMS, op. cit. supra *note 4, at 80 (30 to 60%);* Lumbard, *For Equal Justice—A Public Defender, N.Y. Times, Nov. 2, 1947, § 6 (Magazine), p. 17 (80%).*

evidence to hold the accused, the judge or the justice will commit him to the county jail and will set bail.[15]

If the charge is not of an indictable offense, but is instead a charge of one of many misdemeanors specified by statute, a charge of an offense against an ordinance, or a charge of a violation of any one of several statutes specified by statute, the city judge or the justice has jurisdiction not merely to hold, but to hear and decide.[16] He thereupon tries the case, either with or without a jury.[17]

1. *Proceedings prior to and including the preliminary hearing in an indictable offense.* A person suspected of having committed an indictable offense appears first before a magistrate.[18] As already indicated, in Tompkins County this magistrate is almost always either the city judge or one of the justices. The appearance results from the service of a summons, the execution of a warrant of arrest, or an arrest made by a peace officer or other person without a warrant. The chief functions of this proceeding are to tell the accused what he is charged with, to advise him of his right to the aid of counsel in every stage of the case, and thereafter to examine into the existence of probable cause to hold him for the grand jury.[19]

Our consultants suggest that in the usual case, once an arrest has been made, the arresting officer does not attempt to protect the constitutional rights of his prisoner, such as the right to avoid self-incrimination and the right to obtain the help of counsel. Instead, the officer will question his prisoner about what he did and why he did it, and will suggest that if the prisoner confesses to the magistrate he will "get off" lightly, but that if he does not "come clean" he will be punished harshly. In addition, we are told, it is quite usual for the officer to advise the prisoner to waive his legal right to a preliminary hearing.

Opinions differ concerning the frequency, and the severity, of the use of intimidation short of threats and violence to obtain from the prisoner a statement which may incriminate. A few of our consultants believed they had reliable evidence even of violence or threats of violence. We believe that such abuse is quite infrequent in Tompkins County, if it occurs at all. But far more frequent, we fear, is the use of strong pressure, short of

---

[15] N.Y. CODE CRIM. PROC. §§ *208–10.*

[16] N.Y. CODE CRIM. PROC. § *56;* N.Y. VILLAGE LAW § *182.*

[17] N.Y. CODE CRIM. PROC. § *702.*

[18] N.Y. CODE CRIM. PROC. §§ *146–47.*

[19] N.Y. CODE CRIM. PROC. §§ *188–90.*

violence or threats thereof, to induce a confession. And even where no such pressure is used, the prisoner is rarely, if ever, told of his right to remain silent. Usually he is urged to give a statement, sometimes as the price of a promised favor. In some cases, no copy of this statement ever becomes available to him or to his counsel.

The committing magistrate does not ordinarily impress upon the prisoner the importance of the preliminary examination; instead he usually advises him to save time by either waiving it or "getting it over with." This amounts to suggesting that the prisoner either waive the examination altogether or else allow the People to examine their witnesses before he has a chance to get counsel. The committing magistrate looks upon the preliminary hearing as an unimportant detail, a mere formal step toward the finding of probable cause. The indigent person, who has no counsel at this stage nor any offer of assigned counsel, is most unlikely to withstand the combined pressures from police and magistrate for his waiver of hearing or for a "quick hearing" without counsel.

Here another difference of opinion has to be reported. All but one of our consultants with extensive criminal practice repeatedly stressed the crucial importance to the defense of the preliminary hearing. The People's case appears on this examination. Its weaknesses can then be probed and exploited before the trial. The witnesses are more likely to tell the truth at the hearing than at the trial, because the events are fresher in their memories; hence their later wishful recollections, coached or spontaneous, can more easily be exposed at the trial for what they are. One consultant, on the other hand, thought that defense counsel should usually waive the preliminary hearing, largely on the ground that it facilitates the People's proof of their case if, later on, some witness who has testified at the hearing should become unavailable for the trial. In that event, the transcript of the hearing can be read at the trial, to "plug the gap." He further believed that the record of the hearing is often used unfairly to confuse honest witnesses at the trial.

We submit that the majority view is the more reasonable one. Even allowing that some of the enthusiasm for the hearing stems from that adversary spirit which does so much to pervert our criminal law, still there are important advantages, of a legitimate kind, which inhere in this examination and which make it unfair for an accused to be talked out of it without the advice of counsel. But even if the minority view, that the preliminary hearing is disadvantageous to the defense in most cases, is correct, it would still be vitally important that defense counsel, rather than the accused, decide in the particular case whether the hearing should be waived.

\* \* \* \*

## B. County Court

The grand jury is impanelled by one of the justices of the supreme court, who sit in Ithaca from time to time on circuit. After indictment, all cases, with one rare exception, are transferred to the county court for trial. The exception is first-degree murder cases, which are tried in the supreme court itself. But there has been only one of these in Tompkins County during the last decade. In such cases, the problem of obtaining experienced and skillful legal assistance is not acute because of the statutory compensation allowed[20] and also because of the public's interest in murder cases.

In all other cases the county court arraigns persons charged with indictable offenses, takes pleas from them, and tries them. It also deals, similarly, with any lesser crimes which may be transferred to the county court pursuant to certificate,[21] but such transfers are rare. In addition, the county court hears any appeal from a conviction in a court of special sessions or from a denial of an application for a writ of error in a coram nobis proceeding in such a court.[22]

The county judge, as already noted, is expressly charged by statute with the duty of assigning counsel for any person arraigned before him who, in answer to the judge's inquiry, requests such assistance.[23] All our consultants agree that the county judge is careful and conscientious in his assignment practice. In this court, as distinguished from the justice courts, and to a lesser degree from the city court, assignments are normal and expected.

Although there is good evidence that assignments in county court are made when needed, there is also substantial evidence that they do not entirely fulfill their purpose. The indictable offenses normally carry heavy

---

[20] N.Y. Code Crim. Proc. § 308.
[21] N.Y. Code Crim. Proc. §§ 57–59a.
[22] N.Y. Code Crim. Proc. § 517(3).
[23] N.Y. Code Crim. Proc. § 308.

penalties. And, it would seem, adequate preparation and investigation of many of these cases may require considerable amounts of time and money. The county judge tends to discount this need, saying that most of these cases are comparatively simple, involving local events and persons. But our talks with lawyers and the responses to our questionnaire presented rather impressive evidence to the contrary. On the Tompkins County questionnaire 28 of the 35 respondents who answered the question about funds for preparation thought that the lack of such funds was an inadequacy of the system. Fifteen of them thought this inadequacy serious; only 7 were satisfied. . . .

Sharp disagreement was found among our consultants concerning the helpfulness of the prosecutor in protecting an accused indigent against the possibility of a mistaken conviction. The county judge and the two district attorneys who served in succession during the period of our study told us that the district attorney's office was always willing to open its files and to give all the information and assistance possible, without discrimination between counsel assigned and counsel retained. Some consultants agreed, but a slight majority disagreed. The comments of this majority are in no sense a reflection on the fairness or conscientiousness of any individual district attorney. The criticism goes rather to the nature of the office and to the tendency, inherent in the adversary system, for any district attorney to try to get as many convictions as he can. Those consultants who have been successful in their dealings with the district attorney incline, no doubt, to feel that the prosecutor has been fair; whereas those who have not been so successful incline to be censorious.

Our own conclusion is that the district attorney's claim that he protects the rights of the accused as diligently as the rights of the People is somewhat exaggerated. Some attorneys, particularly in cases where trial seemed inevitable, found it impossible to avail themselves of the district attorney's asserted willingness to open his files to counsel for all defendants. In general, we believe that the district attorney does feel a real responsibility to protect indigent persons against unjust convictions, within the limits allowed by his attitude toward the duties of his office. But we doubt whether his conception of his own function is adequate for the protection of the rights of the indigent—more than half of all those indicted. Under the existing assignment system, the indigent defendant is represented by counsel without pay and without funds, and he is pitted against the county's resources of men and money. It takes little imagination to see his terrifying disadvantage. To compensate, he needs more than a mere passive fairness on the part of the district attorney; he needs his active solicitude to avoid the danger of an unjust conviction.

Another matter of great importance concerning county court assignments is the time at which counsel is assigned. Although assignment is sometimes made by a communication from the county judge to the lawyer either before or after the arraignment, the usual procedure is to make the assignment in open court at the arraignment. But there is some evidence, as already noted, that police officers usually question a suspect before they take him to a committing magistrate for his first hearing, and that they may continue to question him thereafter. This questioning often results in a confession or, at the least, in a statement which will gravely prejudice the defendant's case. We believe that such practices occur frequently enough to be a serious hazard to the fair determination of guilt or innocence. It is a hazard which earlier assignments might alleviate. A few consultants, at least, held strong opinions to the effect that assignment comes too late when it comes after the arrest, hearing, and indictment. It should be made at the first hearing, at the latest, so that counsel can advise about waiving the preliminary examination and can participate in it if it is held. One attorney with much criminal experience insisted that assignments should be made immediately after an arrest.

In view of these expressions of opinion it was surprising that of the 44 respondents to our Tompkins County questionnaire only 3 answered that the usual time of assigning counsel is "very much too late.". . . But it is to be noted that these three respondents handled half of the criminal cases in the county from 1954 through 1956.

The county judge does not maintain any formal roster of assignments. Only 12 of the 44 practitioners who answered the questionnaire had had county court assignments in the years 1954 through 1956. Of the 57 cases assigned to these 12 lawyers during that period, 31 were assigned to two young lawyers with less than five years of practice. In 1956 there were 26 cases assigned. Of these, one lawyer with one and a half years of experience had 15 cases. . . .

The county judge told us that it is his policy to give assignments mainly to young lawyers. In a serious case, however, he assigns a lawyer of greater experience. He gave as a reason for not assigning experienced trial lawyers in most cases the fact that he did not want to impose upon them. It is interesting to note, on the other hand, that some trial lawyers when asked why they never had assignments answered that the judges do not like trials and that if experienced counsel were assigned the judges could be sure there would be trials.

Handling cases without fee is thought by most of our consultants and by 8 of our 44 respondents to be "a serious hardship" on the lawyer. Six of the 8 so answering are among the 9 having extensive criminal experience. Another 19 think it "a hardship but not a serious one." The remaining 9, of the 36 who replied to this question, think it "no hardship at all.". . . It has been reported to us that some years ago resentment against the assignment system induced some of the younger lawyers to meet to plan a protest against the hardships it imposes. But nothing further was done about it.

The county judge told us that it is his practice to ask the accused in open court whether he can afford counsel. At the same time he advises the accused that it will be to his benefit to retain private counsel if he can. But if the accused convinces the judge that he cannot, an assignment is made without further investigation. Knowing the community and its people as he does, the judge feels that he is rarely mistaken about the indigency of a person appearing before him.[24]

Assigned counsel differ as to the way in which they treat the question of the indigency of a client. About half will assume without investigation that the defendant cannot pay. The other half make investigations of their own. If substantial assets or a likelihood of future earnings appear, the attorney may ask the court to relieve him of the assignment or may arrange to receive remuneration without informing the court. . . . There were doubts and differences of opinion as to the correct course to follow.

We have not heard of any case of assigned counsel's "bleeding" the family of an indigent person. This is in striking contrast with what we are told occurs in some large metropolitan areas; there, many assigned lawyers make a business of "squeezing" fees out of defendants and their families and friends.

The county judge told us that in cases where he thinks the accused has enough to pay a modest fee to a lawyer, but not enough to pay a

---

[24] *Respondents to our questionnaire in Cortland County complained in numerous comments that the county judge there failed to make an adequate investigation of indigency. In the light of these complaints it is interesting to note the relatively high proportion of assignments to the total number of criminal cases in this county court as compared to Tompkins County. . . .*

normal fee, he will ask a lawyer to take the case charging a specified fee, possibly from a half to a third of what the lawyer would ordinarily bill. Six of our respondents indicated that they had received cases from the county judge on this "partial assignment" basis. . . .

There are some kinds of indirect compensation for counsel who take assigned cases. One such form arises out of the fact that the county judge in Tompkins is also the surrogate. He is able to reward those young lawyers who take assignments by conferring remunerative appointments as special guardians. He does this as a matter of policy. Opinion is unanimous that he handles this with great fairness and that he does not allow political considerations to enter into his treatment of counsel.

Some of our consultants mentioned another form of indirect compensation for the assignments. This is the publicity that results from appearances in county court to defend indigents in cases that command the public interest and are reported in the local press.

The duties undertaken by assigned counsel without remuneration are not, by and large, as heavy as the above discussion might suggest. It is rare for assigned counsel actually to conduct a trial; not one tenth of his assignments result in trials. It is unheard of for him to conduct an appeal.


## II. EVALUATION

We have noted that most authorities treat it as a triusm that the lot of the indigent defendant in a community such as Tompkins County is less hard than in a metropolis. The usual reasons given are that in a small community people take a friendly interest in one another's affairs; they are more apt to know one another and to know a lawyer.

There is doubtless some validity in this general view. It is a fact, for instance, that the courts of this county are less hurried than those of most urban centers. There is no great pressure, as there is in those centers, to keep up with the case load. The assigning judge can look at the indigent persons before him as individuals, rather than as a mass, because their number is small.

On the other hand, it is our belief that the much vaunted "neighborliness" of the small-town lawyer is overemphasized. The pressure of economic circumstance plays as great a part in the life of the small-town lawyer as it does in the life of his big-town brother. He, like his big-town brother, must weigh every part of his practice from the point of view of its economic reward. He has no more time for "neighborliness" than he would have if he were practicing in Manhattan. Nor is there any evidence that the small-town lawyer has a more compelling sense of duty than his big-city counterpart. The picture of the small-town lawyer as a public spirited benefactor is a popular myth, but we have found no reason to credit it. Our consultants have seemed to us to display about the same level of professional responsibility one would expect from lawyers in a big city. Each has a living to make from practice. Each responds to many motives—only one of which is his professional duty as an officer of the court.

A major reason why the system works as well as it does in this county is the fairness of the judiciary and of the prosecuting officials. This virtue has its drawback, however, in that it depends on the accident of the incumbency of particular individuals.

Major defects of the system are, first, the fact that the prosecutors and the poilce—often because of an eager and tough devotion to their job as they see it—are not sufficiently solicitous of the rights of accused persons or sufficiently awake to the ever-present danger of an erroneous charge; and, secondly, that most of the justices are without legal training and, partly for that reason, are subject to some degree of domination.

*　　*　　*　　*

## III. RECOMMENDATIONS

We present the following recommendations with a keen realization that they are based upon a narrow local study.[25] We make no pretense to

---

[25] *A far broader study, covering many parts of the country, has recently been made by a joint committee of the National Legal Aid and Defender Association and the Bar Association of the City of New York, with financial aid from the Fund for the Republic.* SPECIAL COMM. TO STUDY DEFENDER SYSTEMS, op. cit. supra *note 4. We learned of this project shortly after we had begun our own study. Its sponsors were interested in our work as likely to throw light on an area different in character from areas covered by their own studies. We, on our part, welcomed the opportunity to read their confidential field surveys, and to make our own preliminary report available to them. Their director, Mr. Kenneth R. Frankl, was generous in giving*

finality. We do hope, however, that our views will be sufficiently suggestive to spur others to further studies, and to action in the near future.

Before suggesting any changes, we must be clear about the objective for which they are sought. This we take to be that as few persons as possible, accused of crime and wanting counsel, go without effective legal representation because of poverty.

We propose changes of two sorts, first, those aimed at bringing about a tolerable minimum standard in this field; and, secondly, those aimed at bringing about not merely a tolerable standard but a good one.

## A. A Tolerable Minimum Standard

*First.* Effective legal services should be provided for any indigent accused of any serious misdemeanor or any felony. We see no excuse, other than difficulty and expense, for treating serious misdemeanors in a manner different from felonies. Thus, in New York, for example, we would recommend the adoption of a provision like Section 308 of the Code of Criminal Procedure (now applicable to indictable offenses only) to cover also all serious misdemeanors triable by courts of special sessions.

*Second.* An indigent should be represented by a competent lawyer. Criminal practice is as much a subject for the expert as is, say, surgery. By common consent it can not be learned from the books or otherwise than by doing. Assignment of a recent law graduate, with little or no criminal law experience, should be made only in the rare cases where the appointing judge is absolutely certain that the defendant will in no way be prejudiced thereby. In any but these cases the appointment of an inexperienced lawyer should be coupled with the appointment of an experienced "chief counsel" to guide and advise and, where necessary, be responsible

---

us invaluable help and encouragement throughout. Because their survey was much wider than ours, it furnishes a sounder basis for broad conclusions than does ours. Its detailed and thoughtful recommendations should be of the greatest aid to communities interested in coping with this problem.

Another survey of this subject, and a most intensive one, is being conducted by the American Bar Foundation. See 1 AMERICAN BAR FOUNDATION, THE ADMINISTRATION OF CRIMINAL JUSTICE IN THE UNITED STATES 20, 88–91 (1955). We have had the benefit, through the courtesy of the Foundation's board of directors, of examining the pilot project report of this group, which contains extensive studies in three communities of the defense of indigents accused of crime. This report is not publicly available.

for deciding how much the youngster should do "on his own," how much he should do under supervision, and how much the chief counsel should do himself. This standard also requires that the so-called "office lawyer," who hardly ever goes to court and who pretends to no familiarity with the intricacies of criminal practice, be treated in this area as a novice, and that he not serve without an experienced "chief counsel."

*Third.* In the case of felonies, counsel should be assigned earlier in the proceedings than at present; certainly at the preliminary hearing, if not before.

Meeting these requirements involves, of course, a burden on practicing lawyers far greater than that which they carry now in the defense of the indigent. We do not blink the difficulties; but they have to be met. The burden is one imposed by society for the purpose of satisfying one of its most imperative needs: the just and equal administration of the criminal law. The necessary manpower must be found or created. As a minimum requirement for creating the necessary manpower we recommend the following:

*Fourth.* Reasonable fees should be paid for legal services performed by assigned counsel. The working out of a fair scale, based upon time reasonably required for the services, should not present insuperable difficulties. Many of our consultants and respondents support this suggestion. But some oppose it, believing that it is part of the lawyer's duty to the court and to the public to donate his services when he is assigned. . . .

*Fifth.* Assigned counsel should be allowed all reasonable expenses of preparing a defense and, where necessary, a trial. This recommendation received almost unanimous support from our consultants and overwhelming support from our respondents in all three counties. . . .

The cost to Tompkins County of compensating assigned attorneys (*"Fourth"* recommendation) and reimbursing them for reasonable expenses (*"Fifth"* recommendation) cannot be estimated with much accuracy. Many states do provide compensation for assigned attorneys.[26] Some states do this on a fixed scale. In Iowa, for example, the modest allowance, granted for felony cases, is ten dollars a day as a fee and nothing for expenses.[27] Other states allow amounts which are reasonable, subject to

---

[26] SPECIAL COMM. TO STUDY DEFENDER SYSTEMS, op. cit. supra *note 4, app., provides the most recent compilation of statutory materials on the subject.*

[27] IOWA CODE ANN. § 775.5 (1950).

statutory maxima. In Wisconsin, for example, a county is required to pay an attorney assigned to defend a felony case

such sum as the court shall order as compensation and expenses, not exceeding $25 for each half day in court, $15 for each half day of preparation not exceeding 5 days, $15 for each half day attending at the taking of depositions, and his actual disbursements for necessary travel and other expense, automobile travel to be compensated at not over seven cents a mile.[28]

Other states provide for reasonable payments without statutory maxima.[29] Some states do not distinguish between felonies and misdemeanors,[30] while others do.[31]

Obviously, the cost to Tompkins County would depend on what formula is adopted for compensation and on whether compensation is to be provided for both felonies and misdemeanors or for felonies alone. It would depend, too, on whether Tompkins County is to pay both fees and reasonable expenses, as is done in Wisconsin, or fees only, as in Iowa.

In New York there has been some experience, under Section 308 of the Code of Criminal Procedure, with the reimbursement of "personal and incidental expenses" incurred by counsel in the defense of crimes punishable by death. But unfortunately there is no source of information on the annual aggregate amount thus spent or on the amount spent per case. Therefore, what the cost would be of paying reasonable fees and expenses in assigned felony and misdemeanor cases is highly uncertain. Michigan furnishes a little evidence. There, in the year 1956, in the Recorder's Court of the City of Detroit, the total cost of assigned counsel in felony cases was 176,844 dollars, with an average fee per case of 89.49 dollars.[32] If we use the three-year average to arrive at 20 as the annual number of assignments in the Tompkins County Court, and accept the average fee per case in the Detroit Recorder's Court in 1956, it would cost only about 1800 dollars per year to compensate attorneys assigned to felony cases in Tompkins

---

[28] Wis. Stat. § 957.26 (1958). *Proposed federal legislation has also used the device of reasonable compensation within statutory maxima. See, e.g., H.R. 398, 83d Cong., 1st Sess. (1953), which set $35 a day as the maximum fee for an assigned attorney in districts not having a city of more than 500,000 population, and which also provided for a maximum annual salary of $10,000 for a public defender in larger districts. This bill and other similar proposals have never been enacted.*

[29] Mich. Comp. Laws § 775.16 (1948).

[30] E.g., ibid.

[31] E.g., Iowa Code Ann. § 775.5 (1950).

[32] [1956] Recorder's Court of the City of Detroit, Michigan Ann. Rep. II.

County. No similar estimate can be made, however, of the cost of representing indigents charged with serious misdemeanors, because there is no basis for estimating their number.

*Sixth*. A more effective test of indigency should be instituted. The informal method of determining indigency which is presently in use leaves a great deal to be desired. One possible requirement might be an affidavit showing financial responsibilities, income, assets, and liabilities. Rigid tests, however, should be avoided. Nothing could be more harshly unrealistic, for example, than New York's statutory definition of a "poor person" entitled to an order allowing him to sue in forma pauperis: that his assets not exceed 300 dollars.[33]

What we have so far sketched as a tolerable scheme might never "get off the ground" or might crash after doing so. We have at times wondered whether the assignment system continues to operate only because no one really takes it very seriously. (This is no derogation of the well-meaning judges, justices, lawyers, and police; they carry out their parts in a world they never made.) If taking the present system very seriously, by implementing it as suggested, should indeed break it down, more sweeping changes might then find more support.

### B. A Desirable Standard

In proposing a more ambitious solution of this social problem we have to draw even more heavily upon things which we know only at second hand and on "hunch."

*First*. The best way to "lick" the problem is by an autonomous legal-aid organization with a criminal division. To the extent that it could be financed by private funds, such as a community chest, or contributions from the bar, or both, that would doubtless be the safest way to guard it against abuses. It is our opinion, however, that the important thing is to launch a defender office, regardless of whether it is supported publicly or privately, or partly by public moneys and partly by private.

*Second*. Defenders representing this organization should be available in all criminal courts. This does not necessarily mean that defenders must be employed on a full-time basis. Where there is not enough work to make that efficient, a defender might also practice privately, as many

---

[33] N.Y. Civ. Prac. Act §§ *196, 198–99;* N.Y. Rules of Civ. Prac. *35–37.*

district attorneys ordinarily do. But the defender would be available immediately upon any criminal charge or upon any arrest based on such a charge—as readily and promptly available as a medical doctor in the event of a physical injury.

*Third.* The services of the police, and crime detection equipment, should be freely available to the defender office. The inequality of the contest between officials seeking to convict and counsel seeking to acquit would thus be eliminated—or at least greatly mitigated.

Two major objections often made to changes such as we advocate are that they will create a new sphere of political graft and that they will be expensive.[34] A democratic government which is serious about its ideals, however, must seek to realize them through the most honest and able officials it can enlist. If there is a job that has to be done, risks of official dishonesty cannot excuse leaving that job undone. Difficulties in attaining an ideal which lies at the very heart of our national purpose cannot be sufficient reason to abandon that ideal.

To be sure, the recommendations we have made will require spending money. But can we afford to speak gloriously of human rights, to pronounce our belief in the equality of all men, and at the same time to sit idle while many of our citizens are deprived of fundamental rights because of poverty? The test of our system is in what we do and not in what we say; it is the legal reality and not the legal form which counts.

We cannot better end this article than by quoting from Judge Jerome Frank's dissenting opinion in *United States v. Johnson:*[35]

Such are the coercions of poverty that a decent sensible lawyer may well advise an innocent man, too poor to obtain essential defense evidence, to bargain with the prosecutor to accept a plea of guilty to a lesser crime than that with which the defendant is charged.

For thirteen years, I have been calling attention to this problem and urging a solution. I was most agreeably surprised, therefore, to learn, just the other day, that in Scandinavia it has been the practice, for upwards of seventy years, not only to allow every accused a defense counsel of his choice at government expense, but to place the police department and the office of the

---

[34] *For a recent and fuller discussion of the opposing views as to the desirability of a public defender system for New York State,* compare *Marden,* A Public Defender System for New York State? Yes—With Some Qualifications, 29 N.Y.B.A. BULL. 289 *(1957),* with *Dimock,* No Public Defender System for New York State, 29 N.Y.B.A. BULL. 300 *(1957).*

[35] *238 F.2d 565 (2d Cir. 1956),* vacated, *352 U.S. 656 (1957).*

prosecutor equally at the service of the defense and the prosecution; defense counsel may have these agencies, at government expense, make all necessary investigations, including searches for witnesses and documents and analyses by handwriting, medical or chemical experts; and the prosecution is responsible for producing at trial the witnesses called by the accused as well as all other evidence he wishes introduced—again at government expense.

The federal government and all the states in this country, the richest on the globe, will, I hope, soon emulate the less opulent Scandinavian countries.[36]

---

[36] Id. *at 573* (*dissenting opinion*). (*Footnotes omitted.*)

# Law, Public Opinion, and Mass Media

# THE EFFECTS OF NEWSPAPERS
# ON THE VERDICTS
# OF POTENTIAL JURORS*

*Rita James Simon*

## INTRODUCTION

A few weeks after President Kennedy's assassination, Irving Kupcinet, a Chicago newspaper columnist and television moderator, asked a panel of noted lawyers and judges for their views on the question: Could Lee Harvey Oswald have received a fair trial in Dallas or anywhere in the United States? The consensus of the group was that it would have been extremely difficult, if not impossible, for Oswald to have received a fair trial in any city in the United States.

The events in Dallas, both the assassination of President Kennedy and the trial of Jack Ruby, have given a special relevance to the issues discussed in this paper. The problem under investigation is: Does pretrial publicity by the mass media prejudice a jury's behavior? By prejudice we mean[1]

a disturbance of a juror's impartiality such that his judgment of the issues before him are affected either in favor of or against any party to the trial by the intrusion of material that otherwise would not be accessible to him.

* *Funds for this experiment were obtained from The Lawrence A. Wien Foundation through the efforts of Judge Bernard Meyer of the Supreme Court of the State of New York. The author also acknowledges, with thanks, the assistance of Ray Karon and Emery Sasser in the preparation of the trial and the running of the experiment.*

[1] *This definition was offered by Judge Bernard Meyer of the Supreme Court of the State of New York.*

This article was published as "Murder, Juries, and the Press," in 3 *Trans-action* (1966), 40–42.

Publicity by the mass media prior to and during a trial exposes a conflict betweeen two principles that are deeply embedded in our national consciousness: The principle of a free press and the right to a fair, speedy, and public trial.[2] Many lawyers have expressed the view that the phrase "freedom of the press" has become so deeply embedded in our national consciousness that we have ceased to analyze its purpose and meaning in present-day society and its impact on other institutions and principles in that society. Lawyers who hold this view believe that freedom of the press encroaches and subverts the right to a fair trial.

Judge Hubert Will, one of the participants on the television panel mentioned earlier, commented in a recent article:[3]

Even when the press reports crimes and criminal trials with reasonable thoroughness and accuracy—too often in the very process, it encroaches and subverts the constitutional right to a fair trial by an impartial jury.

Traditionally, the law has a number of safeguards or remedies which when imposed are supposed to insure that a case will be decided only upon the evidence and the law. These remedies can be introduced at different stages of the case. For example, during the pretrial period one of the lawyers may be able to convince the court that a fair and impartial trial cannot be held in the county of the indictment. If the court agrees to a *change of venue*, the trial will be moved to a community that is supposedly less permeated by prejudice. Or, the court may move to *postpone* the trial until the passions of the potential jurors have subsided.

The *voir-dire,* or pretrial examination, is another opportunity for protection against a prejudiced trial. Presumably, in their examination of prospective jurors lawyers can challenge for cause jurors who admit to or who can be shown to have formed an opinion about the case. In exercising his peremptory challenges, a lawyer may eliminate others whom he suspects might be prejudiced against his client.

---

[2] *It is generally estimated that only about 2 per cent of all trials are the target of extensive newspaper and television coverage. But they are usually important cases involving a serious crime or principle of law. Clifton Daniel, managing editor of the* New York Times, *noted that in January 1965, 11,724 felonies were committed in New York City, and of these only 41 were mentioned in the* New York Daily News, *which gives more attention to crime than any other newspaper in the city. Quoted from a statement of Alfred Friendly, managing editor,* The Washington Post, *to Senate Judiciary Committee, August 11, 1965.*

[3] *Judge Hubert L. Will, "Free Press vs. Fair Trial"* Nieman Report, *September 1963, pp. 16–21.*

Once the trial is under way, the judge can continue to question and to instruct jurors about their exposure to newspapers, television, and radio reports about the case. Although most judges are very wary about exercising this prerogative, they can have the jury *locked up* for the length of the trial and until it has rendered its verdict.

Many lawyers doubt the effectiveness of these traditional remedies for preventing publicity from interfering with a fair trial and have urged additional remedies. Their proposals range from prohibiting any publicity about the case outside of the factual account of the crime until the end of the trial, to partial controls which aim specifically at preventing the reporting of any information that the jurors would not be exposed to during the trial because it is inadmissible, to an appeal to the more responsible journalists that they adopt internal constraints appropriate to the problem.

The press's traditional response to the dangers described by a portion of the bench and bar has been that restrictions on freedom of the press would be a greater threat to our basic liberties than any harm that is or might be created under the present circumstances. One of the leading spokesmen for this position is Mr. Justice Hugo Black, who asserted in an interview in 1962 that

the rights set forth in the Bill of Rights, including freedom of the Press, are absolute, subject to no qualifications whatsoever, valid at all times and places, without ifs, buts, or whereases.[4]

As additional support for their position against placing restrictions on the press, newspapermen cite the important role that the press has played historically, in protecting the right of an accused to a fair and speedy trial in an open court, in exposing police corruption, inefficiency, and political influence or domination of the courts. They also point to the help which they claim newspapers provide the police in rounding up suspects and in urging witnesses to come forth and testify.

Ronald Goldfarb, a Washington attorney, stated the case for the press as strongly as anyone has when he offered this challenge:[5]

---

[4] *Quoted from a talk by Judge Emory H. Niles, Chief Judge of the Supreme Bench of Baltimore City, on "The Power of the Court and a Free Press." See Fifth Annual Meeting of the National Conference of State Trial Judges, p. 90.*

[5] Ronald Goldfarb, "Public Information, Criminal Trials: Causes Celebre," Publishing, Entertainment, Advertising Law Quarterly, Vol. III, No. 1 (June 1963), pp. 57–68.

Unless the prejudicial effects of press coverage can be clearly shown to exist, the protection of fair trial at the expense of press freedom may be a loss of liberty without corresponding gain.

At the time of writing a proposal for a large-scale empirical study of the effects of news media on juries' verdicts is being completed. If funds are obtained for conducting the research described in that proposal, the question that Mr. Goldfarb raises—and that all of us who are concerned about protecting individual and institutional freedoms should raise—may receive some definitive answers. The experiment described in this paper is a preliminary empirical inquiry into the same problem. The author conducted the study while working on the more elaborate research proposal.

## RESEARCH DESIGN

Specifically, the problem under investigation in this study is the influence of alternative types of crime reporting on the reactions of potential jurors to a criminal trial. Half of the subjects were exposed to three "sensational" accounts of the events leading up to a murder trial. The other half were exposed to three "conservative" accounts of the same events. The "conservative" stories were modeled after those that might appear in the *New York Times* and the "sensational" stories were of the type that usually appear in the tabloid press. For example the captions in the "sensational" stories, each of which were in half-inch lettering, read:

WOMAN SLASHED TO DEATH IN APARTMENT

COPS NAB TWO FOR HYDE KNIFE SLAYING

KNIFE DISCOVERED IN MURDERERS' ROOMS

The captions on the "conservative" stories, which were about half as large, read:

YOUNG CHICAGO WOMAN KILLED IN APARTMENT

TWO ARRESTED IN SOCIALITE MURDER CASE

NEW EVIDENCE REVEALED IN HYDE CASE

In addition to important stylistic differences between the "sensational" and "conservative" accounts, such as the more elaborate use of adjectives and details in the former, the "sensational" accounts differed from the "conservative" stories in one other crucial respect. The second and third "sensational" stories reported that one of the defendants, Fred Kessler, had a "long-standing criminal record." The second story reported that Kessler had been released from the state penitentiary at Joliet in 1957. In the third story, every time Kessler's name was mentioned it was preceded by the phrase "ex-convict." There was no mention of a prior criminal record for William Anderson, the codefendant in the trial.

In so far as the events surrounding the crime for which the two defendants would eventually stand trial were concerned, there were no differences in the circumstances of the two defendants. One was not described as the accomplice of the other. Except for the mention of Kessler's prior criminal record in the "sensational" stories, the two defendants were treated exactly alike.[6]

After the subjects read the newspaper accounts, ballots were distributed on which they were asked to indicate:

Is Fred Kessler guilty or not guilty of the crime for which he is charged?

Is Bill Anderson guilty or not guilty of the crime for which he is charged?

Before the trial began, the jurors were instructed by the judge as follows:

Ladies and Gentlemen, the recording you are about to hear is a shortened and edited version of the trial that occurred shortly after the last article appeared. After you listen to this case, we shall ask you to render a verdict, as if you were a member of the jury deciding the defendants' fate. Before the trial begins we ask that you lay aside any opinion that you may have formed about the case and that you listen to the testimony and to the attorneys' closing statements with an open mind. The decision that you reach should be based on the *evidence* presented during the trial—not on the speculation of newspapers. We repeat, do not allow the accounts in the newspaper to influence your decision. Let the evidence, the witnesses, all the events during the trial speak for themselves. They are the relevant considerations.

The trial began with the opening statements of the two attorneys. They were followed by three witnesses for the prosecution and four for the defense. Neither defendant took the stand, therefore, there was no

---

[6] *The three newspaper accounts were distributed at the same time and the subjects read them in one sitting.*

reference to Kessler's prior criminal record, nor was any attempt made to differentiate the roles of the two defendants by any of the witnesses. After each attorney made his closing statement, the judge instructed the jurors as to the law that they were to apply. The jurors were told that if they found the defendants guilty, the men could receive the death sentence.[7]

The subjects were then asked to render a verdict for each defendant. In addition, a brief questionnaire was distributed in which the participants were asked to fill out the usual demographic information.


## THE SAMPLE

Subjects for the experiment were drawn from the voter registration lists.[8] Out of the 33,000 registered voters in the community every fortieth name was selected, giving us a sample of 825 names. Each of the 825 persons was contacted by mail. The potential respondent received a letter which described the problem and which made a plea for his cooperation. A self-addressed postcard was included in each mailing. Each person could choose between one of two evenings, if he wished to participate.

The rate of return was disappointing. Only 69 persons, or 8 per cent, of the original sample agreed to participate. A few months later we drew another sample of 400 names from the voter registration lists and again sent letters urging persons to participate. This time, we received only a 7 per cent return, for a total of 28 subjects.

Having first analyzed the two sets of responses separately and having found no difference between the first and second group, we merged the data from the two samples. The tables presented below describe the combined responses of both groups.

Had more funds been available for the study, we would have tried contacting respondents by phone or soliciting their cooperation by going personally to their homes. But since the study was a preliminary inquiry, we decided to analyze the data we had and to report the results. We believe that our findings are of sufficient interest and pertinence that they merit publication, notwithstanding the smallness of the sample.

---

[7] *The recorded trial lasted about thirty minutes.*

[8] *In most large communities persons are usually called for jury duty from the voter registration list.*

# FINDINGS

Of the 97 subjects, 51 were exposed to the "sensational" stories and 46 to the "conservative" stories. The figures in Table 1 describe the subjects' reactions to each defendant after having been exposed to the three newspaper accounts. We mentioned earlier that an important difference between the "sensational" and "conservative" reports was that Kessler's prior criminal record was reported in the "sensational" accounts and omitted in the "conservative" accounts.

TABLE 1. VERDICT DISTRIBUTION BEFORE THE TRIAL BY SENSATIONAL AND CONSERVATIVE NEWSPAPER REPORTS.

| | Sensational | | | Conservative | | |
|---|---|---|---|---|---|---|
| Defendants | Guilty | Not Guilty | No Opinion | Guilty | Not Guilty | No Opinion |
| Kessler | $67_{(34)}$* | $21_{(11)}$ | $12_{(6)}$ | $37_{(17)}$ | $39_{(18)}$ | $24_{(11)}$ |
| Anderson | $53_{(27)}$ | $33_{(17)}$ | $14_{(7)}$ | $37_{(17)}$ | $39_{(18)}$ | $24_{(11)}$ |

*Figures in parentheses are the frequencies.

The figures in Table 1 show that persons were more likely to believe *Kessler* guilty after reading the "sensational" stories than they were after reading the "conservative" stories (67 per cent compared to 37 per cent.)[9] The difference in the per cent who believed Anderson guilty under the two versions is in the same direction (higher under sensational) but is not significant. Table 1 shows several other interesting results. Persons were less likely to have formed an opinion after having been exposed to the "conservative" stories than they were after reading the "sensational" reports. Persons exposed to the "conservative" reports did not differentiate between the two defendants and were less likely to find either defendant guilty.

But the crucial question is how the subjects voted *after* they were exposed to the trial? Were the subjects who were exposed to the "sensational" pretrial reporting more likely to find the defendants guilty than were the subjects who were exposed to the "conservative" accounts? As is usually the case, the "sensational" stories were slanted against the defendants. Table 2 describes the posttrial verdicts.

---

[9] *A difference that attained significance at the .01 level: $x^2 = 8.6$.*

| Defendants | Sensational | | | Conservative | | |
| --- | --- | --- | --- | --- | --- | --- |
| | Guilty | Not Guilty | No Opinion | Guilty | Not Guilty | No Opinion |
| Kessler | 25(13) | 73(37) | 2(1) | 22(10) | 78(36) | — |
| Anderson | 25(13) | 73(37) | 2(1) | 22(10) | 78(36) | — |

The most important findings in Table 2 are the *lack* of differences in verdicts between subjects who were exposed to the "sensational" and "conservative" newspaper stories and the lack of differences in verdicts between the two defendants within each version. We note also that after the trial the proportion of persons who believed the defendants guilty was lower than it was on the basis of the newspaper stories alone, even when the accounts they were exposed to were relatively straightforward, as in the "conservative" reports.

These findings suggest strongly that jurors take seriously the judge's instructions that they lay aside any opinions they may have formed about the case and that they base their decision on the evidence. During the trial both defendants were treated exactly alike. There would have been no basis for differentiation between Anderson and Kessler, and the jurors did not differentiate.

The validity of these findings rests on the assumption that jurors, or persons who are assuming the role of jurors, understand and adhere to the instructions they receive from the bench. In this experiment the judge instructed the jurors to

. . . lay aside any opinion that you may have formed about the case and . . . listen to the testimony and to the attorneys' closing statements with an open mind. The decision that you reach should be based on the *evidence* presented during the trial—not on the speculation of newspapers.

Our results indicate that the jurors obeyed the court's instructions. But the practical question is: Was their behavior typical? Would jurors serving on an actual case behave as the jurors did in this situation? We believe they would. We say this primarily because we found that the behavior of the subjects in this experiment was consistent with the behavior of real jurors in a courtroom situation.

A few years ago a large-scale study of the American jury system was conducted at the law school of the University of Chicago. As part of that study the jury project ran an experiment with an automobile-negligence action in which jurors heard three different versions concerning the defendant's insurance status. In version $A$, the jury heard that the defendant had no insurance. In version $B$, when the defendant stated that his insurance agent instructed him to return to the scene of the accident, the defendant's attorney called for a mistrial. The judge refused to grant a mistrial, but instructed the jury to disregard the defendant's mention of insurance. In version $C$, the defendant made the same reference to insurance but the jury received no instruction to disregard.

TABLE 3. INSURANCE MENTIONS* BY TREATMENT AND IMPLICATION FOR AWARD.

| Defendant's Insurance Status | Implications of Insurance Mention | | | Total | Neutral in Per Cent |
|---|---|---|---|---|---|
| | Raise | Neutral | Lower | | |
| A. No Insurance | 41 | 51 | 27 | 119 | 43 |
| B. Insurance but Instruction to Disregard | 7 | 25 | 4 | 36 | 69 |
| C. Insurance and No Instruction to Disregard | 28 | 24 | 9 | 61 | 39 |
| Total | 76 | 100 | 40 | 216 | 46 |

* An insurance mention is one consecutive burst of speech on the part of a single participant; each mention was recorded and classified according to its tendency to raise, lower, or have no effect upon the award.

The main reason for introducing this variation was twofold: (1) in order to see how the presence or absence of insurance affected the jury's verdict, especially the amount of damages awarded; and (2) to see if the jury obeyed the judge's instructions and disregarded the defendant's mention of insurance. Table 3 describes the number of times the jury mentions insurance in the course of its deliberation under each instruction version; and the implications of the insurance mention on its verdict.[10]

The figures show clearly that the jurors make noticeably fewer references to the defendant's insurance status when they are instructed to disregard the presence of insurance. The references that are made are

---

[10] *Ten juries were exposed to each instruction version.*

much more likely to be neutral in their implications for verdicts. In other experiments conducted by the jury project, the results also showed that the jurors understood and in large measure carried out the court's instructions.[11] The subjects for these experiments were drawn by lot from the jury pools of three large metropolitan areas.

## CONCLUDING REMARKS

Our original question was: Does pretrial publicity by the mass media prejudice a jury's behavior? The results of this experiment indicate that publicity does not prejudice the jurors' verdicts. This is not to say that newspapers fail to influence their readers' opinions. When opinions were solicited on the basis of the newspaper stories alone, we found that persons exposed to the "sensational" publicity were more likely to find the defendants guilty than were persons exposed to the "conservative" reports. We also found the "sensational" reports were more likely to induce opinions than were the "conservative" accounts. But after listening to the trial, differences of opinion between subjects exposed to "sensational" and "conservative" reports disappeared and both groups reported identical verdicts. The posttrial verdicts were more favorable to both defendants than were the tentative verdicts reported on the basis of exposure to pretrial publicity.

If these results can be replicated on a larger sample and in other communities, they should provide strong support for persons who share the views of Mr. Justice Black, Mr. Goldfarb, and members of the press who warn against the protection of fair trial at the expense of press freedom. These results certainly suggest that dangers to fair trial by pretrial publicity have yet to be proven.

One word of caution about the findings reported in this study. In addition to the smallness of the sample, and to possible idiosyncracies in the community in which the study was conducted, the persons who agreed to participate in the study were special in that they represent many of the qualities generally found in a blue-ribbon jury.[12] Although the

---

[11] For a more detailed discussion of jurors' reactions to rules of law see Rita J. Simon, The Jury and the Defense of Insanity (Boston: Little, Brown, 1967).

[12] But we also note that it is a blue-ribbon jury that usually decides the kinds of cases that are likely to receive extensive pretrial publicity.

universe from which our sample was drawn was representative of the adult community, the persons who agreed to participate came primarily from the upper-middle classes. About two-thirds of the subjects were business and professional people with a college education. But, as we indicated earlier, our results are consistent with those found by the Chicago Jury Project, whose subjects were persons drawn by lot from the jury pools of three metropolitan jurisdictions. Nevertheless, when the experiment is replicated in other communities, efforts should be made to secure a more representative sample.

# PARENTAL AUTHORITY:
# THE COMMUNITY
# AND THE LAW

Julius Cohen,
Reginald A. H. Robson,
and Alan Bates

## THE PROBLEM—IN GENERAL PERSPECTIVE

Modern jurisprudential theory has moved steadily in the direction of regarding ends or values as the central problem of the law. Holmes's thrust against blind historicism in law,[1] Pound's Sociological Jurisprudence, the attack by the realists on the arid conceptualism of the Analytic School, the emphasis of Lasswell and McDougal on "policy training" and of Cowan on Experimental Jurisprudence are but a few of the many landmarks along the way.[2] Those theorists and law-makers whose juristic

---

[1] *Holmes was critical of "the way in which tradition not only overrides rational policy, but overrides it after first having been misunderstood and having been given a new and broader scope than it had when it had a meaning."* The Path of the Law in COLLECTED LEGAL PAPERS (1920), 192. *Indeed, he was prompted by his feelings in the matter to write: "I look forward to a time when the part played by history in the explanation of dogma shall be very small, and instead of ingenious [historical] research we shall spend our energy on a study of the ends sought to be attained and the reasons for desiring them." Ibid., 195.*

[2] *Roscoe Pound*, The Scope and Purpose of Sociological Jurisprudence, 25 HARVARD LAW REVIEW 591–619 (1911), 25 HARVARD LAW REVIEW 140–168, 489–516

formulae include the moral sense of the community as an essential ingredient are directly and openly involved with this central problem of value. For what is the moral sense but another name for the values of the community? To state the central problem of law as such gives identity to a large area of jurisprudential thought. However, to hold that the problem must be dealt with intuitively rather than empirically, is to hold what we do not believe—that blindness and aridity, no matter what the jurisprudential school, are the persistent and ineradicable elements of the law.

The moral sense of the community may be viewed normatively as well as existentially; it is both an *ought* and an *is*. It functions normatively as part of an *ought* proposition for those who desire the law to be guided by it as an external standard, but the *content* of the normative standard is nevertheless a fact datum. If, as we have been reminded, the *is* without the *ought* is directionless,[3] then certainly the *ought* without the *is* must be blind. In a very real sense, our research undertaking may be viewed as an attempt to furnish a seeing eye to an otherwise blind *ought* in an area of law where it was felt that techniques of modern social science could be of assistance.

While we do not wish to minimize whatever significance might attach to the specific findings of our study as they pertain to the problem of parental authority, the primary concern of our undertaking has, from the very beginning, been the development of a *method* that could well apply to other areas of the law in which the ascertainment of the moral sense of the community is an essential operative factor. There are issues concerning which the moral sense of the community is felt or ascertained without the need of any special prompting—issues which provoke dramatic headlines, issues which promptly encourage the assertion and identification of forces *pro* and *con* within the community. There are also a host of what may be called "introverted" issues—at points between the morally indifferent (*e.g.*, whether there should be two or three signatures to a will), and the headline issues—points on which the moral sense of the community is operative, but must be coaxed or flushed out if it is to be

---

(*1912*); *Edwin N. Garlan*, REALISM AND JUSTICE (*1941*), passim; *Harold D. Lasswell and Myers S. McDougal*, Legal Education and Public Policy: Professional Training in the Public Interest, YALE LAW JOURNAL 203 (*1943*); *Thomas A. Cowan*, Postulates for Experimental Jurisprudence, 9 RUTGERS LAW REVIEW 404 (*1955*).

[3] *Morris R. Cohen*, LAW AND THE SOCIAL SCIENCES (*1933*), 204–208; *Huntington Cairns*, LEGAL PHILOSOPHY FROM PLATO TO HEGEL (*1949*), 314; *Henry Aiken*, A Pluralistic Analysis of the Ethical "Ought," 48 JOURNAL OF PHILOSOPHY (*1951*), 497.

identified. The method that we have utilized in our pilot undertaking would seem to be especially adaptable to this end. While refinements and improvements in method can and will be made from the experiences of application, we nevertheless offer it at this initial stage as a step in the direction of dealing concretely with a gap that has for some time been recognized theoretically by competent scholars in the field of law. We do not suggest that it is a method that could profitably be employed whenever any *discrete* issue faces a law-maker. There is the question of time, there is the question of expense, and there is the problem of the need for stability in the law. It would obviously be unwieldy in a single instance where the speed of decision is an element of the justice of the case; it would clearly be uneconomical if applied to a narrow, insignificant area of legally controllable activity; and where legal stability is a desired end, it would perhaps be unwise to subject law to the unsettling gyrations of constant polling. However, this does not mean that the method could not be effectively and economically employed to obtain a measure of the community's moral sense with respect to a generic class or classes of important issues, where an immediate decision is not pressing, and where long-range stocktaking is the goal. And, despite obvious institutional differences in the processes, we see no reason why it could not be utilized as much for legislative as for judicial law-making purposes. The establishment of the community's moral sense is clearly seen as a counterpart of much of legislative activity;[4] and, although subject to camouflaging because of the trappings of judicial method, it is operative on the judicial level, either explicitly or implicitly, as a norm to consider or follow in much of judicial law-making activity.

We are aware of the fact that the very novelty of the procedure suggested would itself deter the average law-maker; we are mindful of attitudes of resistance to new empirical data,[5] even assuming the adoption

---

[4] *We recognize, of course, that under our system of representative government, the determination of the community's moral sense is, in effect, delegated to those elected by the constituency. We submit, however, that there is nothing in our system of representative government that would prohibit elected representatives from adopting a method for checking on their own estimate of the community's moral sense.*

[5] *See, for example, the report of the responses by state legislators to an inquiry concerning the impact on law of the Kinsey-Martin-Pomeroy study on* SEXUAL BEHAVIOR IN THE HUMAN FEMALE *(1953). Fowler Harper, Book Review, 63* YALE LAW JOURNAL *(1954), 895–899.*

of the method. If analogy is a method for dulling the sharp edge of innovation, perhaps a moment's reflection would suggest that the quest for the community's moral sense is at least as old as the institution of the jury,[6] and that the quest for method is in tune with the lawman's concern with the ever-present problem of reliability.

There will be those whose resistance to the application of such a method is motivated by a distrust, however honest, of the techniques and claims of the social sciences. To many, research lacking the rigor of the most advanced physical sciences is not sufficiently trustworthy to merit the attention, let alone the respect, of policy-makers. Ancient wisdom would suggest that "It is the mark of an educated mind to seek only so much exactness in each type of inquiry as may be allowed by the nature of the subject-matter,"[7] and modern wisdom would remind us that "no knowledge can be rejected merely on the ground of human fallibility until something better is proposed."[8]

## THE PROJECT

\* \* \* \*

### The Findings

Within the confines of the specific areas of inquiry that were carved out for undertaking, what, then, in summary, are our findings? Briefly, we discovered: There are at least twice as many issues concerning which the community views are in disagreement with the law as there are of those on which the community views and the law are in harmony. Of the 17 issues examined, the community and the existing law would disagree as

---

[6] *When a jury, for example, is instructed to determine whether the conduct of a defendant is that of a "reasonable man," it is, in effect, creating a legal norm, based on its conception of the community's moral sense. "The factor controlling the judgment of the defendant's conduct is not what* is, *but what* ought *to be." Francis H. Bohlen,* STUDIES IN THE LAW OF TORTS *(1926), 603.*

[7] *Aristotle,* NICHOMACHEAN ETHICS *(Wheelwright trans., 1935), III.*

[8] *Edgar S. Brightman, The Relation of Law to Morals, 1* JOURNAL OF PUBLIC LAW *(1952), 271.*

to ten, agree as to five, and perhaps evenly divide as to one; and if, on the last issue of the group of 17, on which the law of the jurisdiction has not yet crystallized, the courts would follow what seems to be the preponderant judicial view throughout the country, there would be an additional instance of a variance between the community's views and the law.

The community does not display the same degree of homogeneity with respect to all the issues presented to it. There are wide variations in the degree of consensus within the community. On some issues, there is virtual unanimity; on others, the divisions within the community, in varying degrees, are quite evident. For some questions the predominant view was held by a substantial majority; for others by a bare majority, and for still others, by less than a majority.

The majority in the community would favor greater legal restrictions on parental authority over the child than the law presently requires. Out of eleven general areas in which the issue of parental authority was raised, a majority would impose greater restrictions upon parents in eight of them than the law does at present; it would be as ready as the present law to restrict parental control with respect to two of them; and it would agree with the law in not restricting such authority only in one instance.

Child autonomy may be conceived as a set of claims which the child can assert, and a set of obligations which he is required to meet. In the specific areas covered, a majority in the community would have the law grant more legally enforceable claims to pre-adolescent children than it now permits. In the smaller number of cases in which we raised the question of legally enforceable obligations of the pre-adolescent child, a majority of the community was in favor of relaxing the requirements of the existing law.

With respect to the question of granting autonomy to the child, the law, by and large, does not distinguish between the pre-adolescent and the adolescent child; with few exceptions, it tends to lump children under 21 into one large, generic category—no matter what the gradations in age. The community, on the other hand, recognizes the need to have the law accord increasing degrees of autonomy as the age of the adolescent child increases—autonomy not only as to claims, but as to obligations as well. To a substantial portion of the community, the age of 18 marks the boundary line between adolescence and adulthood.

Except in the case of marriage, the law does not differentiate between boys and girls in the recognition of claims and the imposition of legal obligations. With respect to this, a majority of the community—on all the issues considered—is in agreement with the position of the law.

To a majority of the community, the problem of the support of indigent parents and indigent, emancipated children is primarily a matter for the family, and secondarily a matter for the government. In this, the community is in accord with the prevailing law.

By and large, there are no *substantial* differences between the views of the members of various social groupings within the community toward the issues we studied, based on such factors as sex, residential area, religion, age, income, parenthood, schooling and occupation. However, in several instances, the small differences in the views of respondents identified with different socio-economic groups do exhibit consistent patterns.

On none of the selected issues involving parent-child relationships does the law *consistently* reflect the views of any particular social group among the ones we studied in the community rather than those of any other.

Of the reasons given for the views expressed by the respondents concerning the issues posed in the Interview Schedule, the predominant one is concern for the welfare of the child. Parental authority is regarded as a means to an end, and there is little hesitance to employ the arm of the law to curb it when its exercise is perceived as being detrimental to the welfare of the child. There is comparatively little sentiment against the intrusion of law or government in what has, for so long a time, been considered the private domain of the family; there is considerable feeling in favor of increased autonomy for the child—especially for the older child.

### Some Suggested Reasons for Our Findings

FINDINGS RELATING TO THE VARIANCE BETWEEN LAW AND THE COMMUNITY'S MORAL SENSE

Why is there so great a variance between the existing law and the community's moral sense in the selected areas of parent-child relationships? We suggest that there are three principal reasons for the difference between the law and what the community thinks the law ought to be: the differences in the impact of tradition upon law-makers and upon the community; the relative lack of pressures exerted upon law-makers to signal the need for change; and the inadequacy of prevailing techniques utilized by law-makers for ascertaining the moral sense of the community.

Judges lay considerable stress upon tradition as a basis for operations in the present; there is a natural orientation toward the past as a guide to present behavior. This orientation is fostered and supported not only by legal principle of long standing, but also by what Dean Pound has called the "taught tradition," that is, by the very training for the profession of law itself. This type of built-in professional conservatism is a force that is not operative in the development of the views of the community as such. With respect to legislators, not only is there an institutional inertia which militates in favor of the *status quo* until countervailing pressures are brought to bear, but, in implementing the need for change, there is a constant search for precedent and analogy—a striving to tie new policy as much as possible to the experiences of the past. The views of the community are, of course, also conservative in the sense that they are influenced by the culture of the society coming out of the past. They are not by any means ordinarily subject to instantaneous change in response to the immediate situation. Particularly is this true where the views being considered relate to a basic and continuing social institution such as the law, in contrast to relatively ephemeral matters such as the choice between opposing candidates in the elections. However, we suggest that when members of the community are asked to give their views as to what the law should be, they are likely to give less weight to the desire that the law should be consistent with the past than are judicial and legislative lawmakers, and are more likely to feel that the law should be consistent with the views gained as a result of their own personal experience. We realize, of course, that law-makers are also members of the community and in their private capacities are subject to the same influences as any other person. What we are stressing here, however, is that the law-maker is subject to the demands of his professional role; as a legislator or judge, his actions are influenced by the feeling that in this role, he should not, generally speaking, depart from tradition. If what we have just been saying is true, then this would serve to maintain a difference between the law and the views of the community, particularly when the latter are changing rapidly.

One of the ways in which pressure to change may be exerted upon the law is through the courts, by the frequent occurrence of litigation. However, so far as the area of parent-child relationships is concerned, the number of disputes which are referred to the law for a decision is relatively small. To the extent that such disputes are brought before the courts, judges are exposed in various ways to the views of segments of opinion within the community on these issues, a process which presumably facilitates continuous modification of the law to conform with such expressions of opinion. When such opportunities for contact with views held by various groups in the community are infrequent, it is to be expected that the law will be less sensitive to the changes in the views of the community.

Another avenue for securing change in the law is through organized pressure upon legislative bodies. However, in the area of parent-child relationships, the intensity and persistence of the demands of organized pressure groups in the legislative forum would seem to be relatively slight. In making this statement, we are aware that there are many individuals and organizations that, at times, represent the interests of the family, including the child, before legislative bodies, but for the specific issues that we studied in this project, it remains true that, relatively speaking, not much organized pressure is brought to bear upon the makers of law. Even in those instances where pressures have been successfully exerted upon legislators by such individuals and organizations, it would not necessarily follow that such pressures did in fact reflect the views of the entire community. The relative scarcity of court cases and organized community pressures on legislative bodies to change the laws in this area may be due to three principal factors: the ability of parents to bring about changes in their relationships with children without recourse to law, the relative inability of children to initiate changes on their own behalf, and the factor of dissenting acquiescence.

It seems highly probable that modern parental behavior already reflects recognition of the change in sentiment by granting more autonomy to the child and by exercising less parental authority in areas that were canvassed in our study—all this without resort to the processes of the law. A behavioral study of family practices—especially those which pertain to parent-child relationships—would be of great value in testing this hypothesis, and would be in keeping with Ehrlich's interest in the "living law." Such an inquiry was, however, beyond the pale of our undertaking.

With respect to the second factor, we suggest that to expect the child to process claims in a court against his parents in order to urge upon the court the need for a change in legal norms is to expect too much. He would not ordinarily have the means or the foresight, and even in those rare instances when both would be present, there would be the problem of the courage needed to challenge parental authority.

The concept of dissenting acquiescence is one seemingly at variance with this oft-quoted statement from the *Report on the Enforcement of the Prohibition Laws of the United States:*

It is axiomatic that under any system of reasonably free government a law will be observed and may be enforced only where and to the extent that it reflects or is an expression of the general opinion of the normally law-abiding elements of the community. To the extent that this is the case, the law will be observed by the great body of the people and may reasonably be enforced to the remainder.[9]

The word "only" in this statement would, however, seem to color it with an undue sense of disproportion. It does not take into account the fact that laws may be enforced even if they do not reflect the moral sense of the community—providing the community is not aroused, as in the case of Prohibition, to a state of fever-pitched opposition. Ordinarily, we submit, acquiescence born of inertia is as operative a force in law-observance as is harmony of the law with the views of the community. Many of the laws of the jurisdiction dealing with parent-child relationships are quite at variance with the community's moral sense, but there is scarcely any evidence that the opposition to the standards of the law is the opposition of an aroused community. We do not know at what point and under what conditions dissenting acquiescence becomes active resistance, but if the experience with Prohibition is a criterion, we are certain that the critical stage has not been reached in the area of the law governing parent-child relationships.

Assuming that law-makers are concerned with making laws accord with the views of the community, variance between the law and the community's moral sense would also seem to be a function of the nature of the techniques that are generally employed by law-makers in endeavor-

---

[9] *House Document No. 722, 71st Cong., 3rd Sess.* REPORT ON THE ENFORCEMENT OF THE PROHIBITION LAWS OF THE UNITED STATES (*January 7, 1931*).

*A similar observation was made by Bertrand Russell in* POWER (*6th ed., 1948*): ". . . the Law is almost powerless when it is not supported by public sentiment, as might be seen in the United States during prohibition, or in Ireland in the '80's, when moonlighters had the sympathy of a majority of the population. Law, therefore, as an effective force, depends upon opinion and sentiment even more than upon the powers of the police. The degree of feeling in favor of Law is one of the most important characteristics of a community."*

ing to establish what the moral sense of the community actually is. Those law-makers who, in seeking to narrow the variance, nevertheless employ unreliable techniques, e.g., hunch, intuition, or reactions only to special segments of the community, are apt wrongly to assume that their objective has been achieved. A variance is neither narrowed nor erased by good intentions alone; it is apt to persist as long as there is a mistaken notion of what the community's moral sense actually is.

\* \* \* \*

### Implications of Our Findings

#### Tool for the Law-Maker

For those law-makers whose juristic philosophy stakes out as an objective a high degree of harmony between the existing law[10] and the moral sense of the community, our findings make it clear that, in the area of parent-child relationships, such harmony exists only to a very limited extent. In fact, with respect to the specific issues that were raised in this area, the law and community opinion were more often in disagreement than in agreement. Those who would desire in a practical way to narrow the gap between the law and the community's moral sense will find detailed and accurate information in our study on the extent of agreement or disagreement between the law and the views of the community. There is also information which identifies the precise areas in which harmony or variance are present.

We realize, of course, that our data do not provide information as to the views of the community on all the issues involving parent-child relationships. By grouping the discrete questions in terms of their common denominators—some, for example, dealt with different aspects of the autonomy of the child, others with the financial support of the family, and so forth—we did endeavor to ascertain the predominant views of the community on more general issues than those raised by the discrete questions themselves. Accordingly, our data include information that will

---

[10] *Throughout this discussion, the reader should keep in mind that in this study we have been concerned with comparing the views of the community with statute law and judicial decision. . . . [W]e realize that the law-in-action may differ in varying degrees from our statement of the law, but we have not dealt with this aspect of the problem in this study.*

enable law-makers to make reasonable inferences as to what community opinion would probably be on a more specific matter based upon our conclusions as to what the views of the community are with respect to the more general issue. For example, we do not have the views of the community on whether the law should hold the child responsible for criminal acts which he might commit, or whether the parents should be held accountable. However, we did conclude from our data that the majority of the community felt that the law should grant a fair degree of autonomy to the child, particularly when he reaches adolescence, and also thought the law should make an older child responsible for his *civil* wrongs. We suggest, therefore, that this information would give law-makers a more informed basis for dealing analogically with the problem of the child's legal responsibility for criminal acts. Our findings yielded other general clusters of community sentiment from which similar analogical extensions could be made.

## THE PROBLEM OF RESPECT FOR THE LAW

Our data showing disagreements between the views of the community and the law suggest questions concerning the possible effects of such a divergence upon the law itself. How far can the two be at odds before the enforcement of the law is adversely affected? To what extent do disagreements between the law and community opinion engender hostility and disrespect toward the particular law and toward law in general? An important instance of the consequences of such a situation was the experience of the country with the Prohibition Amendment. The answer to these questions is obviously not a simple one, and is not within the purview of our undertaking. Our findings do, however, prompt inquiry into the extent to which respect for and obedience to law are affected by such considerations as: the importance of the issue for the community, the frequency with which the issue arises, the complexity of the issue and the degree of consensus within the community concerning the issue.

## THE PROBLEM OF COMPETING MORAL SENSES

Our data indicate that there are a number of issues where there is almost complete agreement in the community as to what the law should be; in these cases, those who feel that the law should be related to the views of the community would have little difficulty in implementing their objective. However, our data also show that there are many issues where community opinion concerning the law's attitude is almost evenly divided between opposing points of view, and still others where the most popular view of what the law should be represents the opinions of less than a majority of the community. In contrast to the situations where there is a high degree of consensus within the community, these data showing substantial disagreement among the population as to what the law should be create certain problems that must be faced by those advocating community opinion as the standard to which law should seek to conform. How is a "community view" to be defined for this purpose? Should law conform to this standard only where there is a high degree of consensus among the population? If so, what should be the law in those areas where there are differences of opinion within the community? Or, if a lower degree of consensus is acceptable, where should the line be drawn? Should law only conform to community opinion where a majority of the population holds the same view, or should it be in harmony with the most popular point of view in the community, even though a majority of the population holds different opinions? These are questions of considerable magnitude as well as of practical importance. Our findings merely point up these questions; they do not purport to answer them. They should, however, help illuminate some of the implications of a juristic theory that seeks a high degree of harmony between law and *the* moral sense of the community.

\* \* \* \*

The Community's Moral Sense and the Law versus the Findings of Science

There are those who would view with concern the application of a juristic formula which erects the moral sense of the community as a norm for the law. This is a political or philosophical issue with which our undertaking is not concerned—our interest, as we have pointed out, being solely with the "then" or implementation phase of an "if-then" proposition. However, it is worth noting that one reason that has been advanced in opposition to this juristic formula is the fact that the community's moral sense might run counter to the findings of science. Those who offer this criticism would prefer to have both the law and the community's moral sense bow ultimately to science as the higher standard. In designing our project, we regarded the answers people gave to our questions as to what the law should be as *means* for achieving certain *ends,* the latter represented by the reasons they gave for their responses. The purpose of this kind of analysis was to try to identify those instances: where there was agreement between the law and the community, both as to the ends to be achieved and the means for achieving them, and where there was agreement between the law and the community as to the ends but disagreement as to means. In both such situations, the relevant consideration for many would be the verdict of social science as to the relative effectiveness of alternative means for achieving the mutually desired ends. While we do not claim to have made a completely exhaustive search of the vast social science literature in the field of family behavior, we do feel confident in stating that, although there is some material that is tangentially related, there is a dearth of material of a sufficiently high degree of reliability that is directly and specifically relevant to the particular problems that we covered. We have an illustration here of the point . . . concerning inter-disciplinary research between law and the social sciences: that, while both disciplines may be interested in the same general area, *i.e.,* the family, up to the present time each field has had a different focus of interest. In the absence of sufficiently reliable scientific data, action, if there must be action, must proceed on the basis of guess. In such a circumstance, the choice is not between reliable knowledge and no knowledge, but between two guesses as to the consequences of the law taking one path instead of another—the law-makers' guess, and the guess that is embodied in the expression of the community's moral sense. When one guess is no more intelligent than the other, the choice between them, when a choice must be made, would put the law-maker's political philosophy to a crucial and revealing test.

\* \* \* \*

# TRIAL
# BY MASS MEDIA?

## Martin Millspaugh

When Judge John B. Gray of the Baltimore Supreme Bench convicted three radio stations of contempt in obstructing the administration of justice,[1] he stated that the function of a jury is to ". . . bring to the case public opinion in the community. . . ." Under this Court's controversial Rule #904, he judged that broadcasts on the arrest and charging of Eugene James for the knife murder of little Marsha Brill ". . . must have had an indelible effect on the public mind." James, a Negro, was deemed to have been deprived of his right to a jury trial when his lawyer was forced to request the substitution of a panel of judges because of publicity given the case.

Judge Gray ruled that the right to due process could take precedence over the guarantee of Press freedom in the First Amendment. The legal point will probably have to be solved by the Supreme Court, but the crucial nature of this case to the communications industry is shown by the activity of both the American Newspaper Publishers' Association and the American Society of Newspaper Editors in behalf of the stations' defense. The prosecution was supported by the Maryland Bar, which favored the Rule.

### PROS AND CONS IN THE BALTIMORE PRESS

Since the press executives themselves have recognized their interest in the matter, it should be interesting to discover how the Baltimore newspa-

---

[1] *Baltimore* Sun, *January 28, 1949, pp. 22, 4.*

Reprinted by permission of the publishers from 13 *Public Opinion Quarterly* (1949), 328–329.

pers, which were not held in contempt, handled the James case. An analysis was made of the way the four important papers (the morning and evening *Sunpapers,* Hearst's *News-Post,* amd the Negro *Afro-American*) reported developments during the eight days which passed between the murder and setting of the date for James's trial. There was no doubt that he had killed the little girl, but the defense was later conducted on the question of his sanity: whether he was criminally responsible and liable for a first degree murder conviction.

The defendant's background, mental condition, home life, etc., were therefore items which might have had material bearing on the case. There were a number of pertinent facts along that line: he had never gone beyond the third grade; he had been hospitalized for a head injury; his family always lived in extreme poverty; and all three of the psychiatrists who examined him agreed that he had schizophrenic tendencies, at least. But the three large dailies gave little attention of these factors, devoting most of their space to accounts of the horror of the crime, the personality of the little girl, and in general contributing to the stereotype of James as an enemy of society.

## DISTRIBUTION OF SPACE

In the analysis the "neutral" facts of the crime itself and of the manhunt were separated from material which supported either the first degree murder prosecution or the defense, and a count was made of the column centimeters devoted to each side. It immediately became apparent that there was only one side of the case as far as the white dailies were concerned. The nine fact-points favorable to the prosecution were reported 21 times, and the seven points in favor of the defense were mentioned six times. Only the *Afro-American,* seeking to compensate for this imbalance, gave the bulk of its space to the points in James's favor. The column centimeters of space given to the crime in each paper are as follows (headlines, text, and pictures were included) [on page 643].

In effect, then, the stimulus which the three dailies presented to potential white jurors was not calculated to bring an impartial public opinion to bear on the trial. That the newspapers were not alone in this position will be indicated by the fact that Governor Lane himself congratulated the Baltimore police on the successful completion of the case before

|                            | Morning Sun | Evening Sun | News-Post | Afro |
|----------------------------|-------------|-------------|-----------|------|
| Neutral                    | 332.1 cm.   | 255.8 cm.   | 778.6 cm. | 20.2 cm. |
| Destructive to James's case | 173.6      | 203.9       | 709.3     | 2.6  |
| Helpful to James's case    | 0.0         | 49.9        | 59.8      | 80.9 |

James had come to trial. The lawyers for both the prosecution and the defense, however, agreed that the story was reported to the defendant's disadvantage.

# Law and Social Change

# LEGAL EVOLUTION

# AND SOCIETAL

# COMPLEXITY[1]

*Richard D. Schwartz*
*and James C. Miller*

[Abstract omitted.]

The study of legal evolution has traditionally commended itself to scholars in a variety of fields. To mention only a few, it has been a concern in sociology of Weber[2] and Durkheim;[3] in jurisprudence of Dicey,[4] Holmes,[5] Pound,[6] and Llewellyn;[7] in anthropology of

---

[1] *The authors are indebted to Arnold S. Feldman, Raoul Naroll, Terrence Tatje, and Robert F. Winch for their helpful comments on this paper. A grant from the Graduate School of Northwestern University aided in the completion of the work.*

[2] *Max Weber*, Law in Economy and Society, *ed. Max Rheinstein (Cambridge, Mass.: Harvard University Press, 1954). For a discussion and development of Weber's thinking on legal evolution see Talcott Parsons, "Evolutionary Universals in Society," American Sociological Review, XXIX (June, 1964), 350–53.*

[3] *Émile Durkheim*, The Division of Labor in Society, *trans. George Simpson (Glencoe, Ill.: Free Press, 1947).*

[4] *A. V. Dicey*, Lectures on the Relation between Law and Public Opinion in England during the Nineteenth Century *(London: Macmillan Co., 1905).*

[5] *Oliver Wendell Holmes, Jr.*, The Common Law *(Boston: Little, Brown & Co., 1881). Holmes's discussion of the place and limitations of historical analysis provides an appropriate background for the present study. "The law embodies the story of a nation's development through many centuries, and it cannot be dealt with as if it contained only the axioms and corollaries of a book of mathematics. In order to know what it is, we must know what it has been, and what it tends to become. But the most difficult labor will be to understand the combination of the*

---

Reprinted from 70 *American Journal of Sociology* (1965), 159–169, by permission of the authors and of The University of Chicago Press. Copyright 1965 by The University of Chicago Press.

Maine[8] and Hoebel;[9] in legal history of Savigny[10] and Vinogradoff.[11]

There are theoretical and practical reasons for this interest. Legal evolution[12] provides an opportunity to investigate the relations between law and other major aspects and institutions of society. Thus Maine explained the rise of contract in terms of the declining role of kinship as an exclusive basis of social organization. Durkheim saw restitutive sanctions replacing repressive ones as a result of the growth of the division of labor and the corresponding shift from mechanical to organic solidarity. Dicey traced the growth of statutory law-making in terms of the increasing articulateness and power of public opinion. Weber viewed the development of formal legal rationality as an expression of, and precondition for, the growth of modern capitalism.

For the most part, these writers were interested in the development of legal norms and not in the evolution of legal organization. The latter subject warrants attention for several reasons. As the mechanism through which substantive law is formulated, invoked, and administered, legal organization is of primary importance for understanding the process by which legal norms are evolved and implemented. Moreover, legal organi-

---

*two into new products at every stage. The substance of the law at any given time pretty nearly corresponds, so far as it goes, with what is then understood to be convenient; but its form and machinery, and the degree to which it is able to work out desired results depend very much on its past" (pp. 1–2). In stressing history as providing an explanation for procedure rather than substance, Holmes points to those aspects of legal development that—in the present study at least—appear to follow highly uniform sequences of change.*

[6] *Roscoe Pound, "Limits of Effective Legal Action,"* International Journal of Ethics, *XXVII (1917), 150–65; and* Outlines of Lectures on Jurisprudence *(5th ed.; Cambridge, Mass: Harvard University Press, 1943). See also his* Interpretations of Legal History *(London: Macmillan Co., 1930).*

[7] *Karl N. Llewellyn,* The Common Law Tradition: Deciding Appeals *(Boston: Little, Brown & Co., 1960).*

[8] *Sir Henry Maine,* Ancient Law *(London: J. M. Dent, 1917).*

[9] *E. Adamson Hoebel,* The Law of Primitive Man *(Cambridge, Mass.: Harvard University Press, 1954).*

[10] *Frederick von Savigny,* Of the Vocation of Our Age for Legislation and Jurisprudence, *trans. Abraham Hayward (London: Littlewood & Co., 1831).*

[11] *Paul Vinogradoff,* Outlines of Historical Jurisprudence, *Vols. I and II (London: Oxford University Press, 1920–22).*

[12] *The term "evolution" is used here in the minimal sense of a regular sequence of changes over time in a given type of unit, in this case, societies. This usage neither implies nor precludes causal links among the items in the sequence. For a discussion of diverse uses of, and reactions to, the term "evolution," see Sol Tax (ed.),* Issues in Evolution *(Chicago: University of Chicago Press, 1960).*

zation seems to develop with a degree of regularity that in itself invites attention and explanation. The present study suggests that elements of legal organization emerge in a sequence, such that each constitutes a necessary condition for the next. A second type of regularity appears in the relationship between changes in legal organization and other aspects of social organization, notably the division of labor.

By exploring such regularities intensively, it may be possible to learn more about the dynamics of institutional differentation. Legal organization is a particularly promising subject from this point of view. It tends toward a unified, easily identifiable structure in any given society. Its form and procedures are likely to be explicitly stated. Its central function, legitimation, promotes crossculturally recurrent instances of conflict with, and adaptation to, other institutional systems such as religion, polity, economy, and family. Before these relationships can be adequately explored, however, certain gross regularities of development should be noted and it is with these that the present paper is primarily concerned.

This article reports preliminary findings from cross-cultural research that show a rather startling consistency in the pattern of legal evolution. In a sample of fifty-one societies, compensatory damages and mediation of disputes were found in every society having specialized legal counsel. In addition, a large majority (85 per cent) of societies that develop specialized police also employ damages and mediation. These findings suggest a variety of explanations. It may be necessary, for instance, for a society to accept the principles of mediation and compensation before formalized agencies of adjudication and control can be evolved. Alternatively or concurrently, non-legal changes may explain the results. A formalized means for exchange, some degree of specialization, and writing appear almost universally to follow certain of these legal developments and to precede others. If such sequences are inevitable, they suggest theoretically interesting causative relationships and provide a possible basis for assigning priorities in stimulating the evolution of complex legal institutions in the contemporary world.

## METHOD

This research employed a method used by Freeman and Winch in their analysis of societal complexity.[13] Studying a sample of forty-eight

---

[13] *Linton C. Freeman and Robert F. Winch, "Societal Complexity: An Empirical Test of a Typology of Societies,"* American Journal of Sociology, LXII (*March, 1957*), *461–66.*

societies, they noted a Guttman-scale relationship among six items associated with the folk-urban continuum. The following items were found to fall in a single dimension ranging, the authors suggest, from simple to complex: a symbolic medium of exchange; punishment of crimes through government action; religious, educational, and government specialization; and writing.[14]

To permit the location of legal characteristics on the Freeman-Winch scale, substantially the same sample was used in this study. Three societies were dropped because of uncertainty as to date and source of description[15] or because of inadequate material on legal characteristics.[16] Six societies were added, three to cover the legally developed societies more adequately[17] and three to permit the inclusion of certain well-described control systems.[18]

---

[14] *This ordering has not been reproduced in other studies that followed similar procedures. Freeman repeated the study on another sample and included four of the six items used in the first study. They scaled in a markedly different order, from simple to complex: government specialization, religious specialization, symbolic medium of exchange, writing. The marked change in position of the first and third items appears attributable to changes in definition for these terms (Linton C. Free man, "An Empirical Test of Folk-Urbanism," [unpublished Ph.D. dissertation, Northwestern University, 1957], pp. 45, 49–50, 80–83). Young and Young studied all six items in a cross-cultural sample of communities, changing only the definition of punishment. Their ordering is somewhat closer to, but not identical with, that found by Freeman and Winch (op. cit.). From simple to complex, the items were ordered as follows: punishment, symbolic medium of exchange, governmental specialization, religious specialization, writing, educational specialization, (Frank W. and Ruth C. Young, "The Sequence and Direction of Community Growth: A Cross-Cultural Generalization," Rural Sociology, XXVII [December, 1962], 374–86, esp. 378–79).*

*In the present study, we will rely on the Freeman-Winch ratings and orderings, since the samples overlap so heavily. The reader should bear in mind, however, that the order is tentative and contingent upon the specific definitions used in that study.*

[15] *Southeastern American Negroes and ancient Hebrews.*

[16] *Sanpoil.*

[17] *Three societies—Cambodian, Indonesian, and Syrian—were selected from the Human Relations Area Files to increase the number of societies with counsel. The procedure for selection consisted of a random ordering of the societies in the Human Relations Area Files until three with counsel were located in geographically separate regions. These were then examined to determine the presence or absence of other legal characteristics. The random search eliminated the possibility of a bias in favor of societies conforming to the scale type.*

*The three societies were quota sampled by region to represent a randomly determined three of the following six regions: Asia, Africa, the Middle East, North*

Several characteristics of a fully developed legal system were isolated for purposes of study. These included counsel, mediation, and police. These three characteristics, which will constitute the focus of the present paper,[19] are defined as follows:

*counsel:* regular use of specialized non-kin advocates in the settlement of disputes.
*mediation:* regular use of non-kin third party intervention in dispute settlement.
*police:* specialized armed force used partially or wholly for norm enforcement.

These three items, all referring to specialized roles relevant to dispute resolution, were found to fall in a near-perfect Guttman scale. Before the central findings are described and discussed, several methodological limitations should be noted.

First, despite efforts by Murdock[20] and others, no wholly satisfactory method has been devised for obtaining a representative sample of the world's societies. Since the universe of separate societies has not been

---

America, South America, and Oceania. Purposely omitted from the sample were Europe and Russia because they were already represented in the "counsel" type in the Freeman-Winch sample. Selection from different regions was designed to avoid the problem, first noted by Francis Galton, that cross-cultural regularities might be due to diffusion rather than to functional interrelationships. For a discussion of the problem and evidence of the importance of geographical separateness in sampling, see Raoul Naroll, "Two Solutions to Galton's Problem," Philosophy of Science, XXVIII (1961), 15–39; Raoul Naroll and Roy G. D'Andrade, "Two Further Solutions to Galton's Problem," American Anthropologist, LXV (October, 1963), 1053–67; and Raoul Naroll, "A Fifth Solution to Galton's Problem," American Anthropologist, Vol. LXVI. . . .

[18] These three—Cheyenne, Comanche, and Trobrianders—were selected by James C. Miller before the hypothesis was known to him. Selection of both the Comanche and Cheyenne is subject to some criticism on the grounds that they were prone to diffusion, but this hardly seems a serious difficulty in view of the difference in their scale positions. At all events, the coefficients of reproducibility and scalability would not be seriously lowered by eliminating one of the two.

[19] The original study also included damages, imprisonment, and execution. These were dropped from the present analysis, even though this unfortunately limited the scale to three items, to permit focus on statuses rather than sanction. Data on damages will be introduced, however, where relevant to the discussion of restitution.

[20] George Peter Murdock, "World Ethnographic Sample," American Anthropologist, LIX (August, 1957), 664–87.

adequately defined, much less enumerated, the representativeness of the sample cannot be ascertained. Nevertheless, an effort has been made to include societies drawn from the major culture areas and from diverse stages of technological development.

Second, societies have been selected in terms of the availability of adequate ethnographic reports. As a result, a bias may have entered the sample through the selection of societies that were particularly accessible—and hospitable—to anthropological observers. Such societies may differ in their patterns of development from societies that have been less well studied.

Third, despite the selection of relatively well-studied societies, the quality of reports varies widely. Like the preceding limitations, this problem is common to all cross-cultural comparisons. The difficulty is mitigated, however, by the fact that the results of this study are positive. The effect of poor reporting should generally be to randomize the apparent occurrence of the variables studied. Where systematic patterns of relationship emerge, as they do in the present research, it would seem to indicate considerable accuracy in the original reports.[21]

Fourth, this study deals with characteristics whose presence or absence can be determined with relative accuracy. In so doing, it may neglect elements of fundamental importance to the basic inquiry. Thus no effort is made to observe the presence of such important phenomena as respect for law, the use of generalized norms, and the pervasiveness of deviance-induced disturbance. Although all of these should be included in a comprehensive theory of legal evolution, they are omitted here in the interest of observational reliability.[22]

---

[21] *On this point see Donald T. Campbell, "The Mutual Methodological Relevance of Anthropology and Psychology," in Francis L. K. Hsu (ed.),* Psychological Anthropology *(Homewood, Ill.: Dorsey Press, 1961), p. 347. This inference should be treated with caution, however, in light of Raoul Naroll's observation that systematic observer bias can lead to spurious correlations* (Data Quality Control: A New Research Technique *[New York: Free Press of Glencoe, 1962]).*

[22] *Determination of the presence of a characteristic was made after a detailed search by Miller of the materials on each society in the Human Relations Area Files. His search began with a thorough reading for all societies of the material filed under category 18, "total culture." (All categories used are described in detail in George P. Murdock et al.,* Outline of Cultural Materials *[4th rev. ed.; New Haven, Conn.: Human Relations Area Files, 1961].) This was followed by a search of the annotated bibliography (category 111) to locate any works specifically dealing with legal or dispute settling processes. When found, works of this kind were examined*

Fifth, the Guttman scale is here pressed into service beyond that for which it was developed. Originally conceived as a technique for the isolation of uni-dimensional attitudes, it has also been used as a means of studying the interrelationship of behavior patterns. It should be particularly valuable, however, in testing hypotheses concerning developmental sequences, whether in individuals or in societies.[23] Thus, if we hypothesize

---

in detail. In addition, materials filed under the following categories were read: community structure (621), headmen (622), councils (623), police (625), informal in-group justice (627), intercommunity relations (628), territorial hierarchy (631), legal norms (671), liability (672), offenses and sanctions (68), litigation (691), judicial authority (692), legal and judicial personnel (693), initiation of judicial proceedings (694), trial procedure (695), execution of justice (696), prisons and jails (697), and special courts (698). If this search did not reveal the presence of the practice or status under investigation, it was assumed absent. The principal sources relied on for these determinations are given in a mineographed bibliography which will be supplied by the authors on request.

A reliability check on Miller's judgments was provided by Robert C. Scholl, to whom the writers are indebted. Working independently and without knowledge of the hypotheses, Scholl examined a randomly selected third of the total sample. His judgments agreed with those of Miller 88 per cent, disagreed 4 per cent, and he was unable to reach conclusions on 8 per cent of the items. If the inconclusive judgments are excluded, the reliability reaches the remarkable level of 96 per cent.

The use of a single person to check reliability falls short of the desired standard. In a more detailed and extensive projected study of the relationships reported here, we plan to use a set of three independent naïve judges. For discussion of the problems involved in judging cross-cultural materials see John W. M. Whiting and Irvin L. Child, Child Training and Personality (New Haven, Conn.: Yale University Press, 1953), pp. 39–62; and Guy E. Swanson, The Birth of the Gods (Ann Arbor: Michigan University Press, 1960), pp. 32–54.

[23] The use of the Guttman scale is extensively treated by Robert L. Carneiro in "Scale Analysis as an Instrument for the Study of Cultural Evolution," Southwestern Journal of Anthropology, XVIII (1962), 149–69. In a sophisticated critique of the Carneiro paper, Ward L. Goodenough suggests that quasi-scales may be needed for charting general evolutionary trends and for treating the traits that develop and then fail to persist because they are superseded by functional equivalents ("Some Applications of Guttman Scale Analysis to Ethnography and Culture Theory," Southwestern Journal of Anthropology, XIX [Autumn, 1963], 235–50). While the quasi-scale is a desirable instrument for analyzing supersedence, Goodenough appears unduly pessimistic about the possible occurrence of approximately perfect scales, see p. 246. Studies that obtained such scales, in addition to the one reported here, include Freeman and Winch, op. cit.; Stanley H. Udy, " 'Bureaucratic' Elements in Organizations: Some Research Findings," American Sociological Review, XXII (1958), 415–18; Frank W. and Ruth C. Young, "Social Integration and Change in Twenty-four Mexican Villages," Economic Development and Cultural Change, VIII (July, 1960), 366–77; and Robert L. Carneiro and Stephen L. Tobias, "The Application of Scale Analysis to the Study of Cultural Evolution,"

that A must precede B, supporting data should show three scale types: neither A nor B, A but not B, and A and B. All instances of B occurring without A represent errors which lower the reproducibility of the scale and, by the same token, throw doubt in measurable degree on the developmental hypothesis.[24] Although the occurrence of developmental sequences ultimately requires verification by the observation of historic changes in given units, substantiating evidence can be derived from the comparative study of units at varying stages of development. The Guttman scale seems an appropriate quantitative instrument for this purpose.

## FINDINGS

In the fifty-one societies studied, as indicated in Table 1, four scale types emerged. Eleven societies showed none of the three characteristics; eighteen had only mediation; eleven had only mediation and police; and seven had mediation, police, and specialized counsel. Two societies departed from these patterns: the Crow and the Thonga had police, but showed no evidence of mediation. While these deviant cases merit detailed study, they reduce the reproducibility of the scale by less than 2 per cent, leaving the coefficient at the extraordinarily high level of better than .98.[25]

---

Transactions of the New York Academy of Sciences, *Series II, XXVI* (1963), 196–207.

*The suggestion that Guttman scales could be used for discovering and testing temporal sequences was made earlier by Norman G. Hawkins and Joan K. Jackson in "Scale Analysis and the Prediction of Life Processes,"* American Sociological Review, *XXII* (1957), 579–81. *Their proposal referred, however, to individuals rather than societies.*

[24] *The developmental inference does not preclude the possibility of reversal of the usual sequence. It merely indicates which item will be added if any is acquired. Cf. S. N. Eisenstadt, "Social Change, Differentiation and Evolution,"* American Sociological Review, *XXIX* (June, 1964), 378–81. *The finding of a scale also does not rule out the possibility that two items may sometimes occur simultaneously, although the existence of all possible scale types indicates that no two items invariably occur simultaneously and that when they occur separately one regularly precedes the other.*

[25] *This coefficient of reproducibility far exceeds the .90 level suggested by Guttman as an "efficient approximation . . . of perfect scales" (Samuel Stouffer [ed.],* Measurement and Prediction *[Princeton, N.J.: Princeton University Press, 1950]). The coefficient of scalability, designed by Menzel to take account of extremeness in the distribution of items and individuals, far exceeds the .65 level*

TABLE 1. SCALE OF LEGAL CHARACTERISTICS.

| Society | Counsel | Police | Mediation | Errors | Legal Scale Type | Freeman-Winch Scale Type |
|---|---|---|---|---|---|---|
| Cambodians | x | x | x | | 3 | * |
| Czechs | x | x | x | | 3 | 6 |
| Elizabethan English | x | x | x | | 3 | 6 |
| Imperial Romans | x | x | x | | 3 | 6 |
| Indonesians | x | x | x | | 3 | * |
| Syrians | x | x | x | | 3 | * |
| Ukrainians | x | x | x | | 3 | 6 |
| Ashanti | | x | x | | 2 | 5 |
| Cheyenne | | x | x | | 2 | * |
| Creek | | x | x | | 2 | 5 |
| Cuna | | x | x | | 2 | 4 |
| Crow | | x | | 1 | 2 | 0 |
| Hopi | | x | x | | 2 | 5 |
| Iranians | | x | x | | 2 | 6 |
| Koreans | | x | x | | 2 | 6 |
| Lapps | | x | x | | 2 | 6 |
| Maori | | x | x | | 2 | 4 |
| Riffians | | x | x | | 2 | 6 |
| Thonga | | x | | 1 | 2 | 2 |
| Vietnamese | | x | x | | 2 | 6 |
| Andamanese | | | x | | 1 | 0 |
| Azande | | | x | | 1 | 0 |
| Balinese | | | x | | 1 | 4 |
| Cayapa | | | x | | 1 | 2 |
| Chagga | | | x | | 1 | 4 |
| Formosan aborigines | | | x | | 1 | 0 |
| Hottentot | | | x | | 1 | 0 |
| Ifugao | | | x | | 1 | 0 |
| Lakher | | | x | | 1 | 2 |
| Lepcha | | | x | | 1 | 3 |
| Menomini | | | x | | 1 | 0 |

*that he generated from a scalability analysis of Guttman's American Soldier data. Herbert A. Menzel, "A New Coefficient for Scalogram Analysis," Public Opinion Quarterly, XVII (Summer, 1953), 268–80, esp. 276. The problem of determining goodness of fit for the Guttman scale has still not been satisfactorily resolved (see W. S. Torgerson, Theory and Methods of Scaling [New York: John Wiley & Sons, 1958], esp. p. 324). A method utilizing $x^2$ to test the hypothesis that observed scale frequencies deviate from a rectangular distribution no more than would be expected by chance is suggested by Karl F. Schuessler, "A Note on Statistical Significance of Scalogram," Sociometry, XXIV (September, 1961), 312–18. Applied to these data, Schuessler's Test II permits the rejection of the chance hypothesis at the .001 level. $x^2 = 60.985$ (7df).*

TABLE 1. SCALE OF LEGAL CHARACTERISTICS. (*Continued*)

| | | | |
|---|---|---|---|
| Mbundu | x | 1 | 3 |
| Navaho | x | 1 | 5 |
| Ossett | x | 1 | 1 |
| Siwans | x | 1 | 1 |
| Trobrianders | x | 1 | * |
| Tupinamba | x | 1 | 0 |
| Venda | x | 1 | 5 |
| Woleaians | x | 1 | 0 |
| Yakut | x | 1 | 1 |
| Aranda | | 0 | 0 |
| Buka | | 0 | 0 |
| Chukchee | | 0 | 0 |
| Comanche | | 0 | * |
| Copper Eskimo | | 0 | 0 |
| Jivaro | | 0 | 0 |
| Kababish | | 0 | 1 |
| Kazak | | 0 | 0 |
| Siriono | | 0 | 0 |
| Yaruro | | 0 | 0 |
| Yurok | | 0 | 1 |

* Not included in Freeman-Winch sample.

Coefficient of reproducibility $= 1 - 2/153 = .987$; coefficient of scalability $= 1 - 2/153–120 = .94$; Kendall's tau $= +.68$.

Each characteristic of legal organization may now be discussed in terms of the sociolegal conditions in which it is found.

### Mediation

Societies that lack mediation, constituting less than a third of the entire sample, appear to be the simplest societies. None of them has writing or any substantial degree of specialization.[26] Only three of the thirteen (Yurok, Kababish, and Thonga) use money, whereas almost three-fourths of the societies with mediation have a symbolic means of exchange. We can only speculate at present on the reasons why mediation is absent in these societies. Data on size, using Naroll's definition of the social unit,[27] indicate that the maximum community size of societies without mediation is substantially smaller than that of societies with

---

[26] *Statements of this type are based on the ratings in the Freeman-Winch study, as noted in n. 14 above. For societies that did not appear in their sample, we have made our own ratings on the basis of their definitions.*

[27] *Raoul Naroll, "A Preliminary Index of Social Development,"* American Anthropologist, *LVIII (August, 1956), 687–720.*

mediation.[28] Because of their small size, mediationless societies may have fewer disputes and thus have less opportunity to evolve regularized patterns of dispute settlement. Moreover, smaller societies may be better able to develop mores and informal controls which tend to prevent the occurrence of disputes. Also, the usually desperate struggle for existence of such societies may strengthen the common goal of survival and thus produce a lessening of intragroup hostility.

The lack of money and substantial property may also help to explain the absence of mediation in these societies. There is much evidence to support the hypothesis that property provides something to quarrel about. In addition, it seems to provide something to mediate with as well. Where private property is extremely limited, one would be less likely to find a concept of damages, that is, property payments in lieu of other sanctions. The development of a concept of damages should greatly increase the range of alternative settlements. This in turn might be expected to create a place for the mediator as a person charged with locating a settlement point satisfactory to the parties and the society.

This hypothesis derives support from the data in Table 2. The

TABLE 2. DAMAGES IN RELATION TO LEGAL FUNCTIONARIES.

|  | No Mediation | Mediation Only | Mediation and Police | Mediation, Police, and Counsel | Total |
|---|---|---|---|---|---|
| Damages | 7 | 17 | 10 | 7 | 41 |
| No damages | 6* | 3 | 1 | 0 | 10 |
| Total | 13 | 20 | 11 | 7 | 51 |

* Includes Thonga, who have neither mediation nor damages, but have police.

concept of damages occurs in all but four of the thirty-eight societies that have mediation and thus appears to be virtually a precondition for mediation. It should be noted, however, that damages are also found in several (seven of thirteen) of the societies that lack mediation. The

[28] *Data were obtained for thirty-nine of the fifty-one societies in the sample on the size of their largest settlement. Societies with mediation have a median largest settlement size of 1,000, while those without mediation have a median of 346. Even eliminating the societies with developed cities, the median largest settlement size remains above 500 for societies with mediation.*

relationship that emerges is one of damages as a necessary but not sufficient condition for mediation. At present it is impossible to ascertain whether the absence of mediation in societies having the damage concept results from a simple time lag or whether some other factor, not considered in this study, distinguishes these societies from those that have developed mediation.

### Police

Twenty societies in the sample had police—that is, a specialized armed force available for norm enforcement. As noted, all of these but the Crow and Thonga had the concept of damages and some kind of mediation as well. Nevertheless, the occurrence of twenty societies with mediation but without police makes it clear that mediation is not inevitably accompanied by the systematic enforcement of decisions.

The separability of these two characteristics is graphically illustrated in ethnographic reports. A striking instance is found among the Albanian tribesmen whose elaborately developed code for settling disputes, Lek's Kanun, was used for centuries as a basis for mediation. But in the absence of mutual agreements by the disputants, feuds often began immediately after adjudication and continued unhampered by any constituted police.[29]

From the data it is possible to determine some of the characteristics of societies that develop police. Eighteen of the twenty in our sample are economically advanced enough to use money. They also have a substantial degree of specialization, with full-time priests and teachers found in all but three (Cheyenne, Thonga, and Crow), and full-time governmental officials, not mere relatives of the chief, present in all but four (Cuna, Maori, Thonga, and Crow).

Superficially at least, these findings seem directly contradictory to Durkheim's major thesis in *The Division of Labor in Society*. He hypothesized that penal law—the effort of the organized society to punish offenses against itself—occurs in societies with the simplest division of labor. As indicated, however, our data show that police are found only in association with a substantial degree of division of labor. Even the practice of governmental punishment for wrongs against the society (as noted by

---

[29] *Margaret Hasluck*, The Unwritten Law in Albania (*Cambridge: Cambridge University Press, 1954*).

Freeman and Winch) does not appear in simpler societies. By contrast, restitutive sanctions—damages and mediation—which Durkheim believed to be associated with an increasing division of labor, are found in many societies that lack even rudimentary specialization. Thus Durkheim's hypothesis seems the reverse of the empirical situation in the range of societies studied here.[30]

## Counsel

Seven societies in the sample employ specialized advocates in the settlement of disputes. As noted, all of these societies also use mediation. There are, however, another thirty-one societies that have mediation but do not employ specialized counsel. It is a striking feature of the data that damages and mediation are characteristic of the simplest (as well as the most complex) societies, while legal counsel are found only in the most complex. The societies with counsel also have, without exception, not only damages, mediation, and police but, in addition, all of the complexity characteristics identified by Freeman and Winch.

---

[30] *A basic difficulty in testing Durkheim's thesis arises from his manner of formulating it. His principal interest, as we understand it, was to show the relationship between division of labor and type of sanction (using type of solidarity as the intervening variable). However, in distinguishing systems of law, he added the criterion of organization. The difficulty is that he was very broad in his criterion of organization required for penal law, but quite narrow in describing the kind of organization needed for non-penal law. For the former, the "assembly of the whole people" sufficed (op. cit., p. 76); for the latter, on the other hand, he suggested the following criteria: "restitutive law creates organs which are more and more specialized: consular tribunals, councils of arbitration, administrative tribunals of every sort: Even in its most general part, that which pertains to civil law, it is exercised only through particular functionaries: magistrates, lawyers, etc., who have become apt in this role because of very special training" (p. 113). In thus suggesting that restitutive law exists only with highly complex organizational forms, Durkheim virtually insured that his thesis would be proven—that restitutive law would be found only in complex societies.*

*Such a "proof," however, would miss the major point of his argument. In testing the main hypothesis it would seem preferable, therefore, to specify a common and minimal organizational criterion, such as public support. Then the key question might be phrased: Is there a tendency toward restitutive rather than repressive sanctions which develops as an increasing function of the division of labor? Although our present data are not conclusive, the finding of damages and mediation in societies with minimal division of labor implies a negative answer. This suggests that the restitutive principle is not contingent on social heterogeneity or that heterogeneity is not contingent on the division of labor.*

It is not surprising that mediation is not universally associated with counsel. In many mediation systems the parties are expected to speak for themselves. The mediator tends to perform a variety of functions, questioning disputants as well as deciding on the facts and interpreting the law. Such a system is found even in complex societies, such as Imperial China. There the prefect acted as counsel, judge, and jury, using a whip to wring the truth from the parties who were assumed a priori to be lying.[31] To serve as counsel in that setting would have been painful as well as superfluous. Even where specialized counsel emerge, their role tends to be ambiguous. In ancient Greece, for instance, counsel acted principally as advisors on strategy. Upon appearance in court they sought to conceal the fact that they were specialists in legal matters, presenting themselves merely as friends of the parties or even on occasion assuming the identity of the parties themselves.[32]

At all events, lawyers are here found only in quite urbanized societies, all of which are based upon fully developed agricultural economies. The data suggest at least two possible explanations. First, all of the sample societies with counsel have a substantial division of labor, including priests, teachers, police, and government officials. This implies an economic base strong enough to support a variety of secondary and tertiary occupations as well as an understanding of the advantages of specialization. Eleven societies in the sample, however, have all of these specialized statuses but lack specialized counsel. What distinguishes the societies that develop counsel? Literacy would seem to be an important factor. Only five of the twelve literate societies in the sample do not have counsel. Writing, of course, makes possible the formulation of a legal code with its advantages of forewarning the violator and promoting uniformity in judicial administration. The need to interpret a legal code provides a niche for specialized counsel, especially where a substantial segment of the population is illiterate.[33]

---

[31] *Sybille van der Sprenkel, Legal Institutions in Manchu China (London: Athlone Press, 1962). See also Ch'ü T'ung-tsu,* Law and Society in Traditional China (*Vancouver, B.C.: Institute of Pacific Relations, 1961*).

[32] *A. H. Chroust, "The Legal Profession in Ancient Athens,"* Notre Dame Law Review, *XXIX (Spring, 1954)*, 339–89.

[33] *Throughout the discussion, two sets of explanatory factors have been utilized. The observed pattern could be due to an internal process inherent in legal control systems, or it could be dependent upon the emergence of urban characteristics. It does seem clear, however, that the legal developments coincide to a considerable ex-*

# CONCLUSIONS

These data, taken as a whole, lend support to the belief that an evolutionary sequence occurs in the development of legal institutions. Alternative interpretations are, to be sure, not precluded. The scale analysis might fail to discern short-lived occurrences of items. For instance, counsel might regularly develop as a variation in simple societies even before police, only to drop out rapidly enough so that the sample picks up no such instances. Even though this is a possibility in principle, no cases of this kind have come to the authors' attention.

Another and more realistic possibility is that the sequence noted in this sample does not occur in societies in a state of rapid transition. Developing societies undergoing intensive cultural contact might provide an economic and social basis for specialized lawyers, even in the absence of police or dispute mediation. Until such societies are included in the sample, these findings must be limited to relatively isolated, slowly changing societies.

The study also raises but does not answer questions concerning the evolution of an international legal order. It would be foolhardy to generalize from the primitive world directly to the international scene and to

---

tent with increased "urbanism" as measured by Freeman and Winch. Evidence for this assertion is to be found in the correlation between the Freeman-Winch data and the legal scale types discerned. For the forty-five societies appearing in both samples, the rank correlation coefficient (Kendall's tau) between positions on the legal and urbanism scales is +.68. While this coefficient suggests a close relationship between the two processes, it does not justify the assertion that legal evolution is wholly determined by increasing urbanism. A scatter diagram of the interrelationship reveals that legal characteristics tend to straddle the regression line for five of the seven folk-urban scale positions, omitting only scale types 2 (punishment) and 3 (religious specialization). This suggests that some other factor might emerge upon further analysis that would explain why roughly half of the societies at each stage of urbanism appear to have gone on to the next stage of legal evolution while the others lag behind. A promising candidate for such a factor is the one located by Gouldner and Peterson in their cross-cultural factor analysis of Simmons' data and described by them as "Apollonianism" or "Norm-sending" (Alvin W. Gouldner and Richard A. Peterson, Technology and the Moral Order [Indianapolis: Bobbs-Merrill Co., 1962], pp. 30–53).

To test whether the legal sequence has a "dynamic of its own," it would seem necessary to examine the growth of legal systems independent of folk-urban changes, as in subsystems or in societies where the process of urbanization has already occurred. The data covered here do not permit such a test.

assume that the same sequences must occur here as there. There is no certainty that subtribal units can be analogized to nations, because the latter tend to be so much more powerful, independent, and relatively deficient in common culture and interests. In other ways, the individual nations are farther along the path of legal development than subtribal units because all of them have their own domestic systems of mediation, police, and counsel. This state of affairs might well provide a basis for short-circuiting an evolutionary tendency operative in primitive societies. Then too, the emergent world order appears to lack the incentive of common interest against a hostile environment that gave primitive societies a motive for legal control. Even though the survival value of a legal system may be fully as great for today's world as for primitive societies, the existence of multiple units in the latter case permitted selection for survival of those societies that had developed the adaptive characteristic. The same principle cannot be expected to operate where the existence of "one world" permits no opportunity for variation and consequent selection.

Nonetheless, it is worth speculating that some of the same forces may operate in both situations.[34] We have seen that damages and mediation almost always precede police in the primitive world. This sequence could result from the need to build certain cultural foundations in the community before a central regime of control, as reflected in a police force, can develop. Hypothetically, this cultural foundation might include a determination to avoid disputes, an appreciation of the value of third-party intervention, and the development of a set of norms both for preventive purposes and as a basis for allocating blame and punishment when disputes arise. Compensation by damages and the use of mediators might well contribute to the development of such a cultural foundation, as well as reflecting its growth. If so, their occurrence prior to specialized police would be understandable. This raises the question as to whether the same kind of cultural foundation is not a necessary condition for the establishment of an effective world police force and whether, in the interest of that objective, it might not be appropriate to stress the principles of compensatory damages and mediation as preconditions for the growth of a world rule of law.

---

[34] *For an interesting attempt to develop a general theory of legal control, applicable both to discrete societies and to the international order, see Kenneth S. Carlston,* Law and Organization in World Society (*Urbana: University of Illinois Press, 1962*).

# LAW
# AND SOCIAL
# CHANGE*

*Yehezkel Dror*

## I. INTRODUCTION

The varied aspects of the relationship between law and social change pose some challenging problems of great significance for an understanding of the role of law in modern societies. These aspects include new modes for changing the law, lag in the development of law behind social change, the use of law as a device to induce social change and others.

Despite the growing recognition of the significance of social change and the great amount of research going on in this area, and the progress being made at the same time in the social study of law[1] and in comparative law, these fields of investigation have been isolated from each other, and relatively little has been done to investigate their inter-relationships. Among the reasons for the lack of research in this area might be the dearth of research personnel trained both in law and the social sciences, the absence of research methods adjusted to investigation of the social

\* *The author acknowledges with appreciation the valuable suggestions of Professor Benjamin Akzin.*

[1] *For surveys of the development of the social study of law (which is largely identical with the discipline commonly known as "sociology of law"), see Gurvitch, Sociology of Law ch. 1 (1947) and Pound, Sociology of Law, in Twentieth Century Sociology 297–341 (1954).*

Reprinted by permission of the author and of the publishers from 33 *Tulane Law Review* (1959), 787–802. Footnotes have been renumbered to run in sequence throughout the selection.

aspects of normative systems such as law,[2] the overconcern of social scientists with the "social control" function of law[3] and the underdevelopment of the social study of law in general.

In exploring some central issues we will first examine some basic concepts; then we shall proceed to a brief discussion of main modes for changing the law, which will lead to a more detailed analysis of the relationship between law and social change. Finally, some implications of our investigation will be examined, especially for their significance for the social study of law, the comparative study of law and the development of the policy-study approach[4] to law making.

At this point some close connections between the comparative study of law and the investigation of the relationships between law and social change should also be noted. On one hand, the methods developed by the comparative study of law provide research methodologies essential for the study of law and social change. The impossibility of conducting controlled experimentation in this area and the inherent limitations of inductions based on the experience of any one society, emphasize the necessity of utilizing comparative research methods; these enable us to gain an insight into legal and social processes by investigating comparable phenomena and problems in different societies and examining the impact of different variables and factors operating in these societies. On the other hand, the continuous development and progress of the comparative study of law depends to some extent on an understanding of the basic processes of the relationships between law and society, which must provide the essential background and perspective for the study of the various legal systems which are scarcely susceptible to meaningful investigation when isolated from their social contexts.

---

[2] *Similarly, sociology of religion is one of the more undeveloped parts of sociology. Here again methods are needed for investigating the relations between normative systems and society, and such methods have not yet been designed. For an interesting discussion of some of these methodological problems see* Introduction to Brandt, Hopi Ethics (1954).

[3] *For a short survey of the view of law by contemporary American sociologists, see* Davis, The Treatment of Law in American Sociology, *in* 42 Sociology and Social Research 99 (1957).

[4] *Following an oral suggestion by Professor Karl N. Llewellyn, I prefer this term to the commonly accepted term "policy science" used by Harold Lasswell. Lerner & Lasswell, The Policy Sciences 3–15 (1951). One may doubt whether the present state of that discipline (or approach) justifies the use of the somewhat presumptuous term "science."*

## II. SOME BASIC CONCEPTS

The two basic concepts of our investigation are social change and law. Society is always undergoing processes of change; human generations follow one another and different persons fulfil various social roles. The concept "social change" does not refer to this constant change in the population of every society, but refers to changes in the society as such, including the various social institutions, roles and status definitions, accepted ideologies, value patterns, pattern variables and value-profiles. In other words, the concept of social change refers to changes in social structure or in culture.

Social change can be initiated by various factors, including changes in the physical environment of the society; changes in the genetic constitution of the population; contact with other societies; internal social change, such as general social movements and new technological or social inventions.[5] One of the characteristics of all contemporary cultures is their high rate of social change; in modern Western societies a high rate of social change, associated especially with changes in technology, has become accepted as a permanent feature of social life, while the various so-called underdeveloped societies which are still relatively static aim at achieving an even higher rate of social change, so as to enable them rapidly to reach the level of technical development characteristic of Western societies. Contemporary sociology devotes much attention to the study of social changes, but as yet its basic pre-conditions and processes are little understood, and very little is known of basic problems, such as whether human societies are able to exist in a state of permanent high rate of social change, and for how long, and how high-rate social change influences the mental stability of the individual.

Society consists of a large number of social institutions and components; social change in most cases begins in some of these institutions or elements, which in turn influence other institutions and elements until the whole of society changes. This raises the problem, of the extent to which certain components of society and culture can change without bringing about changes in other aspects of society, and the extent to which some components of society and culture can remain static despite changes in other aspects.

---

[5] *Barnett, Innovation: The Basis of Cultural Change (1953); Parsons, The Social System 480 (1951).*

This problem is closely related to the more general one, *i.e.,* to what extent do the various aspects of society form an interacting system, every change in one part of which must bring about corresponding changes in all other parts. The more autonomous a certain area is, the more it can be studied in isolation from the other institutions of its society and the easier it is to compare it with parallel areas in other societies. On the other hand, if a certain area of culture or social activity is very closely interwoven with other aspects of the same society, it becomes difficult to study it in isolation and it becomes nearly impossible to compare it by itself and outside its social context with parallel areas in other societies.

The application of these concepts to our field of inquiry becomes clear when we take into account the character of law, which from the point of view of the social sciences constitutes a part of the culture of every society.

However we may define law, it must be regarded for our purpose as a part of the culture of every society. Applying our previous analysis of social change to the relationship of social change and law, the questions arise as to how far it is independent of other parts of culture and society, how far changes in law follow changes in other aspects of society and how far changes in law bring about changes in other aspects of society. In other words, we can define the problem as one of the relative autonomy of law vis-à-vis other components of society. Its central concerns are the processes creating a lag[6] between law and other components of society and culture and the processes adjusting law to society and society to law.

The relationship between law and social change is further complicated by the dual social character of law. The whole of the law of a given society forms a system consistent within itself and with a whole network of internal relationships, which constitutes a subsystem of that society's total culture and is intimately linked with its law making, law-applying and law-enforcing institutions and processes; furthermore, law is a pervasive element of every social institution and plays an important role in all of them. Thus, family law forms a part of the whole of law and cannot be understood in isolation from the legal system as a whole, but family law is

---

[6] *The concept of "lag" as referring to the differential rate of development of various social institutions and the resultant maladjustment between them was mainly developed by W. F. Ogburn, especially in his book,* Social Change *(1922). For a modern discussion of this concept see Wallis,* The Concept of Lag, *29 Sociology and Social Research 403.*

also an internal and essential part of the family institution, and cannot be fully understood without consideration of it.

### III. PROCESSES OF CHANGE IN THE LAW

Three main organs bring about changes in the law: specialised legislative organs, specialised law-applying organs and various law-enforcing and law-using organs and bodies. The existence of differentiated and formally defined legislative bodies which enact statutory law, courts which are in charge of applying the law, and prosecution and police agencies which enforce it, is a characteristic shared by all modern societies (though the law making, law applying and law enforcing activities of various administrative agencies confuse to some extent the social division of work in this respect). In many of the primitive societies, on the other hand, social differentiation of work is less developed, and some or all of the legal functions may be performed by the same body or may be left to the basic units of social action (*e.g.,* the family);[7] but wherever we find law (or pre-law), these basic functions are performed to some extent and serve as the vehicle through which changes in the law occur.

Conscious legislation by a special legislative body constitutes today one of the most important avenues for changing the law.[8] While conscious legislation by a special organ can be found at various periods and in different kinds of societies, it is mainly in Western bureaucratic society (beginning with the period of enlightened absolutism in the seventeenth and eighteenth centuries) that conscious law-making by a central legislative body became of predominant importance and constitutes the main mode for changing the law, though some similar tendencies can be discerned in Rome during the period of the empire.

Concerning the role of the central legislature vis-à-vis the other organs

---

[7] *Gluckman, The Judicial Process Among the Barotse of Northern Rhodesia (1955); Hoebel, The Law of Primitive Man (1954); and Llewellyn & Hoebel, The Cheyenne Way (1941), include some fascinating examples of the operation of the various law-associated processes in primitive societies.*

[8] *This development is perhaps associated with the evolution of the concept of "public policy" and the desire to use legislation as a conscious instrument to achieve the policy objectives. This approach was perhaps best expressed in the writings of Jeremy Bentham.*

of law-changing, two phenomena merit special attention. In a country with a rigid constitution and with an agency authorised to pronounce the validity of legislation in the light of that constitution, the possibilities of changing the law by conscious legislation are limited. Therefore, in such a country the other organs of law-changing bear a special responsibility and fulfil an important role.[9] The United States illustrates the case: the power of Congress to legislate is limited by the Constitution; since the constitution-amending process is rather cumbersome, the courts, especially when interpreting the Constitution, change the law in important areas.[10] In England, on the other hand, where there is no rigid constitution limiting the powers of the central legislature, all parts of the law are susceptible to change by direct legislative action and the responsibility of the courts in this respect is more limited.

Another phenomenon worthy of note is the reliance of the central legislature on secondary legislation. In all modern societies the scope and spread of secondary legislation is growing, despite constant efforts which are made to limit it.[11] In fact, many of the legislative changes of the law are brought about today through delegated legislation by administrative organs. It may well be that one of the reasons for the universal development of delegated legislation is the inability of the central legislature to deal with all needed changes of the law. Coupled with the undesirability or impossibility of leaving the problem to the courts, the only remaining solution lies in the grant of authority to administrative bodies to change the law through secondary legislation. The apparent correlation between the high rate of social change experienced by modern societies and the

---

[9] *Concerning the general problem of the stability of the basic parts of the law included in formal constitutions and their social significance see Lowenstein,* Reflexions sur la valeur des constitutions dans une epoque revolutionnaire, 2 *Revue française de science politique 5–24, 312–34 (1952), and Benjamin Akzin,* On The Stability and Reality of Constitutions, *in 3 Scripta Hierosolymitana 313–30 (1956).*

[10] *The New Deal controversies following the decisions of the Supreme Court of the United States in Panama Refining Co. v. Ryan, 293 U.S. 388 (1935), and Schechter Poultry Co. v. United States, 295 U.S. 495 (1935), and the "court packing plan" illustrate the use of extra-legal means to motivate the courts under extreme circumstances to change the law in cases where the legislature, subject to constitutional limitations, is unable to act.*

[11] *The already classical document on this problem is the Committee on Ministers' Powers,* Report, Cmd. No. 4060 (1932). *Concerning later developments in England, see Report from the Select Committee on Delegated Legislation (1953).*

large extension of the legislative authority of administrative bodies seems to bear out this hypothesis.[12]

An interesting variety of secondary legislation is the grant of quasi-legislative functions to the courts. In addition to the authority of the courts in some Anglo-American jurisdictions to regulate their internal administration and parts of the rules of procedure, there are some special cases of grants of authority to the courts which are very important from our point of view. The concluding sentence of Article 46 of the Palestine Order in Council, 1922, serves as an interesting illustration of a delegation of authority of this kind:

"Provided always that the said common law and doctrines of equity shall be in force in Palestine so far only as the circumstances of Palestine and its inhabitants and the limits of His Majesty's jurisdiction permit and subject to such qualification as local circumstances render necessary."[13]

Here the task of determining the "circumstances" is left to the courts and they are made responsible for adjusting the rules of the common law and equity to conditions in Palestine—a function clearly involving important law-making characteristics and very significant from the point of view of social change. The responsibility for the reception of the common law and equity in Palestine was here squarely and explicitly put on the court.[14]

\*   \*   \*   \*

Historically speaking, the courts, and to some extent administrative agencies, have been the most important organs for shaping and changing

---

[12] *This is only a partial explanation of the phenomenon of widespread delegated legislation. Additional important variables operate and shape the extent and form of delegated legislation in various societies.*

[13] *Drayton, Laws of Palestine 2569. This article laid down the law to be in force in Palestine. After leaving in force most parts of the Ottoman law it directs the courts, in cases of* lacunae, *to apply the common law and doctrines of equity recognized in England, subject to the qualification included in the sentence quoted above.*

[14] *It is interesting to compare the situation in Palestine with the situation in the United States after the revolution. The various colonial charters and state statutes included different rules on the reception of the English common law, but the courts in all jurisdictions assumed the responsibility for deciding which parts*

the law and adjusting it to social change, especially under the Anglo-American system of law.

The courts rely on various well-known mechanisms for changing the law. These vary as between countries which accept the doctrine of binding precedent to various degrees and countries in which courts are not bound by previous decisions. If the courts are not bound by precedent, they may re-interpret the law, relying mainly on contemporary ideas and concepts,[15] or change the law with the aid of legal fictions or constructions. When the courts are bound by precedent, they use, in addition to fictions, various distinguishing techniques, limiting and re-interpreting the *ratio decidendi* of previous decisions.

\* \* \* \*

It would be interesting to consider the extent to which the courts themselves and various segments of the population are aware of the law-making functions of the courts. At certain periods, the function of the courts was regarded as pure law-applying and it was thought that this function did not involve the making of new law, but today legal theory both on the Continent and in Anglo-American jurisdictions tends to recognize and appreciate the creative function of the courts.[16]

Furthermore, whether law-enforcing agencies prosecute or refrain from prosecuting certain offenses affects the impact of the law on society, although the law itself is not changed. Still more important from the view of changing the law are the practices of law-users, such as trade-practices, standard clauses and agreements, which constitute a rather important mode of changing the law—one that reflects rather accurately certain aspects of social change.

---

*of the common law suited conditions in the United States and received only those parts. Ford, The Common Law: An Account of Its Reception in the United States (1951).*

[15] *Renner, Die Rechtsinstitute der Privatrechts und ihre Soziale Function (1925), suggests that the meaning and content of legal concepts (such as "property") changes, while the concepts themselves remain constant. Otto Kahn-Freund, in his introduction to the English translation of Renner's book (1949), and Friedmann, Law and Social Change in Contemporary Britain (1951), tried to apply Renner's analysis to Anglo-American legal developments.*

[16] *For an investigation tracing the developments and discussing the differences between continental and Anglo-American thought in this respect cf. Von Mehren, The Judicial Process: A Comparative Analysis, 5 Am. J. Comp. L. 197 (1956).*

## IV. THE RELATIONSHIP BETWEEN LAW AND SOCIAL CHANGE

There is nearly always a certain difference between actual social behavior and the behavior demanded by the legal norm; the existence of a certain "tension" between actual behavior and legally desired behavior (and between legally required behavior and morally demanded behavior) belongs to the characteristics of law in all societies[17] and does not by itself signify the existence of a lag between law and social change. A lag appears only when there is more than a certain tension, when the law does not in fact answer the needs arising from major social changes or when social behavior and the sense of obligation generally felt towards legal norms significantly differs from the behavior required by law. In other words, while a certain difference between actual behavior and legally required behavior can be found in all societies, the concept of lag applies to law and social change in dynamic situations, after either social change or changes in the law occur and no parallel changes and adjustment processes take place in law or society respectively.

Some illustrations will clarify the concept of lag relative to law and social change. After the invention of the automobile, the totally unsuitable laws developed for horse-drawn carriages were applied.[18] After the industrial revolution the various laws against conspiracy were applied to workers' organizations in a way which constituted a clear lag behind the new social situation, which included both new techniques and ways of economic organization and new public sentiments and ideologies. It took the law in England and other countries a long time to catch up with these social developments and provide answers to the problems raised by them.[19] A contemporary illustration concerns the development of atomic energy and of public international law; public international law lags behind modern developments in nuclear techniques and has not yet adjusted itself to the new situations created by them. When space flight becomes technically feasible, even more urgent and difficult problems of adjustment to technological and social change will be posed before law.

---

[17] Kelsen, General Theory of Law and State 436–37 (1949).

[18] On the necessity of developing special law-making procedures to deal with this problem in France see Sieghart, Government by Decree 267–68 (1950).

[19] Dicey, Lectures on the Relations between Law and Public Opinion in England during the Nineteenth Century (2d ed. 1919). For a critique of Dicey's method and analysis see Stone, The Province and Function of Law 473 (1950).

All these illustrations deal with lag of the law behind social change. Though the very high rate of social change in contemporary societies confronts the agencies in charge of changing the law with difficult problems, the relative ease of legislation and the new modes of changing the law provide rather simple ways of adjusting the law to social change. In some jurisdictions, especially the international society and to some extent countries with rigid constitutions and judicial review powers over the constitutionality of legislation, the use of legislation to adjust the law to social change is somewhat limited; in all countries difficulties are faced concerning the problem of the best way of effecting this adjustment. In general, the use of conscious legislation in modern societies makes the process of adjustment of the law to social change rather easy. At a time when legislative action was not accepted as readily and legislatures were composed of conservative elites generally opposed to social change and averse to corresponding changes in the law, the lag of the law behind social change was very formidable indeed, and the primary responsibility for changing the law was imposed on the courts (themselves often composed of judges opposed on social change). But today the general orientation of nearly all strata and elites is in favor of change, and popular elections in democratic countries as well as support requirements in many a dictatorship assure the necessary sensitivity of the legislative organs and their willingness in general to change the law and adjust it to social change. More and more the issue here becomes one of preserving legal security, which is endangered by the rapid changes in the law, rather than one of preventing lag of law behind social needs and developments.

More novel, both from the theoretical and the practical point of view, is the problem of the lag of society after changes in the law. How far, if at all, can changes in the law be used to bring about social change? The first question is whether it is feasible and possible to change society through changing the law. Classical Marxian theory would answer in the negative. Regarding law as a superstructure on technology and the economy, that theory admitted the possibility of the lag of law behind social change and fully conceived that it might take some time for changes in technology and economy to be reflected in the law; but it would be inconceivable, from a Marxian point of view, for law to bring about changes in the basic technology and economy of society. Today, Soviet jurists recognize the possibility of using law to bring about social change and influence its direction,[20] and in fact Soviet Russia uses law extensively to bring about and regulate social change.[21]

A different argument against the possibility and desirability of using law to bring about social change was made by the historical school of jurisprudence and its founder, Savigny. Savigny, applying to law parts of Hegel's philosophy, regarded law as an organic growth indigenous to every society.[22] Therefore, he opposed legislation, and especially legislation adopting foreign institutions and laws.[23]

These arguments have been clearly overruled by the facts of reality. The growing use of law as a device of organized social action directed toward achieving social change seems to be one of the characteristics of modern society which is in need of intensive study. The relative novelty of the conscious, systematic and large-scale use of law as a device of social action and the apparent contradiction and real tension between the ideology of the rule of law—which regards law as the stable foundation of social order—and the instrumental orientation towards law associated with the utilization of law as a means of social action, may provide a partial explanation for the lack of attention paid to these crucial evolutions in the role of law and law-making in modern society.

Closer analysis of the role of law vis-à-vis social change leads us to distinguish between the direct and the indirect aspects of the role of law.

Law plays an important indirect role in regard to social change by shaping various social institutions, which in turn have a direct impact on society. Thus, a law setting up a compulsory educational system has a very

---

[20] *Kechekyan,* Social Progress and Law, *in 6 Transactions of the Third World Congress of Sociology 42 (1956). The author, a professor at the Moscow Law Institute, recognizes the use of law as an instrument in directing social change.*

[21] *See Hazard, Law and Social Change in the USSR (1913) and Berman, Justice in Russia (1950), where the use of "parental law" as an instrument for changing society through education by the law is discussed.*

[22] *See Savigny, Ueber den Beruf unserer Zeit sur Gestzgebung und zur Rechtswissenschaft (1814).*

[23] *It is interesting to note the influence of Savigny and his students on one of the founders of the social study of law, namely Eugen Ehrlich. Ehrlich, in his book, Grundlegung der Soziologie des Rechts (1913) (translated into English in 1936), accepted the organic theory of law and failed to distinguish clearly between law and other social norms. Consequently he became one of the founders of the Freirechtsschule, and opposed legislative activity. Many contemporary sociologists are still strongly influenced by Ehrlich.*

important indirect role in regard to social change, by enabling the operation of educational institutions which play a direct role in social change. On the other hand, law interacts in many cases directly with basic social institutions in a manner constituting a direct relationship between law and social change. Thus, a law designed to prohibit polygamy has a great direct influence on social change, having as its main purpose the bringing about of changes in important patterns of behavior. This distinction is not free from difficulties, caused mainly by the multiple character of most parts of law, which are both in a direct and in an indirect relationship with social changes. The distinction is not an absolute but a relative one: in some cases the emphasis is more on the direct and less on the indirect impact of social change, while in other cases the opposite is true.

The indirect influence of law on social change is closely interwoven with the functions of the various social institutions of which, as already mentioned, parts of law are an important element. Full examination of the indirect aspect of the role of law in relation to social change requires, therefore, analysis of social institutions outside the scope of this article. We will therefore limit ourselves to citing illustrations designed to clarify this aspect of the relation between law and social change.

To a considerable extent, law exerts an indirect influence on general social change by influencing the possibilities of change in the various social institutions. For example, the existence of a patent law protecting the rights of inventors encourages inventions and furthers change in the technological institutions, which in turn may bring about basic general social change.[24] The absence of freedom to associate and disseminate ideas can prevent, or at least delay, the spread of new social ideas, and thus exert a very important basic influence on the processes of social change in society.[25] The extent to which contact with other societies is limited or encouraged by law regulates one of the basic factors bringing about social change, and so on. Here, law as part of the various institutions (technology, political and social control, external relations) influences the chances

---

[24] *The importance of the role of patent law in this respect has been recognised also in the USSR. Hazard, op. cit. supra note [21], at ch. 8.*

[25] *Rose, The Use of Law to Induce Social Change, in 6 Transactions of the Third World Congress of Sociology 59 (1956). Rose emphasizes the importance of the role of law as a protector of minority groups, since they first adopt change and pass it on to the other members of the society. This article is also important because it is one of the first papers written by a prominent sociologist to recognise the uses of law as a device to induce social change.*

of changes in these social institutions and through them the processes of social change in general.

A somewhat different indirect relationship between law and social change concerns the indirect use of law in directed social change. The legal basis of organized social action in all modern societies—associated as they are with the internal functional needs of large-scale bureaucratic societies[26]—calls for the reliance on legal means as indirect aids for nearly all conscious attempts to bring about directed social change. Thus, if the state desires to set up a public body the functions of which include bringing about certain social changes, it is necessary to use law to set up the body and define its powers; here, law indirectly serves social change by setting up organs which directly try to further various social developments. The act setting up the Tennessee Valley Authority in the United States[27] and the acts dealing with new towns in England[28] illustrate this functioning of law as an indirect factor in social change.

A slightly different illustration of the indirect use of law in organized social action involving social change, is the creation of legal duties which in turn enable direct action to bring about social change. One of the most important instruments of directed social change relied upon in many countries is education. But in order for the educational network to operate effectively it is necessary to create a duty to study in them. Hence, as already mentioned, compulsory education laws indirectly serve the operation of the educational institutions, which in turn function as a direct factor in social change.

A very interesting additional way in which law indirectly serves social change is the role of law in preserving and assuring the operation of a free market economy, which is one of the more important mechanisms of social change in many countries, especially the United States.

Further ways in which changes in the law indirectly serve or reflect social change could be enumerated, but the important fact is the distinction between direct and indirect aspects of the relationships between law and social change. While there are many marginal cases and the difference is often one of degree, this distinction is of primary importance in obtain-

---

[26] Heller, Staatslehre 216 (1934).

[27] 48 Stat. 58 (1933), 16 U.S.C. § 831 (1952).

[28] New Towns Act, 1946, 9 & 10 Geo. 6, c. 68; cf. Town and Country Planning Act, 1947, 10 & 11 Geo. 6, c. 51.

ing a comprehensive and inclusive view of the relationships between law and social change.

Every collection of statutes and delegated legislation is full of illustrations of the direct use of law as a device for directed social change. This is true for all modern societies. But the more interesting and extreme examples of the use of changing the law as a device to bring about social change from which we can hope to study its processes and problems are provided by those cases where a revolutionary or intellectual minority obtains legislative power and uses it in its efforts to bring about extensive changes in social structure and culture. This was the case in Japan and Turkey, where whole parts of Western law were received with the intention thus to further the Westernization of these countries, and this was also the case in Soviet Russia. To some extent the efforts of various colonial powers, especially France, to introduce their law into various territories under their rule was also motivated by the desire to shape the social realities of those places.

Illustrations of the use of law to bring about substantial social change can also be found in modern Western countries. An interesting case illustrating an ambitious effort to shape social behavior through the use of law was the enactment of prohibition in the United States.[29] It was also one of the most conspicuous failures, showing that there are strict limits to the effective uses of law to bring about social change.

Consideration of the conditions for effective use of law as a device for directed social change and the limits of such use, is of the utmost practical and theoretical importance, as such a study provides a key to the development of a policy-study of legislation and to an understanding of some of the basic social processes associated with law and social behavior.

This question can be approached in two principal ways. One possible method would require examination of the psychological and socio-psychological processes through which law operates, and definition of the conditions under which individuals and groups adjust their behavior to new laws and, conversely, definition of the conditions under which new laws do not significantly influence behavior. It is not certain whether the study of psychology and social psychology has developed far enough to permit the use of this method. The role of law within the motivational

---

[29] *For an interesting though outdated description of various efforts to control the consumption of alcohol through various legal devices see Catlin, Liquor Control (1931).*

system of the individual and the psychological processes by which law commands obedience under certain conditions are not understood and are not likely to be thus understood until a great deal of progress is made in the study of more elementary socio-psychological phenomena, about which too little is known. Therefore this avenue to the investigation of the effectiveness of law is closed at present.

Fortunately, there is another way in which this question can be dealt with at least partially, *i.e.,* through a comparative empiric investigation of the effects of attempts to use law to induce social change in various societies. While little research has been done in this direction, published material together with a case-study from Israel, permit suggestion of a preliminary hypothesis concerning some of the independent variables determining the effectiveness of the use of law to induce social change.

Recently published material on the impact of the reception of Western law on society in Turkey[30] clearly brings out two facts: the reception did have a significant influence on some aspects of social life, while certain other aspects were but little influenced by the new laws meant to regulate them. It seems that the aspects of social action of a mainly instrumental character,[31] such as commercial activities, were significantly influenced by new law, while those aspects of social action involving expressive activities and basic beliefs and institutions, such as family life and marriage habits, were very little changed despite explicit laws trying to shape them.

This conclusion from the Turkish experience is reinforced by the failure up to the present time to change family habits of certain immigrant groups in Israel through legal norms. While Israel itself has not received a foreign legal system,[32] the legal pattern of Israel constitutes a new legal environment for the immigrants who came from various oriental and Arab countries; moreover, some laws have been enacted especially in order to bring about social change among them and among the Arab population of Israel. The Marriage Age Law,[33] serves as an interesting illustration.

---

[30] 60 *International Social Science Bulletin* (1956), *includes a series of articles on the reception of foreign law in Turkey, based on a symposium on this subject held by the International Committee of Comparative Law in 1955 at Istanbul.*

[31] Cf. *Parsons,* op. cit. supra *note 5, at 45, for discussion of some of the problems associated with this concept.*

[32] *Akzin,* Codification in a New State, A Case Study of Israel, 5 *Am. J. Comp. L. 44–47 (1956).*

[33] *4 Laws of Israel 158.*

This act sets the minimum age of seventeen for marriage, admitting pregnancy as the only exception, and imposes a criminal sanction on anyone who marries a girl below the age of seventeen without a permit from the district court or who assists in the marriage ceremony. By fixing the minimum age at seventeen, the law tried to impose a rule of behavior strictly opposed to the customs and habits of some of the sections of the Jewish population of Israel which came from Arab and oriental countries, where marriage was generally contracted at a lower age.[34] In relation to this part of the population, as well as in relation to parts of the Moslem and Druze population of Israel, the law constituted a determined effort to bring about social change through law.

In fact, while no systematic field-investigation has been conducted in this matter, it seems that this act has had only limited effect on social action. Those communities which formerly permitted marriage of females at an early age continue to do so.[35] The main impact of the law on social action was to create a situation where many marriages are contracted without formal registration, while the real purpose of the act is not being achieved. At present, the failure of the act to bring the desired social change is generally recognized, and it seems that the law will be amended so as to fix the minimum age of marriage at sixteen and grant free discretion to the courts to permit marriage after the age of fifteen.

It seems that here the Israeli experience supports the conclusion that can be drawn from the Turkish experience and supports our hypothesis that changes in law have more impact on emotionally neutral and instrumental areas of activity than on expressive and evaluative areas of activity. Basic institutions rooted in traditions and values, such as the family, seem to be extremely resistant to changes imposed by law.

Further comparative study is urgently needed to throw more light on the subject and to enable re-examination and elaboration of this basic hypothesis. The difficulties encountered in all countries when trying to use law as an instrument to control economic activities, evidenced by the everpresent phenomenon of the black market in periods of shortage and

[34] *On Jewish marriage laws and customs in various countries and periods see Freeman, Kidushin and Marriage Customs and Law (1945).*

[35] *This information is based on conversations with officials of the Ministry of Religious Affairs and the Ministry of Social Welfare, who are responsible for some aspects of the execution of the law.*

rationing, requires additional study which may well modify our hypotheses in important respects. Additional comparative study of the experience of various countries, including, *inter alia,* the experiences of Japan, Communist China and some of the so-called underdeveloped countries, could provide important relevant material, thus furthering the study of the direct relationship between law and social change and allowing us to grasp more fully the possibilities and limitations of the use of law as a means to induce social change.[36]

## V. CONCLUSIONS AND IMPLICATIONS

Social change and changes in the law are constant and interacting processes, present to a considerable extent in all contemporary societies. From the point of view of the social study of law and the comparative study of law, the investigation of these processes can contribute much to the understanding of the various legal systems within their respective social contexts. On the other hand, the study of these phenomena can contribute much to our understanding of the relationships between law and society and to the policy approach to law and law-making.

The high rate of social change prevalent or aimed at in nearly all contemporary societies seriously challenges the skills and abilities of statesmen, lawyers and social scientists, co-operation between whom is an essential prerequisite for finding at least partial solutions to the difficult problems posed by the dynamic character of modern technological culture. One of the more important devices used to initiate and control directed social change is law, a device the use of which is prima facie (and, in most cases, perhaps mistakenly) believed to be cheaper and quicker than education, economic development and other instruments and ways of directed social change.

This is one of the more significant areas where the comparative social study of law can make a significant contribution to the solution of social problems.[37] By examining and defining the conditions under which law

---

[36] *For an important recent study posing some basic problems of the relationship between law and social change and dealing with them through a close analysis of historical material see Hurst, Law and the Conditions of Freedom (1956).*

[37] *On the tendency to regard the solution of social problems as one of the func-*

can induce social change and by emphasizing the limits upon the use of law to induce social change, a significant contribution can be made to the development of law-making as a main object of policy studies.

---

tions of the social sciences see Lynd, *Knowledge for What?* (1948). For a vigorous counter-attack condemning the policy-orientation, especially in regard to law see Riesman, Towards an Anthropological Science of Law and the Legal Profession, 57 Am. J. Soc. 121–35 (1951).

# INDEX

Accident(s):
  claims, attrition rate, 373
  costs of, 368
Adversary system and expert testimony, 467
*Akins v. Texas,* 361
*American Soldier, The,* 545
Angell, Robert, 7, 65
Anthropological study of law, 220
  present trends, 221
  roots of, 220
Anthropology and law, 110
Applied scientific learning, 142, 145
Arnold, Thurman, 224
Ashmore, Harry, 500
Assigned-council system:
  changes recommended, 607
  evaluation of, 597
Attorneys general:
  aspiration groups, 545
  career patterns, 545
  self-perceptions, 548

Attorneys general (*Continued*)
  Southern, in desegregation decisions, 538
Aubert, V., 223
Aussage tests, 117

Baltimore newspapers, 641
Bankruptcy cases:
  causes, 96
  clinic, 94
  data collected, 97
Bargain-justice, defined, 405
Bargaining processes:
  considerations received, 401
  types reported, 400
Barrett, E. J., 350, 433
Bates, A., 628
Bentham, J., 201
Beutel, F. K., 138, 163
*Birmingham News,* 533
Black, Justice H., 354, 619
Bloustein, E. J., 591

Bohannan, P., 228
Bordua, D., 250
Brandeis, Justice L., 3, 68, 435
Broeder, D. W., 247, 339
Brogan, D., 538
Bromage, A., 541

Callahan, C., 80
Canons of professional ethics, 554, 567
Cardozo, B., 3, 5
Carlin, J., 244, 246, 255
Cassell v. Texas, 359
Cauro, I., 62
Change of venue, 618
Chanin, R. H., 367
Civil Justice Project (Columbia University), 248
Civil Rights Acts:
  1957, 506
  1960, 506
  1964, 535
Civil-rights laws, 250
Clark, J. P., 250, 449
Clinical programs in professional responsibility, 576
  evaluation of, 576
  schools involved, 577
Clinic, bankruptcy, 94
Cohen, J., 628
Cohn, N., 224
Colsen, E., 226
Columbia (University) experiment, 5
Community attitudes and legal rules, 631
Community reactions to desegregation decision, 497, 501, 504

Community's moral sense, 629, 633
Conviction processes, method of study, 343
Cooley, C., 66
Courtroom procedures, recommendations for improvements, 134
Court(s), 42, 247
  as vehicle of change, 667
  See also specific courts
Cowan, T., 138, 141
Cox, Judge H., 518, 529
Criminal courts, 248
Cultural lag, 251
Currie, B., 5
Custom and law, 73

Dahl, R., 212
Danzig, E. R., 80, 83
Dawkins, Judge B. C., 509, 522, 524, 525
Defense of insanity: See Insanity, defense of
Desegregation of public schools, 250
  factors in community reactions, 499
  survey of community responses, 495
Diamond, A. S., 63
Dicey, A. V., 648
Douglas, Justice W. O., 3, 81, 94
Dror, Y., 251, 663
Durkheim, E., 648, 658

Enactment of changes in the law, 174
Ethico-imperatives, 7

Ethics, 59
  *See also* Professional ethics
*Eubanks v. Louisiana,* 355
Experimental jurisprudence:
  changes in the law, 174
  method, 163
  value judgments, 173
Experimentalism and law, 161
Expert testimony (witnesses):
  as decision makers, 326
  juries' evaluation of, 247
  juries' reactions to, 318
  juries' understanding of, 469
  lawyers' reactions to, 316
  qualifications of, 466
  quality of, 468

Family law, public's attitudes, 249
Fourteenth Amendment violations, 363
Frake, C. O., 227
Frank, Judge J., 29, 187, 612
Frankfurter, Justice F., 206, 359
Franklin, M. A., 367
Free press versus fair trial, 618
Freeman, L. C., 649
Freud, S., 147
Freund, P. A., 507
Fuller, L., 199

Gluckman, M., 228, 232
Goldfarb, R., 619
Goldstein, J., 249
Grievance committees, 567
Griswold, E., 305
Guaranteed law, 48

Guilty, plea of:
  attorney's role, 399
  reasons for, 397
Gurvitch, G., 60
Guttmacher, M., 249, 315, 478
Guttman scalogram analysis, 425, 650, 653

Hamilton, C., 250, 506
Hand, Judge L., 206
*Hill v. Texas,* 355
Hoebel, E. A., 155, 231
Hogbin, H. J., 154
Holmes, O. W., 3, 4, 19, 647
Homosexual offenders:
  judges' attitudes, 478
  sentences, 483
  types of offenses, 487
Hutchins, R., 82

Ihering, R., 14
Indigents, defense of, 591
Individual practitioner: *See* Solo practitioner
Insanity, defense of:
  commitment procedures, 464, 472
  who decides responsibility, 463, 471
Insurance, influence on award, 625
Israel, 677

Jaffe, A., 329
Johnson, Judge F. M., 510, 521, 522
Judges:
  attitudes toward jury system, 310
  comparison with juries, 118, 300
  personalities of, 37

Jurimetrics, 138
  contrast with jurisprudence, 184
  subject matter of, 178
Jurisprudence, 56, 178
  analytical, 57
  historical, 57
  present position, 140
  theoretical, 57
  *See also* Experimental jurisprudence; Political jurisprudence; Sociological jurisprudence
Jury, Juries, Jurors:
  comparison with judges, 118, 300
  damages willing to award, 332
  as decision makers, 326
  decisions about damages, 330
  evaluation of expert testimony, 247
  influence of plaintiff's family, 340
  personal standards of evaluation, 93
  prejudice, 617
  psychological processes involved, 91
  quotient verdict, 337
  reactions to psychiatric testimony, 318
  relation between background and opinion, 333
  "representative," 354
  research on, 80
  response to evidence, 83
  understanding of expert testimony, 469
  use of extrarecord information, 334

Jury Project (University of Chicago), 316, 339, 627
Jury system, 246
  and lawyers' fees, 307
  quality of, 293, 299
Jury trials:
  court congestion, 294
  personal-injury cases, 294

Kadish, S., 249
Kalven, H., 247, 293, 329
Kant, E., 201
Kinsey, A., 479
Kort, F., 353
Krislov, S., 251, 537

Ladinsky, J., 245, 275
LaFave, W., 249
Lag, relative to law and social change, 671
Lasswell, H., 82
Law:
  as agency of social control, 193
  defined, 21
  distinction between *is* and *ought,* 30
  distinction between sociological and legal concepts, 46
  evasion of, 114
  factors in directed social change, 675
  forces determining content and growth, 25
  and logic, 25
  method of sociological investigation, 58
  and morals, 19, 22
  scientific theory of, 60, 61

Law (*Continued*)
  and social change, 663
  and the social sciences, 151, 161
  as vehicles of change, 667
Law-firm personnel, 266
  beginning associate, 267
  junior partner, 271
  middle partner, 272
  middle-range associate, 269
  senior associate, 270
  senior partner, 273
Law teachers, 12
Lawyers:
  classified by practice, 557
  fees, 307
  participation in professional or-
    ganizations, 569
  reactions to psychiatric testi-
    mony, 316
  social backgrounds, 288
  survey of, 464
  work of, 264
  *See also* Law-firm personnel;
    Solo practitioner
Legal coercion, 7, 49
Legal dogmatics, 46
Legal ethics, 246
  *See also* Professional ethics
Legal evolution, 647
  patterns of, 649
Legal institutions, evolutionary se-
  quence, 661
Legal justice, 4, 13
Legal norms, 48
Legal order, 53
Legal organization, regularities of,
  648

Legal profession, 244
  *See also* Lawyers
Legal pseudo-science, 11
Legal realism, 44
Legal reform, 82
"Legal relationship," 55
Legal rules:
  social causes, 72
  social effects, 74
  *See also* Law
Legislative lag, 175
Llewellyn, K., 3, 5, 29, 231, 275
Loevinger, L., 138, 178
Lombroso, C., 59

McDougall, M., 82
McQuitty, L., 412
Maine, H., 648
Malinowski, 63, 81, 110, 141, 222
Mansfield, W., 266
Mark, I., 367
Marston, W., 80, 81, 117
Mass media and jury, 617
Merton, R., 138
Meyer, Judge B., 617
Middle range, problems of the, 137
Miller, J. C., 251, 647
Millspaugh, M., 249, 641
*Model Code of Evidence,* 156-157
Moore, U., 79
Moral sense, community's, 629, 633
Mother-right, 111
Mueller, G., 479
*Muller v. Oregon,* 68

Nader, L., 140, 220, 226
National Council of Legal Clinics,
  573

Negro(es):
  exclusion from jury panels, 247
  exclusion from jury service, 354
Negro voting rights, 506
  Bullock County case, 512
  judicial aggressiveness, 515
  judicial enforcement, 508
  judicial resistance, 518
  Macon County case, 511
  Montgomery County case, 513
  refusals against Negro complain-
    ant, 525
Newman, D., 248, 392

Ogburn, W., 251
O'Gorman, H., 244

Parent-child relationships, law and
  community opinion, 637
*Patton v. Mississippi,* 359
Peltason, J., 211, 508
Personal-injury cases:
  extent of litigation, 369
  nationwide survey, 390
  size of recoveries, 378
Petrajitsky, L., 61
Philosophy of law, 158
  doctrine of pragmatism, 160
Piaget, J., 61
Plaintiffs' attorneys in personal injury, 374
Plea of guilty:
  attorney's role, 399
  reasons for, 397
Police, 249
  actions, appraisals of, 452, 454
  interaction with social-control
    agencies, 450

Police (*Continued*)
  isolation, indicators, 449
  practices, 436
  as vehicle of change, 667
Police survey data:
  dispositions, 447
  interrogation and confessions,
    444
  processing of felony arrests, 437
  release rate, 441
  time from arrest to charge, 443
  time from arrest to release, 442
Political jurisprudence:
  basic idea, 203
  criticisms, 213
  position on *is-ought* debate, 216
  relation to judicial realism, 202
  relation to political science, 202
  relation to sociological jurispru-
    dence, 201
  tasks of, 214
Postponement of trial, 618
Pound, R., 3, 9
*Powell v. Alabama,* 591, 593
Prediction in the law, 35
Press:
  coverage in criminal trial, 641
  free, versus fair trial, 618
Primitive law, 111
Pritchett, H., 411
Professional ethics:
  canons of, 554
  compliance with canons of, 567
  conditions leading to unethical
    conduct, 560
  criminal versus civil lawyers,
    565
  lawyers' views, 561

Professional ethics (*Continued*)
  most common unethical practices, 558
  significance of, 554
Professional (legal) organizations, 569
Professional responsibility, training for, 574
Psychiatrists as expert witnesses, 314
  survey of, 464

Quantitative research in legal sociology, 194
Quotient verdict, 337

Realism, legal, 44
Reason, role of, in law, 197
Recovery rates in personal injury:
  affected by attorney's presence, 380
  attorney's role, 377
  delay, 386
  stage of disposition, 381
Reference-group theory, 542
Reisman, D., 223, 224
"Representative" juries, 354
Research, basis for law, 187
Rights, 53
Robsen, R., 628
Roff, M. F., 83
Rose, A., 138
Rosenblum, V., 211
Ross, E. A., 3
Ruby (Jack) trial, 474
Ryan, M. W., 495

Scale types, 655
Schattschneider, E., 211

Schlesinger, D., 82
Schwartz, K., 251
Schwartz, L. B., 479
Schwartz, R. D., 647
Scientific theory of law:
  experimentation, 61
  methods for constructing, 60
  observation, 60
Selznick, P., 139, 190
Shackelford, W., 249, 463
Shapely-Shubik Index, 417
Shapiro, M., 140, 201
Simon, R. J., 249, 314, 463, 573, 617
Skolnick, J., 250
Smigel, E., 245, 264
*Smith v. Texas,* 354
Social backgrounds of lawyers, 278
Social change, 251
Social-control agencies and police, 450
Social justice, 4, 16
Social sciences, effect on law:
  anthropology, 144
  economics, 149
  psychology, 146
  social psychology, 149
Sociological jurisprudence, 143
  founders of, 3
Sociologists' approach to law, 66
Sociology:
  contribution to law, 192
  importance to law, 67
Sociology of law, stages of development, 191
Solo practitioner:
  characteristics, 245
  contrast with firm lawyers, 264
  motivations of, 255

Solo practitioner (*Continued*)
practice of, 262
status within metropolitan bar, 261
training of, 257
*See also* Lawyers
Southern attorneys general and desegregation decisions, 538
*Southern School News, The,* 538
*Speller v. Allen,* 362
State law, 52
Status, 16
Supreme Court, U.S. (Justices):
assignment of opinion writing, 420
attitudes, 248
behavior in racial-exclusion cases, 353
behavior patterns, 408
blocs, 411
number of opinions written by, 418
opinions in civil-liberty cases, 425
political role of, 205, 206
treatment of civil-liberties cases, 409
Sutherland, Justice G., 592

Talbert, Mrs. E. D., 526
Testimonial errors, 118
Thayer, J. B., 153

Thomas, D. S., 81, 94
Timasheff, N., 7, 56
Tompkins County, 591
Trial courts, work of, 41
Trobriand Islands, 111
Truman, D., 210
Turkey, 677

Ulmer, S., 247, 248, 353, 407
Unethical practices: *See* Professional ethics
University of Chicago Jury Project, 316, 339, 627

Venue, change of, 618
*Voir-dire,* 618

Weber, M., 646, 648
Wechsler, H., 208
Weihofen, H., 315
Weld, H. P., 80, 83
Westin, A., 212
Whiting, B., 228
Wigmore, J. H., 117, 153
Will, Judge H., 618
Willcox, B. F., 591
Williams, R., 250, 495
Winch, R., 649
Work histories of solo and firm lawyers, 280
Wood, A., 246, 553